T0191546

Communications in Computer and Information Science 1813

Rationale

The CCIS series is devoted to the publication of proceedings of computer science conferences. Its aim is to efficiently disseminate original research results in informatics in printed and electronic form. While the focus is on publication of peer-reviewed full papers presenting mature work, inclusion of reviewed short papers reporting on work in progress is welcome, too. Besides globally relevant meetings with internationally representative program committees guaranteeing a strict peer-reviewing and paper selection process, conferences run by societies or of high regional or national relevance are also considered for publication.

Topics

The topical scope of CCIS spans the entire spectrum of informatics ranging from foundational topics in the theory of computing to information and communications science and technology and a broad variety of interdisciplinary application fields.

Information for Volume Editors and Authors

Publication in CCIS is free of charge. No royalties are paid, however, we offer registered conference participants temporary free access to the online version of the conference proceedings on SpringerLink (http://link.springer.com) by means of an http referrer from the conference website and/or a number of complimentary printed copies, as specified in the official acceptance email of the event.

CCIS proceedings can be published in time for distribution at conferences or as post-proceedings, and delivered in the form of printed books and/or electronically as USBs and/or e-content licenses for accessing proceedings at SpringerLink. Furthermore, CCIS proceedings are included in the CCIS electronic book series hosted in the SpringerLink digital library at http://link.springer.com/bookseries/7899. Conferences publishing in CCIS are allowed to use Online Conference Service (OCS) for managing the whole proceedings lifecycle (from submission and reviewing to preparing for publication) free of charge.

Publication process

The language of publication is exclusively English. Authors publishing in CCIS have to sign the Springer CCIS copyright transfer form, however, they are free to use their material published in CCIS for substantially changed, more elaborate subsequent publications elsewhere. For the preparation of the camera-ready papers/files, authors have to strictly adhere to the Springer CCIS Authors' Instructions and are strongly encouraged to use the CCIS LaTeX style files or templates.

Abstracting/Indexing

CCIS is abstracted/indexed in DBLP, Google Scholar, EI-Compendex, Mathematical Reviews, SCImago, Scopus. CCIS volumes are also submitted for the inclusion in ISI Proceedings.

How to start

To start the evaluation of your proposal for inclusion in the CCIS series, please send an e-mail to ccis@springer.com.

Wenxing Hong · Yang Weng

Editors

Computer Science and Education

17th International Conference, ICCSE 2022
Ningbo, China, August 18–21, 2022
Revised Selected Papers, Part III

 Springer

Editors
Wenxing Hong ⓘ
Xiamen University
Xiamen, China

Yang Weng ⓘ
Sichuan University
Chengdu, China

ISSN 1865-0929   ISSN 1865-0937 (electronic)
Communications in Computer and Information Science
ISBN 978-981-99-2448-6   ISBN 978-981-99-2449-3 (eBook)
https://doi.org/10.1007/978-981-99-2449-3

This Springer imprint is published by the registered company Springer Nature Singapore Pte Ltd.
The registered company address is: 152 Beach Road, #21-01/04 Gateway East, Singapore 189721, Singapore

Preface

We are pleased to introduce the proceedings of the 17th International Conference on Computer Science and Education (ICCSE 2022), which was held online and offline at NingboTech University in Zhejiang, China, during August 18–21, 2022.

Organized by the China Research Council of Computer Education in Colleges & Universities (CRC-CE) with the technical sponsorship of IEEE Education Society, the conference served as an international forum for presenting state-of-the-art research in the fields of computer science education, engineering, and advanced technology. Focused on rapidly evolving digital literacy and skills, as well as their applications in education practices and digital areas, professors, experts, professionals, and researchers from universities, research institutes, and related industries came together to exchange new research results, ideas, and novel perspectives on a wide range of computer science, especially AI, data science, and engineering, and technology-based education, by addressing frontier technical and business issues essential to the applications of data science in both higher education and advancing e-Society.

We were honored to have three renowned speakers share their latest research works: Ben M. Chen from The Chinese University of Hong Kong, China; Shimin Hu from Tsinghua University, China; and Shihua Li from Southeast University, China. Additionally, ICCSE this year received 510 submissions, of which 168 high-quality manuscripts were accepted in the proceedings. Submissions with the topics of computer science, data science, educational technology, and e-Society or smart society were carefully evaluated through a rigorous double-blind peer-review process (three reviews per submission) by an esteemed panel of international reviewers, comprising the organizing and advisory committee members, as well as other experts in the field from across the world. We express our gratitude to all the authors for their valuable contributions to the conference and their commitment to advancing the field, and to all the reviewers.

Finally, we would like to express gratitude to the program chairs for their wise advice and suggestions on organizing the conference technical program. We are also indebted to the conference organizing committee members, who have all worked extremely hard on the details and activities of this conference.

We sincerely hope that you will find these proceedings instructive and inspiring for further research.

March 2023

Wenxing Hong
Yang Weng

Organization

Honorary Chairs

Clarence de Silva — University of British Columbia, Canada
Hu Zhengyu — NingboTech University, China
Li Maoqing — Xiamen University, China

General Chair

Hu Jie — NingboTech University, China

Organizing Chairs

Hong Wenxing — Xiamen University, China
Lu Dongming — NingboTech University, China
Tang Dandan — Ningbo Association for Science and Technology, China

Program Chairs

Li Xin — Louisiana State University, USA
Luo Shijian — NingboTech University, China
Marcin Kilarski — Adam Mickiewicz University, Poland
Pang Chaoyi — NingboTech University, China
Weng Yang — Sichuan University, China

Publications Chairs

Wang Qing — Tianjin University, China
Xia Min — Lancaster University, UK
Yang Fan — Xiamen University, China
Zhang Bailing — NingboTech University, China
Zheng Tongtao — Xiamen Institute of Software Technology, China

Industry Chairs

Hu Changxing	NingboTech University, China
Li Chao	Tsinghua University, China
Wu Dazhuan	NingboTech University, China

Regional Chairs

Cui Binyue	Hebei University of Economics & Business, China
Cai Liang	NingboTech University, China
Lang Haoxiang	Ontario Tech University, Canada
Li Jingyue	Norwegian University of Science and Technology, Norway

Program Committee

Ben M. Chen	Chinese University of Hong Kong, China
Cen Gang	Zhejiang University of Science and Technology, China
Chen Zhibo	Beijing Forestry University, China
Chen Zhiguo	Henan University, China
Ching-Shoei Chiang	Soochow University, Taiwan
Deng Zhigang	University of Houston, USA
Ding Yu	Netease Fuxi AI Lab, China
Dong Zhicheng	Xizang University, China
Farbod Khoshnoud	California State Polytechnic University, Pomona, USA
He Li	Software Guide Magazine, China
He Liang	East China Normal University, China
Hiroki Takada	University of Fukui, Japan
Hiromu Ishio	Fukuyama City University, Japan
Huang Jie	Chinese University of Hong Kong, China
Jiang Qingshan	Shenzhen Institutes of Advanced Technology, CAS, China
Jin Dawei	Zhongnan University of Economics and Law, China
Jonathan Li	University of Waterloo, Canada
Koliya Pulasinghe	Sri Lanka Institute of Information Technology (SLIIT), Sri Lanka

Zhou Qifeng   Xiamen University, China
Zhou Wei   Beijing Jiaotong University, China
Zhu Shunzhi   Xiamen University of Technology, China

Contents – Part III

Innovative Studies
on Technology-Enhanced Teaching
and Learning

Research on Multi-dimensional Bilingual Teaching Model of Computer Courses Supported by Artificial Intelligence

Changhua Zhao[1,2,3]([⊠]), Chunqiao Mi[1,2,3], and Tangbo[1]

[1] School of Computer Science and Engineering, Huaihua University, Huaihua 418000, Hunan, People's Republic of China
lala_zhao@163.com
[2] Key Laboratory of Wuling-Mountain Health Big Data Intelligent Processing and Application in Hunan Province Universities, Huaihua 418000, Hunan, People's Republic of China
[3] Key Laboratory of Intelligent Control Technology for Wuling-Mountain Ecological Agriculture in Hunan Province, Huaihua 418000, Hunan, People's Republic of China

Abstract. Aiming at the problems of the integration of computer course teaching with international teaching and engineering certification, this study designs a multi-dimensional teaching mode of computer courses through the support of Artificial Intelligence. It analyzes the teaching resources, learning services, teaching process and teaching means involved in computer course teaching. Taking the course of "Computer Introduction" as an example, this study explores the multi-dimensional bilingual teaching mode supported by Artificial Intelligence, trains computer talents who meet the ability requirements of the era of Artificial Intelligence, and provides ideas for the teaching innovation of other courses.

Keywords: Artificial Intelligence · Computer Courses · Multi dimensional · Bilingual Teaching Mode

1 Introduction

Artificial Intelligence (AI) technology is developing continuously. It promotes the reform of teaching methods, teaching tools and teaching environment, and provides new conditions and opportunities for the teaching of computer courses in Colleges and Universities. International talents are strategic resources for countries to improve their comprehensive national strength and international competitiveness. In the international talent competition, China's international talent training and development should adapt to the new situation and new needs of national economic and social opening to the outside world in the new era. This is in line with China's new role and orientation in the process of globalization. It is also "the Belt and Road" construction, which requires new challenges and talents for talents. In addition to professional knowledge and ability, the international talents needed by China should also have the ability to communicate professionally in foreign languages. According to the graduation requirements in the "general standard for engineering education certification", which includes "communication" ability, that is, "be able to effectively communicate and communicate with peers in the industry and the public on complex engineering problems, including writing reports and design manuscripts, making statements, clearly expressing or responding to instructions, and have a certain international vision and be able to communicate and communicate in a cross-cultural context". This means that students can apply it to learning professional knowledge, solving the application of professional literature and cross-cultural communication with peers in the industry. With the support of artificial intelligence, implement diversified and three-dimensional bilingual teaching (Chinese and English) for computer series courses, so that students of this major can be familiar with the language norms of international professional communication, enhance their confidence in completing English tasks in professional fields, and also provide reference for bilingual teaching modes of other engineering majors in the school.

2   Related Research

2.1   Teaching Mode Under AI

As one of the most advanced technologies in the world, AI has brought new opportunities and challenges to the teaching of various courses in Colleges and Universities [1]. The traditional teacher centered classroom has deficiencies in the cultivation of students' comprehensive quality. Students' subjectivity is difficult to give full play, and it is difficult to cultivate college students who meet the requirements of the development of the times by simply reforming the teaching content [2]. Domestic teaching modes mainly include research-based teaching mode, task driven teaching mode, and teaching mode based on virtual simulation platform, micro class, Mu class, etc. The research-based teaching model strives to cultivate students' innovative ability, but this model has high requirements for students' learning foundation [3]. Based on the task driven teaching model, due to the uneven ability of students to complete tasks, the interaction between teaching and learning is also difficult to carry out effectively. The teaching mode based on virtual simulation platform, SPOC and MOOC has deficiencies in personalized teaching needs [4]. In the teaching of computer course, some well-known universities abroad provide students with corresponding reading documents for different teaching contents, conduct in-depth discussion on some classical knowledge points, and add cutting-edge research contents in classroom teaching, so as to increase the breadth and depth of course teaching. We need to cultivate students' practical ability through comprehensive homework [5]. With the development of AI, some foreign schools have explored the intelligent presentation of teaching content in the teaching of computer courses, but the development is not mature enough.

2.2   Application of AI in Bilingual Teaching

With the development of educational informatization, AI technology has had a revolutionary impact on bilingual teaching. The theoretical research and practical achievements of bilingual teaching informatization are increasingly enriched, which has brought bilingual education to a new level [6]. However, at the same time, the in-depth application, integration and innovation of AI technology are not enough, which is mainly reflected in the lack of relevant teaching resources, insufficient international academic exchanges and cooperative research, backward information infrastructure and insufficient teachers' information-based teaching ability [7]. Due to the limited time and energy, teachers mostly imitate the traditional teaching mode and directly apply the PPT template of relevant courses in the teaching process. The application of multimedia resources and tools is only limited to the shallow level. The function and function of AI technology can't be well displayed, and intelligent teaching can't be widely carried out and implemented [8]. The traditional evaluation method can't improve students' learning level. Based on the above situation, taking the ability in the era of AI as the goal, it is a beneficial exploration to carry out multi-dimensional bilingual teaching supported by AI.

3 Construction of Multi-dimensional Teaching Mode of Computer Courses Supported by AI

3.1 Three Dimensional Construction of Teaching Resources

Online Resource Allocation
Online resources are allocated with the help of corresponding platforms, such as network assisted teaching platform, research-based teaching platform, high-quality course construction platform, etc. In the era of big data, the acquisition of teaching resources has long gone beyond national boundaries. For bilingual teaching, it is particularly necessary to select foreign excellent teaching platforms.

Offline Resource Allocation
Computer courses are highly practical, and corresponding experimental practice bases are needed offline. The off campus practice base can be companies, etc., and the experimental sites in the school are generally configured by the school. In addition, the original English version of the teaching materials used can more accurately express professional terms.

Online and Offline Resource Recommendation Service Supported by AI
We can conduct multi-dimensional analysis through AI technology to master the dynamic results of students' habit of using resources, learning track, learning level and learning effect. To solve the problem, we can use the real-time translation provided by foreign electronic resources to recommend appropriate online and offline resources. In this way, the intelligent and personalized content push of the platform can be realized.

3.2 Construction of Three-Dimensional Teaching Service

Teachers Answer Questions Online and Offline
By collecting and understanding the information of each student, we can carry out online Q & A in order to better interact with students and provide personalized services. When

answering questions, we need to analyze the reasons for students' questions, record and summarize them, and give students inspiration and encouragement in learning. Face to face Q & A needs to set themes around the teaching content to enhance the purpose of teaching services.

Discussion and Mutual Assistance among Students

Students discuss and help each other through online Wechat groups and offline centralized counseling. Activities are limited in time and topics are communicated in foreign languages. In this way, the discussion content will be relatively concentrated, exercise oral English and learn more professional terms. Everyone is free to express their views. Through discussion, students can understand each other's strengths and weaknesses and put forward solutions at the same time.

Personalized Teaching Service with the Support of AI

There are differences in students' foreign language level, learning foundation, learning ability and learning preference. Different students have different needs for teaching services. Adopt AI technology to collect and analyze students' learning information, clarify which knowledge points students have mastered and which key and difficult points need to be broken through, and collect students' learning behavior information, so as to teach students according to their aptitude.

3.3 Construction of Three-Dimensional Teaching Process

Diversified Teaching Forms

To achieve the corresponding teaching objectives, teaching forms need to be diversified. In addition to the traditional teaching mode, it also needs to adopt the teaching form designed by teachers and students. Under the guidance of teachers, students independently design learning plans, and then teachers review and implement them. In the teaching process, students need to organize in a foreign language. Through diversified teaching forms, pay attention to fully reflect students' autonomy and effectively stimulate students' interest in foreign languages and professional knowledge. In this way, it can break through the key and difficult points of learning and effectively achieve the ability goal.

Diversified Evaluation Methods

Teaching evaluation is a very important link in teaching. Appropriate evaluation methods play a positive role in promoting teaching. Considering the reasonable setting of evaluation indicators to achieve diversified evaluation, we adopt a dynamic and static evaluation system. On the subject of evaluation, we give full play to the role of students as the main body. Students' self-evaluation and students' mutual evaluation can account for a certain proportion. Through diversified evaluation, let students find their own shortcomings and direction of efforts.

Teaching Process Optimization with the Support of AI

Due to the limited energy of teachers, some repetitive work in the teaching process can be completed by technical means, which needs to make full use of AI assisted teaching means to optimize the teaching process.

4 Artificial Intelligence Technology Helps the Realization of Multi-dimensional Teaching of Courses

4.1 Teaching Solution of Computer Courses by AI Empowerment

Selection of Teaching Resources
Having rich resources does not mean that the teaching objectives of the course can be achieved. We need to choose the right resources from the massive resources. For the bilingual teaching of computer course, we make some specific resources according to the characteristics of students. We analyzed the knowledge system, Chinese and English translation, key and difficult points of the course, what Chinese and English resources support each knowledge point, especially how to break through the difficult problems. Different teaching resources are needed for different ability goals. We need to solve the problem of hierarchical gradient of teaching resources.

Personalized Recommendation of Teaching Resources
We can recommend popular resources and make a ranking list of popular resources according to the frequency of resource use. At the same time, let students participate in the scoring of good and bad resources. After a period of scoring data collection, recommend the resources recognized by everyone. The recommendation methods of teaching resources should be evaluated and analyzed according to the recommendation results, continuously improved, integrated with a variety of methods, and provide a variety of learning programs for students.

Diversification of Teaching Methods
We promote students' interest in learning through diversified teaching forms. By inviting foreign teachers and experts with overseas study background into the classroom to interact with students and conduct special Q & A. Some teaching contents can be completed online through MOOC, breaking through the limitation of course hours and cultivating students' learning ability. Self-learning of traditional teaching materials will make learning boring, and some concepts are difficult to understand and master only by text introduction. We break through some difficulties through diversified teaching resources. For some teaching contents, the teaching form from theory to practice and then back to theory and practice is adopted.

Diversification of Teaching Evaluation
In addition to the traditional evaluation methods, students' use of resources and the degree of participation in curriculum interaction should be included in the evaluation system. Teachers should set evaluation parameters, automatically generate evaluation results by the platform, and construct a diversified evaluation system of computer curriculum through AI technology. Teachers need to actively solve the difficult problems in the evaluation process and treat every student fairly.

4.2   Teaching Realization of Computer Courses by AI Empowerment

This study selects "Computer Introduction" as an example course to carry out the teaching pilot. Firstly, three-dimensional allocation of teaching resources of the course, including online resource allocation, offline resource allocation and online and offline resource recommendation service supported by AI technology. Secondly, build three-dimensional teaching services, including teachers' online and offline Q & A, students' discussion and mutual assistance, and carry out personalized teaching services with the support of AI technology. Thirdly, realize the three-dimensional teaching process, including the diversification of teaching forms, the diversification of evaluation methods, and the optimization of teaching process with the support of AI technology. Finally, through the comparative analysis of the effect, improve the teaching resources and teaching methods (Fig. 1).

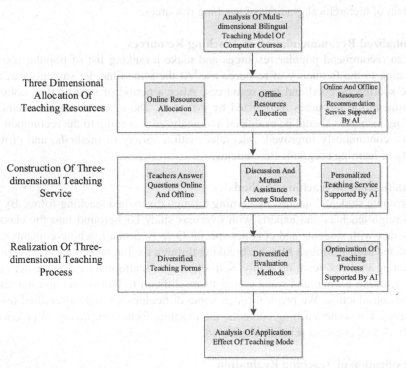

Fig. 1. Implementation Scheme of Multi-dimensional Bilingual Teaching of Computer Course Supported by AI

The specific implementation process is as follows:

Understand the relevant teaching software supported by AI, investigate the bilingual teaching mode of foreign language college, the available foreign teacher resources, and experts with overseas study background and industry background, so as to prepare for the construction of three-dimensional teaching space.

Taking the "Computer Introduction" as an example, select the appropriate teaching resources. First, select offline teaching materials and reference books. The teaching materials are in the original foreign language, with moderate difficulty and recognized by the industry. Then, for online reference resources, select forums and forums closely related to cutting-edge technologies such as big data, AI and Cyberspace Security, such as Ted, new technology release and other resources. Finally, guide students to enter foreign Coursera, EDX and other MOOC platforms to search the public teaching resources of international top universities such as Harvard and MIT, and carry out three-dimensional allocation of teaching resources.

Make full use of AI teaching software to provide students with online and offline Q & A. Establish a special discussion space, publish discussion topics regularly, discuss in English alternately, and solve problems with each other. At the same time, count the students' speeches and mine meaningful and constructive speeches to provide reference for later evaluation. According to the difference of students' individual knowledge level, AI technology is used to provide students with personalized learning services.

Diversified teaching forms are adopted. In addition to the conventional online and offline flipped classroom learning basic knowledge, for the new technology part of the teaching content, the teaching form jointly designed by teachers and students is adopted. Under the guidance of teachers, students independently design learning plans, and let students make presentations in thematic groups. Then teachers review and implement, and pay attention to fully reflect students' autonomy and effectively stimulate students' interest in learning. Let them break through the key and difficult points of learning and effectively achieve their ability goals. Invite foreign teachers into the classroom to practice oral English with students. For cutting-edge new technologies, invite experts with overseas learning background to give special lectures and interact with students.

Set reasonable evaluation indicators and adopt a process evaluation system. The evaluation of the basic knowledge part is carried out by the system, and the topics include Chinese and English. The operation part should pay attention to the use of re technology. In addition, it should also include daily oral evaluation, students' discussion of the topic in the group, etc. On the subject of evaluation, students themselves should also be one of the subjects of evaluation. Students' self-evaluation and students' mutual evaluation account for a certain proportion. Through diversified evaluation, let students find their own shortcomings and direction of efforts.

This study implemented three-dimensional bilingual teaching for Freshmen (2020) in the course of "Computer Introduction". Through the analysis of students' interviews and performance evaluation results, the main results are shown in the following aspects:

Through diversified forms of teaching, students' interest in English learning is stimulated.

Through online and offline resource allocation, the introduction of computer introduction course on foreign Coursera platform has brought a refreshing feeling and made the classroom more vivid and interesting.

The understanding of professional terms is increased through the original textbook. The translation in Chinese textbooks is sometimes obscure and difficult to understand. The understanding of professional knowledge is deepened through the original textbooks.

Through three-dimensional service, discussion and mutual assistance among students, students' oral expression ability is exercised.

Through the personalized recommendation of personalized intelligent software, students can better understand the latest cutting-edge technology in computer and consolidate the professional architecture.

5   Conclusion and Suggestion

Domestic colleges and universities are strengthening cooperation and exchanges with foreign colleges and universities. In the past two years, they have strongly supported teachers to study for doctoral degrees abroad, which provides an opportunity for bilingual teaching in this study. Computer courses are highly dependent on English, so bilingual teaching of computer courses can improve students' international competitiveness. This study takes the course "Computer Introduction" as an example to carry out teaching pilot, and explore the multi-dimensional bilingual teaching of computer course supported by AI. This paper studies the all-round overall design of the teaching content, teaching form, teaching platform, evaluation technology and analysis technology in the bilingual teaching of computer course, so as to create a multi-dimensional bilingual teaching mode of the course. It is of great significance to improve students' innovative and practical ability and adapt to the new needs of the future AI society for the ability of international talents.

Acknowledgement. We are very thankful that this study is supported by the Scientific Research Project of Hunan Provincial Department of Education (Grant No. 21C0646) and Teaching Reform Project of Huaihua University (Grant No. 2021123). This work is also supported in part by the Huaihua University Double First-Class initiative Applied Characteristic Discipline of Control Science and Engineering. We are also very grateful for the helpful suggestions and constructive comments given by the reviewers and editors.

References

1. Li, Z., Jin, H., Liu, Y.: Artificial intelligence opens the new mode of "internet plus education". Telecommun. Netw. Technol. (012), 6–10 (2016)
2. Zhong, Z., Zhong, S., Tang, Y.: Research on the construction of intelligent learning model supported by artificial intelligence. Res. Audio Vis. Educ. **42**(12), 9 (2021)
3. Wang, G.: Research and application of artificial intelligence in computer network technology. Curric. Educ. Res. Res. Learn. Teach. Methods (10), 285–285 (2019)
4. Xie, R.: Internationalization of artificial intelligence - diversified and innovative teaching model. Comput. Educ. (6) (2017)
5. Zou, M.: Research on multi-dimensional teaching mode of computer network course supported by artificial intelligence. Univ. Educ. (3), 4 (2020)
6. Yang, M., Shang, J., Yan, H., et al.: Exploration on bilingual teaching reform of computer network course. Heilongjiang Sci. **11**(11), 2 (2020)
7. Wang, H.: Reform and practice of bilingual course teaching in colleges and universities – taking "the application of MATLAB in physics" as an example. Educ. Obs. (2), 3 (2020)
8. Ning, B., Li, J., Wang, B.: Research on bilingual teaching method of engineering with the support of information technology – taking the bilingual course of radar system as an example. China Electron. Educ. (01), 56–62 (2015)

Research on the Form of "Four-Steps" Open Project Practical Teaching Activities

Gang Cen$^{(\boxtimes)}$, Zeping Yang , Yuefeng Cen , and Zeyu Zheng

Zhejiang University of Science and Technology, Hangzhou, China
gcen@163.com, cyf@zust.edu.cn

Abstract. A "four-steps" open project practice teaching mode is proposed from the perspective of local application-oriented talents cultivation. This mode is constructed for the purpose of improving the comprehensive quality of application-oriented talents, based on the platforms of open innovation and experiments, students' scientific and technological innovation projects, as well as the students' discipline competition, with emphasis on the consolidation and promotion of scientific research results. It is a students' interest-oriented and innovative practical results based mode. Through the forms of "five-autonomies" open project practice teaching, this mode is able to meet the needs of students' personalized practice teaching. In line with the curriculum of professional courses, this mode extends the practical teaching outside the classroom, improves students' scientific and technological innovation ability, and ultimately fosters the education of application-oriented innovative talents.

Keywords: personnel training · "four-steps" · practical teaching · innovative education · construction of teaching environment

1 Introduction

How to improve the education quality of engineering innovation talents has always been the core issue. ZUST (Zhejiang University of Science and Technology) is a provincial university which mainly focuses on cultivating high-level application-oriented talents in China. Exporting high-quality engineering innovative talents is the goal that has been pursued by ZUST [1]. In school teaching, a complete teaching system consists of planned teaching and unplanned teaching. However, the unplanned practical teaching system has failed to fill the vacancy of the high-quality engineering innovation talents. In recent years, although many improvements and gratifying results have been achieved, there are still many areas that can be improved. Systematical improvements of the practical teaching system to increase the output of high-quality engineering innovative talents has become a major issue that schools need to study and solve in the new era [2].

2 The Overall Idea of "Four-Steps" Open Project Practice Teaching

2.1 Several Pedagogical Issues that This "Four-Steps" is Intended to Address

Local application-oriented undergraduate institutions intend to address the emergence of several teaching the following issues.

The Problem of Whole Process Engineering Practice Environment. Currently, the lack of a systematic engineering practice environment outside the teaching program makes it difficult to meet the diversified, comprehensive, personalized, and maximized growth needs of students. For example, students often lack practical experience and skills related to actual engineering projects, as well as interdisciplinary and cross-disciplinary practice environments, which limits their overall quality improvement. In addition, the lack of effective evaluation methods and systems in the practical teaching process also affects the improvement of the practical effect. Therefore, these undergraduate institutions lack a systematic engineering practice environment to meet the needs of students. Outside the curriculum system, students find it difficult to gain practical experience and skills, especially for future career needs. At the same time, this also makes it difficult for students to apply what they have learned in real life, thereby limiting their abilities and creativity. In addition, the lack of effective transformation mechanisms and achievement display platforms also limits the opportunities for students' practical results to be displayed and applied, thereby reducing their confidence and innovative drive.

Systematic Top-Level Design of Practical Teaching Activities. The practical activities such as open experiments, discipline competitions, science and technology projects, paper publications, and patent applications in undergraduate colleges lack integration, resulting in a lack of synergy and weak overall effect. A systematic top-level design is required to promote the sustainable development of students' innovative ability. To achieve this goal, a comprehensive and unified project-based teaching system that combines open experiments, discipline competitions, science and technology projects, paper publications, and patent applications must be established. The design of this system should comprehensively and sustainably promote the development of students' innovative abilities.

Improve the Effectiveness of Practical Teaching. In practical teaching at schools, there are prominent problems such as passive learning and insufficient cultivation of innovation ability, which are also challenges faced by the education sector today. In practical teaching, students are usually passive recipients of knowledge, lacking initiative and creativity, which hinders the effective improvement of their practical and innovative abilities. Therefore, we need to change the traditional "spoon-feeding" education and realize experiential practical education to improve the effectiveness and quality of practical teaching. Students need to play a more active role and become the main body of practical teaching. Through practical activities, students will gain more practical experience, enhance their innovative thinking ability, improve their practical problem-solving skills, and cultivate teamwork spirit.

2.2 The General Idea of "Four-Steps" Open Project Practice Teaching Activity Form

To solve the above problems and improve the engineering innovation level and practical ability of students in application-oriented undergraduate institutions, the group has proposed a "four-steps" project practice teaching activity, which is based on the CDIO (Conceiving-Designing-Implementing-Operating) as shown in Fig. 1.

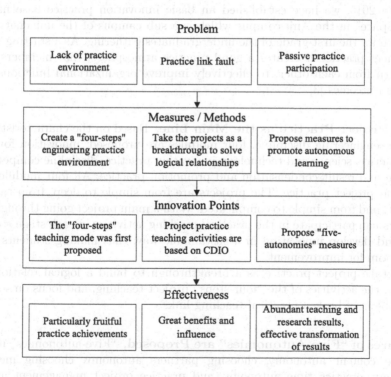

Fig. 1. General idea of the form of project practice activities.

Adopt the CDIO Theory. Create an engineering environment for the "four-steps" open project practice teaching activities. It focuses on solving the problem of lack of engineering practice environment outside the teaching plan, and creates the whole process of "four-steps" engineering environment from the team environment, hardware environment and soft environment.

CDIO upholds the constructivist view of knowledge, emphasizing the active cognitive construction of the subject and the cyclic rise of the carrier, i.e. the cognitive subject is required to develop and apply the product, process and project life cycle from easy to difficult. Based on this idea, and taking into account the structural features and complexity of the project and the characteristics of students in different grades, this paper innovatively takes a project as the main line and hierarchizes the "four-steps" to complement the teaching within the training program. This structure from simple to complex, from validation projects to research projects, facilitates students' targeted project practice, which in turn helps them to gain an integrated learning experience and an overall development of their knowledge and abilities.

Since 2015, we have established an basic innovation practice base named "Blue Space" in the Anji campus which is a sub campus of the university and the place for the first-grade of the undergraduates gathering. As a starting point for project practice it creates a good practice atmosphere, that members help and learn from each other, to effectively improve organizational functions and learning outcomes [3].

Using Project Practice as the Main Line. Based on the characteristics of the new engineering discipline, four modules are proposed: innovation foundation practice, science and technology innovation practice, discipline competition practice and result condensation and promotion practice. All four modules are based on project practice. The projects are from simple to deep, from easy to difficult, and from simple to complicated. With a main project going throughout, students can participate in the practical teaching activities in each stage step by step, and develop innovation in a sustainable way, thus making students have more room for improvement.

We take project practice as a breakthrough to build a logical relationship between the activities of the "four-steps" project teaching, and focus on solving the problem of broken practical teaching links.

Measures of "Five-Autonomies" are Proposed. "Five-autonomies" means practice content autonomy, choosing partners autonomy, choosing mentors autonomy, practice time autonomy, and practice project management autonomy [4].

Practice content autonomy means that the source of practice content can be students' own themes, teachers' research projects, discipline competition projects, enterprise demand projects, etc. Choosing partners autonomy means that members of the practice study group can come from different grades and different campuses. Choosing instructors autonomy means that teachers from different disciplinary backgrounds are available for students to choose as project monitors. Practice time autonomy means that students can choose the starting and ending time of practice according to their own situation, spanning from one to several semesters. Practice project management autonomy means that students manage practice bases and projects independently, making project implementation more convenient and effective [5, 6].

The measures of "five-autonomies" focus on solving the problem of passive learning in practice, allowing students to participate in basic practice, science and technology practice or disciplinary competitions that interest them, giving them a sense of control over their own learning and promoting a practice paradigm that aims at their personalized development.

3 Construction of "Four-Steps" Open Project Practice Teaching Activity Model

3.1 Logical Relations of Activity Forms

Based on CDIO, according to the structure characteristics of the project, the complexity and the characteristics of the students in different grades of schools, with the integration of the open experiment teaching, extracurricular science and technology innovation project achievements of study and practice, college students competition, and achievement condensed promotion, we established an activity patterns and theoretical system named "four-steps". That is, the relatively independent four modules are organically integrated to form a project-based, interrelated and hierarchical practical teaching activity system, as shown in Fig. 2.

3.2 "Four-Steps" Open Project Practice Teaching Activity Format

Basic Project Practice. The purpose of basic project practice is to familiarize students with the "four-steps" activity model. This approach allows students to participate in the "four-steps" process in a progressive and hierarchical manner, starting with simpler projects and gradually moving on to more complex ones. The ultimate goal is to develop students' innovative abilities and provide them with practical experience that they can use in their future careers.

To achieve this goal, it is important to provide students with a supportive learning environment that encourages active engagement and experimentation. One way to do this is through basic training seminars, which can provide students with the foundational knowledge and skills they need to start working on their own projects. In addition, visits to innovation bases and exposure to the practical achievements of senior students can help spark students' interest in project-based learning and motivate them to take on more challenging projects.

Specific implementation: Through publicity and mobilization, organizing visits to innovation bases such as "Blue Space", observing the practical achievements of seniors, and attending the meeting of outstanding seniors, we can guide

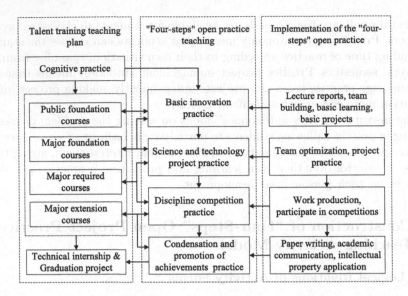

Fig. 2. The logical relationship between the forms of "four-steps" open practical teaching activities.

students to understand CDIO and stimulate their interest in the project practice. Through basic training seminars, students can try to start some small projects and form teams to practice basic projects. In this stage, students mainly practice in innovation bases such as "Blue Space".

Science and Technology Project Practice. The purpose of science and technology project practice is to optimize the team structure and customize the project practice content according to individual interests and strengths. By engaging in innovation project practice, students can enhance their abilities in research, collaboration, design, development, and cooperation.

To achieve this goal, it is necessary to establish a comprehensive system for science and technology project practice that includes project topic selection, project proposal writing, project implementation, and project evaluation. In order to optimize the team structure, students can form teams based on their individual interests and strengths, and can be guided by teachers and industry experts.

During the project practice process, students should be encouraged to think creatively and independently, and to communicate and collaborate effectively with team members. They should also learn to solve practical problems and apply theoretical knowledge to real-world situations.

Specific implementation: With the help of innovative practice bases such as "Blue Space", students can apply for science and technology innovation projects, reorganize or optimize project practice teams, or participate in teachers' research projects. Driven by innovation projects, students further improve their design, development and collaboration skills. The outstanding students can help guide the junior students in this stage, and they can learn from each other to promote the rapid growth of the team.

Discipline Competition Practice. The purpose of the discipline competition practice is to enhance the quality of work and showcase the practical achievements of students based on their mastery of some professional knowledge. This practice is aimed at improving the students' abilities in project management, document writing, speech expression, and more. It also serves as a platform for students to learn from each other and exchange ideas, as well as to promote healthy competition among peers. In this stage, students are encouraged to participate in various discipline competitions and challenge themselves to continuously improve their skills and knowledge in their chosen field of study. Through such competitions, they can also gain valuable experience in teamwork, communication, and problem-solving. The discipline competition practice is an essential component of the comprehensive project practice system and plays a significant role in the cultivation of innovative and practical talents.

Specific implementation: To enhance the practical experience of students and promote their innovation ability, it is crucial to complete the practical part of the discipline competition with the help of innovation bases. The innovation bases provide students with necessary resources, equipment and mentors to carry out their projects. Moreover, students can access a real-world environment to test their innovations and apply theoretical knowledge into practical activities. To achieve the above objectives, students need to select key issues or technologies in the project research results and create or improve them. They can then participate in national or provincial university competitions to showcase their innovative ideas and achievements. During the competition, students have the opportunity to exchange ideas with peers and experts from different universities and disciplines, which can broaden their horizons and stimulate their creativity. Through this combination of competition and learning, students can improve their project management ability, competition ability, and speech and expression ability. They can also gain confidence in their own innovative ideas and learn from the experience of others to enhance their future projects.

Condensation and Promotion of Achievements Practice. The purpose of the condensation and promotion of achievements practice is to improve the ability of writing papers, intellectual property rights application, public speaking and academic communication.

Specific implementation: Summarize and refine the results of the previous project practice, write papers or declare intellectual property rights. Students can choose to attend relevant academic conferences for learning and exchange. Summarize the experience of participating in the "four-steps" activities and guide other students to carry out project practice activities. There is no limitation on the venue for the whole practice process.

4 Implementation of the "Four-Steps" Open Project Practice

4.1 Environment Guarantee

In the process of "four-steps" project practice, we need to mobilize, organize and manage, and provide a good practice environment. It mainly includes the hardware environment and software environment [7]. The hardware environment is that we provide a place for all students to practice independently, the necessary common equipment and instruments, etc. The software environment includes software learning materials, design and development systems and application tools needed for practice. In addition to this, we need all mentors and enthusiastic seniors to be available as assistant mentors.

4.2 Specific Implementation

These four stages have a clear progression from easy to difficult, and from simple to complex, starting with validation projects and moving towards research projects. The stages are not only designed in a logical sequence but are also highly correlated, providing students with a complementary learning experience to the training plan, thereby promoting the integration of knowledge and the comprehensive development of their abilities.

By completing these four stages, students can not only acquire practical skills and knowledge in engineering but also develop problem-solving abilities, creativity, and critical thinking skills. Furthermore, they will gain valuable experience in project management, teamwork, and communication.

4.3 Implementation Cases

Take the "Panda" project practice team as an example, they participated in some small practice activities in the "Blue Space" innovation base practice, and applied for a school level science and technology innovation project to study website design with the theme of "Web-based campus information publishing platform". On the basis of this project, they applied for the national project: "AI-based global tourism detection and dispatching system". After completing the project practice, they entered the third level of project practice. They improved the results of the project and completed works such as "Impression of West Lake" and "Meet West Lake". By participating in the provincial and national university discipline competitions, they achieved the excellent results of second prize in national and provincial competitions. Finally, these works and application techniques are condensed into papers and software publications. The project practice flow of the team is shown in Fig. 3. The main line of the whole team is the "Territorial Tourism Management System", around which the four stages of the "four-steps" process are implemented to achieve a high degree of integration between theory and practice [8].

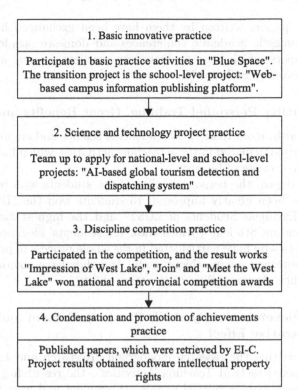

Fig. 3. The case of "four-steps".

5 The Effectiveness of "Four-Steps" Open Project Practice Teaching Activities for Talent Cultivation

5.1 Practice Achievements of Students in Project Practice Teaching

Students have made rich achievements in scientific and technological innovation, discipline competitions and condensation and promotion of achievements. With the establishment of "Blue Space", teachers and students on multiple campuses can communicate better. The open project practice teaching activity has more full vitality and has achieved remarkable results [9].

From 2015 until 2021, 253 practice projects have been initiated by students who have participated in practice activities in "Blue Space", including 26 national-level projects, 56 provincial-level projects, 171 university-level projects, and more than 10 teacher research projects and independent design projects. Students won 319 awards in discipline competitions, including 63 national-level awards, 149 provincial-level awards and 107 university-level awards. They have written and published 87 academic papers, applied for and obtained 15 intellectual property rights of invention patents and 20 intellectual property rights of software works.

Most of the papers written by them have been exchanged in many international and domestic academic conferences and domestic academic journals. There are 4 papers which were evaluated as excellent papers, and 29 papers have been retrieved by SCI and EI.

5.2 High-Quality Personnel Training, Great Benefits and Influence

In terms of breadth, more than 1,000 students of science and engineering majors of the university participated in these teaching activities, which have remarkable results and wide a range of benefits.

In terms of depth, the personal ability of the students who participated in the practice has been greatly improved. 13 students won the "Baosteel Scholarship", "The Excellent Students of ZUST" and the highest award in ZUST named "Outstanding Student", which show the students' elegance. Some postgraduate students who have participated in the whole process of project practice teaching have obtained many achievements. And they have obvious advantages in practical ability, design ability, cooperation ability.

5.3 The Achievement of Symbolic Teaching Reform and Obvious Demonstrative Effect

In addition to writing the research monograph "Research and Exploration on 'Four-Steps' Open Practical Teaching Activities", the research group has also written 25 research papers related to this achievement and won 3 achievement awards at the department level or above. We has established the "'four-steps' project teaching activity results website". The practice results have been promoted and exchanged in the domestic and overseas, and have been highly recognized by peers [10].

6 Conclusion

The "four-steps" teaching model is proposed the first time for the cultivation of application-oriented talents in colleges and universities, which is based on the teaching of planned courses and the design of practical projects in a progressive manner, and these practical projects further feed the professional knowledge. The research and practice of this teaching model has been supported by the Ministry of Education's "Research on Open Practical Teaching in Engineering Education Environment" and other teaching research and reform projects. Through the design, exploration and practice for more than 10 years, the traditional teacher-centered teaching mode has been changed and the student-centered teaching idea has been deeply spread. The "four-steps" project teaching mode provides a novel and effective pathway for the cultivation of engineering application-oriented talents, and is also an important initiative to guide students' scientific and technological innovation and strengthen their practical ability, whose theory and practice are of great significance to high-level application-oriented undergraduate education and teaching reform [11].

Acknowledgment. Thank you for the support of the general planning fund for Humanities and Social Sciences Research of the Ministry of Education (17yja880004) in 2017 and the key project of Teaching Research and Reform of Zhejiang University of Science and Technology "Construction and Practice of a New Generation of Information Technology Innovation Talent Training System based on the College of Artificial Intelligence Industry" (2022-jg15) in 2022.

References

1. Wu, A., Hou, Y., Yang, Q., Hao, J.: Accelerating development and construction of emerging engineering, taking initiative to adapt to and lead the new economy. Res. High. Educ. Eng. (01), 1–9 (2017)
2. Zhang, Y., Fang, H.: From living space to the cultural space: how to implement the modern university academy system. J. High. Educ. **37**(03), 56–61 (2016)
3. Jiang, X., Yu, J., Song, S., Wu, H., Cheng, X.: Innovation and practice on student management and educational pattern under collegiate system - a case study on zust anji campus. J. Zhejiang Univ. Sci. Technol. **28**(02), 153–157+171 (2016)
4. Han, J., Cen, G.: A new environment construction of open project instruction for students' self-management. Res. Explor. Lab. **30**(04), 215–218 (2014)
5. Cen, G., Lin, X., Mo, Y.: Exploration and practice of open-ended practical teaching innovation by 'four steps' - using application-oriented talent cultivation mode of German for reference. J. Zhejiang Univ. Sci. Technol. **27**(05)
6. Cen, G., Wu, S., Jiang, X., Lv, B., Zhu, R., Ding, Z.: Research and exploration on construction management of project practice innovation base based on 'four steps'. Res. Explor. Lab. **40**(07), 244–248 (2021)
7. Chen, J., Zhang, Y., Wei, Y., Hu, J.: Discrimination of the contextual features of top performers in scientific literacy using a machine learning approach. Res. Sci. Educ. **51**(01), 129–158 (2021)
8. Cen, G., Yu, J.: A new environment construction of open project instruction for students' self-management. Res. Explor. Lab. **30**(02), 158–160 (2011)
9. Cen, G.: Teaching research and exploration of open-ended 'four-step' project practice teaching mode in innovative and application-oriented talents training. J. Zhejiang Univ. Sci. Technol. **32**(05), 413–419 (2020)
10. Jiang, X., Zhu, R., Cen, G., Song, S., Li, X., Wang, S.: Design of student affairs management system of 'plam academy' smart campus. J. Zhejiang Univ. Sci. Technol. **32**(02), 139–144 (2020)
11. Cen, G., Lin, X.: Research and exploration of "four steps" open practical teaching activities. China Water&Power Press (2016)

Exploring the Association Between Computational Thinking and Cognitive Abilities of Elementary Students: A Preliminary Study

Shuhan Zhang(✉) [iD] and Gary K. W. Wong [iD]

Faculty of Education, The University of Hong Kong, Hong Kong, China
shuhan@connect.hku.hk, wongkwg@hku.hk

Abstract. Computational thinking (CT) has become a practical skill for everyone. While numerous attempts have been made in defining the term and its components, there is still a lack of consensus on the definition of CT. Aligned with recent empirical studies where the conception of CT was extended to other cognitive domains, more research can be done to enrich the nomological framework of CT. This study aims to unravel the relationship between CT and cognitive abilities at the elementary level. Students from 3rd–4th graders of the primary schools in northern China were invited (n = 246) and assessment tests for CT and general cognitive abilities were administered. Results indicate that CT can be positively predicted by numeracy, visuospatial abilities, and inductive reasoning skills. The study has contributed to the field in both theoretical and practical aspects. Theoretically, the findings enrich our conceptual understanding of CT as an independent psychological construct. Practically, the study indicates the role of general cognitive abilities in the development of CT skills, providing guidance on the design of CT learning resources for elementary education.

Keywords: Computational thinking · Elementary education · Cognitive abilities

1 Introduction

In the digitized era, computational skills have become an increasingly important literacy to live in a world surrounded by advanced technologies. Computational thinking (CT), which originated from "algorithmic thinking" [1], has been popularized since Jeanette Wing proposed the term in 2006, depicting it as an approach to "solving problems, designing systems, and understanding human behavior, by drawing on the concepts fundamental to computer science" [2, p. 33]. Although CT is rooted in computer science (CS), Wing stressed that CT is not an explicit capacity equipped by CS professionals, but instead a generic practical skill for everyone [2].

Standing on Wing's call, CT has permeated into educational fields across the globe [3], and coding, or computer programming, a basic concept in CS, has been used as the medium for CT instructions [4]. While coding provides a practical platform to support CT learning activities, CT is deemed broader than coding and CS for its high applicability to other areas which are not necessarily computer-based [5]. Indeed, CT appeared to be a standalone psychological domain, independent from other cognitive constructs [6].

To enrich our understanding of CT, a plethora of studies strove to define the notion and specify its components [7], yet there is no consensus on a generally accepted definition of CT [8]. In recent years, the line of research in conceptualizing CT has been extended to empirical studies, where the relations between CT and other cognitive abilities were explored (e.g., [7, 9]). These studies help build a nomological network of CT as an independent cognitive construct, underpinning the development of CT instructions and assessments [8]. However, the research area is still in its infancy, and more initiatives can be taken in expanding the conception of CT at different educational levels. To bridge this gap, this study explores the connection between CT and other cognitive domains. As a recent trend can be seen in integrating CT into elementary curricula [10], we aimed to investigate the topic in the elementary school context. Specifically, based on the development of mental processing [11], we focused on the traditional cognitive abilities which can be acquired by young children, namely, quantitative skill, categorical skill, and visuospatial skill. The findings will help provide theoretical support for the design of learning resources for elementary CT education. The study is guided by the following research questions.

RQ1: Does CT associate with other cognitive abilities of elementary school students?
RQ2: To what extent does CT associate with other cognitive abilities of elementary school students?

2 Method

2.1 Sample

Participants were recruited from two public primary schools in northern China. Pupils from Grade 3–4 were invited (age 7–10), and a total of 246 students agreed to participate. Note that the schools administered computer science courses from Grade 3, following the municipal education system, and thus this cohort had been exposed to coding activities to some extent.

2.2 Instrument

Assessments for the CT and cognitive abilities were screened. Based on the characteristics of the sample group, the following tests were selected, and a summary is presented in Table 1.

Computational Thinking Test for Lower Primary (CTtLP). To assess students' CT performance, CTtLP was selected [12]. CTtLP was developed with a principled approach using Evidence-Centered Design, geared towards children aged 6–10. Items were designed with maze interface where computational problems were presented (see Fig. 1), covering CT constructs of sequences, directions, loops, events, and conditionals. The content of CTtLP was validated by expert reviews and cognitive interviews, and psychometric properties were reported via field tests, providing sufficient validity and reliability evidence.

The Comprehensive Test of Cognitive Development (CTCD). To investigate children's cognitive abilities, CTCD was referred to [13]. CTCD aimed to measure individual's cognitive development from early adolescence. The tool has been successfully adopted among adolescents, and adequate psychometric qualities were yielded. This study centered on three basic domains (quantitative skill, categorical skill, and visuospatial skill). As our sample is a younger cohort, to adapt to this study, a selection of sub-constructs of the domains was conducted, and descriptions on the sub-constructs are as follows.

- Numeracy: Quantitative skill is assessed by numerical operations. Arithmetic problems covering the four operations (addition, subtraction, multiplication, and division) were provided. Each problem contains two operations (e.g., 7 + 5–3, 3 + 8 ÷ 2). Fifty problems were displayed with increasing difficulty, with a time limit of 4 min.
- Figure induction: This is a sub-dimension of categorical skill. Raven-like matrices were used to measure students' ability to induce the principles of figure formations (see Fig. 2). Five matrices were selected. Each matrix contains several figures underpinned by a certain pattern, based on which students need to identify the next figure.
- Verbal analogy: This is a sub-dimension of categorical skill. Students were asked to solve five verbal analogy problems where induction of semantic relations was examined (see Fig. 3). The items were displayed in the format of (a: b) → (c: ?), meaning "a is to b as c is to ?". Students were required to reason the relationships between words.
- Class inclusion: This is a sub-dimension of categorical skill. The tasks provided pictures of several objects from mixed classes. Students were required to identify the classes of each object and answer questions such as "Which is more: class A or class B?" (see Fig. 4). Six items were included.
- Image manipulation: This is a sub-dimension of spatial skill. Paper folding tasks were provided to test students' ability to manipulate images mentally (see Fig. 5). Five items were used, where students were asked to identify the output of a piece of paper when it is folded along a certain line.
- Mental rotation: This is a sub-dimension of spatial skill. This task was used to examine students' ability to visualize the output of figure rotation (see Fig. 6). Five items were designed using a clock scenario. A figure was put on one hand, and students were required to imagine the how figure appear to be when the hand rotated to the other hand.

Test of Visual Perceptual Skills-Revised (TVPS-R). As spatial perception (or visual perception) is a distinct dimension of spatial skill [14], which is not covered in CTCD, we adopted TVPS-R [15] to measure the construct. Based on the age bracket of the sample, the visual figure-ground subset was selected. The task is to find the target form from the four forms that are presented under a distracting background (see Fig. 7), aiming to assess students' ability to identify shapes under distractions. The parallel subset has been utilized in Chinese primary school context, and test reliability was verified [16].

Table 1. Summary of Instruments

Test	Construct	Description	Item
CTtLP	CT performance	Computational problems presented by maze interfaces	20
TVPS-R	Visual perception	Problems of finding the target form from the figures with distracting backgrounds	5
CTCD	Numeracy	Arithmetic problems solved by the four numerical operations	50
	Figure induction	Raven-like matrices to identify the next figure based on underlying principles	5
	Verbal analogy	Verbal problems of "a is to be as c is to ?" to identify the word based on semantic relations	5
	Class inclusion	Questions of "which is more: class A or class B?" to gauge categorical skill	6
	Image manipulation	Paper folding tasks to visualize the output of folded paper	5
	Mental rotation	Clock task to visualize the output of a rotated figure	5

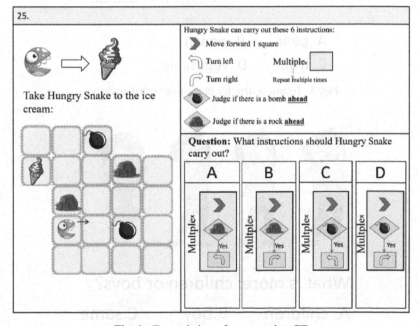

Fig. 1. Example item for measuring CT

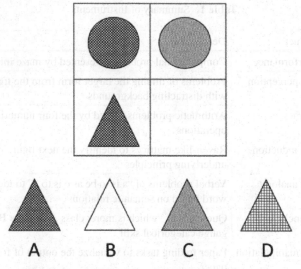

Fig. 2. Example item for measuring figure induction

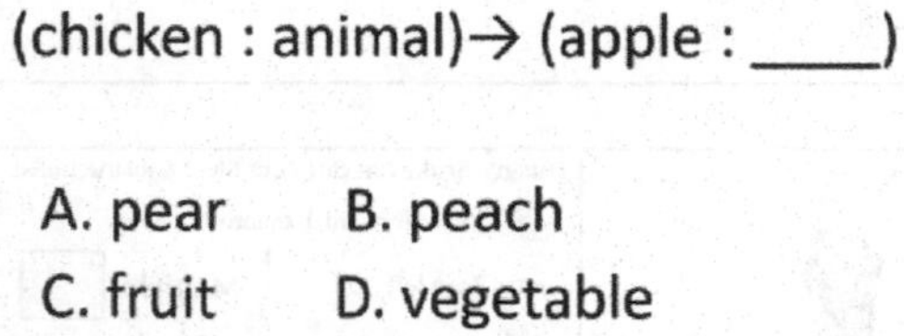

(chicken : animal)→ (apple : _____)

A. pear   B. peach
C. fruit   D. vegetable

Fig. 3. Example item for measuring verbal analogy

What is more: children or boys?

A. children   B.boy   C.same

Fig. 4. Example item for measuring class inclusion

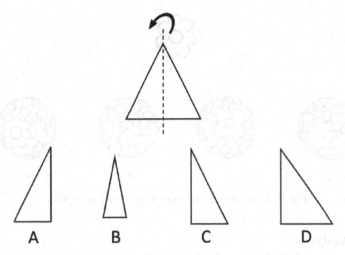

Fig. 5. Example item for measuring image manipulation

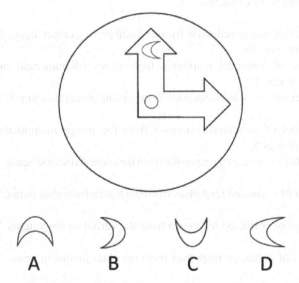

Fig. 6. Example item for measuring mental rotation

2.3 Procedure

All the items were administered in one test. The test was distributed online, and students were invited to the computer rooms at school to complete the tasks under the teacher's invigilation. The numerical items were delivered first via a web page which was automatically closed after 4 min. Then, 40 min were given to complete the remaining items.

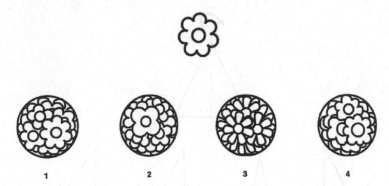

Fig. 7. Example item for measuring visual perception

2.4 Data Analysis

Before performing data analyses, scores for each construct were calculated, where the following variables were extracted:

- CTper: CT performance reflected by the number of correct items in CTtLP. The maximum point was 20.
- Num: Number of corrected responses from items of numerical operations. The maximum point was 50.
- VisPe: Number of corrected responses from visual perception items. The maximum point was 5.
- ImaMa: Number of corrected responses from the image manipulation items. The maximum point was 5.
- MenRo: Number of corrected responses from the mental rotation items. The maximum point was 5.
- FigIn: Number of corrected responses from the figure induction items. The maximum point was 5.
- VerAn: Number of corrected responses from the verbal analogy items. The maximum point was 5.
- ClaIn: Number of corrected responses from the class inclusion items. The maximum point was 6.

To explore the relations between CT skills and the specified cognitive abilities, correlation and regression analyses were conducted with SPSS.

3 Result

3.1 Descriptive Statistics

The descriptive statistics of the variables are presented in Table 2 (N = 246). It can be seen that students performed moderately in CTtLP, showing a mean score of 8.5 out of 20. For cognitive abilities, fair achievement was made in numeracy and visual perceptual tasks, while the categorical tasks (i.e., figure induction, verbal analogy, class inclusion) and spatial tasks (image manipulation, mental rotation) showed slightly weak performance.

3.2 Correlation Analyses

To examine the associations between CT and the specified cognitive abilities, correlation coefficients were calculated with Pearson's r. Results are displayed in Table 3. It indicates that CT had a significant positive correlation with all variables except mental rotation. Moderately high correlates were detected with visual perception (r = .66), figure induction (r = .63), and image manipulation (r = .57), and mild coefficients were yielded with numeracy (r = .29), verbal analogy (r = .44), and mental rotation (r = .30). Unexpectedly, a negative correlation was observed between CT performance and class inclusion, yet not statistically significant.

Table 2. Descriptive Statistics

Variable	Mean	SD	Min	Max
CTper	8.47	4.68	0	19
Num	18.10	7.49	0	48
VisPe	2.09	1.96	0	5
FigIn	1.64	1.46	0	5
VerAn	1.75	1.34	0	5
ClaIn	1.96	1.43	0	6
ImaMa	1.54	1.13	0	4
MenRo	1.27	1.06	0	4

Table 3. Correlations Between CT Performance and Cognitive Abilities

	Num	VisPe	FigIn	VerAn	ClaIn	ImaMa	MenRo
CTper	.29**	.66**	.63**	.44**	−.12	.57**	.30**

Note: ** p < .01

3.3 Regression Analyses

After verifying the correlations between cognitive abilities and CT performance, regression analysis was performed. Multiple linear regression was used with CT scores as the dependent variable, and the measured cognitive constructs as independent variables, where ENTER method was applied. The model summary is reported in Table 4. Results illustrated that the multiple regression model correlates r = .746 with CT performance, indicating that the variables explained 55.6% of variance (F (7,245) = 42.539; p < .001).

In particular, CT performance was significantly positively predicted by, from higher to lower, visual perception (β = .340, p < .001), figure induction (β = .235, p < .001), numerical skill (β = .175, p < .001), and image manipulation (β = .173, p < .001), whereas a negative prediction was observed from class inclusion, yet minimal (β = -.091, p = .045). Collinearity statistics were checked, and results showed that the tolerance values ranged from .412 to .949 and the variance inflation factor (VIF) lay between 1.054 and 2.426, suggesting no collinearity issue [17]. Then, residuals were examined, and normality distribution was confirmed.

Table 4. Summary of Regression Model on CT Performance

	Standardized β	t	R	R^2	Adjusted R^2
Model			.746	.556	.543
Num	.175**	3.949			
VisPe	.340**	5.309			
FigIn	.235**	3.497			
VerAn	.040	.724			
ClaIn	−.091*	−2.015			
ImaMa	.173**	2.946			
MenRo	.016	.328			

Note: * p < .05, ** p < .01

4 Discussion

This study aims to investigate the associations between CT and other cognitive domains in the elementary school context. Through correlation and regression analyses, a strong interplay was found between CT performance and several specific cognitive abilities, bringing both theoretical and practical implications to the CT field.

The findings enriched the theoretical conception of CT as a psychological construct. Specific cognitive abilities could explain more than half of the variance in CT performance, indicating that CT is underpinned by a series of cognitive skills. While a plethora of studies has been done in defining CT and its components in different educational contexts [7, 18], this study has expanded the line of research by adding potential elements (i.e., numeracy, inductive reasoning, visual perception, spatial visualization) to CT operational definitions. Yet as there is still half of the variance that remained unexplained, CT seems to be a standalone psychological construct, independent from the associated abilities. The findings support the idea that there are underlying cognitive processes to scaffold the conceptualization and understanding of CT [19], which chimed with related studies (e.g., [8, 20]).

Practically, explicit cognitive correlates of CT were observed, which could shed light on CT elementary education. Visual perceptual skills were found to be the strongest predictor, indicating that pupils' ability to identify symbols and shapes plays a critical role in developing CT skills, stressing the need for cultivating children's icon-based thought in educational practices [21]. In line with other studies (e.g., [6, 19]), inductive reasoning skills, measured by figure induction tasks, were found to be a profound predictor variable. As fluid reasoning is fundamental to problem-solving [19], the finding helps verify the practical nature of CT as a problem-solving skill, where abstraction and pattern recognition are leveraged [8]. This implicates educationists to underline the instruction on logical thinking and reasoning, where more programming-independent and text-free learning resources can be provided.

In addition, moderate predictions were found from numerical and spatial skills. Aligned with prior research (e.g., 19, 21), quantitative abilities were closely related to CT, in the possible way that both skills use symbols to express relations of ideas-- math uses equations while CT uses computational instructions [22]. This illustrates the importance of mathematical thinking in supporting children's development of CT. More-over, spatial visualization, measured by image manipulation tasks, was also considered a solid influencer of CT performance, corroborating the findings from related studies (e.g., [9, 20]). As the finding tends to be consistent across educational levels [8], a call for embracing spatial training from early CT education is suggested.

5 Conclusion and Future Research

This study examines the associations between CT and the cognitive abilities of primary school students. In particular, three basic cognitive domains were explored (i.e., quantitative, categorical, and visuospatial), where seven specific dimensions were investigated. Based on correlation and regression analyses, CT was explained with more than half of the variance from the seven variables in total, while significant predicting effects on CT performance were found from visual perception, inductive reasoning, numeracy, and spatial visualization. The findings indicate that while CT is a distinct construct from other cognitive disciplines, the underlying process of the skill is supported by traditional cognitive abilities. By extending the conceptual network of CT, the study helps enrich our understanding and conceptualization of CT. Moreover, based on the supportive role these skills play in the development of CT in young children, practical implications can be drawn regarding the integration of these specific skills into the design of learning resources for elementary CT education.

Note that this is a preliminary study that aims to trial multiple variables with a limited number of items for each construct. In our future research, we aim to involve more items to ensure the psychometric properties of the measured constructs. Also, we aim to expand the research on a larger scale, involving participants from broader demographics (e.g., age, learning experience), where the influence of confounding variables can be investigated. Additionally, to more deeply explore the developmental progression of CT and its cognitive correlates, longitudinal studies are suggested, which could help unravel the causal relationships among the variables.

References

1. Papert, S.: Children, computers and powerful ideas. In: Book Children, Computers and Powerful Ideas. Basic Books (1980)

2. Wing, J.M.: Computational thinking. Commun. ACM **49**(3), 33–35 (2006)
3. Bocconi, S., et al.: Developing computational thinking in compulsory education, European commission. JRC Sci. Policy Rep. **68** (2016)
4. Grover, S., Pea, R.: Computational thinking in K–12: a review of the state of the field. Educ. Res. **42**(1), 38–43 (2013)
5. Armoni, M.: Computing in schools computer science, computational thinking, programming, coding: the anomalies of transitivity in K-12 computer science education. ACM Inroads **7**(4), 24–27 (2016)
6. Román-González, M., Pérez-González, J.-C., Moreno-León, J., Robles, G.: Extending the nomological network of computational thinking with non-cognitive factors. Comput. Hum. Behav. **80**, 441–459 (2018)
7. Xu, F., Zhang, S.: Understanding the source of confusion with computational thinking: a systematic review of definitions. In: Book Understanding the Source of Confusion with Computational Thinking: A Systematic Review of Definitions (2021)
8. Tsarava, K., et al.: A cognitive definition of computational thinking in primary education. Comput. Educ. **179**, 104425 (2022)
9. Tsarava, K., et al.: Cognitive correlates of computational thinking: evaluation of a blended unplugged/plugged-in course. In: Book Cognitive Correlates of Computational Thinking: Evaluation of a Blended Unplugged/Plugged-in Course, pp. 1–9 (2019)
10. Rich, P.J., Hu, H., Christensen, J., Ellsworth, J.: The landscape of computing education in Utah. Grantee Submission (2019)
11. Demetriou, A., Spanoudis, G., Mouyi, A.: The Development of Mental Processing. Wiley, Hoboken (2010)
12. Zhang, S., Wong, K.W.G., Pan, G.: Computational thinking test for lower primary students: design principles, content validation, and pilot testing. In: Book Computational Thinking Test for Lower Primary Students: Design Principles, Content Validation, and Pilot Testing, pp. 345–352 (2021)
13. Demetriou, A., Kyriakides, L.: The functional and developmental organization of cognitive developmental sequences. Br. J. Educ. Psychol. **76**(2), 209–242 (2006)
14. Linn, M.C., Petersen, A.C.: Emergence and characterization of sex differences in spatial ability: a meta-analysis. Child Dev. 1479–1498 (1985)
15. Gardner, M.F.: Test of visual-perceptual skills (non-motor): revised manual. Psychological and Educational Publications, Inc. (1996)
16. Wang, S., Hu, B.Y., Zhang, X.: Kindergarteners' spatial skills and their reading and math achievement in second grade. Early Child. Res. Q. **57**, 156–166 (2021)
17. Menard, S.: Applied Logistic Regression Analysis, Sage (2002)
18. Ezeamuzie, N.O., Leung, J.S.: Computational thinking through an empirical lens: a systematic review of literature. J. Educ. Comput. Res. 07356331211033158 (2021)
19. Gerosa, A., Koleszar, V., Tejera, G., Gómez-Sena, L., Carboni, A.: Cognitive abilities and computational thinking at age 5: evidence for associations to sequencing and symbolic number comparison. Comput. Educ. Open **2**, 100043 (2021)
20. Román-González, M., Pérez-González, J.-C., Jiménez-Fernández, C.: Which cognitive abilities underlie computational thinking? Criterion validity of the computational thinking test. Comput. Hum. Behav. **72**, 678–691 (2017)
21. Strawhacker, A., Bers, M.U.: What they learn when they learn coding: investigating cognitive domains and computer programming knowledge in young children. Educ. Tech. Res. Dev. **67**(3), 541–575 (2018). https://doi.org/10.1007/s11423-018-9622-x
22. Sneider, C., Stephenson, C., Schafer, B., and Flick, L.: Computational thinking in high school science classrooms. Sci. Teach. **81**(5), 53 (2014)

Research on the Integration of Digital Literacy Education and Writing Education in Vocational Colleges

Jiayina Jianaer[✉] [iD]

Security School, Xinjiang Police College, Urumqi, China
421894501@qq.com

Abstract. Today's society has stepped into the era of digital economy, so it is urgent to improve the national digital literacy. In 2021, China proposed the Program of Action for Improving the Digital Literacy and Skills of the Whole People, aiming to improve the digital literacy of the whole people and meet the needs of the development of times. As a higher vocational college cultivating high quality technical talents in the era of digital economy, it is bound to face the problem of improving the digital literacy of teachers and students. As a teaching staff of public courses in higher vocational colleges, the author discusses the integration of digital literacy education and writing education from the perspective of writing teaching, and shares thoughts and ideas in the process of education and teaching in order to improve students' digital literacy.

Keywords: Digital Literacy · Higher Vocational Colleges · Writing Education · Integration

1 Introduction

Today's social development has entered the era of digital economy. Through the study and research of the Guidance on Developing Digital Economy Stability and Expanding Employment issued by the National Development and Reform Commission in 2018 and the Advice on Implementing the Construction Plan of High-level Vocational Schools and Majors with Chinese Characteristics issued by the Ministry of Education in 2019, it is not hard to see that in such a new era, China attaches importance to the cultivation of high-end digital talents, and clearly indicates the need to develop and enhance the level of digital literacy of the whole people. Especially in the 2020 pandemic, schools have been able to keep classes open through the emergency nationwide online education program. This pandemic has once again reminded us that to address the transition in the era of digital economy for education field is urgently needed.

Talent is the first resource needed for a country's economic and social development. When the social development enters a new stage of development, namely the era of digital economy, the demand of the whole society for high-quality technical talents to adapt to this stage will increase rapidly. As the main front of cultivating high-quality technical talents in the era of digital economy, higher vocational colleges are bound to face the problem of improving the digital literacy of teachers and students. To a certain extent, the level of digital literacy can fully prove the quality of future talents, their abilities to adapt to the future society, and their abilities to innovate and practice. Therefore, as educators, we all shoulder the mission of the Time to comprehensively improve their own and students' digital literacy. The author thinks that, in addition to the university library which has been responsible for the mission of training digital literacy, the major courses and public basic courses also put the task of improving students' digital literacy on the agenda and create an environment that can truly improve students' digital literacy through the efforts of the whole society, the government, schools and teachers. Under the influence of both explicit education and implicit education, students can quickly improve their quality and be fully prepared for future employment. Here are some thoughts on the integration of writing education and digital education in vocational colleges for your reference.

2   The Definition of Digital Literacy

Digital Literacy consists of two words, "digital" and "literacy". The meaning of "digital" is closely connected to the technologies related to digits, and "literacy" is the ability to adapt to the environment.

There are many explanations of digital literacy at home and abroad, among which Israeli scholar has a comprehensive and objective interpretation of digital literacy. The concept of digital literacy was first formally proposed in 1994 by Professor Yoram Eshet-Alkalai from the Open University of Israel. In his view, the conceptual framework of digital literacy consists of five parts: first is Photo-Visual Literacy, the ability to interpret visual representations; second is Reproduction Literacy, the ability to copy and recreate existing digital information; third is Branching Literacy, the ability to construct knowledge through nonlinear hypertext navigation; forth is Information Literacy, the ability to think critically about digital information; fifth is Socio-Emotional Literacy, the ability to share knowledge and communicate emotions through digital means of communication [2]. It explains the digital literacy refers to the ability to use information technology and digital information confidently, independently, critically and innovatively in study, work, daily life and social life [3]. His conceptual framework provides a relatively clear direction for our teaching research and teaching reform, especially the fourth Information Literacy, that is, the ability to maintain critical thinking on digital information. For teachers training vocational students in the new era, the improvement of this kind of ability and quality is particularly important.

In November 2021, the Central Cyberspace Affairs Commission issued the Program of Action for Improving the Digital Literacy and Skills of the Whole People (hereinafter referred to as the Program of Action). On the premise of fully absorbing relevant international concepts and concept definitions, the Program of Action put forward the concept of digital literacy with Chinese characteristics, and unified relevant discourse expressions as well. Opening chapter of the Program of Action clearly pointed out that digital literacy and skills are the collection of a series of qualities and abilities such as digital acquisition, production, use, evaluation, interaction, sharing, innovation, security and ethics, which the citizens of digital society should possess in their study, work and life, stating "literacy" and "skills" side by side [4].

Although digital literacy has become a hot topic in academic research and discussion, the research on digital literacy in writing education is limited, and there are few studies on the integration of digital literacy education in writing education.

Language education from the perspective of digital literacy pays particular attention to the ways of meaning presentation, interpersonal interaction, digital behavior pattern, communicative values and identity recognition construction. The establishment of these dimensions helps to respond to the important concerns of language education in the age of digital intelligence [3]. Writing education, as a branch of language education, can use this analysis for reference. In other words, writing education from the perspective of digital literacy is not concerned with information and technology in the traditional sense, but with presentation methods, interpersonal communication methods, digital behavior paradigm, communicative values and identity recognition. Therefore, when we integrate digital literacy education into writing education, the focus of teaching reform should be tilted towards presentation methods, interpersonal communication methods, digital behavior paradigm, communicative values and identity.

3 The Basic Situation of Digital Literacy of Vocational College Students

Vocational college students are the darlings of the digital economy era and the aborigines of the information era. The so-called digital literacy of vocational college students is an effective integration of general skills and special skills for future career development, which can facilitate their efficient use of digital technology to study and work, and achieve the goal of talent training. It is a complex group of abilities and traits with dynamic, prospective and powerful occupational context [5]. It must be emphasized here that the digital literacy of vocational college students is not only improved through the professional core curriculum group, but the result of the common education and effective integration of all the public basic curriculum group and professional curriculum group.

In general, the digital literacy of Chinese higher vocational students is not high, which is an urgent problem to be considered and solved by current education circle.

Specifically, the following points can be used to further understand and find problems of the present situation of college students' digital literacy. Firstly, keen on digital internet activities, usually for entertainment; secondly, with certain retrieval ability, but the way to obtain information is single; thirdly, mainly browse digital content, but not integrate into knowledge system; fourthly, digital security awareness is weak and self-control ability is lower; fifthly, poor problem-solving skills and lack of critical thinking [6].

As "digital immigrant" teachers, facing such a "digital indigenous" group, on the premise of constantly improving our digital literacy, we must also study how to improve students' digital literacy through school teaching, so as to make contribution to the construction of digital China.

4   Research on the Integration

On the morning of September 13, 2016, the Conference on the Research Results of Developing Chinese Students' Core Literacy was held in Beijing Normal University. The conference announced the overall framework and basic connotation of Developing Chinese students' core literacy. The conference proposed that Chinese students develop core qualities with "well-developed people" as the core concept, divided into cultural basis, independent development and social participation, which is manifested in six elements, including cultural heritage, scientific spirit, learning to learn, healthy life, responsibility, practice and innovation. The third element "learning to learn" states that the information awareness which college students should possess are the ability to obtain, evaluate, identify and use information consciously and effectively, the ability of digital survival, actively adapt to the "Internet+" and other social information development trend, and the network ethics and information security awareness, etc. [7]. Although the specific requirements and framework of Chinese college students' digital literacy education is not explicitly stated, we can understand the urgent demand and necessity of improving college students' digital literacy in the era of digital economy.

In November 2021, the Central Cyberspace Affairs Commission issued the Program of Action for Improving the Digital Literacy and Skills of the Whole People (hereinafter referred to as the Program of Action). The Program of Action solves a series of important basic issues, such as what is digital literacy, how to improve the digital literacy and skills of the whole people, which is a milestone in the theory and practice of digital literacy in China, and also pulled a starting gun for the systematic and standardized cultivation and promotion of digital literacy in various regions and fields of the country [8].

In order to improve the digital literacy of the whole people, and as the main force of future employment, university students and vocational college students are no doubt the first group to be cultivated and educated with digital literacy in our whole society. School education is the leader of digital literacy education.

The digital literacy education in schools and the improvement of students' digital literacy is a complex goal that requires the participation and linkage of many parties. In order to seize the call of times to improve the digital literacy of students in higher vocational colleges, the society, enterprises, schools, teachers and students must participate in and help schools develop appropriate talent training programs on the basis of market demand, job requirements and professional characteristic. As the main front of improving students' digital literacy, the three-foot platform should be handed over to teachers to design and reform the specific teaching modes and teaching programs in the end. And, of course, programs to improve students' digital literacy are dynamic, since we are in the age of an explosion of information, and there will be higher demands or requirements in the ever-evolving digital economy. The talent training program designed by us is not a constant one, but a dynamic program that carries out irregular evaluation to update according to the needs of the market, enterprises and positions. Eventually, only the vocational college students trained under the joint participation and cooperation of the society, enterprises, schools and new ideas, can truly help the smooth transformation of enterprises and realize the power of digital talents in the future work.

In recent years, as a common course in vocational colleges, writing education is undertaking not only the task of ideological and political teaching reform of the writing course, but also the task of consciously improving the digital literacy of higher vocational students through the teaching of this course. In view of the current situation and problems of college students' digital literacy, firstly, keen on digital internet activities, usually for entertainment; secondly, with certain retrieval ability, but the way to obtain information is single; thirdly, mainly browse digital content, but not integrate into knowledge system; fourthly, digital security awareness is weak and self-control ability is lower; fifthly, poor problem-solving skills and lack of critical thinking. It is necessary for the teaching staff of writing course to conduct in-depth research on the integration of writing education and digital literacy education and formulate a new teaching plan.

The following is to share thoughts on the integration of digital literacy education and vocational college writing education from the level of social, school, enterprise, teacher, student and the reform of specific teaching methods.

4.1 Social Level

Standing at the height of the overall development of the country, The Program of Action has made a global deployment and improved the top-level design for strengthening the digital literacy and skills of the whole people. In the next step, relevant government departments need to carry out the plan to improve college students' digital literacy and skills, build the digital literacy and skills education framework for schools or alliances, and embed the requirements of digital literacy and skills enhancement into the curriculum of school education as soon as possible [8]. Only in this way can school education have more concrete teaching reform ideas.

School libraries, public libraries, cultural centers and other social education institutions should support school education by providing digital infrastructure and digital literacy training resources, focusing on cultivating students' lifelong learning ability and digital adaptability. We need to align our national strategy with the development of times [8]. Aiming at the goal of talent training in vocational colleges, to design specialized digital literacy and skills programs for college students. If all kinds of libraries can truly realize the above functions, it will certainly boost the digital literacy education of all kinds of colleges and universities to a new level. Talent training programs of higher vocational colleges are closely related to social needs. If students can learn from all kinds of libraries and cultural centers in the stage of school education, it will undoubtedly be a successful case that science and technology museum and other social education institutions get the practice opportunity of digital literacy education related to the professional ability of the post.

4.2 School Level

No matter in what era, school education always needs to avoid "closed-door". Higher vocational colleges in the era of digital economy should take the initiative to contact government departments and enterprises to learn about the latest policies, and study the development direction of enterprises and specific job demands, so as to train talents in a targeted way.

Therefore, higher vocational colleges should combine the characteristics of various majors, employment demand and other factors to pay close attention to the study of digital technology application of higher vocational students, and integrate the cultivation of digital literacy and skills throughout the school education system. Let the teachers of specialized courses and public basic courses organically integrate this new educational task into the whole process of classroom teaching, social practice and employment teaching practice.

It must be emphasized that teachers are the practitioners of digital literacy education. Therefore, schools have the obligation to improve the relevant systems of digital literacy of teachers, so as to facilitate teachers to carry out educational practice smoothly. Under the talent training mode of combining work with study in higher vocational colleges, it is a good choice to organize part of the teachers to investigate relevant industry associations and enterprises or carry out various kinds of learning and training at home and abroad. In a word, only when teachers do enough work can digital literacy education be promoted to a higher level.

As the school, in order to meet the needs of times development, must upgrade the hardware in a timely manner of education teaching need upgrading, such as the digital campus construction, formulate the focus of the work for the school to plan and implement, have a combination of hardware and software requirements only under the premise of will succeed to the implementation of the related education teaching activities.

4.3   Enterprise Level

The main position of employment for higher vocational students, enterprises should provide digital skills practice platform based on improving students' digital literacy during their study and internship.

Through the impact of the epidemic on the viability, resilience and innovation capacity of enterprises, it once again provides sufficient foundation for enterprises to adapt to the transformation of the digital economy era. Therefore, for not being eliminated in the future market competition, enterprises must start to cooperate with higher vocational colleges as soon as possible, in order to cultivate high-quality compound talents for their transformation.

Enterprises are required to present the digital ability demand reports of various specific positions for the schools, including quality demand of digital management, application and professional talents, It connects with the corresponding professional groups, even detailed to each major, which runs through the digital talent training program for higher vocational students jointly formulated by the school, and integrates enterprise specific project into higher vocational teaching plan, so that higher vocational colleges have a clear self-understanding of talent training in different fields [9].

4.4   Teacher Level

At the teacher level, it is necessary to improve teachers' digital literacy, which must be regarded as a necessary skill for teachers' education in vocational colleges. The urgent online teaching caused by the 2020 pandemic can fully tell us that the level of teachers' digital literacy can directly affect the quality of digital literacy education and curriculum education.

The most effective way to improve the digital literacy of teachers is to participate in the digital literacy training or professional courses through school assignment or teachers' self-study, to improve the policy basis, theoretical knowledge, latest ideas and basic skills related to digital literacy.

Moreover, teachers need to study new teaching methods, teaching models and innovative teaching practice program in the integration of digital literacy education and writing teaching.

4.5 Student Level

College students are not only the main object of higher education, but also important participants in digital life, as well as the main body of digital work and digital innovation in the future. It can be said that the improvement of college students' digital literacy and skill is of vital importance for China to realize the power of digital talents [4].

Due to the digital age, every subject is in an ocean of information world. College students, in particular, find it difficult to spare time to take additional courses related to digital literacy amid the pressures of studying at school, preparing for graduate and doctoral exams, and finding jobs. An alternative and effective way is to appropriately embed the concepts, models and methods of digital literacy education into the teaching system construction of each basic course and major course [10], this new way of integrated teaching method will be more effective from the perspective of students. That is to say, rather than set up separate professional courses related to digital literacy education, if we can put the digital literacy education concept embedded in each course teaching process, then it can make students get faster improvement in the digital literacy education environment, in order to meet the requirements of the digital era for vocational college graduates.

When we choose teaching methods, we also need to make a comprehensive assessment and analysis of the overall situation of the student group. Students from different starting points, different cultural backgrounds and different regions have certain differences. On the premise that the main teaching method remains unchanged, appropriate adjustment should be made in some links and task-dominated stages. For example, the comprehensive digital literacy, growth environment and learning conditions of students in western China and developed coastal areas are certainly different, so it is an important part for teachers to understand the learning situation.

4.6 Level of Teaching Content

In terms of teaching content, take the professional public course Safety prevention Technology and the course Practical Writing as examples.

First, the school needs to organize specialized faculty to investigate and survey typical positions in industries and enterprises, and establish typical job group which is combined with the school's employment.

Second, the school organizes the modification of talent training programs for this typical job group, in the meantime, the specialized faculty can visit other colleges and study the construction of the same major, also can invite industry or enterprise professionals to participate in the modification of the school's talent cultivation plan, so as to make our plan suit post-employment requirements, targeted to improve the talent training scheme.

Third, focus on creating a batch of curriculum system that meets the needs of the job and aims at completing the project. In other words, the curriculum setting mode of traditional public basic courses, specialized basic courses and specialized core courses should be broken, and the teaching content of this course should be selected according to the completion of specific projects. There will be multiple traditional knowledge and skills in such course content, which can help us cultivate compound application talents.

At last, it is worth noting that we set up new courses with the goal of completing specific projects, so there will be a variety of traditional course content in each new course. Taking Practical Writing as an example, teachers must understand the typical positions and new course structure of this major in advance. Then sort out the content that students must master and the content of the extension part, so that students can master the Knowledge of practical Writing required to carry out the project smoothly.

4.7 Level of Teaching Methods

According to the above ideas, in terms of teaching methods, the author noticed that the students in the digital era are what we call "digital natives". For them, in the choice of teaching methods, as "digital immigrants", we should learn to explore suitable methods from the perspective of students, such as online and offline hybrid teaching mode.

As one of the practitioners of online teaching during the epidemic, the author has some knowledge of students' digital sensitivity and adaptability. Therefore, the author thinks that the fragmentary theoretical knowledge of traditional courses required by each project can be pushed to students before class through the teaching platform-- Wisdom Tree. In the development stage of the project, teachers can guide them to complete the project, and discuss, summarize, expand after class. During the process of completing the project, students' digital literacy can be exercised and improved virtually in every link, which includes students' digital acquisition, production, use, evaluation, interaction, sharing, innovation, security, ethics and other abilities and qualities, rather than setting up separate professional courses to teach students.

The above are the author's thoughts and suggestions on the current integration of curriculum teaching and digital literacy education. The final result can be obtained only after comprehensive evaluation of the whole teaching process and effect through teaching practice. In specific operation, we should first prepare an open class or experimental class, and finally determine the most suitable teaching mode based on the listening experience of experts and scholars from enterprises, schools and students, so as to encourage more teachers to participate in the practical research on the integration of digital literacy and curriculum teaching.

5   Conclusion

Digital literacy education is very complex and must be carried out successfully through multi-party cooperation. This paper, as a "digital immigrant", puts forward a new idea on the integration of curriculum teaching and digital literacy education by combing and referring to the definition of digital literacy at home and abroad and analyzing the current situation and problems of digital literacy of vocational college students in China. The research on digital literacy in the field of language-related specific curriculum education has just started in China. It is hoped that the sharing of this paper can stimulate new academic growth points in the field of linguistics education, and help China's language education explore new directions and build a new ecology.

References

1. Chongde, L.: Research on Core Literacy of Student Development in 21st Century. Beijing Normal University Publishing House (2016)
2. Eshet-Alkalai, Y.: Digital literacy: a conceptual framework for survival skills in the digital era. J. Educ. Multim. Hyperm. **13**(1), 93–106 (2004)
3. Li, Z., Sun, N.: Research on the Integration of Digital Literacy Education and Art Education, China Electronic Education, May, 2017
4. Office of the Central Cyberspace Affairs Commission. The Program of Action for Improving the Digital Literacy and Skills of the Whole People [EB/OL]. http://www.cac.gov.cn/2021-11/05/c_1637708867754305.htm. Accessed 25 Dec 2021
5. Ting, T.: Research on construction and application of evaluation model of students' digital literacy in higher vocational colleges, Master's Thesis, Guangdong Polytechnic Normal University, June, 2021
6. Zhengqiang, L.: Current situation, problems and educational approaches of college students' digital literacy in China. Inf. Theory Pract. July, 2020
7. Core Literacy Research Group. Chinese students develop core literacy, J. Chin. Educ. (2016)
8. Peng, X., Qingxiang, Z.: Road to a powerful country with digital talents: outline of action to improve national digital literacy and skills and strategy of digital literacy education for college students. J. Agric. Libr. Inf. (2022)
9. Hong, T., Ting, T.: Research on logic and direction of cultivating digital literacy of higher vocational students in digital economy era, China Vocational and Technical Education, February, 2021
10. Limei, Z., Lixia, H.: Discussion on collaborative construction scheme of professional curriculum system in colleges and universities oriented by digital literacy education. Intelligence Quest July, 2021

Improving Information Literacy of Engineering Doctorate Based on Team Role Model

Liwei Bao[1(✉)], Lianhong Cai[1], Jinghan Liu[2], and Yongwei Wu[1]

[1] Computer Science and Technology, Tsinghua University, Beijing, China
csbaolw@mail.tsinghua.edu.cn
[2] The Library, Tsinghua University, Beijing, China

Abstract. The goal of engineering doctorate (EngD) training is a unique educational programme in that improves information literacy of a doctoral study with the needs and innovations of the respective industrial sector. Based on the six core concepts of The Framework of Information Literacy in Higher Education, this paper extracted the specific requirements for the literacy of engineering doctoral students, and proposed to improve their information literacy ability from the comprehensive ability (innovation, leadership, execution). In view of the interdisciplinary integration and innovation of EngD students, this paper proposes an information literacy promotion framework based on team role model, which links the knowledge innovation process, information literacy ability and role positioning, and integrates conventional information literacy cultivation methods and promotion methods into the education process of EngD students. This team role model is illustrated through the use of a case study based on the work of AI electron Microscopy.

Keywords: Engineering Doctorate · Information Literacy · Team Role

1 Introduction

In 2011, the Academic Degrees Committee of The State Council issued the Plan for The Establishment of Professional Degrees for Doctor of Engineering, which established the professional degree of engineering doctorate (EngD), marking that the EngD was officially included in the graduate education system of colleges and universities in China. According to the Plan, EngD students should have the ability to carry out engineering technology innovation, organize planning and implement engineering technology research and development [1]. The research engineer (RE) should have strong information literacy ability in the interdisciplinary field of innovation, leadership in the process of organizing and planning technological progress, and executive power in the implementation of engineering technology to solve complex engineering problems in enterprises. Although there have been many studies on the education and training system of REs, no relevant research results have been published on information literacy education.

In 2015, ACRL published the Framework of Information Literacy in Higher Education (hereinafter referred to as the Framework [2]), proposed six core concepts of

W. Hong and Y. Weng (Eds.): ICCSE 2022, CCIS 1813, pp. 42–50, 2023.
https://doi.org/10.1007/978-981-99-2449-3_5

information literacy, proposed the teaching scope and methods of information literacy, and proposed the extended definition of information literacy: It is pointed out that information literacy includes reflective exploration of information, understanding of how information is generated and evaluated, and a series of comprehensive abilities to use information to create new knowledge and participate in community learning [3,4]. The six core concepts can guide all kinds of information literacy teaching plans and curriculum design, but these provisions are not immutable [2].

Although the Framework has expanded the new vision of information literacy education and added new contents, it has not paid enough attention to the improvement of information literacy ability, such as the lack of training mode for team cooperation in the field of interdisciplinary application. More attention should be paid to the library database using methods and query technology, but more needs to be inspired to the retrieval strategy and the formation process of innovative thinking; Classroom education pays attention to technical specialized courses, emphasizes the teacher-led teaching mode, and ignores the communication between teachers and students, especially the interaction with the authoritative experts in the field. Lack of social culture, economic management and other comprehensive literacy and organizational leadership training [5]. In order to better serve the national innovation-driven development strategy, this paper proposes a role-based information literacy promotion framework for EngD students, aiming at fostering innovation, leadership, and execution in the engineering field.

2 Information Literacy that Should be Possessed by Professional Students

Information literacy educators pay most attention to the change and renewal of training content. The Framework only puts forward six interrelated core concepts of information literacy, but does not provide a specific list of learning skills. Therefore, this paper attempts to reorganize the core concepts of the Framework according to the characteristics of EngD and extract the literacy requirements that should be required for RE ability improvement.

2.1 Six Concepts and Abilities of Information Literacy

1. *Searching as Strategic Exploration* revolves around the process, characteristics and strategies of information retrieval. Searching is not simply to find information, but to train students to design and customize retrieval strategies by rational use of divergent and convergent thinking, and to select searching tools that match information needs and retrieval strategies. Gradually understand the organization of information system, and can flexibly use different types of searching language, reasonable use of various retrieval approaches; The searching process and results can be effectively managed by adjusting retrieval questions and improving searching strategies based on retrieval results [2].

2. *Information Creation as a Process* revolves around recognizing the forms and types of information resources. Information resource collection is not only a process, it is

important to train workers, realized the innovation process is different, the functions and features of information will have limitations, the need to different stages, different form of judging the value of information product, quality, and combined with its information needs to choose and use of all kinds of information products [4].

3. *Scholarship as Conversation* revolves around the exchange and collaboration of information in scientific research. Communication is not a brief communication, but to train the students to master the research methods and demonstration paradigms of the discipline, so that they have the ability to participate in academic communication; When participating in academic exchanges, it is necessary to abide by the information ethics and moral norms of relevant fields, rationally judge the value of specific academic works, summarize the development and change of specific topic views, and push academic exchanges further.

4. *Authority Is Constructed and Contextual* revolves around the evaluation or value judgment of information resources. It is important to identify the authoritative information in the field scene. It is necessary to cultivate the students to learn to use relevant standards, terms, indicators and other research tools to find and discover the authoritative views and suggestions, and at the same time to hold a reserved attitude towards the authority system and its creation process, and grasp the relevant factors that may affect the judgment of information value. In the process of information creation, we strive to establish our own authority, pursue the accuracy and reliability of information, and respect intellectual property rights and academic ethics and norms.

5. *Research as Inquiry* is the concept of research around the whole process of scientific research information activities, including problem discovery, exploration and research, formation of new cognition, research results and so on. Exploration is not simply to come up with solutions, but to train students to find gaps or problems that need to be solved within and between disciplines, re-question and review existing research results, explore the use of more advanced research methods, more diversified disciplinary perspectives, and propose solutions to the problem in the whole process of information activities.

6. *Information Has Value* revolves around the social and economic value of information. To train the students to understand the basic connotation of intellectual property rights, the meaning and characteristics expressed by the knowledge of fair use of copyright, open access and public domain; Understand how the various values of information products affect their generation, dissemination and access, understand the reasons why information is easy or difficult to obtain, and the reasons why information products of individuals or groups are ignored or marginalized; Understand the rights and obligations of individuals to participate in information activities, and master citation norms and reference rules in academic writing [4].

2.2 Training Framework for Information Literacy

The ultimate goal for REs is to improve their comprehensive abilities, namely, innovation, leadership and execution, which is closely related to the concept of information literacy: Searching as Strategic Exploration and Information Creation as a Process. Because innovation needs through retrieving found himself thought, theory, method and technology has been put forward, or a similar idea. Only by constantly changing retrieval strategies, researching, creating, and modifying information can we create new information. Scholarship as Conversation emphasized the leadership authority comes from the scene, created by the information also need to communicate constantly enrich, extend, and confirmed that these exchanges and mentor, not only to students, more needs to be recognized authority in the field, good leadership is not to let others to obey, but to persuade and inspire others to follow your act together. This article emphasizes the exploration that is research and information have value to reveal the importance of executive force, light has innovative ideas and good leadership, no exploration cannot obtain the final results, discovering problems, explore research, research achievements, the formation of new cognitive access to all need the spirit of perseverance, but also want to consider the social and economic value of the information, It needs to be protected during execution. The cultivation of information literacy is the foundation of the improvement of comprehensive ability and an important factor to improve the training quality of vocational and doctoral students. The relationship between innovation, leadership and execution and information literacy concepts is shown in Fig. 1.

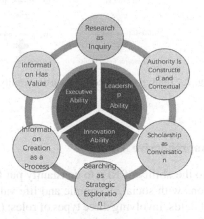

Fig. 1. Comprehensive ability and information literacy training framework for EngD students

The cultivation of EngD students must be closely combined with the solution of major national needs and important engineering and technical problems. It is an urgent problem to implement the cultivation and promotion of individual innovation, leadership, and executive ability so that they can solve profound frontier theories and broad interdisciplinary problems in a short time.

3 Role-Based Framework for Improving Information Literacy of EngD

In order to grow into leading innovative talents, RE need to take on various roles in innovation, organization and implementation of major tasks. They show and improve their abilities by constantly changing roles. Literature [6] proposed that the CRIE model was adopted to represent the four roles of engineering doctoral students, namely, consultant, researcher, innovator and entrepreneur. The model emphasized the improvement of individual ability and did not consider the collaborative knowledge innovation of the team. We analyzed the relationship between team role and comprehensive ability, and based on the team role theory proposed by Dr. Belbin, former director of Industrial Training Department of Cambridge University [7], we created a framework for improving information literacy based on team role, as shown in Fig. 2. In this framework, innovation, leadership and execution are supported by different roles. And in the training process, let the students consciously realize the role they should assume and the role of ability demand, can achieve faster ability improvement.

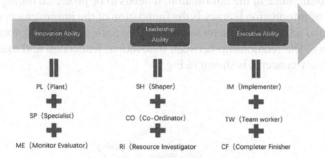

Fig. 2. Team role and comprehensive ability

3.1 Team Role and Comprehensive Ability

Innovation ability refers to the ability of REs to constantly put forward new ideas, new methods and new inventions with social, economic and life values in various practical activities and professional fields, involving three types of roles: (1) Plant (PL): they have strong creative ability, offer suggestions for the progress and development of the team, and are innovators and inventors of the team. Sometimes, however, their ideas are so radical that they risk being ignored in implementation. Even so, they are independent, intelligent, original providers of ideas; (2) Specialist (SP): They focus their attention on what they are good at and pay less attention to other fields. (3) Monitor Evaluator (ME): Be critical and good at making wise decisions after careful consideration. A person who has the quality of supervising people usually makes no wrong decisions.

Leadership ability is a series of activities and behaviors, we can see leadership in many places, it is the core of everything we do well. There are three types of roles involved: (1) Coordinator (CO): able to pool the strength of the team to work towards the common goal, and achieve the team goal by knowing and using people well. (2) Resource Investigator (RI): they are not only good at interpersonal communication and exploring new opportunities, but also good at exploring available and usable resources. (3) Shaper (SH): They challenge others and care about winning. When encountering difficulties during the operation, I will actively find solutions.

Executive ability, for individuals, means to complete their tasks on time, with good quality and quantity; For the team, it means achieving the team's strategic goals within a specified time frame. Leaders not only need to be able to make strategies and plans and give instructions, but more importantly, they need to be able to execute. Three types of roles are involved: (1) Implementer (IM): they attach their loyalty and interests to team goals and pay little attention to individual needs. (2) Team worker (TW): They have staying power and drive, attach importance to details, are not influenced by external motivation or pressure, and like to complete all tasks by themselves. (3) Completer Finisher (CF): strong observation, good at communication.

A role can correspond to multiple students, tutors or project participants, and a PhD student can also correspond to multiple roles. The role model can expand the information literacy framework oriented to individual learning to the information literacy framework oriented to team collaboration, which is more suitable for the characteristics of EngD training.

3.2 The Framework for Improving Information Literacy

The comprehensive ability of industry, medical and biological engineering is manifested in engineering innovation, leading the team to implement transformation and application, solving major national needs, and completing major national projects. Considering the characteristics of engineering doctoral training, colleges and universities have independently formulated the training program for EngD students. However, due to the lack of communication among REs due to part-time, the improvement of information literacy has been affected. Based on the information literacy framework of EngD based on team roles model, this paper designs the information literacy improvement framework, as shown in Fig. 3. This framework organically combines the training objectives of EngD students with ability training and team role, and puts forward a series of measures to improve information literacy on the basis of conventional training.

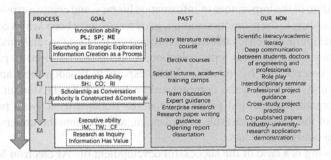

Fig. 3. The framework for improving information literacy

In the three links of knowledge innovation, the concept of information literacy is needed to provide guidance for different roles. The role bearers here are not only REs, but also other personnel, such as library educators, RE tutors, and other project members, who are integrated into the team-oriented information literacy framework as monitors, motivators, and cohesion persons.

Knowledge acquisition (KA) phase is important to cultivate students' innovation ability, the team members the ability to analyze and put forward the idea that team members with clear roles and responsibility, through searching strategy, develop skills at the same time, the process to create information should be enhanced and the retrieval ability, regularly attend lectures, academic training camp to better fit for role.

At the stage of knowledge integration (KI), leadership should be cultivated to strengthen team cooperation, coordinators and resource experts should have a clear understanding of research problems, and motivators should inspire others to form a new knowledge system based on practical problems. For these three roles, students need to actively participate in interdisciplinary seminars and in-depth communication with professionals to increase their knowledge. The authority comes from the scene, to broaden their horizons and master the forefront of the industry, engineering cases and management concepts.

In the stage of knowledge application (KA), executive ability should be cultivated. Completer Finisher and implementer should realize the final goal unremittingly. Team worker should understand intellectual property rights, master copyright, and learn to use them to realize knowledge innovation. For the three types of roles, the idea that information has value and exploration is research should run through all aspects of the application field. The whole should be seen and the phased achievements should be considered, such as invention patents, high-quality papers, project awards, and international, national, or industrial standard recognition can all be regarded as the achievements of knowledge application.

4   Case Study

Since 2012, our department has recruited more than 100 EngD students. In the years of educational affairs, we first urged students to complete the training program, and at the same time assisted the tutor to improve the training quality of EngD students, strengthen the understanding of the importance of information literacy, and create a cross-integration platform. According to the promotion model, good results have been achieved. For example, add special literature retrieval lectures, hire experts to teach the relationship between literature retrieval and doctoral topic selection; Students are required to participate in cutting-edge presentations by interdisciplinary experts to broaden their approaches to problem solving; Strengthen the communication between EngD students and Ph.D. students by organizing doctoral forum; Encourage students to actively participate in the forefront of the research institute organization, and promote the understanding and understanding between students.

The following is a case of the successful development of "AI electron Microscopy" [6] by the interdisciplinary team of EngD students in Tsinghua University. There were three REs, S1 from scanning electron microscope, S2 from materials and S3 from artificial intelligence, carried out their development work under the guidance of professor T1 (ME). They tried to understand their pain points and bottlenecks in the hope of looking for consolidation, in the field of class a few people in-depth exchange on the habitat artificial recognition of the problem of the great error in electron microscopy, At the same time, S4 (PL) attracted a lot of ideas, through the analysis and integration of a large number of literature, proposed to graft intelligent image recognition technology into the electron microscope. With the encouragement and support of S2 tutor T2 academician and S3 tutor T3 (SH and CO), the team used deep learning algorithm to process high-resolution photos collected by electron microscopy, and solved the bottleneck problem of lack of representation of micro-scale representation results at macro scale. Team to contact the R1 (TW) of iron and steel research institute, he has provided the material sample and the experimental data, such as S3 (IM) through the analysis of the applications of artificial intelligence to the development of new materials characterization, to establish the relationship between material "gene" and performance, shorten the material research and development cycle, in addition, the team members got writing guidance published high quality paper [7]. In the process of developing AI electron microscope, RE undertook and completed the corresponding work according to the role.

5 Conclusion

As a special group of graduate students, the EngD students play an extremely important role in engineering technology innovation, organizational planning and technology implementation by improving their information literacy, and then improving their innovation, leadership and executive ability.

This paper presents an information literacy framework based on team role model, which combines professional development needs with research and innovation activities through nine roles they assume in the team, and integrates information literacy education into three stages of interdisciplinary, cross-integration and innovation of industrial and industrial universities and research institutes. Information literacy concept model based on role ACRL framework by personal accomplishment will improve the whole complementary to ascend, extend the accomplishment for the team through the group roles and literacy concept mapping relationship between well solves the problem of innovation and interdisciplinary, accelerate the work gave birth to the understanding of the concept of academic disciplines to each other, make its rapid involved in research and development process, to build a good environment for knowledge innovation, In addition, we can provide timely professional help such as expert guidance and teacher support to improve students' ability to solve practical problems.

Innovation is inseparable from the understanding of information, and the information literacy shown in the evaluation, understanding and utilization of information is particularly important. In the years of teaching and educational administration work, accompanied by the implementation of school unified training program, some beneficial exploration has been made around improving students' information literacy. The training case proves once again that the information literacy framework based on role model is more conducive to cross-field crossover and integration. Both EngD students and information literacy educators can use this framework to discuss the establishment of information literacy training programs and find course collaborators to jointly design research links and engineering projects closely combined with technological innovation.

References

1. Academic Degrees Committee of the State Council.Notice on Printing and Distributing the Program of Professional Degree Establishment of Doctor of Engineering - government portal of the Ministry of Education of the People's Republic of China. http://www.moe.gov.cn/src site/A22/moe_833/201103/t20110308_117376.html
2. Savard, D.: Seeing through the network: a focus on interdisciplinary student research and information discovery. Ref. Serv. Rev. **46**(1), 4–15 (2018)
3. Julien, H., Gross, M., Latham, D.: The information literacy framework: case studies of successful implementation. J. Educ. Lib. Inf. Sci. **62**, 107–108 (2020)
4. Ince, S., Hoadley, C., Kirschner, P.A.: The role of libraries in teaching doctoral students to become information-literate researchers a review of existing practices and recommendations for the future. Inf. Learn. Sci. **120**(3–4), 159–172 (2019)
5. Kerr, C.I., Ivey, P.C.: The Engineering Doctorate model of consultant/researcher/innovator/entrepreneur for new product development - a gas turbine instrumentation case study. Technovation **23**(2), 95–102 (2003)
6. Engineering degree in the center. Cross-border | cross fusion innovationinnovation leader in engineering. Tsinghua university doctoral case.
7. Ju, Y., Li, S., Yuan, X., et al.: A macro-nano-atomic–scale high-throughput approach for material research. Sci. Adv. **7**(49) (2021)

Reflections and Countermeasures on Open Project-Based Practical Teaching at Universities Under the Epidemic Situation

Jiajie Wang, Gang Cen[✉], Shuhui Wu, Kaihui Wu, Yi Jin, and Chenjie Zhu

Zhejiang University of Science and Technology, 318 Liuhe Road, Xihu District, Hangzhou, Zhejiang, China
gcen@163.com, s.wu@zust.edu.cn

Abstract. Recently, the practical teaching based on open project has gained great progresses in the practice and exploration of talent training at applied universities. In this paper, we have studied the practical teaching under the epidemic situation. There are four affecting factors in terms of that have been considered, which are schools, teachers, students, and the practice environment, with focused on the practice teaching form of independent open projects. By comparing the situation before and under the epidemic, the corresponding countermeasures are proposed. After being evaluated the actual effect and promotion, it is worthy developing and application at other applied universities.

Keywords: Open project · Practical activities · Epidemic situation

1 Introduction

Nowadays, the education mode is changing dramatically. The traditional teacher-centered teaching mode can not meet the education requirements of industries and modern society. As a new inquiry teaching mode, the open project-based practical teaching aims to equip students with the ability of creation, innovation and cultivation. Thus, the students will graduate with excellent comprehensive quality. Consequently, it meets social needs as well as closely follows the pace of China's national development strategy of "Innovative Country". The epidemic situation has heavy effects on the teaching activities, in particular the offline teaching. In order to alleviate the impact of the epidemic and fill in the vacancy of offline teaching, the online teaching has been adopted to the of open project-based practical teaching so as to achieve the purpose of mixed teaching [1].

W. Hong and Y. Weng (Eds.): ICCSE 2022, CCIS 1813, pp. 51–61, 2023.
https://doi.org/10.1007/978-981-99-2449-3_6

2   Independent and Open Project-Based Practical Teaching Activities

2.1   Independent and Open Project-Based Practice Teaching Form

Independent and open project-based practice is one type of teaching activities, which is under the guidance of the cooperative learning theory. It regards the projects as its objective tasks and aims to mobilize project students' team autonomy learning. This teaching mode has been extended to the second classroom to promote the all-round development of students.

Independent and open project-based practical teaching can not only help students learn how to discover new ideas from different perspectives but also enhance students' individual creative ability. Through the practical teaching activities of the open project, students are promoted to learn in stages and improve their ability and deep their understanding. It can be seen that the independent and open project practical teaching is a very effective way to cultivate applied talents [2].

2.2   The Characteristics of Independent and Open Practice Project

The independent and open practice project has five properties that are openness, autonomy, diversity, teamwork and individuality [3]. Hereafter, we will introduce each of them in detail.

Openness: For the practice of independent and open project, the first prime property is that it is open to all students. Any freshmen of various majors at university can be recruited for the project as long as students are interested in practice project. The second one is that the practice content is open to all different kinds of scientific problems. Students can choose their own practice content. In the practice base, students just learn practical methodology or develop technique skills in order to create a new project. Last but not least, the time is open. The practice base is open to students all the time. Students can use any their spare time to practice the practical teaching activities.

Autonomy: The five aspects of autonomy of open projects are fully demonstrated during the practice of independent and open practice projects, which are independent choosing of team members, independent choosing of practice content, independent choosing of practice time, independent choosing of tutors, and independent choose project management.

- The practice project team is set up by students freely. The team members can come from different majors and different departments.
- Regarding the theme of the practice project, students can decide according to their own interests and the requirements of the project as well as the methodologies and technique tools can also be chosen independently.

- Regarding the schedule of practice time, the team members flexibly use their time to work on the project according to their own curriculum arrangements. The during time of the entire practice project can be one or more than one semester.
- According to the content of the practice project, the team can independently choose one or more tutors or experienced senior students to guide and assist them.
- The whole practice project process is managed by students independently, which enriches students' practice experience and makes students' practice more convenient, effective and flexible [4].

Diversity: Tutors from the science and technology innovation base use various ways to teach and guide students, including online and offline interviews, lectures, mobilization meetings, summary reports, and other ways.

Teamwork: The progress of practice project is inseparable from the cooperation of the team. The team members learn together and work together driving by the same project objective, and aim to complete the project through collaborative creation.

Personalization: The project practice can be carried out on the basis of students' own individual interests and practical ability. And they do personalized learning according to their own abilities and conditions.

2.3 The Role of Practice of the Independent and Open Projects

The independent and open practice projects' teaching activities are based on the guiding ideology of the student-centered. This teaching activities are converted the teaching activities to the outside of the classroom so that the curriculum teaching activities are integrated with the extracurricular science and technology practice. It could avoid the disadvantages of the teacher centered teaching and studying purely for the exam. In addition, it forms distinct teaching properties. Through the five autonomies to stimulate students' interest in learning, improve students' comprehensive application ability in finding and solving problems, enhance students' innovative thinking, and improve students' scientific research ability.

3   Analysis of Influencing Factors of Independent and Open Practice Project

There are four factors directly affect the progress of project practice activities of the practical teaching activities of open practice projects at universities [5]. These four factors are university, teachers, students, and practice environment.

As the main participants of the practice project teaching activities, the students' knowledge and skilled are playing a decisive role of the results of the project. In practice, a good environment ensures the smooth progress of the practice project activities. In addition, the innovative construction of the university and the guidance of tutors also are the contributive for the progress of the projects.

The relationship of the influencing factors is shown in the following diagram (Fig. 1).

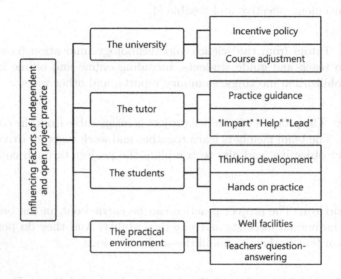

Fig. 1. Influencing factors of independent and open practice project.

3.1   The University

Nowadays, as far as undergraduate education in our country's universities, the universities' undergraduate students focus on learning curriculum knowledge. The learning is mainly about on the fundamental and professional knowledge. Under the examination-oriented education, there is a lack of practical skills training in the four-year curriculum plan, which constraints students' practical and innovative thinking to a certain extent [6]. In addition, other forces, such as college students' innovative practice competitions, are limited by their counterpart majors. Thus, most students cannot participate in these competitions. It is very difficult to implement the beautiful vision of cultivating students' creative thinking and improving students' practical abilities. Therefore, universities should attach importance to the development of students' open project practice teaching. To improve this situation, universities should establish incentive policies for innovative practice and a set of reward systems for innovative credits to fully intrigue students' enthusiasm [7]. In terms of curriculum design, Chinese universities should learn from the foreign teaching models. Hence, universities not only impart cultural knowledge to students but also attach importance to innovate practical activities. For example, the dual system mode of Germany is known as the model of the vocational education around the world. One of the dual systems is that the education of theory and professional knowledge by university. Another system is the vocational skills training of enterprises [8]. This model allows students to absorb theoretical knowledge in the mean while provide them the opportunity to learn skills.

3.2 The Tutor

As disseminator of knowledge, teachers should pay more attention to the development of extracurricular teaching activities in addition to imparting book knowledge in the classroom. Teachers could use their own professional ability to support students in the practice projects and guide students correctly when students encounter problems. Consequently, students' creatively thinking and practical ability can be improved. Teachers should also provide opportunities for project practitioners and their senior students from the same major to get to know each other. In addition, most senior students have more experience and deeper understanding. Thus, they can provide certain help and guardians. In fact, the senior students can be regarded as teaching assistants. Their roles in the complementation of the open practice project are passing, helping, guiding, which are part of tutor's function.

3.3 The Students

Nowadays, it is quite common that undergraduates are trapped in the limited content of their majors. Consequently, most of undergraduates have a relatively narrow range of knowledge, which means their knowledge is not broad enough knowledge from different disciplines. It is particularly common among freshmen and Sophomores. As a results, their inspiration unusually can not be fulfilled in practice since their knowledge lacks horizontal connection and vertical depth. Therefore, students should actively mobilize their subjective initiative and fully participate in the second classroom of innovative practice to create more opportunities for hands-on practice and to improve their own abilities [9]. Gradually, they will gain more achievements then they will start to enjoy these open practice projects.

3.4 The Practical Environment

According to the 'Four Elements' of the Constructivism, the construction of the environment plays an important role during the teaching [10]. For universities, the construction of the environment for students' practice project is quite important. In addition, the universities should provide students with a relatively quiet and open environment, which is the innovation base. The base is helpful for students to communicate and think deeply about the project in a team form.

The base is equipped with necessary practical equipment and sufficient teaching materials, which are very helpful for the efficient development of the students' open practice project. What is more, the base should also be equipped with practical instructors to solve the problems encountered by students during the practice of the open practice projects.

4   The New Problems Under the Pandemic Situation

In recent years, the practice in the campus science and technology innovation base has adopted the implementation of the independent and open project practice mode constantly. So far, it has achieved remarkable teaching results. In the spring of 2020, the sudden outbreak of the epidemic caused all universities across the country to postpone the start of semester. The isolation leads to the online teaching at home, which heavily affected the offline development of project practice teaching. Particularly, the three factors of teachers, students, and practice environment have been greatly restricted.

4.1   The Situation Before and After the Epidemic

Team Formation: Prior to the pandemic: The innovation base of our university has adopted a way of meeting in person. The freshmen would take this opportunity to meet and get familiar with each other. During the meeting, students usually introduce themselves to each other about in term of technical skills and their interests. By this way, it is not difficult for students to find like-minded peer students. Once they have gained a preliminary understanding of each other, they could contact each other privately to decide whether they could set up their own team together. By this way, it is quite easy to set up their theme of open practice projects.

During the pandemic: In order to take the spread of the pandemic under control, the offline meetings can not take place as often as before. During this time, the most students keep a "classroom-dormitory-canteen" life schedule. This situation heavily constrained their social circle. There are less opportunities to meet students from other majors, which leads to a thorny problem in formation during the pandemic. Some teams have been affected heavily by the pandemic. Their team members' enthusiasm has become much weaker. In the worst cases, some team members even quit.

Tutor Selection: Prior to the pandemic: The project team can get to know their tutor through the regular summary meetings held by the science and technology innovation base. In the meeting, students can communicate with tutors face-to-face. Based on these meetings, students can contact the tutors in the form of one-to-one or one-to-many. Usually, they could maintain a good relationship.

During the pandemic: At university, most students' communication with major teachers is limited to classroom. Except few familiar major teachers, students usually have no extra channels to know major teachers' information and their expertise areas During the process of practice project, students will inevitably encounter situations that they cannot solve problems by themselves. It is not easy at all that students can find suitable tutors when offline lectures and other teaching activities are difficult to carry out.

Communication: Prior to the pandemic: The science and technology innovation base of our university has provided a good offline environment for students to collaborate on their open practice projects. In this base, students can communicate their opinions and ideas about the project. Once they have some new ideas, they can communicate with other team members conveniently, which is very important on enriching and improving the content of the project.

During the pandemic: All the communication between team members takes place online. Since team members' different schedule, it is almost impossible that the message from come team members can be answered instantly. It leads to a sharp decrease in the frequency of communication and then there are a loose connection between team members. Furthermore, comparing with the offline communication, online communication easily leads to some misunderstandings when they try to express their inspiration on the projects. This situation could cause an unexpected effect for the project progress.

Project Design: Prior to the pandemic: Based on the offline teaching mode, students can conduct on-the-spot investigations under the guardian of their tutors to understand the project background, and propose the corresponding functional modules quickly and efficiently. For the overall structural design of the project, the team leader generally informs other team members of his ideas by hand-painting. In the creative practice of the project, the team leader assigns different tasks for different team members according to their knowledge and technique skills of team members. Taking code writing as an example, some team members are responsible for the front-end and others are responsible for back-end of the web page. Then, an appointment time will be set to write and run the code together in the innovation base to solve the code loopholes and differences in a timely and efficient manner.

During the pandemic: Because the offline surveys can not be carried out, the project do not have firm foundation from questionnaires' date. Thus, they may consider the problem unilaterally. The project theme lacks scientific basis and credibility. What is more, it is very difficult to accurately work out the real pain point. All in all, the core competitiveness of the project is weak. Besides, as far as the integration of ideas, the communication among members is disordered since it is not inconvenient to record the communication. So it is difficult to obtain effective opinions. In terms of project practice, code design ideas cannot be clearly and precisely expressed and only code comments cannot reach an ideal agreement.

4.2 Project Practice Countermeasures Under the Pandemic Situation

In the pandemic situation, each technology innovation base can use the Ding-Talk APP with better functional integration to build groups. Students communicate with each other online to express their intention to find teammates and the direction of the project practice. By understanding its technical basis and future development direction, students can choose appropriate partners to form a team.

Each tutor clearly indicate his/her professional direction and participation experience in the group. Students can independently select the tutor according to the project direction by viewing their message and then have some personal communication to outline their own project. After obtaining the teacher's consent, determine him/her as the tutor of the project.

In terms of project communication, team members can still choose Ding-Talk APP as a communication medium. They can create a new project communication group, which integrates multiple functions such as online documentation and task assignment to facilitate the communication and work assignment between team leaders and team members. In order to better coordinate, the group leader can set up a group announcement to notify the group members to upload their personal timetable to the group Afterwards, the group leader will make overall arrangements to determine the follow-up group meeting time. After the meeting time is set, each team member needs to complete his/her personal work, summarize and organize their personal thoughts on the current stage of the project, express their opinions in the meeting. During the meeting, team members speak in turns. The group leader edits the online document to record all the discussion content. After all members express their opinions, they will review the online documents together, review all ideas, take the best and get rid of the dross.

Some people in the team are responsible for the collection of information on the project background, which can be obtained through scientific papers and documents, news, mentor contact, and consultation. Determining the project goals and agreeing on the specific function distribution requires the team leader to lead the members to vote through the Ding-Talk meeting. After completing the above preliminary preparations, the team of the project is set up properly.

Students should focus on the data flow level, decompose from top to bottom, use structured analysis methods to establish system processing flow, and draw project structure diagrams. Furthermore, in order to solve the problem of writing, students can familiarize and understand the writing format through the editing function of the Mock multi-person collaborative interface in the early stage. After being proficient, the project developers in the group will jointly edit and write and in a three-day cycle, the Api interface will be iterated and maintained in time. The choice and design of the database type is critical to a project. Databases are divided into relational databases and non-relational databases, such as MySql, MongoDB and other different types of databases need to be determined according to the project structure. In database design, students use ER diagrams, combined with data flow diagrams and data tables of various functions to build a conceptual layer data model, which lays a solid foundation for subsequent code writing and function optimization.

In the project practice, students can use the combination of Git + Gitee to build a local warehouse and synchronize the code to the remote warehouse, realize the self-management of the code, and reduce the inconvenience caused by mutual viewing of the code. Students complete the priority definition of the interface document based on the data flow basis obtained in the previous planning, and write the Mock data according to the interface document. The Mock framework enables front-end and back-end personnel to develop at the same time, greatly shortening the project cycle. In order to improve the efficiency of code integration, students can purchase a cloud server on Alibaba Cloud in advance as a project deployment site. During the project development process, the team members can write the relevant code into two versions: Test and Main. Through coordination of time, formulate an update cycle, deploy the stable version of the code on the cloud server, and find and solve problems in time. Students can create a dedicated test file for each functional module, and use the test data for trial operation, effectively understand the gap between the actual output and the expected operation from the unit test, and continuously improve the code quality in the process of refactoring and debugging.

5 Case Comparison

At the very beginning of the epidemic, the number of scientific and technological innovation projects has dropped significantly comparing with the same period in previous years. Regarding the implementation of project practice strategies in the context of the epidemic, we use the WYB Team and Broken-Sky Team of the BLUE ZONE innovation base from our university school as a case study.

5.1 The Team of WYB

During the epidemic, the students of the WYB maintained the previous way. They still adopted the traditional open project practice teaching mode for project development. They were not ready for the adoption of the online management of open projects. In terms of team formation, the number of members has dropped from the six to four due to the lack of good and sufficient communication. The team possesses limited subject teacher resources. And this tutor need to assist multiple teams at the same time so that his guidance is not efficient. During the process of project implementing, since mainly relying on the offline communication and lacking a rigorous development process, there are many communication problems. For example, misunderstanding of themes and overlapping work assignments occur from time to time, as a result, the project process is stagnant. In terms of team internal communication, the online communication through social software is chaotic so that the communication is low efficient and misunderstand of each other. For summarizing and reviewing, they usually need to review the previous chat records, which is time-consuming and laborious.

5.2   The Team of Broken-Sky

On the other hand, the 2019 Broken-Sky Team of BLUE ZONE can be regarded as a good example case of the practice of open projects [11]. The Broken-Sky Team is composed of three students from different departments and majors when they were in the sophomore year. The team members have broader majors knowledge and technique skills. At the very beginning the epidemic, the open project practice was rather heavily affected. The three members were instructed by their tutor and reorganized the original team.

During the period of isolation at home, these three members of the Broken-Sky kept in touch with senior students through the online group of the Innovation Base. They agreed to discuss the project from 2 pm to 5 pm every day. What is more, the team leader did review and summarize the discussion content from time to time. With the help of senior students with advanced technical experience, this team creatively developed an orderly manner on project management and creation. After two months of online collaborative team working on project development, they won the third prize in the national competition.

After the epidemic is under control, they returned to the university. Based on the experience and insights of the online project practice, they have expanded the number of the team with the help of the good study environment provided by the innovation practice base. Thereafter, the team members made fully use of the Internet technology to make preliminary preparations for the filming of micro-movies during the holidays. The Broken-Sky Team chose Jinyun Xiandu to shoot and create a micro-movie. As a result, they have gained the provincial second prize that marked a great achievement to their tour.

5.3   Achievement Comparison: As Shown in Fig. 2:

Team	Awards under the epidemic
"WYB"	One scientific and technological innovation project: One university-level project.
"Broken-Sky"	Six scientific and technological innovation projects: One national project, One provincial project and four university-level projects; Participated in computer Design Competition for Chinese college students and other disciplines, won one national prize, two provincial prizes and one university prize; One academic paper was published and retrieved by EI-c.

Fig. 2. Results Comparison.

6 Conclusion

Under the epidemic situation, the open project-based practice teaching activities at university have made up for the shortcomings of the single offline model, and have been improved to a certain extent. The practical teaching mode of the project takes advantage of the convenience of Internet technology and digital information transmission, with online assistance and offline, so that students can get rid of site restrictions and smoothly carry out project cooperation and practice. The obtained practical achievements is worthy continuously promoting. The practical method of teaching activities is not only suitable for the epidemic environment but also for the collaborative creation of students across multiple campuses. It has high practical significance and is worthy of widespread implementation and application.

Acknowledgements. This work was supported in part the Humanities and Social Sciences Research Program Fund of the Ministry of Education of China (No. 17YJA880004), the Innovation and Entrepreneurship Training Program for Chinese College Students (No. 202011057014), and the Zhejiang Xinmiao Talents Program (No. 2020R415009).

References

1. Burki, T.K.: COVID-19: consequences for higher education. J. Lanc. Onco. 758–758 (2020)
2. Gang, C., Xuefen, L., Yi, F.: Research on training mode reform for engineering application-oriented personnel-Taking "four steps" training mode of ZUST as an example. J. Zhejiang Univ. Sci. Technol. 135–139 (2016)
3. Gang, C., Xuefen, L.: Open-ended project instruction research. J. Zhejiang Univ. Sci. Technol. 375–380 (2010)
4. Gang, C., Sifan, W., Xingfei, J., Binbin, L., Runkai, Z., Zhaojie, D.: Research and exploration on construction management of project practice innovation base based on "four steps". J. Res. Explor. Lab. 244–248 (2021)
5. Jiaping, H., Gang, C.: Study and exploration of student self-managed open practical teaching bases. J. Res. Explor. Lab. 215–218 (2014)
6. Tao, G., Xingwen, Z., Xiaozi, S., Xiaojuan, W., Kun, X.: Significance of initiating practice and innovation activities in universities. J. Xidian Univ. 107–110 (2010)
7. Santucci, V.G., Cartoni, E., Silva, B.C.D., Baldassarre, G.: Autonomous open-ended learning of interdependent tasks. J. Adv. Mater. Res. **2076**, 2194–2198 (2012)
8. Juan, W.: Thoughts and enlightenment of dual system education in Germany. J. China's Hum. Resour. Soc. Secur. 26–27 (2021)
9. Burnham, J.A.J.: Skills for success: student-focused, chemistry-based, skills-developing. Open-Ended Project Work. J. Chem. Educ. **97**, 344–350 (2020)
10. Gang, C., Xuefen, L., Yunfeng, M.: Exploration and practice of open-ended practical teaching innovation by "four steps"-using application-oriented talent cultivation mode of German for reference. J. Zhejiang Univ. Sci. Technol. 371–375 (2015)
11. Gang, C.: Teaching research and exploration of open-ended "four-step" project practice teaching mode in innovative and application-oriented talents training. J. Zhejiang Univ. Sci. Technol. 413–419 (2020)

Withdrawals Prediction in Virtual Learning Environments with Deep Self-paced Learning

Xianyue Li[1], Wei Xu[2(⊠)], and Shuo Xie[2]

[1] School of Marxism, Shanghai University of Political Science and Law, Shanghai, China
lixianyue@shupl.edu.cn
[2] School of Communication and Electronic Engineering, East China Normal University, Shanghai, China
wxu@sist.ecnu.edu.cn, 51215904098@stu.ecnu.edu.cn

Abstract. Withdrawals prediction in virtual learning environments aims to predict student dropout by modeling student behaviour when utilizing e-learning platforms. Classic machine learning approaches lack sufficient expression ability. Deep learning methods are inclined to get stuck in the local minimum. In addition, there is not any public source code platform to comprehensively compare all the baselines. In this paper, we propose a new Withdrawals Prediction method in virtual learning environments with Deep Self-Paced Learning (WPDSPL) to deal with these two problems. Specifically, WPDSPL overcomes the bad local minimum problem by introducing self-paced learning into LSTM to gradually add data from easy ones to more complex ones during the training procedure. In addition, we deal with the inconvenient comparison problem by releasing the source code to comprehensively compare all the baselines. Comprehensive experiments demonstrate the superiority of our proposed approach.

Keywords: Withdrawals prediction · Virtual learning environments · Deep learning · Self-paced learning

1 Introduction

The specific objective of withdrawals prediction in virtual environment is to analyze student dropout by modeling student behaviour when interacting with online platforms [1]. With the development of network and in the context of the COVID-19 pandemic, online learning has becoming the main learning platform. Without withdrawals prediction, online students have a much higher chance of dropping out than those attending conventional classrooms, which is a great waste of learning resources for institutions and leads to the problem of lacking proper learning courses for the learners. Therefore, it is of significant importance to increase the withdrawals prediction in virtual learning environments.

Early methods [2–4] utilized classic machine learning approaches, while they lack sufficient expression ability. Deep learning methods [5–8] have sufficient expression ability, while they are inclined to get stuck in the local minimum when optimizing the objective function, especially with limited information. In addition, there is not any public source code platform to comprehensively compare all the baselines.

Self-Paced Learning (SPL) [9] is effective in dealing with the local minimum problem for optimizing complex objective functions. SPL aims to gradually add easy data to more complex data during the learning process. It is the curriculum [10], the easy to hard learning order, that leads the model to be evolved from naive to mature. Therefore, introducing SPL into previous deep learning based methods can obtain a more reliable model.

In this paper, we propose a new Withdrawals Prediction method in virtual learning environments with Deep Self-Paced Learning (WPDSPL) to deal with these two problems. Specifically, WPDSPL overcomes the bad local minimum problem by introducing SPL into LSTM [7,8] to gradually add easy samples to complex samples during the training procedure. In addition, we deal with the inconvenient comparison problem by releasing the source code (https://pan. baidu.com/s/1PeigGkllR81RHoNkkG73TA) to comprehensively compare all the baselines. Our methodology has been meticulously crafted to address these two problems, thereby enabling acquisition of a better model. The veracity of our hypothesis has been ascertained in the experimental section.

There are three contributions in our paper: (1) We propose a first self-paced learning base method for withdrawals prediction. (2) Our work is also the first one to comprehensively compare all the baselines with public source code. (3) Experiment results imply the superiority of our proposed method.

2   Related Work

2.1   Withdrawals Prediction

Withdrawals prediction in virtual learning environments aims to predict student dropout by modeling student behaviour when utilizing online platforms. Early works [2–4] mainly adopted classic machine learning algorithms. For example, Taylor et al. [2] utilized logistic regression to model dropout. Amnueypornsakul et al. [3] trained an SVM classifier based on the RBF kernel for each of their two models (i.e., specific and general case models). Al-Radaideh et al. [4] employed the Decision Trees. While all the above methods lack sufficient expression ability.

Recently, with the effectiveness of deep learning [11–20], numerous deep learning based algorithms [5–8] have been proposed. For example, Waheed et al. [5] built an ANN method. Qiu et al. [6] propose DP-CNN to deal with the student dropout prediction problem. Hassan et al. [7] and Mubarak et al. [8] introduced LSTM based methods.

However, all the above deep learning methods are inclined to get stuck in the local minimum. Our WPDSPL is the first work to introduce SPL into deep learning based methods for withdrawals prediction to tackle this local minimum optimization problem. In addition, WPDSPL is also the first work to comprehensively compare all the baselines with public source code.

2.2 Self-paced Learning

SPL [9], which aims to gradually add easy data to more complex data during the learning process, is Inspired by the learning process of human. Based on [9], various kinds of supervised SPL theories [21–27] and applications [28–30] are proposed. Jiang et al. [21] incorporated the information of diversity into the curriculum by introducing a nonconvex regularizer into SPL; they also proposed a method called SPCL [22] to learn the curriculum by jointly taking into account of SPL and prior knowledge; Meng et al. [25] provided a theoretical understanding of SPL. In [31–34], Xu introduced SPL into person re-identification, multi-task learning, multi-model learning and learning with privileged information, respectively. Jiang et al. [29] utilized SPL for skin disease recognition; Xiang et al. [30] proposed a two-level curriculum plan to solve the long tail problem in the task of image classification.

As SPL is effective in solving complex problems, it is also employed in other machine learning methods [35–42]. In the aspect of unsupervised learning, Ghasedi et al. [29] proposed a SPL clustering framework. In the aspect of weakly supervised learning, Zhang et al. [37] proposed a collaborative SPCL clustering framework. In the aspect of semi-supervised learning, Yang et al. [43] established an easy-to-hard graph by sorting the difficulty of points and edges of the graph neural network. Cascante et al. [44] directly applied SPL into the pseudo-labeling method and selecting the confident unlabeled samples according to the distribution of prediction scores of unlabeled samples.

However, there have been no studies to exploit the curriculum learning in the task of withdrawals prediction. To our best knowledge, our WPDSPL is the first work to introduce SPL into the task of withdrawals prediction in virtual learning environments.

3 Method

Figure 1 presents an overview of our WPDSPL method. The feature of student click information is sent into our WPDSPL to obtain the final model parameter w. Our WPDSPL includes two processes: the model learning process with learned curriculum and the curriculum learning process with learned model. These two processes are alternatively optimized until the final curriculum is obtained.

3.1 Notation

Suppose the training dataset is $\{(x_i, y_i)|i = 1, \ldots, n\}$, where x_i represents the i-th sample, the feature of student click information, and y_i is its label. For the curriculum, $\mathbf{v} = [v_1, \ldots, v_n]$ denotes the importance weights of all the samples. We aim to learn to find a new predictor $f(x_i, w)$ and w is its model parameter. Some key notations used in this paper are listed in Table 1.

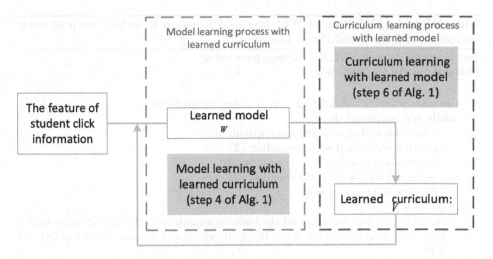

Fig. 1. Overview of our WPDSPL method. The feature of student click information is sent into our WPDSPL to obtain the final model parameter w. Our WPDSPL includes two processes: the model learning process with learned curriculum and the curriculum learning process with learned model. These two processes are alternatively optimized until the final curriculum is obtained.

Table 1. Important notations used in this paper.

notation	description
x	the feature of student click information
y	label
v	the importance weights of samples
w	model parameter
f	predictor

3.2 Problem Formulation

The objective function of WPDSPL is:

$$\min_{w,v} \sum_{i=1}^{n} v_i L(y_i, f(x_i, w)) + g(w, \lambda_w) + g(\mathbf{v}, \lambda_{\mathbf{v}}) \tag{1}$$

$$\text{s.t.} \quad \mathbf{v} \in [0,1]^n.$$

Here $g(\mathbf{v}, \lambda) = -\lambda \sum_{i=1}^{n} v_i$ [33,34] represents the self-paced regularizer, λ represents the age parameter and the training loss L is utilized for measuring the hardness of samples. In our task, the L is cross-entropy and the f(x,w) is an LSTM [45] based network. Its specific structure is mentioned in the training details part of the experiment section.

Algorithm 1. Algorithm of Withdrawals Prediction in virtual learning environments with Deep Self-Paced Learning

---

input: input dataset $D(X, Y)$, learning pace set Q
Output: model parameters w

1: Initialize $\mathbf{v}^* = [1]^n$, $\lambda = 0.1$, $\mu = 0$. //assign the start values
2: **while** not converged **do**
3:      // model learning with learned curriculum
4:      update w with fixed $\mathbf{v}^*$ via equation (2)
5:      //curriculum learning with learned model
6:      update $\mathbf{v}$ with fixed w^* via equation (3)
7:      //update the learning pace
8:      $\mu = \mu + 1$
9:      Sort training loss value for all the training examples in the ascend order to get a set TR, then we can get $\lambda = TR(Q(\mu))$, which sets λ value to the top $Q(\mu)$ of TR.
10: **end while**
11:
12: **return** $w = w^*$

3.3 Optimization

We deal with (1) by alternatively optimizing parameters w and $\mathbf{v}$. Algorithm 1 presents the detailed steps. More concretely:

1) Model learning with learned curriculum–optimize w under fixed $\mathbf{v}^*$: Under this condition, (1) degenerates to the following form:

$$\min_{w} \quad \sum_{i=1}^{n} v^*_i L(y_i, f(x_i, w)) + g(w, \lambda_w) \tag{2}$$

Equation 2 is a weighted supervised deep learning based objective function, which can be optimized with standard deep learning toolbox.

2) Curriculum learning with learned model – optimize $\mathbf{v}$ under fixed w^*: The sample importance is highly related to the loss function: $L(y_i, f(x_i, w^*))$. When w^* is fixed, the form of v_i is:

$$v_i = \begin{cases} 1, & \text{if } L(y_i, f(x_i, w^*)) < \lambda \\ 0, & \text{otherwise .} \end{cases} \tag{3}$$

4 Experiments

4.1 Datasets, Baselines and Training Details

Datasets. The utilized dataset is the same as [7], which is selected from OULA [46]. However, [7] doesn't mention the train-test split. Inspired by [5], we utilized the first 70% as the training set. The remaining data sets are the test set.

Baselines. We adopt three commonly used metrics, accuracy, precision and recall to evaluate the performance of withdrawals prediction. Higher values indicate better performances. The utilized baselines methods are: (1)LSTM [45]. The input dimension is 20, the three hidden layers are 50, 20, 10 and the output dimension is 2. The activation function is tanh (2) ANN [5]. The input dimension is 500, the three hidden layers are 50, 20, 10 and the output dimension is 2. The activation function is relu. (3) SVM [47], RBF kernel based SVM is utilized and the input dimension is also 500.

Training Details. For all the deep learning based baselines, we train them for 60 epochs. The batch size of 1250 for WPDSPL and 50 for ANN, the initial learning rate of 1e-3 and Adam optimizer with step decay learning method are also utilized. We set the Learning pace set parameter Q to be $\{\frac{1}{2}ANum, \frac{10}{18}ANum, \frac{11}{18}ANum, \ldots, ANum\}$. Here $ANum$ is the number of all the training samples. Q includes 10 elements and we train 6 epochs for each self-paced steps. For the hyper-parameters of SVM, default values are utilized.

4.2 Experimental Results

Table 2 shows comparison results of different baselines on the dataset OULA [46]. Our WPDSPL outperforms all the baselines under all the weeks. Moreover, SVM achieves the lowest performance, which indicates the effectiveness of deep learning based methods. In addition, LSTM is better than ANN, which implies the importance of sequential learning. What's more, WPDSPL is better than LSTM, which reflects the usefulness of self-paced learning.

4.3 Model Analysis

The Effectiveness of Sequential Learning. To analyze the effect of sequential learning, we also conduct experiments of some simple versions of our WPDSPL. They are WPDSPL without considering the sequential learning. For example, ANN(SPL) and SVM(SPL) represents the methods that extend ANN and SVM to their SPL version, respectively. The comparison results are presented in Fig. 2. This figure shows that LSTM is better than ANN and SVM and WPDSPL is better than ANN(SPL) and SVM(SPL), which implies the usefulness of sequential learning.

The Effectiveness of Self-paced Learning. Figure 3 presents the effectiveness of self-paced learning. As can be found, all the SPL methods are better than their associated methods without considering the curriculum, which indicates the usefulness of self-paced learning. Moreover, the performance improvement caused by self-paced learning is larger when the task is more difficult(according to the performance to the baseline method), which reflects the advantages of utilizing SPL in early weeks.

Table 2. Comparison results of all methods

Method	Weeks	Accuracy%	Precision%	Recall%
SVM [47]	5	71.94	60.10	72.29
	10	82.58	70.13	83.16
	15	83.70	81.53	83.99
	20	87.18	87.20	85.46
	25	92.33	90.19	90.80
ANN [5]	5	75.2	62.7	78.5
	10	85.32	72.14	87.34
	15	86.45	82.20	87.72
	20	92.87	87.98	93.27
	25	93.02	90.87	94.62
LSTM [45]	5	80.18	63.26	84.41
	10	86.24	72.88	90.31
	15	89.65	83.20	90.67
	20	93.10	89.21	93.49
	25	95.38	91.89	96.68
WPDSPL-Ours	5	86.58	70.26	89.79
	10	90.14	78.38	92.31
	15	91.85	85.70	93.82
	20	94.17	89.91	94.67
	25	**95.89**	**92.59**	**97.17**

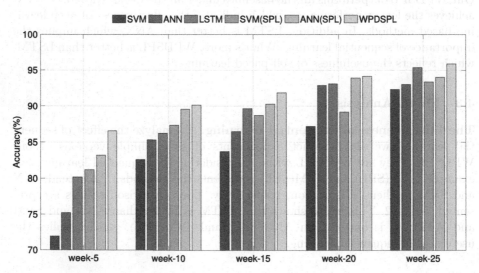

Fig. 2. The effectiveness of sequential learning

4.4   Policy Implications

As observed from above experiments, our WPDSPL outperforms other base-lines, especially, in the early stages, whose information is limited. The improved predictability of our WPDSPL is correlated with many crucial decisions and

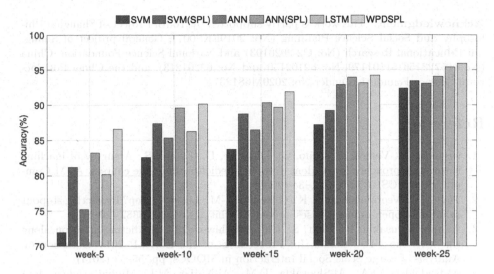

Fig. 3. The effectiveness of self-paced learning

policies. Although student withdrawals are mainly influenced by three main factors: the student factor, the course factor and the environmental factor [48], only the course factor can truly decrease the rate of student withdrawals during the learning process. This is due to the fact that the student factor and the environmental factor is almost static during the learning process, it can be estimated before the course, which will recommend unsuitable students not to enroll in this course.

For the course factor, as the university consists of three groups of people: administrations, academic institutions and individual teachers, we will analyze the associated policies for these three groups, respectively. Specifically, firstly, administrations utilize our WPDSPL to find students at risk and arrange technique corporations to build online communication systems for teachers to help these students. Secondly, academic institutions should teach the common prerequired knowledge and answer the common learning questions for all the students at risk. In the end, after the course, each individual teacher should give each at risk student support, especially, for some difficult parts, such as research projects.

5 Conclusion

A new withdrawals prediction algorithm is proposed by introducing SPL into LSTM to gradually add data from easy ones to more complex ones during the training procedure. In addition, we also release the source code to comprehensively compare all the baselines. Given that our method has been purposefully crafted to deal with two problems of previous methods, a more accurate withdrawals prediction model can be learned. Comprehensive experiments indicates that our WPDSPL performs well in withdrawals prediction tasks.

Acknowledgment. This work is partly supported by Youth Project of Shanghai Philosophy and Social Science Planning (No: 2019EKS007), General project of Shanghai Educational Research (No: C2-2020103) and National Science Foundation, China (No:615723156151101179, No: 62102150 and No: 62201213), and the China Postdoctoral Science Foundation under No: 2020M681237.

References

1. Prenkaj, B., Velardi, P., Stilo, G., Distante, D., Faralli, S.: A survey of machine learning approaches for student dropout prediction in online courses. ACM Comput. Surv. (CSUR) **53**(3), 1–34 (2020)
2. Taylor, C., Veeramachaneni, K., O'Reilly, U.-M.: Likely to stop? Predicting stopout in massive open online courses. arXiv preprint arXiv:1408.3382 (2014)
3. Amnueypornsakul, B., Bhat, S., Chinprutthiwong, P.: Predicting attrition along the way: the UIUC model. In: Proceedings of the EMNLP 2014 Workshop on Analysis of Large Scale Social Interaction in MOOCs, pp. 55–59 (2014)
4. Al-Radaideh, Q.A., Al-Shawakfa, E.M., Al-Najjar, M.I.: Mining student data using decision trees. In: International Arab Conference on Information Technology (ACIT 2006), Yarmouk University, Jordan (2006)
5. Waheed, H., Hassan, S.U., Aljohani, N.R., Hardman, J., Alelyani, S., Nawaz, R.: Predicting academic performance of students from VLE big data using deep learning models. Comput. Hum. Behav. **104**, 106189 (2020)
6. Qiu, L., Liu, Y., Quan, H., Liu, Y.: Student dropout prediction in massive open online courses by convolutional neural networks. Soft. Comput. **23**(20), 10287–10301 (2019)
7. Hassan, S.U., Waheed, H., Aljohani, N.R., Ali, M., Ventura, S., Herrera, F.: Virtual learning environment to predict withdrawal by leveraging deep learning. Int. J. Intell. Syst. **34**(8), 1935–1952 (2019)
8. Mubarak, A.A., Cao, H., Ahmed, S.A.M.: Predictive learning analytics using deep learning model in MOOCs' courses videos. Educ. Inf. Technol. **26**(1), 371–392 (2021)
9. Kumar, P., Packer, B., Koller, D.: Self-paced learning for latent variable models. In: NeurIPS, pp. 1189–1197 (2010)
10. Bengio, Y., Louradour, J., Collobert, R., Weston, J.: Curriculum learning. In: ICML, pp. 41–48 (2009)
11. Wei, X., Qiu, S., Huang, K., Liu, W., Zuo, J., Guo, H.: Image deraining with adversarial residual refinement network. J. Vis. Commun. Image Represent. **77**, 103133 (2021)
12. Guo, H., Xu, W., Qiu, S.: Unsupervised low-light image enhancement with quality-task-perception loss. In: 2021 International Joint Conference on Neural Networks (IJCNN), pp. 1–8. IEEE (2021)
13. Qiao, Z., Xu, W., Sun, L., Qiu, S., Guo, H.: Deep semi-supervised learning for low-light image enhancement. In: 2021 14th International Congress on Image and Signal Processing, BioMedical Engineering and Informatics (CISP-BMEI), pp. 1–6. IEEE (2021)
14. Xu, W., Chen, X., Guo, H., Huang, X., Liu, W.: Unsupervised image restoration with quality-task-perception loss. IEEE Trans. Circuits Syst. Video Technol. **32**(9), 5736–5747 (2022)

15. Zhang, Y., Zhang, J., Guo, X.: Kindling the darkness: a practical low-light image enhancer. In: Proceedings of the 27th ACM International Conference on Multimedia, pp. 1632–1640 (2019)
16. Xu, K., Yang, X., Yin, B., Lau, R.W.H.: Learning to restore low-light images via decomposition-and-enhancement. In: Proceedings of the IEEE/CVF Conference on Computer Vision and Pattern Recognition, pp. 2281–2290 (2020)
17. Yang, W., Wang, S., Fang, Y., Wang, Y., Liu, J.: Band representation-based semi-supervised low-light image enhancement: bridging the gap between signal fidelity and perceptual quality. IEEE Trans. Image Process. **30**, 3461–3473 (2021)
18. Zamir, S.W., et al.: Learning enriched features for fast image restoration and enhancement. arXiv preprint arXiv:2205.01649 (2022)
19. Wang, Y., Wan, R., Yang, W., Li, H., Chau, L.-P., Kot, A.: Low-light image enhancement with normalizing flow. In: Proceedings of the AAAI Conference on Artificial Intelligence, vol. 36, pp. 2604–2612 (2022)
20. Xu, X., Wang, R., Fu, C.W., Jia, J.: SNR-aware low-light image enhancement. In: Proceedings of the IEEE/CVF Conference on Computer Vision and Pattern Recognition, pp. 17714–17724 (2022)
21. Jiang, L., Meng, D., Yu, S., Lan, Z., Shan, S., Hauptmann, A.: Self-paced learning with diversity. In: NeurIPS, pp. 2078–2086 (2014)
22. Jiang, L., Meng, D., Zhao, Q., Shan, S., Hauptmann, A.: Self-paced curriculum learning. In: AAAI, pp. 6–14 (2015)
23. Li, H., Gong, M.: Self-paced convolutional neural networks. In: IJCAI, pp. 2110–2116 (2017)
24. Ren, Y., Zhao, P., Sheng, Y., Yao, D., Xu, Z.: Robust softmax regression for multi-class classification with self-paced learning. In: IJCAI, pp. 2641–2647 (2017)
25. Meng, D., Zhao, Q., Jiang, L.: A theoretical understanding of self-paced learning. Inf. Sci. **414**, 319–328 (2017)
26. Ren, Z., Dong, D., Li, H., Chen, C.: Self-paced prioritized curriculum learning with coverage penalty in deep reinforcement learning. IEEE Trans. Neural Netw. Learn. Syst. **29**(6), 2216–2226 (2018)
27. Wang, K., Wang, Y., Zhao, Q., Meng, D., Liao, X., Xu, Z.: SPLBoost: an improved robust boosting algorithm based on self-paced learning. IEEE Trans. Cybern. **51**(3), 1556–1570 (2019)
28. Zhou, S., et al.: Deep self-paced learning for person re-identification. Pattern Recognit. **76**, 71–78 (2017)
29. Yang, J., et al.: Self-paced balance learning for clinical skin disease recognition. IEEE Trans. Neural Netw. Learn. Syst. **31**(8), 2832–2846 (2019)
30. Xiang, L., Ding, G., Han, J.: Learning from multiple experts: self-paced knowledge distillation for long-tailed classification. In: Vedaldi, A., Bischof, H., Brox, T., Frahm, J.-M. (eds.) ECCV 2020. LNCS, vol. 12350, pp. 247–263. Springer, Cham (2020). https://doi.org/10.1007/978-3-030-58558-7_15
31. Xu, W., Chi, H., Zhou, L., Huang, X., Yang, J.: Self-paced least square semi-coupled dictionary learning for person re-identification. In: 2017 IEEE International Conference on Image Processing (ICIP), pp. 3705–3709. IEEE (2017)
32. Wei, X., Liu, W., Chi, H., Huang, X., Yang, J.: Multi-task classification with sequential instances and tasks. Signal Process. Image Commun. **64**, 59–67 (2018)
33. Wei, X., Liu, W., Huang, X., Yang, J., Qiu, S.: Multi-modal self-paced learning for image classification. Neurocomputing **309**, 134–144 (2018)
34. Wei, X., Liu, W., Chi, H., Qiu, S., Jin, Yu.: Self-paced learning with privileged information. Neurocomputing **362**, 147–155 (2019)

35. Ghasedi, K., Wang, X., Deng, C., Huang, H.: Balanced self-paced learning for generative adversarial clustering network. In: CVPR, pp. 4391–4400 (2019)
36. Zhang, D., Meng, D., Li, C., Jiang, L., Zhao, Q., Han, J.: A self-paced multiple-instance learning framework for co-saliency detection. In: CVPR, pp. 594–602 (2015)
37. Zhang, D., Han, J., Zhao, L., Meng, D.: Leveraging prior-knowledge for weakly supervised object detection under a collaborative self-paced curriculum learning framework. Int. J. Comput. Vision 127(4), 363–380 (2019)
38. Zou, Y., Yu, Z., Kumar, B.V.K., Wang, J.: Unsupervised domain adaptation for semantic segmentation via class-balanced self-training. In: ECCV, pp. 289–305 (2018)
39. Zhang, W., Dong, X., Ouyang, W., Li, W.: Self-paced collaborative and adversarial network for unsupervised domain adaptation. IEEE Trans. Pattern Anal. Mach. Intell. 29, 7834–7844 (2019)
40. Lin, L., Wang, K., Meng, D., Zuo, W., Zhang, L.: Active self-paced learning for cost-effective and progressive face identification. IEEE Trans. Pattern Anal. Mach. Intell. 40(1), 7–19 (2017)
41. Tang, Y.-P., Huang, S.-J.: Self-paced active learning: query the right thing at the right time. In: AAAI, pp. 5117–5124 (2019)
42. Lyu, G., Feng, S., Wang, T., Lang, C.: A self-paced regularization framework for partial-label learning. IEEE Trans. Cybern. 52(2), 899–911 (2020)
43. Yang, L., Chen, Z., Gu, J., Guo, Y.: Dual self-paced graph convolutional network: towards reducing attribute distortions induced by topology. In: IJCAI, pp. 4062–4069 (2019)
44. Cascante-Bonilla, P., Tan, F., Qi, Y., Ordonez, V.: Curriculum labeling: revisiting pseudo-labeling for semi-supervised learning. In: AAAI, pp. 3062–3069 (2021)
45. Schmidhuber, J., Hochreiter, S., et al.: Long short-term memory. Neural Comput. 9(8), 1735–1780 (1997)
46. Kuzilek, J., Hlosta, M., Zdrahal, Z.: Open university learning analytics dataset. Sci. Data 4(1), 1–8 (2017)
47. Chen, D., Wu, Q., Ying, Y., Zhou, D.: Support vector machine soft margin classifiers: error analysis. J. Mach. Learn. Res. 5(9), 1143–1175 (2004)
48. Lee, Y., Choi, J.: A review of online course dropout research: implications for practice and future research. Education Tech. Research Dev. 59(5), 593–618 (2011)

A Study on Game Teaching in Python Programming Teaching for Middle School

ZhiWei Qu[1], Xue Wang[2], and Wei Zhang[1(✉)]

[1] College of Computer and Information Technology, Mudanjiang Normal University, Mudanjiang, China
zhangwei706@126.com

[2] College of Western Languages, Mudanjiang Normal University, Mudanjiang, China

Abstract. With the rapid development of information technology, the impact of video games on teenagers is becoming increasingly prominent. Due to the support of the game learning theory, students will have more learning interest and efficiency when video games were integrating into learning. In this paper, a game teaching mode which is suitable for teenagers' programming learning was developed, and it is designed based on the sandbox game Minecraft. Moreover, the author has designed some teaching activities, learning strategies and teaching cases. According to following practice, this teaching method has been proven to enhance the effectiveness of teaching python programming in middle schools, especially in enhancing students' interest in programming.

Keywords: Game Teaching · Python Education · Middle school · Programming Education

1 Introduction

Game-based teaching is the integration of game elements and design concepts into the teaching process to stimulate students' learning motivation and make them actively participate in the classroom so as to promote students' learning effect [1]. With the development of information technology and the update of game-based teaching theory, teachers can create a relaxed and happy teaching situation by adding reasonable game elements into the teaching design, and fully mobilize students' intrinsic motivation, so as to achieve the purpose of improving the teaching effect [2]. At the same time, experiments have been conducted to prove that gamification has a significant positive impact on computer subjects [3].

Under the influence of national strategic development requirements, Chinese primary and middle schools are actively implementing programming courses, aiming to cultivate innovative talents with hands-on skills and computational thinking. Through a questionnaire survey of a sample of primary and middle schools nationwide, it was found that 93.49% of middle schools offer AI-related courses, such as programming courses, robotics courses, and maker courses [4]. However, the programming teaching

W. Hong and Y. Weng (Eds.): ICCSE 2022, CCIS 1813, pp. 73–85, 2023.
https://doi.org/10.1007/978-981-99-2449-3_8

system offered by most schools needs to be improved, teachers mostly adopt traditional teaching methods in teaching programming, and teachers' teaching ability of programming education needs to be improved. Therefore, how to design and conduct an effective programming classroom, combine programming education with students' cognitive characteristics, and design interesting teaching activities to stimulate learning motivation is the current problem that needs to be solved in middle school programming education.

Python is one of the most popular programming languages today, with features such as simple syntax, intuitive and easy to learn, and support for rich third-party libraries, which is suitable for beginners to learn programming. At present, Python language has become an important part of learning in China's middle IT education, and is the mainstream language for middle programming education [5].

In primary and middle school programming education, children at the elementary school level mainly use Scratch, a graphical programming software from MIT, to learn programming. Scratch has a clear and concise interface and uses a modular command language that allows students to create simple animations and interactive games, making it an enlightening tool for children's programming education [6]. The Python language, on the other hand, is a new addition to middle school programming education in recent years. It is difficult to learn from the experience of teaching programming at the elementary school level, and the specialized Python teaching system at the higher education level cannot be applied to adolescents at the middle school level, and in general, middle school Python programming education has just started recently and is still at the stage of development in exploration [7].

For the application of Python teaching in Minecraft, Sun,D and Li,Y selected 20 seventh grade students in Hangzhou, China, who had never been exposed to programming before, and randomly divided the 20 students into 10 groups of two students for pair programming to write, debug, and run the python language in Minecraft. The results of the study showed that students' creativity, critical thinking, and their attitudes toward programming improved after learning to program in the python language in Minecraft [8]. Andrei Grigorivich uses the Minecraft game environment for python language programming to learn loops and discusses the possibility of using python programming in primary and middle schools [9]. This shows that there are advantages of Minecraft in teaching programming and that there is a possibility of applying Minecraft to teaching programming in middle school.

In this context, based on the investigation of the current situation of middle school programming education, this paper uses the sandbox game minecraft as a teaching tool and applies it to middle school python programming education based on gamification teaching theory. Using minecraft game to design the framework and content of middle school programming teaching activities, attract students' interest in learning, stimulate learning motivation, and cultivate middle school students' computational thinking, creative thinking and problem solving ability. This paper uses gamification instead of traditional teaching to provide new directions and ideas for middle school programming education exploration, thus achieving the purpose of promoting the development of middle school programming education.

2 Teaching Design of Python Programming in Middle School Based on Minecraft

2.1 Teaching Objectives and Content Analysis of Python in Middle School

Based on the series of high school information technology textbooks published by Shanghai Education Edition of China, the teaching objectives of programming at the middle school level can be summarized as enabling students to use a programming language to write programs, implement simple algorithms, experience the whole process of computer problem solving, and improve the ability of using information technology to solve problems [10].

The teaching content of Python programming language in the book includes the following Table 1:

Table 1. Main Contents of Python Programming Teaching in Middle School

Teaching Topics	Teaching Content
Understanding programs and programming languages	1. Programs and characteristics 2. Program design and its general process 3. The basic structure of a program
Design simple numerical data algorithm	1. Data type arithmetic operator 2. Loop structure: for statement while statement 3. Relational and logical operators 4. Select structure if statement
Design batch data algorithm	1. Batch data and its representation and operation 2. Function definition and call 3. Nested and modular design

It can be seen that the teaching of Python in middle school includes the basic understanding of programming, the basic syntax and functions of python, nested modularization and so on.

2.2 Gamification Teaching Environment Design

To carry out minecraft programming in the middle school, we first need to build a teaching environment, including a multimedia teaching environment, a game platform environment and a code editing environment.

The multimedia teaching environment is the place where teachers and students communicate with each other and issue tasks. You can use software such as Tencent conference or electronic classroom management system.

Game platform environment is the environment that supports python programming in minecraft, including minecraft game, java runtime environment, minecraft bukkit server, and RaspberryJam plugin [11].

The code editing environment is the Python programming environment, including python and pycharm.

2.3 Gamified Teaching Activity Design

Game-based teaching design is to integrate game elements into the classroom teaching process with the understanding of teaching contents and purposes, so that students can learn in an interesting and educational teaching environment and thus enhance the teaching efficiency [12]. In this paper, the specific design of game-based teaching activities includes four parts: introduction, teaching, practice and evaluation. The details are shown in the Table 2:

Table 2. Design of Game Programming Teaching Activities

Teaching activities	Teacher activities	Student activities
Introduction before class	Create game scenarios to clarify learning tasks	Understanding learning objectives
Teach knowledge	Demonstrate and explain new knowledge	Learn new knowledge
Practice consolidation	Supervise and solve doubts	Independent inquiry, practical operation
Summary and evaluation	Teacher evaluation and summary	Student evaluation and review

2.4 Gamification Teaching Task Design Outline

Based on the middle school python teaching objectives and content, combined with the characteristics and knowledge of minecraft game, the following programming teaching task outline is designed. The details are shown in the Table 3:

3 Gamified Teaching Evaluation Design

Gamified programming teaching activities based on minecraft are different from traditional classroom teaching. Traditional teaching evaluation emphasizes learning the mastery of objective knowledge and cultivating learners' ability to integrate cognition, which pays too much attention to the results and does not reflect objectively and comprehensively on teaching evaluation. Game-based learning not only focuses on the mastery of learning contents, but also emphasizes students' interest, problem-solving ability, and computational thinking [13]. Therefore, the evaluation of this gamified programming teaching is carried out in the following three aspects.

Table 3. Game Programming Teaching Task Design Outline

Number	Teaching Theme	Class Hour	Teaching Objectives
1	Understanding the world	1	Understand the basic operation of minecraft and the functions of pycharm interface
2	Hello classroom!	2	Understand the three-dimensional coordinate system, learn the basic structure of the program, constants, variables and print functions
3	Ten chickens forever	3	Learn data types, libraries, arithmetic operators, and while loops
4	Pyramid	2	For loop, nested
5	Artificial rainbow	3	Definition function, batch data, list
6	Empty walk	3	Select structure,if statement
7	Resist zombies	2	Use the knowledge learned to improve the problem-solving ability
8	Work evaluation and explanation	2	Consolidate knowledge, evaluate and summarize

3.1 Questionnaire Survey on Students' Interest in Programming

In this paper, we refer to Deng Rui's "Computer Students' Interest in Learning Scale" from Hunan Normal University for the design of the questionnaire, including pre-test and post-test. This questionnaire has been tested and modified by Si-Xin Gao and Yu-Yue-Wen for many times with good reliability and validity, and it is a mature test scale [14]. The questionnaire was divided into five response levels using the Likert option, i.e. 1. strongly disagree 2. disagree 3. neither agree nor disagree 4. agree 5. strongly agree. Reliability and validity analyses were conducted before the use of the questionnaire. The pre and post test questionnaires are specified in the following Table 4 and Table 5.

3.2 Student Python Performance Evaluation

The python language paper is divided into five types of questions: multiple choice, judgment, program reading, program fill-in-the-blank, and program design, for a total of 15 questions and 100 points [15].

3.3 Student Interviews

The purpose of designing follow-up interviews with students is mainly twofold: first, to understand students' interest in the gamified learning course through direct communication and to understand students' interest in learning python. Second, the students who participated in the teaching case study will inevitably have certain learning experiences

Table 4. Questionnaire on Students' Interest in Programming (pre-test)

Dimension	Title number	Subject
Emotion	1	Learning a programming language is by my own choice and it will help me in my future studies and work
Emotion	2	I am confident that I can master a programming language
Cognition	3	I feel that I have potential in computing
Cognition	4	I realize that programming can help me solve complex mathematical problems when I encounter them
Cognition	5	I realize the importance of programming and that it is essential in many aspects of my life
Behavior	6	When I use computers in my daily life, I think about how these functions are implemented
Behavior	7	I pay attention to information, videos, games, etc. related to programming in my daily life
Behavior	8	When programming classes are offered at school, I am happy to learn them

Table 5. Questionnaire on Students' Interest in Programming (post-test)

Dimension	Title number	Subject
Emotion	1	After learning Python, I think this language will help me in my future study and work
Emotion	2	In addition to Python, I would like to master another programming language
Cognition	3	Books and courses related to programming will interest me
Cognition	4	When someone around me discusses programming-related issues, I am interested in the conversation
Cognition	5	I think it is important to work with programming in real life
Behavior	6	I will consider using the programming methods I know to implement some of the functions I want
Behavior	7	I will pay attention to information, videos, games, etc. related to programming
Behavior	8	When people are talking about programming, I want to know what they are talking about

generated in the learning process, so it is important to understand their feelings about the learning process from the students' perspective and ask their opinions about the teaching design, so as to provide reference for the subsequent teaching improvement. The student interviews were conducted in three main dimensions: firstly, students' feelings about this gamified programming teaching, whether they had unique effects and feelings under the new teaching method; secondly, we investigated students' process situation in this gamified teaching, including difficulties and knowledge mastery; and thirdly, the impact of gamified teaching on students' interest in learning programming in the future. The outline of the interview is shown in the following Table 6.

Table 6. Student Interview Outline

Dimension	Title number	Content
Feelings	1	What did you learn about programming after taking the course?
	2	Did you like the combination of games and learning in the class?
	3	Which learning style made you more efficient than the traditional course?
Process	4	Have you mastered all the knowledge in this course? To what extent?
	5	What difficulties did you encounter in the learning process? How did you solve them?
Interest	6	Are you looking forward to the new course?
	7	Do you want to learn new programming languages and programming knowledge?

4   Analysis of the Implementation and Results of Teaching Python Programming in Middle Schools Based on Minecraft

4.1   Implementation of Teaching Activities

The gamified programming teaching activity was conducted in L city. The experiment was conducted as an online interest class during the winter break due to the coronavirus, and the number of experimental students was controlled to 50, with gender parity of students as much as possible. Due to the ample time available during the winter break, each student was able to learn the entire course systematically. The course implementation process followed the instructional activity design and task outline. The subjects were randomly divided into two classes, A and B. Class A was randomly selected as the control group and class B as the experimental group. Class A was taught with traditional Python programming and class B was taught with gamified programming. In order to reduce errors and control irrelevant variables, both class A and class B were taught by the author as the teacher.

The teaching experiment was conducted using a quasi-experimental research method, and the study used a pre- and post-test experimental design with an experimental group and a control group. The details are shown in the Table 7:

The research process was divided into three main steps.

Table 7. Experimental Design

Group	Pre-test	Experimental treatment	Post-test
Control group A	O1	C	O2
Experimental group B	O3	X	O4

Pre-experimental Test: The subjects were randomly grouped, informed of the experimental purpose and experimental requirements, and issued programming interest questionnaires for the pre-test.

Experimental Process: According to the activity design and task outline of minecraft-based middle school python programming teaching, the experimental group B was taught. The project-based teaching was conducted for the control group A according to the Shanghai version of the high school IT textbook. The total duration of teaching was 18 class hours, 45 min per class, divided into three weeks.

Experimental Post-test: The same set of high school python language test papers were distributed to control group A and experimental group B at the end stage of the course, post-test programming interest questionnaires were distributed, and student interviews were conducted.

4.2 Teaching Case Presentation

This part of the author chose the fourth teaching theme of Pyramid to demonstrate the educational case, due to the whole lesson time is long, the following will be a brief demonstration of the teaching process.

Introduction Before Class: Teacher leads students into a virtual campus in Minecraft and tells them the legendary story of the Egyptian pharaohs and the pyramids and the unsolved mystery of how the ancient Egyptians built the pyramids. The teacher briefly introduces the structure of the pyramids, asks students to recall the way they placed gold blocks in minecraft using Python code, and thinks about how to build pyramids in minecraft using python programming.

Teach Knowledge: Teacher explains the for loop structure in Python and demonstrates the use of for loops to print all integers between 1 and 99. After students have basic knowledge of the syntax of the for loop, the teacher again explains the structure of the pyramid, shows the Python code that uses the for loop to build the pyramid, and explains to students the meaning of each line of code:

```
import mcpi.minecraft as minecraft
import mcpi.block as block

mc = minecraft.Minecraft.create()
pos = mc.player.getTilePos()
for y in range(10):
    width = 9-y
    for x in range(pos.x-width,pos.x+width+1):
        mc.setBlock(x,pos.y+y,pos.z-width,block.GOLD_BLOCK.id)
        mc.setBlock(x,pos.y+y,pos.z+width,block.GOLD_BLOCK.id)
    for z in range(pos.z-width+1,pos.z+width):
        mc.setBlock(pos.x-width,pos.y+y,z,block.GOLD_BLOCK.id)
        mc.setBlock(pos.x+width,pos.y+y,z,block.GOLD_BLOCK.id)
```

Practice Consolidation: Teacher guides students to build their own pyramids using different cube materials. In this process, students conduct independent investigation and practice, and the teacher gives timely guidance to students' problems.

Summary and Evaluation: Teacher randomly selects students to run the programs they have written and then shares the results with the group, organizes other students to comment on them, and students compare and reflect on the programs they have written and improve them. Finally, the teacher will summarize the learning of the lesson.

4.3   Analysis of the Results of Teaching Activities

Analysis of Students' Programming Interest Results: In order to test the significance of the differences between the three dimensions of the pretest data of control group A and experimental group B, the author conducted independent samples t-test on the pretest data of the three dimensions of programming interest of control group A and experimental group B. The scores of the three dimensions of programming interest, affective, cognitive, and behavioral, overall, were 10, 15, 15, and 40, respectively. The specific data analyzed are shown in Table 8.

In order to test the significance of the difference between the three dimensions of post-test data of control group A and experimental group B, the author conducted an independent sample t-test on the post-test data of three dimensions of programming interest of control group A and experimental group B. The overall scores of the three dimensions of programming interest, emotion, cognition and behavior, are 10 points, 15 points, 15 points and 40 points respectively. See table for specific analysis data. The specific data analyzed are shown in Table 9.

The mean values of each dimension are shown in the table, and the analysis of the results shows that the post-test mean value of each dimension has increased to different degrees compared to the pre-test mean value, with the cognitive dimension increasing the most, by 1.2 points, and the behavioral dimension increasing the least, by 0.76 points.

From the analysis results, it can be seen that the overall p-value of programming learning interest is 0.000, which is much less than the 0.05 significant level, which can

Table 8. Pre-test Data Analysis of Programming Interest of Control Group and Experimental Group

Dimension	Group	N	Avg	σ	df	t	p
Emotion	Control group	25	8.040	1.098	48	0.383	0.703
	Experimental group	25	7.920	1.115			
Cognitive	Control group	25	11.040	1.398	48	−0.097	0.923
	Experimental group	25	11.080	1.525			
Behavior	Control group	25	10.960	1.457	48	−0.287	0.775
	Experimental group	25	11.080	1.497			
Total	Control group	25	30.040	2.605	48	−0.048	0.962
	Experimental group	25	30.080	3.226			

Table 9. Post-test Data Analysis of Programming Interest of Control Group and Experimental Group

Dimension	Group	N	Avg	σ	df	t	p
Emotion	Control group	25	8.360	0.994	48	−2.803	0.007**
	Experimental group	25	9.080	0.812			
Cognitive	Control group	25	11.280	1.458	48	−3.048	0.004**
	Experimental group	25	12.400	1.118			
Behavior	Control group	25	11.160	1.545	48	−1.888	0.065
	Experimental group	25	11.920	1.288			
Total	Control group	25	30.840	2.173	48	−4.053	0.000***
	Experimental group	25	33.400	2.291			

prove that there is a significant difference in students' programming learning interest before and after the experiment of gamified programming teaching. The behavioral dimension p = 0.065 has increased but not significantly, while the affective dimension $p < 0.01$ and the cognitive dimension $p < 0.01$ have increased significantly.

Analysis of Student Performances: In this study, the python language test was administered to students in control group A and experimental group B through high school python language test papers, and further independent sample t-tests were conducted on the python test scores of the two experimental groups, and the results of the analysis are shown in the following Table 10.

The results of the independent sample t-test for the results of the experimental group of the control group showed that the mean value of the results of the control group was 83.76 and the mean value of the results of the experimental group was 83.16, $p > 0.05$,

Table 10. Data Analysis of Python Performance of the Experimental Group in the Control Group

Dimension	Group	N	Avg	σ	df	t	p
Achievement	Control group	25	83.760	6.200	48	0.368	0.715
	Experimental group	25	83.160	5.304			

the difference was not significant, indicating that the results of the python results of the experimental group of the control group were similar and did not change significantly.

4.4 Student Interview Analysis

The student interviews were conducted by online voice after the course, and the interviews were recorded and analyzed descriptively. Ten students were randomly interviewed in the experimental group, and the interviews focused on three aspects: feelings, process, and interests.

In terms of feelings, the interviews showed that the students had a strong interest in programming and a new understanding of it after the teaching activities, and they highly approved of the game-based teaching method. "It feels fun to learn programming in a game". Students said that learning in a game environment greatly increases their learning autonomy, that they pay high attention to the teaching objectives arranged by the teacher, and that they have more autonomy in learning compared to traditional teaching.

In terms of process, the interviews showed that the students basically mastered the programming knowledge in the course and could recall the basic parts of the class, but when it came to the difficulties in the learning process, some of them mentioned that "the learning content was increased because there were more game operations in the course." The introduction of games as an educational medium in the teaching process makes it difficult to grasp the depth and breadth of the teaching content compared to traditional teaching, and slightly increases the learning task of students, which is a key issue to be addressed in the future to improve the teaching of game-based programming.

In terms of interest most of the students expressed their expectation for the new curriculum of gamified programming and said they would pay attention to courses and books about programming in their lives and hope to master the new programming language and work in programming-related jobs in the future. It significantly reflects the role of gamification teaching in promoting students' interest in learning.

5 Conclusion

Due to the current situation that some teachers lack of appropriate teaching methods in middle programming education, the author use Minecraft to develop the teaching of python programming which based on the theory of gamification teaching in middle schools. According to the analysis of the results of the teaching experiment, compared with those who received traditional teaching, students who received gamification teaching have approximately equal scores in python class, while they are more interested in learning, especially in the affective and cognitive dimensions. And they have a new understanding of programming learning and a willingness to work in programming in the future, which proves the feasibility and effectiveness of gamification teaching in the field of middle school programming education. Applying the concept of gamification in the process of programming teaching and making students learn driven by game tasks can improve the teaching effect and students motivation. This game teaching mode provides a new idea for middle school programming education and shows the great potential of applying gamification teaching in programming education, which is important for the development of middle school programming education.

Acknowledgment. This work was supported by "Graduate innovation program of Mudanjiang Normal University", "Doctoral Research Fund of Mudanjiang Normal University" (Grant No.: MNUB202009), "Education Teaching Reform Project in Heilongjiang Province" (Grant No.: 20-XJ21035).

References

1. Kapp, K.M.: The gamification of learning and instruction: game-based methods and strategies for training and education. Pfeiffer, San Francisco (2012)
2. Zhang, L., Hu, R., Zeng, J., Shang, J.: How to design scientific, effective and fun educational games—research on MathGame design from an interdisciplinary perspective of learning science. E-educ. Res. (10), 75 (2021)
3. Li, Y., Song, J., Yao, Q.: Research on influence of gamification learning method on students' learning effect: meta-analysis based on 35 experiments and quasi-experimental studies. E-educ. Res. (11), 60 (2019)
4. Zhang, J.: A first look at building a middle school artificial intelligence curriculum. IT Education in Primary School and Middle School, no. 12, pp. 62–24 (2019)
5. Yuan, T.: Exploring the python road of middle school information technology. Comput. Knowl. Technol. (23), 254–255 (2021)
6. Zhang, X., Yue, Y., Liang, Y.: An empirical study on cultivating computational thinking of senior high school students by digital game teaching in python course. E-educ. Res. (07), 91–92 (2021)
7. Sun, L., Zhou, D.: Design and construction of scratch-based teaching model for children's programming education: a case of elementary science. E-educ. Res. (06), 76–77 (2020)
8. Sun, D., Li, Y.: Improving junior high school students creativity, critical thinking. In: International Conference on Game-Based Learning (2019)
9. Sidenko, A.G.: Studying the while loop in teaching Python programming with gamification elements in Minecraft. Bulletin of Moscow City Pedagogical University. Series: Informatics and Informatization of Education, no. 1, pp. 94–97 (2019)
10. Zheng, J.: Information technology compulsory 1 data and computing. Shanghai Science and Technology Education Publishing House, Shanghai (2020)
11. O'Hanlon, M., Whale, D.: Learn Minecraft programming from scratch. Posts and Telecommunications Press, Beijing (2015)
12. Zhang, J., Fu, G., Zheng, X., Zhang, H.: Gamification in the field of educational technology: a learning catalyst of beyond gaming. E-educ. Res. (04), 20–21 (2019)
13. Lu, Z., Hu, M., Shang, J.: A qualitative study of game-based learning experiences. Distance Education in China, no. 03, pp. 39–40 (2020)

14. Yu, Y.W.: Design and implementation of Minecraft-based Python programming teaching activities. Zhejiang University (2019)
15. Hu, Q.: Research on the practice of online Python language teaching based on minecraft. Shanghai Normal University (2021)

Research on Practice of P-PMCP Double Closed-Loop Hybrid Teaching Model—Taking Course of "Big Data Visualization" as an Example

Peipei Gao , Hong Zhao(✉), Sai Liang, and Huiting Xiang

Nankai University, Tianjin 300071, China
watersky@nankai.edu.cn

Abstract. Under the current trend of education reform in China, educational concepts and teaching models are evolving around the "Student-Centered" approach. How to develop a philosophy of education that is in line with this theme and how to design a teaching model that is in line with this philosophy becomes an important issue for teachers to produce innovative results. To address this issue, this paper proposes a P-PMCP hybrid teaching model that incorporates the general laws of human cognition into the design of the learning objectives and activities for each cognitive stage. Taking the course Big Data Visualization as an example, online and offline hybrid teaching was carried out based on the P-PMCP model. The paper illustrates the effectiveness of the method through the comparison of the student's performance and questionnaire analysis.

Keywords: Student-centered · Cognitive Law · P-PMCP · Hybrid Teaching · Big Data Visualization

1 Introduction

World-class universities generally place the quality of undergraduate education in an important position. The current education reform of universities in China should realize "two changes", namely, the change of education concept from "discipline-based" to "student-based" and the teaching model from "teacher-centered" to "student-centered". These "two changes" revolve around a single theme—"student- centeredness" [1, 2]— and are followed by the exploration of new teaching concepts and teaching models.

To achieve a "student-centered" teaching philosophy, the cognitive patterns of learning should be explored. Hu, RP, and Shao, M in 2018 proposed that "Cognitive theory has a subtle influence on the teaching methods. To fully activate students' motivation and initiative, improve the students' learning ability and achieve the harmonious unity of teaching and learning, the teachers should grasp the students' cognitive features and changing regularity. [3]" The general cognitive learning pattern of humans is "Knowing–Exploring–Innovating", and the research and practice in teaching would only be effective when we follow this law.

© The Author(s), under exclusive license to Springer Nature Singapore Pte Ltd. 2023
W. Hong and Y. Weng (Eds.): ICCSE 2022, CCIS 1813, pp. 86–97, 2023.
https://doi.org/10.1007/978-981-99-2449-3_9

In order to achieve the "student-centered" teaching mode, we should study the teaching methods that are suitable for the current teaching trend and that have strong generalization ability. Hybrid teaching [4, 5]—a teaching method that embraces the advantages of both traditional offline learning and online learning—is considered to be a powerful tool to realize the "student-centered" goal and is an important way to produce innovative results in education. Through the dynamic combination of these two strategies, the learners can explore the learning contents gradually and deeply. Some researchers have integrated the method of BOPPPS(Bridge-in, Objective, Pre-assessment, Participatory Learning, Post-assessment, Summary) [6] into online teaching and constructed the teaching model of HBOPPPS. Through comparative study, it is found that "HBOPPPS is likely a more effective teaching model and useful for enhancing the effectiveness of Physiology teaching. This is attributable to the reproducibility and flexibility as well as the increased learning initiatives [7]". However, the exploration of what kind of learning process can fully reflect the students' subjective status and the teacher's leading role is still lacking. Current research also includes the study of the effect of combining the online and offline learning sessions: "Using online in the tenth to fifteenth, twenty-fifth to thirtieth, and fortieth to forty-fifth min of classroom teaching (50 min in total) can effectively increase students' interest and engagement in learning [8]", However, there is still a lack of data to support the impact of fragmented learning time on learning efficiency. Moreover, scholars have proposed the "Prediction—Observation—Quiz—Explanation" (POQE) procedure for the hybrid teaching design [9]. Nevertheless, such studies tend to focus on empirical learning while neglecting the development of students' creative ability as well as the ability to independently identify and solve problems.

Based on these aspects, this paper integrates the general cognitive law of "Knowing–Exploring–Innovating" into hybrid teaching, proposes the P-PMCP teaching model to design corresponding learning objectives and activities for the three cognitive stages of "Knowing", "Exploring" and "Innovating", highlighting the concept of "student-centeredness" in the process, and illustrates the application and effect of the P-PMCP teaching model with the course "Big Data Visualization".

2 P-PMCP Hybrid Teaching

The P-PMCP model consists of five parts (Fig. 1):

Pre-class + MOOC + Class + Practice

Project (Integrated Innovation Projects)

Fig. 1. The five parts of P-PMCP model.

P-PMCP has a double closed-loop structure, where each lecture goes through a PMCP process, forming an inner closed loop; "Project" refers to a comprehensive and innovative project that runs through the entire course, forming an outer loop. The form of the P-PMCP model is progressive, and the interconnected links fully reflect the goal progression and the step-by-step implementation of the model.

These five sessions are divided into 3 modules.

The study sessions "Pre-Class Push" and "MOOC Self-Study" happen before class, using the MOOC and SPOC platform, constituting the "Knowing" module;

The study session "Class Participation" takes place during class and the study session "Practice & Exploration" is carried out after class, these two sessions constituting the "Exploring" module using the enterprise practice platform and SPOC platform;

The study session "Project" is carried out throughout the whole semester, where students unlock the "Innovating" module through the practice of integrated innovation projects, using the competition platform.

As illustrated in Fig. 2, the P-PMCP model emphasizes pre-class instructional design by determining the teaching objectives of each session and implementing them step by step, and ultimately reaching the goal of instruction.

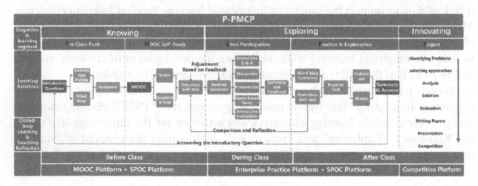

Fig. 2. P-PMCP hybrid teaching model.

2.1 Pre-class

The goal of this part is to ask questions. Before the class, the teacher would push the introductory learning material via the online platform, presenting the problems to be solved and clarifying the role of this module in the overall knowledge system. The teacher assigns the MOOC videos, graphics, and other materials as guidance for students to self-study with questions in mind. Then, students explore and investigate the learning content step by step according to the guidance. This process helps students to stimulate their interests and motivates them to investigate issues related to their own majors.

2.2 Mooc

The goal of this part is to clarify the problem–solving methods. Students work in groups before class to complete the online collaborative learning. Each student learns a part of the MOOC materials and explains the content to other students, increasing their knowledge retention rate and learning rate through this process. Teachers upload the pre-class self-test questions, and students can test themselves to check the result of independent learning. Teachers can also beware of the learning condition of the class in advance. At the same time, teachers can conduct pre-class Q&A session online to address possible problems promptly. Moreover, teachers may review the results of the pre-test to adjust the focus in the class.

2.3 Class

The goal of this part is to solve the problems posed before the class. The course is organized in groups, using offline participatory learning methods. Various forms of participatory learning are carried out step by step according to the level of participation to guide students to get solutions to their problems, making students the main body of independent learning. The first level of interaction is not named, such as pop-ups and posts; the second level of interaction is named, such as online interactive quizzes and group discussions; the third level of interaction is active, such as group presentations, game-based study and interactive evaluation, etc. At the end of the class, the groups are invited to summarize the learning outcomes of the current learning unit.

2.4 Practice

The goal of this part is to submit a problem-solving report and further practice the acquired knowledge in depth. Learning groups answer the pre-class introductory questions, allowing the learning unit to form a closed loop. Teachers assign post-class self-test questions and practices, using real data and cases as much as possible. Students can further practice and consolidate their knowledge of the unit, considering both teaching requirements and workplace needs. Both teachers and students can compare the scores of the post-test with the pre-test to check the effectiveness of learning.

2.5 Project

To achieve the teaching objectives of the course, a group project is carried out throughout the whole semester. The project helps to develop students' awareness and ability to innovatively solve complex problems by implementing the knowledge they have acquired comprehensively. It forms a closed-loop process of identifying problems, selecting approaches, analysis, finding solutions, evaluation, writing papers and presentation. As an effective examination method, the project can be used to determine the student's level of achievement throughout the course. In addition, activities such as "Innovative Project Competition" are organized to promote learning and stimulate students' interest.

3   A Case Study of P-PMCP Hybrid Teaching

3.1   The Knowledge Framework of the Big Data Visualization Course

The course *Big Data Visualization* is designed based on the Outcome-Based Education (OBE) philosophy with three progressive levels of teaching objectives: "Basic Visualization Theory"–"Theory-based Visualization Practice"–"Integrated Visual Analytics Project Development". The course follows the problem-solving logic of visual analytics, implementing the theory of the "knowledge puzzle" [10] when designing the course framework, with each piece of the puzzle solving one problem in visual analytics. The course carries out comprehensive innovation projects according to the bottom-up hierarchy of "Basic Awareness– Data Access–Task Analysis–Visual Mapping–Visual Interface". The framework of the course is shown in Fig. 3.

3.2   P-PMCP Hybrid Teaching in Big Data Visualization

Nankai University's general education course Big Data Visualization is offered to all students and is designed with the P-PMCP double-closed-loop model. Each learning unit is organized according to the model as the inner closed-loop and the integrated innovation project as the outer closed-loop. In the following parts, Lec5 Visualize Frameworks & Graph (Network) in Big Data Visualization is used to illustrate the application of P-PMCP hybrid teaching.

The knowledge objectives of this lecture include: understanding what a data visualization framework is, to be able to describe the relationships among its various components, to be able to use the techniques and tools available, and to comprehend what graph structure (network structure), graph data, and graph attributes are as well as to understand the scope of application of graph structure visualization.

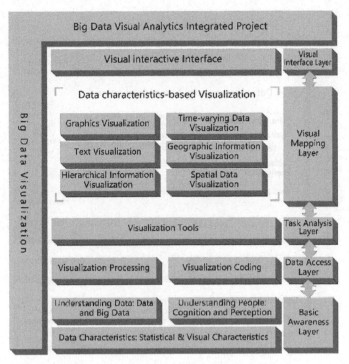

Fig. 3. Big data visualization course framework.

The capacity objectives of this lecture include: being able to use SaCa DataViz, a data analysis (BI) platform, to build model and visualize the social network structure using graphs, and to draw conclusions concerning the characteristics of social relationship by comparing, analyzing and discussing the results.

Pre-class. The question posted previous to this lecture is "How can we visualize and analyze social networks in our 'social circle of friends'?". The teacher presented the knowledge puzzle of the lecture so that students know "what I have already learned", "what I am learning" and "what I will learn". The position and role of this module in the overall knowledge system was also presented according to the puzzle. The knowledge puzzle of Lec5 is shown in Fig. 4.

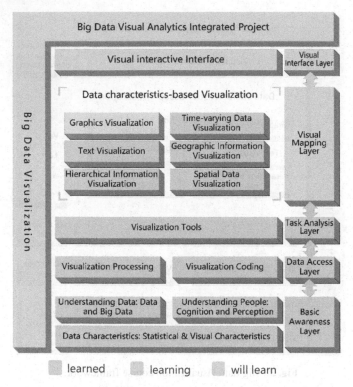

Fig. 4. Knowledge Puzzle of Lec 5.

MOOC Students worked in groups to collaborate online before class and complete the pre-class self-test questions. Students would study the MOOC videos and graphics online using WeChat and complete the self-test questions using "Rain Classroom", a smart teaching platform that supports posting question and Q&A sessions. The pre-class courseware is shown in Fig. 5.

Class. Classes were conducted offline for participatory learning, with guidance and support from the teacher. Students worked in groups to solve the "social circle of friends" visualization problem, discussed the key points of each step of the social network visual analysis, and proposed a solving plan. The task was approached following the process of "social network data acquisition–data cleansing and organizing–visual mapping–visual analysis–conclusion". Each group presented a report on their solution and conclusion, which was evaluated by the other groups and the teacher respectively. Eventually, the learning group concluded with a summary of their social network visualization and further expanded to the general process of visualization.

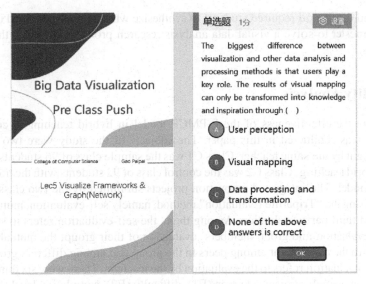

Fig. 5. Pre-class Push (partial).

Practice. After class, practice materials were sent to students, which were authentic data and cases from industry. The course used SaCa DataViz, a visual data analysis platform, to provide students with real-life work experience and online collaborative visual analysis training to consolidate and improve their ability to solve industry problems. A comparison of the post-class self-test and the pre-class self-test is shown in Fig. 6.

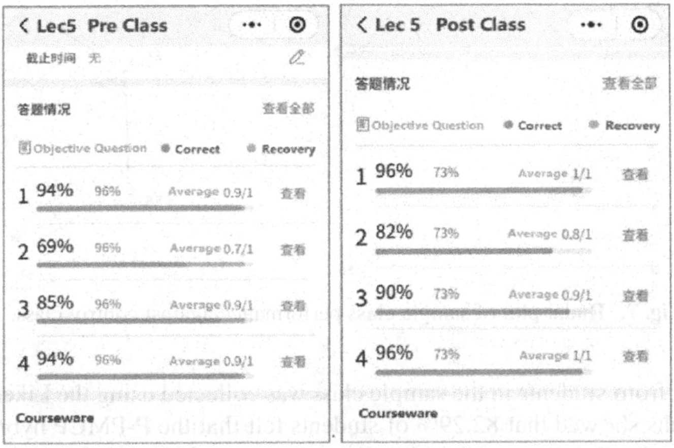

Fig. 6. Comparison of self-test before and after class.

Project. The final assessment for the Big Data Visualization course required students to work in groups to complete a visualization research project. The project had a certain breadth and depth, and required students to synthesize what they have learned through-out the semester to solve a visual data analysis research problem related to their own disciplines.

4 Validity Analysis

To evaluate the effectiveness of the P-PMCP model in hybrid teaching, a compara-tive study was conducted in this paper. The subjects of the study were two parallel classes taught by the same teacher. Class C1 was the sample class of 96 students with P-PMCP hybrid teaching; Class C2 was the control class of 92 students with the traditional teaching model. The integrated innovation projects submitted by the two classes were assessed using the "Tripartite Evaluation" method, namely self-evaluation, mutual eval-uation, and third-party evaluation. Among them, the self-evaluation refers to students' own self-evaluation and group members' evaluation of their group; the mutual evalua-tion refers to the assessment among peers in the group and among different groups; the third-party evaluation refers to the evaluation by the teachers. There were six dimensions of evaluation, namely project selection (E1), difficulty (E2), completion level (E3), dis-cipline/industry application value (E4), innovation (E5), and presentation performance (E6). The average performance of the sample class and the control classes is shown in Fig. 7, which demonstrates that the sample class has a significant advantage in the dimension of E1, E2, E4, and E5.

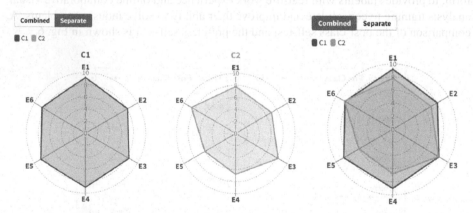

Fig. 7. Radar plot of sample class performance against control class.

Feedback from students in the sample class was collected using the Likert scale [11, 12]. The results showed that 82.29% of students felt that the P-PMCP hybrid teaching helped them to develop awareness and ability to detect professional problems; 78.13% of students felt that they had improved their problem-solving skills through group learning; 92.71% of students felt that the course had stimulated their interest in learning and that they would actively use visual analytics to solve professional problems in the future; 83.34% of the students were satisfied with the learning experience and the outcome of the course. The results of the questionnaire are shown in Fig. 8.

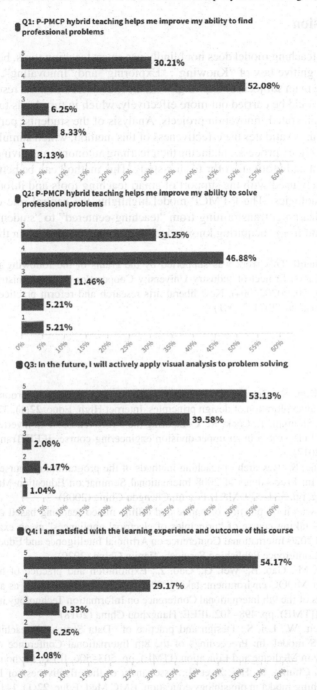

Fig. 8. Results of the questionnaire, the distribution of answers on Q1, Q2, Q3 and Q4.

5 Conclusion

The P-PMCP teaching model does not blindly use smart teaching tools, but conforms to the general cognitive law of "Knowing", "Exploring" and "Innovating", allowing students to be the main subjects of learning. With the assistance of online resources, offline explorations would be carried out more effectively, which in turn leads to the output of high-quality integrated innovation projects. Analysis of the students' performance and the questionnaires validates the effectiveness of this method, which stimulates students' interest in the inquiry process, enhancing their learning autonomy and giving them a sense of achievement and motivation for further study. This method can be better interpreted and more widely used with the support of smart teaching tools and information-based teaching technologies. The P-PMCP model highlights the central role of students in teaching and learning, transforming from "teaching-centered" to "student-centered" in the process, and from "acquiring knowledge" to "having the ability" in the result.

Acknowledgement. This work was supported by the grants of the following programs: Collaborative Education Project of Industry University Cooperation of the Ministry of Education (202002021001, 202002021004), New liberal arts research and reform practice project of the Ministry of Education (2021020001).

References

1. Kim, M., Kim, S., Getman, J.: The experience of three flipped classrooms in an urban university: an exploration of design principles. Internet High. Educ. **22**(1), 37–50 (2014)
2. Mason, G., Shuman, T., Cook, K.: Comparing the effectiveness of an inverted classroom to a traditional classroom in an upper-division engineering course. IEEE Trans. Educ. **56**(4), 430–435 (2013)
3. Hu, R., Ming, S.: Research of teaching methods of the programming course based on cognitive law. In: Proceedings of 2008 International Seminar on Education Management and Engineering, pp. 534–539. M&D Forum, Chengdu China (2008)
4. Shi, L.: Research on practice of online and offline mixed teaching based on wisdom tree platform — taking course of "principles of electrical appliances" as an example. In: Proceedings of 2020 International Conference on Artificial Intelligence and Education (ICAIE), pp. 76–78.Conference Publishing Services, Tianjin China (2020)
5. Lu, H., Ye, M., Gao, B., Wei, G., Gao, Z.: Exploration and practice of hybrid teaching mode under MOOC environment: taking "Database System Principle" as an example. In: Proceedings of the 9th International Conference on Information Technology in Medicine and Education (ITME), pp. 498–502. IEEE, Hangzhou China (2018)
6. Li, Q., Chen, W., Lei, S.: Design and practice of "Data Structure" teaching class based on BOPPPS model. In: Proceedings of the 8th International Conference on Information Technology in Medicine and Education (ITME), pp. 503–506. IEEE, Fuzhou China (2016)
7. Xiaoyu, L., Chunm, L., Hui, Z, et al.: Assessment of the effectiveness of BOPPPS-based hybrid teaching model in physiology education. BMC Med. Educ. **22**(1), 1–10 (2022)
8. Sabine, Z., Uta, L., Timo, G.: Web-based and mixed-mode cognitive large-scale assessments in higher education: an evaluation of selection bias, measurement bias, and prediction bias. Behav. Res. Methods **53**(1), 1202–1217 (2021)

9. Chiruei, J.H., et al.: The effect of the "prediction-observation-quiz-explanation" inquiry-based e-learning model on flow experience in green energy learning. Comput. Educ. **133**(1), 127–138 (2019)

10. Peipei, G., Yuanhong, Z., Mingxiao, L.: A new teaching pattern and evaluation system of knowledge point puzzle in massive online computer courses. In: Proceedings of the 15th International Conference on Computer Science & Education (ICCSE), pp. 103–106. IEEE (2020)

11. Reiser, R., Maron, A., Visintin, L., Abeijon, M., Kreinovich, V.: Relation between polling and likert-scale approaches to eliciting membership degrees clarified by quantum computing. In: Proceedings of 2013 IEEE International Conference on Fuzzy Systems, pp.1–6. Hyderabad, India (2013)

12. Hornbeck, H., Alim, U.: UofC-Bayes: a Bayesian approach to visualizing uncertainty in Likert scales. In: Proceedings of 2019 IEEE Conference on Visual Analytics Science and Technology (VAST), pp.130–131. Vancouver, BC, Canada (2019)

KAP: Knowledge-Graph Based Auxiliary Platform for Outcome-Based Python Education

Wanchun Jiang[✉], Zhibin Sun, Jintian Hu, Ping Zhong, and Mingming Lu

School of Computer Science and Engineering
Central South University, Changsha, China
jiangwc@csu.edu.cn

Abstract. Outcome Based Education (OBE) is currently a popular approach, but quantifying students' learning outcomes remains a challenge. To address this issue, this paper proposes the development of a Knowledge-graph based Auxiliary Platform (KAP) for outcome-based Python education. KAP facilitates manual organization of knowledge points by teachers according to the expected learning outcomes and associates relevant questions with each point. This feature allows for automatic qualification of students' mastery of knowledge by monitoring their progress within the question bank in KAP. Moreover, the discrepancy between the targeted and achieved levels of knowledge mastery can guide teachers in adjusting their teaching process in a timely manner. To implement KAP, we utilized the model-view-controller design pattern and incorporated it into the Python programming course for sophomores at Central South University in China. Results from one semester demonstrate that KAP is a valuable tool for both teaching and learning. Objective and subjective evaluations confirm that KAP is a suitable platform for outcome-based Python education.

Keywords: Outcome Based Education · Knowledge-graph · Python

1 Introduction

Outcome-Based Education (OBE) has gained popularity as an approach that distinguishes itself from traditional education methods by incorporating three key elements: theory of education, a systematic structure for education, and a specific approach to instructional practice. OBE aims to organize the entire educational system towards achieving essential learning outcomes.

In the OBE model, what students learn and their success in doing so is considered more important than how and when they learn. As such, teachers must have a clear understanding of students' abilities and adjust their teaching progress in a timely manner based on students' outcomes. In university education, there is often a focus on course content and teaching time, leading to a potential loss of sight of what students actually take away from the class. OBE can help address this deficiency.

To realize OBE in university education, teachers must be able to track and update students' mastery of knowledge in a timely manner. Knowledge-graphs are a potential tool for OBE teaching. As a graph structure, they can store the relationships between various knowledge points and customize node attributes to provide feedback to the teacher on the students' achieved degree of mastering knowledge.

In this paper, we develop KAP, which has the following characteristics

- Use the knowledge-graph to organize the knowledge framework of related courses, which is clearer and more intuitive.
- Use the OBE education model to help college students master the relevant knowledge of the course.
- Use the knowledge-graph to feed back the Achieved degree of mastering knowledge to teachers, which is time-sensitive.
- Integrate the functions of auxiliary teaching, automatic test, student management, automatic test, etc.

KAP has been implemented in the Python programming course for sophomore students at Central South University in China. After one semester, the results showed that KAP was beneficial to the teaching and learning process. Both the objective and subjective evaluations confirm that KAP is a suitable platform for outcome-based python education.

2   Background and Related Work

2.1   Outcome Based Education

Outcome Based Education (OBE) is a kind of goal-oriented, student-oriented, and reverse-thinking approach to the construction of a curriculum system. OBE aims to improve the final outcomes achieved by students [4]. During the educational process, OBE emphasizes outcomes, that is, what students achieve in the teaching process. Specifically, the achievement is usually reflected in whether students have the corresponding ability, and the ability is closely related to the degree of mastering knowledge. Therefore, teachers always set the Target degree of mastering each knowledge point before the classes and quantify the Achieved degree of mastering knowledge point by students during the class. The quantification of the Achieved degree of mastering knowledge is based on the collection and analysis of the training results such as homework and final exam. In this way, the difference between the Achieved degree and the Target degree of mastering knowledge is used to guide the adjustments of the teaching process. Furthermore, as the number of students enrolled in courses increases, it becomes more difficult for teachers to understand students' Achieved degree of mastering knowledge. In addition, there is no clear standard for the quantification of outcomes, and it is difficult to define the degree of mastering knowledge in the traditional teaching model [7]. Therefore, the effective application of the OBE concept to all aspects of teaching requires the help of auxiliary platforms.

2.2   Online Education

In online learning platforms, such as MOOCs [8], Tronclass [1], and digital reading, teaching materials are shared over the internet, providing students with ample opportunities to gain knowledge. However, surveys [3] have shown that students who actively use social media may perform better in digital reading, but their digital reading performance may be inversely related to their use of ICT-based social media. Furthermore, most online platforms cannot provide analysis and feedback on the students' Achieved degree of mastering knowledge, which makes it difficult for teachers to know students' mastery of outcomes. Therefore, it is impossible to adjust their teaching progress and teaching plan in time according to the students' Achieved degree of mastering knowledge, which is difficult to achieve the goals of OBE. Moreover, platforms with low media richness [10] rarely establish clear relationships between knowledge points and homework questions, making it difficult for both students and teachers to understand the outcomes of the course and quantify the results of OBE in a timely manner.

2.3   Education Based on Knowledge-Graph

The concept of knowledge-graph was first proposed by Google in 2012, it can link heterogeneous data from different fields to each other. With the maturity of knowledge-graph technology, it is not only used in Internet companies but also in the field of education. Z. Yang et al. [9] found that in in-group cooperation, the use of knowledge-graph to coordinate knowledge construction can not only improve the efficiency of knowledge acquisition but also enhance the effect of communication and interaction, increase the degree of participation in learning, and improve the learning effect. P. Chen et al. [2] developed KnowEdu to automatically build a knowledge-graph according to courses and use neural networks to extract teaching data to better fit the relationship between various knowledge points.

However, above works only store course knowledge points discretely and without using knowledge-graphs to capture and display logical relationships between knowledge points for users. Therefore, Shaw R S [6] studied the relationship between knowledge graph construction methods and academic performance in programming language learning, and the study showed that applying knowledge graphs to programming language teaching will significantly improve academic performance. Moreover, the learning methods and knowledge graph structures are crucial to improving learning satisfaction. Besides, S. Li et al. [5]proposed a knowledge point organization model based on AND/OR Graph, which stores knowledge points in the database in the structure of knowledge-graph and decomposes the knowledge structure of teaching into various subgraphs.

In summary, the application of knowledge graphs in education is mostly used to construct course knowledge points. Although some work realizes that the reflection of the logical relationship of knowledge points is helpful for course learning, feedback on the Achieved degree of mastering knowledge and the OBE goals is missed.

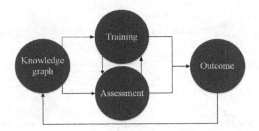

Fig. 1. Basic Idea

2.4   Discussion

As mentioned above, knowledge-graph is helpful to education and the organization of course knowledge. With the help of a clearer knowledge context, students can learn the knowledge better. Therefore, we believe that knowledge-graph will be of great help to the quantification of outcomes in OBE. The specific advantages are as follows:

- The knowledge of the course is stored in the knowledge-graph in the form of nodes, and the attributes in the nodes can store the information of students' Target degree of mastering knowledge.
- The assignments are arranged according to the knowledge-graph, which is connected with the knowledge nodes. This can help to feedback on the students' Achieved degree of mastering knowledge.

Summarize the above OBE teaching methods and knowledge-graph. We propose a knowledge graph-based auxiliary platform for outcome-based Python education.

3   KAP

3.1   Basic Idea

Knowledge-Graph. Under the condition of limited class hours, teachers use knowledge-graph technology to make Python programming courses cover a wide range of knowledge points. They build the knowledge-graph based on the Target degree of mastering knowledge, which is derived from the OBE (Outcomes-Based Education) goals. The knowledge-graph is intended to assist teachers in OBE teaching and help students understand the outcomes they need to master in class. Additionally, students train through KAP to improve their Achieved degree of mastering knowledge. KAP assesses students' training results, and the assessment results are fed back to teachers through the knowledge-graph.

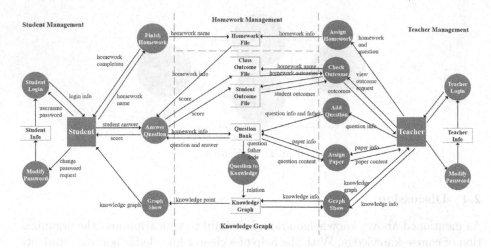

Fig. 2. Framework of KAP

Training. Teachers can use KAP to conduct targeted training for students. If the Achieved degree of mastering knowledge does not meet the Target, then teachers can arrange training items for the knowledge points in the knowledge-graph corresponding to the Target to help students fully understand and achieve it. KAP can also help teachers cultivate students' outcomes, that is, teachers can arrange training content according to the Target degree of mastering knowledge, and help students achieve it more efficiently.

Assessment. To assess students' degree of mastery of the target knowledge, KAP will automatically calculate their scores after training and convert them into their achieved degree of mastering knowledge using a specific method. Then, the results will be fed back to the teacher through the knowledge-graph. Based on the assessment results, teachers can decide whether additional training is needed for this target.

Outcomes. The focal point of OBE teaching is Outcome, which represents the ability students can master through the course. KAP helps teachers to judge whether students' Achieved degree of mastering knowledge has reached the Target degree of mastering knowledge. If most students do not reach the goal, teachers need to adjust their teaching progress and the structure of the knowledge-graph, and re-explain the knowledge points related to the outcome.

3.2 Framework and Functions

Based on above basic ideas, we design KAP, whose framework are shown in Fig. 2. KAP has two kinds of users: one is students and the other is teachers. It provides users with interfaces and functions to interact with the database. Users submit their own data and requests to KAP, and KAP operates the database according to the user's request, such as adding, deleting, modifying, and querying the database. The center of KAP is the database, which records the content of the homework and saves the knowledge-graph and question bank. Based on the above content, KAP is mainly divided into four parts, as shown below.

Knowledge-Graph. Compared with the application of knowledge-graph in Sect.2, the knowledge-graph in KAP should be used to display the specific knowledge details of Python courses. Because the knowledge-graph is based on the teacher's teaching content, different from KnowEdu [2], the knowledge-graph of KAP should not be automatically generated, but should be manually entered by the teacher, only in this way can the knowledge-graph play a good auxiliary role in the teaching content.

KAP needs to reflect the logical relationship in the course knowledge, which requires knowledge as a node and a logical relationship as an edge to store in the graph. Furthermore, in order to assist teachers in OBE teaching, knowledge points in the knowledge-graph should timely feedback on students' Achieved degree of mastering knowledge. When designing the knowledge-graph, teachers need to do it according to the outcomes they expect students to master.

Homework Management. As an auxiliary teaching system, KAP needs to reduce the workload of teachers, that is, to realize the automation of homework assignments and reviews. Therefore, the question bank needs to be maintained in the system that includes the content and answers to the questions. In order to feedback on the completion of students' homework in the knowledge-graph, the questions in the question bank need to be linked with the knowledge-graph. Additionally, the system needs to be able to randomly assign diverse homework. The number of assignment questions is set by the teacher, but the assignments are different for each student. Furthermore, KAP sets deadlines and completion time limits on assignments to ensure teachers can get timely feedback from students.

Student Management. Since the system serves multiple users from the student side, the database needs to store the information of each student. When students access the system independently and complete their homework, the system needs to be able to match each student with their homework completion records one-to-one and display the information on the student side after the student logs in. Additionally, the system should be able to reflect the Achieved degree of mastering knowledge of each student for teachers to adjust the target outcome.

Teacher Management. As the administrator of the entire system, teachers should have more permissions than students, including the management of knowledge-graph, question banks, and homework. As the core of KAP, the

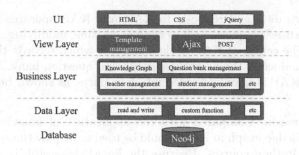

Fig. 3. Basic structure

teacher can view the Achieved degree of mastering knowledge from each student in the entire class.

3.3 Implementation

Basic Structure. We use the popular Model-View-Controller (MVC) design pattern in our system. Different functional modules in the business layer to implement OBE. We divide the system as a whole into five layers, as shown in Fig. 3. The following will introduce the most important two layers: Database, and Business Layer.

The **database** uses the neo4j graph database, which is a high-performance NOSQL graph database. The knowledge-graph is stored in the database, which is manually entered by teachers. The nodes of the knowledge-graph are not only related to the course content but also to the outcomes that teachers want students to master. Question banks are also stored in the database.

The **business layer** is the part where the front end interacts with the back end. Mainly responsible for the classification and implementation of system functions, corresponding to the View in Django, including how each function is implemented. By calling the data layer to realize the interaction with the database, the low coupling effect of the project is achieved.

Knowledge-Graph. We applied KAP to the author's Python Data Processing and Programming course. The links between knowledge in the course can form a knowledge-graph. Each chapter continues to stratify knowledge into sections and knowledge points. So we divide the knowledge into three types of nodes and store them in the knowledge-graph. Their relationship is: *chapter → section → knowledge point*

Each knowledge node contains nine attributes. The type and meaning of each attribute are shown in Table 1. Among them, Mastery can be fed back to teachers in real-time as the outcomes of OBE.

There is also a connection between each question node and the knowledge-graph, which is used to feedback on students' answers and the Achieved degree of mastering knowledge.

Table 1. Attributes of knowledge node

Name	Definition
Type	The type of the node, the unified value is 'Chapters' or 'Section' or 'Knowledge Point'
Title	The name of the node
Difficulty	The difficulty of the node
Importance	The importance of the node
Weights	The weights of the node in this course
Teached	0 for the node has not been taught, 1 for the node has not been taught
TestNum	The times of question node related to this node appears in all assignments
RightNum	The times of question node, which gets right by students, related to this node appears in all assignments
Mastery	The class's mastery of this knowledge point

Homework Management. The homework comes from the question bank, and the completion of the homework will be fed back to the knowledge-graph, which is helpful for the realization of OBE. The question node in the question bank is an addition to the knowledge-graph and is a child node of the knowledge point node. The attributes of question nodes are similar to those of knowledge nodes, but with content attributes and answer attributes.

The completion of each homework is fed back to the knowledge-graph through relation 'question_hfile' and relation 'kpoint_question', and the attributes of the corresponding nodes in the knowledge-graph are updated after each homework is completed.

Student Management. Students are stored in the database as nodes, which are attached to the knowledge-graph, and the relationship between student nodes and question nodes is used to store the completion of homework.

When the student completes a certain homework, the system will establish an edge between the student's node and the corresponding question node in the homework. At the same time, the system will also find the corresponding subgraph containing the question node in the knowledge-graph, and update the attributes of the knowledge node in the subgraph, such as TestNum, TestRightNum, Mastery, to feedback the Achieved degree of mastering knowledge of the students.

Teacher Management. Teachers can view the learning situation from the three dimensions of homework, class, and individual students, and promote the realization of OBE by obtaining feedback.

Table 2. Visit times of KAP in the lastest six weeks

Week	1th	2nd	3rd	4th	5th	6th
Times	300	429	380	396	327	368

The student's learning information includes the student's personal student number, name, the score of each assignment, the number of questions done, the total number of correct questions, etc. Class learning information includes each student's score for each homework, the mastery of knowledge points in the class, etc. In the information of the homework, we can see the specific content of each question of this homework, how many people got it right, how many people got it wrong, and the score of each student, etc.

Deployment. We deployed the system on Alibaba Cloud. The server has one CPU core and the memory size is 4G. Since we have no more than 200 students in this course, the server resources are sufficient.

4   Results

4.1   KAP in Class

The system is used in the author's "Python Data Processing Programming Course", which has approximately 110 students per year. Currently used in teaching in the spring of 2022, a total of seven assignments were assigned before the completion date of the essay, 64 assignments were not submitted, and the assignment submission rate reached 91.69%. According to the statistics of the access system data, the total number of visits to the system is 2222, the average number of visits per day is 52, and the most frequent day was visited 194 times. The Table 2 shows the weekly visits for the last six weeks. From the statistical data, about half of the students use the system every day on average, which also shows that the system has improved students' enthusiasm and self-learning ability.

4.2   Using Cases

Now, we show how the KAP system is used in the Python Programming classes. In detail, the education process of the first chapter "Basic Grammar" is shown as an example.

Determine the Outcome. The course has only 32 class hours. Teachers need to combine the main teaching content and knowledge-graph to refine the outcomes that students need to master, mainly including *Use of Operators*, *Use of Comments, Familiarity with Keywords* and *Understanding of Python Built-in Functions*. Teachers will teach and assign homework according to the defined outcomes, so as to get the students Achieved degree of mastering knowledge points.

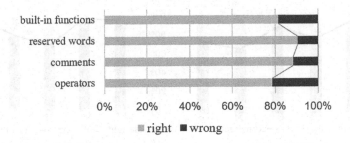

Fig. 4. Correct rate of each knowledge point

Assign Homework. When the teacher completes the offline teaching, the homework will be assigned. The homework questions need to be set to cover all the learning needs that the teacher expects the students to get in this lesson and obtained from the KAP question bank to easily measure the achievement of the students' mastery. We focused on the four results mentioned above in the first lesson, so this assignment will focus on them. Of these, there are 5 questions for each result, for a total of 20 questions.

Finish Homework. At this stage, students need to complete the teacher's homework on time, which is usually one week before the next class. In this homework, a total of four outcomes are involved, the four knowledge points related to these four outcomes are named: operators, comments, reserved words, and built-in functions.

Assessment. Teachers can check the students' or the entire class's Achieved degree of mastering knowledge through the assessment function provided by KAP. In this homework, a total of 105 people completed the homework on time. Statistics of this 105 homework are shown in the Fig. 4 .

It can be seen that the entire class has a good mastery of these four outcomes, all above 60%. Among them, the mastery of the three outcomes, namely the *Use of Comments, Familiarity with Keywords* and *Understanding of Python Built-in Functions*, is greater than 80%. Teachers can simply think that the entire class has basically mastered these three outcomes.

Figure 5 shows the correct rate of the topics contained in these four outcomes, it can be seen that the correct rate of almost every question is above 60%, and even some questions have a correct rate of more than 95%, indicating that the students have a good mastery of knowledge. The teacher can decide whether to choose questions with a lower accuracy rate to explain in the next class according to the results of KAP's analysis of the degree of outcomes mastered by students.

Teaching Adjustment. In this assignment, the teacher knew through KAP that the student's mastery of the Outcome on *Use of Operators* did not reach the 80% goal, so in the next week's teaching, the teacher helped the students to

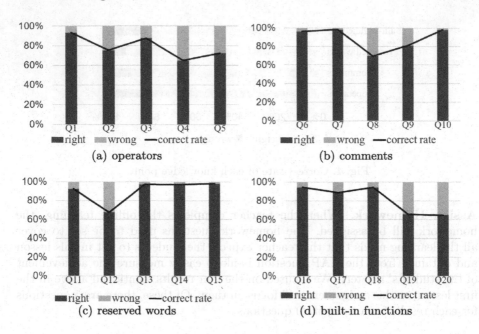

(a) operators   (b) comments

(c) reserved words   (d) built-in functions

Fig. 5. Correct rate of four outcomes

review the knowledge points related to operators. At the same time, the teacher explained the five questions of Q4, Q8, Q12, Q19, and Q20 with a correct rate of less than 70% in this assignment to help students better master the outcome.

4.3 Subjective Results

Teacher. Through KAP, the way teachers assign homework has changed from handwritten documents to electronic versions. Previously, they used to write questions based on course knowledge, but now they only need to find the corresponding questions in the question bank according to the knowledge-graph. After students submit homework, teachers do not need to spend more time judging whether students' homework is right or wrong, KAP will automatically help teachers complete homework correction and analyze statistics. Teachers are able to devote more time to the teaching process.

Students. We distributed 100 questionnaires to the students who participated in the course study and received 90 valid questionnaires, which proves that the promotion of KAP has attracted the attention of the students, and the statistical results of the questionnaires are reliable.

The distributed questionnaire consists of three parts and a total of eight questions, respectively counting the feedback of students' learning performance, learning satisfaction, and learning enthusiasm after using KAP to find out whether KAP has achieved better results in assisting all aspects of OBE teaching

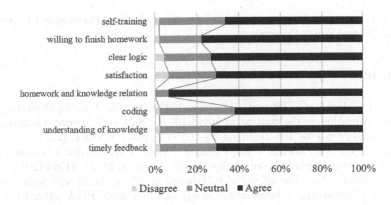

Fig. 6. Statistics on student usage of KAP

work. Q1–Q3 Statistical KAP experience in students' Training and Assessment, such as: whether the practice results are timely feedback, practical programming training, etc. Q4–Q6 counted students' feedback on the auxiliary effect of KAP in the teaching process. Q7 and Q8 investigated the influence of KAP-assisted OBE teaching mode on students' learning enthusiasm. For example, Q4 counts the degree of fit between the system homework and the teaching content perceived by students, and basically no students objected to KAP. From the perspective of Q5, less than 7% of students still take a wait-and-see attitude towards the integration of KAP into curriculum teaching.

From the final statistical results, nearly 25% of students feel that KAP needs to be further strengthened and improved related functions, and more than 70% of students are satisfied with the overall performance of KAP, which shows the effectiveness of OBE teaching based on knowledge-graph.

5   Conclusion

We propose KAP, a knowledge-graph-based auxiliary platform that assists teachers for outcome-based python education. It can analyze the achieved degree of mastering knowledge of students and use it as feedback to guide the adjustment of the teaching plan. We have already applied this system to a course at Central South University, and the results showed that teaching was more efficient. Besides, through the experience of using KAP, we found that KAP can not only help students to master knowledge better but also stimulate their enthusiasm and motivation to learn. In future work, we will further improve KAP and provide more convenient functions for teachers' teaching.

Acknowledgement. The authors sincerely thank the reviewers for their helpful comments on this paper. This work is partially supported by the key research and development project of Hunan province under grant No. 2022SK2107 and the academic research project on education of central south university. In addition, this work was also carried out in part using computing resources at the High Performance Computing Center of Central South University.

References

1. Alves, P., Morais, C., Miranda, L., João V Pereira, M., Vaz, J.: Digital tools in higher education in the context of covid-19. In: 2021 16th Iberian Conference on Information Systems and Technologies (CISTI), pp. 1–6. IEEE (2021)
2. Chen, P., Lu, Yu., Zheng, V.W., Chen, X., Yang, B.:Knowedu: a system to construct knowledge graph for education. IEEE Access **6**, 31553–31563 (2018)
3. Jie, H., Rushi, Yu.: The effects of ICT-based social media on adolescents' digital reading performance: a longitudinal study of PISA 2009, PISA 2012, PISA 2015 and PISA 2018. Comput. Educ. **175**, 104342 (2021)
4. Ismail, A.M., Zakwan, F., Ismail, R., Ismail, B.N.: Implementation and assessment of outcome based education (OBE) in the faculty of civil engineering at universiti teknologi mara (UITM). In: International Congress on Engineering Education (2011)
5. Li, S., Li, X., Wang, L.: Knowledge points organization model based on and/or graph in ICAI. In: 2010 Sixth International Conference on Natural Computation, vol. 4, pp. 2121–2124. IEEE (2010)
6. Shaw, R.-S.: The learning performance of different knowledge map construction methods and learning styles moderation for programming language learning. J. Educ. Comput. Res. **56**(8), 1407–1429 (2019)
7. Varghese, A., Kolamban, S., Prasad, J., Nayaki. S.: Outcome based assessment using fuzzy logic. Int. J. Adv. Comput. Sci. Appl. **8**(1) (2017)
8. Wu, W., Bai, Q.: Why do the MOOC learners drop out of the school? - based on the investigation of MOOC learners on some Chinese MOOC platforms. In: 2018 1st International Cognitive Cities Conference (IC3) (2018)
9. Yang, Z., Pan, W., Wang. Y.: Group cooperative learning model and its application based on group knowledge graph. In: 2021 IEEE 3rd International Conference on Computer Science and Educational Informatization (CSEI), pp. 324–327. IEEE (2021)
10. Zhao, Y., Wang, A., Sun, Y.: Technological environment, virtual experience, and MOOC continuance: a stimulus-organism-response perspective. Comput. Educ. **144**, 103721 (2020)

Learning Comparative Analysis of Teaching Models Based on Smart Platforms——Takes ERP Principles and Applications as Example

Jieru Cheng, Gening Zhang, and Jimei Li[✉]

Beijing Language and Culture University, College Road No. 15 in Haidian District of Beijing, Beijing, China
ljm@blcu.edu.cn

Abstract. Based on the background of big data technology and the post-epidemic era, the introduction of online teaching has become an inevitable development trend. Hybrid teaching is a feasible way to improve teaching quality in the teaching reform, and it is important to explore the effect of online and offline hybrid teaching mode. This paper has analyzed the data of an example course—ERP principles and applications, on the EduCoder practice smart platform in a visual form in order to compare learning behaviors and results between hybrid teaching mode and self-learning online mode. Then it has made significance tests and established the teaching quality evaluation model of the course. At last, this paper has given some suggestions on how to improve the online learning ability and results.

Keywords: Online and Offline · Teaching Mode · Blended Learning · Comparative Analysis · Smart Platforms

1 Introduction

At this stage, China's epidemic prevention and control is still on the way. How to balance online teaching and traditional teaching mode has become a major problem in society. How to innovate in education mode has also become a concern of many educators. In this context, it is of great significance to make a comparative study of pure online teaching mode and online and offline mixed teaching mode.

Online learning refers to the mode of online learning or online learning through online learning platform. Online and offline mixed teaching mode means that learners should not only accept learning in the online and offline classroom like the traditional mode, but also carry out operation practice, classroom check-in, discussion, fill in questionnaires and hand in materials on the online platform. The score recorded on the platform is component of the final score of the course.

This paper introduces the conceptual framework, evaluation criteria, verification process and research conclusions of hybrid teaching effectiveness evaluation, realizes the integration of classroom teaching evaluation and online learning evaluation, and establishes the factor composition model of hybrid teaching effectiveness.

W. Hong and Y. Weng (Eds.): ICCSE 2022, CCIS 1813, pp. 111–122, 2023.
https://doi.org/10.1007/978-981-99-2449-3_11

This paper aims to compare the differences between pure online teaching mode and online and offline mixed teaching mode in learning behaviors, learning achievement and learning quality, analyze the reasons for the differences, and finally give reasonable suggestions. This study attempts to analyze how the teaching participants in the online and offline integrated teaching build a new network interaction under the complex mode, explore the interactive relationship between the participants in the hybrid teaching construction, and promote the effective transformation of the digitization of higher education in China.

2 Literature Review

Technology-enabled blended learning, combining online and offline, is deconstructing the traditional one-size-fits-all model of teaching and learning. Since the late 1990s, the concept of blended learning, often referred to as 'blended' or 'inverted' learning, has evolved through a focus on information technology and a combination of traditional and online teaching models, teacher-directed and backstage design and transformation, and more 'student-centred' teaching and coaching. From the late 1990s to the present day, the concept of blended learning has evolved through three stages, focusing on information technology and combining traditional and online teaching models, the design and transformation of teacher-directed and backstage classroom organisation, and the blending of "student-centred" teaching and tutorial approaches [1]. In qualitative terms, blended learning must be a deliberate integration of purely face-to-face and online teaching; In quantitative terms, the proportion of online teaching in blended learning should be in the range of 30%–79%, usually around 50%. If the amount of time spent online in a course is greater than or equal to 80% of the total number of hours taught, the course is fully online and not blended.

Modern education has gone through a process of development from offline teaching to distance learning and then to online teaching. Online teaching refers to the process of teaching activities that takes place in an online teaching environment where teachers and students are separated remotely under the guidance of theories such as distance education and online learning. The development of distance learning has been influenced by the work of Borje The early thinking on online teaching, represented by Borje Holmberg, considered online education to be one of the advanced forms of distance learning. The use and spread of Massive Open Online Course (MOOC) technology has led to a transition from distance learning to online teaching and learning. With further research, a more suitable online teaching model for higher education has emerged, namely the SmallPrivate Online Course (SPOC). In contrast to the large-scale and open characteristics of MOOC, SPOC has the characteristics of small scale and privacy.

With the further maturation of technologies such as mobile internet, artificial intelligence and virtual reality, online teaching has been widely used in various fields. Wang Wen and Han Xibin point out that compared to traditional face-to-face teaching, online teaching focuses on "any time, any place" learning and the multiple interactive features of learning, with learners mainly using technology to access learning content, effectively breaking through the limitations of learners in time and space. The purely online mode of teaching also meets the requirements of national strategies to improve the relevance, adaptability and effectiveness of the training of skilled personnel. It can effectively alleviate the problems of insufficient teachers and teaching resources and student diversity caused by large-scale expansion, and achieve "no lowering of standards, multiple modes and flexible study systems".

Existing research focuses on the following online teaching models: ① MOOC (or SPOC) + domestic online teaching platform model. For example, MOOC + Rain Classroom model, SPOC + Tencent Classroom model, etc. ② MOOC, SPOC or MOOC + SPOC model. ③ Domestic online teaching platform model and its combination. For example, Super Star Learning Pass model, Rain Classroom model or Tencent Classroom + Rain Classroom model, etc. Online learning resources are designed with problems or tasks as the guide, PPT and videos as the carrier, discussions and assignments as the channel, using the immediacy of the online platform to motivate learners and guide students to explore and think and complete their learning tasks. Regarding online teaching modes, Wei Wei and Zhang Xuefeng put forward three common features, ① Live mode. Known as live teaching mode, live mode is a teaching mode that uses online video conferencing and online teaching" platforms such as Tencent Conference, Nail and Super Star Learning Pass to transmit and display images and sounds of teachers and students in real time. ② Recording mode. The recording mode is an online teaching mode in which teachers record the images and voices of the course in advance and students learn anytime and anywhere through the online learning platform. ③ Audio-visual mode. Voice and text mode is an online teaching mode in which the teacher provides real-time teaching information to students by means of continuous voice short messages on voice chat platforms such as WeChat groups and QQ groups, and at the same time assists in sending information such as graphics, and students and teachers complete interactive discussions within the chat groups. Many scholars have actively explored different online teaching models in their own contexts, and have achieved some results.

However, in general, the following shortcomings exist in previous research on online teaching models: ① there are more case studies on a particular online teaching platform, but there is a lack of horizontal comparison studies on different online teaching models or platforms; ② there are more quantitative studies on the influencing factors and teaching effects of existing online teaching, but there is a lack of real-life experience analysis combined with specific teaching situations; ③ the existing studies do not give teachers sufficient suggestions and strategies for teaching.

With regard to blended teaching, some studies have proposed a "two-line integration" type of blended teaching under the concept of co-construction classroom ecology, using technology platforms as support for online and offline interaction [2]. Zhang Qian and Ma Xiupeng propose to create a co-temporal, multi-step blended teaching process [3]. Diao Yajun and Liu Shizhen point out that the change of teaching mode inevitably requires teachers to prepare lessons taking into account the preparation of online resources and their effectiveness, depth and breadth as well as the extent of students' utilization [4]. Fengjuan Jiang use the UTAUT model to conclude that the factors influencing behavioural intentions to learn in a blended learning environment are: mobile self-efficacy > effort expectations > performance expectations > social influence > achievement goals [5]. Chen Xifeng takes the "Psychology of Advertising" course, which is a blended teaching course, as an example, to study the effect of blended teaching in this course, mechanism and many other problems. Li Minhui and Li Qiong find that the "convergent interactive" blended teaching model can be divided into five categories from the perspective of the field, namely "recorded courses, online learning", "recorded courses, offline learning", "live courses, offline learning" and "live courses, offline learning". ", "live courses, offline learning", "live courses, online and offline dual-teacher teaching", "offline classroom, online and offline learning". Its teaching effectiveness is influenced by the teaching field of the lecturer, the learning field of the students and the supplementary teaching field of other teaching participants. Guan Enjing proposes that the effectiveness of blended teaching can be further explored in three ways: the optimisation of blended teaching evaluation indicators and methods, the validation of the blended teaching effectiveness evaluation system and the expansion of the scope of blended teaching implementation.

3 Course Design and Application of ERP Principles and Applications

The course "ERP Principles and Applications" is characterised by the "principle of application" and the objective of the course is to train students to apply their knowledge in the practical operation of ERP and to master the processes and operations of ERP systems. Through the simulation of various functional positions in the enterprise, familiar with the functions of the ERP system, to clarify the processing of different types of business processes, and the responsibilities, rights and benefits of each position in the enterprise environment. Through the simulation of the enterprise process environment, students are able to systematically combine economic business deepening theory and practice in a comprehensive manner, using the enterprise business process as the connecting thread, to gain a deeper appreciation of the relationship between an enterprise's part and whole, and to understand the enterprise's process-based operation model. Supported by the ERP U8 platform built with UFIDA on the EduCoder Smart platform, students have mastered the principles and methods used in theoretical teaching and then simulated and analysed the business management processes of various departments of an enterprise through demonstration sets of accounts and simulated date. It enables students to practically appreciate the systematic and applied value of ERP.

There were 63 learners in our case study course, including both purely online and mixed learners, with 16 purely online learners and 43 mixed learners. There were 44 online practical exercises, 9 weekly quizzes, a final exam, a group business design and lab report, and a final group defence and submission of materials in the course design (Table 1).

3.1 Online Teaching Design and Application

Online teachers have provided learning resources, formula course delivery and assessment arrangements, set time points and issued learning tasks. Students were mainly self-learning and could access them anytime and anywhere via their computers and mobile phones. The online teaching platform would provide the teacher with the appropriate learning statistics.

Table 1. Comparison between online teaching model and blended teaching model.

Elements		Online Teaching Model	Blended Teaching Model
Teaching objects		Students should master principle and practise skills	Students should master principle and practise skills
Teaching content		Multimedia resources like courseware, cases, tests, etc	Multimedia resources like courseware, cases, tests, etc
Teaching environment		Network teaching platform+Data operational environment	Data operational environment+Physical classroom
Teaching methods		Case teaching method, independent studying	Case teaching method, independent studying, group discussion, presentation
Teaching evaluation		Behaviors of online learning+Achievement of online learning	Behaviors of offline classes+Offline tests+Behaviors of online learning+Achievement of online learning
Teachers and students activities	Before class	Students should complete online preview tasks	Students should complete online preview tasks
	During class	Students learn through network teaching platform autonomously	Teachers give classroom teaching and interact with students
	After class	Complete tasks after class+Group discussion	Complete tasks after class+Group discussion

The online learning resources were modularised according to the knowledge points involved in ERP principles and the rules in application operations, such as basic terminology, system management login, account management, user management and role and authority management. The teachers' main course knowledge points were formed into recorded videos, which were uploaded to the online platform by the teaching assistants. Once the online resources were published, students could access the resources and downloaded the text at any time, even after the course had finished. At the same time, the platform technology allowed online teaching resources to be adapted at any time and their origin or expansion could be visualized.

3.2 Design and Application of Blended Learning

The blended teaching model is completed by a lead teacher and a teaching assistant, using online practical training and quizzes as a bridge between offline courses and online summaries and practice to complete a two-way teaching flip. The instructor uses the multidisciplinary and comprehensive nature of the ERP course to provide students with certain knowledge of management, computing and finance, such as production operations management, management practices, management information systems and accounting principles.

The teacher offline uses half of the teaching time to narrate learning points and relative ideological and political education. The other half of the time is spent on practical training. Students can analyse specific problems and shift their thinking models from theory to practice through practical training. Feedback sessions are also set up online so that teachers could keep abreast of students' needs and plan their teaching as required. The organic integration of online and offline teaching plays an important role in it.

4 Online Practical Teaching Design

4.1 Instructional Mode

The principle and application of ERP adopted two teaching methods. One of them was online teaching model, students firstly watched teaching video through MOOC platform or EduCoder, and then practised and operated independently on EduCoder. Another method was online and offline blended teaching, students attended offline classes and operated practical training on online platform in the meantime.

4.2 Functions of Teaching Platform

Students can check in and complete unit testing through EduCoder platform, which provides a virtual environment for students to complete practical training, questionnaires. It also supports shared teaching materials, discussions, online video resources uploading, gathering statistics of personal scores and learning time and efficiency analysis. This platform has functions like class ranking and analyse conditions of whole class as well.

5 Analysis of Case Curriculum

5.1 Analysis of Learning Behaviors

In the original approximately 912 data items, 46 practical training completion data, 9 quiz data, and total final grade data were included. We studied more than 100 previous practical training records of the enterprise application platform so as to make comparisons. In the learning behavior analysis process, we filtered the desensitized data and then manually performed secondary calculations. We researched on following targets, average times of measurement, average time of practical training, average ratio of on-time passed/unpassed/late submission, efficiency of passing stages, evaluation efficiency, to analyse learning behaviors.

$$\text{Average times of measurement} = \frac{Sum\ of\ practical\ training\ times}{The\ number\ of\ users} \tag{1}$$

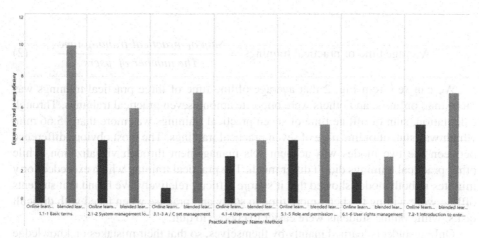

Fig. 1. Average times of measurement

Judged on Fig. 1, average times of measurement of online and offline blended learners were higher than online learners. Online learning mainly depended on students' learning autonomously, which lacked interaction between teachers and students, students' learning initiative and motivation reduced relatively.

Although online curriculum break through limitations of traditional classroom teaching that students have flexible time to learn, and online video resources can be watched repeatedly. However, online learners can't set up links between students and students, students and teachers, students and teaching resources through watching video resources and scanning courseware [6]. Therefore, students couldn't have a good command of knowledge as well as key and difficult points, and then they didn't have enough initiative to complete challenges.

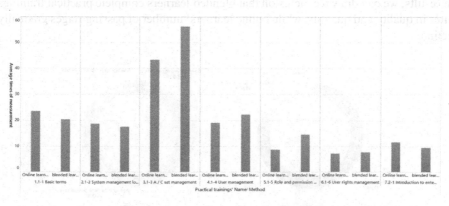

Fig. 2. Average time of practical training

$$\text{Average time of practical trainings} = \frac{Sum \; of \; practical \; training \; time}{The \; number \; of \; users} \quad (2)$$

We can see from Fig. 2 that average offline time of three practical trainings was more than online's, and others were opposite among seven practical trainings. Through calculation, sum of offline time of seven practical trainings was more than 15.66 min, which was sum of online time of seven practical trainings. The most obvious difference between the two modes was account sets management through visualization, while other practical trainings didn't differ much. The practical training which exceeded forty minutes in both modes showed that it's more difficult relatively. We found that students offline were willing to spend more time to study and practise when faced with difficult tasks, while online students were easier to choose to quit.

Online students learned mainly by themselves, so that their mistakes on knowledge understanding couldn't be corrected on time, their questions on teaching content couldn't be answered timely during learning process, and lagging information feedback couldn't satisfy demands of different levels of students.

In comparison, the platform presents testing results after offline learners complete practical trainings. Students' questions can be solved on time through the process and teachers can effectively supervise students' study conditions. Teachers can also adjust teaching plans timely according to visualization data feedback, letting students absorb knowledge easier, increasing classroom efficiency and making teaching process have more individualization and precision [7].

Online learners' ratio of passing stages on time was lower than fifty percent basically, while ratio of not passing stages on time was more than fifty percent on the whole, and ratio of delay of passing stages was tiny, which could be ignored.

In contrast, blended learners' ratio of passing stages on time was ninety percent or so while ratio of not passing stages and delay of passing stages was pretty tiny. Based on the results, we can draw a conclusion that blended learners complete practical trainings better in quality and quantity, while online learners' number of passing stages gradually decline.

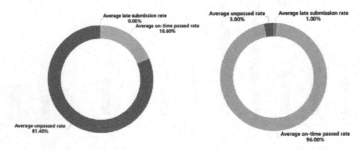

Fig. 3. The average ratio of on-time passed/unpassed/late submission

After calculation, Fig. 3 shows online learners had 81.4% not passing stages and 18.6% passing on time in every practical training, while blended learners had 3% not passing stages and 96% passing on time in every practical training.

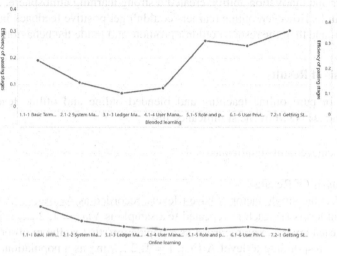

Fig. 4. Efficiency of passing stages

$$\text{Efficiency of passing stages} = \frac{\text{Number of finished stages}}{\text{Used time}} \quad (3)$$

Based on Fig. 4, online learners completed a maximum number of 0.1 levels per unit of time, and their efficiency gradually declined. The completion efficiency of offline learners' level exceeded 0.3, which fluctuated slightly in the early stage. With the growth of training experience, the efficiency increased substantially after about four training, and basically remained above 0.25. At the same time, the number of assessments (evaluation efficiency) per unit time was calculated, and the overall evaluation efficiency of online learners was not as good as that of offline learners.

$$\text{Evaluation efficiency} = \frac{\text{Average times of measurement}}{\text{Average number of levels completed}} \quad (4)$$

Finally, we calculated the evaluation efficiency. It's found that online learners have basically exceeded 10 from the fourth level, that is, it took ten times to pass a level on average, while offline learners were basically less than five times. At the beginning of the course, there's no big efficiency difference between online students and offline students, there's no big difference in learning ability. The problem was that the tracking and feedback in the later stage of the course were not in place, resulting in a decline in learning enthusiasm and a sharp decline in efficiency. This suggested that online learning couldn't produce a resulting chain of positive feedback. In the ERP principle and application courses, verification experiments accounted for a large proportion, and students needed to test the theoretical knowledge learning results through practical training. EduCoder platform calculated the star students, got positive feedback, stimulated students' learning motivation [8], offline learners group collaborated to complete the homework, exercised diversified thinking mode through discussion, improved knowledge transfer and innovation ability, created a strong learning atmosphere, and formed a virtuous circle. However, online learners couldn't get positive feedback in the overall environment, and then the results couldn't promote and guide the behavior.

5.2 Analysis of Results

The results of pure online teaching and blended online and offline teaching were compared and analyzed by the significance test.

1) Test of achievement significance

① Analysis Of Results

Let the single factor A have r levels, recorded as $A_1, A_2, \ldots A_r$, under different levels (i), each m repeated test sample is $Y_{ij}(i = 1, 2,\ldots, r; j = 1, 2,\ldots, m)$, each level can be regarded as a population, that is, the m observed sample set corresponding to level A $\{Y_{ij}, j = 1, 2,\ldots, m\}$ as a population, a total of r populations. Suppose, here each population is normally distributed N $(\mu i, \sigma i2)$, each population variance $(\sigma i2)$ is equal, and all test samples are independent of each other.

② The original and alternative assumptions are based on the overall distribution of the two teaching modes.

Original hypothesis H0: There is no significant difference between the performance of pure online learning and those of mixed online and offline learning.

Hypothesis H1: There is a significant difference between the scores of pure online learning students and those of mixed online and offline learning students.

At the significance level = 0.05, the minimum significance level p-value for rejecting the null hypothesis was 1.36267E−9, and $p < 0.05$, so we reject the original hypothesis.

③ Get significant differences in the results of these two learning modes.

5.3 Teaching Quality Evaluation Model

This course follows the principle of "combining process evaluation with result evaluation, and combining online activity evaluation with offline activity evaluation" [9]. According to the requirements of the relevant documents of the school curriculum examination and the actual situation of the course, the quality evaluation model is established as follows:

$$Z = G + 0.5Q + 0.3C + 0.2A \tag{5}$$

Z represents the total score of the course and the final score; G represents the attendance, assigned points according to the regulations of the school, Q represents the process assessment score, C represents the quiz score, and A represents the defense score.

In the actual operation process, we quantify each training task; Quiz results were directly quantified, namely unit test scores; Defense scores were directly calculated by the teacher; Attendance was directly deducted from the sum of process assessment results and quiz scores and defense scores. In conclusion, this model is a quantifiable model and is operable.

6 Conclusion and Strategic Suggestions

6.1 Conclusion

After analysis, online and offline mixed learners were far better than pure online learners in learning behavior, academic performance and learning quality. The "fusion and interactive" blended teaching mode combines online and offline teaching through information technology to create a field-based interactive relationship between teachers, students and other teaching participants. Improve the efficiency of students' self-construction of knowledge system, and promote the further transformation of higher education to digitization and modernization. The case presents the advantageous "fusion and interaction" blended teaching mode 10 [10].

6.2 Suggestions

In the post-epidemic era, we will face comprehensive changes in teaching concepts, teaching platforms, teaching methods and teaching relations.

For educators, teachers should have the teaching concept of keeping pace with The Times, abandon the traditional concept of "teaching for learning", and cultivate and stimulate students' independent learning motivation and consciousness [11]; and establish an equal, active and democratic atmosphere of classroom, encourage students to actively participate in classroom activities, reasonably set and arrange classroom teaching content and related knowledge modules, so that students can easily and actively complete the course learning.

In terms of online courses themselves, course content organization requires modular, time fragmentation and diversified knowledge acquisition [12], while independent learning resources should meet the needs of new era learners with fragmented, mobile and interactive characteristics. More importantly, we should highlight the interaction design [13], and use the question answer and theme forum to strengthen the communication and interaction in the learning process, so that the teaching effect will be better.

Finally, colleges and universities should increase the investment of network resources and campus learning culture construction, to provide a learning atmosphere and environment that can guarantee college students' online independent learning. Only by firmly establishing the dialectical development concept that online teaching triggers the profound reform of college teaching, and accurately grasping the problems that need to be solved in different development stages of online teaching, can we achieve better results [14]. In the era of promoting the development of education formalization, we should create a benign ecological environment for the high-quality development of online teaching.

Acknowledgment. This work was partly supported by Research on International Chinese Language Education of the Center for Language Education and Cooperation "Research on identification and influence of teaching methods of International Chinese Education based on classroom video" (No. 21YH11C), by New Liberal Arts Program of Ministry of Education (No. 2021180006), by New Engineering Program of Ministry of Education (No. E-SXWLHXLX 20202604), by the Cooperative Education Program of the Ministry of Education (NO. 202101110002), and by the Science Foundation of Beijing Language and Cultural University (supported by "the Fundamental Research Funds for the Central Universities") (No. 22YJ080004).

References

1. Zou, Y., Feng, T., Wang, Y.: Curriculum design and practice of blending teaching: a case study of ERP sand table business simulation course. Account. Res. (07), 181–189 (2020)
2. Shao, Z.: The value implication, action mechanism and practice path of "dual-line integration"realization——is based on the perspective of co-built classroom ecology. Vocat. Tech. Educ. China (08), 23–31 (2021)
3. Zhang, Q., Ma, X.: Construction and suggestions of integrated teaching model in universities in post-epidemic period. Jiangsu High. Educ. (02), 93–97 (2021)
4. Diao, Y., Liu, S.: Practical exploration of blended teaching in subject English from the perspective of ideological and political curriculum. J. Foreign Stud. (06), 89–93 (2021)
5. Jiang, F.:A study of influencing factors of college students' behavior intention to learn in blended teaching environment. Audio-Vis. Educ. Res. **42**(06), 105–112, 128 (2021)
6. Sun, Y., Li, Q.: Research on the effect of middle school students' learning experience on learning effect inblended teaching—— takes MOOC teaching in Hubei universities as an example. J. Hubei Univ. Econ. (Humanit. Soc. Sci. Ed.) **19**(02), 146–150 (2022)
7. Lu, G., Yue, X., Jiang, Z.: Application of online and offline hybrid teaching in computational thinking class. Theor. Res. Pract. Innov. Entrepreneurship **4**(23), 56–58 (2021)
8. Quan, L., Zhu, Y., Wei, Y., et al.: The application of online and offline mixed teaching in college teaching today. Sci. Technol. Wind (31), 121–123 (2021)
9. Qin, S., Zhong, C., Zhang, X.:Construction of an online and offline hybrid teaching quality evaluation system model. Econ. Res. Guide (05), 104–106 (2022)
10. Li, M., Li, Q.: Exploration of the "integrated interaction" modes of online teaching from the field perspective. Mod. Educ. Technol. **31**(09), 120–126 (2021)
11. Larson, R., Falvo, D.C.: Elementary Linear Algebra, 6th edn. Houghton Mifflin Harcourt Publishing Company, New York (2009)
12. Wu, Y., Xiao, Q., Mou, X., et al.: The exploration of online and offline hybrid teaching mode in the "computer-aided design" course. Anhui Archit. **28**(11): 85–86, 137 (2021)
13. Zhang, Q., Wang, A.:The design of new blended teaching mode based on flipped classroom. Mod. Educ. Technol. (4), 27–32 (2014)
14. Chai, J., Tian, Y.: Open, shared, diverse and individualized university internet education. J. Chifeng Univ. (Chin. Philos. Soc. Sci. Ed.) **40**(9), 147–149 (2019)

Research on Hierarchical Teaching Using Propensity Score Weighting-Based Causal Inference Model

Jiacheng Kang[1]([✉]) and Yang Weng[2]

[1] Sichuan University, Chengdu, Sichuan 610064, China
727939731@qq.com
[2] Sichuan University, Chengdu, Sichuan 610064, China
wengyang@scu.edu.cn

Abstract. The "double reduction" policy is an important initiative of the Party Central Committee to build a strong education country. In this context, how to reduce the burden without reducing the quality has become a hot topic of discussion among educators, so the tiered teaching model has gradually come into view. The research on the effectiveness of the tiered teaching model is not available in domestic educational experiments and foreign data are not in line with China's national conditions, so it is of great significance to explore the effectiveness of the tiered teaching model based on statistical methods. The goal of this paper is to analyze the effectiveness of hierarchical teaching based on a causal inference model. Based on the performance data of three grades in a middle school in Chengdu since the enrollment in 2019, this paper first analyzes the potential factors affecting class performance through a causal inference model with propensity score matching-teacher level and the subject of headteacher. Then uses a hybrid model of propensity score matching method and double difference method to eliminate the mutual interference between the two influencing factors as much as possible and judge their degree of influence; finally, sets the above two influencing factors as weights and builds a causal inference model through the propensity score weighting method to obtain the conclusion of the effectiveness of the tiered teaching model. The main contributions of this paper are: firstly, this study verified that the two factors-teacher level and the subject of headteacher have significant effects on class performance through causal inference model, and the effects of the effects were calculated. Secondly, this study built the first weighted causal inference model in the context of educational randomized trials. Finally, it came to the important conclusion that the tiered teaching model is effectively better than the general teaching model, which presents an important data support and reference for the development of education in China.

Keywords: Causal inference model · Hierarchical teaching · Propensity score · Difference in difference · Weighting

W. Hong and Y. Weng (Eds.): ICCSE 2022, CCIS 1813, pp. 123–135, 2023.
https://doi.org/10.1007/978-981-99-2449-3_12

1   Introduction

In recent years, the State has put forward the requirement of "double reduction", which refers to the effective reduction of the excessive burden of homework and off-campus training on students in compulsory education. In order to effectively improve the standard of education in schools and to reduce the burden but not the quality, we need to rely on a long-term mechanism as a guarantee. In this context, the tiered teaching model has become a hot topic of discussion. The tiered teaching model is both an innovative educational idea and a new exploration of quality education methods, with important pedagogical implications.

Tiered teaching refers to the scientific and rational division of students into groups of students with similar levels of proficiency, after the school has first randomly divided the administrative classes and the teachers have tested and assessed the students' current knowledge, ability levels and potential tendencies in various ways.

Experts in education in China are divided on whether the tiered teaching model is effective, but unfortunately, research on tiered teaching in China has remained almost exclusively at the theoretical stage. Prior to 2002, there was little rigorous evaluation of the effectiveness of educational reform in the United States, and evaluators often tended to use surveys or small-scale qualitative case studies to judge the merits of a reform. In China, policy makers and educators are eager to know whether the tiered teaching model does indeed have a significant impact on improving student achievement, even if they are limited by the paucity of research data and restricted research methods. In the absence of reliable research findings, it is often difficult for policy makers to replicate a novel educational reform on a large scale. If a large number of studies confirm the effectiveness of tiered teaching, policy makers may try to pilot this model in the province or even nationally, if conditions permit, which would play an important role in the development of education in China.

This study is a study established under a randomized controlled experiment, and the specific experiments and control group settings will be described in Sect. 2. In order to control as much as possible for the effects of other factors on class performance, and to find more clearly the causal relationship between the tiered teaching model and performance, it was necessary to verify whether teacher rank and classroom discipline did have a significant effect on performance, and to control as much as possible for such an effect.

The first step in the study was to construct separate causal inference models of propensity scores for teacher rank and classroom teacher subject based on changes in mean scores in multiple examinations in classes at a grade level that was not tiered, to infer and calculate the effects of teacher rank and classroom teacher subject background on student achievement, and then to discuss the interactive effects of the two. In examining these two influences, the study first estimates the propensity scores for each sample using logit regression, secondly matches the propensity scores obtained, then verifies the degree of influence of these two factors, and finally verifies the interaction between these two influences. In the second step, the propensity scores were recalculated from the factors validated in the first step, based on the achievement data of a tiered grade, and then fitted to the new propensity score weighting model using inverse probability weighting to verify that the tiered model contributed significantly to student achievement and classroom performance. In a final step, the results of the model were generalized by incorporating the performance trends of the first cohort of students after the "double reduction".

The main contributions of this paper are: firstly, based on the data source secondary school examination results for class 2019, it was verified that both teacher level and the subject of the headteacher do have an effect on class performance. Mean intervention effect values were calculated and estimated from the mean intervention results for the experimental and control groups, with larger mean intervention effect values indicating a larger effect of this one intervention. It was found that the impact of teacher level was greater than the impact of the classroom teacher's discipline. Secondly, based on student test data from the class level tier of the Class of 2020 (the year in which tiered instruction was conducted), the impact factors that passed validation were set as weights using the inverse probability weighting method to try to control for the impact of other factors on achievement and it was found that the tiered teaching model also had a significant positive impact on classroom performance. Thirdly, the causal relationship between the tiered teaching model and student achievement progress was verified based on examination data from the 2020 student tier, while reasonable speculations were made as to the causes of the tiered teaching model on individual student heterogeneity. Finally, the findings of this study were validated in the examination results of the school's class of 2021, adding to the statistical research on the effectiveness of the tiered teaching model in China, providing reliable statistical theoretical support for further educational reform and laying the foundation for subsequent educational randomized experiments based on statistical methods.

In order to study the causal relationship between layered teaching and student achievement, we should first understand what causation is. The human inquiry into unknown things is the source of driving force of social development. From ancient Greek philosophy to the causal cycle of Chinese Buddhism, it contains human inquiry into the causes of all things in the world and the consideration of causal relationship [5]. Causal relationship refers to the relationship between two events, usually one of events B (i.e. "result") is the result of another event a (i.e. "cause"). Unlike the correlation, variable or event a is a cause of B, and when and only when a is changed, the other conditions remain unchanged. Causal inference is a discipline which is developed on the basis of statistical discipline, which is used to study the causal relationship between things. After continuous development and evolution, causal inference is widely used in various fields of social science, including sociology, econometrics, epidemiology and biostatistics.

Causal relationship is often confused by the correlation between things, and the correlation is only the existing distribution characteristics between the two factors. Causality emphasizes a certain intervention. This operation effectively causes the change of another observation variable, strictly distinguishes the "cause" variable and the "result" variable, and plays an irreplaceable role in revealing the occurrence mechanism of things and guiding intervention behavior. Human beings discover the laws of nature through observation, and then realize the ultimate goal of exploring the causal relationship between natural things. Einstein believed that "western science is based on formal logic based on the law of causality".

Since Galton [7] put forward the concept of correlation coefficient in 1888, "the problems involving causal inference have entangled the heels of statistics from the beginning" [8]. In 1911, Pearson proposed using contingency table to analyze causality, in 1921. Wright proposed path analysis model, in 1934. Neyman proposed potential result model, in 1935, Fisher proposed randomized experimental method, and in 1974, Rubin [9] proposed a virtual fact model for observational research, Pearl [10] and Spirtes [11] proposed a causal network diagram model, gradually pushing causal inference to the climax of scientific research.

Experimental research and observational research are important research methods to realize causal inference. Experimental research, known as the randomized experiment of the golden rule, is the most reliable method of causal inference. However, in order to infer the effect of the cause on the result, it is necessary to determine the cause factor before the randomized experiment, which itself is a big problem. Moreover, many limitations of the actual situation often do not allow randomized experiments. The experimental cost is huge, the technology has limitations, and it is extremely difficult to find a large number of the same other variables or instrumental variables not affected by confounding factors in a limited space. However, only one phenomenon can be observed in a single individual, and the applicability is too low. Researchers hope that simple observation data can infer the causality of the research object.

Observational research is based on the existing and observable data. It is simple, efficient and easy to understand. It is mainly applied through the cause and effect diagram model and the potential result framework. The prediction based on general correlation is not generally applicable. The invasion of external intervention factors can easily change the current correlation and overall distribution of each variable. The causality diagram model based on the prediction method of causality mechanism can intuitively connect causality inference with the theory of probability independence, predict the future intervention results of external intervention factors, and realize that it only acts on the subject without hindering the normal operation of other factors, which is more realistic and universal. Most of the causal inference research on causal graph models is based on the data generation mechanism model of directed acyclic graph, namely Bayesian network. At present, Bayesian network model is mostly used to study the causal relationship between multiple factors. Jansen R. [13] first proposed the method of predicting the interaction between proteins by Bayesian network in biology in 2003. Friedman n. [14] discussed the application of Bayesian network in gene network construction in 2004, Sachs K. [15] discussed the structural learning of protein regulatory networks using a variety of experimental data and causal network methods. Causal inference based on Bayesian network emphasizes the use of small sample data to build a powerful data network and extract causality from the data. The core of the potential outcome model is to apply the same research object with and without intervention respectively, and compare the result difference between the intervention group and the control group. This difference is the final effect of receiving the intervention relative to not receiving the intervention. To some extent, observational research is a pseudo random experiment. But for the same research object, researchers can only observe one of the phenomena, and can not virtual a parallel world to experiment simultaneously. Therefore, for the subjects receiving the study, the state of non intervention is a virtual state of "anti fact" under the premise of accepting intervention; Under the premise of not accepting intervention, the accepted intervention is a virtual state of "anti fact", so the potential result model is also called the anti fact framework.

In practice, many methods of causal inference are more likely to be realized by extracting causal relationship. The weighted algorithm is based on the bias of choice caused by the different data distribution between the intervention group and the control group. By properly reweighting each sample data, a pseudo population is created to eliminate the interference of some confounding factors, which makes the data distribution of the experimental group and the control group tend to be the same. Finally, the causal relationship is evaluated according to the weighted results. The layered algorithm divides the whole experimental group into sub groups, and each sub group has some intervention groups and control groups. Under the same test conditions, the intervention results are weighted average of the measurement results of each sub group. Matching algorithm, double difference algorithm and tree model are all important experimental methods for causal inference.

Pedagogy is a complex social problem, which is influenced by social, economic, cultural and other factors [16]. In order to reduce the influence of many factors on the experimental results, Frederick Mosteller and Howard Hitt and others presided over a conference on the status of educational research in 1999, and put forward the application of causal inference model to educational experiments [17]. By establishing causal inference model, researchers can analyze whether an intervention has an impact on potential results.

After opening the door to apply causal inference model to educational experiments, the United States Congress passed the "No Child Left Behind Act" in 2001, and established the Institute of Education Sciences, aiming to create a new scientific foundation for educational research. During the first decade of its establishment, ies funded more than 175 large-scale randomized controlled experiments, and obtained a large number of experimental data of random education [18]. These experimental data also got many interesting conclusions under the support of causal inference model. Through the investigation, it is found that in the same school and the same grade, the difference between class and class will change obviously with the passage of time. Besides the influence of the external society, the teacher setting within the class will also have an impact. These potential influences also have an impact on the accuracy of experimental results. How to control these effects, Tobias Kurth [20] summarized five common methods to control confounding factors in the real problem background in 2006: multivariate regression model adjusting confounding factors, building regression model after matching tendency scores, regression model adjustment tendency scoreInverse probability weighting and standard death ratio weighting method. Unfortunately, the educational concepts and teaching modes are quite different under different national conditions. The educational experimental conclusions of foreign countries do not necessarily conform to the education situation in China. Therefore, to discuss whether the layered teaching model is effective in domestic education, researchers must choose appropriate models and methods to analyze based on the domestic education data.

There are different opinions on whether the layered teaching mode is effective or not. Unfortunately, the domestic research on layered teaching is almost in the theoretical stage. Cook [20] proposed that the conclusions of education evaluation not based on random experiments and statistical analysis are unreliable. Before 2002, the United States rarely strictly evaluated the effectiveness of educational reform, and evaluators tend to use the methods of investigation or small-scale qualitative case study to judge the merits and disadvantages of a reform. In China, even if limited to the lack of research data and limited research methods, policy makers and educators are eager to know whether layered teaching model is really helpful to improve students' performance. Without reliable research results, it is difficult for decision makers to popularize a new educational reform in a large area. If a large number of research results confirm the effectiveness of layered teaching, decision makers can try to carry out the experiment of educational reform in the whole province and even the whole country under the condition of the conditions, which will play an important role in the development of education in China.

2   Model and Method

This study is based on the randomized controlled experiment to control the interference of many uncertain factors in the educational experiment. Based on the randomized controlled experimental design, the causal inference model can better process the experimental data of this experimental method. In order to study the causal inference conclusion of randomized controlled trials better, Rubin [1] proposed using the average intervention effect value to estimate the impact degree of an intervention. Average Treatment Effect is the most commonly used measure in causal model. It defines the mean value of the difference between the potential results of the experimental group and the control group in a group of randomized controlled experiments.

$$ATE = E\left[Y(T = 1) - Y(T = 0)\right] \tag{1}$$

Rubin [2] proposed the method of introducing propensity score into the causal inference model. The goal is to eliminate the different factors of users in the experimental group and the control group in the observational study as far as possible, so as to obtain a more accurate estimation of causal effect. For example, whether a drug can reduce a person's blood pressure, in theory, researchers always hope to have two time lines parallel to time and space. One line is that the person took the medicine and the other line is that the person did not take the medicine. If different experimental interventions bring different experimental results, it is natural to judge the impact of this kind of drug on this person. Further taking the average value of multiple samples can judge the impact of this drug on a wide range of people. But in reality, researchers cannot do so. Based on this idea, the researchers consider to carry out the control experiment by finding the samples as close as possible in the experimental group and the control group. In order to reduce the potential or inevitable experimental errors, this method can match two very close classes in the experimental group and the control group, so that the impact of an intervention can be compared more clearly. For many known or unknown influencing factors, Raudenbush [3] proposed that increasing the weight is an important strategy to solve this series of influencing factors. The core idea of propensity score weighting method is to use propensity score to weight, and adjust the attributes of the objects in the experimental group and the control group to be consistent with the target objects. This study hopes to set the two factors of teacher level and head teacher subject as the weight to control their impact on students' performance, and better discuss the impact of hierarchical teaching mode on students' performance.

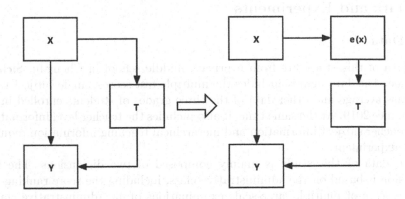

Fig. 1. Propensity score weighted causal inference model.

In the experiment of studying the effectiveness of the intervention of layered teaching, the two factors of teacher level and head teacher discipline are added as weights. When studying the impact of different factors on class performance, researchers set the model into a two-tier structure and embed class J into grade K. Generally speaking, it can always be assumed that these classes are independent of each other [4]. This study defines whether class J in Grade K receives intervention measures in a randomized controlled experiment: $T_{jk} = 1$ means the class J accepts the intervention; $T_{jk} = 0$ means the class J never accepts the intervention. On this basis, the potential results of class J in Grade K after intervention are set as $Y_{jk}(t), t \in \{0, 1\}$. More intuitively, researchers can directly observe the potential results. The model is:

$$Y_{jk} = Y_{jk}(1) + (1 - T_{jk})Y_{jk}(0)$$
$$= \mu_{0k} + \beta_k T_{jk} + \varepsilon_{jk}$$
(2)

Here, $\beta_k = W_{jk}(t)\mu_{1k} - (1 - W_{jk}(t))\mu_{0k}$, $W_{jk}(t)$ represents the weight of class J in Grade K about intervention effect T, β_k represents the average intervention effect of intervention measures in grade K weighted by propensity score. In this study, the inverse probability weighting method is adopted. The weight of this method is determined based on the tendency score. Since there is an independent tendency score for each class, its weight will also be different:

$$W(t = 1) = \frac{1}{e(X_t)}, W(t = 0) = \frac{1}{1 - e(X_t)}$$
(3)

Further, in the experiment on student achievement data, this study nested another layer based on the class level model: student level i. As before, it is also defined $T_{ijk} = 1$ means the student i has accepted an intervention. If he has not accepted an intervention, $T_{ijk} = 0$.

3   Data and Experiments

3.1   Data

The data of this study are from a private middle school in Chengdu, Sichuan Province. The data mainly includes the multiple test scores, single subject ranking, class average and other data of the three grades of students enrolled in the school since 2019. At the same time, it also includes the teacher level information, head teacher subject information and hierarchical teaching information required by the experiment.

The data of this study is mainly composed of two dimensions. The first dimension is based on the administrative class, including the score ranking and average score of multiple large-scale examinations of 43 Administrative classes in three grades, as well as the subjects taught by the head teacher and the level of class mathematics teacher. The large-scale examination includes the half-term and final examinations of each semester; The second dimension is based on students, including the scores and rankings of 682 students in 2020. Due to the different admission time of the three grades, the number of large-scale examinations is also different. The data source of this study provides data at the end of January 2022. Therefore, ten test scores in five semesters of level 2019, six test scores in three semesters of level 2020 and two test scores in one semester of level 2021 are collected.

The fifth line is the bar chart of all students' multiple test scores and the comparison chart of normal distribution curve. Through the analysis of bar chart

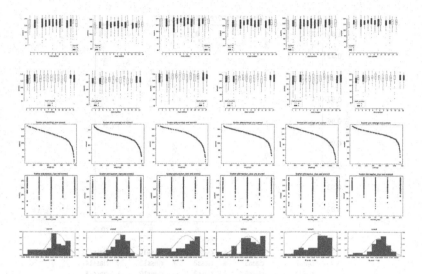

Fig. 2. Student achievement summary and analysis.

and normal distribution line chart, it can be basically seen that except for the third exam, the other exams basically conform to the normal distribution, but also show a slightly right deviation.

If the most basic point of educational experiment is often the performance of each student, but researchers can hardly guarantee that there will be no interaction between students in one way or another. Researchers generally believe that the same teaching model and teaching methods will not be effective for all students, so it may be difficult to study whether the impact of hierarchical teaching on individual students is positive or negative by virtue of causal inference model. This is what people often call the importance of teaching students according to their aptitude. However, this study starts from each administrative class, which is very different. Generally speaking, the development of mathematics achievement in a class is only related to the students and teachers in the class, and will not be affected by the students and teachers in other classes. In other words, the improvement of class A's mathematics performance must not be because class B has adopted better teaching modes and methods. In this way, we can ensure that the grades of each class are independent of each other, and the influence of each other can be ignored.

3.2 Experiments

According to the maximum normalization algorithm, the maximum normalized score of each class in each examination can be obtained:

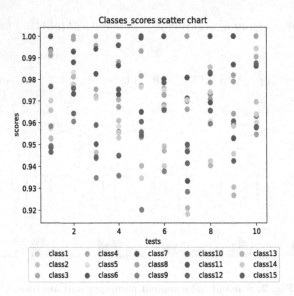

Fig. 3. Normalized score of class grades.

The horizontal axis in the figure represents the number of tests, while the vertical axis represents the maximum normalized score of each class in each test. The closer it is to 1, the better its class score.

After obtaining the maximum normalized score, this study attempts to analyze the impact of teachers at all levels on class performance and calculate the average maximum normalized score μ_D of teachers at all levels in each academic year, where D represents the teacher level. The calculation results are shown in the following table:

Table 1. Average maximum normalized score on teacher level

Teacher level	First year	Second year	Third year
Primary(μ_{D_1})	0.958	0.956	0.956
Deputy primary(μ_{D_2})	0.969	0.937	–
Intermediate(μ_{D_3})	0.967	0.959	0.962
Deputy senior(μ_{D_4})	0.987	0.979	0.980
Senior(μ_{D_5})	–	–	0.964

By calculating the difference of the influence of teachers at adjacent levels on class performance, it can be found that the influence gap between the lowest level and secondary level teachers on class performance is small, and the gap between secondary level and secondary level teachers shows great fluctuation over time. The reason for such experimental results is very likely that the small number of secondary primary teachers leads to certain fluctuation of experimental results; The difference between intermediate teachers and sub senior teachers has remained above 0.02 for a long time. Since the normalized scores are less than 1 and generally between 0.95–0.98, the difference of 0.02 can be regarded as a large difference.

This study uses the same way to study the impact of head teacher subjects on class performance. Similarly, the average normalized scores of math teachers and non math teachers can be calculated:

Table 2. Average maximum normalized score on head teacher subjects

	First year	Second year	Third year
Math teachers	0.992	0.984	0.977
Non math teachers	0.964	0.956	0.961

In the first academic year, the average normalized score of mathematics head teachers was 0.028 higher than that of non mathematics head teachers, which was almost maintained in the second academic year, but the gap was reduced to 0.016 in the third academic year. Whether this kind of fluctuation has a significant positive impact on the mathematics teacher's performance.

After verifying the influence of teacher level and head teacher discipline on class performance, they are set as weight for modeling. The propensity score $P_{jk}(H)$ of 2020 class samples to the hierarchical teaching model is calculated by logit regression model, $P_{jk}(H) = 1/(1 + e)$. Thus, the propensity score of each class can be estimated:

Table 3. Propensity score estimation on Hierarchical Teaching

Class	1	2	3	4	5	6	7	8	9	10	11	12	13	14
Propensity score	0.62	0.99	0.39	0.28	0.90	0.69	0.56	0.57	0.93	0.19	0.92	0.66	0.66	0.62

Based on the propensity score weighting algorithm, the normalized score of the score change of each class in 2020 under the weighted estimation can be obtained, and the average treatment effect can be further calculated:

$$ATE = \frac{1}{n} \sum y_{jk}(1) - \frac{1}{n} \sum y_{jk}(0) = 0.01. \tag{4}$$

It is worth reminding that the important index for evaluating the class performance in this study is the normalized score of the class. This value is obtained from the average score of the class in each exam by the highest average score of the grade. In the process of calculating ate, the change value of the average normalized score of each class in six exams is calculated first, and then divided by the weight given by the inverse probability weighting method, Therefore, the final ate can only infer that there is a strong causal relationship between the layered teaching mode and the progress of class performance, that is, it has a significant positive impact on class performance. The average normalized score of all classes is between 0.96–0.98, so 0.01 can be regarded as having a great impact. To sum up, the layered teaching mode has a significant impact on the improvement of class performance.

4   Conclusion

As a promising pedagogical research, this study is limited by the small amount of randomized controlled experiment data in the experimental process, and can not draw more accurate general conclusions in many details. At the same time, it is difficult for researchers to explain the specific practical significance of the weighted normalized score or standardized score, but it can be seen from the experimental results that the layered teaching mode has a significant positive impact on students than the non layered teaching, and the average score of the experimental group is significantly higher than that of the control group. This effect is obviously very remarkable.

On the whole, in order to estimate whether the layered education model has a significant positive impact on students' performance, a model based on propensity score matching and weighting is used to estimate the ate value of the average intervention effect. It is found that layered teaching has a significant impact on the improvement of class performance.

References

1. Rubin, D.B.: Comment: which ifs have causal answers. J. Am. Stat. Assoc. **81**(396), 961–962 (1986)
2. Rosenbaum, P.R., Rubin, D.B.: The central role of the propensity score in observational studies for causal effects. Biometrika **70**(1), 41–55 (1983)
3. Raudenbush, S.W., Martinez, A., Spybrook, J.: Strategies for improving precision in group-randomized experiments. Educ. Eval. Policy Anal. **29**, 5–29 (2007)
4. Hong, G., Raudenbush, S.W.: Evaluating kindergarten retention policy: a case study of causal inference for multilevel observational data. J. Am. Stat. Assoc. **101**(475), 901–910 (2006)
5. Pearl, J.: Causality: Models, Reasoning, and Inference. Cambridge University Press, New York (2000)
6. Cook, T.D.: Randomized experiments in educational policy research: a critical examination of the reasons the educational evaluation community has offered for not doing them. Educ. Eval. Policy Anal.**24**(3):175–199 (2002)
7. R. E. Fancher.: Introduction to Galton (1889) co-relations and their measurement, chiefly from anthropometric data. In: Kotz, S., Johnson, N.L. (eds) Breakthroughs in Statistics. Springer Series in Statistics. Springer, New York (1997). https://doi.org/10.1007/978-1-4612-0667-5_1
8. Holland, P.W.: Statistics and causal inference. J. Am. Stat. Assoc. **81**, 945–970 (1986)

9. Donald, B.R.: Estimating causal effects of treatments in randomized and non-randomized studies. J. Educ. Psychol. **66**, 688–701 (1974)
10. Pearl, J.: Causality: Models, Reasoning, and Inference. Cambridge University Press, New York (2009)
11. Spirtes, P., Glymour, C., Scheines, R.: Causation, Prediction, and Search. MIT Press, New York (2000)
12. Greenland, S., Robins, J.M., Pearl, J.: Confounding, and collapsibility in causal inference. Stat. Sci. **14**(1), 29–46 (1999)
13. Jansen, R., et al.: A Bayesian networks approach for predicting protein-protein interactions from genomic data. Science **302**(17), 449–453 (2003)
14. Friedman, N.: Inferring cellular networks using probabilistic graphical models. Science **303**(5659), 799–805 (2004)
15. Causal protein-signalling networks derived from multiparameter single-cell data: K. Sachs, O. Perez, D. Pe'Er, D. A. Lauffenburger, and G. P. Nolan. Science **308**, 523–529 (2005)
16. Bloom, H.S., Richburg-Hayes, L., Black, A.R.: Using covariates to improve precision for studies that randomize schools to evaluate educational interventions. Educ. Eval. Policy Anal. **29**, 30–59 (2007)
17. Holland, P.W.: Causal inference, path analysis, and recursive structural equations models. ETS Research Report 1, 1–50 (1988)
18. Spybrook, J., Shi, R., Kelcey, B.: Progress in the past decade: an examination of the precision of cluster randomized trials funded by the U.S. Institute of Education Sciences. Int. J. Res. Method Educ. **39**(3), 255-C-267 (2016)
19. Robins, J.M., Miguel ngel Hernán, M., Brumback, B.: Marginal structural models and causal inference in epidemiology. Epidemiology **11**(5), 550–560 (2000)
20. Tobias, K., Alexander, M.B.: Results of multivariable logistic regression, propensity matching, propensity adjustment, and propensity-based weighting under conditions of nonuniform effect. Am. J. Epidemiol. **163**(3), 262–270 (2005)

Research on Experimental Teaching Reform of Computer Principles Course Based on Logisim Simulation Software

LiPing Yang$^{(\boxtimes)}$, GuoLiang Li, Li Qin, and FuChuan Ni

College of Informatics, Huazhong Agricultural University, Wuhan, Hubei, People's Republic of China

Abstract. On the basis of analyzing the current existing problems in the experimental teaching of computer principles course, Logisim virtual simulation software is introduced to reform the experimental system. Four experimental projects have been designed in the simulation environment Logisim, including data coding experiment, the experiment on the arithmetic unit composition, memory composition experiment, and MIPS processor design experiment. We have also introduced ITC platform to achieve the openness and sharing of the experiments. It is convenient for students to spend more time after class to fully digest the content of this experiment according to their own situation. Moreover, the extracurricular big project homework based on the simulation environment has been set up reasonably. Through the practice of experimental teaching reform, it is proved that it has a good effect on training students' system ability.

Keywords: Computer Principles Course · Virtual Simulation Experiment · Logisim · Reform in Education

1 Introduction

Computer Principles Course is a core professional basic course of various computer majors. It mainly discusses the basic composition principle of the major computer functional components and the interconnection technology of the whole machine. Through the study of this course, students can fully understand the composition, structure and principle of the computer system, so that they can establish a clear concept of the whole computer, thereby improving their ability to analyze and apply computer systems as well as their ability to design and develop the computer system [1]. This course is highly theoretical, with many abstract concepts. Students generally find it difficult to learn and master the essence of the course. It is far from enough for teachers to achieve the teaching objectives of the course only by relying on theoretical teaching, and teachers must also cooperate with the practical teaching stages that can well support theoretical teaching [2].

Moreover, in recent years, many newly-opened computer majors in universities have cut down the hardware basic courses severely, so the students' hardware foundation is

W. Hong and Y. Weng (Eds.): ICCSE 2022, CCIS 1813, pp. 136–143, 2023.
https://doi.org/10.1007/978-981-99-2449-3_13

not good before learning the computer principles course. Under this background, how to improve the mode and experimental environment of the experimental course, to train and improve students' computer system ability in a very limited class time, is a subject that needs to be explored vigorously.

2 The Present Situation of Experimental Teaching of This Course

As recorded [2], at present, the practical teaching methods of computer principles course in domestic universities mainly have the following forms.

- Traditional experimental box form: In some colleges and universities, the experimental teaching of this course is to connect the separation devices through wires to form a system, and then students can check the function of the system by turning the switch and observing the signal lights. This way enables students to establish intuitive logic device concepts, but the reliability of the experimental system is very low, and there are many force majeure factors in the experiment. Therefore, students are likely to have severe frustration in the experiment. Moreover, this kind of experiment is mainly replication experiment, which seems to be a "complex" system that can only compose of hundreds of wires, but its design connotation is very simple. The experiment cost is high, the consumption is high, the site requirement is high, the workload of equipment maintenance is heavy, and the improving of the experiment box is slow. The form can't meet the actual requirements of modern electronic system design.
- The form of FPGA development board: Hardware design is simulated by hardware description language, and then debugged and run on the development board. The experimental content is mainly hardware design. This real way of hardware design can stimulate students' interest in hardware learning and improve their ability to design hardware. However, this experimental method is limited by hardware conditions. The simple design experiment is mainly realized by means of the components provided by the experimental system, and the content is largely biased towards verification, which is insufficient to build the concept of a complete computer system and support the design of CPU. Moreover, the experimental process is very complex, requiring students to choose a series of processes such as circuit mode first, which wastes a lot of students' time and also affects the experimental results [3]. Another serious problem is the programming of hardware design. Students always feel that they are doing programming experiments instead of designing hardware, and it is difficult for them to establish the corresponding relationship between hardware design and the underlying circuit, which resulting in students not having a deep understanding of hardware design [1].

Because the above two schemes are not ideal, it is difficult to improve students' system ability. Therefore, by learning the advanced experience of other universities, we have adopted *Logisim* virtual simulation software in the experimental platform of this course for the students majoring in Big Data in our university.

3 Experimental Teaching Reform Based on Logisim Software

3.1 Design of Experimental Content in Simulation Environment

Logisim is a Java-based application that supports any platform in a Java environment. It adopts graph-based interface, which is easy to learn and get started. Circuit diagram design and simulation in Logisim are very convenient and efficient, and Logisim can run completely without hardware environment [3]. Logisim software occupies little computer resources, which is easy for students to install and use on their own computers. The experiment is flexible, free from time and space restrictions, and it is very convenient for teachers to check and accept the experimental results in Logisim. At present, hundreds of universities around the world are using the simulation software, including the CS61C course at the University of California, Berkeley. National University of Defense Technology, Huazhong University of Science and Technology and other well-known key universities in China are also using the software to carry out the experiments of the computer composition course [2].

In combination with the practical course based on Logisim simulation software written by Professor Tan Zhihu's course group of Huazhong University of Science and Technology [4], we have written the experiment guide book of 5 experimental projects for the students majoring in Big Data of our university. In these experiments, except for the first experiment "Logisim novice on the road", which is equivalent to the preparatory experiment, the other experimental projects focus on the goal of capability output, gradually realize the circuit of each major component in the computer system, and finally make students can integrate and design a complete MIPS CPU.

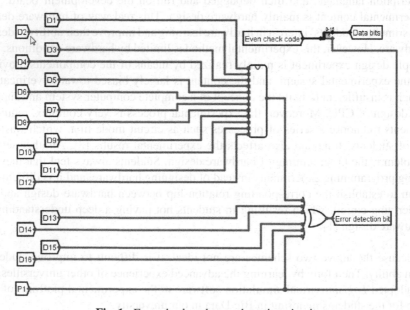

Fig. 1. Even check and error detection circuit.

Data Coding Experiment. The purpose of this experiment is to make the students master the coding rules of location code, machine code and font code in Chinese character coding. The objective is to enable students to build Chinese character code display circuit in Logisim by using Chinese character coding principle. In this experiment, students should master the coding rules of parity check codes, and design the parity code and error detection and test circuit in Logisim.

Based on these experiment purposes, in the 4 class hours arranged in this experiment, students are required to design and complete the circuit of converting the machine code of Chinese character into location code in Logisim. The students need design parity coding circuit of 16-bit data coding, and be familiar with the function of transmission test circuit of 17-bit parity coding.

In fact, this experiment is also a foundation for the subsequent storage system experiment, because the storage system experiment involves the storage expansion of Chinese character database, so students need to first through this experiment to have a comprehensive understanding of Chinese character coding and character database.

Finally, the parity check error detection circuit designed by students in Logisim is shown in Fig. 1.

Experiment on the Arithmetic Unit Composition. The purpose of this experiment is to make the students master the coding rules of location code, machine code and font code in Chinese character coding. The objective is to enable students to build Chinese character code display circuit in Logisim by using Chinese character coding principle. In this experiment, students should master the coding rules of parity check codes, and design the parity code and error detection and test circuit in Logisim.

Based on the experiment purposes mentioned above, the content of this experiment is arranged to require students to design 8-bit controllable adder and subtracter circuit in Logisim. Students are required to design and implement 4-bit and 16-bit fast adders using 4-bit carry-ahead CLA74182 circuit. An unsigned 5-bit array multiplier is required to design and implement in Logisim.

For those students who has the ability to learn more, additional experimental project can be arranged, such as the design of 32-bit ALU unit, so that students can integrate all kinds of arithmetic operation components and logic operation components into the circuit of an ALU unit.

Memory Composition Experiment. The purpose of this experiment is to let the students understand the basic principles of bit expansion and character expansion in the storage system, so that the students can use the relevant principles to solve the problem of Chinese character database storage expansion. Let students know the basic principle of MIPS register file, so that students can use Logisim decoder, multiplexer and other components to finally build MIPS register file. Based on the register file, students should understand the working process of writing and reading data in RAM, which lays a good foundation for the subsequent processor experiment.

Based on the experiment purposes mentioned above, the content of this experiment is arranged for 4 class hours, and students are required to use capacity expansion to build Chinese character database in Logisim. Students should use Logisim decoder and other components to achieve a MIPS register file, and test error for the register file.

During this experiment, it should be noted that each student must be able to understand the working principle of reading and writing data in the RAM of MIPS register file, so as to lay a good foundation for the design of the data path of the register in the next experiment about processor.

MIPS Processor Design Experiment. This experiment is a synthesis of all the previous experiments. The purpose of the experiment is to require students to master the basic methods of CPU hard-wired controller design. In Logisim, students are required to design and implement a hard-wired 32-bit MIPS processor circuit with 8 core instructions in a single cycle. And the final implementation of the MIPS processor can run a bubble sort program. Through this experiment, students should master the general process of MIPS monocycle CPU design and deepen their understanding of the working principle of the hard-wired controller.

Based on the experiment purposes mentioned above, the content of this experiment is arranged to require students to construct data paths by using the functional components completed in the leading experiments, design the hard-wired controller, and finally complete MIPS monocycle hard-wired controller CPU that supports the simple instruction system which includes 8 core instructions.

This experiment is very comprehensive and difficult, so it is better to assign students to preview before the experiment class, otherwise students may not be able to complete the whole MIPS CPU circuit in 4 class hours. The circuit diagram of the monocycle hard-wired controller CPU designed by excellent students in Logisim is shown in Fig. 2.

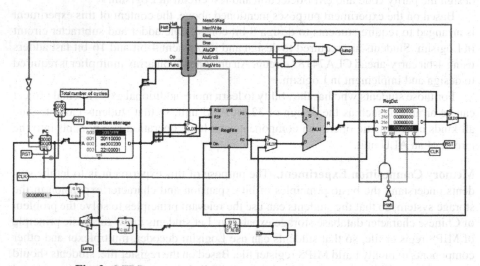

Fig. 2. MIPS monocycle hard wired controller designed in Logisim.

3.2 Introducing ITC Platform to Achieve the Openness and Sharing of Experiments

Under the traditional experimental course mode of computer composition principle, students generally have to go to the computer room to complete experiments on computers or experimental boxes. This mode limits the time and place of the experiment, and the experimental conditions are not open enough and too limited, which can't meet the needs of modern college students for flexible learning and fragmented learning anytime and anywhere.

Because our experiment course adopts Logisim simulation environment, and no physical experiment box is needed, after our university introduced ITC platform of Beihang University, we conveniently arranged the simulation experiment environment on ITC virtual machine. In this way, even if students haven't fully implemented the experimental contents in the computer room in class, they can also log in to the ITC platform after class and continue to do experiments online. Moreover, the circuit resource files required for each experiment can also be uploaded to the online experiment page for sharing in advance, which is convenient for students to download resource files to carry out experiments anytime and anywhere so that the experimental time in class can be effectively extended to after class. It is convenient for students to spend more time after class to fully digest the content of this experiment according to their own situation, which really realizes the openness and sharing of the course experiment and helps students to cultivate their system ability.

3.3 Extracurricular Big Project to Stimulate Students' Autonomy

In-class experiments of this course are provided to students with an experimental instruction book prepared by the teacher. The instruction book contains detailed experimental steps, so that students can finish the whole experimental content within a very limited time in class. Although in this mode, students can generally finish the experiment on time, but students are very dependent on the experimental steps in the instruction book. It is difficult to stimulate students' learning autonomy and initiative without giving them space to play.

Therefore, in order to better improve students' system ability, we extend in-class experiments to extra-curricular activities, make full use of students' extra-curricular time, and arrange students to complete big projects that are more designed and more complicated than in-class experimental projects.

At the beginning of the semester, we assign students the big project for extra-curricular experiments, and ask them to finish it step by step in their spare time, and then hand it in at the end of the semester. There is no specific limit to the content of the big project, and students can choose freely according to their own interests within the scope of Chapter 1 to Chapter 3 in reference [4]. We encourage students to think independently and consult reference materials independently to complete the big project. This kind of unlimited project content can give students a lot of free play space. Some students with strong ability have completed several design experiments that they are interested in, which greatly cultivates students' design ability and is also a useful supplement to the in-class experiment system. After-class project also makes students have a more comprehensive and profound understanding of the whole computer system.

4   Effect of Experimental Reform

According to the experimental content designed by us around system ability training, after several rounds of teaching exploration, in terms of students' teaching evaluation feedback, our virtual simulation practice teaching reform has achieved good results.

First of all, the experimental content is progressive, from easy to difficult, which helps to gradually cultivate and improve students' system ability. Each experiment has clear requirements for the level that students must reach, so that students can gradually develop a system view in the process of learning step by step, and finally most students can have a higher level of system design ability.

Secondly, a little bit and gradually increasing difficulty of experiments makes students less afraid of difficulties, and the completion rate of each experiment is high, which enhances their sense of accomplishment, implements the system ability training objectives that this course should undertake, and meets the requirements of computer engineering education certification.

Finally, the experimental contents that students need to do themselves make the boring theoretical lectures in the course vivid. In the theoretical teaching, we also introduce the knowledge and skills related to the experiments, which make students more willing to have theoretical classes, let practice feed back theory, and make students more aware of the importance of theoretical study. It also promotes them to actively learn theory and principle knowledge.

5   Conclusion

Because the computer principles course is a core course to cultivate system ability of students majoring in computer science, we have reformed the experimental platform and content of this course around the practical course goal of cultivating students' system ability. *Logisim* virtual simulation software has been adopted, and experiments have been carried out with the virtual machine environment of ITC platform. However, at present, the relevant exploration has only been carried out among two grades of students, and the experimental content and mode are not perfect enough. In the future, how to improve the experimental curriculum system and further plan the supporting experiment of each chapter of the curriculum is a problem that we need to further explore and improve in the future teaching.

Acknowledgments. This work is supported by the second batch of new engineering research and practice projects of the Ministry of Education (Program No. E-JSJRJ20201327).

References

1. Chen, W., Liang, Z., Tang, Y., et al.: Experimental exploration of computer principles course. Comput. Educ. **15**, 23–27 (2014)
2. Hu, D., Tan, Z., Wu, F.: Research on the virtual simulation experiment teaching for principle of computer organization course. J. EEE **40**, 113–116 (2018)

3. Shao, X., Ye, Z., Ou-Yang, Y., et al.: Discussion on the principles of computer composition course teaching based on system ability training. Comput. Educ. **11**, 140–144 (2018)
4. Tan, Z., Qin, L., Hu, D.: Practical Tutorial on Computer Composition Principles--from the Logic Gate to the CPU. Tsinghua University Press, Beijing, pp.163–164 (2018)
5. Jiang, L., Cheng, W.: Exploration of project-driven computer composition principle teaching method based on OBE concept. Comput. Educ. **10**, 76–80 (2021)
6. Zhang, Q., Liu, S., Li, X.: Experimental teaching design of computer composition principle for engineering education accreditation. Comput. Educ. **9**, 141–144 (2020)
7. Zhao, Z., Ning, F.: Exploration on teaching reform of computer composition principle course based on OBE concept. Wirel. Internet Technol. **18**, 49–151 (2021)
8. Liu, S., Xu, L., Zhang, Q., et al.: A hybrid teaching organization model based on computer composition principle of engineering education accreditation. Comput. Educ. **3**, 104–107 (2021)
9. Huang, L., Lv, C., Shi, Y., et al.: A engineering education accreditation oriented study of teaching reform on computer organization course. Educ. Teach. Forum. **12**, 260–262 (2018)

Hierarchical and Diverse Cultivation of Data Thinking Capability in College Based on New High School Curriculum Standards

Jie Zhang ⓘ, Ying Jin(✉), Li Zhang, Ye Tao, and Ping Yu

Department of Computer Science, Technology of Nanjing University, Nanjing, China
{zhangj,jinying}@nju.edu.cn

Abstract. Starting from the national demand for big data talent cultivation, universities have problems such as insufficient understanding and content mismatch in Cultivation of Data Thinking Capability. In particular, according to the cultivation requirements and contents of data thinking capability in the information technology curriculum of new high school Standards, this paper puts forward the reform of the cultivation system of data thinking capability in universities, including the exploration and Realization of course series, curriculum content, evaluation system and so on.

Keywords: new high school standards · college · data thinking capability

1 Background

In the "Action Plan for Promoting Big Data Development", the government proposed that big data is a "new driving force, new opportunity, and new method" [1] to "promote economic transformation", "reshape national competitive advantage", and "improve government governance capability". The government has also established a policy mechanism for personnel training." Big data talents are the talents engaged in big data related work, mainly including core talents engaged in research and development, analysis work, and composite talents with both industry background and big data skills." [2] The talent gap is expected to reach more than 2 million in 2025. Colleges and universities need to take the quality and effectiveness of talent development as the fundamental standard for working performance assessment, not forgetting the original intention of establishing moral education, remembering the mission of nurturing people for the Party and the

---

1. Association of Fundamental Computing Education in Chinese Universities, Teaching re-search project of 2021-College Computer Basic Curriculum Reform Based on new high school curriculum standards. 2. University Computer Course Teaching Steering Committee of the Ministry of Education, Research on the reform of university computer empowerment edu-cation in the new era project- Research on the reform of university computer empowerment education in New Liberal Arts. 3. Computer Education Research Association of Chinese Universities, Projects in the direction of education in 2021 - Research on the connection be-tween universities and K12 information technology teaching

© The Author(s), under exclusive license to Springer Nature Singapore Pte Ltd. 2023
W. Hong and Y. Weng (Eds.): ICCSE 2022, CCIS 1813, pp. 144–154, 2023.
https://doi.org/10.1007/978-981-99-2449-3_14

country, and not only focus on the in-depth training of professional talents, but also pay more attention to the exercise of composite talents.

The cultivation of computer technology talents is the demand of all industries in the information age, and the development of new technologies of cloud computing, big data, Internet of Things, and artificial intelligence has put forward the requirements for the cultivation of computer technology talents in-depth and breadth. However, the content of the university curriculum generally lags behind the development of the technology of the times, so the rapid development of computer information technology-related courses needs to keep pace with the times to reform and improve. The information technology curriculum standards for high school developed by the Ministry of Education were newly revised in 2017, and many courses were offered at the high school level to improve students' information technology knowledge and skills, enhance information awareness, develop computational thinking, improve digital learning and innovation skills, and establish a correct sense of worth and responsibilities in the information society. Students have already acquired information technology training in the high school period, but the learning objectives and knowledge composition in the high school do not support it to meet the requirements that society needs. Therefore, it is necessary to re-enhance students knowledge structure and skills through the cultivation of literacy, ability, and thinking at the university level.

Data is a resource, and the understanding and use of data affect all professions and industries. This paper discusses the development of data thinking capability from high school connection to college.

2 Cultivation of Data Thinking Capability in High School it Courses

The latest high school IT curriculum standards, i.e. the new standards, propose the core literacy of high school IT subjects, including four components: information awareness, computational thinking, digital learning and innovation, and information social responsibility. The four core literacies are influencing each other to support each other and jointly cultivate students' information literacy. The development of information awareness in the first one requires students to have sensitivity to information and judgment of its value. In turn, this aspect of competence needs to be acquired through proper analysis of data [3].

The high school information technology curriculum includes two compulsory courses, six optional compulsory courses, and two elective courses, totaling ten courses. There is one compulsory course named" Data and Computing", including data and information, data processing and application, algorithms and programming modules, and four optional compulsory courses named" Data and Data Structure"," Data Management and Analysis" and" Preliminary Artificial Intelligence". Data and Data Structures"," Data Management and Analysis", and" Preliminary Artificial Intelligence" are four courses related to data. Including data, data structure, data requirements analysis, data management, data analysis, and other contents.

The optional compulsory courses are more of a deep dive and expansion of the compulsory courses, starting not only with data modeling, data abstraction, and code implementation, but also learning to collect and use the right analysis and mining methods from the massive amount of data, and understanding the powerful weapons for making scientific decisions. All need to recognize the importance of data, and the importance of data thinking capability development.

3   University Level Requirements for Data Thinking Capability

In the Basic Requirements for Teaching Basic University Computer Courses [4], it is mentioned that the development of basic university computer teaching should not only conform to the discipline's own rules of development, but also actively adapt to the needs of national economic and social development. China has made remarkable achievements in information technology construction and has established a large network environment, and is now in the historical development stage of strengthening independent innovation research to utilize the power of this large network. The deep integration of computer and information technology into various fields of economy and society, and the formation of a new form of economic development with the Internet as the infrastructure and realization environment are not only the macro strategy of the country, but also the basic vision that every university student should have when entering the society.

In such a historical period, basic university computer teaching faces great opportunity: it will take up the main task of cultivating the ability of computational thinking, which is one of the three pillars of scientific thinking; it will prepare the necessary knowledge and application ability for the cross-fertilization of computer disciplines with other disciplines, and it will cultivate information society citizens who have the literacy of computational thinking and are familiar with computer applications. Therefore, the development trend of basic university computer teaching in the next decade will show more significant characteristics.

The content of basic university computer education is divided into the following three fields: system platform and computing environment, algorithm foundation and program development, and data management and information processing. Among them, the field of data management and information processing: involves the basic techniques and methods of applying computer systems for data analysis and information processing, typically database technology, multimedia information processing technology, intelligent technology, etc. Its subfields are data organization and management, multimedia information processing, analysis, and decision making. The cources related with data are database technology, statistical analysis of data, data mining, artificial intelligence, etc. There is a certain continuity with the courses in high school.

Both the core literacy requirements of the new high school curriculum and the basic requirements of the university basic computer courses have the same goal in data thinking development requirements. But due to the knowledge structure and immature worldview of high school students, it is impossible to meet the goals of universities for talent development in terms of achieving the same literacy development. As shown in Table 1 below, 2 dimensions were selected to compare the requirements of high school standard IT and college basic computer courses.

In terms of curriculum content requirements, high schools are more likely to use" application cases" and" life cases" and then use words such as" experience"," feeling"," understanding" and" awareness" to describe the extent to which students have mastered knowledge.",," understanding",," awareness" and other words to describe the degree of students' mastery of knowledge. In contrast, the requirements of universities for similar contents are more focused on the mastery on" methods",," strategies" and" theories". Therefore, universities need to try to provide a more in-depth curriculum system for the cultivation of data thinking and computational thinking talents.

Table 1. I Comparison between the content requirements of high school it teaching and the requirements of university basic computer courses

content in High school standard	high school requirements	content in universities	universities requirements
Data and Computation Algorithm and Program Implementation	Outline the concepts and characteristics of algorithms from real-life examples, and represent simple algorithms using appropriate description methods and control structures. Acquire the basic knowledge of a programming language and implement simple algorithms using a programming language. Experience the basic process of programming through solving practical problems, feel the efficiency of algorithms, and master the methods of debugging and running programs. Describe the process of creation and development of programming languages and understand the functions and features of different types of programming languages	Algorithm Fundamentals and Program Development Algorithm and Programming	Understand the concept of algorithm and program; master the basic methods of iteration and recursion; understand the strategy of solving algorithms for typical problems; understand the concept and role of common data types and data structures; understand the idea of the modular design of programs, as well as the design ideas of module decomposition and compounding; understand the concepts of information encapsulation, interface, etc., as well as the ideas of reusability and reliability; understand the basic methods and ideas of program testing

(*continued*)

Table 1. (*continued*)

content in High school standard	high school requirements	content in universities	universities requirements
Data Management and Analysis Data Analysis	Understand common data analysis methods, such as comparative analysis, group analysis, average analysis and, correlation analysis, etc.; use appropriate data analysis tools in practice to analyze, present and, interpret data. Use digital learning to understand new developments in data management and analysis techniques; combine appropriate case studies to recognize the importance of data mining for problem solving and scientific decision-making in the information society	Data Management and Information Processing Analysis and Decision Making	Understanding of information representation and basic analysis methods in data analysis and decision making; statistical analysis, decision support systems, statistical analysis techniques, decision trees, association rules, an overview of artificial intelligence, an overview of data mining

4 Data Thinking Capability Cultivation System

Guided with the "3–3" undergraduate teaching reform, Nanjing University has been adjusting the basic computer education curriculum system after several rounds of reform, aiming to better align with the undergraduate teaching mode. Basic computer education to cultivate computational thinking as a whole extends to different fields of computing, in which the cultivation of data thinking has become one of the most important contents and goals of basic computer education in our university. This paper focuses on several aspects of the course series, course content, and evaluation system.

4.1 Course Series

For the needs of the students at different levels, we arrange general basic courses, elective courses, innovation and entrepreneurship courses in the data thinking course series. The basic course is offered as a compulsory course for science and engineering departments as well as arts and science departments, and students from art departments are encouraged to take it as an elective. Figure 1 shows the proportion of the students from the departments that arrange the Python course as elective course, in which includes all kinds of departments of arts and sciences in the university.

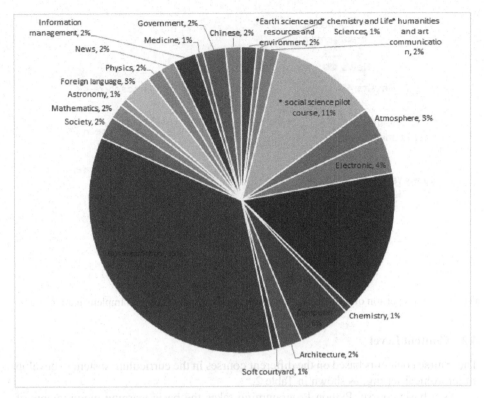

Fig. 1. The proportion of cross-platform course enrolment in Python programming courses

Elective courses are offered to all students, in principle, regardless of arts departments or sciences departments. But generally, students will choose courses that interest them or can improve their capability in depth and breadth. The elective courses related to data thinking development include Database Technology, Data Science, Data Processing Using Python, etc. Most of them are the extension for the content of the basic courses.

The innovation and entrepreneurship course is an important part of the "five-in-one" innovation and entrepreneurship teaching system of Nanjing University, and it is the main channel to promote innovation and entrepreneurship education in the university. It is offered to all students in Nanjing University. Figure 2 shows the proportion of students in the course, mainly in science and technology, including students from computer science and School of AI.

The curriculum series meets the requirements of talent cultivation in Nanjing University. The first stage is the general education stage for freshmen. The second and third years education focus on the specialization cultivation, and the fourth year for diversification cultivation.

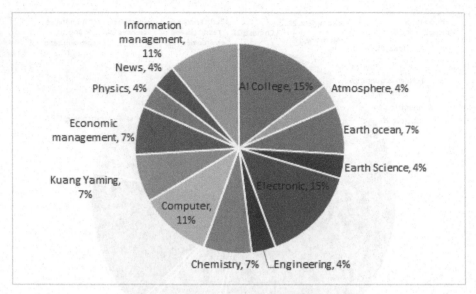

Fig. 2. The proportion of students in Introduction to Big Data and Python Implementation course

4.2 Content Level

The course content is based on the different courses in the curriculum system to develop a hierarchical setting, as shown in Table 2.

As a basic course, Python Programming takes the basic learning requirements of programming languages as a starting point. In addition, the using of scientific data processing libraries and the learning of basic methods of data processing are also added to this course. The aim is to enable the students to use Python to do data analysis and to support their research. In this course, we use IDLE or anaconda as the programing environment.

The elective courses on data processing in Python and R language focus on the process of data processing and analysis, i.e., data acquisition, data statistics, data mining. The course" Data Processing Using Python" focuses on the implementation of Python in the whole process of data processing, from data acquisition locally or from the web, how to represent data, to pre-processing, exploring, analyzing and visualizing data, and finally to representing and processing data through a simple GUI interface. In this course, we use engineering platform tools such as pycharm, vscode, etc.

In the innovation and entrepreneurship course Big Data Introduction and Python Implementation, which opens for the whole school, the course focuses more on industrial implementation and application. It includes the overview of big data, big data technology, big data analysis process, Python implementation, platform practice, big data industry application, and big data infrastructure. Both theoretical knowledge and cases are included in this course. It also includes practice on industry big data platform with real case study. Combining with industry hotspots and frontiers, this course enhances students' understanding and experience of innovation and entrepreneurship. Through the cultivation of the ability of comprehensive application of knowledge, students will be prepared to go deeper into the industry and solve practical problems. The curriculum resources are built in collaboration with external forces and based on industry-university

Table 2. Comparison of course content and tool platforms for the three levels

Course Level	Course Name	Course content related to data processing	Use of tools or platforms
Basic Course	Python Programming	SciPy, the scientific computing ecosystem; numpy library, pandas library, matplotlib library	IDLE, anaconda, etc
Elective Courses	Data Processing Using Python	Data acquisition: Local and Network Data Acquisition; Powerful Data Structures and Python Extension Libraries: extension libraries SciPy, numpy, pandas; Python data statistics and mining: Python convenient data acquisition and preprocessing, Python data statistics mining and applications (including cluster analysis, Python in science and technology, and humanities and social sciences applications). Object-oriented and graphical user interfaces (including the use of GUI libraries)	anaconda, pycharm, VS code, etc
Innovation and Entrepreneurship Class	Introduction to Big Data and Python Implementation	Big data overview, big data technology, big data analysis process, Python implementation, platform practice, big data industry applications, big data infrastructure	pycharm, VS code, FineBI, pandasBI, etc

research projects. In this course, besides of Python, students need to choose data analysis platforms and visualization platforms that can be practically applied in industrial applications, such as FineBI, etc.

For students who have spare capacity for learning, they are organized into teams to discuss the scientific research based on real data. The outcome should also be linked with industry demands. Students are also encouraged to attend college student innovation competition programs. Then we could study from the competition program to refine the course designing.

The hierarchical diversification of course contents is set following the theory of talent cultivation in Nanjing University. In the diversified cultivation stage, students need to be divided into three directions - the specialization cultivation direction, the composite talent cultivation direction, and the innovative for employment direction. They are each designed for the students who are willing to continue to study along with their current major, students who want to study across the major, and students who want to start their own business in the future.

The whole series of courses and all the levels of course content for the cultivation of data thinking for non-CS major students have been set to improve the system of talent cultivation, which is in line with the training objectives of computer basic education for students to take basic courses. The courses also help the hierarchical students to carry out targeted improvement, which is in line with the objectives of cultivating inter-disciplinary talents, and enable students on innovation and entrepreneurship.

4.3　Evaluation System

The evaluation system is designed to support the hierarchy for different courses. The evaluation of the basic course examines the fundamentals, so it is divided into closed-book exams, project design, and course assignments. It examines not only the mastery of basic knowledge, but also the ability to solve practical problems with teamwork. The course project mainly focuses on examining students ability in data processing.

For example Fig. 3, students chose instant noodles as the research object and found over 3,000 instant noodles data from Japan, China, and Korea. The analyzed the data in multiple dimensions such as flavor, packaging, and origin distribution. Then they created word cloud based on the flavor level of different instant noodles types. Students analyze the data by their interests and from real life scenario, and finally visualize the results. Thus helps them to fully understand how to use Python to support real-life problems.

Fig. 3. Instant noodle types word cloud by favor level

The elective course evaluation is also contains closed-book exams and project design, but in which the requirements for project design have been increased. The students not only need to implement the data processing, but also to master some algorithms such as data mining or artificial intelligence machine learning.

Since the goal of the Innovation and Entrepreneurship class is to cultivate innovative and entrepreneurial talents, the evaluation of the course is mainly based on the practical assignments about Python programing and the using of big data platforms. It also requires the students to study the papers on the application of big data in related industries, and finish the course paper for evaluation. More attention is paid to students' understanding and practice of practical cases of industry applications.

For example, the students used the SVM method for customer churn prediction based on a cleaned dataset, which contains thousands of cell phone program customer churn information in Fig. 4. And then analyzed the impact of different parameters on overfitting, as shown in the Fig. 5 below.

```
# 3. Training SVM classifier
classifier = svm.SVC(C=2,kernel='rbf',gamma=0.01)
classifier.fit(train_data, train_label.ravel())
# ravel function defaults to row order first when downscaling. ravel function
does not affect the result without adding, but there will be a red warning.
# 4. Calculate the classification accuracy
print("training set: {:.2%}".format(classifier.score(train_data, train_label)))
print("Test set: {:.2%}".format(classifier.score(test_data, test_label)))
```

Fig. 4. Part of the code of the project in the student's thesis

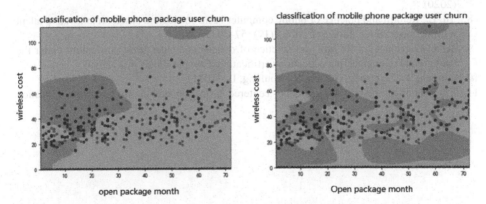

Fig. 5. Comparison of some visualization results of the projects in the student's thesis

The evaluation of university students' innovation and entrepreneurship projects is more open. Its evaluated by comparing the result with the goal set when applying the project. Thus to improve the real-life problem-solving capability through research-based learning approach.

5 Summary

The whole series of courses and all the levels of course content for the cultivation of data thinking for non-CS students have been set to improve the system of talent cultivation, which is in line with the training objectives of computer basic education for students to take basic courses, but also for the hierarchical students to carry out targeted improvement, which is in line with the objectives of cultivating interdisciplinary talents, and enable students on innovation and entrepreneurship.

However, there is still room for improvement in the overall course content design, especially how to deal with the gap between the content setting and the actual ability of students.

References

1. An action outline to promote big data development (GF [2015] No. 50)
2. China's big data industry development white paper (2019)
3. The 2017 edition of high School Information Technology Curriculum Standards
4. Basic Requirements for the teaching of College Computer Basic course 2015. Higher Education Press, Beijing (2015)
5. Fuliang, G., Gang, Z., Yongjie, L., Liangzhong, C., Hui, G.: Practical exploration on the curriculum reform of college computer foundation under the new syllabus. Comput. Eng. Sci. **41**(S01), 4 (2019)
6. Zhang, J., Jin, Y., Tao, Y.: Exploration on the construction of big data basic course for non computer major. In: 2020 15th International Conference on Computer Science and Education (ICCSE) 2020
7. Meijuan, W., Hui, L., Jingli, H., Changyou, Z., Yuanyuan, J.: Research and practice of college computer basic curriculum reform based on computational thinking. Comput. Educ. **3**, 5 (2020)
8. Yu, L.: Reform and practice of public computer basic curriculum based on innovative talent training mode. Educ. Modernization **7**(17), 57–59 (2020)
9. Yong, O., Hong, L.: Reform and practice of college computer basic curriculum under the background of engineering education certification. Comput. Educ. **4**, 4 (2019)
10. yunyun, W., Zenggang, X., Xia, K., Youfeng, L.: (2021)
11. Exploration on the reform of student - centered basic computer course Computer education (10), 5

Design and Production of Intelligent Practical Teaching Robot

Wei Jiahan[1]🆔, Xue Wen[1](✉)🆔, Jin Zhaoning[2]🆔, and Wang Yuexi[1]🆔

[1] Chinese-German Institute for Applied Engineering, Zhejiang University of Science
and Technology, Hangzhou, China
xuewen@zust.edu.cn

[2] School of Information and Electronic Engineering, Zhejiang University of Science
and Technology, Hangzhou, China

Abstract. The inconvenience caused by time and space could be solved
by service-oriented robots in people's daily life. In this paper, an intelligent interpretation robot for science and technology museums, which
can provide visitors with real-time inquiry services and back-end management control of technicians, was designed. The system used in this
robot integrates and innovates voice interaction technology, sensing technology, radar scanning, autonomous detection and positioning, and aerial
download technology, providing an effective solution for the design of an
intelligent interpreter for science and technology museums.

Keywords: Robot · Information technology · Intelligent interpretation

1 Introduction

With the development of robot sensing technology, artificial intelligence and
other technologies, intelligent robots have gradually integrated into our lives.
In the field of service oriented robots, four iconic products: fire rescue robots,
surgical robots, intelligent public service robots and intelligent nursing robots,
and promoting the serialization of professional service robots and the commercialization of personal and family service robots are primarily developed. At
present, a number of public cultural facilities represented by "robot museums"
are established in China. Many of these museums are for science education to
the public, such as the Chaoyang District Youth Science and Technology Center in Beijing and the Suzhou Robotics Science and Technology Museum. The
lack of innovation in the robots and understanding of user needs leads to a poor
educational effect. With the tendency of commercialization of service-oriented
robots, intelligent interpretation robots in science and technology museums have
come into being. The application and promotion of intelligent robots in science
and technology museums can effectively cultivate students' interest in exhibits,
expand their scientific and cultural knowledge, improve their scientific literacy,
as well as promote the popularization and development of intelligent robots in
China, which has important social significance [1].

W. Hong and Y. Weng (Eds.): ICCSE 2022, CCIS 1813, pp. 155–166, 2023.
https://doi.org/10.1007/978-981-99-2449-3_15

In this paper, an intelligent interpretation robot is designed using image processing, speech recognition module, distance sensor, WIFI module, OTA and STM32 controller for research. The robot achieves data collection and data analysis by connecting to the science and technology museum database. By analyzing the data results, the database and system can be continuously optimized. After being updated and synchronized to the robot by OTA, it can provide better services to the visitors. It enables visitors to learn abundant knowledge of science and technology. The robot contains fully automatic and semi-automatic working modes, and can be applied to public places such as science and technology museums.

For the characteristics of the currently existing intelligent interpretation robot, new design concepts and solutions are proposed from three aspects: technology, theory and design concept respectively. By using OTA, forwarding server and other technologies, the integration of IoT technology and interpretation robot can be achieved.

1) The robot adopts OTA technology, cutting-edge technologies and their corresponding data and information. By analyzing the current situation of domestic and foreign research, the feasibility of the intelligent interpretation robot design for science and technology museums based on the "Internet of Things" model is elaborated from theory and practice respectively.
2) Targeted on the current low degree of intelligence of science and technology museums in China, a designed scheme of intelligent interpretation robot for science and technology museums based on the "Internet of Things" model is proposed, and its working principle, structural composition and main functional modules are introduced in detail. The original information is provided for more scholars' research.
3) Shape design is fully considered in the anthropomorphic design. Content design focuses on the development of science and technology museum interpretation function, breaking the stereotypical influence of students on the content of science and technology museum. With this technology, students' interest in the "Internet of Things" in science and technology museums could be stimulated, the quality of service and educational significance could be improved. At the same time, the science elements are taken into account, so that the exhibits and knowledgeable are interesting and are able to be educated and to have fun. In addition, it can also increase the interactive experience and strengthen the communication between students and robots.

In Sect. 2 of this paper, we described the whole design framework of our solution. Section 3 provided the hardware design. Section 4 gave the software design. The tests and analysis were provided in Sect. 5. At last, the conclusions and future were given in Sect. 6.

2   Overall Solution Design

2.1   Introduction to the Overall Design

The group's overall design of the robot is shown in Fig. 1.

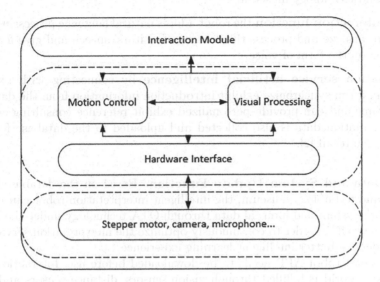

Fig. 1. Overall Design.

2.2   Function Introduction

Exhibit Identification Function. Gray scale identification sensor or camera are used to scan the identification code to identify different exhibits. After recognition, the exhibits are automatically played with the most recent synchronized voice from the database.

Visitor Identification Function: The human infrared identification sensor is used to confirm whether there are visitors who need intelligent robot services, and the ultrasonic distance measuring sensor is used to complete the identification of visitors' position related to the robot and the robot's position related to the displayed case. Based on these two data, the robot adjusts its position related to the visitors and the showcase. It can improve the safety of the robot's travel route.

Tour guiding function based on the radar scan independent detection and positioning of the building map, the robot would give corresponding guidance according to the needs of visitors through the voice interaction, so that visitors can quickly find the destination. This function means visitors can choose their own destinations, including rest areas, exhibition areas and restrooms in the science and technology museum.

Voice interaction function the robot adopts natural language processing technology to analyze and process the content of visitors' speech and give feedback to visitors in the form of voice.

Information service artificial intelligence by connecting with external database, it can synchronize exhibit introduction information from the database in real time and can provide personalized exhibit reference consulting service. The consultation data is also collected and uploaded to the database for easy analysis and recall [2].

OTA Data and System Update Function. Based on the database of the science and technology museum, the intelligent interpretation robot can update the robot's system and internal data through OTA technology under the operation of the staff, in order to continuously optimize the interpretation service and give students a better intelligent learning experience.

The smart robot APP needs to be downloaded before use. Interaction with the outside world is fulfilled through vision sensors, distance sensors and voice modules. The smart robot itself has certain information processing capabilities, which can process and classify the data collected by the sensors. The robot would record the interaction data with students, which facilitates the staff to optimize the services of the intelligent interpretation robot through big data. Therefore, when the exhibition hall is providing informatic technology services, intelligent robots can be used to complete some of the more repetitive tasks like the explanation of exhibits. This saves human resources significantly.

2.3   Design Process

The design process for developing an intelligent interpretive robot for science and technology museum with scenarios includes four stages.

Determine the tesearch content investigating and studying the scientific, advanced, practical and production feasibility of the robot, and determining the research focus and the main content of the research and production of the robot.

Determine the solution collecting the relevant information of each part of the module and the main controller, and developing the solution according to the existing technology.

Design and Production. Research, design and produce robot solutions.

Operational Testing. After aggregation and performing the field tests, problems are identified and analyzed so that the robot are improved. The overall design flow of the robot is shown in Fig. 2.

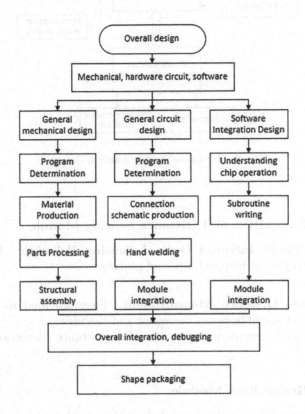

Fig. 2. Overall design process.

3 Robot Hardware Solution Design

The entire hardware design scheme of the robot was studied, and it was decided to use Raspberry Pi as the central processor and to use STM32 as the main controller with corresponding hardware modules to achieve the functions including ranging, moving, positioning, and broadcasting. The total hardware design scheme is shown in Fig. 3.

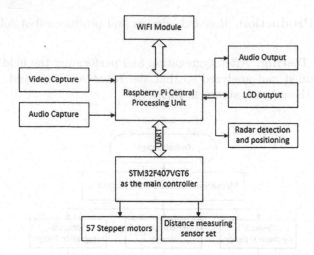

Fig. 3. Hardware master solution design.

3.1 Body Recognition and Distance Sensing Module

The Human Body Infrared Optical Sensing Principle. It is used to achieve the detection of human body and objects.

The Ultrasonic Distance Measurement. They are used to measure the related movement speed between the robot and the visitor.

Combined with microcontroller, the long-distance detection could be completed.

3.2 Robot Recognition Module

Grayscale recognition sensor module it detects the color scale value near the recognition exhibit for recognition judgment.

Camera module the basic information corresponding to the exhibits is pre-stored in the robot. The robot calls the corresponding explanation voice by recognizing the specific ID of different exhibits. The ID can be numbers, bar codes, QR codes or other identification marks.

3.3 Radar Scanning Autonomous Detection and Positioning Module

The information about the obstacles around the robot is collected by radar. The data is sent to the microcontroller for processing and analysis to obtain the corresponding location coordinates, which are subsequently displayed on the computer display as two-dimensional or three-dimensional images to achieve coordinate conversion and create a local map to eventually create a global map [3].

3.4   Speech Recognition Module

This module integrates speech recognition, speech synthesis, RF (radio frequency) function, and voice (MP3) on demand, infrared, and other functions. It has a high recognition rate over long distances and uses a non-specific voice recognition control module as an independent voice processing control center to recognize and process incoming voice commands.

3.5   IOT Interface Module

The robot can be connected to the STC server through the RMII protocol using a network cable with RJ45 interface to realize the IoT. The abstraction description of the device is used to achieve the purpose of service-oriented resource devices [4]. The abstraction description process is carried out at three main levels: devices, resources and services. The above three-level design achieves the purpose of differentiating heterogeneous devices, determining the type of resources, and sterilizing the resources respectively [5].

3.6   The WIFI Module

The WIFI module and STM32 microcontroller are connected through serial port. The WIFI module receives data and outputs through serial port; serial port receives data and outputs through WIFI module. The robot and data are synchronized with the database of the science and technology museum through OTA technology for wireless update.

3.7   LCD Output Module

This module is responsible for the display of the user interface and its debugging.

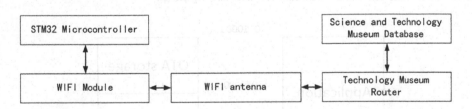

Fig. 4. WIFI module diagram.

4 Robot Software Solution Design

4.1 Two Important Statements of Speech Recognition Function Application

The Important Statement in the Subroutine. BSR_Teain(int Comm andID, int Train Mode):Command ID is the training command number, and Train Mode represents the number of exercises. Different training results will produce different return values, and the training program could handle the corresponding return values appropriately.

The Most Important Function in the Subroutine. BSR_GetResult(): the main purpose is to get data in the recognizer. Different values can be generated according to the change of the machine recognition. When the voice data is obtained, a res value will be generated after machine recognition. When no command can be identified, the res=0; when the recognizer is not initialized or the recognition function is not enabled, the res=-1; when the recognition of abnormal commands, the res=-2; when the recognition is completed, the serial number of the command is returned.

4.2 Forwarding Server Technology

To enable cross-network monitoring of the robot, the information sent from each client is transmitted to the server side in real time by using a combination of HTTP protocol and TCP/IP protocol, and the server returns the corresponding control data, thus ensuring stable and efficient operation between the nodes [6].

4.3 Over-the-Air Download Technology (OTA)

The Robot Will Continuously Record User Feedback in the Service. So that the STC can optimize the robot backend data, and synchronize the robot and data with the STC database for wireless updates.

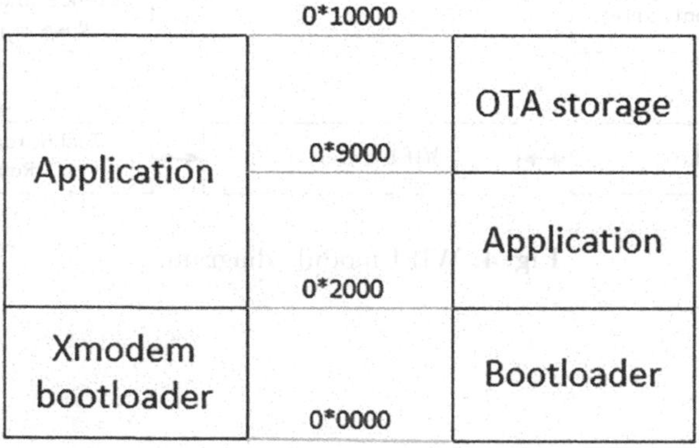

Fig. 5. Application loader schematic.

The Robot Gets the Firmware Upgrade File from the Server Through OTA Technology. The backup upgrade is determined to achieve OTA. The schematic diagram of the application bootloader is detailed in Fig. 5. [7].

The application bootloader runs as shown in Fig. 6.

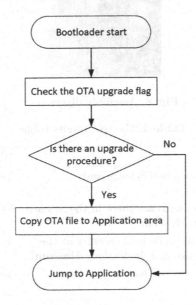

Fig. 6. Application bootloader runtime flow.

5   Robot Assembly and Test

The commissioning system is divided into five parts:

5.1   Robot Assembly

The overall appearance of the completed design of the group is shown in Fig. 7. and Fig. 8.

Fig. 7. Renderings.

Fig. 8. Assembly diagram.

Table 1. the test results table

No.	question	Whether accurately
1	Introducing Zhengzhou Science and Technology Museum.	Yes
2	What exhibition halls are there in the Science and Technology Museum?	Yes
3	What events have been held recently at the Zhengzhou Science and Technology Museum?	Yes
4	What functions do you have?	Yes
...	...	...

The test found that the overall response of human-computer interaction is good, but there is a certain distance limitation, when the sound source exceeds 200cm, the recognition result error is larger.

5.2 OTA System Test

The device side uploads the version number to the OTA cloud. The cloud determines the requirements to upgrade and sends the upgrade to the device. The device side updates the program after downloading through the communication protocol (receiving the upgrade package), uploads the current version number, and the cloud checks the version number and finds the update. The system runs well and can update data in time through OTA technology.

Based on the above four tests of B to E, the robot's guided tour function, explanation function and intelligent question and answer function have been basically realized.

6   Conclusions and Future Work

In terms of technology the designed robot is able to explain and guide the tour basically through laboratory tests and field tests at the science and technology museum. It foreshadows the feasibility of replacing docents with intelligent robots in the future.

In terms of function the robot can basically meet the personalized needs of different visiting objects, such as guiding tours, explaining the background of exhibits, and simple human-machine interaction.

In Terms of Educational Effect. The intelligent interpretive robot can stimulate visitors' interest in knowledge and assist them to further understand the information of exhibits. It fully demonstrates the convenience brought by future intelligent life and work.

This design is expected to provide a reference and experimental basis for the development of educational robots.

However, there are some shortcomings to overcome in next stage, including: 1) the robot's radar scanning autonomous detection and positioning system needs to be further improved. 2) the background information and database of the exhibits are limited that may lead to the robot answering questions that are not asked. The following work will be carried out in this regard.

The realization of the basic functions of the robot provides the basic information and experimental data for the next step of optimizing the interpretive robot, which can be used as a reference to design intelligent interpretive robots for other exhibits to achieve the popularity of the interpretive robot. In the future, the popularization of different science and technology museum interpretive robots also expands the database of human-computer interaction information, which can promote the interpretive robot to improve its functions in the form of positive feedback.

Making full use ofscience and technology museum network resources, design and build multiple science and technology museum venues to share resources system. Cost saving at the same time can also improve the efficiency of science education and achieve better publicity effects.

Language category expansion, such as the expansion of multilingual language packages to achieve the ability of robots to meet foreigners.

Paying more attention to the demand response, optimize products and services, grasp the product needs of fixed groups and various types of exhibition halls accurately, and maintain long-term close contact with them to provide "tailor-made" customized products. Establishing a good reputation to enhance product awareness. Based on a clear market positioning, the integrated use of various communication media as a means of communication would be used to maximize the effect of information dissemination.

Acknowledgements. Acknowledgements would be sent to Zhejiang Institute of Science and Technology for funding the projects of: Extracurricular Science and Technology Innovation and Practice for College Students in 2021 (Spring Sprout Project); Entrepreneurship Training Program (2021cxcy180); National Student Innovation and Entrepreneurship Training Program (2022cxcy49). Acknowledgement would also be sent to Zhengzhou Science and Technology Museum and Zhengzhou Creators Space.

References

1. Xiaoxia, X., Yafan, C., Shannon, C., Chung, H.C.: Social innovation and health-related well-being of left-behind children: evidence from an Intell. Robot Proj. China J. **4**, 1–21 (2020)
2. Jianye, Z., Vijayalakshmi, S.: Reform and innovation of artificial intelligence technology for information service in university physical education. J. Intell. Fuzzy Syst. **4**, 3325–3335 (2021)
3. Xiaolong, C., Jian, G., Xiaoqian, M., Zhigao, W., Ningbo, L., Guoqing, W.: Multi-Dimensional Automatic Detection of Scanning Radar Images of Marine Targets Based on Radar PPInet. Remote Sens. **13**, 3856–3856 (2021)
4. Qiu, G., Zheng, Z., Xu, Y.C., Deng, Y.: Development of personalized IoT mobile applications using MIT app inventor 2. In: 2021 4th International Conference on Computer Science and Software Engineering (CSSE 2021), pp. 175–179 (2021)
5. Yanhong, G.L., Chenghao, W., Cui, L.Y: Research on production big data acquisition and transmission system in intelligent Jobshop. In: Proceedings of the 33rd Chinese Control and Decision Conference (CCDC 2021), vol. 7, pp. 71–76 (2021)
6. Zhiliang, L.: Research on the implementation of streaming media forwarding server in distance education: Intell. Comput. Appl. **11**, 153–155 (2017)
7. Peng, C., Mei, X., Chuanshu, Z., Wei, Y.: Bus OTA implementation and vehicle CAN communication design. Autom. Electr. Appl. 4–6 (2022)

Language Vitality Assessment Based on Cyberspace Data: A Case Study and Future Research Prospects

Qingzhen Chen[1] and Huanghai Fang[2(✉)]

[1] Overseas Education College, Xiamen University, Xiamen, China
[2] School of Foreign Studies, Suqian University, Suqian, China
fanghuanhai@xmu.edu.cn

Abstract. According to an Objective Language Vitality Assessment Scale, this paper uses cyberspace data to evaluate the objective language vitality of Chinese in San Jose, California. It can be found that the low instrumental value of Chinese in the field of work, the lack of institutional support in the field of education and media, as well as the impact of the US government's language policy, are the main reasons for the low level of language vitality of Chinese in this city. It was proposed that by collecting a large amount of sample data and using machine learning technology to adjust indicators and weights, an optimal formula, that is, the most stable language vitality prediction model, can be obtained. This predictive model can be used to predict the future language vitality.

Keywords: Chinese · Second language · Language vitality assessment · Machine learning

1 Introduction

As a basic work of language resource protection projects, language vitality assessment has been widely concerned and valued by UNESCO and scholars around the world (Giles et al. 1977; Bourhis et al. 1981; Fishman 1991; Landweer 2000; Lewis & Simons 2010; Ehala, Ehala 2010; McEntee-Atalianis 2011; Soo et al. 2015; Lee and Van Way 2016; Mufwene 2017; Fitzgerald Fitzgerald 2017; Laurentia and Ioanna 2018; Fang 2020). The earliest language vitality assessment framework was proposed by Giles et al. 1977, which included three types of structural variables: the Status, Demographic and Institutional Support (Giles et al. 1977). In 1991, Fishman proposed the Graded Inter-generational Disruption Scale (GIDS) which divided language endangerment into eight levels (Fishman 1991). Lewis and Simons (2010) designed a 13-level Expanded Graded Intergenerational Disruption Scale (EGIDS) on the basis of three evaluative systems, and argued that "any known language, including those languages for which there are no longer speakers, can be categorized by using the resulting scale". In addition, UNESCO classified language vitality into six levels (UNESCO 2003) and in 2012, after further discussion, the Towards UNESCO Guidelines on Language Policies: a Tool for Language Assessment and Planning (Final version) was published (UNESCO 2012).

With the rapid development of Internet technology, the vitality of world languages in cyberspace have attracted the attention of scholars (Paolillo 2005; Pimienta 2009; Ronen et al. 2014; Guo and Shen 2019) in recent years. Ronen et al. (2014) used big data, including book translations, language use of Wikipedia and twitter, to provide a concept of language importance that goes beyond simple economic or demographic measures. S. J. Guo and J. Shen (2019) designed a quantitative evaluation system composed of five indicators: Economy, Demographic, Web content languages, Social media and Knowledge dissemination by using the four data --- language use in Wikipedia and twitter, GDP and demographic --- published by MIT Media Lab and the data, "Usage statistics of content languages for websites", from W3techs. The paper analyzed the order of world language vitality in cyberspace and its causes (Guo and Shen 2019). Their researches demonstrate a new approach to assessing language vitality by using the big data of virtual linguistic landscape and world language use.

However, there is still room for improvement in the current language vitality evaluation framework (Fan 2006; Mufwene 2017; Fitzgerald 2017; Fang 2020), for example, the indicator number in some framework is too small, some indicators are difficult to quantify resulting in weak operational applicability.

In view of this, we proposed the Objective Language Vitality Assessment Scale, which includes four main headings: Social, Economic, Political and Cultural factors. Social factors mainly include demographic, social status of ethnic groups, language use in media and education, etc.; Economic factors basically include economic status of ethnic groups, language use in the field of work and international trade, international tourists, etc.; Political indicators include political status of ethnic groups, language services for public affairs and language use of official media; Cultural indicators are essentially the language use of books and films (Fang et al. 2021).

It is generally believed that the Assessment Scale can be used to evaluate the language vitality of Chinese -- with the spoken form of Mandarin Chinese, and the written form of both simplified and traditional Chinese characters -- as a second language in overseas communities by learning from the best-known assessment systems (Giles et al. 1977, Fishman 1991, UNESCO 2003, Lewis and Simons 2010) and taking into account the data of language vitality in both social and virtual space (Paolillo 2005; Pimienta 2009; Ronen et al. 2014; Guo and Shen 2019).

2   Chinese Language Vitality in San Jose

For the research of language vitality assessment of Chinese as a second language, it is considered that San Jose, California, is a typical case study. As a highly diversified immigrant city, approximately 57.6 percent of San Jose citizens speak an ethnic language other than English at home (please refer to American Community Survey). According to American Community Survey 2018, the Hispanic immigrants account for 32.4 percent of the total population of San Jose, and the Asian immigrants account for 35.8 percent of the total population, including 10.7 percent of Vietnamese and 8.2 percent of Chinese.

On the basis of the Objective Language Vitality Assessment Scale (Fang et al. 2021), a survey had been conducted from April 2020 to April 2021 and all results, mainly focusing on 2018 data, had been calculated by the following process:

- Firstly, standardize the original data, that is, take the English data of each indicator as the denominator 1, and convert the Chinese data into percentages.
- Concerning the reverse indicators, such as "educational attainment" and "median household income", are calculated as "vi = 1-x" where vi is the vitality value of the indicator, and x is the original standardized data.
- Finally, average the percentage data of all indicators in each category, and then the average value of the four categories are weighted by the following weight distribution: economic factors account for 40%, political factors account for 30%, social factors account for 20%, and culture factors account for 10%.

The evaluation results shows that the objective language vitality value of Chinese in San Jose is 20.81 percent, indicating a low level of language vitality. As can be seen in Table 1,The highest vitality of Chinese language is in the economic field, with language vitality value of 41.25 percent, while the lowest vitality is in the cultural field, with vitality value of only 2.98 percent. This result reflects the impact of China's rapid economic development on the global economy and the strong penetration of American culture in the multi-directional flow of cultural globalization.

Table 1. Evaluation results of Chinese objective language vitality in San Jose (2018)

Category	Subdirectory	Indicator	Vitality Value
Social	Demography	Proportion	33.51%
		Concentration	25.50%
		Language spoken at home	16.78%
	Social status	*Education attainment (reverse indicator)	−31.04%
		Proportion of executives in major industries (represented by Silicon Valley high-tech companies)	14.34%
	Mass media	Television channel	6.67%
		Newspaper	7.55%
		Radio	1.61%
		Google trend- "human language - Chinese VS English"	26.58%
		Google trend -"learning Chinese VS learning English"	26.58%
		Usage of content languages for websites	2.51%
		Language usage of knowledge base website (represented by Wikipedia)	3.68%
		Language use in social media (represented by Twitter)	0.18%

(continued)

Table 1. (*continued*)

Category	Subdirectory	Indicator	Vitality Value
	Education	Number of language programs (mainly private)	51.28%
		Number of language programs in public primary and secondary schools	3.81%
		Enrollment of language courses in public primary and secondary schools	0.81%
		Number of AP programs in public secondary schools	4.26%
		Enrollment of AP course in public secondary schools	0.36%
Economic	Economic status	Number of ethnic firms	19.14%
		Revenue of ethnic firms	17.36%
		Average income of employees in ethnic firms	87.34%
		*Median household income (reverse indicator)	−6.42%
	Work filed language	Number of jobs requiring ethnic language	1.24%
		Proportion of high-paid jobs requiring ethnic language	0.92%
	International trade	Trade volume with ethnic countries	139.96%
	International visitors	Number of visitors from ethnic countries	32.01%
		Visitor spending from ethnic countries	79.73%
Politics	Political status	Ethnic proportion of senior government officials	2.52%
		Proportion of government employees in ethnic groups with above middle-income	9.99%
	Government services	Language options in City Call Center / online services	6.06%
		Translation needed in government call center (represented by 911)	0.12%
		Language available in government website	12.23%
		Language use of government documents	2.47%
	Official media	Language use of government social media (represented by YouTube)	1.05%

(*continued*)

Table 1. (*continued*)

Category	Subdirectory	Indicator	Vitality Value
		Language preference of government social media audience (represented by YouTube)	12.61%
		Language use of government emergency resources	8.33%
Culture	Books	Book Translation	2.85%
		Language collections in public library	5.07%
	Movie	Box office of movies from ethnic country	1.03%
Weighted sum ($VI = \sum p\,\bar{x}$)			20.81%

3 Analysis of Evaluation Results

3.1 Social Indicators

Considering the universality of bilingual and even multilingual users in contemporary society and the possibility of language shift in overseas communities where Chinese is a second language, the indicator of "Language spoken at home" has been added in addition to the "Proportion" and "Concentration" in Demography. San Jose's Chinese language vitality was relatively good in terms of Demography, in which the value of "Proportion" reached 33.51 percent, and the values of "Concentration" and "Language spoken at home" also reached 25.5 percent and 16.78 percent respectively.

Both "Education" and "Mass media" in Social indicators belong to the Institutional Support factors proposed by Giles et al. (1977), and they are also included in the areas where the language with highest vitality is widely used in Fishman's GIDS (Fishman 1991). The language vitality of Chinese was relatively low in the fields of education and mass media in San Jose, among which the field of education was the worst. The vitality values of the four indicators related to language programs and enrollment of public schools were as low as 0.36 percent (Enrollment of AP courses in public secondary schools), 0.81 percent (Enrollment of language courses in public primary and secondary schools), 3.81 percent (Number of language programs in public primary and secondary schools) and 4.26 percent (Number of AP programs in public secondary schools). In academic year 2016–17, only three public schools in San Jose opened Chinese programs (please refer to Santa Clara County Office of Education website), although this number increased to eight in two years, according to the data from California Department of Education, in academic year 2018–19, only 665 students enrolled in Chinese courses in San Jose public schools, and only two middle schools opened AP Chinese program with merely 12 students enrolled that year.

Obviously, Chinese language does not have institutional support advantages in public education system of San Jose City and Santa Clara County. We believe that this weakness is one of the most important reasons for the low language vitality of Chinese in San Jose.

3.2 Economic Indicators

The Chinese language vitality of San Jose performed best in the economic field, in which the vitality value of "Trade volume with ethnic countries" has reached 139.96 percent. Nevertheless, the average language vitality value of Chinese in the economic field was only 41.25 percent. In 2018, Chinese accounted for 5.07 percent of the international visitors in San Jose, while reaching 13.51 percent of the international tourist spending (please refer to *Team San Jose 2018 Annual Report*). However, the relatively small number of tourists made Chinese language vitality value in this field far lower than that of Spanish, which is also a second language.

Among the economic factors, the lowest vitality value of Chinese was in the indicators of "Work field language". In the variables of the number of jobs and the proportion of high-paid jobs with Mandarin Chinese requirements, the language vitality value was as low as 1.24 percent and 0.92 percent respectively.

This means that only a very small number of jobs required Mandarin Chinese in San Jose and it will most likely not add value to job candidates to master this language skill. When a language does not bring economic benefits to learners or help them achieve a utilitarian goal, learners' second language learning motivation may be greatly affected (Wee 2003), and for members of the language group, this social reality may bring more possibilities of language shift.

3.3 Political Indicators

"Government services" is included in the Institutional Support factors proposed by H. Giles, R. Y. Bourhis and D. M. Taylor in 1977, and its related indicators were one of the areas where Chinese language vitality performed most poorly, with a vitality value of 6.15 percent only, in San Jose. Among them, the lowest one was the indicator of "Translation needed in government call center (represented by 9-1-1)", the vitality index was as low as 0.12 percent. This data reflected the real language usage in San Jose, that is, most immigrants in San Jose are bilingual or multilingual users, which may also serve a sign of the language shift process of immigrants in the United States.

There is no language policy that clearly defines the status of different ethnic languages in San Jose. However, the Language Access Guidelines and Procedures from Santa Clara County states that:"Departments distributing or creating documents for the public should endeavor to make available those documents, at a minimum, in Spanish and Vietnamese language. Departments are also encouraged to translate documents into additional languages, such as, traditional Chinese or Tagalog, as appropriate."

In addition, Sect. 48985 of the California Education Code states that if 15 percent or more of the pupils enrolled in a public school speak a single primary language other than English, all notices, reports, statements, or records sent to the parent or guardian of any such pupil shall be written in both English and the primary language.

From the two regulations above, the following conclusions can be drawn:

- English is the undoubted primary working language in high-level fields such as government, education, employment and media, in California;
- The government has made certain priorities for language services other than English;

• The language services available to ethnic groups in public schools are related to their population and concentration.

This may explain why most of the important information on government official websites only provide Spanish translation rather than Chinese translation.

This phenomenon is more intuitive in public signs in San Jose. For example, as we can see in VTA (Santa Clara Valley Transportation Authority) bus stations in San Jose, both the bus stop and the ticket machine provide English, Spanish and Vietnamese version.

According to VTA's call center data, during calendar year 2014, 56.7 percent of all callers requested assistance spoke Spanish. Mandarin speakers represented 22.7 percent of all calls, Vietnamese speakers 12.9 percent. In calendar year 2015, it was 56.4 percent in Spanish, 22.8 percent in Mandarin and 13.4 percent in Vietnamese. Although the number of calls from Mandarin speakers has exceeded that of Vietnamese speakers by about 10 percentage points for two consecutive years, only Spanish and Vietnamese, in addtion to English, are used on bus stops and ticket machines.

Similarly, the dominant language on public signs in San Jose City Hall is English. On the day of the field investigation, October 16, 2020, there were several "City Hall is Closed" notices, using English, Spanish and Vietnamese, posted on the glass doors. On the department signs inside the City Hall, each department name was composed of three languages: English, Spanish and Vietnamese, of which English was on the first line with a larger font, while Spanish and Vietnamese on the second and third lines, respectively, with smaller fonts.

As Landry and Bourhis (1997) pointed out: "It is through its language policy for government signs that the state can exert its most systematic impact on the linguistic landscape of the territory under its jurisdiction." Conversely, the language choice and language use on government signs also reflect language policy and language attitude of the government.

3.4 Cultural Indicators

It is often believed that cultural globalization is based on economic globalization. Over the past decades, the rapid development of science and technology has shortened the space and time distance between countries and provided the material foundation for cultural globalization. Werner Sollors (2009) pointed out that: "In the past, teaching American students to be fluent in other languages was concentrated in the most important living European languages (French and German) and of Latin, the acquisition of which was a sign of being educated. The newer forms of bilingualism are directly related to migratory flows of people and cultural products, have stimulated the study of heritage and minority languages, have made Spanish also by far the most popular foreign language taken by students in the United States, and have led to the establishment of courses like 'Beginning Chinese for Native Speakers'."

This shows the impact of migratory flows of people and cultural products on stimulating minority language learning. In the process of cultural globalization, the cultures of various countries flow in multiple directions around the world, however, there remain different influences among different cultures, some are stronger, while others are weaker.

During Christmas 2017, China produced two-thirds of the world's Christmas trees; 80 percent of Christmas products from a factory in Yiwu, China, were exported to Europe, and many of Christmas decorations and Santa Claus dolls in New York came from China. These Christmas products with new designs and new ideas from China decorated the Christmas of different families in different countries and regions. Nonetheless, the core of this is still Western culture. This may allow us to understand why products with the label of "Made in China" spread all over the world in the past few decades, but the Cultural indicator was the field where Chinese language has the lowest vitality in San Jose, with a vitality value of only 2.98 percent.

The great success of Hollywood films in the world shows an important symbol of the export of American culture. According to Annual Report on Development of Global Film Industry (2018), as of December 31, 2017, all the top ten grossing films of all time in the world were produced in Hollywood; In addition, a number of Hollywood films, such as Star Wars: Episode VIII - The Last Jedi, The Fate of the Furious, Beauty and the Beast, Despicable Me 3, Pirates of the Caribbean: Dead Men Tell No Tales, Murder on the Orient Express and Coco won the box office champion in 2017 in many countries and regions. Even if screenwriters use cultural stories from other countries, the films produced by Hollywood usually end up with a distinct "Hollywood mark" and are mostly in English, such as Coco in 2017 and Mulan in 2020.

Book translation is also an important way of cultural transmission. Although there is no clear evidence to show the inevitable connection between literature and language spread, the fact that several internationally renowned language communication institutions --- Goethe-Institut from German, Instituto Cervantes from Spain, Dante Alighieri Society from Italy, for instance --- all choosed to name themselves in the name of their own literary giants, shows the importance of national language and literature to language transmission and the maintenance of language vitality. According to Index Translationum, from 1979 to 2019, there were 40,187 books translated from English into Chinese in China, while only 1,362 books translated from Chinese into English in the United States.

Due to the natural functions of cultural products, such as carrying cultural consciousness and values, and the way of expressing opinions, the prevalence of books and movies has undoubtedly played a role in promoting language communication. "Even when accessed in one's own language, books and films originating in the United States can be a cultural and linguistic lesson" (Wright 2016). The unequal flow of cultural products between the United States and China also reflects the strong spread of English around the world and the hardships of maintaining and developing Chinese language in English-speaking countries. As a language with approximately 1.12 billion speakers worldwide(please refer to Statista), what is true of Mandarin Chinese is even truer of other languages with much fewer users.

4 Prospects for Future Research

4.1 Creating a More Accurate Formula

In this paper, we use the Objective Language Vitality Assessment Scale with 38 indicators proposed by Fang, Shen and Chen in 2021 as foundation to measure Chinese language vitality in San Jose, California.

From a mathematical perspective, using 38 indicators to predict a vitality value is basically creating a linear function to combine and convert those 38 indicators into a vitality value. Linear function means combining values using constant weights. For example $Y = aX + bZ + c$ is a linear function, where we're using X and Z indicators to calculate the value of Y. a and b are constant values called weights. If a is much larger than b then that means X is more important to Y than Z is to Y. c is a constant value that helps us adjust the range value of Y. It plays a mathematical role but not important in our context.

So far, our approach to measure a language's vitality is totally logical, based on some measurements and assumptions, but it has 3 potential pitfalls:

- Is the weight distribution of the 38 indicators optimal? (problem #1)
- Are those 38 indicators sufficient to reliably predict a language vitality? (problem #2)
- Does each indicator be significantly independent of one another? (problem #3)

These 3 potential issues can be addressed by having a lot of data and employing a computer science technique called Machine Learning. Machine Learning is a vast domain. What we need here is one of the simplest forms of Machine Learning. Figure 1 below describes the problem we are trying to solve visually.

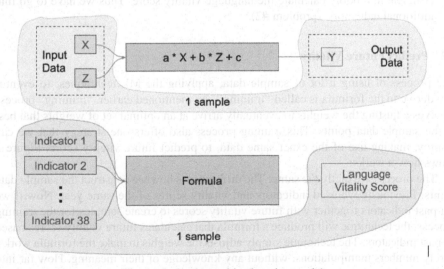

Fig. 1. A simple machine learning model

Before discussing the solution, we will add a few terminologies to help us describe it.

- The indicators together are input data.
- The formula is what we are trying to create.
- The vitality score is the output data.
- A set of input data and output data together is called a sample data point.

With this definition, it means the research on this paper has been about one single sample data point. One class of problem that Machine Learning (ML) can solve is when given a lot of sample data points, say vitality data for hundreds of cities, the technique will help us create a formula that works the best for all cases. What really happens is the technique adjusts the weights until they seem to work best for all the samples. (For more information please see Linear classifier in Wikipedia).

After applying the ML technique we would have 2 possible outcomes:

1. It found a formula that works well and gives us the formula in terms of weights for each indicator.
- We can look at the weights and tell how important each indicator is to the vitality score, relatively. (problem #1)
- The weight for some indicators might go close to zero, that means they do not matter at all, and we can drop them. (problem #1)
- There are additional techniques that can tell how related the indicators are. We only need to keep the fundamental indicators and drop those that are strongly related to them, which does not add any value by themselves. (problem #3)
1. It could not derive a stable formula. This means the set of indicators we have is not sufficient to reliably calculate the language vitality score. Thus we have to go find additional indicators. (problem #2).

4.2   Predict Future Vitality

The process of using a lot of sample data, applying the ML techniques, to eventually derive to the formula is called "training". As mentioned earlier, "training" process involves adjusting the weights to eventually arrive at an optimal set of weights that best fit the sample data points. This training process also offers one strategy that we can employ, making use of the exact same data, to predict future vitality score. Figure 2 shows how it works:

The process is exactly the same. The difference is how we construct the sample data points. Previously we used indicators and vitality scores of the same year. Now if we put past indicators together with future vitality scores to create samples for the training process, the technique will produce a formula that calculates future vitality scores based on past indicators. The technique simply adjusts the weights to make the formula works, purely numbers manipulations, without any knowledge of their meaning. How far into the future we want to predict is depending on how we construct the samples, offsetting by how many years.

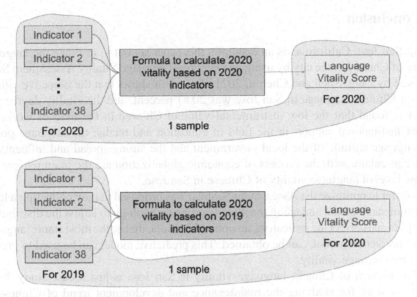

Fig. 2. Machine Learning Model for Predicting Future Language Vitality

As with all ML training, this future prediction strategy is only reliable if we train it with a lot of sample data points. There are additional ML techniques that can drastically improve the formula's reliability over time but also require even more data, over a longer period of time. This is about using "past" to predict the "future" -- the more history we learn the more likely that we can make a more accurate future guess. And with this comes pitfalls too.

- There will be new indicators that never exist that start influencing the outcome. For example, the formula for 1980s never needs to factor in the internet usages of a language, now that indicator is one of the most crucial one to calculate the vitality score.
- Some indicator will become obsolete over time.
- Many one time societal or natural events that have no historical pattern can throw our prediction totally off -- for example COVID-19.
- There are political events and policies changes that alter the dynamics of the system too.

The list above is not comprehensive, it is, in fact, barely a few examples. The accuracy of the proposed formula depends heavily on the reliability of the data. If an indicator changes drastically over the year without a clear pattern, it will throw the formula off too. In such a case we should drop that indicator. We simply can not predict anything without a pattern. Computer science disciplines offer tools for us to inspect, improve, and calculate language vitality. They are, in themselves, not the solution.

5 Conclusion

Taking San Jose, California, as an example, this paper set out to evaluate the language vitality of Chinese in the city by using an Objective Language Vitality Assessment Scale proposed by Fang, Shen and Chen in 2021. The result shows that the objective vitality value of Chinese language in San Jose was 20.81 percent, and the vitality degree was low. It is found that the low instrumental value of Chinese in the field of work, the lack of institutional support in the field of education and media, the language policy and language attitude of the local government and the strong spread and influence of American culture with the process of economic globalization are the main reasons for the low level of language vitality of Chinese in San Jose.

In order to optimize the Assessment Scale, it was proposed that by collecting a large amount of sample data and using machine learning technology to adjust the distribution of weights and correct the indicators, an optimal formula, that is, the most stable language vitality prediction model, can be obtained. This predictive model can be used to predict the future language vitality.

Our research of Chinese language vitality in San Jose is just a case study, but it is a basis work for studying the maintenance and development trend of Chinese as a second language in overseas communities. In future research, subjective language vitality, language attitude and language behavior of the local Chinese community can be included in discussion, and the goal of predicting the future language vitality through the past data could be realized by the proposal above. In this process, the development and changes of language roles, language status and linguistic capital displayed in virtual space should also be considered.

Acknowledgements. This work is supported by the Foundation of Center for Language Education and Cooperation (21YH019CX2). We aregrateful to the workmates for their comments.

References

Bourhis, R.Y., Giles, H., Rosenthal, D.: Notes on the construction of a 'subjective vitality questionnaire'for ethnolinguistic groups. J. Multilingual Multicultural Dev. 145–155 (1981)

Ehala, M.: Ethnolinguistic vitality and intergroup processes. Multilingua **29**(2), 203–221 (2010)

Fishman, J.A.: Reversing Language Shift: Theoretical and Empirical Foundations of a Assistance to Threatened Languages. Multilingual Matters, Clevedon (1991)

Fitzgerald, C.M.: Understanding language vitality and reclamation as resilience: a framework for language endangerment and 'loss'(Commentary on Mufwene). Language **93**, e280–e297 (2017)

Giles, H., Bourhis, R. Y., Taylor, D.M.: Towards a Theory of Language in Ethnic group relations. Language, Ethnicity and Intergroup Relations. Academic Press, London, pp. 307–348 (1977)

Lewis, M.P., Simons, G.F.: Assessing endangerment: expanding fishman's GIDS. Revue Roumaine de Linguistique **2**, 103–120 (2010)

Lee, N.H., Van Way, J.: Assessing levels of endangerment in the catalogue of endangered languages (ELCat) using the language endangerment index (LEI). Lang. Soc. **45**(2), 271–292 (2016)

Landweer, M.L.: Indicators of ethnolinguistic vitality. Notes Sociolinguistics **5**(1), 5–22 (2000)

Landry, R., Bourhis, R.: Linguistic landscape and ethnolinguistic vitality: an empirical study. J. Lang. Soc. Psychol. **16**, 23–49 (1997)

McEntee-Atalianis, L.J.: The value of adopting multiple approaches and methodologies in the investigation of ethnolinguistic vitality. J. Multiling. Multicult. Dev. **32**, 151–167 (2011)

Mufwene, S.S.: Language vitality: the weak theoretical underpinnings of what can be an exciting research area. Language **93**, e202–e223 (2017)

Schreiber, L., Sitaridou, I.: Assessing the sociolinguistic vitality of istanbulite romeyka: an attitudinal study. J. Multiling. Multicult. Dev. **39**, 1–16 (2018)

Paolillo, J., Pimienta, D., Prado, D.: Measuring Linguistic Diversity on the Internet. UNESCO, Paris (2005)

Pimienta, D., Prado, D., Blanco, Á.: Twelve Years of Measuring Linguistic Diversity in the Internet: Balance and Perspectives. UNESCO, Paris (2009)

Ronen, S., Goncalve, B., Hu, K.Z., et al.: Links that speak: the global language network and its association with global fame. Proc. Natl. Acad. Sci. U.S.A. **111**(52), E5616–E5622 (2014)

How, S.Y., Chan, S.H., Abdullah, A.N.: Language vitality of Malaysian languages and its relation to identity. GEMA Online J. Lang. Stud. **15**(2), 119–136 (2015)

Sollors, W.: Multilingualism in the United States: a less well-known source of vitality in American culture as an issue of social justice and of historical memory. Nanzan Rev. Am. Stud. **31**, 59–75 (2009)

UNESCO. Language Vitality and Endangerment. UNESCO, Paris (2003)

UNESCO. Towards UNESCO Guidelines on Language Policies: A Tool for Language Assessment and Planning. UNESCO, Paris (2012)

Wee, L.: Linguistic instrumentalism in Singapore. J. Multiling. Multicult. Dev. **24**(3), 211–224 (2003)

Wright, S.: Language Policy and Language Planning: From Nationalism to Globalisation. Palgrave Macmillan, United Kingdom (2016)

Fang, H.H., Shen, L., Chen, Q.Z.: Study on Chinese vitality assessment under the vision of international chinese education: taking San Jose, California as an example. J. Res. Educ. Ethnic Minorities **32**, 146–156 (2021)

Guo, S.J., Shen, J.: The vitality and distribution reasons of world languages in the cyberspace. Appl. Linguis. **01**, 27–36 (2019)

Fang, X.B.: From Language Vitality to Language Resilience. Journal of Yunnan Normal University (Humanities and Social Sciences Edition), vol. 52, pp. 22–31 (2020)

Fan, J.J.: Language vitality and language endangered assessment. Mod. Foreign Lang. (Quarterly) **29**, 210–213 (2006)

Lu, B., Niu, X.Z., Liu, Z.S.: Annual Report on Development of Global Film Industry. Social Sciences Literature Press, Beijing (2018)

Design and Implementation of a Cloud-Native Platform for Financial Big Data Processing Course

Ping Yu[✉], Ye Tao, Jie Zhang, and Ying Jin

Department of Computer Science and Technology, Nanjing University, Nanjing, China
{yuping,taoye,zhangj,jinying}@nju.edu.cn

Abstract. With the advent of big data, financial technology steps into a more intelligent era. The demand for big data-related financial application development and operation continues to expand. Hadoop and Spark are popular parallel computing frameworks that are adopted as big data processing platforms, but the time cost of their environment deployment is a significant expense for beginners. BDKit, a big data application development and operation platform based on container cloud, is proposed in this paper, aiming to provide customized and scalable cloud service solutions for teaching practice. It is based on Kubernetes ecosystem and relies on the powerful self-repair and load balancing capability provided by Kubernetes to ensure the stable operation of users' virtual clusters. At the same time, BDKit encapsulates a variety of Docker images to achieve the construction of big data application development and operation environment according to the components required by different users. The services provided by BDKit can greatly reduce the pressure of preparing big data processing environment and help to achieve the purpose of teaching students according to their aptitude.

Keywords: Big Data · Fintech · Kubernetes · Docker · Cloud-Native

1 Introduction

In recent years, artificial intelligence, big data, cloud computing and other computer technologies have been widely applied in the financial industry, making financial technology to step into a more intelligent and digital era. At the same time, a large number of universities began to train interdisciplinary talents in the field of computer science and financial engineering. Interdisciplinary major of computer science and financial engineering focuses on the integration of economics, finance, computer technology and other disciplines. It mainly aims to cultivate students to master fintech and data science, with knowledge in data processing, data mining, programming, software engineering and artificial intelligence.

As one of the major compulsory courses for junior students, financial big data processing course focuses on big data technologies (Hadoop [1], Spark [2], HBase [3], Hive [4], etc.) and their applications on large volume of financial data. It requires students to have mastered the fundamentals of computer science, such as programming languages

W. Hong and Y. Weng (Eds.): ICCSE 2022, CCIS 1813, pp. 180–193, 2023.
https://doi.org/10.1007/978-981-99-2449-3_17

(C++, Java or Python), data structure and algorithm, data base and distributed computing. Different from any course offered by financial engineering majors or other basic computer courses, it is a comprehensive course with an emphasis on practice. It aims to systematically cultivate students' capability of big data processing program design, development, and parameter tuning through a series of experiments. It challenges students because most of them lack training on large-scale computer systems. Due to the particularity of big data processing technology requiring multiple machine nodes, it is very difficult to set up a parallel computing cluster both technically and in terms of manpower and material resources. It costs students and teaching assistants much time on the first step of installing and configuring big data processing platforms, such as Hadoop and HBase, even in pseudo distributed mode. Based on three years of teaching experience, we find it is necessary to provide an online platform for students to rapidly access the big data processing cluster environment.

Cloud computing provides utilities for using computing resources without installing and maintaining them on-premises [5]. Most of the existing large cloud service providers only provide basic system level services, but users still need to build and configure their own environment. Even large cloud service providers such as Ali Cloud and Tencent Cloud, which provide parallel computing environment images such as Hadoop for direct deployment, are mainly oriented to high-performance computing needs of enterprises and large-granularity requirements of direct executing applications rather than teaching and learning purposes, so the granularity of services provided is too large. It is not suitable for individual learners in terms of performance and price. At present, some scholars and teaching staff have carried out exploration in the construction of big data experimental platform [6–8]. However, these big data development and training platforms for teaching are uneven in technology, and generally have the following problems: (1) Some platforms are oriented to web services with high level abstraction, which is often just the executor of Hadoop and Spark programs, so that users lose the opportunity to access the underlying cluster. It is difficult for users to debug and tune their programs. (2) Some platforms are based on VM images and the resource usage is high and the performance is low. The number of cluster nodes and software components is usually fixed, and the degree of customization and extensibility is low. For example, it is difficult to efficiently process streaming financial data on the platform that lacks stream computing components such as Apache Storm [9] or Flink [10].

Therefore, we hope to propose a cloud-native solution named as BDKit for financial big data processing course. It can provide services at appropriate levels of abstraction, so that on the one hand, it can build a customized virtual cluster according to the needs of students to provide the parallel computing environment, and on the other hand, it can ensure students to have fully independent operation of the cluster environment. Besides big data practice, students also get the opportunity of learning about cloud computing technology if they wish.

This paper provides the following contributions:

- We propose a big data teaching platform based on container cloud. It supports the creation of Hadoop/Spark clusters and the online development, running, and monitoring of big data applications such as MapReduce, Spark, and Hive. With the help of BDKit, students can put more efforts on big data program design and optimization.
- We design a series of basic experiments and some comprehensive projects for students to apply big data technology in financial big data processing. Students are more confident with the technology needs of the fintech after course training.
- The cloud-native solution has stimulated students' interest in big data and cloud computing. Based on students' feedback, it proves to be effective for interdisciplinary major of computer science and financial engineering.

2 Platform Design

2.1 Requirements

With the maturity of open-source big data frameworks like Hadoop and Spark, and the ecosystem of big data components built around them, it's getting easier to develop applications that can handle massive amounts of data. However, the hardware acquisition, environment construction and state management of the cluster are still quite tedious and difficult. Even if a user has enough hardware to build a cluster, setting up a cluster and configuring the environment can be a huge and complex task, especially for beginners, if the user is not familiar with Linux commands or other related tools.

Based on three years of teaching practice, we found that the junior students have common difficulties in preparing big data clusters. They were puzzled by various system-level problems and had to put much time on solving them. The frustration diminished their interest in learning big data technology even though they were good at programming and algorithms. After investigation, the most frequent problems are summarized in Table 1.

In fact, solving these problems is not the key point of this course. In order to simplify the construction and deployment of the big data framework and provide users with a real distributed environment with convenient access and rich computing components, it is particularly important to build an integrated online platform for teaching and practicing.

With specific consideration on financial scenarios, financial data generally has the characteristics of "stream data" and needs to be processed quickly in a short time. It is necessary to include streaming computing components in the supporting platform. However, there are different frameworks available in the big data community, including Spark streaming, Storm and Flink. The platform is thus expected to be open for different frameworks. In addition to this, operability of the platform is also important. As big data technology is strongly connected with cloud computing, a cloud-native platform will be user-friendly to students to understand the combination of these two mainstream technologies.

Table 1. Common problems

No.	Problem	Possible Cause
1	Name Node disappears after restarting computer	The fold of *hadoop.tmp.dir* disappears after restart
2	Name Node disappears after starting HDFS	The configuration of *hdfs-site.xml* is wrong
3	Resource Manager disappears when executing MapReduce task	VM or docker does not allocate enough memory or computer has not enough memory
4	MapReduce or spark task stucks	Computing resources are insufficient
5	No hbase master found when shutting down HBase	The *pid* file is deleted by operating system
6	HMaster can not start	HBase environment setting has error

2.2 Platform Overview

BDKit is based on Kubernetes ecology [11, 12], which can automatically reschedule, restart and replication, thus has strong self-repair capability. At the same time, it relies on the Docker [13–15] virtualization technology and abstracts each node as a pod. A virtual Hadoop/Spark cluster consists of multiple nodes. Each user can create more than one node according to different application scenarios. On the one hand, it greatly saves system resources compared to the virtual machine method. It provides a more fine-grained computing needs of cloud services to users. On the other hand, users can control the virtual cluster that belongs to oneself completely through a web-based terminal with root authority. In this way, students can get more in-depth exposure to the cluster, and customize the cluster at a higher level. With different images prepared in advance, we can provide instances of different environments according to users' requirements, so that users can select Hadoop and Spark ecological components on demand. In addition, BDKit also provides a shared data set, which can be mounted by disk to facilitate all users of the platform to directly access the data set prepared by the platform administrator, generally the teacher or teaching assistants, for experiments according to their teaching needs. Finally, it also integrates popular web-based interactive code editor services (e.g., VsCode code-server [16] and Jupyter notebook [17]) and UI components of Hadoop and Spark monitor for online development and monitoring. To facilitate code management, BDKit adopts Git [18] service to enable pulling code from remote repositories and pushing modified code. Even if one deletes his/her cluster, all application codes are still available in the his/her remote repository.

2.3 Layered Architecture

As shown in Fig. 1, BDKit consists of four logical layers, bottom-up namely virtualization layer, business layer, API interface layer and view layer.

(1) **Virtualization Layer:** BDKit runs on top of a Kubernetes cluster, relying on Kubernetes for cluster management. It exposes all ports through the abstraction of services. To meet the differentiated needs of users, BDKit provides various docker images pre-installing a variety of big data development components. Users can directly choose the appropriate image when creating a cluster, or compose different components on demand to get a customized cluster. For example, a user can get a cluster of the last version of Hadoop and Spark frameworks together with a specific version of Anaconda [19] and Jupyter notebook.

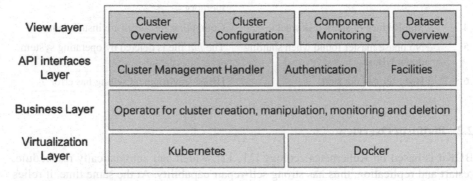

Fig. 1. Layered architecture of BDKit

(2) **Business Layer:** It is the kernel part of BDKit. We design and implement a big data processing cluster operator based on Operator SDK [20]. The operator defines the controller of Hadoop/Spark cluster and all relevant cluster resources. It is in charge of creating, manipulating and deleting clusters.

- *Cluster Architecture*: The architecture of Hadoop/Spark cluster created by BDKit refers to the master-slave mode of Hadoop, that is, it contains one master node and multiple slave nodes. The master node, including Name Node and Resource Manager, manages metadata of the HDFS and scheduling tasks. Slave nodes include Data nodes and Node Managers. They store actual data and manage the single node. Based on the master-slave mode, the master and slave nodes are deployed to run in independent pods. On the Kubernetes platform, the communication between pods is handled by a service. A headless service of the same name is deployed for each pod in the cluster. In addition, the cluster also sets up NodePort service for the master pod to expose the pod interior for Web UI viewing, and Hadoop/Spark cluster management. Figure 2 shows the logical architecture of the cluster.
- *Cluster Operator*: Kubernetes allows developers to extend the Kubernetes API with CustomResourceDefinition (CRD). Each custom resource requires a controller to perform specific operations. Operator SDK is a toolkit to manage Kubernetes native applications, called Operators, in an effective, automated, and scalable way [20]. Based on the operator framework, BDKit defines big data

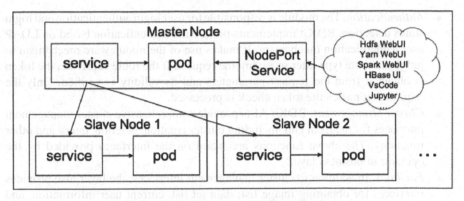

Fig. 2. Logical architecture of Hadoop/Spark cluster

CRD for Hadoop/Spark cluster resources, and constructs a controller to operate Hadoop/Spark cluster resources at business layer, e.g., automatic deploying and monitoring of cluster resources. Figure 3 shows the workflow of the cluster controller to construct a Hadoop/Spark cluster. When the cluster instance is available, it creates PVC and Git container as needed and create a master pod with relevant services. It checks whether the number of exiting slave pods (foundNum) equals the expected slave node number (expectNum) defined by the user. If not equal, the controller will create or delete slave pods to ensure foundNum is the same as expectNum.

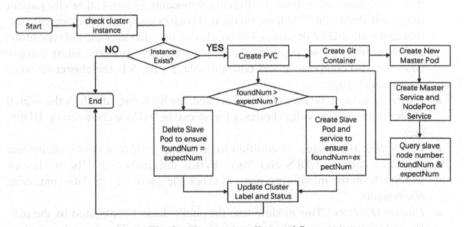

Fig. 3. Cluster controller workflow

(3) **API Interface Layer:** To separate concerns of front-end and back-end, BDKit designs an API interface layer to define APIs to listen to GET/POST requests from front-end clients, and invoke back-end API handlers to process the requests including cluster creation, deletion, etc. Its functions include:

- *Authentication*: The module is responsible for user login authentication and login status detection. BDKit implements permission authentication based on LDAP user authentication mechanism. It makes use of the middleware mechanism to judge the route type after receiving the request. If the route is private, the token is obtained from the request parameters and its validity is verified. Only the request that passes the token check is processed.
- *Cluster Management*: BDKit APIs provide comprehensive cluster management interfaces for the front end, including cluster creation, deletion, query and other functions. The above functions are based on the interfaces provided by the operator in business layer.
- *Facilities*: In addition to cluster management interfaces, the layer also provides interfaces for obtaining image list, data set list, current user information, and cluster container status, etc.

(4) **View Layer:** As a cloud service, BDKit provides web UI which is platform independent. Users can access it anytime from any device through a web browser. The view layer hides complex cluster deployment details for users, and provides concise and efficient operation and intuitive monitoring of big data related tasks, thus improves users' development efficiency. It is based on React development framework and Ant Design Pro UI framework to design web interfaces and implement the acquisition and display of back-end data. Its modules are as follows:

- *Cluster Configuration*: If there is no cluster instance, the homepage displays a list of available images for the user to select. It also allows users to customize their own image by composing different components. Figure 4 shows the page of image self-definition. When the image is chosen or composed, the user can customize the number of slave nodes in the cluster, the address of the Git repository, and the public data set provided by the platform. Big data computing components are also composable and customizable. Figure 5 is the cluster resource configuration page.
- *Cluster Overview*: When a cluster is created, the homepage displays the overall cluster status and provides shortcuts for accessing VsCode code-server, HDFS, etc.
- *Component Monitoring*: In addition to providing ports to access management interfaces such as HDFS and Yarn, BDKit integrates web UIs of Hadoop and Spark on the monitoring page to check the status of big data computing components.
- *Dataset Overview*: This module lists the public dataset configured by the platform administrators (e.g., the teacher or teaching assists). They have the privilege to upload experimental dataset to the platform. Students can only browse and mount the dataset to their cluster.

Fig. 4. Image self-definition page

Fig. 5. User cluster resource configuration page

3 Experiments

The teaching objectives of financial big data processing course includes letting students: (1) be more in-depth understanding of the basic principles of big data processing; (2) be more familiar about emerging technologies in the field of big data; (3) be more confident with finance technology needs.

To achieve the objectives in a semester with 72 class hours in total, we arrange the teaching contents into five stages, accompanied with four experiments and one final project.

3.1 Experiments Design

Table 2 shows the class teaching contents and corresponding experiments in the last semester. The last column defines the experimental environment options.

Table 2. Experiments design

Stage	Teaching Contents	Experiments	Environments
1	Introduction to Hadoop and HDFS	Installing Hadoop in a standalone mode and learning HDFS operations	Standalone
2	Basic and advanced MapReduce Programming	Massive text data processing with inverted index and word co-occurrence in MapReduce	Distributed Cluster or BDKit
3	Introduction to NoSQL database, HBase and Hive	Learning HBase/Hive operation and programming	Distributed Cluster or BDKit
4	Introduction to Spark ecosystem and stream computing	Massive data aggregation and classification in Spark	Distributed Cluster or BDKit
5	Introduction to financial big data processing	Individual loan default forecast (final project)	Distributed Cluster or BDKit

- **Experiment 1:** After introduction of Hadoop and HDFS, we assign an experiment of Hadoop installation and HDFS operation. As a first step to big data technology ecosystem, we require students to install Hadoop in standalone mode in their own computers. Linux is recommended as the default operating system. After that, we suggest them to install Hadoop and HDFS in pseudo distributed mode. For the students who are interested in parallel computing, we suggest them to construct a distributed cluster by means of virtual machine or docker.
- **Experiment 2:** The most important part of this course is training big data processing skills. We put many efforts on teaching how to design MapReduce programs with a series of examples, such as wordcount, sorting, word co-occurrence, inverted indexing, page rank, etc. After basic programming training, we introduce how to design parallel machine learning algorithms for big data analysis with MapReduce framework. In the second experiment, we ask students to process massive text data (e.g., Shakespeare's collected work) to accomplish the tasks of inverted indexing and word co-occurrence. Since Hadoop is implemented in Java, Java is the recommended programming language. Python is also allowed if the students are not familiar with Java.
- **Experiment 3:** NoSQL is a new scheme of database design that enables the storage and querying of data outside the traditional structures in RDBMS [21]. In the third stage, we clarify the principles of NoSQL database and compare NoSQL with SQL, taking an example of HBase. HBase is built on top of HDFS that provides a way of storing sparse data sets, which is commonly used in many big data applications. We also introduce Hive which is a data warehouse in the Hadoop ecosystem. Hive facilitates reading, writing, and managing large datasets residing in distributed storage by using SQL. To let students better understand NoSQL database and data warehouse,

we assign the tasks of creating big tables, storing data in HBase and Hive, manipulating and querying data with a series of operations.

- **Experiment 4:** Spark is a unified engine for executing data engineering, data science, and machine learning on single-node machines or clusters [2]. It is now the most widely-used computing engine for big data. In this stage, we introduce the fundamental principles of Spark and its important libraries, including Spark SQL, Spark ML, GraphX and Spark Streaming. We ask students to do massive data aggregation and classification by use of Spark ML. By collecting streaming data with a data sever such as Kafka [22], students are able to complete the stream computing task with Spark Streaming.

- **Final Project:** Financial innovation upgrades the need of making full use of big data technology and practicing big data thinking. In the end, we discuss big data applications in financial field with some real-world cases, such as credit risk forecasting, insurance fraud identification, bank customer portrait. We design a final project which derives from a big data competition. It takes personal credit in financial risk control as the background, and predicts the possibility of default according to the information of the loan applicant, so as to judge whether the loan is approved or not. The training data selected in this project is the default record data of a network credit loan product. The project consists of four tasks which involve data statistics (MapReduce and Spark programming), data online analytical processing (Hive or Spark SQL) and machine learning (Spark ML). In the past semesters, we have chosen different topics for the final project, including sentiment analysis of securities news, prediction of e-commerce returned customers, etc.

Except the first experiment, all other work should be done in a distributed cluster. BDKit provides convenient computing environment for the students who have difficulty in setting up a cluster with sufficient resources.

3.2 Experiments Feedback

In the end of last semester, we made a survey among the students about the time spent in each experiment and got some feedback about BDKit. In the class, 12 students (Group 1) finished all work by using their own computers. 20 students (Group 2) learned to use BDKit after a short tutorial given by the teaching assistant. They did Exp. 2–4 and the final project (Exp. No. 5 in Table 3) based on BDKit. Table 3 shows the average time costing on each experiment by the two groups. It shows that BDKit can help students to save much time and effort, especially on cluster setting up and framework configuration. Figure 6 is a snapshot of Kubernetes pods creating by BDKit. Each student was assigned at least three pods to execute big data processing tasks. Among Group 2, only two students selected Jupyter notebook as the code editor, all others chose VsCode. In the terminal of VsCode, they could control their Hadoop/Spark cluster with command line tools.

Table 3. Time cost (hour)

Exp. No	Expected Time	Average Time without BDKit (Group 1)	Average Time with BDKit (Group 2)
1	2	6.8	/
2	6	16.3	7.4
3	4	8.1	3.2
4	6	8.9	5.1
5	12	19.3	10.3

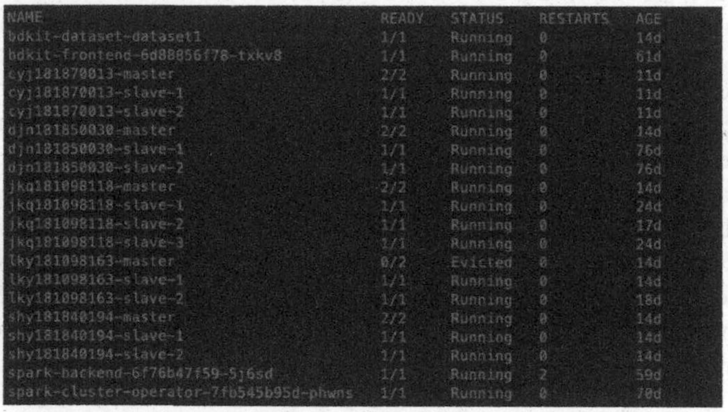

Fig. 6. Snapshot of pods created by BDKit

4   Evaluation

BDKit is deployed in cs-cloud, which is a cloud supercomputing platform of Nanjing University. BDKit runs in a Kubernetes cluster with 1 master node and 2 worker nodes. The master node is allocated 48 core CPU and 128 GB memory. Each worker node has 8 core CPU and 16 GB memory. The cluster is scalable by easily adding or removing worker nodes. Due to the access restriction, it can only be visited from campus network now. User accounts are registered by teaching assistants in advance.

4.1   Performance Evaluation

To verify that BDKit works as we expect, we use BDKit for the most basic WordCount MapReduce task to test its performance under different volumes of inputs. The experimental design is as follows: The user first created a Hadoop cluster containing one master and two slaves on BDKit, and then processed the text files of different sizes as input for WordCount. The time command in Linux was used to measure the actual experience time of the user. The size of the text files varied from 1MB to 800 MB. When the input file size is 800MB, the actual execution time on BDKit is about 100s. Moreover, it can be seen from Fig. 7 that the processing time increases linearly with the input size, indicating that the BDKit platform can meet the performance requirement of teaching and learning.

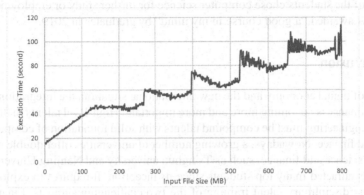

Fig. 7. WordCount execution time on BDKit

4.2 Comparison

There are mainly two types of big data platforms on the market: commercial cloud platform and educational training platform.

Compared with commercial cloud platform such as Amazon EC2 and Ali Cloud, BDKit provides students with customizable experiment environment. They are free to compose different components on demand. All datasets used in the experiments can be uploaded in advance. cStor is a popular educational big data platform [23]. Its technology stack largely overlaps with BDKit, but differs in the actual experience. cStor only provides SSH remote login interface and VIM for users. It does not support specific component and resource customization. BDKit provides VsCode and integrates with complete compilation packaging environment and code version control system. Jupyter Notebook is also available for Python developers. BDKit is more friendly to students. As a platform based on a new technology stack, it is also open for research objectives.

4.3 Teaching Effect

Financial big data processing course was initiated in 2017. It is a compulsory course of computer and finance interdisciplinary experimental class. We started to develop BDKit in late 2019 based on the requirements collected from three classes of students (2017–2019). It was put into use in September 2020. During two semesters of trial, we got some bug reports and improvement suggestions from students. Most students gave their approval to BDKit in their final semester report. Two students from business school and department of mathematics took this course as an elective one. They said that they wouldn't have finished the experiments without BDKit. It is worth mentioning that three students from the experimental class took part in the development and maintenance of BDKit. They had more interest in software technology than financial engineering. They learned to develop and test cloud-native applications in their spare time. BDKit helps to achieve the purpose of teaching students according to their aptitude.

Based on the graduation report from two classes of students (2020 and 2021), at least one third of the students chose computer science for further study or employment. This course was awarded "a good course in my mind" by graduates in 2019.

5   Conclusion

In the era of digital economy and the new international situation, the integration of computer and finance is becoming more and more important. High-level talents in the field of financial engineering must be compound talents with solid foundation of computer technology and finance. Nowadays, a growing number of universities offer double majors in computer science and finance, such as Tsinghua university and Nanjing University. The project has attracted many top students since its inception. It requires to explore a new path of interdisciplinary talent training of the two challenging subjects. Financial big data processing course is an attempt to blend the two disciplines, as a teaching program with fintech features. It focuses on training students to apply big data processing skills in financial data analysis.

To overcome the problems of complex big data computing cluster and high threshold of operation, this paper designed and implemented an online experimental platform named BDKit. It is a container cloud-based platform for developing and running big data applications. It supports the creation of Hadoop/Spark clusters and the online development, running, and monitoring of big data applications. It can realize personalized cluster configuration and minute-level cluster creation, greatly reducing the workload of big data application developers. BDKit needs to pursue higher stability and security while ensuring its functional availability. In the next step, we will upload some typical financial data processing cases to the platform as learning materials. User registration will be open when we deploy it on a public cloud.

Acknowledgements. This work is supported by the National Natural Science Foundation of China (Grant No. 62072225) and the reform of university computer empowerment education in the new era project (Research on the reform of university computer empowerment education in New Liberal Arts) founded by University Computer Course Teaching Steering Committee of the Ministry of Education.

We would also like to thank all the students who participated in the development of BDKit. They are Kai Wang, Manjie Yuan, Yitong Zhao, Maidi Wang, Dongyu Wang and Haogang Wang.

References

1. Hadoop. http://hadoop.apache.org
2. Spark. http://spark.apache.org
3. HBase. http://hbase.apache.org
4. Hive. http://hive.apache.org
5. Cloud Computing. https://www.ibm.com/cloud/learn/cloud-computing

6. Rabkin, A., Reiss, C., Katz, R., et al.: Experiences teaching MapReduce in the cloud. In: 43rd ACM Technical Symposium on Computer Science Education, pp. 601–606. ACM Press, New York (2012). https://doi.org/10.1145/2157136.2157310

7. Eckroth, J.: Teaching big data with a virtual cluster. In: 47th ACM Technical Symposium on Computer Science Education, pp. 175–180. ACM Press, New York (2016). https://doi.org/10.1145/2839509.2844651

8. Ngo, L.B., Duffy, E.B., Apon, A.W.: Teaching HDFS/MapReduce systems concepts to undergraduates. In: 2014 IEEE International Parallel & Distributed Processing Symposium Workshops, pp. 1114–1121. IEEE Press, New York (2014). https://doi.org/10.1109/IPDPSW.2014.124

9. Apache Storm. http://storm.apache.org

10. Apache Flink. http://flink.apache.org

11. Brewer, E.A.: Kubernetes and the path to cloud native. In: 6th ACM Symposium on Cloud Computing, p. 167. ACM Press, New York (2015). https://doi.org/10.1145/2806777.2809955

12. Kubernetes. https://kubernetes.io/docs/concepts/overview/kubernetes-api/

13. Docker. https://www.docker.com

14. Bhimani, J., Yang, Z., Leeser, M., Mi, N.: Accelerating big data applications using lightweight virtualization framework on enterprise cloud. In: 2017 IEEE High Performance Extreme Computing Conference, pp. 1–7. IEEE Press, New York (2017). https://doi.org/10.1109/HPEC.2017.8091086

15. Shah, J., Dubaria, D.: Building modern clouds: using docker, kubernetes & Google cloud platform. In: 9th Annual Computing and Communication Workshop and Conference, pp. 184–189, IEEE Press, New York (2019). https://doi.org/10.1109/CCWC.2019.8666479

16. VS Code in the browser. https://github.com/coder/code-server

17. Jupyter Notebook. https://jupyter.org

18. Git. https://git-scm.com

19. Anaconda. https://www.anaconda.com

20. Operator SDK Integration with Operator Lifecycle Manager. https://sdk.operatorframework.io/docs/olm-integration/

21. NoSQL Databases. https://www.ibm.com/cloud/learn/nosql-databases

22. Apache Kafka. https://kafka.apache.org

23. cStor. http://www.cstor.cn/proTextdetail_13713.html

High-Speed Emotional Analysis of Free-Descriptive Sentences Using an Emotional-Word Dictionary

Yonghui Huang[1], Kenshin Tsumuraya[1], Minoru Uehara[1], and Yoshihiro Adachi[2(✉)]

[1] Graduate School of Information Sciences and Arts, Toyo University, Saitama 3508585, Japan
{s3B102200084,s3B102200130,uehara}@toyo.jp
[2] Research Institute of Industrial Technology, Toyo University, Saitama 3508585, Japan
adachi@toyo.jp

Abstract. Information and Communications Technology (ICT) is greatly used from basic to higher education, and research on ICT education is actively conducted. As part of our educational support research using ICT, we have been conducting research to analyze (classify, search, visualize, etc.) student questionnaire responses in class at high speed. In this paper, we report a technique for high-speed emotional analysis of free-descriptive sentences using an emotional-word dictionary. Each element of the emotional dictionary is a pair that consists of an entry and an 11-dimensional vector that represents the emotional category to which the entry belongs. To date, we have created a Chinese dictionary that contains approximately 13,000 words and a Japanese dictionary that contains approximately 8,000 words. Our emotional expression analysis system that uses these emotional-word dictionaries analyzes the emotions contained in the analyzed sentences at high speed (10,000 sentences in approximately 1.5 s). This system has functions for negative word and degree adverb processing. The emotional expression analysis method using the emotional-word dictionary described in this paper can be applied not only to Chinese and Japanese but also to the emotional analysis of free-descriptive sentences written in many other languages.

Keywords: Emotional Analysis · Emotional-word Dictionary · 4-Value Emotional Analysis · Chinese Text Analysis · Japanese Text Analysis

1 Introduction

ICT is greatly used from basic to higher education in many countries, and research on ICT education is actively conducted. As part of our educational support research using ICT, we have been conducting research to analyze (classify, search, visualize, etc.) student questionnaire answer sentences in class at high speed [1]. By obtaining information about questions, opinions and requests regarding the lesson from questionnaire answers during the class, it is possible to proceed with a lesson that reflects the understanding status and requests of the students. Free-descriptive sentence analysis (classification and search) can be broadly divided into topic-based approaches and emotion-based

© The Author(s), under exclusive license to Springer Nature Singapore Pte Ltd. 2023
W. Hong and Y. Weng (Eds.): ICCSE 2022, CCIS 1813, pp. 194–207, 2023.
https://doi.org/10.1007/978-981-99-2449-3_18

approaches. From the viewpoint of the analysis technique, it can be classified into a method using a dictionary and a method using machine learning. We have studied free-descriptive sentence analysis techniques and their applications using these approaches and techniques [1–3].

Techniques for analyzing emotions in text include a method that uses an emotional word dictionary to detect emotions from words in the target text, and a method that uses a machine learning model (BERT [4], SVM, etc.) learned from a corpus of sentences labeled with emotions. Emotional analysis using an emotional-word dictionary requires labor to create the dictionary, but emotional analysis can be performed relatively accurately and at a very high speed. Machine learning models, particularly the BERT method, have the potential to achieve considerable emotional analysis accuracy if a sufficient teacher-labeled text corpus is collected. However, their analysis speed is very slow, and it is difficult to analyze students' emotions in real time during class. In recent years, studies on the application of emotional analysis and Web services have been actively conducted [5–8]. Much of this is about sentiment analysis that categorizes sentences into positive, neutral, and negative, or coarse-grained emotional analysis that classifies sentences into a few emotional categories.

We created emotional-word dictionaries for Chinese [9] and Japanese [2, 10]. They contain emotional words as their entries and 11-dimensional vectors that represent the emotional categories of {joy, anger, sadness, fear, shame, like, dislike, excitement, peacefulness, surprise, request} to which each word belongs as their meanings. We proposed the request emotion category in [10], which is an indispensable category for the analysis of class questionnaire response and review sentences. The 10 emotion categories, excluding 'request,' were proposed in the book "Emotion Expression Dictionary" by Akira Nakamura [11], and are standard in Japanese emotional analysis research. We developed a method using our Chinese and Japanese dictionaries to detect emotions in free-descriptive sentences at very high speed.

In this paper, we describe the emotional analysis method for free-descriptive sentences using the emotional-word dictionary, mainly for Chinese. It includes a method for generating an emotional word dictionary, an emotional analysis algorithm using a generated dictionary, and an emotional analysis system that implements this algorithm.

2 Emotion Expression Analysis Using Dictionary

A great deal of effort is required to create and update the emotional-word dictionary for emotional analysis, but it can provide a delicate and flexible emotional analysis function by taking account of negative words and degree adverbs. In modern AI, there is a strong demand for explainable AI that can explain the reasons for drawing its conclusions. With emotional analysis using an emotional-word dictionary, it is possible to easily implement an explanatory function for the analysis results based on information such as emotional words, negative words and degree adverbs detected from sentences.

Emotional-word dictionaries include WordNet-Affect [12], which manually assigns emotional labels corresponding to WordNet synsets, and EmoSenticNet [13], which assigns a WordNet-Affect emotional label to the SenticNet concept. A research group at Dalian University of Technology published "情感词汇本体第2版" (Emotional Vocabulary Body 2nd Edition) [14] as a Chinese dictionary of emotional words. It includes, for example, emotional words as its entries and the part of speech of each emotional word, the emotional categories to which they belong, and the emotional intensity in their meaning data, and classifies emotions into seven major categories and 21 minor categories. A study [15] has been reported in which the impressions of 'Weibo' users on diabetes treatment drugs were analyzed using this dictionary.

We established a method for generating an emotional-word dictionary and a high-speed emotional analysis method using a generated dictionary. Then, based on these methods, we implemented an Emotional-word Dictionary Management System (EDMS) and Emotional Expression Analysis System (EEAS) for Japanese [2]. We can directly apply these methods to emotional analysis using an emotional-word dictionary for Chinese.

2.1   Emotional-Word Dataset

We created the Toyo University Chinese Emotional-word Dataset (TU-CED), which contains approximately 13,000 emotional words, with reference to [14]. It is represented by a table (Excel sheet) that consists of emotional words, emotion categories to which each emotional word belongs, and emotion intensity. Note that in TU-CED, a word can belong to several emotion categories. Part of TU-CED is shown in Fig. 1.

単語	情感分類	強度
碍手碍脚	ND	5
碍事	NN	3
碍事	NE	3
碍足碍手	ND	5
唉声叹气	NB	5
唉呀呀	PH	3
暧昧不明	NN	3
碍眼	ND	5
碍眼	NN	3
安厝	NB	5
安的什么心	NA_	5
安定	PE	5
安堵乐业	PE	5
安堵如故	PE	7
安分	PH	5
安富恤贫	PE	5
安富尊荣	PE	5
安故重迁	NN	5

Fig. 1. Part of TU-CED

2.2   Chinese Emotional-Word Dictionary Management System

The Chinese EDMS (CEDMS) implemented using the morphological analyzer Jieba [16] generates a Chinese Emotional-Word Dictionary (CEWD) from TU-CED. Each element of the emotional-word dictionary has an emotional word as an entry and the emotion category vector to which it belongs as a meaning. The emotion category vector for a word is an 11-dimensional vector corresponding to {joy, anger, sadness, fear, shame, like, dislike, excitement, peacefulness, surprise, request}, and each component of the vector is set to 1 if the word belongs to the emotion category corresponding to that component, and 0 otherwise.

The procedure for generating an emotional-word dictionary performed by the CEDMS is as follows:

Step 1.1: Read the TU-CED Excel data.

[Perform the operations from Steps 1.2 to 1.4 below for each element of the TU-CED.]

Step 1.2: Analyze the emotional word of the element using Jieba and convert it into a list of morphological prototypes.

Step 1.3: Generate a dictionary entry by joining the elements of the prototype list obtained in Step 1.2.

Step 1.4: From the emotion category labels to which the emotional word belongs, obtain an 11-dimensional vector corresponding to that word.

Step 1.5: From the vectors for each entry obtained in Steps 1.2 to 1.4, synthesize the emotion category vector of the entry. (Take the maximum value for each corresponding component of the vectors.)

Step 1.6: Output a table consisting of a pair of entries obtained in Step 1.3 and the corresponding emotion category vector obtained in Step 1.5 to a CEWD Excel file.

Using the above procedure, the number of entries consisting of one prototype was 11,409, two prototypes was 928, three prototypes was 567, four prototypes was 104, five prototypes was 52, six prototypes was 28, seven prototypes was 33, eight prototypes was 12, nine prototypes was 5, ten prototypes was 2, eleven prototypes was 0, and twelve prototypes was 1. Additionally, in total, the generated CEWD had 13,141 entries. Figure 2 shows part of CEWD.

'碍事' (bothersome) was defined in two categories of the NN (belittle) class and NE (bored) class in Fig. 1. Because the NN class corresponds to the 'anger' category and the NE class corresponds to the 'dislike' category, [0, 1, 0, 0, 0, 0, 1, 0, 0, 0, 0] was obtained as the emotion category vector of the entry '碍事' as shown in Fig. 2.

2.3 Chinese Emotional Expression Analysis System

The Chinese EEAS (CEEAS) uses the Python dictionary object 'dict' to quickly analyze the emotions expressed by free-descriptive sentences based on CEWD.

The CEEAS emotional analysis procedure is as follows:

Step 2.1: Read the CEWD file and store it in a dictionary object. (Its entry is the key and its emotion vector is the value.)

Step 2.2: Analyze the target sentence in Chinese with Jieba and convert it into a list of morphological prototypes.

[Repeat Steps 2.3 and 2.4, reducing n from 12 to 1.]

Step 2.3: Slice the prototype list obtained in Step 2.2 in order from the beginning to the end by n words, concatenate the sliced partial list to create a search term, and match it with the entries of CEWD. If matching is successful, extract the emotion category vector corresponding to the matched entry.

感情語	乐	怒	哀	怖	耻	喜	厌	激
碍手碍脚	0	0	0	0	0	0	1	0
碍事	0	1	0	0	0	0	1	0
碍足碍手	0	0	0	0	0	0	1	0
嗳声叹气	0	0	1	0	0	0	0	0
暧昧不明	0	1	0	0	0	0	1	0
碍眼	0	1	0	0	0	0	1	0
安厝	0	0	1	0	0	0	0	0
安定	0	0	0	0	0	0	0	0
安堵乐业	0	0	0	0	0	0	0	0
安堵如故	0	0	0	0	0	0	0	0
安分	1	0	0	0	0	0	0	0
安富恤贫	0	0	0	0	0	0	0	0
安富尊荣	0	0	0	0	0	0	0	0
安故重迁	0	1	0	0	0	0	1	0
安国富民	0	0	0	0	0	0	0	0
安好	0	0	0	0	0	0	0	0
安家乐业	0	0	0	0	0	0	0	0
安静	1	0	0	0	0	0	0	0
安安稳稳	1	0	0	0	0	0	0	0
安居	1	0	0	0	0	0	0	0
安居乐业	1	0	0	0	0	0	0	0
安乐	1	0	0	0	0	0	0	0
安良除暴	1	0	0	0	0	0	0	0
安全	0	0	0	0	0	0	0	0

Fig. 2. Part of CEWD

Step 2.4: If matching in Step 2.3 is successful, check the prototype list to determine whether there are any negative words/degree adverbs before and after the sliced list. Modify the emotion category vector based on the rules defined if there are negative words/degree adverbs.

Step 2.5: Synthesize the emotion category vectors extracted from the sentence to be analyzed. (Take the maximum value for each corresponding component of the emotion category vectors.)

Step 2.6: Convert the emotion vector obtained in Step 2.5 into emotion category words.

Step 2.7: Convert the emotion vector obtained in Step 2.5 into a polarity value.

Because the CEWD entry is stored as the key of the 'dict' object and is hash-searched, matching between the search term and the CEWD entry in Step 2.3 is executed very quickly. In Step 2.7, the conversion from the emotion category vector of the analysis target sentence to the polarity value is performed as follows: CEEAS calculates the polarity value by adding the values obtained by multiplying the component corresponding to {joy, like, peacefulness} of the emotion category vector by 1 and the component corresponding to {anger, sadness, fear, shame, dislike} of the emotion category vector by -1; that is, each emotion of {joy, like, peacefulness} is considered as a positive emotion, each emotion of {anger, sadness, fear, shame, dislike} is considered as a negative emotion, and each emotion of {excitement, surprise, request} is considered as a neutral emotion.

CEEAS has an interactive processing mode and file processing mode. In the former mode, when a Chinese sentence is entered on the CUI, the analysis result is output instantly. By contrast, in the latter mode, the sentence data to be analyzed are read from an Excel file (or text file), and the analysis result processed in a batch is output to an Excel file.

Figure 3(a) shows a snapshot of the execution of interactive emotional analysis using CEEAS and Fig. 3(b) shows a translation of its content into English. Lines 17–23 show that CEEAS detected and processed a negative word. Additionally, lines 25–31 demonstrate how CEEAS processed double negation. Lines 33–39 show that CEEAS detected multiple emotions in a sentence. These lines also show that CEEAS detected degree

```
 1 请输入文本内容（输入q结束）
 2 >> 我喜欢化学。
 3
 4 情感表现: [['喜欢']]
 5 情感向量: [0, 0, 0, 0, 0, 1, 0, 0, 0, 0]
 6 情感分类: ['喜']
 7 极性值: 1、极性: positive
 8
 9 请输入文本内容（输入q结束）
10 >> 我希望你上课慢一点。
11
12 情感表现: [['希望']]
13 情感向量: [0, 0, 0, 0, 0, 0, 0, 0, 0, 1]
14 情感分类: ['望']
15 极性值: 0、极性: neutral
16
17 请输入文本内容（输入q结束）
18 >> 我不喜欢化学。
19
20 情感表现: [['不', '喜欢']]
21 情感向量: [0, 0, 0, 0, 0, 1, 0, 0, 0, 0]
22 情感分类: ['厌']
23 极性值: -1、极性: negative
24
25 请输入文本内容（输入q结束）
26 >> 我不是不喜欢化学。
27
28 情感表现: [['不是', '不', '喜欢']]
29 情感向量: [0, 0, 0, 0, 0, 1, 0, 0, 0, 0]
30 情感分类: ['喜']
31 极性值: 1、极性: positive
32
33 请输入文本内容（输入q结束）
34 >> 我非常喜欢化学，但我有点讨厌物理。
35
36 情感表现: [['非常', '喜欢'], ['有点', '讨厌']]
37 情感向量: [0, 0, 0, 0, 0, 1, 1, 0, 0, 0]
38 情感分类: ['喜', '厌']
39 极性值: 0、极性: neutral
```

(a) Snapshot of interactive processing in CEEA

```
 1 Please enter a sentence (enter q to end)
 2 >> I like chemistry.
 3
 4 Emotional expression: [['like']]
 5 Emotional vector: [0, 0, 0, 0, 0, 1, 0, 0, 0, 0]
 6 Emotional category: ['like']
 7 Polarity value: 1, Polarity: positive
 8
 9 Please enter a sentence (enter q to end)
10 >> I want you to take lessons more slowly
11
12 Emotional expression: [['want']]
13 Emotional vector: [0, 0, 0, 0, 0, 0, 0, 0, 0, 1]
14 Emotional category: ['request']
15 Polarity value: 0, Polarity: neutral
16
17 Please enter a sentence (enter q to end)
18 >> I don't like chemistry.
19
20 Emotional expression: [['do not', 'like']]
21 Emotional vector: [0, 0, 0, 0, 0, 1, 0, 0, 0, 0]
22 Emotional category: ['dislike']
23 Polarity value: -1, Polarity: negative
24
25 Please enter a sentence (enter q to end)
26 >> I'm not that I don't like chemistry
27
28 Emotional expression: [['do not', 'do not', 'like']]
29 Emotional vector: [0, 0, 0, 0, 0, 1, 0, 0, 0, 0]
30 Emotional category: ['like']
31 Polarity value: 1, Polarity: positive
32
33 Please enter a sentence (enter q to end)
34 >> I like chemistry very much, but I hate physics a little.
35
36 Emotional expression: [['very', 'like'], ['a little', 'hate']]
37 Emotional vector: [0, 0, 0, 0, 0, 1, 1, 0, 0, 0]
38 Emotional category: ['like', 'dislike']
39 Polarity value: 0, Polarity: neutral
```

(b) English translation of the content of 3(a)

Fig. 3. Interactive emotional analysis using CEEAS

adverbs in the sentence. Degree adverb information is used in the 4-value emotional analysis processing described in Sect. 4. CEEAS output the emotion categories detected from the input sentence and the detected emotional words, negative words, and degree adverbs as the emotional expressions for determining the emotion categories. The output of this emotional expression can be considered as an explanatory function of CEEAS.

3   Performance Evaluation

Seven collaborators attached emotion category vectors to each of 3,784 sentences collected from Chinese news and review sites. Each component of the teacher vector of each sentence was determined by the majority vote of each component of the seven attached vectors, and a CEEAS evaluation dataset consisted of the collected sentences and teacher vectors.

3.1   Accuracy of Emotional Analysis

Table 1 shows the accuracy of emotional analysis for the CEEAS evaluation dataset.

Table 1. Accuracy of emotional analysis for the CEEAS evaluation dataset

	number	accuracy	precision	recall	F1score
joy	1,186	0.88	0.77	0.87	0.82
anger	496	0.88	0.55	0.67	0.60
sadness	265	0.96	0.77	0.55	0.64
fear	25	0.99	0.34	0.84	0.48
shame	4	1.00	0.23	0.75	0.35
like	492	0.91	0.60	0.85	0.70
dislike	1,174	0.85	0.79	0.72	0.75
excitement	14	0.99	0.40	0.71	0.51
peacefulness	94	0.97	0.45	0.82	0.58
surprise	44	0.97	0.28	0.68	0.40
request	315	0.96	0.69	0.91	0.78

The 'number' column in Table 1 is the number of sentences that belonged to each emotion category in the CEEAS evaluation dataset. Some sentences belonged to multiple emotion categories, and the sum of these numbers exceeded the number of dataset sentences. As shown in Table 1, emotion detection was performed relatively accurately for the emotion categories of {joy, anger, sadness, like, dislike, peacefulness, request}, which had many data sentences.

3.2 Speed of Emotional Analysis

Figure 4 shows the measurement of the calculation speed of the CEEAS evaluation dataset in file processing mode. The analysis time of 1,000 to 10,000 sentences was measured by cutting out or copying and increasing the data. The measurement environment was an Intel Core i7-1068NG7 CPU @ 2.30 GHz and 16 GB memory. As shown in Fig. 4, CEEAS analyzed the emotions of 10,000 Chinese sentences in approximately 1.5 s. The emotion classification of 10,000 sentences using BERT took approximately 300 s (50 s with a GTX 1660TI GPU) for one emotion category [17].

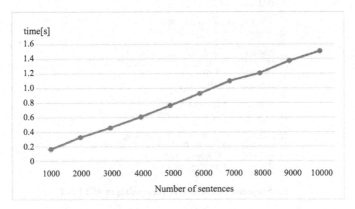

Fig. 4. Processing time of emotional analysis by CEEAS

4 4-Value Emotional Analysis

Humans usually communicate fine-grained emotional expressions, using degree adverbs such as 'very' or 'a little.' We created a 4-value emotional-word dictionary using a 4-value emotion category vector that mapped $\{0, 1, 2, 3\}$ to $\{$no emotion, a little emotional, emotional, very emotional$\}$. Using the 4-value emotional-word dictionary and a degree adverb processing function, we implemented 4-value CEEAS (4CEEAS) for the high-speed 4-value emotional analysis of Chinese sentences. 4CEEAS performed a more fine-grained emotional analysis of free-descriptive sentences. An example of executing interactive emotional analysis using 4CEEAS is shown in Fig. 5.

As shown in line 5 of Fig. 5, in 4CEEAS, when there was an emotion, the component of the emotion category vector corresponding to the emotion was 2. As shown in line 13, the component of the corresponding emotion category vector was 3 when there was a strong emotion, and as shown in line 21, the component of the corresponding emotion category vector was 1 when there is a weak emotion. As lines 25–31 show, 4CEEAS detected and processed multiple emotional words with negatives and degree adverbs from a single sentence. As mentioned in Subsect. 2.3, 4CEEAS calculated the polarity value by adding the values obtained by multiplying the component corresponding to $\{$joy, like, peacefulness$\}$ of the emotion category vector by 1 and the component corresponding to $\{$anger, sadness, fear, shame, dislike$\}$ of the emotion category vector by -1.

```
1 请输入文本内容（输入q结束）
2 >> 我喜欢化学。
3
4 情感表现：[['喜欢']]
5 情感向量：[0, 0, 0, 0, 0, 2, 0, 0, 0, 0, 0]
6 情感分类：['喜']
7 极性值：2、极性：positive
8
9 请输入文本内容（输入q结束）
10 >> 我很喜欢化学。
11
12 情感表现：[['很', '喜欢']]
13 情感向量：[0, 0, 0, 0, 0, 3, 0, 0, 0, 0, 0]
14 情感分类：['非常喜']
15 极性值：3、极性：positive
16
17 请输入文本内容（输入q结束）
18 >> 我有点讨厌物理。
19
20 情感表现：[['有点', '讨厌']]
21 情感向量：[0, 0, 0, 0, 0, 0, 1, 0, 0, 0, 0]
22 情感分类：['有点厌']
23 极性值：-1、极性：negative
24
25 请输入文本内容（输入q结束）
26 >> 我非常喜欢化学，但我有点讨厌物理。
27
28 情感表现：[['非常', '喜欢'], ['有点', '讨厌']]
29 情感向量：[0, 0, 0, 0, 0, 3, 1, 0, 0, 0, 0]
30 情感分类：['非常喜', '有点厌']
31 极性值：2、极性：positive
```

(a) Snapshot of interactive processing in 4CEEAS

```
1 Please enter a sentence (enter q to end)
2 >> I like chemistry.
3
4 Emotional expression: [['like']]
5 Emotional vector: [0, 0, 0, 0, 0, 2, 0, 0, 0, 0, 0]
6 Emotional category: ['like']
7 Polarity value: 2. Polarity: positive
8
9 Please enter a sentence (enter q to end)
10 >> I like chemistry very much.
11
12 Emotional expression: [['very', 'like']]
13 Emotional vector: [0, 0, 0, 0, 0, 3, 0, 0, 0, 0, 0]
14 Emotional category: ['very like']
15 Polarity value: 3. Polarity: positive
16
17 Please enter a sentence (enter q to end)
18 >> I hate physics a little.
19
20 Emotional expression: [['a little', 'hate']]
21 Emotional vector: [0, 0, 0, 0, 0, 0, 1, 0, 0, 0, 0]
22 Emotional category: ['a little dislike']
23 Polarity value: -1. Polarity: negative
24
25 Please enter a sentence (enter q to end)
26 >> I like chemistry very much, but I hate physics a little.
27
28 Emotional expression: [['very', 'like'], ['a little', 'hate']]
29 Emotional vector: [0, 0, 0, 0, 0, 3, 1, 0, 0, 0, 0]
30 Emotional category: ['very like', 'a little dislike']
31 Polarity value: 2. Polarity: positive
```

(b) English translation of the content of 5(a)

Fig. 5. Interactive emotional analysis using 4CEEAS

5 Differences Between the Chinese and Japanese Analysis

We implemented the EDMS for Japanese using Steps 1.1 to 1.6 and the morphological analyzer MeCab [18]. Using the EDMS, we generated a 4-value Emotional-Word Dictionary for Japanese (4EWD) that contained approximately 8,000 emotional entries from a 4-value Japanese emotional-word dataset. Then, using 4EWD, we implemented the 4-value EEAS for Japanese (4EEAS) using Steps 2.1 to 2.7 that analyzes Japanese sentences at very high speed [2, 10].

An important processing difference between 4CEEAS and 4EEAS is how to search for negative words and degree adverbs in Step 2.4. 4CEEAS mainly searches for negative words and degree adverbs on the front side of the slice list (emotional words), whereas 4EEAS searches for negative words on the back side of the slice list and searches for degree adverbs on the front side of the slice list.

First, the processing of negative words and degree adverbs for Chinese sentences in 4CEEAS is explained using specific examples. The list of morphological prototypes of the Chinese sentence "我不喜欢物理 (I don't like physics)" is ['我', '不', '喜欢', '物理'], and the negative word '不' is in front of the emotional word '喜欢.' Similarly, the list of morphological prototypes of "我非常喜欢化学 (I like chemistry very much)" is ['我', '非常', '喜欢', '化学'], and the degree adverb '非常' is in front of the emotional word '喜欢.' In Chinese, a few negative words come after emotional words, such as '才怪 .' Figure 6 shows an example of the processing of negative words and degree adverbs in 4CEEAS. In Fig. 6, the morpheme prototypes in line 20 that are difficult to translate into English are marked with * in the English translation line.

Next, the processing of negative words and degree adverbs for Japanese sentences in 4EEAS is explained specifically. The list of morphological prototypes of the Japanese sentence "私は物理が好きではない (I don't like physics)" is ['私', 'は', '物理', 'が', '好き', 'だ', 'は', 'ない', 'だ'], and the negative word ['だ', 'は', 'ない', 'だ'] is after the emotional word '好き ' By contrast, the list of morphological prototypes of "私は化学が非常に好きです (I like chemistry very much)" is ['私', 'は', '化学', 'が', '非常', 'に', '好き', 'です'], and the degree adverb ['非常', 'に'] is in front of the emotional word '好き.' Figure 7 shows an example of the processing of negative words and degree adverbs in 4EEAS. In Fig. 7, among the morpheme prototypes in lines 4, 12, and 20, those that are difficult to translate into English are marked with * on the corresponding English translation lines.

```
1 请输入文本内容（输入q结束）
2 >> 我不喜欢化学。
3
4 情感表现：[['不'，'喜欢']]
5 情感向量：[0, 0, 0, 0, 0, 0, 0, 2, 0, 0, 0, 0]
6 情感分类：['厌']
7 极性值：-2、极性：negative
8
9 请输入文本内容（输入q结束）
10 >> 我很喜欢化学。
11
12 情感表现：[['很'，'喜欢']]
13 情感向量：[0, 0, 0, 0, 0, 3, 0, 0, 0, 0, 0, 0]
14 情感分类：['非常喜']
15 极性值：3、极性：positive
16
17 请输入文本内容（输入q结束）
18 >> 过于死板的教育，学生们会喜欢才怪。
19
20 情感表现：[['过于'，'死板'], ['喜欢'，'才怪']]
21 情感向量：[0, 3, 0, 0, 0, 0, 2, 0, 0, 0, 0, 0]
22 情感分类：['非常怒'，'厌']
23 极性值：-5、极性：negative
```

(a) Processing of negative words and degree adverbs

```
1 Please enter a sentence (enter q to end)
2 >> I don't like chemistry.
3
4 Emotional expression: [['do not','like']]
5 Emotional vector: [0, 0, 0, 0, 0, 0, 2, 0, 0, 0, 0]
6 Emotional category: ['dislike']
7 Polarity value: -2. Polarity: negative
8
9 Please enter a sentence (enter q to end)
10 >> I like chemistry very much.
11
12 Emotional expression: [['very','like']]
13 Emotional vector: [0, 0, 0, 0, 3, 0, 0, 0, 0, 0, 0]
14 Emotional category: ['very like']
15 Polarity value: 3. Polarity: positive
16
17 Please enter a sentence (enter q to end)
18 >> If education is rigid, students will not like it.
19
20 Emotional expression: [[*, 'rigid'], ['like', *]]
21 Emotional vector: [0, 3, 0, 0, 0, 0, 2, 0, 0, 0, 0]
22 Emotional category: ['very anger', 'dislike']
23 Polarity value: -5. Polarity: negative
```

(b) English translation of the content of 6(a)

Fig. 6. Processing of negative words and degree adverbs in 4CEEAS

```
 1 文を入力してください。(終了は q)
 2 >> 私は物理が好きではない。
 3
 4 感情表現: [['好き', 'だ', 'は', 'ない', 'だ']]
 5 感情ベクトル: [0, 0, 0, 0, 0, 0, 2, 0, 0, 0, 0]
 6 感情カテゴリ: ['厭']
 7 極性値: -2, 極性は: negative
 8
 9 文を入力してください。(終了は q)
10 >> 私は化学が非常に好きです。
11
12 感情表現: [['非常', 'に', '好き']]
13 感情ベクトル: [0, 0, 0, 0, 0, 3, 0, 0, 0, 0, 0]
14 感情カテゴリ: ['非常に好']
15 極性値: 3, 極性は: positive
16
17 文を入力してください。(終了は q)
18 >> 私は化学が非常に好きですが物理は少し嫌いです。
19
20 感情表現: [['非常', 'に', '好き'], ['少し', '嫌い']]
21 感情ベクトル: [0, 0, 0, 0, 0, 3, 1, 0, 0, 0, 0]
22 感情カテゴリ: ['非常に好', '少し厭']
23 極性値: 2, 極性は: positive
```

(a) Processing of negative words and degree adverbs

```
 1 Please enter a sentence (enter q to end)
 2 >> I don't like physics.
 3
 4 Emotional expression: [['like', *, *, *, *]]
 5 Emotional vector: [0, 0, 0, 0, 0, 0, 2, 0, 0, 0, 0]
 6 Emotional category: ['dislike']
 7 Polarity value: -2, Polarity: negative
 8
 9 Please enter a sentence (enter q to end)
10 >> I like chemistry very much.
11
12 Emotional expression: [['very', *, 'like']]
13 Emotional vector: [0, 0, 0, 0, 0, 3, 0, 0, 0, 0, 0]
14 Emotional category: ['very like']
15 Polarity value: 3, Polarity: positive
16
17 Please enter a sentence (enter q to end)
18 >> I like chemistry very much, but I hate physics a little.
19
20 Emotional expression: [['very', *, 'like'], ['a little', 'hate']]
21 Emotional vector: [0, 0, 0, 0, 0, 3, 1, 0, 0, 0, 0]
22 Emotional category: ['very like', 'a little dislike']
23 Polarity value: 2, Polarity: positive
```

(b) English translation of the content of 7(a)

Fig. 7. Processing of Japanese negative words and degree adverbs in 4EEAS

6 Conclusions

In this paper, we mainly described an emotional analysis method using an emotional-word dictionary and CEEAS implemented based on this method for Chinese. CEEAS uses the Python object 'dict' as the internal expression of the emotional-word dictionary, and implements its entries as its keys and the emotion word category vectors as its values. The search for the emotional-word dictionary entry is very fast because it uses a hash function, and adding a new emotional word to the emotional-word dictionary has almost no effect on the processing speed of CEEAS. CEEAS has a function to explain why a particular emotion category was found in the sentence being analyzed, which greatly supports the addition, deletion, and modification of the emotional-word dictionary. Our emotional analysis method can be expanded to multiple languages, including English. We are also studying emotional analysis using machine learning models from BERT and its successors. CEEAS using the emotional-word dictionary can analyze the emotions of sentences very quickly. BERT is relatively accurate, but it takes a long time to analyze sentences [17]. For these reasons, it is preferable to use CEEAS for the analysis of free-descriptive sentences that require real-time performance, such as the questionnaire responses of students during class and questionnaire responses of participants during large-scale meetings. By contrast, it is more suitable to adopt emotional analysis using BERT, which has relatively high accuracy, for information that may take a long time to analyze, such as public opinion on SNS and review sentences.

A future task is to update the emotional-word dictionary to further improve the analysis accuracy based on the results of emotional analysis by collecting a large number of free-descriptive sentences with teacher labels. Emotional words continue to evolve over time because they are influenced by factors such as the rise of digital culture such as SNS; thus, updating the emotion categories is also a major issue.

References

1. Adachi, Y., Negishi, T.: Development and evaluation of a real-time analysis method for free-description questionnaire responses. In: IEEE Proceedings of the 15th International Conference on Computer Science and Education (2020)
2. Adachi, Y., Kondo, T., Kobayashi, T., Etani, N., Ishii, K.: Emotion analysis of japanese sentences using an emotion-word dictionary. J. Vis. Soc. Jpn. **41**(161), 21–27 (2021). (in Japanese)
3. Tsumuraya, K., Takahashi, H., Adachi, Y.: Emotion analysis and topic analysis of Japanese sentences by BERT. In: Proceedings of the 84th National Convention of IPSJ (2022). (in Japanese)
4. Devlin, J., Chang, M.W., Lee, K, Toutanova, K.: BERT: pre-training of deep bidirectional transformers for language understanding. arXiv:1810.04805 (2018)
5. Sailunaz, K., Alhajj, R.: Emotion and sentiment analysis from Twitter text. J. Comput. Sci. **36**, 101003 (2019)
6. Huang, C., Trabelsi, A., Zaïane, O.R.: ANA at SemEval-2019 task 3: contextual emotion detection in conversations through hierarchical LSTMs and BERT. arXiv:1904.00132 [cs.CL] (2019)
7. Yang, L., Li, Y., Wang, J., Sherratt, R.S.: Sentiment analysis for E-commerce product reviews in chinese based on sentiment lexicon and deep learning. IEEE Access **8**, 23522–23230 (2020)
8. Acheampong, F.A., Wenyu, C., Nunoo-Mensah, H.: Text-based emotion detection: advances, challenges, and opportunities. Eng. Rep. **2**(7), e12189 (2020)
9. Huang, Y., et al.: Chinese emotional word dictionary and Chinese emotional expression analysis system. In: Proceedings of the 84th National Convention of IPSJ (2022). (in Japanese)
10. Seyama, Y., Astremo, A., Adachi, Y.: Extraction of "request" intentions for review analysis on social media and e-commerce sites. In: Proceedings of the 20th Forum on Information Technology (2021). (in Japanese)
11. Nakamura, A.: Kanjyou hyougen jiten [Emotion Expression Dictionary]. Tokyodo Shuppan Co. Ltd. (1993). (in Japanese)
12. Strapparava, C., Valitutti, A.: WordNet-Affect: an affective extension of WordNet. In: Proceedings of the 4th International Conference on Language Resources and Evaluation (2004)
13. Poria, S., Gelbukh, A., Cambria, E., Hussain, A., Huang, G.B.: EmoSenticSpace: a novel framework for affective common-sense reasoning. Knowl.-Based Syst. **69**, 108–123 (2014)
14. Linhong, X., Hongfei, L., Yu, P., Hui, R., Jianmei, C.: Constructing the affective lexicon ontology. J. China Soc. Sci. Tech. Inf. **27**(2), 180–185 (2008)

15. Dun, X., Zhang, Y., Yang, K.: Fine-grained sentiment analysis based on Weibo. Data Anal. Knowl. Discov. 1(7), 61–72 (2017)
16. jieba. https://github.com/fxsjy/jieba. Accessed 14 Apr 2022
17. Yang, H., Adachi, Y.: BERT niyoru tyuugokugobun no kaiseki [Analysis of Chinese sentences by BERT]. 2021 Research Presentation Abstracts, RIIT Toyo University (2022). (in Japanese)
18. MeCab: Yet Another Part-of-Speech and Morphological Analyzer. https://taku910.github.io/mecab/. Accessed 16 Apr 2022

Teaching Practice of E-Learning Teaching Mode in Big Data Course Ideology and Politics

Mingyou Liu[1]([✉]), Yingxue Zhu[1], Li Li[1], and Zhaofang Zhang[2]

[1] School of Biology and Engineering, Guizhou Medical University, Gui'an New District, Guiyang, Guizhou, China
liumingyou@gmc.edu.cn

[2] Cost Consulting Department, Taiheyun Engineering Consulting Co., LTD., Guanshanhu District, Guiyang, Guizhou, China

Abstract. Pandemic of the COVID-19, it has brought a huge impact on all walks of life, especially the education industry. Because of the large number of people involved, considering multiple factors such as the health status of students, it is the general trend to innovate traditional education methods. Therefore, this project intends to introduce the latest e-learning teaching methods into the teaching process, and carry out the practice of ideological and political teaching reform in big data courses. Through the introduction of the e-learning learning mode, students can transcend geographical limitations and complete the learning of big data online. At the same time, the case-based ideological and political teaching method enables students to master big data, and also be able to think deeply about the connotation of big data, and make your own contribution to the country and society in the future work in the big data industry. The introduction of the e-learning teaching model not only enriches the traditional teaching model, but also brings about the reform and innovation of the education industry.

Keywords: Big data course teaching · e-learning · Ideological and Political · "Rain Classroom" technology

1 Introduction

The COVID-19 pandemic has had a great impact on all walks of life, especially the education industry, where governments and educational institutions are studying how to migrate education to online [1]. Therefore, it is of great practical significance to carry out online e-learning education in colleges and universities. At present, our country pays great attention to the cultivation of big data talents, and many scientific research institutions have set big data majors and big data related courses [2]. During the big

Funded: Guizhou Medical University Undergraduate Teaching Content and Curriculum System Reform Project: (No.3: JG2022029), Provincial Health Commission Science and Technology Foundation of Guizhou (No. Gzwkj2023–590), Guizhou Medical University National Natural Science Foundation Cultivation Project (No. 21NSFCP40), 2021 Guizhou Medical University "Ideological and political course" Construction Project: (No.1: SZ2021045, No.2: SZ2021046).

data educations, it is necessary to guide students from a higher level, so that students can learn to think about big data ideological and political content independently, and students have a deeper understanding of big data technology. Therefore, from the perspective of curriculum ideology and politics, in the teaching process of big data courses, this project introduces the e-learning teaching model that it allows students to transcend geographical restrictions, overcome the impact of the COVID-19 pandemic, and conduct learning and teaching exchanges anytime, anywhere.

2 Methodology

During the e-learning [3] teaching, supported by computer network, online teaching is carried out remotely, and the classroom is moved online, so that students and teachers can communicate online without barriers, In the whole teaching process, this paper used the current relatively advanced "Rain Classroom" technology to deeply integrate mobile terminals with classroom teaching. Through this technology, teachers can timely understand the learning status of students, whether it is teaching interaction in the course of classroom teaching, or in the Q&A after the class and the preview before the class, teachers can understand the learning status of students, and the students can also give feedback to the teacher [4].

2.1 Clarify the Teaching Objectives

In the teaching of big data courses, in addition to focusing on cultivating students' big data thinking ability, students are required to master big data processing ability. At the same time, in the form of cases, the ideological and political elements are integrated into the teaching content, and the ideological and political concepts are integrated into the big data. In this way, while mastering big data technology, students know how to control, manage and reasonably handle big data, especially the security challenges brought by big data, which need to be considered from multiple perspectives and cultivate students' creative thinking, not only from a personal perspective, but also at the national level.

2.2 Adjust the Teaching Plan

In the whole teaching process, guided by cases, introduce technical explanations step by step, give full play to the advantages of e-learning teaching mode, let students express their opinions, ask questions, solve problems in the learning process, and resonate with other students, The e-learning advantage of the teaching mode is that students can overcome nervousness, speak freely on the Internet, and participate in the discussions of ideological and political cases without any barriers. The advantage of "Rain Classroom" teaching technology is that the questions raised by teachers in the course of class can be fed back to the multimedia teaching platform in real time by students, so that teachers can know the understanding level of students in real time. The technology that integrates teaching technology drives the innovation of e-learning teaching mode, thereby affecting the entire teaching process through e-learning. The specific teaching plan is shown in Fig. 1.

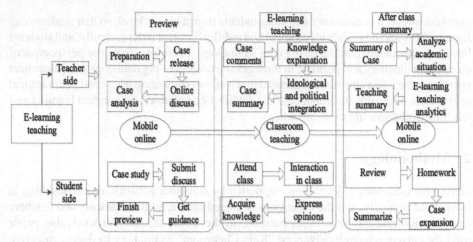

Fig. 1. E-learning teaching plan

2.3 Big Data Integration Ideology and Politics

According to the big data system, the teaching is decomposed, and the ideological and political teaching thinking is carried out from different levels. Big data talents are divided into different levels, and the teaching content and teaching focus of each level are different, and the teaching training is carried out according to the actual needs.

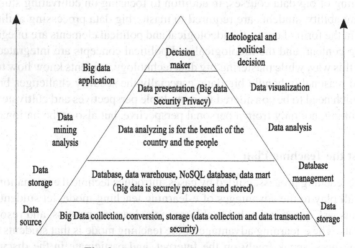

Fig. 2. Big data knowledge architecture

As can be seen from Fig. 2, the bottom layer is the big data collection module. It is necessary to pay attention to the security of big data and to distinguish sensitive information. The second layer is the big data processing module. Students should know that they must make contributions to the people of the country after mastering big data technology, In the later data visualization process, it is necessary to focus on protecting personal privacy, and all big data analysis decisions need to be used in practical and key areas.

Theoretical e-Learning Teaching Reform. In the teaching process of the eLearning theory course, the emphasis is on online resources. All courses are delivered online. Unlike traditional offline teaching, online teaching cannot be conducted face-to-face in terms of teacher-student interaction. In order to create a teaching environment that crosses geographical barriers for students, it is necessary to carry out teaching reforms in the latest teaching methods, used the latest teaching methods, introduced the "Rain Classroom" technology in the teaching process, and incorporate mobile terminals commonly used by students into the teaching system, forming the latest e-learning teaching mode, in this mode, students can participate in the whole teaching process through the "Rain Classroom" applet integrated in the mobile terminal; at the same time, whether uploading assignments to the online teaching platform or students can complete online experiments through the virtual laboratory. Online teaching platform completes offline case discussion, and submission the research results, online virtual experiment platform completes e-learning online experimental teaching.

Experiment e-Learning Teaching. The traditional experimental teaching is completed offline, while e-learning requires students to complete the experimental operation online. The big data experiment benefits from the fact that the resources used are computer clusters, which can be deployed online, and students can remotely enter the experimental module to complete the experimental content. Students' experiments are not subject to geographical restrictions and can be carried out anytime, anywhere.

2.4 Improve the Teaching Plan

Improve e-Learning Theory Teaching. As the focus of ideological and political teaching in big data courses, theoretical teaching requires students to discuss and think about cases in the course of class. Through e-learning teaching methods, students can achieve online barrier-free interaction discussion. In the teaching practice of more than 140 h in multiple classes, a large amount of data of students' learning has been statistically analyzed, so that the e-learning teaching process can be analyzed more scientifically. Large number of students participated in the teaching practice of e-learning in the big data ideological and political course as shown in Fig. 3.

Students e-learning statistics

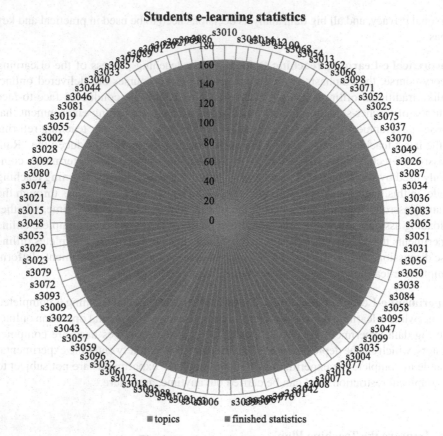

Fig. 3. Students e-learning statistics

As can be seen from Fig. 3, it found that each student has a different degree of participation in e-learning. Active students participate in many times, and some students participate less, but they are generally more active than offline teaching participation. The main reason is that students are more relax and be more active in online teaching.

Without face-to-face embarrassment, students can speak freely without worrying about the feelings of other students, and can express their thoughts more truthfully.

E-Learning Online Resources. The advantage of the e-learning teaching mode is that it can provide a large number of online resources. After learning, students can continue to learn online according to their own shortcomings. Teachers can also publish supplementary teaching content on the online teaching platform for students to learn. Especially for big data ideological and political cases, students need to check the materials first, then submit their own opinions and discuss the case, all of which are applicable to the e-learning teaching mode.

2.5 E-Learning Experimental Platform

The big data experiment platform is a comprehensive training system that deploys cluster resources to the cloud to meet the needs of students for online experiments. During the experiment, each student completes an experimental content according to the teaching requirements of the teacher. Some students who complete the experiment in advance can also choose the experimental project they are interested in according to their own interests. The advantage of e-learning experiment is that the laboratory is always open, experimental exercises can be carried out anytime and anywhere, and teachers can also see the experimental operation of each student online and give timely guidance.

Experiment time		Experimental progress rate		Number of experimental students	
2020-05-02 12:14	--	100%	8-1	11	
2020-05-11 14:11	--	100%	8-1	5	
2020-05-01 17:07	--	100%	8-1	5	
2020-04-29 14:54	--	100%	8-1	6	
2020-05-09 09:34	03:24:51	20%	3-1	10	
2020-04-29 09:25	03:24:49	13%	2-1	3	
2020-05-10 21:42	--	100%	8-1	3	
2020-05-09 09:57	03:24:48	13%	2-1	2	
2020-05-09 09:45	--	100%	8-1	3	
2020-05-13 10:27	03:24:41	27%	3-2	1	
2020-05-09 10:57	03:24:28	0%	0-0	3	
2020-05-11 23:41	03:24:28	0%	0-0	1	
2020-05-09 10:56	03:24:18	87%	6-1	2	monitor
2020-05-11 10:38	--	100%	8-1	1	
2020-05-09 16:22	--	100%	8-1	4	

Fig. 4. Big data e-learning experiment platform

The experimental process of student e-learning is shown in Fig. 4. The number of students participating in each experiment is different, which reflects the different points of interest of students. Students can conduct experiments online at the same time. Teachers can enter the experimental environment of each student to view students' experimental arrangements and problems encountered. The experimental time and number of experiments of each student are recorded by the platform, which also provides raw materials for the statistical analysis of teachers in the later stage.

2.6   Case-Based Teaching Methods

The traditional knowledge point teaching method limits students' thinking ability to a certain extent. In the process of ideological and political teaching of big data courses, the use of case-based teaching methods can arouse students' thinking and allow students to actively participate in case discussions. To complete the integration of ideological and political teaching in the discussion, and also merge the case to the entire teaching module, so as to achieve the purpose of moisturizing things silently.

3   Results

In order to explore the learning effect of e-learning, analyzed and counted the students' e-learning student situation data, to gain a better understanding of the students' learning status. During the entire e-learning teaching process, various measures are used to provide teaching feedback, including questionnaires, after-class discussions, etc. Teachers adjust teaching methods, update teaching methods, and dynamically adjust the teaching process according to students' feedback.

3.1   Teaching Statistics Research

Through the survey, it was found that most of the students' e-learning learning times were about 30 times, which was related to the number of teaching development. However, it was also found that some students' learning times reached more than 80 times, which was more than twice that of other students. A lot of learning was done. There are also some students who study less frequently, which provides a basis for the later teacher's guidance and intervention, and also provides a reference for the later assessment. Teachers can contact students after class to understand the specific situation and find solutions in time. Part of the reason is that the students e-learning learning conditions are not met, and some students are absent from e-learning for special reasons. The students' learning statistics times are shown in the Fig. 5.

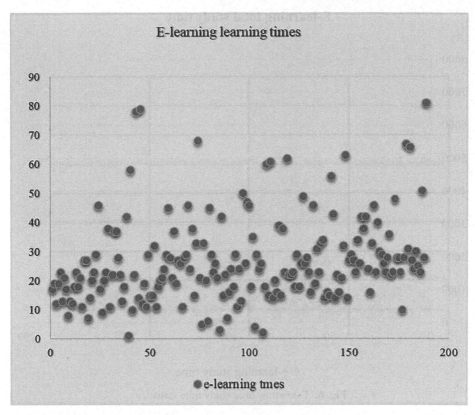

Fig. 5. Online teaching platform learning statistics

In addition to counting the number of students' study, the students' study time can also be counted, in this way, teachers can understand the students' learning, including whether they are serious about studying through e-learning, or whether the study time meets the requirements, etc., as shown in Fig. 6.

As can be seen from Fig. 6, the total study time of some students has reached more than 7,000 min, indicating that students have a high degree of participation and interest in big data ideological and political courses, and have conducted a lot of after-school learning, and some students have a small amount of learning, which is in line with the statistics in Fig. 5 above. If the e-learning learning conditions of students are not met, online learning cannot be taught temporarily, but the advantage of e-learning is that they can continue learning after meeting the conditions. This is an offline teaching institute does not come with.

E-learning total study time

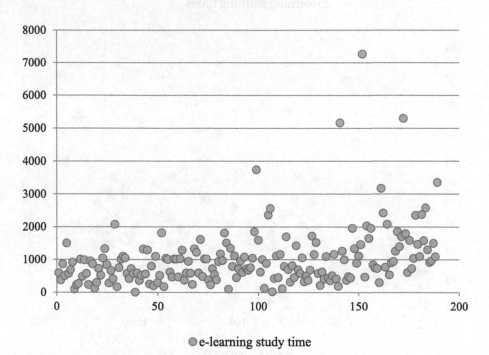

●e-learning study time

Fig. 6. E-learning total study time statistics

3.2 E-Learning Teaching Feedback

Through questionnaires, we can understand the teaching effect of the e-learning teaching mode, students will evaluate the current teaching satisfaction, and teachers will know the whole teaching situation in time after receiving the results, so as to provide theoretical support for the next stage of teaching adjustment.

Theoretical Teaching Effect. Through the method of issuing and returning questionnaires, it reported the students' recognition of the teaching mode. Students generally accept the e-learning teaching mode. Generally speaking, the current teaching mode meets the students' learning needs, as shown in Fig. 7.

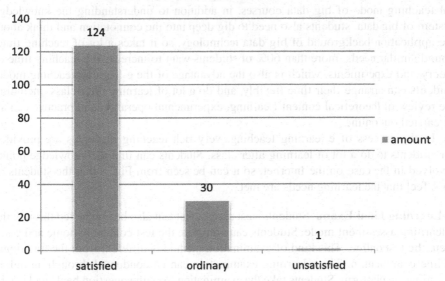

Fig. 7. E-learning satisfaction statistics

As can be seen from Fig. 7, most students agree with the current e-learning teaching mode, the current teaching model meets the needs of students' learning, and some students do not accept this teaching mode temporarily because they do not meet the e-learning teaching conditions.

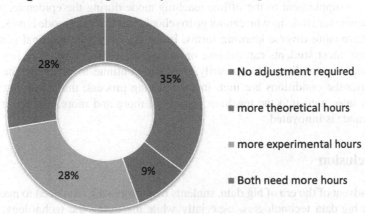

Fig. 8. Big data ideological and political teaching analysis

Big Data Ideological and Political Teaching Analysis. In the ideological and political teaching mode of big data courses, in addition to understanding the knowledge system of big data, students also need to dig deep into the connotation and think about the application background of big data technology, so it takes a lot of teaching time. Found similar needs, more than 60% of students want to increase the teaching time of theory and experiments, which is also the advantage of the e-learning teaching mode, students can arrange their time flexibly, and do a lot of learning after class, including the review of theoretical content Learning, experimental operation and practice can all be carried out online.

In the process of e-learning teaching, very rich teaching resources are provided for students to do a lot of learning after class. Students can find the knowledge points involved in the case on the Internet, so it can be seen from Fig. 8 that the students of 35% feel that the learning needs are met.

E-Learning Final Exam. Students' test assessment can also be conducted through the e-learning assessment mode. Students can complete the test content at home and complete the test online. This kind of examination method is different from the traditional offline examination. The e-learning examination can be conducted through an online examination platform. Students take the examination from the question bank, and teachers can understand the students' examination through the online invigilation system. This type of examination is more flexible and solves the problem. During the epidemic, students could not come to school to take the exam.

4 Discussion

The e-learning teaching mode, as a new teaching mode based on computer network, can be used as a supplement to the offline teaching mode during the epidemic, providing online teaching for students who cannot go to school. This teaching mode is more flexible, students have more diverse learning forms. In the era of mobile terminal general film applications, most students can achieve online e-learning learning. Very few students cannot meet the conditions temporarily, they can continue to complete the learning content after the conditions are met. In the teaching process, the e-learning teaching method is integrated into the teaching process of more and more, and the traditional teaching mode is innovated.

5 Conclusion

With the advent of the era of big data, students majoring in big data need to master more and more big data technologies, especially while mastering the technology, students need to dig deeper into the technical connotation, so the course ideology and politics are introduced into big data through the case-based teaching mode, students can learn the development direction and application direction of big data in the future while learning big data, especially the industries that are urgently needed by the country. In view of the serious impact of the current epidemic, many students cannot come to the school to study normally, so this course introduces the idea of e-learning teaching mode and moves the classroom to online, so that students can learn the content of big data anytime, anywhere.

Acknowledgments. We would like to thanks the Funded Project: 2021 Guizhou Medical University "Ideological and political course" Construction Project: (No.1: SZ2021045, No.2: SZ2021046), Guizhou Medical University Undergraduate Teaching Content and Curriculum System Reform Project: (No.3: JG2022029), Provincial Health Commission Science and Technology Foundation of Guizhou (No. Gzwkj2023-590), Guizhou Medical University National Natural Science Foundation Cultivation Project (No. 21NSFCP40), National Natural Science Foundation of China (No. 32160668).

References

1. Adedoyin, O.B., Soykan, E.: Covid-19 pandemic and online learning: the challenges and opportunities. Interact. Learn. Environ. 1–13 (2020)
2. Yan, Y.: Research status of big data and education informatization in China—study based on biliometric and content analysis (2010–2019). In: 2020 International Conference on Big Data and Informatization Education (ICBDIE), pp. 99–104. IEEE (2020)
3. Khan, M.A., Vivek, Nabi, M.K., Khojah, M., Tahir, M.: Students' perception towards E-learning during COVID-19 pandemic in India: an empirical study. Sustainability **13**, 57 (2021)
4. Guo, J., Zhu, R., Zhao, Q., et al.: Adoption of the online platforms Rain Classroom and WeChat for teaching organic chemistry during COVID-19. J. Chem. Educ. **97**(9), 3246–3250 (2020)
5. Chun-ling, T., Rui-xing, C.: Research on the challenges and countermeasures of ideological and political education in colleges and universities under the background of big data. J. Jiamusi Voc. Inst. (2017)
6. Di, W., Yun, L., Jia, C.: Research on the innovation and development model of ideological and political education in we-media environment based on big data. Revista de la Facultad de Ingenieria **32**(16), 351–357 (2017)
7. Huang, X., Zhao, J., Fu, J., et al.: Effectiveness of ideological and political education reform in universities based on data mining artificial intelligence technology. J. Intell. Fuzzy Syst. **40**(2), 3743–3754 (2021)

An Experimental Case Study for the Course of 'Testing Technology and Data Processing'

Siliang Lu[1]($\boxtimes$) iD, Xiaoxian Wang[1] iD, Bin Ju[1] iD, Yongbin Liu[1] iD, Feng Xie[1] iD, and Min Xia[2] iD

[1] Anhui University, Hefei 230601, People's Republic of China
silianglu@ahu.edu.cn

[2] Lancaster University, Lancaster LA14YW, UK

Abstract. 'Testing Technology and Data Processing (TTDP)' is one of the core courses for the undergraduates in mechanical engineering subject. This paper designs an experimental case to improve the students' abilities in signal acquisition, preprocessing, feature extraction, and artificial intelligence (AI)-based pattern recognition. The case study is based on an internet of things (IoT) node that integrating with accelerometer, microphone, and magnetic sensors. The order tracking algorithm and a double-layer bidirectional long short-term memory (DBiLSTM) model are used to process the multi-sensor data for condition monitoring and fault diagnosis of a motor. The students' feedback demonstrates that the designed case improves their interests to this course, and also improves their abilities in engineering practice.

Keywords: TTDP course · Case study · AI · IoT · DBiLSTM · Condition monitoring and fault diagnosis

1 Introduction

'Testing Technology and Data Processing (TTDP)' is one of the core courses for the undergraduates in mechanical engineering subject. The teaching modules and chapters of the TTDP course typically include signal and its description, testing devices, sensitive elements and sensors, signal conditioning and acquisition, signal processing, instrumentation and peripheral interface. The teaching objective of this course is to make students understand the working principle of sensor, signal processing method and its applications in engineering.

Experimental case study integrates several knowledge points of the course, and uses an intuitive and vivid demonstration means to show the hidden knowledge points of the course behind the case to students. Compared with the traditional knowledge points teaching by chapters, case study teaching usually starts from the engineering application objectives, and designs the experimental or simulated prototypes to meet the engineering needs by integrating course knowledge. Case study teaching can effectively mobilize students' enthusiasm, improve their interest in learning, and promote students to better understand the application of knowledge points in engineering. How to design an

W. Hong and Y. Weng (Eds.): ICCSE 2022, CCIS 1813, pp. 220–230, 2023.
https://doi.org/10.1007/978-981-99-2449-3_20

interested prototype that involves the knowledge points of sensors and signal processing methods is important for case study teaching of the TTDP course.

The internet of things (IoT) and artificial intelligence (AI) technologies developed rapidly and have been intensively used in industrial applications in recent years [1–3]. In an IoT node, the data from multiple sensors are acquired and transmitted to a cloud server. The data are proposed to extract the features, and then the AI algorithms are introduced to feature fusion, classification, and pattern recognition [4]. In this study, an experimental case is designed based on the IoT and AI for the TTDP course. In this case, a IoT node with the accelerometer, microphone, and magnetic sensor are installed on a motor, and the multiple sensor data are acquired and analyzed. Considering that the motor may work under varying-speed conditions, the rotation angle of the motor is estimated from the magnetic leakage signal, and then the vibration and sound signals are resampled using the order tracking algorithm. Finally, a double-layer bidirectional long short-term memory (DBiLSTM) model is design to fuse the signals for motor fault recognition and classification. The feedback from the students demonstrate that the designed case improves their interests to this course, and also improves their abilities in engineering practice.

The rest of this paper is organized as below. Section 2 introduces the experimental prototype. Section 3 introduces the signal processing algorithms and the DBiLSTM model. Section 4 introduces the procedures and results. Section 5 introduces the teaching arrangement of the case study. Section 6 draws the conclusions.

2 Experimental Prototype

The experimental prototype for the case study is shown in Fig. 1. An IoT node (STEVAL-STWINKT1B, STMicroelectronics Inc.) is installed on the side of the motor housing. The IoT node consists of a micro controller unit (MCU) with type of STM32L4, two accelerometers with types of IIS3DWB and ISM330DHCX, two microphone sensors with types of IMP23ABSU and IMP34DT05, a magnetic sensor with type of IIS2MDC.

The accelerometers can simultaneously measure the data on three-axis. Hence, total 9 channels of data are acquired and storage on a TF card on the IoT node. Wireless signal transmission can also be conducted by installing a Bluetooth or Wi-Fi module on the IoT node. In this case, the motor is set with different healthy or fault conditions and the signals are processed to identify the motor's condition. 10 types of motor conditions are configured as shown in Table 1. When a fault occurs in a motor, the signatures of the vibration and sound signals will be different from those in healthy condition. Hence, the motor condition can be monitored by analyzing the motor signals.

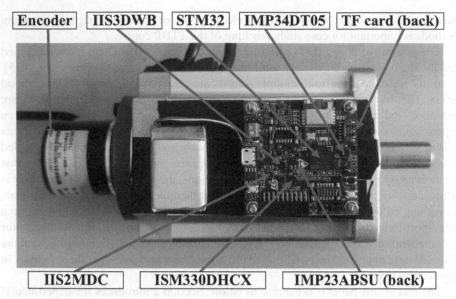

Encoder **IIS3DWB** **STM32** **IMP34DT05** **TF card (back)**

IIS2MDC **ISM330DHCX** **IMP23ABSU (back)**

Fig. 1. Experimental prototype.

Table 1. Motor Fault Type and Label

Label	0 (HRC)	1 (HSF)	2 (HEA)	3 (IN05)	4 (IN10)
Condition	High resistance connection	Hall sensor fault	Healthy	Bearing inner raceway fault (0.5 mm)	Bearing inner raceway fault (1 mm)
Label	5 (IN15)	6 (RA)	7 (OU05)	8 (OU10)	9 (SC)
Condition	Bearing inner raceway fault (1.5 mm)	Rotor asymmetry	Bearing outer raceway fault (0.5 mm)	Bearing outer raceway fault (1 mm)	Stator winding short circuit

3 Signal Processing and AI Methods

In this case, the magnetic leakage signal is first processed to estimate the rotation angle of the motor and then the vibration and sound signals are resampled on angular-domain to avoid the influence of motor speed fluctuation. Afterward, the pre-processed signals are inputted into the DBiLSTM model for fault recognition.

3.1 Rotation Speed Estimation and Order Analysis

The magnetic leakage signal is denoted as $S_M[i]$, $i = 1, 2, ..., M_1$, and $M_1 = fsm \times T$ represents the number of sampling points, fsm is the sampling frequency of the magnetic signal, T is the duration of signal acquisition. The instants of signal sampling are denoted as $t_1[i]$, $i = 1, 2, ..., M_1$. The vibration and sound signals are denoted as $VA_k[j]$, $j = 1$,

2, ..., M_2, and $M_2 = fsva \times T$ is the number of sampling points, $fsva$ is the sampling frequency, $k = 1, 2, ..., 8$ represents the kth channel of vibration or sound signal. The sampling instants are denoted as $t_2[j], j = 1, 2, ..., M_2$. Because $fsm < fsva$, numerical interpolation is conducted on the magnetic leakage signal to extend its length as:

$$IM[j] = interp1(t_1[i], S_M[i], t_2[j]), j = 1, 2, ..., M_2 \tag{1}$$

where $interp1()$ is a one-dimensional interpolation function in MATLAB.

Next, the phase of the magnetic signal is calculated as:

$$p[j] = \arctan\left\{ \frac{\text{Im}(\mathcal{H}(IM[j]))}{\text{Re}(\mathcal{H}(IM[j]))} \right\} \tag{2}$$

where $\mathcal{H}()$ represents the Hilbert transform, Re() and Im() represents the real and image parts of the signal, respectively. The rotation angle of the motor rotor can then be calculated as:

$$\beta[j] = \frac{180°}{\pi \times np} \times \left(unwrap(p[j]) - p[1] \right) \tag{3}$$

where np is the number of the motor pole pairs, $unwrap()$ is a built-in MATLAB function used for signal unwrapping. The term $-p[1]$ guarantees that the $\beta[j]$ starts from zero.

Subsequently, the vibration and sound signals are resampled in accordance with the rotation angle curve as shown below [5]:

$$RVA_k[j] = resample(VA_k[j], \beta[j]) \tag{4}$$

where $resample()$ is the built-in MATLAB function that resamples the signal $VA_k[j]$ according to the new vector $\beta[j]$. Finally, the spectrum of the resampled signal $RVA_k[j]$ is calculated and used as the input time series of the DBiLSTM model.

3.2 Fault Recognition Based on DBiLSTM

After extracting the features of multi-channel vibration and sound signals, the DBiLSTM deep neural network model is established in this paper to realize feature fusion and motor fault pattern recognition. As shown in Fig. 2, the DBiLSTM model is a serial structure composed of input layer, two BiLSTM layers, fully connection layer, Softmax layer and classification layer.

The features' dimension of input layer signal is $8 \times M_2$, that is, the number of channels of is 8, and the frequency spectrum length of each channel is M_2. BiLSTM is a bidirectional long and short-term memory network, whose input and output are time series, as shown in the lower subgraph of Fig. 2 [6]. BiLSTM network is composed of forward LSTM network and backward LSTM network. For input time series $(x_0, x_1, ..., x_{M2-1})$, the output time series of the forward LSTM is expressed as $(h_{L0}, h_{L1}, ..., h_{LM2-1})$, the output time series of backward LSTM is expressed as $(h_{R0}, h_{R1}, ..., h_{RM2-1})$. Combining the forward and backward output sequences, the time series output of BiLSTM is expressed as $([h_{L0}, h_{R0}], [h_{L1}, h_{R1}], ..., [h_{LM2-1}, h_{RM2-1}])$.

DBiLSTM model

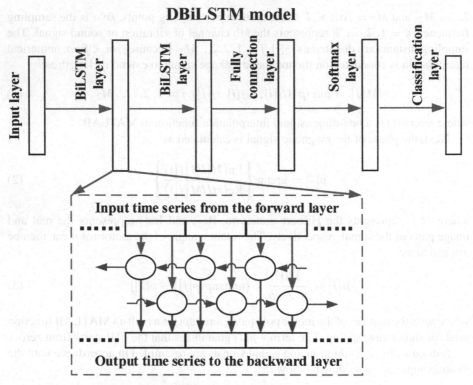

Fig. 2. DBiLSTM model.

4 Implementation Results

In this section, the results of the designed case study are introduced as shown below.

4.1 Results of Signal Processing

The motor bearing fault signal is analyzed to illustrate the performance of the signal processing method. The vibration signal that acquired by the accelerometer and its envelope spectrum are shown in Figs. 3(a) and 3(b), respectively. Because the motor rotates at varying speed condition, the fault indicators cannot be found in the envelope spectrum.

The synchronously sampled magnetic signal is shown in Fig. 4(a). It can be seen that the amplitude of the magnetic leakage signal fluctuates with the speed when the motor rotates, so the magnetic leakage signal can reflect the speed of the motor. The signal waveform is not smooth enough due to the low sampling frequency of the magnetometer. A partial magnification also shows sharp curves at the peaks and troughs. To improve the accuracy of motor angle estimation, cubic spline curve interpolation is performed on the magnetic signal, and the obtained results are shown in Fig. 4(b). By comparing Figs. 4(a) and 4(b), it can be seen that the curve becomes smooth after interpolation, and the waveform is close to a sine wave. Then, the cumulative rotation curve of the motor is estimated and calculated from the interpolation signal, and the results were shown in Fig. 4(c). The motor has experienced a process of first deceleration and then acceleration in a period of 0 to 2 s.

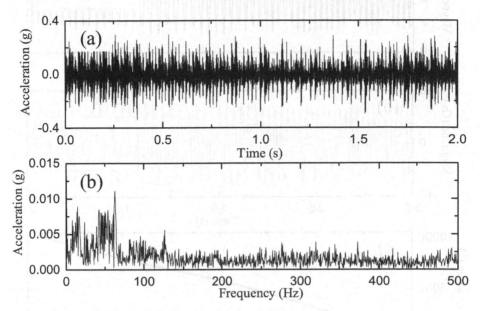

Fig. 3. (a) The vibration signal and (b) its envelope spectrum.

The cumulative rotation angle curve in Fig. 4(c) is used for resampling of the vibration signals in Fig. 3(a), and the results are shown in Fig. 5. After resampling, the original time-domain signal converts to an angular domain signal, and the envelope order spectrum is shown in Fig. 5(b). The characteristic orders related to bearing faults can be clearly distinguished from the envelope order spectrum. By comparing Fig. 3(b) and Fig. 5(b), it can be seen that after order analysis, the non-stationary feature of the original time-domain signal becomes approximately stationary in the angular domain signal. The order of these fault characteristics is closely related to the fault type of the motor, and the signal after order analysis can better characterize the operation condition and fault type of the motor.

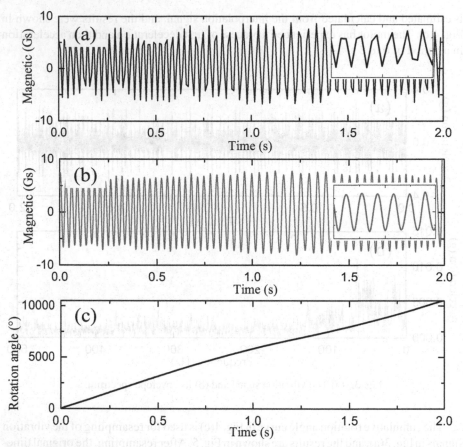

Fig. 4. (a) The magnetic signal, (b) the signal after interpolation, and (c) the calculated motor rotation angle.

4.2 Results of Fault Pattern Recognition Based on DBiLSTM

After resampling the 8 channels of signals with 10 different types of motor faults, the DBiLSTM deep neural network model is built according to Fig. 2 for feature extraction and fault pattern recognition. The feature dimension of each training sample is 8×5000, and the training sample size of 10 motor fault types in each group is $8 \times 5000 \times 10$. A total of 50 groups of samples are used for training.

The learning rate of the training was set to 0.001, and the number of iterations is set to 125. The hardware platform configuration for network training is as follows: Processor Intel I9-0900, memory 32 GB, operation system 64-bit WIN10, NVIDIA RTX3070 8 GB, environment MATLAB 2021a. The curves of loss and accuracy in the training process are shown in Fig. 6. With the increase of the number of iterations, the loss approaches 0 and the accuracy approaches 100%.

After the DBiLSTM model training was completed, the validation data set is verified. The classification results of 10 motor health and failure types are shown in Fig. 7. For

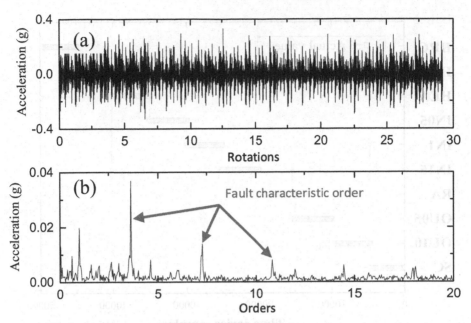

Fig. 5. (a) The resampled vibration signal and (b) its envelope order spectrum.

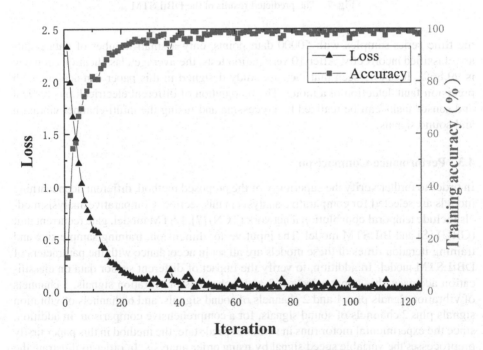

Fig. 6. The training process of the DBiLSTM.

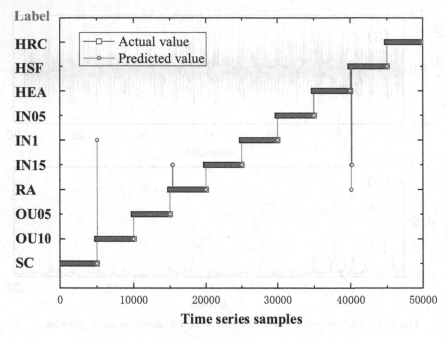

Fig. 7. The predicted results of the DBiLSTM.

the time series samples with 50000 data points, only a small number of data points are classified incorrectly. After 10 verification tests, the average classification accuracy is 99.86%. It can be seen that the case study designed in this paper can achieve high precision fault detection of a motor. The recognition of different electrical, mechanical and sensor faults can be realized by processing and fusing the multi-channel vibration and sound signals.

4.3 Performance Comparison

In order to further verify the superiority of the proposed method, different deep learning models are selected for comparative analysis in this section. Comparative analysis models include temporal convolutional network (TCN) [7], LSTM model, gate recurrent unit (GRU) [8] and BiLSTM model. The input vector dimension, training sample size and training iteration times of these models are all set in accordance with the parameters of DBiLSTM model. In addition, to verify the impact of different sensor data on classification accuracy, this paper selects 1, 2 and 3 channels of vibration signals, 3 channels of vibration signals plus 1 and 2 channels of sound signals, and 6 channels of vibration signals plus 2 channels of sound signals, for a comprehensive comparison. In addition, since the experimental motor runs in variable speed state, the method in this paper firstly preprocesses the variable speed signal by using order analysis. In order to illustrate the necessity of preprocessing, the direct feature extraction and analysis of the original signal are also carried out in the contrast experiment. Each combination of sensors and methods is tested for 10 times, and the average test accuracy is shown in Table 2.

Table 2. Comparative Experimental Results (Unit: %)

Method/Sensor channel		6 Vibration + 2 Sound	3 Vibration + 2 Sound	3 Vibration + 1 Sound
TCN	No process	97.55	96.03	95.68
	Resample	98.13	96.38	95.99
LSTM	No process	86.98	79.73	77.47
	Resample	88.47	80.46	78.49
GRU	No process	76.63	71.44	69.90
	Resample	78.35	71.65	70.63
BiLSTM	No process	91.69	86.75	84.88
	Resample	94.14	88.78	85.88
DBiLSTM	No process	99.63	99.29	97.34
	Resample	99.86	99.82	98.44
Method/Sensor channel		3 Vibration	2 Vibration	1 Vibration
TCN	No process	91.85	80.66	62.57
	Resample	92.42	89.59	74.22
LSTM	No process	66.34	59.76	35.14
	Resample	76.67	64.15	41.81
GRU	No process	62.32	50.10	33.05
	Resample	69.01	54.41	34.56
BiLSTM	No process	77.55	70.05	53.91
	Resample	81.68	76.41	50.06
DBiLSTM	No process	95.15	50.55	45.18
	Resample	96.38	68 .50	49.88

Three conclusions can be drawn from the comparative analysis results in Table 2, as follows: 1) For the same model and pretreatment method, multi-channel and multi-sensor data can improve the accuracy of fault identification. 2) For the same data type and model, the signal preprocessed by order analysis has higher classification accuracy. 3) The highest motor fault identification accuracy can be obtained under the same conditions by stacking BiLSTM model. Hence, the designed case that preprocesses the variable speed signals and designs a deep neural network is suitable for motor fault diagnosis under variable speed conditions.

5   Teaching Arrangement of the Case Study

The teaching case designed in this paper involves a variety of sensors, testing methods and signal processing methods, which needs to be carried out after students have learned the basic knowledge of TTDP course. The case study will consolidate the knowledge they have learned and further broaden their vision and thinking ability. In the teaching process for the undergraduates in the Department of Mechanical Engineering of Anhui University, this case study is arranged in the last few weeks of the semester in the form of seminar. The case can be arranged by 3 lessons according to the actual situation.

The sensors and hardware chips on the IoT node can be introduced in the first lesson. The principles, parameters, and peripheral interfaces of the relative humidity and temperature sensor, absolute pressure sensor, accelerometer and gyroscope, vibration sensor, motion sensor, magnetometer, and microphone are introduced and discussed. The signal processing algorithms such as signal filtering algorithm, signal interpolation algorithm, Fourier transform, Hilbert transform, signal resampling algorithm, can be introduced in the second lesson. The AI models such as TCN, GRU, LSTM and its variants can be introduced in the third lesson. The signal processing and AI algorithms can be implemented using the MATLAB or python language on their familiar integrated development environment.

6 Conclusions

This paper designs an experimental case for the TTDP course to help student better understand the knowledge points such as sensors and data processing methods. The hardware platform, signal processing algorithms, AI models specific to the IoT nodes are introduces. Examples and teaching arrangement suggestions are also provided to facilitate the use of this case. The feedback from the students indicate that the designed case can effectively mobilize their enthusiasm, improve their interest in learning, and promote them to better understand the application of knowledge points in engineering.

References

1. Xia, M., Shao, H., Williams, D., Lu, S., Shu, L., de Silva, C.W.: Intelligent fault diagnosis of machinery using digital twin-assisted deep transfer learning. Reliab. Eng. Syst. Saf. **215**, 107938 (2021)
2. Wang, X., Lu, S., Huang, W., Wang, Q., Zhang, S., Xia, M.: Efficient data reduction at the edge of industrial Internet of Things for PMSM bearing fault diagnosis. IEEE Trans. Instrum. Meas. **70**, 3508612 (2021)
3. Lu, S., Qian, G., He, Q., Liu, F., Liu, Y., Wang, Q.: *In situ* motor fault diagnosis using enhanced convolutional neural network in an embedded system. IEEE Sens. J. **20**, 8287–8296 (2020)
4. Zhou, X.Y., Wu, X.L.: Teaching mode based on educational big data mining and digital twins. Comput. Intell. Neurosci. **2022**, 9071944 (2022)
5. Lu, S., Yan, R., Liu, Y., Wang, Q.: Tacholess speed estimation in order tracking: a review with application to rotating machine fault diagnosis. IEEE Trans. Instrum. Meas. **68**, 2315–2332 (2019)
6. Zhou, L.X., Zhang, Z.Y., Zhao, L.J., Yang, P.L.: Attention-based BiLSTM models for personality recognition from user-generated content. Inf. Sci. **596**, 460–471 (2022)
7. Yang, W., Yao, Q., Ye, K., Xu, C.-Z.: Empirical mode decomposition and temporal convolutional networks for remaining useful life estimation. Int. J. Parallel Prog. **48**(1), 61–79 (2019). https://doi.org/10.1007/s10766-019-00650-1
8. Nie, X.Y., Xie, G.: A novel framework using gated recurrent unit for fault diagnosis of rotary machinery with noisy labels. Meas. Sci. Technol. **32**, 055107 (2021)

Video-Based Sentiment Analysis of International Chinese Education Online Class

Jimei Li[⊠], Haotong Li, Liangyu Zhu, Chenglong Lin, and Ruoxi Xiang

School of Information Science, Beijing Language and Culture University, Beijing, China
{ljm,rxxiang}@blcu.edu.cn

Abstract. In the era of COVID-19, online teaching has gradually become an indispensable part of the education systems in countries around the world and a major direction of research for educators. This emerging educational approach has both advantages and disadvantages. In the absence of observing students' learning status and emotions, the assessment of students' learning emotions as well as class efficiency have become a major challenge. This paper used Chinese international education class videos as the data source and adopted a semi-automatic method to construct a student emotion data-set, which can overcome the difficulty of insufficient class teaching video resources and fill the gap of student emotion data in international Chinese education online class. Also, this paper creatively used a segmentation method to research students' emotions within each teaching behavior segment, which would provide a reference for future research on students' emotion analysis and teaching behavior.

Keywords: International Chinese Education · Online class · Emotion Recognition · Learning Status

1 Introduction

Since January 2020, the COVID-19 has spread all over the world, and the impact has been tremendous. For International Chinese Education, the epidemic is a huge challenge [1]. Fortunately, modern technology, with the Internet as the core, has fully supported Chinese teaching [2]. In the international Chinese education class, non-verbal behaviors are always parts of the teacher-student interaction. Due to the problem of language differences, facial expressions would gradually become the main way for international students to express their learning emotions and express their inner thoughts. Therefore, to study students' emotions will pay a significant role in assisting professor to teach in the online class of international Chinese education [3].

The common research method for students' learning status in international Chinese education is to conduct a questionnaire survey on students after the class [4]. But the return rate of the questionnaire and the objectivity of the survey are difficult to guarantee because the students participating in the class come from different countries and regions, who are diverse in many factors such as time difference, network conditions and students' personal situations. This paper analyzed the students' emotional states in the online class videos of international Chinese education, and constructed an emotional positivity algorithm based on emotional classification, which can greatly improve the feasibility and objectivity of assessing students' learning states.

Aiming to help the teachers in related fields to analyze effectively the learning status of international students, this paper investigated the learning emotions of international Chinese education students in online class based on the emotion classification method. In Sect. 2, we summarized previous research on emotion classification and learning status of students in international Chinese education. In Sect. 3, we constructed a data-set of student emotions in international Chinese education online class videos based on emotion classification methods, and realized automatic classification of student emotions based on deep learning methods. In Sect. 4, we divided the online class videos of international Chinese education into segments based on the teaching behavior classification method, and obtained key frame images for each segment of teaching behavior and perform image restoration process. Then in Sect. 5, a comprehensive emotion positivity algorithm was constructed based on the emotion labeling method to fit students' emotions in the class and then analyze students' learning status. At last, we give a summary and the future development trend.

2 Related Works

There was no more mature theory related to online Chinese teaching [5] since it emerged in 2002 when the SARS virus spread. It was a relatively short period of time and there were relatively few studies on class interaction in online Chinese teaching. Jin Liu has used the Flanders Interaction Analysis System (FIAS) and its modified version to study class teaching. There are many domestic and international studies that apply the theory of teaching behavior to analyze class content. However, it can only reflect the verbal behaviors of teachers and students in the class, but not other important factors affecting teaching quality, such as the non-verbal behaviors of teachers and students, making the evaluation conclusions incomplete [6].

With the progress of research, scholars at home and abroad began to pay attention to nonverbal behaviors in the process of teaching international Chinese education. Taking the Confucius Institute of Abdelmalek Essaâdi University as an example, Juan Du studied the nonverbal expressions of teachers in the process of teaching Chinese as a foreign language, and analyzed the auxiliary role of nonverbal behaviors in teaching [7]. However, due to the different purposes, the subjects of the paper analyzing the issuance of nonverbal behaviors were teachers, not students. Unlike the offline class context of that research, the online class became the primary teaching and learning scenario for international Chinese education after the outbreak of the COVID-19. Many of the nonverbal behaviors mentioned in that paper, including gestures and postures, occurred less frequently in the online class.

Sheng Chen et al. used students' expressions as the research content to analyze students' emotional changes in the learning process, so as to fit students' learning states [7, 8] and proposed an emotional classification method based on the learning state space. After that, the research method of analyzing students' learning states using students' emotions as the research content has gradually been improved. But the context of the paper was still the offline class, and the class situation and teacher-student interaction were not consistent with the online class.

Based on teaching behavior theory and emotion classification theory, this paper has constructed a data-set of students' emotions for international Chinese education online class according to student emotions in international Chinese education online class and designed algorithms to fit students' emotional positivity in the class.

3 Construction of Data-Set and Implementation of Sentiment Classification Function

At this stage, research on student emotions usually uses publicly available databases such as fer2013 for facial expression recognition. However, a common data-set of student emotions in online class of international Chinese education has not yet appeared, and there is a lack of research basis in analyzing the online learning status of international students.

In this paper, we use positive, neutral, and negative as classification labels, and have set out a program to capture images and manually classified them to construct initially an online class emotion data-set for international Chinese education.

3.1 Emotion Classification Method

There are many ways to classify emotions; Ekman Paul first suggested classifying emotions into six main categories, which are boredom, fear, fright, anger, happiness, and disappointment [9]. In order to further make instructional improvement measures for various emotional states, Chen Sheng et al. classified emotions into positive, negative, and calm categories based on the learning state space.

This paper focused on students' nonverbal expressions of physical emotions and used students' class emotions to fit students' class learning status. The class video recording of student expressions used in the research occurred mainly in contexts where the student was asked to interact with the teacher, when the student's emotions significantly responded to his mastery of the class content and his understanding of the teacher's requirements. On account of this study, we have come to a conclusion that the positive, neutral, and negative emotion classification models can effectively establish a mapping of students' emotions to their learning status. Positive emotions include emotions that play a positive role in learning such as happiness and surprise; negative emotions include emotions that play a negative role in learning such as sadness, anger and disgust; and neutral emotions include all emotions that do not play a significant role in learning such as calmness.

3.2 Construction of Student Emotion Data-Set for International Chinese Education Online Class

In our research, the data sources are the three online classes teaching videos of International Chinese Education which were selected for the International Chinese Language Education online class emotion data-set. There are two classes of Economic and Trade

Reading, and one class of News Reading in the fall semester of the 2020–2021 academic year.

The process of constructing the student emotion data-set of international Chinese education online class in this paper consists of two main steps. The first step is to set out a python program to capture and save the expression images in the videos. And the second step is to select manually the images that match the expression classification features into the data-set.

Automatic Capture. Firstly, we have made a python program to automatically annotate the video, capture the face images of people in the video and save them to the specified folder. The program can read in the video at the specified file location, read the images in the video frame by frame within the specified frame number, use haarcascade _frontal-face_default.xml as the face detector, frame out the face images containing more than 10 face key points, save them as image files to the folder at the specified location, and automatically capture the face in the video.

Manual Selection. After the facial images of the students were saved, the images that meet the needs of the data-set are manually selected, and the images are classified according to the classification requirements for image emotion and screened into the data-set. In principle, images of the questioned student's facial video being projected to the main screen with a clear portrait are used. The facial emotion of the person in the image should meet the above emotion classification rules and can be clearly categorized as positive, neutral or negative. In principle, five images at least of each student were selected for each category with slightly different emotions but belonging to the same emotion category.

There are 491 valid pictures obtained, including 202 pictures in the neutral category, 149 pictures in the positive category, and 140 pictures in the negative category.

3.3 Implementation of Emotion Classification Function

Model Training. We have trained the Res-Net residual neural network based on the constructed data-set with the resnet34-pre network in the PyTorch deep learning framework [10], with the aim of implementing an automatic classification function for portrait images.

The residual network is a convolutional neural network proposed by four scholars from Microsoft Research, which has the advantages of being easy to optimize and can improve accuracy by adding considerable depth. The residual blocks inside the network use jump connections to alleviate the problem of gradient disappearance caused by increasing depth in deep neural networks [11].

We have used 182 images of neutral category, 135 images of positive category, and 126 images of negative category, totaling 443 images, as the training set; 20 images of neutral category, 14 images of positive category, and 14 images of negative category, totaling 48 images, as the validation set, for 20 training rounds to obtain the automatic class emotion classification model.

Classification Ability Test. To verify the classification ability of the classification model, 50 images of students' faces with clear image content and clearly distinguishable emotions were manually captured in the source video, and the emotion categories were manually labeled according to the emotion classification criteria. The trained model was used to perform the classification and check whether the manual annotation matched with the model classification results. Of the 50 images used to test the classification ability, 20 images in the positive category, 20 images in the neutral category, and 10 images in the negative category. The precision and recall of the emotion classification procedure for each class could be obtained from the confusion matrix in Table 1.

Table 1. Confusion Matrix of Emotion classification

Confusion Matrix		Classification results		
		Active	Neutral	Negative
Manual label	Active	19	1	0
	Neutral	0	20	0
	Negative	1	2	7

List the precision and recall of each class in the confusion matrix of Table 1 into Table 2. It can be concluded that the above model can classify the students' class emotions within the source videos more accurately. Limited by the size of the data-set, the classification model currently has limited ability and accuracy to classify emotional images that are not included in the data-set and where the picture environment differs significantly from the class environment of the data source video.

Table 2. Precision and Recall of Emotion classification Confusion Matrix

Category	Active	Neutral	Negative
Precision	95%	91%	100%
Recall	95%	100%	70%

4 Video Data Processing

4.1 Video Segmentation

In the video used for the research, the class content consists of the teacher interacting with the students individually. Given some reasonable assumptions are: (1) the teacher's interactions with each student are independent of each other, (2) the paragraphs of teacher-student communication can be viewed as a continuous string of teaching behaviors, and (3) students' performance within each teaching behavior is independent of each other.

We have used the classification of teaching behaviors as the basis for classifying class videos into teaching behavior paragraphs based on teaching behavior characteristics [12]. The classification criteria and characteristics of teaching behaviors used in this paper are shown in Table 3 which we have built in reference [12].

In this paper, we divided the videos into different teaching behavior segments according to the order of teacher-student communication. From the class videos, we have found that: (1) each teaching act has a clear start and end time, (2) there is no break between every two teaching acts, i.e., the end time of the previous teaching act is the start time of the next teaching act. The exception is when the teacher performs multimedia operations (such as locks or unlocks the screen), so that the subject of the screen is no longer the student, while there is still verbal communication between the teacher and the student in the video.

4.2 Key Frame Capture

We have draw the conclusions from the class videos that are: (1) students' performance within each instructional behavior segment is relatively independent, (2) within each teaching behavior phase, students' emotions are relatively stable, and (3) the emotional state of students in this teaching behavior can be fitted with a certain number of key-frame images captured over the same time interval. The number of key-frames within a teaching behavior and the time interval of capturing key-frames are positively correlated with the duration of that teaching behavior.

In this paper, the key-frame capture method is as follows: if the duration of a teaching act is taken as an integer in seconds as t, the number of key-frames within the teaching act and the time interval x for capturing key-frames are calculated as

$$x = \sqrt{t} \tag{1}$$

In Eq. (1), t is the duration of the teaching act, rounded to the nearest second.

The images obtained according to this frame extraction method can effectively represent the students' emotions, postures, movements and other physical states during the stage of that teaching behavior, and do not rely on subjective judgment of the students' physical states in the video. The number of key frames extracted within each teaching act is related to the duration of the teaching act, and is relatively objective in terms of the number of key frames extracted.

4.3 Image Recovery

Image recovery can use algorithms including image graying, filtering, histogram equalization, and geometric changes [13] to eliminate or weaken useless information in the image and retain or recover as much useful information as possible.

In the context of this paper, factors such as environment and equipment may lead to image degradation and under-recognition. There are some examples: (1) operations (such as video transmission and extraction of key frames) cause pepper noise in the images, (2) students' class environment and the different equipment used cause the problem of insufficient contrast and clarity in the images, (3) factors (such as skin color, appearance, clothing, and environment) interfere with the color information in the images due to the different ethnicities of the students.

Table 3. Classification and characteristics of teaching behaviors

Course Structure	Behaviors		Characteristics
Before class	Highlights Review		Review of the content of the previous lesson
	Attendance		
During class	Classroom Organization		Discourse that organizes the beginning and end of the class, as well as discourse designed to maintain the quality and flow of the class and fluency of the discourse, stage transitions of teaching behaviors
	Unrelated Language		Language unrelated to the content that does not interfere with teaching
	Abnormal Behavior		
	Practical Operation		Perform hands-on exercises, such as teacher-led reading of texts and words in unison
	Teachers	Lecturing	
		Mentoring	Includes guided questioning, using words to instruct students
		Positive Feedback	Affirmation of student responses
		Negative Feedback	
		Asking Questions	Does not contain leading questions (leading questions: teacher knows the answer to the question)
		Retelling	Repeating student discourse
		Content Presentation	Play multimedia aided teaching
		Display of Student Works	Includes critique of student work
		Instruction	Issue instructional language, such as "Please open the textbook."
	Students	Discussing	
		Answering	Includes answers to questions from the instructor and other students
		Feedback	Response to teacher's class organization
After class		Asking Questions	Includes questions for teachers and other students
		Presentation	Presenting their own work, such as reading aloud essays, acting out dialogues

To resolve the above problems and meet the processing needs at the same time, we make out the technology path as follows. Firstly, the images are grayed out to remove the color information, while the effect of highlighting the location information related to the key facial expressions was achieved. Then the images are filtered several times to eliminate the noise in the images. Since the noise composition embodied in the data is not complex, and the overall effect of pretzel noise is presented, one or two median filtering processes are used to basically eliminate these noise disturbances. However, the resulting image may cause the problem of insufficient contrast and clarity because of the different class equipment of each student, and after grayscale and filtering processing, it may further aggravate the lack of contrast and clarity, so finally the picture needs to be histogram equalization to improve its contrast and clarity, and avoid the interference of the picture too bright, too dark and blurred factors on information extraction.

The main tool used in our work for digital image processing is Open-CV (Open Source Computer Vision Library), a cross-platform computer vision and machine learning software library distributed under the Apache 2.0 license (open source) that can be built on Linux, Windows, Android, and Mac OS operating systems. It is lightweight and efficient - consisting of a set of C functions and a small number of C++ classes - and provides interfaces to Python, Ruby, MATLAB, and other languages to implement many common algorithms for image processing and computer vision. Open-CV is a common tool in the field of computer vision and has a very powerful and wide range of functions.

In this paper, Open-CV is used as the core, and some minor adjustments are made to ensure that the recovering is done as quickly as possible in a short time to achieve the required response time and processing effect in the actual application.

Digital image processing algorithms improved the distortion of images due to light and video compression to some extent. However, the image after the above digital image processing is a single-channel grayscale image, which is not consistent with the three-channel input format required by the classification model, and the subsequent paper still uses the unrestored three-channel image for emotion classification. Considering the implementation capability of the algorithm, the digital image processing algorithm currently used in the study is only applicable to the processing of contrast, recognition, etc. Deep learning [13, 14] methods will be used in the future.

5   Assessment of Students' Emotional Motivation

Feedback on students' learning status in the class is an important part in the evaluation of class efficiency in online Chinese education. Previous literature has made many attempts in this area, and the methods used are post-class questionnaires and post-class video face-to-face communication between teachers and students. For the questionnaire method, it can give teachers an objective and accurate feedback on students' class status under ideal conditions, but the return rate of the questionnaire and the objectivity of the questionnaire results are difficult to guarantee considering the time difference and students' personal situations; for the post-class video face-to-face communication method, it is too costly and inefficient to obtain feedback on all students' learning status.

Based on the experience of previous studies, the original emotion positivity algorithm of this project can give teachers more intuitive and objective feedback on students' learning status in time after each class, which is helpful for teachers to grasp students' learning situation.

5.1   Classification to Obtain Facial Image Emotion Scores

The trained residual neural network emotion automatic classification procedure was used to classify the key frame student clear images. If the classification result is POSITIVE, the emotion positivity score of the image is 1; if the classification result is NEUTRAL, the emotion positivity score of the image is 0; if the classification result is NEGATIVE, the emotion positivity score of the image is -1.

5.2 Calculation of Emotion Positivity Score for Teaching Behaviors

It could be concluded that the class can be viewed as a continuous string of teaching behaviors and that the calculation of students' class emotion positivity scores can be decomposed into the calculation of emotion positivity scores for each teaching behavior. To approximate the students' emotions in class, a trained emotion classification function was used to score each key frame image within a given teaching act after digital image processing. Positive emotions were scored as 1, neutral emotions as 0, and negative emotions as -1. The emotion positivity score of the nth image was represented by i_n.

The affective positivity score of each teaching behavior is equal to the average of the affective positivity scores of all key-frame pictures within that teaching behavior. Using P to represent the emotion positivity score of an instructional act, the emotion positivity score of a single teaching behavior is calculated as

$$P = \left(\sum\nolimits_{i=1}^{x} i_n\right)/x \tag{2}$$

In Eq. (2), x is the number of key-frames that fall in a teaching behavior.

The score of each key frame can only take three values of -1, 0 and 1, so the domain of each teaching behavior emotion positivity score value is $[-1, 1]$.

5.3 Calculation of the Overall Student Motivation Score

The study concluded that each student's overall positivity was related to two factors: the emotion positivity score for each teaching behavior and class participation. The higher the student's emotion positivity score across teaching behaviors, the higher the student's emotion positivity in teaching behaviors. The higher the number of key frames captured, the higher the student's class participation. Then, the calculation of students' overall positivity can be divided into two parts, the calculation of class emotion positivity score and the calculation of class participation score. Using S for the student overall positivity score, Se for the student class emotion positivity score, and Sc for the student class participation score, then.

$$S = Se + Sc \tag{3}$$

Calculation of Class Emotion Positivity Score. Using the number of key frames corresponding to each teaching behavior as the weight, a weighted average was calculated for the emotion positivity score of all teaching behaviors in which a student participated as one student's class emotion positivity score. Then

$$Se = \sum\nolimits_{j=1}^{y} P_m * x_m / \sum\nolimits_{j=1}^{y} x_m \tag{4}$$

In Eq. (4), y is the number of instructional acts in which a particular student participated and x_m is the number of key frames under the mth instructional act.

Each teaching behavior emotion positivity score interval is $[-1, 1]$, then the class emotion positivity score value domain for a particular student is $[-1, 1]$.

Table 4 shows the results of teaching behavior segmentation, key frames and teaching behavior positivity scores of one of the students involved in the experiment of this paper. According to the method of calculating the class emotion positivity score, in Table 4 the student's class emotion positivity score is $(0.71 * 7 + 1 * 2 + 0.4 * 5 + 0.5 * 2 + 0.57 * 7)/(7 + 2 + 5 + 2 + 7) /(7 + 2 + 5 + + 7) \approx 0.61$.

Calculation of Class Participation Score. It is found that student participation in the class is positively correlated with the length of student-teacher interaction, i.e., the number of key frames captured.

In a real class scenario, the number of key frames captured for each student does not differ by more than two orders of magnitude, i.e., the number of key frames captured for a student in a whole class is generally between $[2, 50]$ with an interval of 48. The number of key frames captured for a student is squared to 48 and taken as the base number of 7. According to the calculation, $\log7 (2) \approx 0.35$ for the minimum number of frames 2, and $\log7 (48) = 2$ for the maximum number of frames 48, the current value range of the equation is $[0.35, 2]$. And it is known to be $[-1,1]$ which is the domain of values of class emotion positivity score for a particular student.

The above calculation is multiplied by 0.5 in order to balance the effect on the overall positivity score between the value of the class participation score and that of the class emotion positivity. As a result, the equation for calculating the student class participation score is then

$$Sc = 0.5 * \log_7 \left(\sum_{j=1}^{y} x_m \right) \tag{5}$$

In Eq. (5), x_m is the number of key frames under the mth teaching behavior for a particular student, y is the number of teaching behavior in which a particular student participated.

For example, the student in Table 4 had 23 key-frames captured, so his class participation score was $0.5 * \log7(23) \approx 0.8$.

In a conclusion, the student's class emotion positivity score (Se) ranges from $[-1, 1]$ and the class participation (Sc) score is $[0.18, 1]$, so the student's overall positivity score (S) ranges from $[-0.72, 2]$.

For instance, the student in Table 4 has a overall positivity score of $0.61 + 0.8 = 1.41$, which is in the top 20% of the score range. Considering that the student's overall positivity score approximately follows a normal distribution, the student's score would rank higher than 20%. It is consistent with his actual performance.

In the actual class according to the class videos, the student was very positive. He shared with the teacher his story about being trapped in Vietnam due to the epidemic and unable to return to Beijing, and gave the teacher and classmates a welcome to visit Vietnam.

The calculation and video verification have shown that the above algorithm can approximate the performance of students in the source video and can help teachers

Table 4. Teaching behavior segmentation and emotional positivity Score of a student

Student Number	7									
Teaching Behavior	Students:Answering (1)		Teachers:Asking Questions (1)		Students:Answering (2)		Teachers:Positive Feedback (1)		Students:Answering (3)	
Beginning/End	Beginning	End	Beginning	End	Beginning	End	Beginning	End	Beginning	End
Time	45:50	46:45	46:45	46:50	46:50	47:15	47:15	47:20	47:20	48:10
Key Frame Count	7		2		5		2		7	
Teaching Behavior Emotional Positivity Score	0.71		1		0.4		0.5		0.57	

assess the class performance of international students. However, the algorithm has limited ability to assess the class environment and student learning beyond the video data source since the current data source contains a small number of students and the class format is relatively homogeneous.

6 Summary and Improvement

In the research, we start from video data sources, then construct an international Chinese education student emotion data-set to achieve automatic emotion classification, and then divide class video paragraphs according to the teaching behavior classification guidelines and capture the key frames into images, proceedingly repair and classify the images to obtain emotion positivity scores. At last, we have constructed the algorithms to evaluate students' overall positivity and analyzed students' learning status.

We have found that the question of evaluating students' overall positivity in the online class can be split into two subquestions of evaluating students' class participation and students' class emotion. The algorithm to evaluate student class participation can be designed to compare the length of student-teacher interaction. And evaluating students' class emotion can be done by segmenting the video, capturing key frames according to paragraph duration, and finally transforming it into the problem of classifying emotion for each key frame portrait picture.

The future works for improvement are as follows.

- To expand the student emotion data-set and improve the classification accuracy of the emotion classification model by introducing more online class video data source of international Chinese education.
- To obtain images of different students' emotions at the same moment in the class in order to analyze the teacher's approach to adjusting the class atmosphere to the students' learning status.
- A higher degree of objectivity and reproducibility would be achieved by automatically segmenting class paragraphs through techniques such as semantic analysis in natural language processing.

Acknowledgment. This work was partly supported by Research on International Chinese Language Education of the Center for Language Education and Cooperation "Research on identification and influence of teaching methods of International Chinese Education based on classroom video" (No. 21YH11C), by New Liberal Arts Program of Ministry of Education (No. 2021180006), by New Engineering Program of Ministry of Education (No. E-SXWLHXLX 20202604), by the Cooperative Education Program of the Ministry of Education (NO. 202101110002), and by the Science Foundation of Beijing Language and Cultural University (supported by "the Fundamental Research Funds for the Central Universities") (No. 22YJ080004).

References

1. Cui, X.: Teaching Chinese in the context of global public health emergencies. World Chin. Lang. Teach. **34**(03), 291–299 (2020). (in Chinese)

2. A compilation of views on the impact of the New Guan epidemic on international Chinese language education. World Chin. Lang. Teach. **34**(04), 435–450 (2020). (in Chinese)

3. Wu, Y.: Exploring the role of nonverbal behavior in Chinese language education for foreigners. Drama House (01), 210+212 (2017). (in Chinese)

4. Ren, Y.: Investigation and reflection on online teaching of Chinese as a foreign language in the context of the epidemic, p. 52. Shenyang Normal University (2021). (in Chinese)

5. Chang, S.: A study on online Chinese class interaction based on flanders interaction analysis system. Hunan Normal University (2021). (in Chinese)

6. Liu, J.: The application of flanders interaction analysis system in Chinese as a foreign language class. Northwest Normal University (2016). (in Chinese)

7. Du, J.: Investigation and research on non-verbal behavior of teachers of integrated foreign Chinese courses, p. 113. Jilin University (2021). (in Chinese)

8. Chen, S.: A study on class teaching based on dynamic identification of students' emotions. China Educ. Informatization (13), 33–36 (2019). (in Chinese)

9. Wang, Z.: A case study of Don't Lie to Me based on Paul Ekman's facial expression theory, p. 66. Henan University of Technology (2015)

10. Wei, S.-B.: Research on facial expression recognition based on multiple features. Hefei University of Technology (2019).(in Chinese)

11. Zhang, C.: Face recognition and simulation platform based on residual neural network. J. Xuzhou Eng. Coll. (Nat. Sci. Ed.) **34**(01), 33–37 (2019). (in Chinese)

12. Li, J., Li, C., Xiang, R.: A preliminary study on the recognition of speech acts performed by international chinese teachers in class based on deep learning. In: The 16th International Conference on Computer Science & Education (ICCSE 2021), pp. 937–942, 18–20 August 2021

13. https://github.com/WZMIAOMIAO/deep-learning-for-image-processing

14. Su, J., Xu, B., Yin, H.: A survey of deep learning approaches to image restoration. Neurocomputing **487**, 46–65 (2022)

Design of Process Management Platform for Project Practice Teaching

Jin Zhiqi, Cen Yuefeng, Wang Xinjie, Xu Jiachen, and Cen Gang(✉)

Zhejiang University of Science and Technology, HangZhou, China
`cyf@zust.edu.cn, gcen@163.com`

Abstract. In order to solve the problems arising during the students' project practice teaching, a project practice process-oriented management platform is designed by the project team. A process management of students' project practice is realized by the constructing of project teaching environment and tracking students' project practice process, thus leading to improvement of the project practice effect in universities.

Keywords: Project teaching · Practical teaching · Process management · Platform design

1 Introduction

With the development of Chinese industry, the demand for application-oriented talents is increasing, so higher education institutions are paying more and more attention to the cultivation of application-oriented talents [1]. In this regard, the national "Excellent Engineer Training Education Program" has set high requirements for colleges and universities to cultivate applied talents with innovative thinking. Universities have been exploring new modes of cultivating applied talents to meet the needs of national development.

Zhejiang University of Science and Technology draws lessons from Germany's application-oriented talent training plan and combines with the training experience of many domestic universities to carry out project practice teaching activities, focusing on improving students' comprehensive ability and practice level [2]. By exploring the method of project practice teaching, the school adopts a new teaching mode of students' active participation, independent collaboration and exploration and innovation to guide students to solve practical problems, think deeply and make continuous innovation in project learning, which has achieved certain results in the cultivation of applied talents [3].

Although the mode of project practice teaching has obtained great positive significance and effect, there are still some difficulties and challenges. In order to improve the effect of project practice, the project team combined with the method of improving students' comprehensive ability, designed a process management platform for project practice teaching to help students carry out project practice activities smoothly, so as to promote the cultivation of applied talents.

W. Hong and Y. Weng (Eds.): ICCSE 2022, CCIS 1813, pp. 244–254, 2023.
https://doi.org/10.1007/978-981-99-2449-3_22

2   The Proposal of Project Practice Teaching Process Management Platform

Problem Analysis. Since the implementation of Zhejiang University of Science and Technology project practice teaching activities, students have improved significantly in terms of comprehensive ability and achieved good results. However, the project team discovered through investigation and analysis that there was still a lot of room for improvement and summarized the following problems.

- Before the beginning of the project, students' understanding of project practice teaching activities is insufficient, which affects their enthusiasm for project practice.
- When preparing for the project, students have some trouble selecting the topic of the project and finding suitable partners, which affects project practice.
- Students focus on project creation rather than project completion in the project process. It appears that students actively declare their projects, but disregard the implementation of the project practice, resulting in a haphazard closing, which affects the quality of the project closing [4].
- In the process of practice, the information interaction between students and the instructor is not timely, which affects the impact of the instructor on the guidance of students [5].

According to the above problem, the project team want to create a collaborative learning platform that supports interaction, communication and collaboration among students, and enhances the learning of teamwork skills to achieve a seamless transition between students' theory and practical application.

2.1   Project Process-oriented Management Model

The application of the concept of process management in project practice is mainly reflected in guiding students' project practice and supervising the whole project process. The characteristic of process management is to highlight the project process in order to achieve high efficiency in project development and maximize project results. Another one is to start from the expected results of the project, deduce the process of project practice according to the conditions that the results need to satisfy, and realize the project planning. In this mode, the team designs the project plan according to the actual situation of the project, changing the focus from the project results to the project practice process, and improves the efficiency of students in the project practice process and the quality of the project results.

In the implementation of the project, it is hard for the project practice team and the tutor to master the project process timely and to carry out overall control and long-term planning of the project. Therefore, the process management model requires all team members to work towards a common goal and enhance the tutor's role in guiding the team. Otherwise, the team motivation and project efficiency would be undermined by the conflicting goals and confusing planning.

2.2 System Proposed

The project process management improves the effectiveness of student project practice. Accordingly, the project team proposed to incorporate the concept of project process management into the platform, and designed the project practice process management platform through integration and innovation with new technology, so as to promote the implementation of project teaching activities.

Systematic process management regards all stages of student projects as a process, including the pre-project preparation stage, the project implementation stage and the project summary stage, focusing on the continuity of project teaching activities. The concept of process throughout the entire project, emphasizing the results of the entire project process instead of the results of sub-projects and tasks, and requiring the results of the current stage to serve the next stage of the project.

Students may not understand the teaching connotation of the project or the way of project management, and only pay attention to the declaration, conclusion and results of the project, and the conclusion and results of all projects are inseparable from the process of project practice. As a result, the system splits the projects on a time scale to improve project efficiency.

3 System Design

3.1 Design Ideas

The project practice process management platform assists project teaching management and performs a guiding and supervising role in the project teaching process. The system combines the learning theory of constructivism and builds up an open practice environment [6], provides students with project guidance, project management and achievement improvement services, and divides the student project practice process into three stages.

Project Planning Stage. The system uses achievement incentives, project recommendations and project planning to guide students to start project practice and do preparation work before the project is carried out (see Fig. 1).

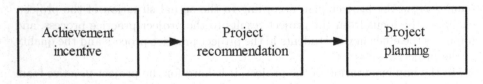

Fig. 1. Approach to the project planning stage.

Project Implementation Stage. The system assists students to form project teams, and supervises them in a variety of ways to ensure the quality of student project practice process and comprehend the process management of each process in different projects (see Fig. 2).

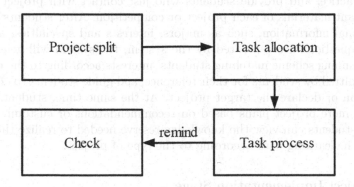

Fig. 2. Approach to the projects implementation stage.

Achievement Summary Stage. The system utilizes systematic guidance and mentoring to extend students' practical results(see Fig. 3).

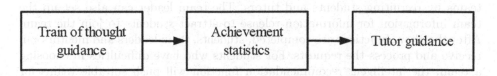

Fig. 3. Approach to the achievement summary stage.

4 Project Process Management Design

The system distinguishes different users as students, teachers, and administrator identities. The different functions in the system are closely related to each other, providing personalized services for students and auxiliary management for each process of project practice. It realizes the project training of students in three stages, promotes project teaching activities, and improves the effect of students' project practice.

4.1   Project Planning Stage

The goal of the project planning stage is to realize project guidance and study planning for students. The system will show students excellent project practice teams and their achievements, so as to stimulate students' enthusiasm for project practice, and provide students who just contact with project practice with relevant materials of each project or competition. After students set their own personal information, such as majors, interests and specialties, and complete the questionnaire generated by the system, the system will generate the project planning scheme matching students' interests according to the questionnaire submitted by students for their reference, and guide students to choose the competition or declare the target project. At the same time, students can set up one or more project plans based on recommendations or customization. In addition, students can view the knowledge reserve needed to realize the project and plan the learning path according to the type of project.

4.2   Project Implementation Stage

The goal of the project implementation stage is to assist students with project practice and help teams with project supervision to improve the effectiveness of student project implementation. The system helps students to form teams for different projects and implement project management. In the process of building a team, students can become team members, browse the specific information of students, teams and tutors in the team list, and join the team to build a team. Students can also create teams and become team leaders. It is easy to build teams by recruiting students and tutors. The team leader can also set up the team information for information release to attract students to join the team. After the above functions are completed, students, team leaders and mentors can receive and process the requests. For students who have difficulties in choosing a team, the intelligent recommendation function will push suitable teams for students based on their interests, strengths and practical intentions, improving the rationality of their team selection(see Fig. 4).

Based on the existing project experience, we designed some basic project templates, so that students can more easily understand, and practical use. Once the student project team is formed, the system helps students break down the project into detailed and quantifiable tasks. The task information includes the task leader, deadline and task content. The system integrates all the tasks created by the students and generates a schedule of the entire project tasks and timelines. After the student submits the task, the team mentor will receive the information and review the task submitted by the student to determine if the task meets the standard. When the task submission time exceeds or the task deadline is approaching, the system will remind the person in charge of different degrees according to the task deadline. At the same time, teachers can also remind students, urge team members to complete tasks on time, and realize the supervision of the project. Students can also write logs to summarize the project

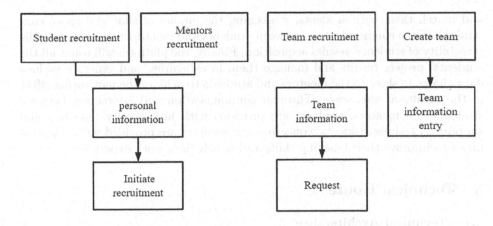

Fig. 4. The way and process of team formation.

process while the project is progressing. The system enables the transfer of documents between the team and the instructor and the storage of project process data for easy access and review of documents during the project. If the project is not progressing well, students can make changes to the overall project plan based on the project situation(see Fig. 5).

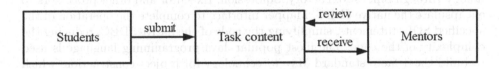

Fig. 5. Form of project supervision.

This stage realizes personalized team recommendation, and highly combines the process management concept with the task-driven idea, using a combination of student self-management and teacher supervision and management to realize the project supervision.

4.3 Achievement Summary Stage

The goal of the achievement summary stage is to expand the project results. Students can learn detailed conditions for obtaining software publications, papers, patents, etc. and other relevant information about the enhancement of project results in the system, which guides them to realize the results. After determining the direction of result enhancement, students can select and seek guidance from their mentors according to their needs and get real-time advice from them on the summary of project results. Mentors can post guidance materials in the system and match them with students, weakening the impact of time and space constraints on the communication between students and mentors and increasing the possibility of students' results acquisition. Finally, the platform will count all the students' project results and manage them in categories, and generate various data charts to show to the mentors and students to achieve the motivating effect of the results at this stage. Through communication and interaction between students and mentors, students are provided with high-quality resources and support to address students' concerns, and mentors are provided with opportunities to improve their teaching skills and enrich their work experience.

5　Technical Route

5.1　Technical Architecture

The system adopts a lightweight framework jQuery, which makes the code concise and easy to expand later, combined with bootstrap framework to achieve a responsive interface layout, to ensure a unified interface style. At the same time, the system uses the Echarts open source visual chart design tool to draw charts to achieve data visualization. System through Ajax technology to achieve front and back-end data transfer to achieve connection of front and back-end data.

The back end of the platform adopts JavaWeb technology, MySQL relational database, and the most widely used ORM framework in China. Mybatis technology through SqlSessionFactory, SqlSession, Executor and other processors to encapsulate the native JDBC. Mapper interface to complete the operation of the specified SQL statements, simplifying the code of the native JDBC, reducing the complexity of the code. The most popular Java programming language is used to build the defacto standard Maven technology for project construction, which is convenient for the management and development of back-end code, and the use of Tomcat technology to build web servers.

5.2　Core Algorithm

The platform uses a hybrid collaborative filtering algorithm [7], in which the target students can fill in the project practice questionnaire form [8] when they first log in, combine the obtained large amount of student data and use the cosine formula to find the top 10 users with the highest similarity (excluding those with exactly the same interests) to form a set, select and accumulate and average the intended contests in the user set that are different from the target students, and select the five contests with the highest similarity among them. The five contests with the highest similarity are recommended to the target students. If students do not fill in the project practice questionnaire, the platform will recommend the five competitions with the highest popularity. The platform records the implicit feedback from users and tags them with behaviors, such as: students' browsing, clicking, searching and other activities in the platform, and filters out the contests with the most behavioral tags as new contests for students. The above screening

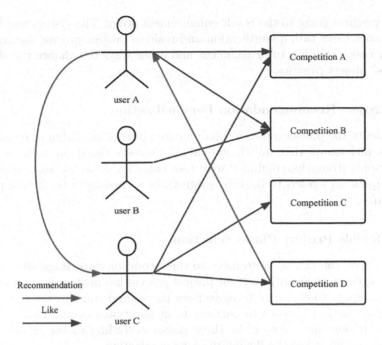

Fig. 6. Schematic of the collaborative filtering algorithm.

process is repeated to achieve dynamic student contest recommendations. Below is a schematic of the collaborative filtering algorithm(see Fig. 6).

$N(u)$ is the set of items preferred by user u, and $N(v)$ is the set of items preferred by user v. The following is the formula for calculating Jaccard similarity as follows:

$$w_{uv} = \frac{|N(u) \cap N(v)|}{|N(u) \cup N(v)|} \tag{1}$$

Find the k users that are most similar to the target user u from the database, and represent them by the set $S(u,k)$, extract all the items that the user likes in S, and remove the items that u already likes r_{vi} denotes the degree of liking of user v to i, and the system defaults to its value of 1. For each candidate contest i, the degree of interest of user u to it is calculated by the following user interest degree formula:

$$P(u,i) = \sum_{v \in S(u,k) \cap N(i)} w_{uv} \times r_{vi} \tag{2}$$

6   System Features

6.1   Project Management Process

The platform divides the project into three stages, starting from the project training planning stage to the project progress stage. Then it evolves from the project progress stage to the result enhancement stage. The system assists each project to achieve task quantification and realizes project process management through task reminder, tutor comment and other ways to enhance the effect of students' project practice.

6.2   Project Recommendation Personalization

For students, the platform uses a collaborative filtering algorithm to recommend projects and teams that match individual interests based on users' interests and personal strengths, combined with user behavior data; for teams, this platform helps team leaders to flexibly assign tasks according to the actual project situation.

6.3   Flexible Project Phase Selection

Students have the flexibility to move to the second or third stage after making some progress on their project. If the project process has made some progress, the person in charge may choose to move from the second stage to the third stage. If the team project chooses to participate in additional competitions while in progress, it can enter any of the three stages according to the team's needs, which greatly improves the flexibility of stage selection.

7   Test Result

Based on the results of the current system trial run, the platform has expanded the number of students' participation in the project teaching activities, met the information construction needs of universities for project teaching environment. Through feedback from students and teachers after the trial, we summarize the following advantages of the system.

- The system's intelligent recommendations use collaborative filtering algorithms to recommend competitions and teammates that may be of interest to users, reasonably helping students plan their projects and achieve team formation.
- With the increase of system users, the accuracy of personalized recommendation is also improving.
- The system enables project process management, which makes the management of students' projects more reasonable and convenient, and improves the quality of students' project completion.
- The implementation of the platform is evaluated through a variety of evaluation methods, including learning achievement, student evaluation, teacher evaluation, etc., in order to confirm the effectiveness and sustainability of the platform.

Below is an illustration of some of the features of the platform(see Fig. 7 & Fig. 8).

Fig. 7. A partial interface diagram of the platform.

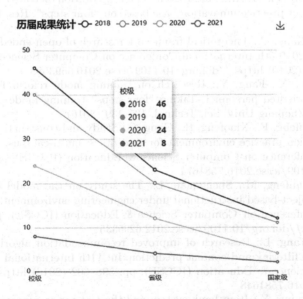

Fig. 8. A partial interface diagram of the platform.

8 Conclusion

In view of the problems and challenges existing in the current project practice teaching activities, the project team combined with the concept of project process management, using modern information technology to develop a project practice process management platform, to solve the problems such as the difficulty in building teams and supervising projects.

The establishment of the system provides an auxiliary role for project practice teaching, constructs an online network environment for project practice teaching, and provides high-quality, interdisciplinary practical education resources to promote the development of students 'learning and innovation ability. We believe that this project will have the potential to be extended in the future, and also provide feasible suggestions and programs for scientific research institutions and educational institutions to promote the development and innovation of practical education.

Acknowledgements. The author of this paper would like to thank the Zhejiang Xinmiao Talents Program (No. 2022R415001) in 2022 for supporting us to complete this research.

References

1. Zeng, L., Zhang, C., Lu, Y., Ma, N.: On the training mode of applied talents in universities from the perspective of excellent teaching. Res. Higher Educ. Eng. 19–23 (2016)
2. Cen, G., Wu, S., Jiang, X., et al.: Research and exploration on construction management of project practice innovation base based on "four steps". Res. Explor. Labor. 54–55 (2021)
3. Xuefen, L., Gang, C.: Theoretical framework research of open-ended project-based instruction. 2010 5th International Conference on Computer Science & Education, pp. 438–441 (2010) https://doi.org/10.1109/iccse.2010.5593588
4. Cen, G., Lin, X., Fang, Y.: Research on training mode reform for engineering application-oriented personnel -Taking "four steps" training mode of ZUST as an example. J. Zhejiang Univ. Sci. Technol. 135–139 (2016)
5. Xuan, C., Yufeng, F., Xiaofeng, H., Gang, C.: Study and construction on independent innovation practice environment for students at multi-campus. In: 11th International Conference on Computer Science & Education (ICCSE) (2016). https://doi.org/10.1109/iccse.2016.7581674
6. Gang, C., Yunfeng, M., Shengquan, L.: The study on the model of open-ended practical project-based instructional under engineering environment. In: 7th International Conference on Computer Science & Education (ICCSE), pp. 1444–1448 (2012) https://doi.org/10.1109/iccse.2012.6295335
7. Jiang, W., Yang, L.: Research of improved recommendation algorithm based on collaborative filtering and content prediction. In: 11th International Conference on Computer Science & Education (ICCSE). pp. 598–602 (2016) https://doi.org/10.1109/iccse.2016.7581648
8. Yan, S., Guoxing, Y.: Item bank system and the test paper generation algorithm. In: 2012 7th International Conference on Computer Science & Education (ICCSE), pp. 491–495 (2012). https://doi.org/10.1109/iccse.2012.6295121

A Study on the Dynamic Development of Chinese Second Language Learners' Oral Lexical Competence from the Perspective of International Chinese Education

Surinah[1] and Huanhai Fang[2(✉)]

[1] Xiamen University, Xiamen 361005, China
[2] Suqian University, Suqian 223800, China
fanghuanhai@xmu.edu.cn

Abstract. This paper employs the complex dynamic system theory (CDST) from the standpoint of interdisciplinary research, we use relevant computer technology to employ quantitative research methods to investigate the dynamic relationship between the development of lexical competence and its influencing factors on Indonesian learners' oral Chinese. This study explains and demonstrates the close relationship between various abilities in language learning, as well as the importance of guiding vocabulary learning strategies and the specific issues that must be addressed in international Chinese teaching.

Keywords: Lexical Competence · Lexical Variation · Lexical Sophistication · Lexical Errors · Chinese Language

1 Introduction

Lexical competence has been valued in the field of second language acquisition for a long time. There are an increasing number of studies in the field of Chinese second language acquisition that use empirical methods to investigate lexical competence. The research on the development of Chinese second language lexical competence started relatively late. Considering the development of lexical competence as a single dimension or only studying one of the dimensions, the results of dynamic and systematic investigation of lexical competence development are quite rare. From the perspective of international Chinese education, this study investigates the dynamic and systematic study of lexical competence in the oral expression of Indonesian Chinese learners in China, with important implications for Chinese L2 practitioners and researchers.

Since the end of the twentieth century, the academic community has conducted research on lexical competence from various perspectives and dimensions, gradually reaching a consensus that learners' lexical competence is a dynamic development process rather than a static state. The dimensions were observed separately (Meara [1], Chapelle [2], Henriksen [3]), and many relevant domestic and foreign literatures were integrated (Meara [4], Chapelle [2], Henriksen [3]; Qian [5]; Zhang and Wu [6], Dóczi and Kormos

© The Author(s), under exclusive license to Springer Nature Singapore Pte Ltd. 2023
W. Hong and Y. Weng (Eds.): ICCSE 2022, CCIS 1813, pp. 255–265, 2023.
https://doi.org/10.1007/978-981-99-2449-3_23

[7]), which can be roughly classified into four dimensions: lexical variation, lexical sophistication, lexical errors, and lexical density, and have become one of the focuses of research on oral and written expressions in recent years.

The research on lexical competence in Chinese as a second language mainly focuses on the development of lexical variation, lexical sophistication, and lexical density. Most studies on lexical competence in writing, such as Huang and Qian [8], Wu [9], Zhou [10], and others, have paid little attention to research on oral lexical competence. Among them, Sun [11], Chen and Li [12] only studied lexical sophistication, while Huang and Qian [8] explored the correlation between lexical sophistication and lexical errors, especially Chen and Li [12], Ding and Xiao [13] who conducted a longitudinal case study on the degree of lexical variation. Furthermore, Zhou [10] added observations on the meaning of words in addition to observing the degree of lexical variation in her longitudinal study. Wu [9] discovered that the composition of intermediated and advanced students is more dense in terms of lexical density. There was no significant difference in lexical density, especially in oral language output. Surinah [14] found that the lexical density of junior and intermediate students in monologue expression decreased significantly, but there was no significant difference in dialogue and composition performance.

To sum up, research on second language acquisition of Chinese vocabulary focuses on the influence of a single factor, which leads to difficulties in understanding or explaining the real situation of Chinese lexical competence development. We have noticed that academia has begun to have an interdisciplinary perspective, and studies on Chinese lexical production ability using the perspective of complex dynamic systems are emerging. For example, Zheng [15] and Dóczi & Kormos [7] used linguistics, psychology, and multiple research perspectives, such as linguistics and sociocultural studies, to explain the development of lexical competence in second language learners. The current research mostly focuses on its "dynamic" research and ignores its "complexity", and it lacks the case study of nationalized Chinese lexical competence. In light of this, this article intends to take an interdisciplinary approach based on the national characteristics of learners, employing quantitative research methods and using Indonesian Chinese learners as a case study to investigate the characteristics of Chinese lexical competence development and its development. The influencing factors attempt to investigate and interpret more thoroughly.

2   Research Design

2.1   Research Questions

What are the developmental features of lexical variation, lexical sophistication and lexical errors in Chinese spoken by Indonesian learners?
What is the dynamic relationship between the various dimensions of lexical competence in Chinese spoken by Indonesian learners?
What is the dynamic relationship between vocabulary learning strategies (VLS) and lexical competence in Chinese spoken by Indonesian learners.

2.2 Research Framework

Because there is insufficient evidence to show that vocabulary density is a core indicator of Chinese L2 lexical competence, the issue of vocabulary density is not considered for the time being in order to explore the multidimensional components of the learners' Chinese lexical competence development system. This study regards the development of lexical competence of Indonesian learners as a complex system, and only observes the dynamic relationship between three dimensions of lexical competence and the dynamic relationship between learners' vocabulary learning strategies and lexical competence development.

2.3 Participants and Data Collection

This study follows the tradition of cross-sectional studies and uses the spoken samples. The participants of the study were Indonesian undergraduates majoring in Chinese language education from one university in Fujian who came to China to learn Chinese, including 28 boys and 62 girls, all aged between 19–22.

After taking into account the total amount of study time, final exam scores, and HSK test scores, they are divided into three grade levels of Chinese proficiency: beginner (G1), intermediate (G2) and advanced (G3). Each grade includes 30 students. It should be noted that all participants were informed of our research objectives and agreed to participate in the corpus construction project for free.

2.4 Data Collection

The source of the corpus is based on two quantitative data. The first is about lexical competence. For this purpose, the data is based on one by one natural dialogue between the researcher and the participants, with the same topic for each participant, and familiar to them, such as school activities, difficulties in learning Chinese (especially in vocabulary learning strategies) and how they adapt, or what they describe China. All conversations were recorded. The second is about the learners' vocabulary learning strategies using. For this purpose, the data is based on Schmitt's Vocabulary Language Strategies Questioner (VLSQ), which has five subscales, including determination, memory, metacognitive, cognitive, and social strategies.

2.5 The Measures

Lexical Variation. First, the new base lists for Indonesian Chinese L2 learners were extracted. On the basis of the collated oral database, word segmentation is carried out through the Chinese corpus word segmentation and part-of-speech tagging software "CorpusWordParser" which developed by the Language Application Research Institute of the Ministry of Education of China. Second, the samples were submitted to the "LanguageData" software (the online Chinese reading grading index software, we can fine it in https://www.languagedata.net/editor/,) to count the number of words and the total words.After that, the sample can be analyzed for the degree of lexical variation. In measuring the degree of lexical variation, we adopted the calculation method of root type-token ratio (RTTR) proposed by Guiraud (in Lu [16]) because The Ratio of Class Characters (RTTR) is the most reliable calculation. The specific calculation method as below:

$$LV = Token/The\ square\ root\ of total\ words. \tag{1}$$

Lexical Sophistication. This study took the lemma of word types as its unit and measured lexical sophistication as below:

$$LS = Number\ of\ the high\ level words\ /Total\ number\ of\ the\ word \times 100\% \tag{2}$$

First, we used "LanguageData" software to classify vocabulary levels., the software automatically compared the samples against HSK vocabulary lists and generated the Learners' Oral Vocabulary List. The vocabulary list comprised in four sub-lists, which divided in "low", "middle", "high" and "others" word level list.The first three lists enumerate words in the samples covered by HSK word list, while the last one words not counted by the HSK word lists. Second, the number of high level word types and their percentages in the number of word types in each oral sample were calculated for each grade level. The lexical sophistication of each grade level was calculated thereafter.

Lexical Errors. This study used the lexical errors rate to examine the accuracy of learners' vocabulary use. The higher lexical errors rate, the lower lexical accuracy, and vice versa. The specific calculation method as below:

$$LE = Number\ of\ wrong\ words/\ Total\ number\ of\ words \times 100\% \tag{3}$$

Lastly, we use SPSS 22 log-likelihood (LL) tests to measure whether differences in lexical variation, lexical sophistication and lexical errors were statistically significant across grade levels.

3 Result

Table 1 shows the descriptive statistics for the performance of lexical variation, lexical sophistication, and lexical errors in the spoken language of Indonesian international students at the beginner (G1), intermediate (G2), and advanced (G3) levels.

The development of lexical competence in the three dimensions is dynamic and unbalanced, as shown in Table 1, and the degree of difference within each dimension is inconsistent. The analysis is carried out separately below.

Table 1. Descriptive Statistics for The Main Variables of Lexical Competence

Variable	Grade	N	Mean	SD
Lexical variation	G1	30	38.99	11.53
	G2	30	50.33	11.23
	G3	30	58.06	11.34
Lexical sophistication	G1	30	18.9888	4.94161
	G2	30	18.6068	3.62284
	G3	30	20.4535	5.74731
Lexical errors	G1	30	16.8358	11.30598
	G2	30	10.9167	6.62449
	G3	30	6.9084	4.10693

3.1 Lexical Variation

From Table 1, the degree of lexical variation gradually increases from the beginner to the advanced grade and generally shows a stable development trend. Following testing, it was discovered that the data met the prerequisites for one-way ANOVA, and the analysis revealed that there were significant differences in the degree of lexical variation among Indonesian Chinese learners of various Chinese levels ($F = 7.679$, $df1 = 2$, $df2 = 87$, $p = 0.001$). The LSD test further showed that: G1 and G2 learners ($r = 11.335$, $p = 0.000$), G2 and G3 learners ($r = 7.734$, $p = 0.01$), G1 and G3 learners ($r = 19.070$, $p = 0.000$). It can be seen that there is a significant ($0.001 < \alpha < 0.01$) development in the lexical variation degree of learners from the beginner to the advanced learners.

3.2 Lexical Sophistication

Table 1 shows that the average of lexical sophistication of learners' spoken language is 18.9888 in beginning stage, then increased to 18.6068 in intermediate stage, and also continued to increase to 20.4535 in advanced stage. Based on the results, one-way ANOVA was performed, and it was found that there were no significant differences in learners' lexical sophistication with different Chinese proficiency ($F = 1.212$, $df1 = 2$, $df2 = 87$, $p = 0.303$). Then, the LSD test was carried out to show that the ratio between G1 and G2 learners ($r = 0.38203$, $p = 0.761$), G2 and G3 learners ($r = 1.84665$, $p = 0.144$), and G1 and G3 learners ($r = 1.46461$, $p = 0.245$), and that there is no significant difference ($\alpha > 0.05$). It was discovered that there is no significant development of the learners in terms of lexical sophistication dimensions after approximately three years of study time. It also suggested that learners have a relatively weak grasp of using intermediate and advanced level vocabulary in dialogue, which is consistent with the findings of Shen [17], Sun [11], and Mo [18].

3.3 Lexical Errors

Table 1 depicts the quantitative evolution of the lexical errors in the research subjects' oral language output. It can be seen that the average lexical errors rate of the primary learners is 16.8358, which decreased to 10.9167 in the intermediate stage, and continued to drop to 6.9084 in the advanced stage. Further one-way ANOVA results showed that the lexical errors rate of learners at different stages was significantly different (F = 11.904, df1 = 2, df2 = 87, p = 0.000). The LSD test showed that there was a significant difference in lexical errors between G1 and G2 level learners (r = 5.91904, p = 0.005), and between G1 and G3 learners (r = 9.92743, p = 0.000), but between G2 and G3 learners there was no significant difference (r = 4.00839, p = 0.053). This indicates that the lexical errors of intermediated to advanced level learners have plateaued, but the lexical errors have decreased significantly over the course of 3–4 years of learning. In other words, the lexical accuracy of Indonesian Chinese learners' spoken vocabulary shows "fast and then slow" development trends.

3.4 Internal Dynamics correlations of Lexical competence in Learners' Oral Chinese

There is also a weak interrelationship among the subsystems of the learner's lexical competence system in the dialogue, and only the lexical variation degree has a strong correlation with other lexical competence variables. The variables in the basic level stage are independent of each other and have no significant correlation, but in the middle and high level stages, there is a significant correlation between lexical variation and lexical errors of middle stage learners (r = -0. 459, p = .011). In addition, there was a significant correlation between lexical variation and lexical sophistication (r = 0.540, p = 0.002) (Table 2).

Table 2. Correlations between LV, LS and LE

M	c	G1(n = 30)		G1 (n = 30)		G3 (n = 30)	
		LS	LE	LS	LE	LS	LE
LV	r	.346	−.041	.294	−.459*	.540**	−.242
	p	.061	.831	.115	.011	.002	.198
LS	r	1	−.030	1	−.243	1	.112
	p		.874		.196		.556

Note: M = Measures, c = correlation indexs LV = Lexical Variation, LS = Lexical Sophistication, LE = Lexical Errors. ** p < 0.01; * p < 0.05 (all two-tailed tests)

3.5 External Dynamics Relationship of Learners' Oral Lexical Competence

Table 3 presents the results of the cumulative check correlation analysis. It can be seen from the table that the lexical competence of learners at different stages and with different variables is affected by learners' vocabulary learning strategies with different degrees. Among them, the lexical variation degree of learners in G1 was significantly correlated with metacognitive strategies ($r = 0.375$, $p = 0.041$), lexical sophistication was related to memory strategies ($r = 0.405$, $p = 0.027$), metacognitive strategies ($r = 0.426$, $p = 0.019$), and the total frequency of strategy use ($r = 0.388$, $p = 0.034$) were significantly correlated. Lexical variation degree of G2 was significantly correlated with the overall vocabulary learning strategy uses ($r = 0.418$, $p = 0.022$). The lexical sophistication of G3 learners was also significantly correlated with the overall vocabulary learning strategy frequency uses of VLS ($r = 0.388$, $p = 0.034$). This indicates that the VLS of Indonesian learners have a significant impact on Chinese spoken vocabulary output, especially in the lexical variation and lexical sophistication dimensions.

4 Discussion

The three dimensions of lexical competence of oral Chinese in Indonesian learners have different development trends. During the three to four years of study in China, the vocabulary capacity produced only has a significant development trend in two dimensions: lexical variation and lexical errors, but there is no significant development trend in lexical sophistication. On the other hand, we know from internal interconnection data that lexical variation is significantly correlated to the other dimensions of lexical competence, particularly at the intermediate and advanced levels. Although there is a dynamic correlation between the internal variables, each dimension of lexical competence does not grow at the same rate. This shows that there are different characteristics between the dimensions of lexical competence subsystems, which lead to different development trends, and its development shows a non-linear trend. This discovery of the "Connected Growers" is consistent with the findings of Spoelman and Verspoor [19], Caspi and Lowie [20], and Tan [21].

The stagnation state experienced by Indonesian students studying abroad is a systematic "attraction state". According to Zheng [15], from the perspective of complex dynamic systems, "stagnation" or "rigidity" in the development of learners' L2 can be regarded as the attraction of the dynamic system in the process of lexical variation development. This "stagnation" state is not the same as a permanent stationary state, but it has the potential to develop (Larsen-Freeman [22]). This is because each dynamic system has different interactive factors, and entering the "stagnation" state is only an "attraction state" of a single system. However, the autonomous system between the system or the interaction between the system may be able to stimulate the stagnation state to turn to the next development phase (Zheng [15]).

We discovered lexical sophistication of Indonesian students in spoken discourses in this study, indicating a "stagnation" development state that requires external intervention to move it to the next stage of development. The "stagnation" in lexical sophistication development may be caused by learners' preference to speak up with high-frequency and low-level vocabulary in conversation, so external intervention should be focused on this. Furthermore, the slow growth of lexical errors in the intermediate to advanced phases requires external intervention to ensure that it is developed in a sustainable manner.

From the perspective of internal interconnection data, lexical variation is significantly related to the other dimensions of lexical competence, especially at the intermediate and

Table 3. Correlations Between VLS, LV, LS and LE (n = 30)

G	M	c	Vocabulary Learning Strategy (VLS)					
			Det	Mem	Cog	Met	Soc	Total
G1	LV	r	.273	.102	.151	.375*	.342	.269
		p	.144	.593	.425	.041	.065	.151
	LS	r	.258	.405*	.225	.426*	.349	.388*
		p	.168	.027	.232	.019	.059	.034
	LE	r	−.214	−.092	−.028	−.084	.089	−.086
		p	.256	.629	.884	.66	.64	.65
G2	LV	r	.059	.058	.252	.137	.207	.418*
		p	.755	.76	.178	.471	.272	.022
	LS	r	.082	−.155	−.167	−.132	−.145	−.118
		p	.667	.413	.377	.486	.444	.534
	LE	r	.043	−.008	−.052	−.026	−.084	.127
		p	.821	.965	.783	.891	.66	.503
G3	LV	r	.043	−.171	.013	.189	.182	.269
		p	.822	.365	.945	.316	.335	.151
	LS	r	.016	.035	.144	.34	.18	.388*
		p	.933	.855	.448	.066	.34	.034
	LE	r	−.157	−.295	−.08	−.119	−.299	−.086
		p	.406	.114	.673	.53	.108	.65
G1	LV	r	.273	.102	.151	.375*	.342	.269
		p	.144	.593	.425	.041	.065	.151
	LS	r	.258	.405*	.225	.426*	.349	.388*
		p	.168	.027	.232	.019	.059	.034
	LE	r	−.214	−.092	−.028	−.084	.089	−.086
		p	.256	.629	.884	.66	.64	.65
G2	LV	r	.059	.058	.252	.137	.207	.418*
		p	.755	.76	.178	.471	.272	.022
	LS	r	.082	−.155	−.167	−.132	−.145	−.118
		p	.667	.413	.377	.486	.444	.534
	LE	r	.043	−.008	−.052	−.026	−.084	.127
		p	.821	.965	.783	.891	.66	.503
G3	LV	r	.043	−.171	.013	.189	.182	.269

(continued)

Table 3. (*continued*)

G	M	c	Vocabulary Learning Strategy (VLS)					
			Det	Mem	Cog	Met	Soc	Total
		p	.822	.365	.945	.316	.335	.151
	LS	r	.016	.035	.144	.34	.18	.388*
		p	.933	.855	.448	.066	.34	.034
	LE	r	−.157	−.295	−.08	−.119	−.299	−.086
		p	.406	.114	.673	.53	.108	.65

Note: G = Grade; M = Measures; c = correlation index Det = Determination, Mem = Memory, Cog = Cognitive; Met = Metacognitive, Soc = Social, Total = Overall vocabulary learning strategy use. ** $p < 0.01$; * $p < 0.05$. (all two-tailed tests)

advanced stages. This means that the lexical variation improvement can also indirectly improve the lexical sophistication, and vice versa. From the relevant data of the learner's vocabulary strategy and lexical competence, the meta-cognitive strategy is significantly correlated to the lexical variation and lexical sophistication. This means that metacognitive strategies are crucial for Indonesian learners who are mature enough to plan and structure their learning. Therefore, in order to obtain the development of more efficient vocabulary capabilities, we may consider to increase the metacognitive strategy application training (e.g., spaced-word practice). According to Schmitt [23], metacognitive strategy means that learners strengthen vocabulary understanding and use through monitoring and managing their learning strategies, reflecting the ability of learners to find vocabulary learning strategies that suits for them, such as using movies or music to study pronunciation and remember new word and routine make some vocabulary exercises. Otherwise, the teacher can guide students through the process of creating a Chinese language environment and introducing them to a Chinese learning conversation platform. Because Indonesian students prefer to learn using electronic devices, an app that can be used to increase the use of high-level vocabulary and improve pronunciation would be very useful, especially for intermediate and advanced learners.

In addition, data on correlations between VLS and lexical competence show that in the intermediate and advanced grades, the overall frequency of VLS use has a significant correlation with lexical competence, implying that training on the use of VLS based on the characteristics of each student is extremely important.

5   Conclusion

According to complex dynamic system theory, Indonesia's Chinese learners' spoken vocabulary is a complex dynamic system that is affected to varying degrees by internal and external resources of the learners' vocabulary system. As the influence of external resources, it leads to different development trends, which presents nonlinear development characteristics of their vocabulary. Therefore, the study vocabulary capacity of learners is assessed using a multidimensional and multi-factor approach.

By quantifying this study: First, after studying for 3–4 years, Indonesian learners show significant development in spoken Chinese, but the development trend is not the same for each dimension. As we know in lexical variation, it develops steadily, but in lexical accuracy it develops slowly, and in lexical sophistication it develops stagnantly. Second, the development of lexical variation has higher correlation with lexical sophistication and lexical errors, especially in intermediate and advanced grades. Third, learners' learning strategies have different implications for lexical competence at different stages, with metacognitive strategies and overall VLS using frequency having the most influence on Indonesian learners' Chinese vocabulary.

Based on these findings, there are several pedagogical implications for Chinese vocabulary teaching. First, in order to improve learners, particularly in the use of natural dialogue, school teachers can begin with meta-cognitive vocabulary learning strategies, guiding learners to form a more systematic and effective learning strategy through monitoring and self-management. Second, teachers can provide more language application training and create more Chinese social platforms. Third, teachers should raise students' awareness of the importance of understanding and using high-level vocabulary.

Acknowledgement. This work is supported by the Foundation of Center for Language Education and Cooperation (21YH019CX2). We are grateful to the workmates for their comments.
*Corresponding Author: Huanhai Fang, School of Foreign Studies, Suqian University.

References

1. Meara, P. : The Dimensions of Lexical Competence. In G. Brown, M. Kirsten and J. Williams (eds.). Performance and Competence in Second Language Acquisition., Cambridge University Press, Cambridge, 35–53 (1996)
2. Chapelle, C.: Construct definition and validity inquiry in SLA research. In: Bachman, L.F., Cohen, A.D. (eds.) Interfaces Between Second Language Acquisition and Language Testing Research, pp. 32–70. Cambridge University Press, Cambridge (1999)
3. Henriksen, B.: Three dimensions of vocabulary development. Stud. Second. Lang. Acquis. 21(2), 303–317 (1999)
4. Meara, P.: Designing vocabulary tests for English, Spanish and other languages. In Butler, C.S. de los Gómez-González, M., Doval-Suárez, S.M.(Eds) The Dynamics of language use, Benjamins, Amsterdam, pp. 271–286 (2005)
5. Qian, D.D.: Investigating the relationship between vocabulary knowledge and academic reading performance: an assessment perspective. Lang. Learn. 52(3), 513–536 (2002)
6. Zhang, W., Wu, X.: A cognitive psychological model of L2 lexical competence development in the classroom setting. Mod. Foreign Lang. 4, 373–384 (2003)
7. Dóczi,B. and Kormos, J.: Longitudinal Developments in Vocabulary Knowledge and Lexical Organization. Oxford University Press,New York, 144 (2016)
8. Huang, L., Qian, X.: An inquiry into Chinese learners' knowledge of productive vocabulary: a quantitative study. Chinese Lang. Learn. 01, 56–61 (2003)
9. Wu, J.: Research on lexical richness development in CSL writing by English native speakers. Chinese Teach. World 01, 129–142 (2016)
10. Zhou, L.: A longitudinal study on the dynamic development of CSL learners' lexical semantic system. Chinese Teach. World 34(01), 98–114 (2020)

11. Sun, X.: A study on development model of productive vocabulary of foreign students. J. Res. Educ. Ethnic Minor. **4**, 121–123 (2009)
12. Chen, M., Li, Y.: Complexity of Chinese oral speeches by Korean native speakers. Appl. Linguis. **4**, 61–70 (2016)
13. Ding, A., Xiao, X.: On the development of oral lexical competence of Italian Chinese language learners. Chinese Teach. World **30**(02), 239–252 (2016)
14. Surinah: A Study on the Development of Indonesian Students' Lexical Competency in Chinese Language Learning Based on Complex Dynamic Perspective, Ph.D. Dissertation, Xiamen Univesity, 119 (2020)
15. Zheng, Y.: Longitudinal study on free productive vocabulary development from the dynamic systems theory perspective. Foreign Lang. Teach. Res. **47**(2), 276–289 (2015)
16. Lu, X.: The relationship of lexical richness to the quality of ESL learners' oral narratives. Mod. Lang. J. **96**(2), 190–208 (2012)
17. Shen, H.: Size and strength: Written vocabulary acquisition among advanced learners. Chinese Teach. World **29**(02), 71–85 (2009)
18. Mo, D.: A comparison of the effects of different input modality on incidental vocabulary acquisition. Chinese Lang. Learn. **06**, 87–95 (2017)
19. Spoelman, M., Verspoor, M.: Dynamic patterns in development of accuracy and complexity: a longitudinal case study in the acquisition of Finnish. Appl. Linguis. **31**(4), 532–553 (2010)
20. Caspi, T., Wander, L.: A dynamic perspective on L2 lexical development in academic English. In: Rubén, C., Christián, A., Maria del Mar, T. (eds.), Insights into Non-native Vocabulary Teaching and Learning. Multilingual Matters, Bristol, pp. 41–58 (2010)
21. Van Geert, P.: A dynamic systems model of cognitive and language growth. Psychol. Rev. **98**(1), 3–53 (1991)
22. LarsenFreeman, D.: The emergence of complexity, fluency and accuracy in the oral and written production of five Chinese learners of Chinese learners of English. Appl. Linguis. **27**(4), 590–619 (2006)
23. Schmitt, N.: Vocabulary learning strategies. In: McCarthy, M. (ed.) Vocabulary: Description, Acquisition and Pedagogy, pp. ,199–227. Cambridge University, Cambridge (1997)

Effectiveness of Strategy Instruction on EFL Learners' Listening Comprehension via a Web-based Virtual Community of Practice

Ping Liu[1] and Wen Zhou[2](✉)

[1] Foreign Languages College, Zhejiang Wanli University, Ningbo, China
[2] School of International Studies, NingboTech University, Ningbo, China
allwin_idc@sina.com

Abstract. For EFL learners, the mastery of listening skill comes first before the skills of speaking, reading and writing in the process of language acquisition. Listening strategy instruction, with the establishment and implementation of a web-based virtual community of practice, is helpful to EFL learners' improvement on their listening comprehension. In this empirical study of 62 students for two semesters, through the analyses of the results of two questionnaire surveys and the scores of three tests, the following conclusions could be drawn: strategy instruction is effective in improving EFL learners' listening comprehension, 2) there is a positive relationship between listening strategy training and listening proficiency, and 3) a web-based virtual community of practice could be an effective and efficient way of enhancing language proficiency, especially in the COVID-19 pandemic era.

Keywords: Strategy instruction · EFL learners · Web-based virtual community of practice

1 Introduction

Listening comprehension is a fundamental skill for EFL learners. The mastery of listening skills comes first before the skills of speaking, reading and writing in the process of language acquisition. [1] Ever since Joan Rubin published her research on language learning strategy research in 1975 [2], issues related to language/listening learning strategy have attracted many well-known scholars [3–6]. Although there have been debates over the effectiveness of explicit listening strategy instruction [7, 8], many researches, especially in recent years, support the positive effects of listening strategy instruction on EFL learners' listening comprehension [2, 9].

The COVID-19 pandemic has been changing the learning processes and practices drastically. Thanks to the availability of Internet and web-based social and learning platforms, lockdown of a city or even a whole country, although does shut down schools and university campuses, does not mean the end of students' learning process. With the

Supported by a teaching reform research project from the Department of Education, Zhejiang Province (Project No. jg20190584).

help of some web-based virtual community of practice, students could still improve their language proficiency. The term "community of practice" was first used by Jean Lave and Etienne Wenger in 1991, which was later defined as "groups of people who share a concern or a passion for something they do and learn how to do it better as they interact regularly" [10]. Over the years, more and more researchers have become interested in the concept of CoP [11, 12]. When CoP is expanded online, new practices emerge in curriculum innovation in nursing [13], STEM [14], and higher education as a whole [15]. Based on all these researches, this study aims to evaluate the effectiveness of strategy instruction on EFL learners' listening comprehension via a Web-based Virtual CoP.

2 Methodology

2.1 Samples

Participating in this research were two classes (altogether 62 students) of English majors (aged between 17 and 19) of Year 2019 at Zhejiang Wanli University, with 30 students in the control class (26 girls and 4 boys) and 32 in the experimental class (26 girls and 6 boys). The majority of the students come from Zhejiang Province, indicating that they have the similar social and cultural backgrounds. At the beginning of the research, both classes had similar English listening proficiency, which could be proved by statistical analysis of scores obtained through a listening diagnostic test (Test 1) done when the students just began their studies.

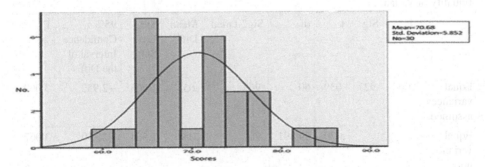

Fig. 1. Normal distribution curve of control class scores in Test 1

As is shown in Figs. 1 & 2 and Table 1 above, the mean scores of the two classes are the almost same: out of the total 100 points, the control class is 70.68 points and the experimental class 70.63 points. Besides, according to the Independent Samples T Test in Table 2 below, Levene's Test for Equality of Variances F = 0.08, P = 0.927, so the variance is neat (equal). In the Equal Variance Assumed, t = 0.039, Sig(2-tailed) = 0.969 (>0.05), 95% Confidence Interval of Difference is between −2.952 and 3.069, which includes 0 and shows that there is no significant difference with 0. Therefore, there is no distinct difference in students' listening comprehension between the two classes at the start of the research.

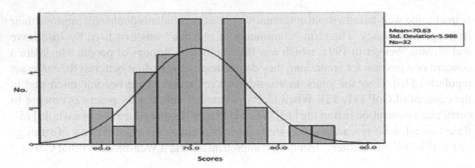

Fig. 2. Normal distribution curve of experimental class scores in Test 1

Table 1. Group statistics of Test 1.

Class	No	Mean	Std. Deviation	Std. Error Mean
Control class	30	70.68	5.852	1.068
Experimental class	32	70.63	5.988	1.059

Table 2. Independent samples test of Test 1

Levene's Test for Equality of Variances		t-test for Equality of Means							
F	Sig	t	df	Sig2-tailed	Mean Diff	Std. Error Diff	95% Confidence Interval of the Diff	F
Equal variances assumed	.008	.927	.039	60	.969	.058	1.505	−2.952	3.069
Equal variances not assumed			.039	59.891	.969	.058	1.504	−2.950	3.067

2.2 Materials and Instruments

This research is based on a quantitative analysis of a questionnaire (done twice) and the scores of three tests.

The Questionnaire. The questionnaire of the research is based on O'MAlley and CHamot's framework (1990), in which the 26 strategies are divided into three categories: Metacognitive strategies (10 in number), Cognitive strategies (11) and Social/Affective

Table 3. Reliability of the questionnaire.

	Cronbach's Alpha	No. of Items
The whole Questionnaire	.842	26
Metacognitive strategies	.761	10
Cognitive strategies	.686	11
Social/Affective strategies	.626	5

strategies (5) [5]. The following are the results of the reliability of the Questionnaire Table 3:

The Cronbach alpha data of the whole Questionnaire is 0.842, and that of Metacognitive strategy is 0.761. Both of them are more than 0.7. Cognitive strategy Cronbach alpha data is 0.686, and Social/Affective strategy Cronbach alpha data is 0.626, being a little bit less than 0.7, but much more than 0.5. According to Qin Xiaoqing, while the generally acceptable data of Cronbach alpha should not be less than 0.7, the data of Cronbach alpha tend to be lower when measuring emotional or affective factors, and the less-than −0.7 data are also acceptable [16]. Therefore, it can be concluded that the Questionnaire is reliable.

All the 62 students are required to fill out the Questionnaire twice. The first was done before Test 1, when the students had just entered the university. The second was after 32 teaching weeks, when the students had learned listening courses for two semesters and was going to take Test 3 (final exam of Semester 2). All strategies in the Questionnaire are written in the first person. A five-point scale is used, in which "1" indicates "never or almost never true of me", "2" for "usually not true of me", "3" for "sometimes true of me", "4" for "usually true of me", and "5" for "always or almost always true of me". The numbers they selected indicate the frequency at which they used a strategy. Thus, the larger the number is, the more frequent they use the strategies. For each survey, all 62 copies of the Questionnaire were collected.

The Three Tests. The scores of three tests are used in this study: Test 1, as has been shown earlier, demonstrates the students' initial level of listening comprehension; Test 2 is the final exam for Semester 1 (after 16 weeks of listening course learning), designed to show the effects of "blind" strategy training; Test 3 is the final exam for Semester 2 (after 32 weeks of studies), designed to show the effectiveness of "informed" listening strategy training with the help of web-based virtual CoPs.

Variables. In terms of teaching contents, both classes were using the same text book with similar teaching schedules. However, students in the control class were taught in the traditional model while those in the experimental class were trained with some listening strategies. For example, they were asked to investigate the background information of the listening materials, study in groups, write learning summary, etc.. But in Semester 1, they were not explained the significance of these activities by the teacher. Thus, through analyzing the scores of Test 2, the effects of the "blind" strategy training can be determined. In Semester 2, "informed" strategy training was provided to the experimental class, when the teacher explained the significance of learning strategies to the students, and encouraged and guided them to use the strategies in their web-based virtual CoPs. Thus, a typical teaching session is like what Table 4 displays:

Table 4. A typical teaching session.

Learning materials	The control class	The experimental class
Warming-up exercise	Teacher introduces information about London traffic conditions, Hampstead, etc. (10 min)	Students introduce information about London that they've collected before class. (10 min)
Dialogue 1	Students listen to the dialogue twice and finish exercises. Teacher checks their answers. (5 min)	Students listen twice, meanwhile taking notes. Then students discuss and finish exercises in group. (8 min)
Dialogue 2	Students listen twice and finish exercises. Students read out their answers. Teacher corrects them. (10 min)	Students listen twice while taking notes, then imitate the dialogue to make up a new one. (8 min)
Passage	Teacher introduces the information of Barbican Centre, tourism and entertainments in London. (5 min) Teacher explains vocabulary. (5 min) Students listen to the passage twice and finishing the exercises (5 min) Teaching corrects students' exercises. (5 min)	Acting as a guide and some tourists, Students introduce the tourism and entertainments about London they've collected. (5 min) Students listen to the passage (1 min) Students discuss in groups about the "unknown points" of the passage and the exercises (5 min) In turn each group read out one answer of the exercises, and tell reasons of their choice, and meanwhile each group tell their guessing results of "unknown points", teacher corrects the answer (8 min)

*based on the textbook X. Shi. *A Listening Course.* 2017

Learning Strategy Training via Web-Based Virtual CoP. On a voluntary basis, students in the experimental class were divided into learning groups of 4 at the beginning of the first semester. Most group members were dormitory roommates, which made it easier for them to collaborate in their studies. One of the group activities they were asked to finish before class was to investigate background information of the topics in texts. In each semester, each group was responsible for reporting the background information of two topics, which they presented in class by the means of debate, role-play, speech, etc. within 10 min. This is a kind of the "top-down" process training, which allows students to learn to employ background knowledge or information in memory in comprehending the meaning of a message [3]. The "top-down" process training lasts 32 teaching weeks (two semesters), while in Semester 2, most of the preparations were done through each group's web-based virtual CoP.

The COVID-19 pandemic led to campus lockdown for the first two months of Semester 2, and the study groups in the experimental class, now dispersed in cities, towns and villages around the province, had to set up web-based virtual CoPs. Most of them (6 out of 8) were using the popular WeChat platform, where they could easily form chat groups and share questions, views, materials (text, picture, voice, video and even web page links) in it. Two remaining study groups used QQ chat groups, where they collaborated as well as the other groups. In these web-based virtual CoPs, besides the Cognitive strategy training mentioned above, students were encouraged to undergo Metacognitive strategy training: making their own after-class listening plans and sharing them among group members, monitoring each other's listening process and finding out obstacles that prevent their understanding, evaluating each other's behaviors in group study, which became part of their formative evaluation. Thus, students' self-evaluation, peer evaluation and teachers' evaluation were organically combined and diversified students' academic evaluation, which could reflect students' academic development more objectively [17].

3   Results and Analysis

3.1   The Questionnaire

The questionnaire results include the average usage frequency of the 26 strategies in O'Malley and Chamot's framework (1990) [5] (Table 5), a synchronic comparison of the strategy usage frequency between the two classes in the first and second questionnaire surveys (Figs. 3 & 4), and a diachronic comparison of the usage frequencies survey results in the two classes (Figs. 5 & 6).

Table 5. Average strategy usage frequency in questionnaire.

Results Strategy	The control class		The experimental class	
	Survey 1	Survey 2	Survey 1	Survey 2
1	2.9	2.6	2.4	3.3
2	3.1	3	2.7	3.8
3	3.3	3.2	2.8	3.8
4	2.8	3	2.7	3.6
5	3.2	3.7	2.9	3.9
6	2.6	**2.6**	**1.9**	**3.6**

(*continued*)

Synchronic Comparison. The following is synchronic comparison of the strategy usage frequency between the two classes in the first and second questionnaire surveys.

Table 5. (*continued*)

Results Strategy	The control class		The experimental class	
	Survey 1	Survey 2	Survey 1	Survey 2
7	2.5	2.8	2.3	3.9
8	3.4	4	3.4	3.8
9	3.6	4.1	3.5	3.9
10	3.3	3.3	3	4.1
11	3.2	3.7	3.2	3.8
12	3.5	3.7	3.3	3.8
13	3	2.6	2.3	3.7
14	3.3	3.6	3.3	4.1
15	3.3	3.4	3.5	4.2
16	3.2	3.4	3.3	3.9
17	3.1	3.2	3.4	4
18	3	3.1	3.2	3.6
19	3.3	**2.5**	2.8	**3.9**
20	3.3	3.6	3.5	3.8
21	3	3.6	3.5	4
22	2.9	4.1	3.5	3.8
23	3	2.7	2.8	3.8
24	3.2	2.9	2.7	3.8
25	2.6	2.6	2.6	3.8
26	2.3	**2.8**	2.8	**4.4**

* Bold numbers will be quoted in the following analysis

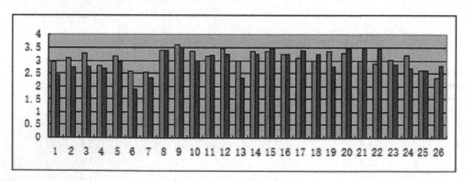

Fig. 3. Strategy usage frequency for the FIRST questionnaire (left bars indicating results of the control class, and right bars the experimental class)

In Fig. 3, it is obvious that at the beginning of the research, there is not much difference in the average usage frequency of listening learning strategies between the two classes. Relatively speaking, students in the control class are better in using Metacognitive strategies than those in the experimental class. However, students in the experimental class are slightly better in using Social/Affective strategies.

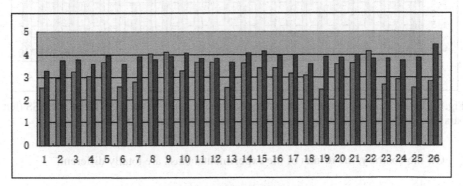

Fig. 4. Strategy usage frequency for the SECOND questionnaire (left bars indicating results of the control class, and right bars the experimental class)

Figure 4 shows very different results. It is very obvious that in almost every item, the usage frequency in the experimental class is higher than that in the control class, especially in Strategy Items No. 6, No. 19 and No. 26. Item No. 6 is the strategy of plan-making, the average usage frequency of the control class is 2.6 and that in the experimental class is 3.6, and the difference means students in the experimental class are much better in making learning plans. Item No. 19 is about dividing the sense groups of listening materials, which is one of the most important listening strategies. The average usage frequency in the control class is 2.5, and that in the experimental class is 3.9. The differences show that students in the experimental class master better the strategies after one year's training. Item No. 26 is about group study, the average results are 2.8 for the control class and 4.4 for the experimental class, which means that after 32 teaching week's training, students in the experimental class participate more frequently in group studies than those in the control class.

Diachronic Comparison. Revealing as the synchronic comparison seems, a diachronic comparison of the usage frequencies survey results in the two classes turns out to be more telling.

Obviously, there is not much difference between the two times survey results in the control class. That means even after two semesters of English major study, students in the control class still use the same learning methods as before in their listening. They still like to enrich their extracurricular listening learning by listening to English songs and watching English movies, and they still think focusing-attention is the most useful strategy in listening.

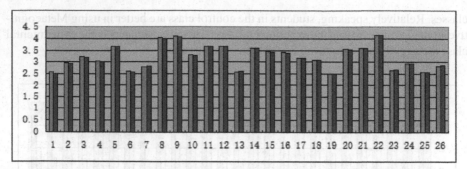

Fig. 5. Diachronic comparison of the strategy usage frequency of the **CONTROL CLASS** (left bars indicating results of the first questionnaire survey, right bars are that of the second)

On the contrary, the results of the experimental class are totally different.

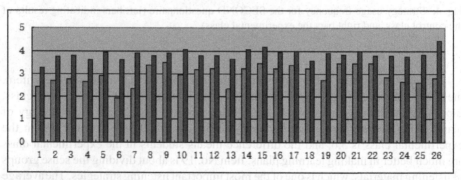

Fig. 6. Diachronic comparison of the strategy usage frequency in the **EXPERIMENTAL CLASS** (left bars indicating results of the first questionnaire survey, and right bars are that of the second)

It is very obvious that there is much difference in the usage frequency between the first and second surveys in the experimental class. The biggest changes are in strategy Items No. 6 and No. 26. In the Questionnaire, Item No. 6 is about making the study plan. It is mentioned previously that plan-making is one of the most important strategies applied in the experimental class. It could be seen that the average usage frequency for this strategy from the first survey is 1.9, and the result for the second survey is 3.6, which means after the strategy training, students in the experimental class realize the importance of plan-making, and use this strategy in their studies consciously.

Item No. 26 is about the strategy of group study. Students in the experimental class formed study groups in Semester 1, but they followed the teacher's instructions "blindly". In Semester 2, the teacher emphasized the importance of learning strategy training, such as background information investigation and peer evaluation among group members in web-based virtual CoPs, which seem to take effect. The results show that in the first survey, the average usage frequency for this item is 2.8, and for the second survey is 4.4, which means that students in the experimental class have benefited from this strategy and they would like to use it in their studies.

3.2 The Tests

As the analysis of the Questionnaire results shows, students in the experimental class used listening strategies more frequently than those in the control class. Does this make any difference in the students' test scores? As Test 1 has already been discussed in the *Samples* part, the following analysis will focus on Tests 2 and 3. The results of Independent sample T-test of these two tests are as follows.

Table 6. Group statistics of Tests 2 and 3

Test	Class	No	Mean	Std. Deviation	Std. Error Mean
Test 2	Control class	30	74.3833	8.59700	1.56959
	Experimental class	32	78.2813	9.10152	1.60894
Test 3	Control class	30	78.9000	8.89537	1.62406
	Experimental class	32	87.3750	5.49927	.97214

Table 7. Independent samples test of Tests 2 and 3

		Levene's Test for Equality of Variances		t-test for Equality of Means						95% Confidence Interval of the Diff	
		F	Sig	t	df	Sig. 2-tailed	Mean Diff	Std. Error Diff		Lower	Upper
Test 2	Equal variances assumed	.105	.747	-1.731	60	.089	-3.898	2.252		-8.402	.607
	Equal variances not assumed			-1.734	59.996	.088	-3.898	2.247		-8.394	.598
Test 3	Equal variances assumed	4.88	.031	-4.544	60	.000	-8.475	1.865		-12.206	-4.744
	Equal variances not assumed			-4.478	47.768	.000	-8.475	1.892		-12.281	-4.669

Analysis of Test 2. Figures 7 & 8 show that students' scores of Test 2 in both classes are normally distributed. The average score of the control class is 74.38 (Fig. 7), and that of the experimental class is 78.28 (Fig. 8). Table 7 shows the Equal Variance Sig (2-tailed) $= 0.088$, which is still slightly greater than 0.05. But the Sig (2-tailed) of Test 1 is 0.969

(Table 2), which is much greater than 0.05. The Sig (2-tailed) of Test 1 (0.969) is also much greater than that of Test 2 (0.088). So, it can be concluded that in Test 2, there is some difference in the students' listening levels between the two classes, though it is not so obvious. As has been pointed out, in Semester 1, the listening strategy training in the experimental class was "blind": students were trained to use some strategies but were not informed of the significance of the usage of the strategies. The test results confirm that the blind training of strategies do help students improve their listening proficiency, but the space of improvement is quite limited.

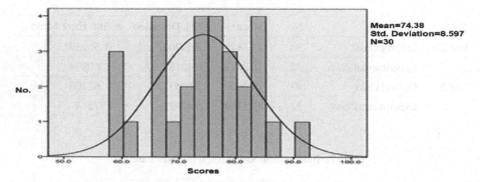

Fig. 7. Normal distribution curve of control class scores in Test 2

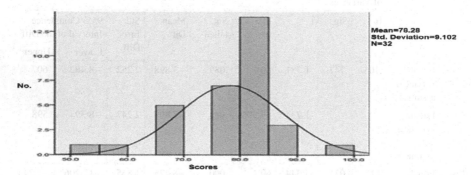

Fig. 8. Normal distribution curve of experimental class scores in Test 2

Analysis of Test 3. Figures 9 & 10 show that students' scores of Test 3 in both classes also appear normal distribution. In Table 6, the average score in the control class is 78.9, and that of the experimental class is about 87.38. In Table 7, Equal Variance Assumed, Sig (2-tailed) = 0.000(<0.05), which means that in Test 3, the difference between the two classes is very obvious.

As has been discussed earlier, in Semester 2, the listening strategy training in the experimental class was "informed": the students were told the importance and signif-icance of the strategies they were asked to use. The figures confirm that this kind of training has achieved remarkable effects. Table 8 shows that the Standard Error Mean of the three tests in the control class and the Std. Error Mean of Tests 1 and 2 in the experimental class are all greater than 1, which mean that the difference between the classmates in the same class is large; but the Standard Error Mean of the experimental class in Test 3 is only 0.97214, which is less than 1. It means the difference between the classmates in the experimental class is becoming much narrower after two-semester's strategy training. The students in the experimental class have improved their listening proficiency. The strategy training benefits almost everyone in the class.

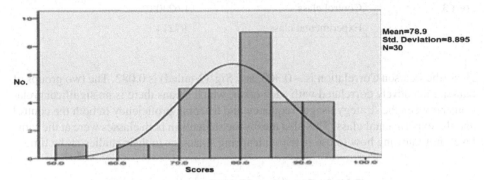

Fig. 9. Normal distribution curve of control class scores in Test 3

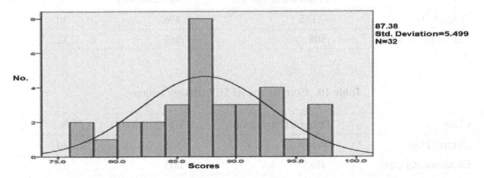

Fig. 10. Normal distribution curve of experimental class scores in Test 3

Correlational Analyses of Strategy Usage Frequency and Listening Level. The analyses above conclude that students in the experimental class use listening strategies more frequently than those in the control class, and that they have got better listening proficiency after 32 weeks' studies. Is there any relation between the strategy usage frequency and listening level? The Pearson Correlation method is run here in order to find the inner relationship between the frequency and the scores of Test 1 and Test 3 in the two classes.

Correlations before and after Strategy Training. Table 9 shows that the Pearson Correlation in the control class is −0.135, and Sig. (2-tailed) is 0.476. In the experimental

Table 8. Standard error mean of the three Tests

	Class	Standard Error Mean
Test 1	Control class	1.068
	Experimental class	1.059
Test 2	Control class	1.56959
	Experimental class	1.60894
Test 3	Control class	1.62406
	Experimental class	.97214

class, the Pearson Correlation is −0.308, and Sig. (2-tailed) is 0.082. The two groups of data are negatively correlated with each other, which means there is no significant relations between the strategy usage frequency and listening proficiency in both the control and the experimental class. This also means the students in both classes were at the same level, not knowing how to use listening learning strategies in their studies at the time.

Table 9. Correlations BEFORE strategy training.

Class	Pearson Correlation	Sig. (2-tailed)	N
Control class	−.135	.476	30
Experimental class	.308	.082	32

Table 10. Correlations AFTER strategy training.

Class	Pearson Correlation	Sig. (2-tailed)	N
Control class	−.109	.565	30
Experimental class	.488**	.005	32

Table 10 shows the correlations when the students in both classes had had two semesters' (32 weeks') listening studies. In the control class the Pearson Correlation is −0.109, Sig. (2-tailed) is 0.565, which mean there is still no significant relations between strategy usage frequency and listening proficiency in this class. However, in the experimental class, the Pearson Correlation is 0.488**, Sig. (2-tailed) is 0.005. According to Qin Xiaoqing (2003: 238), when the Pearson Correlation is between ± 0.40 and ± 0.70, it means the two groups of numbers are significantly positively correlated with each other [18]. So, it can be concluded that when the students in the experimental class have finished their 32-week's strategy training, they've learned the methods of using listening strategies in their listening learning.

Table 11. Correlations of metacognitive, cognitive and social/affective strategy.

Strategy	Pearson Correlation	Sig. (2-tailed)	N
The Metacognitive strategy	.468**	.007	32
The Cognitive strategy	.202	.267	32
The Social/Affective strategy	.515**	.003	32

Correlations Between the Listening Level and Learning Strategies in the Question-naire, there are 3 categories of learning strategies, with the first 10 being metacogni-tive strategies, the next 11 belonging to cognitive strategies and the last 5 belonging to social/affective strategies. The following are the correlational analyses of the con-nections between the scores of test 3 in the experimental class and the average usage frequencies of the three categories of learning strategies.

The data in Table 11 show the Pearson correlation coefficient of the Metacognitive strategy is 0.468**, Sig. (2-tailed) is 0.007, which mean that the scores of Test 3 of the experimental class are significantly correlative to the Metacognitive strategy training, such as plan-making, and it shows that this kind of training is effective.

However, in this table, the Pearson correlation coefficient of the cognitive strategy is 0.202, Sig. (2-tailed) is 0.267. According to Qin Xiaoqing, when it is less than 0.4, it shows there is not significant correlation [18]. So, the scores of Test 3 of the experimental class are negatively correlated with the usage frequency of the cognitive strategy. But the Pearson correlation coefficient of the experimental class is -0.308. Comparing the two data (0.267 and -0.308), it is very clear that the students in the class have tried to use some cognitive strategies in their studies, though the effects are not so obvious.

The Pearson correlation coefficient of the Social/Affective strategy is 0.515**, Sig. (2-tailed) is 0.003, which show the highest relevance between the strategy training and the listening proficiency. Considering the many activities via web-based virtual CoPs in the experimental class, this result is not surprising at all.

Therefore, after the strategy training, students have learned to use some useful strate-gies in their EFL listening comprehension course. Among the strategies, group study via web-based virtual CoPs is the most helpful one. Some other strategies like plan-making are also useful.

4   Conclusions and Discussions

The present research focuses on the listening strategies training for EFL learners. The following findings could be obtained from the data and analysis:

First, strategy training is very helpful for students to improve their listening pro-ficiency, especially with the help of well-running CoPs (web-based if necessary). The Pearson correlation analyses in the research prove that there are positive correlations between strategy training and the improvement of listening level.

Second, strategy training should be informed. The data analyses of Test 2 and Test 3 in the experimental class show, there are obvious different results between "blind" and "informed" training of strategies. Only when students are informed of the significance of strategy training and the methods of strategy applications can they achieve the best results in learning.

Third, a web-based virtual CoP could be an effective and efficient way of enhancing language proficiency, especially in the COVID-19 pandemic era, when face-to-face communication becomes impossible.

References

1. Owolewa, O.O., Olu, O.: Effects of listening strategies' instruction on students' attitude to listening. Eur. J. Educ. Stud. **3**, 624–642 (2017)
2. Rubin, J.: What the "good language learner" can teach us. TESOL Q. **9**, 41–51 (1975)
3. Rubin, J.: A review of second language listening comprehension research. Mod. Lang. J. **78**(2), 199–221 (1994)
4. O'Malley, J.M., Chamot, A.U., Küpper, L.: Listening comprehension strategies in second language acquisition. Appl. Linguis. **10**(4), 418–437 (1989)
5. O'Malley, J.M., Chamot, A.U.: Learning Strategies in Second Language Acquisition. Cambridge University Press, London (1990)
6. Rubin, J., Thompson, I.: How to be a More Successful Language Learner. Foreign Language Teaching and Research Press, Beijing (2009)
7. Cross, J.: Effects of listening strategy instruction on news videotext comprehension. Lang. Teach. Res. **13**, 151–176 (2009)
8. Milliner, B., Dimoski, B.: Explicit listening strategy training for EFL learners. J. Asia TEFL **16**, 833–859 (2019)
9. Al-Shammari, H.G.: The impact of strategy instruction on Iraqi EFL learners' listening comprehension and metacognitive strategy use. MEXTESOL J. **44**, 1–12 (2020)
10. Lave, J., Wenger, E.: Communities of Practice: Learning, Meaning, and Identity. Cambridge University Press, Cambridge (2011)
11. Hightower, G.L.: A Community of practice for enriched English language development. Doctoral dissertation, Arizona State University, Arizona (2009)
12. Gull, K. A.: Mainstream teachers' perspectives on secondary, English learner engagement in inclusive classrooms: communities of practice. Doctoral dissertation, Hood College, Frederick, Maryland (2021)
13. McAllister, M., Moyle, W.: An online learning community for clinical educators. Nurse Educ. Pract. **6**(2), 106–111 (2006)
14. Russell, L.: Can learning communities boost success of women and minorities in STEM? Evidence from the Massachusetts Institute of technology. Econ. Educ. Rev. **61**, 98–111 (2017)
15. Swichard, F.L.: Creating a sense of community in higher education online learning environments through asynchronous communication using video and social learning platform. Doctoral dissertation, Evangel University, Springfield, Missouri (2020)
16. Qin, X.: Methods of Questionnaire in Foreign Language Teaching. Foreign Language Teaching and Research Press, Beijing (2009)
17. Zhang, B.: Construction of diversified academic evaluation system of history teaching theory. Adv. Higher Educ. **4**, 185–186 (2020)
18. Qin, X.: Quantitative data analysis in foreign language teaching research. Huazhong University of Science and Technology, Wuhan (2003)

Course Homework Reform in Universities Based on Extended Reality

Jinrong Fu[1], Yiwen Liu[1,2,3(✉)], Chunqiao Mi[1,2,3], Xiaoning Peng[1,2,3], and Jianhua Xiao[1,2,3]

[1] School of Computer and Artificial Intelligence, Huaihua University, Huaihua 418000, Hunan, People's Republic of China
lyw@hhtc.edu.cn
[2] Key Laboratory of Wuling-Mountain Health Big Data Intelligent Processing and Application in Hunan Province Universities, Huaihua 418000, Hunan, People's Republic of China
[3] Key Laboratory of Intelligent Control Technology for Wuling-Mountain Ecological Agriculture in Hunan Province, Huaihua 418000, Hunan, People's Republic of China

Abstract. In view of the serious issues commonly existing with coursework in Chinese universities at present, such as its original function weakening or being suppressed, its form being too abstract and lack of elaborate design. In order to resolve these problems observed in usual homework, this paper proposes a reform scheme for cloud coursework based on Extended Reality and Bloom model. It mainly includes five key parts, such as interaction, scene, comprehensive evaluation, digital twin and data analysis. In addition, the reform's effectiveness is illustrated through amassing and comparing the feedback of college students for teaching.

Keywords: Extended Reality · Cloud Platform · Virtual Reality · Mixed Reality · Augmented Reality

1 Introduction

The Implementation Opinions on the Construction of First-class Undergraduate Curriculum (JG [2019] No. 8) issued by the Ministry of education pointed out that "courses are the core elements of talent training, and the quality of courses directly determines the quality of talent training". The common "shortboard, weakness and bottleneck" in Chinese universities exist in its curriculum. However, the function weakening and function inhibition [1] exposed by the course homework that has not been carefully designed all show that it has become a "short board among the short boards" [2]. The main reason is that Chinese colleges and universities do not pay enough attention to the course homework, do not realize the importance of homework, and lack the careful design of homework, which makes the homework guide learning, consolidate knowledge, train students to find problems The function of analyzing and solving problems is infinitely weakened. In contrast to the center of higher education in the world today, American

W. Hong and Y. Weng (Eds.): ICCSE 2022, CCIS 1813, pp. 281–288, 2023.
https://doi.org/10.1007/978-981-99-2449-3_25

colleges and universities with their "scientific, reasonable and effective homework system" [3] enable students to always learn the most valuable information and continuously improve the quality of talent training.

The combination of XR technology and course homework can make abstract concepts more intuitive, dynamic and concrete display, so that students can experience the knowledge scene and logical reasoning of three-dimensional application in the learning process, break through the limitation of time and space, and create an immersive learning space of "unity of body and environment" [4].

2 Related Work

2.1 Extended Reality

Extended Reality (XR) is the development trend of virtual technology in the future. It includes Virtual Reality (VR), Mixed Reality (MR), Augmented Reality (AR) and everything between them [5]. The following Figure (Fig. 1) shows the characteristics and differences among VR, MR and AR.

Comparison Item	Virtual Reality	Mixed Reality	Augmented Reality
Common display devices	VR glasses ,HMD helmet	MR glasses, Holographic projection	Phone,Projector
Common auxiliary interactive equipment	Handle, eye tracker, motion capture equipment	Hand capture	Not necessarily required
Current limitations	Fixed display space layout and positioning equipment are required	The software needs to be installed in the user's mobile phone in advance	The sense of immersion is weak, the motion capture is unstable.
Main advantages at present	Widely used and mature technology	It has broad development prospects, is not limited by space, and has a better user experience	It is not limited by space, portable, low cost and easy to promote

Fig.1. Comparison Among VR/MR/AR

Since Ivan Sutherland, the father of computer graphics, designed the first head mounted AR and VR combined display (HMD: Head Mounted Display) in 1968, it has always been human's dream to recreate a world. Although the concept of XR was put forward many years ago, it has been limited by computer software and hardware, and XR technology has not been well developed and applied. Nowadays, the development of digital twins, computer graphics, human-computer interaction and other technologies have paved the way for the advent of the virtual world. XR technology has gradually entered the public's vision and has been applied into various fields. Based on the increasing popularity of Virtual Reality (VR) and Augmented Reality (AR) applications, on March 7th, 2022, Professor Georgios Minopoulos and Professor Konstantinos E. Psannis revealed the necessity of implementing Extended Reality (XR) to users and proposed a simplified Tangible XR system to solve Opportunities and Challenges of Tangible XR Applications for 5G Networks and Beyond. On February 10th, 2022, Professor BaoTrinh and Professor Gabriel-Miro Muntean proposed a resource management scheme for SDN-MEC supporting XR application, based on deep reinforcement learning.

2.2 Bloom Model

B.J.Bloom, an American educational psychologist, divides educational goals into three fields [6]: cognitive field, emotional field and operational field, which constitute the educational goal system. In the field of cognitive learning, the teaching objectives are divided into eight levels which include memorization, understanding, application, analysis, synthesis, evaluation, design and innovation from the lowest to the highest. Although the traditional course homework also adopts a similar model, Bloom model pays more attention to the role and relationship of these eight levels, which is more in line with the blended teaching structure once required by the "Golden class". Under the background of "Internet+ education", scholars at home and abroad have focused on blended teaching, and the course assignments realized by expanding reality and blended teaching based on Bloom theoretical model will become a new trend of contemporary education development in the future.

3 Research Resign

3.1 Course Homework Based on XR Technology

In the implementation opinions on the construction of first-class undergraduate courses (JG [2019] No. 8), it is pointed out that "eliminating water courses, creating golden courses and building first-class undergraduate courses". Despite the weaknesses, course homework, which combine knowledge, ability and quality, are working as an important fundamental part of first-class undergraduate curriculum construction. They not only consolidate knowledge, but also play a huge role in developing students' comprehensive abilities to solve complex problems and advanced thinking skills. In addition, course homework need to keep pace with the times, with the content being cutting-edge and up-to-date, and the form reflecting interactivity and advancement. In this way, the learning outcomes are personalized and research-oriented, students' individual characteristics are excavated, and their inquiry skills are developed.

The definition of XR emphasizes creating a virtual environment for human-computer interaction, that is, natural-oriented human-computer interaction [7]. This interaction uses people's most direct senses to interact with the virtual world of the computer through instinct. Combining XR technology with course homework, XR technology can show abstract concepts more intuitively and dynamically, and promote data visualization, information interaction and computer education. The course assignment of Principle of Computer Composition realized by Extended Reality (XR) digitizes the physical elements of the physical world under the background of digital twins, realizes the seamless connection between the physical world and the virtual world, and makes students realize the course knowledge of vivid image, virtual real interaction and immersion.

3.2 Course Homework Based on Cloud Platform

Taking Principle of Computer Composition as an example, the main teaching contents are decomposed based on Bloom model. There are some problems in traditional course homework, such as too abstract concept, repeated and rigid content, single evaluation method and so on. Here, we divide the Bloom model into four layers [8]. The first layer is to remember and understand; Application and analysis of the second layer; The third level is comprehensive evaluation; The fourth layer is design and innovation. Based on the characteristics of XR technology, different interaction methods are designed in terms of this course. This paper designs different applications of VR, MR and AR according to the course content and the characteristics of Extended Reality technology, and explores the differences between the three in course feedback, interaction mode [9], display effect and usage scenarios. The specific frame design is shown in Fig. 2.

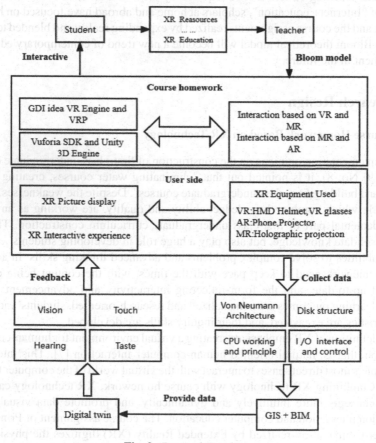

Fig. 2. Research Roadmap

4   Research and Analysis

4.1   Interaction Derived from VR and MR

With cloud XR technology as the core to establish the teaching practice course operation platform, teachers assign tasks before class, and students conduct pre Class Autonomous Learning through cloud XR platform. The "Extended Reality oriented" hybrid teaching mode is adopted, and the hybrid teaching structure based on bloom model is combined with the actual situation of students in the learning process and the content of the course Principle of Computer Composition to design the course homework that meets the requirements of the "golden course". Through Extended Reality (XR) technology, design course assignments that show abstract concepts and build models independently. For example, three-dimensional simulation based on 3D Engine Unity 3D shows the abstract concept, and adding GDI idea VR Engine and VRP can add the three-dimensional data of computer composition structure into the immersive VR and MR interactive system, break the inherent abstract concept, and enable students to achieve the first level of memory and understanding. For example, three-dimensional simulation based on 3D Engine Unity 3D shows the abstract concept, and adding GDI idea VR Engine and VRP can add the three-dimensional data of computer composition structure into the immersive VR and MR interactive system, break the inherent abstract concept, and enable students to achieve the first level of memory and understanding.

4.2   Scenes Presented in AR and MR

The course assignments designed in this paper based on extended reality enable students to basically master basic knowledge points through online learning, while traditional teaching listens to students' expressions and communicates with them in class after the teacher makes up for the shortcomings and key breakthroughs based on the feedback of offline learning results. However, XR-based course work has high interaction and performance, and its core is supported by digital twin technology, which restores teaching model one-to-one and collects students' learning data.MR devices allow students to see real images through semi-permeable lenses, which reflect projections and overlay computer-rendered images onto real images.MR devices can also draw pictures based on real scenes and allow users to see three-dimensional images through left and right eye parallax. Students can control computers through gestures, voice, etc. In the teaching activities of participatory learning, timely targeted examination of the effect of students' learning, and through AR model scenes to guide students to draw analogs and consolidate what they have learned. By starting with the course information and computer model data, the AR technology is used to process the data into text, 2d image, 3D model and video with the help of VuforiaSDK and Unity3D engine to achieve the design and development of online computer hardware model interactive teaching system based on AR technology. After class, according to the different learning effects of each student, after-class homework should be adjusted accordingly, and online and offline learning content and teaching methods should be adjusted according to the learning results of students to maximize the learning effect. In line with level 2 application and analysis and level 4 design and innovation.

4.3 Comprehensive Evaluation

The cloud XR platform records the course work progress and standards achieved by each learning module, pays attention to the students' learning process, evaluates the students' process, evaluates the students' online learning, and evaluates the students' learning effect through examinations and tests. The course assignment is provided with exercises and tests of different difficulties. According to the teaching difficulties, all levels of knowledge of computer composition principles are integrated to make the learning content modular and facilitate students' selective learning according to their own needs. Abstract concepts and abstract contents are expressed through XR technology to enhance students' learning acceptance and deepen knowledge understanding. In the teaching design, from the perspective of students, reflect the student-centered teaching idea, and design the teaching that conforms to the law of students' cognition and the law of multimedia design. During teaching, we should pay close attention to the feedback of students by designing interactive communication, timely adjust the teaching contents and teaching strategies, and guide students to get answers to questions in time through active and active thinking and creative exploration activities. The teacher summarizes and analyzes the problems left in the students' course homework before class, and explains these problems in simple terms in class. After class, teachers arrange homework with different difficulties to facilitate students at different levels to review, consolidate and apply the knowledge points learned, timely grasp the completion of students' homework, reasonably design subsequent teaching contents and teaching methods, and help each student maximize the learning effect from the perspective of teaching students according to their aptitude. The assessment content carries out diversified process evaluation, and evaluates the students' mastery of course knowledge, emotional attitude and comprehensive ability. The learning objectives are evaluated by layers and levels, and the evaluation index system of students' learning effect of advanced mathematics courses and teachers' teaching process is established around the standards of high-level, innovation and challenge of "Golden Courses".

4.4 Combination of XR and Digital Twin

Digital twinning and Extended Reality technology can digitize the physical elements of the physical world. Based on the existing concept of digital twin, GIS + BIM technology [10] is used to collect image data and entity modeling, so as to provide the rapid generation and display of two-dimensional and three-dimensional target data of the course Principle of Computer Composition. The application object of BIM is often a single detail model. Using the function of GIS on the macro scale, the application scope of BIM can be extended to the assignment model of Principle of Computer Composition. GIS + BIM information technology is used to unify and integrate data from multiple sources, different formats and different spatial scales, and to establish management, browsing, query and spatial analysis functions for data and hardware involved in the Von Neumann architecture, CPU operation mode and principle, disk structure, I/O interface and control mode, interrupt mechanism, etc., displaying and analyzing data more effectively and comprehensively, and providing informative and comprehensive basic data support for the operation management and joint scheduling of the cloud XR platform.

4.5 Data Analysis

By analyzing the interview data of more than 1000 registered students, 134 students completed all the surveys. The survey includes the following aspects: the acceptance and access to future use of XR, the proportion of completing assignments independently, how to treat the existing course assignments, the effectiveness of current teaching interaction, the depth of teaching content and so on. As shown in Fig. 3.

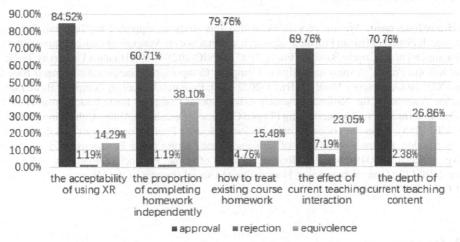

Fig. 3. Statistical table of student data survey

It is assumed that the XR technology-based coursework cloud platform constructed in this paper can play a leading role in course assignments. It helps teachers improve the class attendance and participation rates of Principle of Computer Composition, and the independent completion rate of homework, achieving effective teaching and meeting the standard of of gender equality in the construction of "Golden Course". Students' participation in online independent learning can achieve flexible learning, guide students' learning, consolidate their knowledge, and cultivate their ability to find, analyze and solve problems. It can stimulate the motivation of college students to learn this course, improve their self-learning ability and maximize the learning effect. Based on the Bloom model, we decompose the main teaching contents, integrate the Extended Reality technology with education teaching, change the way teachers "teach" and students "learn", promote the reform and innovation of course assignments, and provide reference for the reform of college computer related courses in theory and practice.

5 Conclusion and Suggestion

At this stage, VR /AR /MR has many problems, such as high investment cost in computer teaching, lack of unified operation and management mechanism and so on. Looking ahead, in the 5G and 6G era, the arrival of cloud XR will subvert the teaching method of computer teaching, reduce and reduce the cost of user terminals, unify the content of teaching resources, and the ultra-high-speed network experience will bring a qualitative and quantitative leap to computer teaching.

It is believed that in the near future, especially with the popularization of 5G communication technology, the reduction of data delay and the increase of bandwidth, as well as the research and development of high-performance graphics processor, the hardware of XR technology can enter the stage of mass production and enter thousands of households like smart phones; Computer science will also usher in a new era with the support of new technology.

Acknowledgement. We are very thankful that this study is supported by Teaching Reform Research Project of Hunan Province" Research and Practice on Assignment Design Framework of Computer Theory Course Based on Fuzzy Test" (H-NJG-2021-0919); Huaihua University Teaching Reform Project" A study on Design of Computer Composition Principles Assignments Based on CC2020 Competency Model "(HHXY-2022-068); Research Project on Computer Basic Education Teaching of the National Research Association of Computer Basic Education in Higher Education Institutions "A Questioning Flipped Classroom Oriented to Ability Cultivation " (2021-AFCEC-255); Project of Hu-nan Provincial Social Science Foundation "Research on the Digital Construction and Inno-vation Path of Zhijiang Peace Culture in the Perspective of Immersive Experience" (21JD046). Scientific Research Project of Hunan Provincial Department of Education (19B447); General program of Humanities and social sciences of the Ministry of Education of China (19YJC880064).

References

1. Wu, Y.: BuildingChina's 'Golden Course.' China Univ. Teach. **12**, 4–9 (2018)
2. Tan, X.: Assignment design in American universities—taking assignment library as an example. Stud. Foreign Educ. **48**(5), 70–83 (2021)
3. Xu, Z.: Introduction and enlightenment of computer programming courses in American colleges and universities. Comput. Educ. **12**, 169–172 (2019)
4. Zhao, Q.: A brief survey on virtual reality technology. Sci. Technol. Rev. **34**(14), 71–75 (2016)
5. Lee, M.J.W., Georgieva, M., Alexander, B., et al.: The State of XR and Immersive Learning Outlook Report:2020Edition. https://immersivelrn.org/ilrn2020/
6. Bloom, B.S., Englehart, M.D., et al.: Taxonomy of educational objectives: the classification of educational goals. Handbook 1. Cognitive domain, pp. 201–207 (1956)
7. Samsung: The Next Hyper--Connected Experience for All. https://chinaflashmarket.com/Upl oads/Report/20200714145321809946.pdf
8. Myrden, A., Chau, T.: Effects of user mental state on EEG-BCI performance. Front. Hum. Neurosci. **9**, 308 (2015). 10.3389hum.2015.00308
9. Rashkov, G., Bobe, A., Fastovets, D., Komarova, M.: Natural image reconstruction from brain waves: a novel visual BCI system with native feedback. bioRxiv. 2019
10. Meouche, R.E., Rezong, M., Hijazi, I.: Integrating and managing BIM in GIS software review. ISPRS-Int. Arch. Photogramm. Remote Sens. Spatial Inf. Sci. **1**(2), 31–34 (2013)

One Case of THOUGHT: Industry-University Converged Education Practice on Open Source

Zhiyi Yu[1], Chao Li[2,3]([✉]), Chaochen Hu[2,3], Zhen Chen[4], Yandong Yao[5], Jiang Wu[6], Hao Wang[5], Jialun Du[5], Min Guo[4], Haoyu Wang[4], Weimin Li[7], Xiu Li[2], Xiaodong Ma[4], Yisong Zhangi[4], and Shuangshou Li[4]

[1] Information Engineering, Beijing University of Posts and Telecommunication, Beijing, China
[2] Department of Computer Science and Technology, Tsinghua University, Beijing, China
li-chao@tsinghua.edu.cn
[3] BNRist, Tsinghua University, Beijing, China
[4] iCenter, Tsinghua University, Beijing, China
[5] R&D, yMatrix Inc., Beijing, China
[6] R&D, Openpie.com., Beijing, China
[7] R&D, Co., Ltd., Beijing 2861, China

Abstract. Nowadays, more and more data are produced in our life. The rapid development of big data and intelligent computing industry has put forward new demands for talents, while colleges and universities with limited industry experiences are striving to promote the talent cultivation. Therefore, the "Innovative Community of Industry-Education Convergence", named THOUGHT (innovaTive Hub for the cO-development of indUstry and hiGHer educaTion) [1], was founded in 2019. THOUGHT aims to improve education cooperation between teaching staff and industry professionals in the related field. The industry-university converged courses are different from technical trainings in enterprises or the speeches of the leaders. In order to cultivate talents, both sides of industry and education cooperate closely in nearly every aspects in course building, e.g., targets, contents, methods, and assessments. And it is necessary to make the courses systematic for learners in terms of knowledge transmission, ability training and value shaping, so as to make them more competent for challenging work in the future of big data and AI. The industry-university converged courses focus on breaking the barrier of the traditional campus. Compared with the emphasis on theories and ideal experiments of traditional campus, it focuses more on practices and applications. Therefore, it needs to rely on a bridge which is convenient for both sides to participate in. Compared with traditional tools of business platforms, open source platforms are better choices. And open source makes it easier for more learners to stand on the giants' shoulders. This paper shares the experience of a case of THOUGHT: the industry-university converged course "Foundamentals and Application of Distributed Data System" jointly built by Tsinghua University and Greenplum open source community. The target, team, organization, structure and contents, practice project, and future work of this course are all introduced in this paper, which may be a vivid case for professors and professionals in this field.

Keywords: Industry-university converged education · Industry-education convergence · Innovation community · Open source · Case study · Greenplum · Distributed data system · Big data · Intelligent computing · THOUGHT

© The Author(s), under exclusive license to Springer Nature Singapore Pte Ltd. 2023
W. Hong and Y. Weng (Eds.): ICCSE 2022, CCIS 1813, pp. 289–303, 2023.
https://doi.org/10.1007/978-981-99-2449-3_26

1 Introduction

With the proposal of "deepening the convergence of industry and education" in the report of the 19th national congress of China, more and more colleges and universities have begun the running mode of "industry-university converged education practice". In order to improve the quality of talent cultivation, universities and enterprises carry out in-depth cooperation. Relying on their own core resources and strong points, both sides adhere to the "win-win" principle, and implement the shared responsibility. As a bridge between universities and enterprises, the industry-university converged education can help strengthen the functions of both sides. The basic principle of THOUGHT Community is "technology-led, industry-driven, education-based, and talent-innovative". Thereby it promotes the organic connection between the education chain, the talent chain, the industrial chain and the innovation chain [1]. At the same time, the cooperation of industry and education can give valuable support to the future career planning of college/university graduates. It can stimulate students' creativity and innovation, and create opportunities for the combination of career planning and study, so as to promote the healthy development of life-long education [2].

Based on the latest needs of industrial technology development in big data and intelligent computing, the THOUGHT Community reforms the talent training program in the education sector.

As "the Outline of the 14th Five-Year-Plan and Long-term Goals for 2035" released by China mentions: "… Support the development of innovative organizations such as digital technology open source community, improve open source intellectual property rights and legal systems, and encourage enterprises to open software source code, hardware design and application service." Since the rise of the open source in the 1980s, it has changed the developing model of the software industry and reshaped the pattern of the software industry. In 2019, Black Duck audited a sample of 2000 commercial software and showed that up to 99% of them used open source components. Software monopoly Microsoft also joined the Open Invention Network Community in 2018, contributing more than 60000 patents to Linux Open Source Community [3]. In the last 15 years, the core technologies of emerging industries such as cloud computing, mobile Internet, big data, artificial intelligence and block chain have all been built based on open source software. Open source is not only a business model, but also an ecological construction method, a complex method of system development. Open source contains a spirit. It is a spirit of sharing and co-governance:open source means a spirit of breaking monopoly, openness and innovation; and open source also implicates a spirit of dedication. Researchers will open their scientific research achievements, so as to make it easier for more people to stand on the giants' shoulders, which can help to stimulate their creativity and promote the technological progress of mankind. If the spirit of "Atom Bombs, Hydrogen Bombs and Man-made Satellites" in China is the dedication of researchers to the country, then the spirit of open source is the dedication of researchers to the industry. The concept of "Community of Shared Future for Mankind" is the best embodiment in the field of information technology [4].

The industry-university converged course not only emphasizes on theory, but also focuses more on practice, which is a breakthrough compared to the traditional style on campus. Therefore, it needs to rely on a bridge which is convenient for both sides to participate in. Open source is such a suitable choice, making it easier for more learners to take advantage of valuable experiences from senior professionals. Compared with traditional business platform tools, open source platforms enable learners to have access to more useful learning resources for free, so we also choose an open source platform. With the intrinsic free and open-source features, the distributed database Greenplum [5] is able to adapt to the special needs of open-source developers through its own free and open-source features.

As a classic representative of education field, Tsinghua University has the world's top research team and education resources. While, with its shared nothing MPP(Massive parallel processing) architecture, Greenplum ranks third in Gartner 2019 for its high cost-performance and availability. Based on all of these, in this industry-university converged education practice case, we take Greenplum as a distributed data system solution for massive data management and analysis. Taking project cooperation, technology transfer and joint development as the carriers, we conducted research and development on open source based on industry-university converged education practice.

With the joint efforts of Tsinghua University and Greenplum Open Source community, we set up a course named "Foundamentals and Application of Distributed Data System", which is a practice case of THOUGHT. The paper will be organized as follows: Sect. 2 is about the case study, including course target, industry-university team members, brief introduction of the course, the course structure and contents, and one practice project of the course; Sect. 3 discusses the future work; and we give the conclusion in Sect. 4; after the reference list, part of the results of the course project are shown in the Appendix section.

2 Case Study

2.1 Course Target

By helping students understand the development process and technical trend of big data management and analysis, the course equips students with basic knowledge and ability in this field, such as key concepts, classic methods, hands-on practice, technology selection/analysis/judgment abilities, etc. By constructing a reasonable curriculum system, this course could help learners to leverage the education resources of various majors. Based on the Trinity philosophy of education, it tries to integrate "knowledge transmission, ability training and value shaping" into the course.

To establish the foundation of understanding, thinking and problem-solving abilities in the related field for students, the course also tries to broaden the vision for them, lays the cornerstone of development, and cultivates practical ability. With the proposal of "deepening the convergence of industry and education" in the report of the 19th national congresevels of headings should be numbered. Lower level headings remain unnumbered; they are formatted as run-in headings.

2.2 Course Team

Our course team consists of twelve core members, including 6 lecturers, 1 counselor, 1 teaching assistant and 4 course-supporting assistants. Most of the members are from

Tsinghua University and Greenplum Open Source Community, who have more than 10 years working experiences in this field. For the constraint of pages, we just list these professionals from industry and education in Fig. 1 (everyone makes distinctive contributions, and the list is in no particular order). All the members have reasonable and clear responsibilities according to their own expertise, and cooperate efficiently.

▶ Lecturer: Yao Yandong, Wu Jiang, Du Jialun, Wang Hao, Chen Zhen, Li Chao

▶ Counselor: LV Zhenghua

▶ Teaching assistant: Hu Chaochen

▶ Course-supporting assistants: Wang Haoyu, Guo min, Ma Xiaodong, Zhang Yisong

LV Zhenghua
Alumni of Tsinghua University, R&D engineer of Greenplum

Li Chao
Associate researcher, BNRist DCST, Tsinghua University

Yao Yandong
Founder of Greenplum open source community in China, Founder of ymatrix

Hu Chaochen
Master candidate, Department of Computer Science and Technology, Tsinghua University

Chen Zhen
Deputy director of administration, iCenter, Tsinghua University

Wu Jiang
Alumni of Tsinghua University, Senior product manager of Greenplum

Ma Xiaodong,
Project teaching of cloud computing and artificial intelligence, Tsinghua University

Min Guo
Project teaching of machine learning and robotics, Tsinghua University

Wang Hao
Senior database expert of ymatrix, Former member of Greenplum R&D department

Zhang Yisong,
Project teaching of intelligent hardware and artificial intelligence, Tsinghua University

Wang Haoyu
Project teaching of artificial intelligence and data management, Tsinghua University

Du Jialun
Core member of Greenplum open source community, Engaging in kernel research and development

Fig. 1. Core Members of the Course team

2.3 Course Brief Introduction

"Foundamentals and Application of Distributed Data System" is an introductory level course, which is related to the field of big data and artificial intelligence and does not need lots of fundamentals or advanced-placement courses. Thus, the course can provide service for a wide range of learners, which is featured by practical application and the industry-university convergence. Based on the open source distributed database, the course aims at almost all the key parts of the life cycle of big data, e.g. ETL, management, query, processing, analysis and machine learning. And it does not involve complex database development and kernel development.

2.4 Course Contents and Structure

This course is organized in 10 chapters: History of Data Processing, A Glance of Greenplum, Greenplum Installation and Fault Diagnosis, The Foundation of Distributed SQL, Greenplum Data Types and Processing, Advanced SQL, Data loading and Export, Visualization, Introduction to Advanced Analysis, Trends and Cases. The specific course system is shown in Fig. 2.

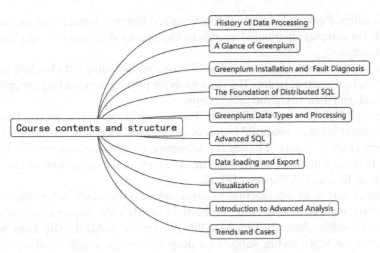

- History of Data Processing
- A Glance of Greenplum
- Greenplum Installation and Fault Diagnosis
- The Foundation of Distributed SQL
- Greenplum Data Types and Processing
- Advanced SQL
- Data loading and Export
- Visualization
- Introduction to Advanced Analysis
- Trends and Cases

Course contents and structure

Fig. 2. Course Contents and Structure

1) The first chapter is the brief introduction of the history of data processing, which can help learners to get the whole picture in this field, understand and think about the disciplines and motivations of its development. And the prospect and future are also discussed in this chapter.

2) The second chapter is a glance(brief introduction) of the open source distributed database Greenplum, which introduces its key concepts, supporting technologies, core architecture, features, highlights and prosperous software ecosystem. This chapter can also help students understand the relevant knowledge of distributed databases /data systems in general.

3) The third chapter takes Greenplum as an example, illustrating the installation and fault diagnosis operations of distributed data systems, which are oriented from the practical operations to the common concepts behind. It explains the installation logic of different Greenplum distributed nodes, initialization and its common configurations. And it also introduces the "one-click installation" of super-converged time series database MatrixDB [6] based on Greenplum.

4) The fourth chapter is the foundation of distributed SQL. Based on the brief review of basic SQL,this chapter leads learners to distributed SQL specific for the queries/operations on distributed relational databases. Through studying the track and diagnosis of basic problems on Greenplum, students can quickly get started with SQL and be familiar with basic operations such as adding, deleting, modifying and checking.

5) The fifth chapter is data types and data processing. This chapter takes Greenplum as an example, introducing different data types, which are roughly divided into basic data types, complex data types and user-defined types. This chapter also discusses the core elements of data types, their application scenarios, and some considerations for technical choices.

6) The sixth chapter is advanced SQL. The main contents include aggregation functions,nested queries, CTE (Common Table Expressions),window functions and

data cubes. Equipped with these functions and features, learners can use advanced SQL for complex distributed queries or exploratory data analysis, just "one-stop" in databases.

7) The seventh chapter is data loading and export, including data loading tools and Greenplum external tables. The main tools for parallel data loading are gpfdist and gpload, and data migration tool gpcopy.

8) The eighth chapter is visualization. Through vivid examples, we use Greenplum to support big data analysis/ business intelligence. Learners can not only have a general understanding of business intelligence and visualization tools, but also can get familiar with some of the visualization tools in the ecosystem of Greenplum, such as Tableau [7], Superset [8], etc.

9) Chapter nine is an introduction to advanced analysis, which is for advanced data analysis and machine learning in the field of AI. This chapter also contains the use of machine learning tool MADlib [9](Apache MADlib: Big Data Machine Learning in SQL) and its support for deep learning, in which serial examples are used to illustrate the scenarios and usages of it.

10) Chapter ten talks about future trends by several classic cases, which introduces both application demands/challenges and future development trend.Through case studies, this chapter helps learners to understand the increasingly promising prospects in the upcoming era.The core content summary of the course is shown in Fig. 3.

2.5 Course Practice Project

Description of project task. The course practice project is to give learners a chance to do the comprehensive training, in which the core elements of big data,from data ETL(Data Extraction,Transformation and Loading), modeling, querying, analyzing, visualization, problem locating, estimating… to evaluating, etc. are all included. Here we just list one of the project tasks in the Autumn semester in 2021:

--Theme: Recovery of Urban Vitality After Epidemic from the Perspective of Human Activities on Internet.

--Data Source: The DaaS(Data as a Service) [10] is an Internet perception big data system based on AI, which is built by "Think Tank 2861 Project Team". This is an Internet-area, data-based, and neural feedback system for the Internet information in China. It takes Internet activities as the input, and processes through AI algorithms and machine learning framework to generate the output, based on which building the real-time macro economics and society big data for about 9.8 million grids in China and its intelligent applications.

Based on DaaS, the training task is specified to investigate the vitality recovery of 50 major cities after the epidemic. The data from DaaS is selected and divided into three dimensions--space, time and item:

1) In terms of space dimension, we select the grid data of key urban districts in 50 major cities as representatives, which covers the data from central cities/edge cities, coastal cities/inland cities, developed cities/developing cities;

2) In terms of time dimension, the data of November 2019 before the epidemic and November 2020 after the epidemic are selected as representatives;

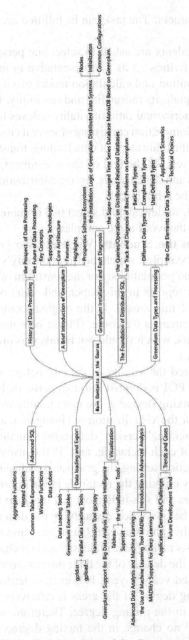

Fig. 3. Core Members of the Course team

3) In terms of item dimension, we select populations, traffics, POIs (Point Of Interests) and other quantitative indicators to reflect the vitality of the cities.

--Task Tips for the Learners: The task can be fulfilled according to two levels, basic level and advanced level:

For the basic level, students are asked to select one perspective (e.g. traffics, populations, entertainment activities...) as a representative to measure the urban vitality. They should give the definition and calculation model of vitality index to this specific single perspective, and explain its rationality and feasibility. Besides, they are asked to visualize the parallel and horizontal ratio of vitality indexes for 2 to 50 cities. And they should select an urban agglomeration consisting of several cities for quantitative analysis and visualization. Finally, the main steps of data loading, transformation, processing and visualization should be given. At the end of the assignment, students are supposed to give the main observations and conclusions, list the contributions of every team member, and summarize/conclude the whole work.

For the advanced level, student should select two or more perspectives to fulfill the above tasks, which makes the work more complex.

Some Examples from the Students. We select two groups of students' course practice project results as examples, which measures the city's vitality after the epidemic from the aspects of POIs and populations. For the constraint of pages, we just put several fragments of their project reports in this paper, and some of the results are listed in the appendix at the end of this article. If the original complete reports are required for reference, contact via email is welcome. (Please note that all these results are just observations by the students, which should not be taken as professional views from the economists or sociologists.)

The first group measured the vitality of the city before and after the epidemic by POIs. The comprehensive POI is divided into two parts, including POI mixing degree and POI density. So the mixing degree is the main vitality index and the density is the auxiliary vitality index. For the visualization of Guangzhou and Shenzhen, they used a tree diagram. In the tree diagram, "Version" defines the structure of the tree, "POI mixing degree" defines the color of each rectangle, and "POI density" defines the size of each rectangle. Through the function setting, the group also realized function of drilling down data in the tree diagram. By clicking the rectangle in the figure, the users can drill down to query the main indicators and sub-indicators that make up the POI mixing degree.

The results are shown below. When quantifying the data of Beijing-Tianjin-Hebei, the three districts showed the same trends as Guangzhou and Shenzhen. In other words, in these districts, there exists an increase in density and no change in the mixing degree. As can be seen from Fig. 4, the density of the three districts increased year-on-year, while the mixing degree decreased year-on-year. However, in terms of the specific numbers, the reduction in the mixing degree of the areas is relatively small. As a result, it can be regarded as no change in the mixing degree. Therefore, assuming that there exists an increase in density and no change in the mixing degree, it can be concluded that the recovery of both districts shows a positive trend. In addition, as the Fig. 4 shows, the three districts' growth rates of the main indicators all show the same trends, and the growth rates are also similar numerically. It is concluded that people's consumption preferences in different districts are alike.

The second group measured the vitality of the city before and after the epidemic by populations. Population is an important evaluation dimension to reflect the vitality of a

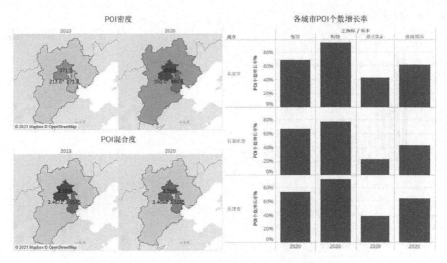

Fig. 4. Growth Rate of POI in Each City

city, which can effectively measure the state and potential of a city after the epidemic. The number of business people during the daytime can reflect the resumption of work and production after the epidemic. And the change of the labor force reflects the city's potential for resumption of work and production in the future. In this study, they defined the labor force as the labor from age 22 to 65. And the business people during the daytime was defined as the number of people engaged in business activities within this grid during the daytime. The resulting data is put into Tableau for visualization.

As the Fig. 5 shows, considering the ratio of commercial and residential population, the number of cities rising and falling year-on-year is almost the same. Considering that the total population will not change significantly in a short time, the year-on-year increase and decrease of the commercial and residential population can reflect the flow of business population. Therefore, the epidemic has changed people's choice of workplace. As a result, the population has shifted from cities to cities.

From the perspective of population, the epidemic has had a severe impact on urban vitality. Among them, Central China, Northeast China, and South China don't recover well in terms of current population vitality and recovery potential, which need to be focused on. Because the number of jobs in large and medium cities has decreased after the epidemic, the labor force index of small and medium cities is better than that of big cities. According to the previous analysis, the vitality of China's epidemic cities has not fully recovered to the level before the epidemic, but the recovery potential is still large.

2.6 Course Results

After a semester of study, the students have learned a lot of knowledge related to distributed systems and big data, and also have the ability to deal with data processing generally, all through the classroom lectures and practices with the open source Greenplum. The students have gained a lot:

横比图：商住人口比

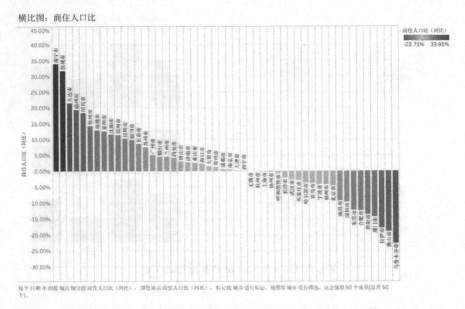

Fig. 5. Ratio of Commercial and Residential Population in Different Areas

1) From the perspective of knowledge, the students master plenty of relevant technical methods.

2) From the perspective of development, the students understand the evolution process and technical trend of big data.

3) Based on their respective majors, students equip themselves with basic ability in the cross direction of big data and machine intelligence. By improving relevant value literacy, they can use relevant technologies to solve common problems in their majors.

In the process of learning, students generally regard this course as an unusual course. Due to their different majors, some of the learners lack the foundation of big data, some of them feel it hard to learn relevant knowledge regarding the distributed database. However, the curriculum design pays attention to the interaction between teachers and students. The learning curve is arranged by our team carefully. As a result, students are neither limited to their comfortable area, nor afraid of too much fresh new contents.

The students also gave comments on the course. Many students rated it as an innovative and interesting course, which is very suitable for students interested in distributed database at entry level. From the students' feedback, we can see that the course has changed the original teaching model of simply teaching the theoretical knowledge, and pays more attention to practice. It also provides students with an opportunity to understand the history/motivation/prospects/trends/demands of the industry, which may be a good career stepping stone in the field of big data for them.

3 Future Work

The course "Fundamentals and Application of Distributed Data System" (based on open source Greenplum) is featured by the convergence of industry and education, which already runs two semesters. In the near future, we will further develop the course in these aspects:

1) Standardize the course contents, publish teaching materials such as text books, experiment handbooks and teaching aids, share teaching resources on and off the campus;

2) Develop online courses, in order to provide services for both the blended teaching style in the classrooms and the online learners out of the classrooms;

3) Based on the two points mentioned above, make services more extensive, so that this course bred in Tsinghua can share more values and provide more services for more teachers, students and online/off-campus learners; and form a virtuous circle, make more people in industry and education participate in, and do it better in the development of curriculum and related supporting resources.

4 Conclusion

With the new talent development model of industry and education convergence, this paper introduces one case of THOGHT based on open source. In the process of cooperation, the course team members from Tsinghua, Greenplum, and DaaS work together to build teaching goals, course content system, and related exercises, homework and practice projects. The feedbacks from students show that they have gained understandings about distributed data system and big data processing through the course "Foundamentals and Application of Distributed Data System". At the end of the course, in 2021 autumn semester, they completed the course practice project "Recovery of Urban Vitality After Epidemic from the Perspective of Human Activities on Internet ". In our future plan, we will publish textbook, supporting materials and online courses, which we hope can contribute more values for other universities and learners outside of campus.

Acknowledgement. The course "Foundamentals and Application of Distributed Data System" is supported by several institutes/departments/teams from Tsinghua University including RIIT, BNRist, iCenter, DCST,and 2861 team; and several organizations from industry including THOUGHT, 1024 Foundation, Greenplum Open Source Community, and MatrixDB. The related work is also supported by the SRT (Student Research Training) project "Research and Practice on Big Data Process and Analysis III" and education reformation project "Design of Data Visualization Experiments in Data Science Teaching" of Tsinghua University. The cloud service hosting Greenplum database for daily practice/homework is supported by iCenter-Cloud of Tsinghua University. Part of the data source for the course practice project is supported by DaaS, which has got granted "Big data industry development pilot demonstration project (2020)" from Ministry of Industry and Information Technology (Field 2/Direction 4 innovative application of livelihood big data/No.54).

Appendix

Part of the results regarding the course project are shown in the appendix below.

As Fig. 6 shows, Guangzhou and Shenzhen both have high year-on-year growth in POI density. In terms of mixing degree, Guangzhou increased year-on-year and Shenzhen decreased year-on-year. However, due to the small number of increase and decrease, we assume that the mixing degrees of the two cities have not changed a lot year-on-year. Both cities showed a trend of "increase in density and no change in mixing degree", which means they recover well. Comparing Guangzhou and Shenzhen side by side, Shenzhen has higher density than Guangzhou in both 2019 and 2020, but Shenzhen is far inferior to Guangzhou in terms of mixing degree.

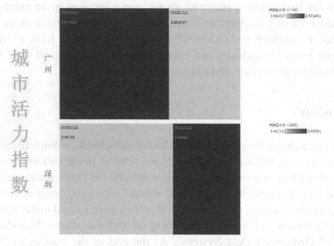

Fig. 6. Urban Vitality Index of Guangzhou and Shenzhen

Figure 7 is a scatter bubble chart, reflecting the year-on-year change in the number of business people and workers in the workforce. As the scatter plot shows, the relative changes of these two indicators are positively correlated. And most cities with large business population are concentrated in the third quadrant. In other words, the business population and the labor force reduced in the same ratio. The distribution of these two indicators is not a normal distribution, but it has a certain degree of discrimination and representativeness.

Figure 8 shows the number of business people in 50 cities during the day and its year-on-year change. It can be seen that the business population in most cities has declined year-on-year. While in districts with large business population, the business population has basically shown a year-on-year decline. In a horizontal comparison, the business population in Jiangsu, Zhejiang and Shanghai has the best year-on-year growth trend. Although Chongqing had a large business population before, it has experienced a significant year-on-year decline. The number of business people in the southern and north-eastern regions, as well as the coastal regions of South China, basically showed a downward trend.

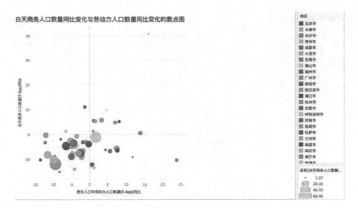

Fig. 7. Scatter Bubble Chart Regarding the Population Change

Fig. 8. Business Population and its Year-on-Year Change During Daytime

Figure 9 shows the number of labor force and its year-on-year change. The figure shows that the labor force in most cities has decreased year-on-year, but the overall situation is better than that of the business population during the daytime. In a horizontal comparison, the labor force in Jiangsu, Zhejiang, Shanghai and the coastal areas of South China show the best year-on-year growth trend. And the labor force in Shanghai showed an upward trend particularly. The South, Central China, and North-east regions all show a downward trend in terms of business population and labor force.

Figure 10 shows the ratio of commercial and residential population in urban agglomerations. The Yangtze River Delta has the highest increase among the five urban agglomerations, followed by Sichuan-Chongqing Urban Agglomeration. While the other three urban agglomerations have declined in different degrees. For the migration of business people from labor-intensive cities to neighboring second-tier cities, different urban agglomerations show different changes regarding the commercial and residential population.

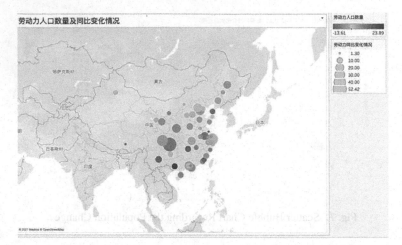

Fig. 9. Labor Force Population and its Year-on-Year Change

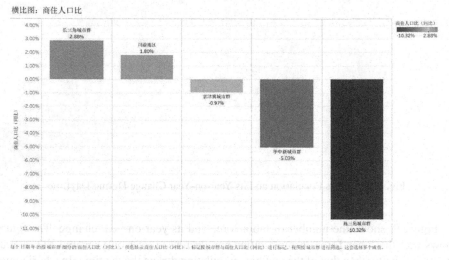

Fig. 10. Ratio of Commercial and Residential Population in Agglomeration

The comprehensive evaluation of urban vitality after the epidemic cannot only rely on one indicator. Population and POI are used as different aspects to measure urban vitality, and the conclusions in the analysis have similarities and also differences. In terms of the overall trend, the POI shows a positive trend in the cities studied, but the population shows the overall trends of the 50 cities are still not as good as those before the epidemic. What's more, it requires the participation of human beings. The indicators of business activities during the daytime show that people's willingness to take part in business activities has not recovered to the level before the epidemic. But the indicators of labor force are better than those of business activities, proving that the recovery potential is still great. On the whole, the epidemic still has a certain impact on the vitality of the city, which is reflected through the decline of the business population and the POI mixing degree. But the recovery potential remains optimistic, which is reflected through the labor force and POI density.

References

1. THOUGHT community: innovaTive Hub for the cO-development of indUstry and hiGHer education. https://thought.idatapark.com/
2. Hong, W., Li, C., Wang, Q.: Technology-inspired smart learning for future education. In: 29th National Conference on Computer Science Technology and Education, Springer Communications in Computer and Information Science book series (CCIS, volume 1216)
3. Open Invention Network: About OIN. https://openinventionnetwork.com/
4. Bao, Y: Spirit of Open Source, Communications of China Computer Federation, April 2021, pp. 1345–1397
5. Greenplum Database:Multi-cloud and Parallel Big Data Open Source Platform, https://cn.greenplum.org/
6. YMatrix:A Super-Converged Database, https://ymatrix.cn/
7. Tableau:We're on a mission to create a data literate world. https://www.tableau.com/community/academic
8. Apache Superset:A Modern Data Exploration and Visualization Platform Spirit of Open Source, Communications of China Computer Federation https://superset.apache.org/
9. Apache MADlib:Big Data Machine Learning in SQL. https://madlib.incubator.apache.org/
10. Lyu, Z.: Internet-perception society big data systems based on AI. In: IEEE BIG DATA 2021, 2021 IEEE International Conference on Big Data (Big Data), pp. 5960-5962 (2021)

On the Current Situation of the English Autonomous Learning of Middle School Students: A Case Study of the Students of Yinzhou Foreign Language Middle School in Ningbo

Li Jia[1,2], Chen Ou[1(✉)] (iD), and Jingyan Zhang[1]

[1] School of International Studies, NingboTech University, Ningbo, China
ocean79ou@163.com
[2] University of Nottingham Ningbo China, Ningbo, China

Abstract. The English Curriculum Standards for Compulsory Education (2011 edition) is the basis for the preparation of teaching materials, teaching, assessment and examination questions in China's compulsory education. The standard mentions "developing autonomous learning ability" in the general objective of the curriculum and advocates autonomous learning, which requires in-class teaching to pay attention to the cultivation of students' autonomous learning ability. How is the English autonomous learning ability of students in compulsory education? What is the situation of students' autonomous learning? In this paper, an investigation is conducted to study the current situation of first grade students' English autonomous learning in Yinzhou Foreign Language Middle School in Ningbo City. This paper first reviews the concept and related theories of autonomous learning. Then, the author uses the questionnaire and the interview to investigate the English autonomous learning situation of the first-grade students in Yinzhou Foreign Languages Middle School, and analyzes the data collected from the questionnaires and the interviews. The results show that the students' English autonomous learning ability is at the medium level. There are differences in the students' autonomous learning abilities, and this difference is related to their English level. Based on the above results, this paper puts forward corresponding suggestions to stimulate students' learning motivation, improve students' learning methods, and help students to learn to evaluate and adjust themselves.

Keywords: Autonomous Learning · English · Middle School

1 Introduction

As the basis for textbook compilation, teaching, evaluation and examination propositions in China's compulsory education stage, English Curriculum Standards for Compulsory Education (2011 edition) mentions "developing autonomous learning ability" in the overall curriculum objective, advocates learner autonomy, and requires that English classroom teaching should pay attention to the cultivation of students' autonomy in English learning [1].

The concept of "learner autonomy" was first proposed by Holec in the field of language teaching and was defined as the ability to take charge of one' s own learning [2]. After the concept of "learner autonomy" was put forward, many scholars have carried out many discussions on the definition of autonomous learning. According to Legutke and Thomas, autonomous learning is a kind of ability [3]. In addition, Benson defines learner autonomy as the learners' ability to control their own learning [4]. However, according to Littlewood, autonomous learning is both an ability and a willingness to independently make and implement choices that affect their actions [5]. Learner autonomy is influenced by many factors, which can be divided into internal factors and external factors. Internal factors include learners' learning motivation, learning strategies, learning motivation, learning methods, learning time, learning reflection, learning plan, learning results [6–9], while external factors include cultural factors. Learning content and learning situation and so on [9–11]. This paper investigates the current situation of English autonomous learning among the first-year students in Yinzhou Foreign Language Middle School on the basis of theories and researches of autonomous learning at home and abroad. It also provides relevant suggestions for English teaching at this stage.

2 Methodology

2.1 Subject

The research subjects are students from Yinzhou Foreign Language Middle School, which is a public school in Ningbo. Students do not have to take a selection test to enter this school, so the students can possibly be seen as representatives of middle school students in general. Three hundred students from the first-year students are randomly selected to take part in a questionnaire survey, ten of which are randomly selected to participate in interviews.

2.2 Materials and Instruments

Questionnaire Survey. The questionnaire is derived from the "autonomous learning" questionnaire used by Peng and Xu [12, 13] with some modifications according to the characteristics of the research object.

The questionnaire used in this study is composed of two sections. Section one collects the basic information of the students, requiring them to answer questions concerning their class, name, gender, age, and the latest English midterm test score. Section two consists of 27 questionnaire items concerning students' English autonomous learning. These items are divided into six small parts, which are shown in Table 1. It can be seen form the table that each part corresponds to one of the dimensions of autonomous learning. Items 1–4 correspond to students' learning motivation. Items 5–7 correspond to students' learning plan. Items 8–11 correspond to students' self-monitoring. Items 12–18 correspond to students' learning strategies. Items 19–21 correspond to external influences. Items 22–27 correspond to students' self-evaluation and adjustment. A brief description of the questionnaire items is shown in Table 1:

Table 1. The Content of the Questionnaire

Dimensions	Items
Basic Information	
Learning Motivation	1–4
Learning Plan	5–7
Self-monitoring	8–11
Learning Strategies	12–18
External Influence	19–21
Self-evaluation and Adjustment	22–27

Interview. Following the questionnaire, interviews are conducted as a qualitative research to help the author collect students' thoughts and attitudes toward autonomous learning, obtain an in-depth understanding of their situation of English autonomous learning, and finally provide some support to the whole investigation. Ten students are interviewed. Each interview is conducted in Chinese, so that the students are able to express their ideas fully. There is no videotape in the interview scene to record the procedure so that the interviewees can feel free to express themselves.

Data Collection. Questionnaires were printed out and sent to students in classes for them to fill in. Altogether 300 copies of questionnaires were distributed and finally 300 copies were collected, so the questionnaire return rate was 100%. There were a total of 286 valid questionnaires and 14 invalid questionnaires, with a valid return rate of 95.3%. After the paper questionnaire was recovered, the author noted down the questionnaire results into Excel and then imported them into the SPSS26.0 software. The author also interviewed 10 students and collected and sorted out the information. To ease the students' nerves, the interviews were not recorded. The interview with each student lasted about 6–10 min.

Data Analysis. All the options of quantitative questions adopt Likert five-point Scale for the ease of statistics. They rank from 5 to 1. For some options, five is assigned to A (strongly agree). Four assigned to B (agree). Three is assigned to C (neither agree nor disagree). Two is assigned to D (disagree). One is assigned to E (I strongly disagree with this statement). For the other, five is assigned to A (always). Four is assigned to B (often). Three is assigned to C (don't know). Two is assigned to D (rarely). One is assigned to E (never).

Before further analysis of the data, the author also analyzed the reliability and validity of the questionnaire, which are shown in Table 2 and Table 3. The Cronbach's alpha value shown in Table 2 is 0.949. It is higher than 0.9, a figure indicating high reliability [14]. It can be seen from the Table 3 that the KMO value is 0.951, which meets the requirement of factor analysis [15].

Table 2. Reliability of the Questionnaire

Cronbach's Alpha	Number of Students
0.949	286

Table 3. Validity of the Questionnaire

Kaiser-Meyer-Olkin Measure of Sampling Adequacy		.951
Bartlett's Test of Sphericity	Approx. Chi-square	4249.915
	Df	351
	Sig	0.000

3 Results

3.1 Overall Situation of Students' English Autonomous Learning

As mentioned above, five to one are assigned to options from A to E, the middle value of 3 is taken as the reference value. On this basis, a mean value below 3 indicates weak autonomous learning ability, 3–4 is at a medium level, and 4–5 indicates strong autonomous learning ability. The higher the mean value is, the stronger the students' autonomous learning ability is. The mean value of the overall data is 3.71, which is presented in the Table 4. It shows that the students' autonomous learning ability is at a medium level, which means they have a certain ability to learn autonomously, but not to a good degree.

Table 4. Overall Situation of Students' English Autonomous Learning

Dimension	Minimum Value	Maximum Value	Mean	Standard Deviation
Overall data	1	5	3.71	1.05

3.2 Students' Motivation to Learn English

In this module, the authors explore the students' motivational attitudes toward learning English. The meaning of each item is as follows. Item 1 asks students whether they are interested in learning English. Item 2 asks them whether they are very confident in learning English well. Item 3 is about the time students spend on English study after class every day. Item 4 investigates their motivation to complete the English tasks that interest them (Table 5).

The middle value of 3 is also taken as the reference value. From the table, it can be seen that the overall mean value of learning motivation dimension is 3.95, which

Table 5. Students' Motivation to Learn English

Dimension	Item	Minimum Value	Maximum Value	Mean	Overall Mean
Learning Motivation	1	1	5	4.12	3.95
	2	1	5	4.02	
	3	1	5	3.58	
	4	2	5	4.09	

is at the medium level. Specifically, the mean values of item 1 and item 2, are higher than 4, which are 4.12 and 4.02 respectively. This means that most students are still interested in English and are confident in learning it well. The mean value of item 3 is the lowest compared with the value of other three items. Its mean value is between 3 and 4, indicating a medium level. It shows that many students are willing to spend time studying English after class. The mean value of item 4 is higher than 4. It means that students' motivation to learn is closely related to their interest in learning, which may be affected by factors such as the contents, arrangement and presentation of learning tasks.

During the interviews, most of the students interviewed felt that they could learn English well. Some of these students said they did not feel that learning English brought them much pressure and were willing to spend time after school to learn English, such as reading English texts, memorizing English words and learning to sing English songs and so on. Only one student was worried about his English study and was not very confident in English learning. From this, it can be seen that, in general, students are relatively well motivated to learn English. However, there may be some students who are not sufficiently motivated to learn English.

3.3 Students' Learning Plan

This module contains three items, item 5, item 6, and item 7. Item 5 asks the frequency of students setting English learning goals. Item 6 investigates whether they consciously learn and review English words step by step. Item 7 is about how often students adjust the study plans according to the actual situation.

Table 6. Students' Learning Plan

Dimension	Item	Minimum Value	Maximum Value	Mean	Overall Mean
Learning Plan	5	1	5	3.62	3.60
	6	1	5	3.62	
	7	1	5	3.58	

The overall mean value of this module is 3.6, which is at the medium level. As is shown in Table 6, the mean value of each individual item is between 3 and 4, which is the middle level. It means that many students have the certain awareness to develop English study plans. But during the interviews, some students said that they didn't assign English study plans. One student even said that he had never made any English study plans. They tended to complete the tasks assigned by teachers, such as doing exercises. And they did not take the initiative to review English words if their English teacher did not dictate them. From here it can be seen that, though the overall mean of this dimension is at the medium level, some students do not have the habit of making personal English study plans on a regular basis, let alone adjust them.

3.4 Students' Self-monitoring in Learning English

This module contains four items about students' self-monitoring in learning English. The questions represented by each of the three items are shown below. Item 8 asks whether students can control their English study time. Item 9 explores whether students check the completion of the plan. Item 10 probes the question of whether they can correct their mistakes in time. Item 11 enquires about whether students can overcome negative emotions in the process of learning English.

Table 7. Students' Self-monitoring in Learning English

Dimension	Item	Minimum Value	Maximum Value	Mean	Overall Mean
Self-monitoring	8	1	5	3.98	3.89
	9	1	5	3.88	
	10	1	5	3.86	
	11	1	5	3.83	

According to Table 7, the mean value of each individual item is at the medium level. The overall mean value is also at the medium level. It means that students have a certain degree of self-monitoring awareness during English study. However, six of ten students interviewed indicated that their self -monitoring ability was weak. They would not consider improvement unless someone else pointed out the problem, and sometimes they had trouble controlling their negative emotions while learning English. This shows that despite of the result that the overall mean value of this dimension is at the medium level, the students still have problems with self-monitoring and many of them lack a sense of ownership in the learning process.

3.5 Students' Learning Strategies in Learning English

Item 12 asks students whether they preview or review after class. Item 13 investigates the frequency students listen to texts' recordings after class. Item 14 is designed to know students' taking notes situation in class. Item 15 explores students' participation in class. Item 16 is set to know whether students recite texts and memorize English words. Item 17 is proposed to see students' initiative to complete the corresponding exercises. Item

18 is about students' awareness of learning and accumulating English learning methods (Table 8).

Table 8. Students' Learning Strategies in Learning English

Dimension	Item	Minimum Value	Maximum Value	Mean	Overall Mean
Learning Strategy	12	1	5	3.77	3.84
	13	1	5	3.35	
	14	1	5	4.18	
	15	1	5	3.60	
	16	1	5	4.07	
	17	1	5	4.14	
	18	1	5	3.76	

It can be seen that the overall mean value of this dimension is 3.84, at the medium level. The mean values of item 12, item 13, item 15 and item18 are also between 3 and 4, which are at the medium level. Besides, the mean values of item 14, item 16 and item 17 are all higher than 4, which means that the students are doing well in these areas. According to the interviews, most students tend to take notes carefully in class. Most of them can also complete exercise books after class. But most of them stated that the strategy for learning English was just a matter of finishing the homework or completing the tasks assigned by teachers. Some students also mentioned that it's enough to listen to the teacher carefully and take good notes during English class. It thus can be seen from the combination of questionnaire survey and interviews that though the mean value of this dimension is at the medium level, many students don't seem to be aware of what English learning strategies are or how to apply them in the process of English learning.

3.6 External Influences on Students' English Learning

This module is about the external influences on students' English learning, that is, their use of resources outside the classroom to learn English. Item 19 is about students' use of the English language learning tools. Item 20 is set to know students' initiative to look for English learning materials. Item 21 enquires how often students watch English videos after class.

As is seen in Table 9, the overall mean is 2.99 which is lower than 3. This dimension has the lowest mean value of all the dimensions, compared with mean values of other dimensions, with item 21 having the lowest mean value of 2.39. This shows that they do not often use resources outside the classroom for English learning. This is also evident from the students' narratives in the interviews. Five of ten interviewees seldom watch English videos after class. Besides, some students think that looking for English materials on their own is a waste of time. Therefore, it shows that there is still room for improvement in students' use of extra-curricular resources for English learning. If students only learn English through textbooks, their knowledge of English will not be comprehensive, which is not conducive to developing their ability to apply English and to long-term English learning.

Table 9. External Influences on Students' English Learning

Dimension	Item	Minimum Value	Maximum Value	Mean	Overall Mean
External Influence	19	1	5	3.18	2.99
	20	1	5	3.40	
	21	1	5	2.39	

3.7 Students' Self-assessment and Adjustment in English Learning

This dimension consists of six items. Item 22 investigates whether students reflect on what they have learned within a certain period of time. Item 23 is about students' self-reflection to find gaps with others after exams. Item 24 is designed to know whether they look for problems if they are not doing well in learning English. Item 25 probes into students' self-learning style adjustment. Item 26 is set to see whether they will encourage themselves when encountering difficulties. Item 27 is aimed at knowing the students' willingness to seek help from others (Table 10).

Table 10. Students' Self-evaluation and Adjustment in English Learning

Dimension	Item	Minimum Value	Maximum Value	Mean	Overall Mean
Self-evaluation and Adjustment	22	1	5	3.27	3.70
	23	1	5	3.99	
	24	1	5	3.95	
	25	1	5	3.79	
	26	1	5	3.86	
	27	1	5	3.34	

The overall mean value of this dimension is also at the medium level. The mean values of item 23 and item 24 are higher than 3.9, which shows that many students can use English exams as a measure of self-evaluation and adjustment. They use English scores to find gaps and analyze the causes for adjustment. It is quite clear from item 22 (mean value of 3.27) that students are probably lack the awareness to reflect their English learning. It is evident from item 25 that students can still improve in changing their learning methods and learning strategies. The mean values of items 26 and 27 are 3.86 and 3.34 respectively, which means that students could do better in encouraging themselves and asking for assistance from others. Some statements from students in the interviews can't be ignored. Six of ten students don't take the initiative to find the gap between themselves and others unless they are asked to. And three students are not used to asking teachers or parents for help in English learning. Though the data show that students' self-evaluation and adjustment in English learning is at the medium level, it can be seen from the interviews that some students lack the awareness of self-evaluation and adjustment.

3.8 Comparative Analysis

This part discusses the relationship between students' autonomous learning ability and English level. In order to study this problem, the students' midterm English scores are taken as a reference for students' English level. The English mid-term exam is a 100 point system. The students' autonomous learning was discussed in groups based on the mean value of different dimension. The first group consists of 161 students who score 100–90 in English. The second group consists of 100 students who score 89–70 in English. The third group consists of 25 students who score 69 or less in English. As for D1, D2, D3, D4, D5 and D6, they represent items such as "learning motivation", "learning plan", "self-monitoring", "learning strategy", "external influence", and "self-evaluation and adjustment" respectively (Table 11).

Table 11. Comparison of Students with Different Levels of English

Group	D 1	D 2	D 3	D 4	D 5	D 6	Overall Mean
Group 1	4.15	3.83	4.09	4.08	3.18	3.96	3.88
Group 2	3.79	3.42	3.71	3.62	2.80	3.47	3.47
Group 3	3.35	2.96	3.28	3.19	2.57	2.95	3.05

Comparing the overall mean values of the three groups, it can be seen that the group with the higher academic performance also has a higher mean value. For the other individual dimensions, the same pattern is also found. Five to one are assigned to options from A to E. On this basis, the higher the mean value is, the stronger the students' autonomous learning ability is. Therefore, a conclusion can be drawn that students' English level is correlated with students' English autonomous learning ability. The better the student's English performance is, the better the student's autonomous learning ability is. From another perspective, it can also be concluded that good English autonomous learning ability can have a positive impact on students' English learning.

4 Suggestions

Dong points out that students are not born with autonomous learning ability. In general, the more guidance, supervision, and inspiration given by the adults with whom students interact in the learning process, the more learning experiences students gain from it.

Students are then able to become more explicitly aware of, direct, and regulate their own learning processes [16]. Therefore, teachers play a very important role in developing students' autonomous learning ability in English. From the above data analysis, it can be seen that students' good English autonomous learning ability has a positive impact on English achievement. In addition, students' overall English autonomous learning ability is at a medium level, and there is still room for improvement in six dimensions mentioned above. On this basis, the following three suggestions are put forward, which combine the six dimensions affecting autonomous learning ability.

4.1 Motivating Students to Learn English

It can be seen from the above that students' learning motivation is an aspect that affects students' autonomous learning and teachers can improve students' learning motivation by improving students' English learning interest.

In order to enhance students' interest in learning, teachers could pay attention to curriculum design and extracurricular guidance. In curriculum design, teachers could design interesting class activities according to different teaching contents, such as singing English songs, playing English games, and performing English dramas. Extracurricular activities can be more flexible than classroom activities. For example, teachers could explore a variety of activities, such as seeing English films, organizing English poetry recitation contests and so on. It should be noted that in this process, teachers are advised to pay attention to designing multi-level activities so that students with different English levels can participate in them. Through these activities, students can not only improve their motivation, but also deepen their impression of the learning content, thus improving their efficiency in learning English.

4.2 Guiding the Students to Find Appropriate Learning Approaches

First, teachers could let students know what learning strategy is and the importance of applying learning strategies in the process of English learning. Then they could encourage students to make learning plans purposefully and consciously to improve the efficiency of English learning. Second, teachers could help students find suitable learning approaches. In this process, teachers could summarize the learning methods of students who have performed well, so as to provide reference for other students in their learning methods.

4.3 Guiding Students in Self-evaluation and Adjustment

Teachers could assign students the task of self-reflection and summarize their experiences. They could provide targeted guidance to each student and give them suggestions. It is also suggested to organize students to share and discuss in small groups. During the exchange process, students are encouraged to reflect, learn from each other's experiences, and offer suggestions to each other.

5 Conclusion

After reviewing the concepts and influencing factors of English autonomous learning, the author conducted a questionnaire survey and interview. It is concluded that students' English achievement is related to students' English autonomous learning ability. Besides, students' overall English autonomous learning ability is at the medium level, which means that there is still room to improve their English autonomous learning ability. On this basis, corresponding suggestions are put forward for teachers to carry out better teaching.

Acknowledgments. The authors gratefully acknowledge the research projects supported by the Zhejiang Provincial Planning Office of Philosophy and Social Science (Grant Number: 23NDJC347YB) and by the Major Humanities and Social Sciences Research Projects in Zhejiang higher education institutions (Grant Number: 2023QN052). This work was also supported by the Zhejiang Higher Education Teaching Reform Project for the 14th Five-Year Plan Period (Grant Number: jg20220689), the 2022 Key Project for Professional Comprehensive Reform at NingboTech University (Construction of International-Communication-Capacity-Oriented Experimental Teaching System and Cooperative Education Mechanism for New Liberal Arts) and the 2022 Project for Professional Comprehensive Reform at NingboTech University (Exploration and Practice of College English Teaching Model from the Perspective of New Engineering and New Liberal Arts Majors).

References

1. Ministry of Education of the People's Republic of China: English Curriculum Standards of Compulsory Education 2011 Edition (in Chinese). Beijing Normal University Press, Beijing (2011)
2. Holec, H.: Autonomy in Foreign Language Learning. Pergamon Press, Oxford (1981)
3. Legutke, M., Thomas, H.: Process and Experience in the Language Classroom. Longman, London (1991)
4. Benson, P.: Teaching and Researching Autonomy in Language Learning. Pearson Education Limited, Harlow (2001)
5. Littlewood, W.: Autonomy: an autonomy and a framework. System **24**(4), 427–435 (1996)
6. Spratt, M., Humphreys, G., Chan, V.: Autonomy and motivation: which comes first? Lang. Teach. Res. **6**(3), 245–266 (2002)
7. Shao, R.Z.: Educational Psychology (in Chinese). Shanghai Foreign Language Education Press, Shanghai (1988)
8. Zimmerman, B.J., Martinez-Pons, M.: Construct validation of a strategy model of student self-regulated learning. J. Educ. Psychol. **80**(3), 284–290 (1998)
9. Chen, M.H.: Elements of English autonomous learning of college students under the network environment (in Chinese). Foreign Lang. Teach. **3**, 33–36 (2007)
10. Hedge, T.: Teaching and Learning in the Language Classroom. Oxford University Press, Oxford (2000)
11. Cortazzi, M., Lixian, J.: English teaching and learning in China. Lang. Teach. **29**(2), 61–80 (1996)
12. Peng, J.D.: A study on learner autonomy in college English teaching (in Chinese). Foreign Lang. World **89**, 15–19 (2002)

13. Xv, J.F., Peng, R.Z., Wu, W.P.: Investigation and analysis on autonomous English learning ability of Non-English Majors (in Chinese). Foreign Lang. Teach. Res. **36**, 64–68 (2004)
14. Qin, X.Q.: Quantitative Data Analysis in Foreign Language Teaching Research (in Chinese). Huazhong University of Science and Technology Press, Wuhan (2004)
15. Kaiser, H.: An index of factorial simplicity. Psychometrika **1**, 31–36 (1974)
16. Dong, Q., Zhou, Y.: On the self-monitoring of students' learning (in Chinese). J. Beijing Normal Univ. (Soc. Sci.) **1**, 8–14 (1994)

Case Teaching of Programming Course Integrating Professional Characteristics Under the Idea of OBE

Pingzhang Gou, Yuyue Han[✉], and Xinyue Hu

College of Computer Science and Engineering, Northwest Normal University, Lanzhou, China
736979136@qq.com

Abstract. Combining computational thinking + information technology empowering professional learning, taking Python programming as an example, according to the characteristics of different majors, the teaching design of Python course based on the OBE concept is carried out. Combined with the course content to carry out case teaching that integrates professional characteristics, the muti-subject, polymorphic, formative evaluation, and summative evaluation are adopted to form a closed-loop continuous cycle improvement mechanism. Teaching practice has proved that the implementation of the case teaching of Python programming based on the OBE concept integrating professional characteristics can effectively improve students' learning effect and cultivate students' computational thinking ability and innovation ability.

Keywords: OBE · Python programming course · Integration of professional characteristics · Case teaching · Diversified teaching evaluation

1 Introduction

In recent years, many schools have carried out in-depth research, reform and implementation on the curriculum content system oriented to computational thinking, the classification and hierarchical curriculum system integrating the characteristics of majors has been formed, which promotes the cross-integration and practical teaching of information technology empowerment, improves students' information literacy, strengthens students' computational thinking, and cultivates students' ability to apply information technology to solve disciplinary problems. As a general course of computational thinking + information technology empowering professional learning, Python programming enables students to master a programming language with wide application value through the study of the basic programming methods, the whole syntax system of Python and the application of Python. [1] The "New Engineering" talent training plan proposes to build a "broad, specialized and integrated" university computer curriculum system characterized by cross-integration and intensive practice. [2] The core task and goal of the school-wide programming course is how to enable the Python programming course to empower professional learning, carry out the cross-integration of computer and other

© The Author(s), under exclusive license to Springer Nature Singapore Pte Ltd. 2023
W. Hong and Y. Weng (Eds.): ICCSE 2022, CCIS 1813, pp. 316–324, 2023.
https://doi.org/10.1007/978-981-99-2449-3_28

disciplines, and form a Python programming course that integrates professional characteristics. By understanding programming languages and application methods, students can master the ability to use computers to solve problems in professional fields and cultivate computational thinking. In addition, students can exercise their hands-on ability through experiments.

The engineering education professional certification follows three basic concepts "results-oriented, student-centered and continuous improvement". The OBE (Outcome-Based Education) also emphasizes the three elements of "results-oriented, learner-centered, and continuous improvement". Therefore, the OBE concept has been gradually recognized by colleges and universities as the implementation approach for engineering education certification, [3, 4] and will be applied to Python programming courses to transform the teaching from traditional teacher-centered to student-centered. The course will be oriented to the cultivation and development of students' ability, carrying out curriculum design, teaching and evaluation. In order to better carry out professional integration, the teaching design of Python programming course integrating professional characteristics is carried out under the concept of OBE. According to the characteristics of different majors, different professional cases are designed for case teaching, so as to enhance inter-professional integration, increase students' practical opportunities, and cultivate their practical ability.

In order to ensure the effective operation of the continuous cyclic improvement mechanism under the OBE concept, the whole activity adopts diversified teaching evaluation. The main purpose is to explore how to effectively improve the teaching effect of Python programming language under the integration of professional characteristics. Through the teaching design of programming courses based on the OBE concept and the case-based teaching research integrating professional characteristics, the teaching methods of programming courses for the whole school will be explored to enable students to use programming to solve professional problems and cultivate students' computational thinking ability, problem-solving ability, innovation ability and sustainable development ability.

2   Teaching Activity Design

Compared with traditional education philosophy, OBE philosophy emphasizes student-centered and learning-results-oriented, focuses on the cultivation and development of students' abilities, and pays attention to the sustainable development of students' abilities. A closed-loop continuous feedback and improvement is required throughout the teaching process. [5] Compared with traditional teaching design, OBE-based teaching design emphasizes reverse teaching design guided by expected learning results. Python programming requires the development of computational thinking in conjunction with programming skills. The concept of OBE emphasizes the transformation of students' knowledge, skills, thinking attitude and values, which is suitable for Python and other programming courses that require thinking and skills training. [6] Chandrama Acharya's theory is highly recognized among OBE concepts, which holds that the implementation of OBE education mode mainly consists of four steps: defining learning outputs, realizing learning outputs, evaluating learning outputs and using learning outputs. It can be briefly summarized as: What are the expected student learning outcomes? How to help students achieve learning outcomes? How to effectively know that students have achieved these learning outcomes? How do students really use their learning results?

Starting from the four steps of Chandrama Acharya's OBE education model, combined with the analysis of the teaching situation of the course and the situation of students. To design teaching activities, first set the expected learning results according to the professional characteristics, and then reverse design guided by the expected learning results. Throughout the process of teaching design, teaching content, links and scenarios are organized around the expected learning results. Finally, according to the instructional design, the teaching activities are carried out and the teaching effect is evaluated. The OBE concept pursues the results that students can achieve and expect after a period of learning, and students can really use the learning results. Python program design course is a general course, which is oriented to different majors. In order to achieve better teaching results and enable students to truly use learning results. According to the characteristics of students of different majors, the expected learning outcomes are analyzed and determined. According to the requirements of different majors empowered by Python programming, classify and formulate the expected learning outcomes, formulate the teaching syllabus, build the content system of course classification, design teaching cases that integrate professional characteristics, and adopt the form of online + offline mixed case teaching mode. In the OBE teaching paradigm, evaluation exists throughout the teaching activity. This ensures the entire teaching activity can form a closed-loop network that can be improved repeatedly [5].

The traditional evaluation of teaching activities is mostly a means of selection and evaluation, and mostly a test is used to measure students' ability level. Emphasizes the test-taking ability of the students, pays attention to the learning results, and ignores the all-round development of the students. However, teaching activity is a kind of dynamic behavior activity, which needs to consider many elements. A single teaching evaluation can't meet the consideration and evaluation of the whole teaching activities. Under the OBE concept, effective evaluation is crucial to the Python course teaching design and the operation of the closed-loop continuous feedback improvement network for the OBE teaching paradigm.

Therefore, through the related research on teaching activities and teaching evaluation under the OBE concept, and comprehensively considering various factors involved in teaching activities, a diversified teaching evaluation framework process is constructed as shown in Fig. 1. Diversified evaluation system includes summary, multiple forms, formative evaluation and summary evaluation. Multi-subject is teachers, students, peer teachers and so on participate in teaching evaluation. Multi-form data is collected in various forms, such as online network platform test, online independent learning duration record, program design evaluation, real-time evaluation and offline survey. "Online + offline" data are collected to form data sets as daily scores. Formative evaluation is to reflect students' independent learning duration and test through MOOC (Massive Open Online Course) + SPOC (Small Private Online Course) online, and conduct modular programming practice test on other online learning resource platforms such as EduCoder practical teaching platform. Offline evaluation is mainly based on rain classroom teaching, and students can timely feedback classroom problems through rain classroom. The summative evaluation is based on the teaching resources platform and the Python paperless exam of different majors as the final grade consideration.

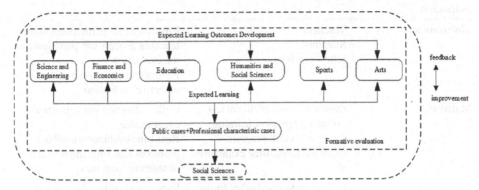

Fig. 1. Research framework flow.

The specific contents and uses of diversified evaluation are shown in Table 1. In order to provide comprehensive, effective and timely feedback and evaluation for teaching activities and promote teaching improvement, a closed-loop continuous feedback improvement network is used, as shown in Fig. 2.

The teaching method adopts the case teaching method, from the student-centered point of view, to increase the opportunities for students to practice, so that students can master the method of using program design to solve problems. Through the study of this course, students can master the basic concepts, basic syntax and programming methods of the Python programming language, and have the ability to use the Python language to solve professional practical computing problems. This develops students' computational thinking skills, enables information technology to empower professional learning, and makes students able to use computer skills proficiently to solve problems in professional fields. To this end, after the basic grammar system and basic program design teaching content of Python, professional categories such as engineering, finance, education, humanities, social sciences, sports and art are combined with. Targeted use of standard libraries and Python third-party libraries to design several cases, design teaching content hierarchically and separately, and ensure that computational thinking and information literacy can be trained and displayed in teaching activities. Among them, science and technology majors focus on the application of Advanced Python programming, and cases of artificial intelligence, Internet of Things, data mining and other aspects in corresponding majors can be selected to cultivate students' computational thinking ability and problem solving ability. Finance and economics majors are oriented by data analysis and processing ability. Appropriate professional cases related to big data application are designed to cultivate students' programming ability based on data processing and analysis.

Education majors mainly focus on the research in the field of education and teaching, and face the problems in the fields of education and teaching of various disciplines or academic research. Considering the subject nature of education majors and the future development direction of students, case design can analyze the current development

Table1. Detailed table of diversified teaching evaluation.

Diversified teaching evaluation	The specific content	Use
Multisubject	Teachers Students fellow teachers	Ensure that all participants in the teaching process can participate in the evaluation Ensure comprehensive and objective evaluation
Multiform	Online network platform test, online independent learning duration record, program evaluation, real-time evaluation, etc	Collect data to form datasets as usual grades Real-time evaluation feedback promotes real-time improvement of teaching activities
	Offline survey and other forms of data collection (such as evaluation scale, questionnaire, interview, etc.)	Survey and collect the attitudes and suggestions of teaching participants
Formative evaluation	Online students learn independently through MOOC + SPOC and other online learning resource platforms (such as EduCoder platform for modular programming exercises and tests)	Collect students' autonomous learning duration and test situation to understand students' initiative in autonomous learning and their mastery of teaching content
	Offline teaching based on "rain classroom"	Students can timely feedback the evaluation of problems in the classroom through the rain classroom, and teachers can also understand the situation of the students in the classroom in real time and make adjustments through the feedback of the students
Summative evaluation	On-campus teaching experiment resource platform paperless exam	According to the characteristics of different majors, the paperless Python exam will be considered as the final grade

trend of education, class performance and other cases by combining basic data statistics or visual analysis of data. For students majoring in humanities and social sciences, they tend to design some cases such as word frequency statistical analysis, word cloud map, long text interpretation analysis or content extraction analysis. Students majoring in sports can carry out cases related to sports events, and use Python to simulate games and predictions to design cases. Art students can choose cases such as graphic and image

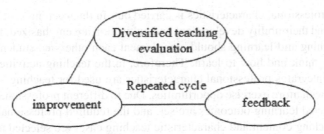

Fig. 2. Closed-loop continuous feedback improved network.

drawing, processing, etc. Professional case design should pay attention to practicality and entertainment, on the basis of stimulating students' interest in learning and creativity, to ensure that the case has a certain application space.

In terms of the teaching form, the traditional classroom instruction combined with the boring Python teaching practice is difficult to stimulate students' interest in learning, and the final teaching effect is poor. In the concept of OBE, teaching is the auxiliary means, and students' knowledge, skills, attitudes and values are the center. The elements of the whole teaching support each other, forming a closed-loop network of "student-centered + diversified evaluation of continuous feedback improvement ". In order to increase students' practice opportunities and exercise their hands-on and practical programming abilities, the teaching adopts the mode of online and offline mixed teaching, and adopts MOOC + SPOC preview and review + classroom teaching + programming exercise + classroom discussion + extracurricular tutoring, so as to facilitate students' active learning and teaching evaluation feedback. The class adopts the mode of group assistance, the class is divided into groups of five to six people. The same group can communicate with each other, help each other, which cultivates students' teamwork spirit and the ability to solve problems independently.

Group members play the role of mutual evaluation in the process of evaluation. Online evaluation tables are distributed to group members, which are evaluated in the form of a percentage system, mainly including the following four aspects: the completion of the program code accounts for 30%, the integrity and operation of the code accounts for 30%, the correctness of the code results accounts for 25%, and the personal innovation accounts for 15%. After the completion of the evaluation, the group members submitted the data, the online evaluation results will be recycled for statistics, and the average evaluation results of the group members will be taken as the score of the evaluated students. The final score of the student is composed of 50% student evaluation score + 50% teacher evaluation score, thus ensuring the fairness and objectivity of the grade evaluation.

3   Teaching Practice

In the teaching practice, the teaching goal is always to integrate the training of computational thinking ability with different majors, stimulate students' interest in programming courses, and cultivate the ability of computational thinking to solve problems in various professional fields. Under the concept of OBE, the case teaching of Python program course with professional characteristics is carried out. In the teaching process, students are centered and their ability development and cultivation are emphasized. In classroom teaching, teaching and learning should complement each other and students should be taught how to think and how to learn. Therefore, in the teaching activities, a number of cases that integrates professional characteristics are used for teaching, so as to provide students with more exercise opportunities. Due to different professional categories, different expected learning outcomes are set, and the required professional knowledge and skills, teaching content and characteristic teaching cases are selected and arranged according to the expected learning outcomes. In terms of teaching form, the "online + offline" mixed teaching mode is adopted. Online teaching is mainly about students learning through MOOC + SPOC. Offline is mainly based on rain classroom teaching. At the same time, online learning resource platforms are made full use of for programming exercises and examinations, such as EduCoder practical teaching platform and paperless examination platform.

3.1 Public Cases

Common Foundation Cases are designed for students of all majors to learn the basic syntax system and basic programming methods of Python. The selected cases should be of a public nature. Temperature conversion and turtle function drawing are selected as basic cases in teaching. From temperature conversion cases to continuous value questions, text progress bar, body mass index BMI, basic statistics calculation and sorting, which helps students understand functions, strings, program branch structure, loop structure, etc. From the turtle function graph to drawing seven-segment digital tube, drawing Koch Snowflake Small Package, which helps students to master the code reuse, modular design, etc. From programming based on formulas to programming based on computational thinking, such as Monte Carlo home. Through the teaching practice of these public cases, it explains the syntax elements and programming mode of Python to students, helps them establish the general concept of Python programming, and enables students to have a comprehensive understanding and mastery of solving problems by using computer programming. Guide students to transition from the pre-structure stage and the single-point multi-point structure stage to the associative and extended abstract structure stage.

3.2 Cases that Integrate Professional Characteristics

Through the teaching of the basic contents of Python, the students have the programming ability based on the basic syntax system of Python. On this basis, the students of different majors are taught with professional special cases.

For different majors in science and engineering, select extended cases that can be designed to be integrated with the major. Such as fractal geometry based on recursive function, extension of Caesar cipher, automatic trajectory drawing, dimensionality reduction of high-dimensional data, scientific computing of matrix operations and broadcast functions, data visualization, scientific coordinate drawing, Holland personality analysis radar chart, Fourier transform, signal processing, machine learning method toolset, Web information extraction, web crawler and other extended cases, expand the use of

Python third-party libraries such as JSON, numpy, matplotlib, requests, and beautiful-soup4 for students. Financial and economic case making tends to be data analysis, such as using matplotlib to make high-quality two-dimensional data visualization, statistical data visualization, scientific coordinate graph drawing, Holland personality analysis radar chart, Fourier transform and other extended cases. Considering that most of the students majoring in education will be engaged in the education industry in the future, Python practice cases related to teaching management should be selected in the case selection, using dictionary contents and the call of the jieba library to make keyword statistics on the text data, using pandas to carry out a certain class grade analysis, and using matplotlib to plot for data visualization. Humanities and social science is mainly text analysis, using dictionary content to count the word frequency of a certain paragraph, so as to further learn to call the jieba library, which can count the word frequency of keywords in texts, literature or famous works, process the tool set of PDF files, and create or update the practical cases of the third-party library of Microsoft Word files. The jieba and wordcloud can also be used to make word clouds. The sport disciplines select the analysis of sports competitions, which allows students to understand the program design process, how to carry out modular design, top-down design, and how to analyze the rules of a certain sports competition through computer programs to simulate competitions between opponents of different levels and levels in thousands of games by simulating some attributes in sports competitions. Art majors can use examples of graphic and image processing to interest students. After learning the basic data types, students will learn regular two-bit data - images, and then how to use PIL library for photo manipulation will be introduced, or students can draw their own work by using turtle. It can be further extended to graphic art, rose drawing and other cases.

3.3 Evaluation and Analysis of Diversified Teaching Effects

The course adopts the form of diversified teaching evaluation, and records and preserves the students' learning process in real time through the online teaching platform and offline programming experiments, including online preview MOOC courses, unit tests through SPOC, on-machine experimental training, using the modular programming exercises and tests on EduCoder practical teaching platform to summarize and analyze. It is used as the formative assessment that accounts for 60% of the total score of the students, and the paperless exam for the final exam accounts for 40% of the total score of the students. According to the data collected from the formative evaluation and summative evaluation as well as students' programming, most students can conscientiously complete the case programming of case-based teaching, with a completion rate of over 95%. Some students can spread their thinking and make their ideas on basic programming to show better results. In the learning process, students can take the initiative to use the knowledge to combine with the characteristics of the major and solve some major-related problems by using third-party library programming. Through the questionnaire survey of peer teachers and students, 185 teaching questionnaires were distributed to students, 183 were recovered, and the evaluation rate was 98%. Both students and peer teachers are more than 90% satisfied with the course, but they also put forward a lot of feedback. Through relevant opinions and feedback, relevant problems can be improved in a timely manner.

4 Conclusion

Empowering information technology to professional learning, forming programming courses with the integration of professional characteristics, so that students of different majors can understand and apply programming to solve related problems in professional fields through learning. Under the concept of OBE, taking the teaching of Python programming courses as an example, combining the Python course content and the preset professional learning outcomes to carry out case teaching that integrates professional characteristics. In teaching practice activities, diversified teaching evaluation is adopted to ensure the objectivity, fairness and effectiveness of evaluation, and timely feedback of evaluation results, so as to promote the improvement of teaching activities and form a good closed-loop continuous cycle improvement network. Through the teaching practice, it has been proved that under the concept of OBE, the case teaching of programming courses integrating professional characteristics can achieve good teaching effects in teaching activities, and students' thinking ability and practical ability are cultivated. After a period of study, students will be able to achieve the expected professional learning outcomes and can solve problems in the professional fields through programming.

Acknowledgment. This work is supported by University-Industry Collaborative Education Program of China (Grant No 202002021009) and the Education Research Project of AFCEC (Grant Nos 2020-AFCEC-150, 2021-AFCEC-464, 2022-AFCEC-143).

References

1. Zhai. Y., Ao, Z.: Exploration of mixed teaching mode in python programming cours. Dev. Pedagogy **2**(12), 172–173 (2021)
2. Wang, D., Liang, J.: Research on computer curriculum system for "new engineering" based on python language. Ind. Inf. Educ. (05), 29–33 (2020)
3. Wang, G., Lu, X., Jin, X., et al.: Research on the construction of new engineering general education system based on the results-oriented education concept. High. Eng. Educ. Res. (04), 29–34 (2021)
4. Zhang, N., Zhang, L., Wang, X., et al.: Understanding OBE: origin, core and practice boundary -- on the paradigm shift of professional education. High. Eng. Educ. Res. (03), 109–115 (2020)
5. Gou, P., Han, Y., Zhang, W.: Diversified teaching evaluation of python programming based on OBE concept. In: 16th International Conference on Computer Science & Education (ICCSE), pp. 402–406 (2021)
6. Liu, M., Li, J., Guan, C.: A hybrid teaching method for python programming language based on OBE concept. Comput. Eng. Sci. **41**(S1), 203–206 (2019)

Exploring Contested Issues with MOOCs and MOOCs' Practical Status in Chinese Local Undergraduate University

Xiaoyan Bu[✉]

NingboTech University, Ningbo 315100, China
bessie@nbt.edu.cn

Abstract. Massive Open Online Courses (MOOCs) have been one of the most focused issues in higher education. It is heatedly discussed whether they could challenge the traditional higher education and bring disruptive transformation to it. This study attempts to present such a debate, and explore the current practical status of MOOCs in higher education, especially in the teaching context of Chinese local undergraduate university. The study finds though MOOCs have innovative characteristics and practical impact on Chinese higher education, they still have not fully demonstrated the power to cause a revolution in higher education at present. If given more time and space for development, MOOCs may have the potential to play a more crucial role. Finally, some suggestions are also provided for the improvement of MOOC teaching in Chinese local undergraduate university.

Keywords: MOOCs · massiveness · openness · online · course · Chinese higher education

1 Introduction

Massive Open Online Courses (MOOCs) have cut a figure in the global higher education in the past decades. Many world first-class universities, such as Stanford University, Harvard University, King's College London, have already created various MOOC platforms and launched their own MOOCs. Chinese universities have also been involved in this strong wave of MOOCs. They not only regard MOOCs as an innovative online education mode, but also as an important opportunity to promote the quality of higher education [1]. According to Xinhua Net's survey in 2020, the number and scale of Chinese MOOCs have ranked first in the world, with more than 34,000 MOOCs and 540 million enrollments [2]. However, the rapid emergence of MOOCs in higher education leads to wide concern and heated discussion as well. For some educators, MOOCs are labeled as a coming "campus tsunami" [3], "the most important education technology in 200 years" [4], "a new textbook in the 21st century" [5]. They assert MOOCs are a disruptive technology, or even a disruptive innovation to transform the current higher education, challenging the traditional higher education and bringing revolutionary changes to it. In contrast, some scholars present different views, arguing that MOOCs are somewhat traditional teaching courses coated with the sugar of online technology and are not mature enough to bring about a disruptive revolution in higher education at present [6, 7]. Such a polarized debate may stimulate the following questions. What roles do MOOCs play in higher education now? Can MOOC teaching mode be the alternative to traditional offline teaching mode? What impacts do MOOCs virtually bring to higher education? Accordingly, the current study is expected to present a debate about these puzzles as well as to explore the current practical status of MOOCs in higher education, especially in a specific teaching context, such as that of Chinese local undergraduate university.

2   MOOCs: Definition and Main Characteristics

MOOCs are online courses characterized by a huge number of participants and open access [8]. They are usually individual web-based courses that can be obtained by all [9]. To be more specific, they are "online courses that allow a massive and open participation on certain platforms, whose main components are as follows: a collection of videos of recorded classes mostly by a renowned professor from a prestigious university, links to material support, automated assessments, discussion forums and peer reviews, providing greater accessibility to a flexible and ubiquitous education" [10]. Therefore, MOOCs are neither Open Educational Resources, nor traditional e-learning courses. They are generally specific courses based on network, freely or low-costly available for a global population.

In order to make a better understanding of MOOCs, some scholars insist MOOCs can be chiefly characterized as what their name implies.EUA Council considers MOOCs' main features are massiveness (i.e. unlimited participation), openness (i.e. no requirement for entry) and online (i.e. available through networks) [11]. Similarly, Atiaja and Guerrero-Proenza [9] point out that MOOCs' characteristics lie in their name: for MASSIVE learners; OPEN to anyone; through ONLINE services; COURSES. It seems the spelling of MOOC itself indicates its main characteristics and helps unlock the secret of MOOCs' connotation to a large extent. Thus, the main characteristics of MOOCs might be generalized as: 1) massive: MOOCs can satisfy the learning desire of a large-scale of diverse participants to learn at the same time, with immense supply of courses. 2) open: anyone can join MOOCs without registration requirements or fee. 3) online: no matter where learners are, they can have lectures at any time through the Internet. 4) course: MOOCs contain educational plans with pedagogical approaches and fulfill the educational function.

However, as part of an innovative educational technology, these four features, though, provide MOOCs with distinctive advantages and make them stand out of various educational forms in higher education, they also make MOOCs fall into a vortex of being questioned. It is said that every letter of MOOC can be negotiable [12].

3   Some Contested Issues with MOOCs in Higher Education

As noted above, though the four letters of MOOC can present the main characteristics of MOOCs, they are also negotiable and contested. So the following discussion will be developed based on these four main characteristics.

3.1 Issues with Massiveness

Massiveness is a marked feature of MOOCs. This wide-range nature of MOOC is reflected in both global participants and the large number of MOOC courses given by a large number of universities [13].

However, such a massive population of MOOC participants poses a big challenge to assessment and feedback of MOOCs. For the sake of avoiding the huge task of artificial feedback, MOOCs rely much on automated online grading system in assessment, so it is difficult for MOOCs to offer diverse assignments, such as short-answer question or essay [14]. Besides, some learners may cheat or plagiarize through learning or in assessment, resulting in inaccurate learning evaluation results. Even though some techniques, like signature track, are adopted to identify learners, these skills are still in experimental period, far from being widely used [9].

Furthermore, though there are millions of MOOC courses online, MOOC teaching mode is not necessarily suitable for all the courses. For example, hand-on courses are difficult to complete in MOOCs and require detailed guidance in reality. Moreover, the quality of massive MOOC courses is uneven, which is also a very unstable factor in MOOC system. As a rising star in education, MOOC has unique pedagogical characteristics. Teachers need not only to grasp professional knowledge and teaching skills, but also to improve their information literacy of producing and operating MOOCs. Researchers stress even though many MOOCs are founded by elite universities, it does not mean these courses are bound to high quality [13]. Only when MOOC instructors are fully capable of delivering MOOCs, can MOOCs successfully meet learners' needs.

3.2 Issues with Openness

Apart from certification fee of few MOOCs, MOOCs are free courses for all types of learners, without any entry requirements. Such unconditional openness of MOOC has alleviated the imbalance of educational resources, as learners from all corners of the world can enjoy massive educational resources, including those resources of world-famous universities. Also, at low or no cost, MOOCs expand access to education, which makes a big step forward in the realization of lifelong education.

However, openness is not equal to diversity. Lane and Kinser [15] state MOOCs are the "McDonaldization of higher education", which refers to "thousands of students across the world taking the same course, with the same content, from the same instructor", regardless of the differences in language, culture, backgrounds, learning styles. Due to the low level of foreign language proficiency, digital proficiency and hardware facilities, students from developing countries or backward regions may be handicapped in MOOC learning. In addition, MOOC resources of top universities may lack local relevance, and thereby "cultural translation" is needed [16], otherwise they are detrimental to local and indigenous knowledge development. These barriers may be the reasons why the majority of MOOC participants are highly educated ones from more advanced countries while only about 2.7% of MOOC learners are from the least developed countries [17]. Furthermore, since the mainstream MOOC platforms are dominated by elite universities in the Western world [18], there is a new worry that MOOCs will lead to digital neocolonialism in higher education. Lockley [19] argues that MOOCs' promise of "education for all" is an illusion, which makes education a public product but threatens marginalized knowledge and the global education system. Thus, how to meet the different needs of learners might be a further consideration in the design of MOOCs.

3.3 Issues with Online

Online is the technical condition to ensure "massiveness" and "openness". With the support of network, learners can participate in MOOCs whenever and wherever they want, so they will fully enjoy the flexibility of MOOC learning, which becomes a strong attraction of MOOCs. Besides, such flexibility also makes the interaction between learners and teachers asynchronous and much easier. Now, learners can just leave questions on forums or social interaction platforms and wait for teachers' answers, instead of queuing up to consult teachers after class.

Unfortunately, there are also contradictory views on MOOCs in online environment. Zakaria [20] illustrates MOOCs are no more than huge online lecture halls, still dominated by traditional teaching mode of one-way knowledge transmission. Additionally, without real-time interaction between teachers and students, the instant feedback mechanism is damaged. Even in some synchronous MOOCs, it is impossible for instructors to answer all the questions on time, since the learners are far more than instructors. According to a survey from Coursera MOOC platform, the interval time between raising a question and getting a response on forums is 22 min on average [21]. Meanwhile, learners in virtual interaction only can leave messages on forums or social interaction platforms where there is no classroom atmosphere, which reduces social participation and ultimately hurts the learners' enthusiasm to study. Therefore, the teaching quality of MOOCs will be greatly influenced by the non-timeliness of interaction.

Moreover, such virtual interaction also influences the depth of education as well as the relationship between teachers and learners. The nature of university learning is a kind of "apprentice-like activity" [22]. It is not only a matter of acquiring knowledge, but also a matter of cultivating character, behavior, viewpoint and professional spirit of learners, which need to be developed through getting along with teachers and classmates. At present, MOOC learning is mostly reflected in the teaching of knowledge, while teaching also involves other content, including the emotional communication, the influence of values and the conflicts of thoughts [23]. So the sophisticated interaction in real class is hard for machines to replace.

3.4 Issues with Course

As non-traditional courses, MOOCs have unique pedagogical features and provide opportunities of autonomous learning. A MOOC is usually composed of several short video lectures together with some exercises or quizzes. For one thing, the time span of each short video lectures are 10–20 min on average, which helps learners make full use of fragmentation time. For another, if students do not fully grasp a knowledge point, they can replay the video and review it time and again. In other words, MOOC learners can arrange their study according to their own learning pace, style and preferences. Another innovation in MOOC teaching is the application of real-time 'big data' analysis. MOOCs can gather the data about learning behavior of each learner for analysis, and then provide learning feedback for learners to enrich their personalized learning experience and for teachers to improve their course designs respectively. Meanwhile, many MOOCs begin to offer services as certification of completion and even credit granting at the end of courses. This advantage might soon have a disruptive impact on higher education [24].

In contrast, the orientation of autonomous learning and personalized learning look like a double-edged sword. It is found that successful MOOC participants are usually those who have strong motivation, independent learning ability, and high self-discipline [25]. Free from the supervision and management of teachers, lots of MOOC learners cannot maintain strong motivation or high self-regulation of learning. Drowned in massive information and complex network, they cannot adhere to MOOC study, which will inevitably affect their completion of MOOCs. As a result, low completion rate almost becomes the most critical issue of MOOCs. According to statistics, the completion rate of many MOOCs even decline to less than 10% [10]. While some researchers doubt the educational quality of MOOCs due to this index, others defend the low completion rate, saying that it does not necessarily indicate the ineffectiveness of MOOCs. MOOC analysis report by Harvard and MIT releases the low completion rate is associated with high registration rate [26]. Perhaps learning with no charge will reduce learners' sense of responsibility, just as "free" is often regarded as "worthless". Learners need not make a learning commitment at the beginning of the course, so the filtering of inactive learners is delayed to the next stage [27]. Other researches have shown that this phenomenon is mainly because learners have diverse motivations to participate in MOOCs. Some of them want to get certificates, some want to look for certain specific knowledge, while others may just want to gain an experience [9].

The validity of MOOC certification and credit has also been questioned. MOOCs have not established a strict evaluation standard and mechanism so far. The threshold of obtaining certifications is still low, so few enterprises value them much in employment [28]. When it comes to credit granting, it is crucial for platforms to raise MOOCs' value and take measures to prevent students from plagiaristic behaviors like "replacing learning" and "cheating in exams". Therefore, how to establish and improve MOOC accreditation and credit granting system and how to increase the social approval of MOOC certification should be resolved in no time.

4   A Case Study: The Status Quo of MOOCs in Teaching Practice of Chinese Local Undergraduate University

In China, the government direct intervention and support have played an important role in improving the construction and development of MOOCs. Early in 2011, China Ministry of Education (MOE) launched a project entitled "Construction of National Excellent Open Courses", and many universities, whether leading ones or local ones, began to build MOOCs of all levels, from undergraduate to postgraduate [29]. In order to display the situation of MOOCs in Chinese higher education, especially in Chinese local undergraduate universities which represent the majority of Chinese universities, let's take NingboTech University (NBT) as an example and explore the above contested issues with MOOCs in a real teaching context.

NingboTech University is an average local undergraduate university in Ningbo with approximately 10,000 students. The university has formally joined the MOOC tide primarily by two means: both as a MOOC customer and as a MOOC producer. As a customer, NBT has chosen several MOOCs from big domestic platforms for students as public optional courses; as a producer, the university organizes teachers to create MOOCs.

4.1 Issues with Massiveness

In NBT, MOOCs are chiefly used as public optional courses. 2–4 MOOCs are launched each term. In the latest three academic years, the most frequently given MOOCs are *Art Appreciation, Foundation of College Students' Entrepreneurship* and *Chinese Silk Culture.* The choice of MOOCs depends on two reasons: insufficient teacher resource and students' lack of specific knowledge. According to "The Evaluation Index System for Undergraduate College in Zhejiang Province", the local undergraduate universities have to offer art optional courses. Lack of art teachers, NBT turns to MOOCs for help and offers the MOOC course *Art Appreciation* for students. *Foundation of College Students' Entrepreneurship* is chosen to help improve the students' competitive ability in innovation and entrepreneurship, because MOE encourages to train College Students' Innovation and Entrepreneurship and students need professional instruction in this aspect. Similarly, the choice of *Chinese Silk Culture* aims to increase students' knowledge of "Maritime Silk Road", responding to the call to build the "21st Century Maritime Silk Road". Consequently, the massive MOOCs prove themselves a good complement to the teaching resources of local universities and a useful support to students' comprehensive development. Yet, it is worth noting that all these chosen MOOCs are used as optional courses in NBT and belong to general education curriculum, which partly confirms MOOCs are more suitable to some basic introductory courses.

The final grade of these courses is made up of video watching (50%), exercises or quizzes (20%), number of discussion or course visits (5%) and final exam (25%). For exercises, quizzes and exams, the platforms only provide multiple choice question as the only assessment instrument. Apparently, the problem of single evaluation model is still unsolved in practice, but just as what the teacher in charge of NBT optional courses said, this may well be the most efficient way to address MOOC assessment presently. Cheating and plagiarism are still headaches for platforms and universities. In order to overcome this deficiency, platforms supervise every student's learning process. Abnormal records of learning will be cleared to zero. If it happens twice, the student will be disqualified. As a result, the dropout rate caused by cheating or plagiarism is lower than 1% in recent three academic years. Though there are some limitations in MOOC assessment, it is proved that most students can get high grades in these MOOCs. For example, NBT students' average grade of the above three MOOC optional courses in the latest three academic years are above 92. This is likely to be the first reason for the popularity of these MOOCs.

NBT teachers also involve in MOOC production. The university has joined the provincial program of "Constructing 100 Excellent MOOCs within Five Years (2016–2020)", aiming to establish student self-learning resource database, to practice teachers' ability to teach online and to select well-built MOOCs to assist the MOOC construction of higher-levels. Most of these MOOCs are put on a provincial platform—ZJOOC. Nevertheless, despite a sum of financial reward and a technical team to shoot videos, teachers lack training of how to design or make MOOCs, so most of them have to grope for ways to make MOOCs. Furthermore, limited by the undergraduate training plan which advocates interactions and face-to-face instruction in major courses, these MOOCs never replace their offline counterparts and are just used as supplementary learning resource. With little training and feedback from the real MOOC teaching practice, it is hard for traditional teachers to change into professional MOOC instructors and produce qualified MOOCs. They may gain some experience in producing MOOCs, but they still have a long way to go in fulfilling the pedagogical ownership.

4.2 Issues with Openness

Thanks to the rich MOOC resources, students of this common local university also can enjoy the excellent courses. No matter whether they serve as optional courses or are used as supplementary materials, all the MOOCs are free for students. Therefore, MOOCs provide a feasible way to cultivate students' awareness of lifelong learning. Next, most of the MOOCs that NBT launches as optional courses are from two popular Chinese MOOC platforms: Chaoxing and Treenity, which could minimize the barriers of language and culture. In addition, the teacher in charge of optional courses in NBT explains these two big platforms contain a large amount of MOOCs made by Chinese first-class universities, which is also the main reason for NBT to choose them. For example, most frequently given MOOCs in NBT mentioned above are created by Peking University, Tsinghua University and Zhejiang University. Apparently, MOOCs of elite universities are still more popular in China. These schools occupy superior educational resources and take a leading position in MOOC education. In this case, the phenomenon of "the strong ones become stronger, whereas the weaker ones become weaker" might appear in future MOOC education [30]. Hence, ordinary local universities must improve the quality of their MOOCs, otherwise they have to face an increasingly competitive pressure in the MOOC market.

4.3 Issues with Online

MOOC optional courses are warmly welcomed by the students. In each term, when the MOOC optional courses are offered for students to select, all the elective places are soon filled in a flash. One reason is that MOOCs have their own flexibility for students to have their classes freely, independent of time and place. For teaching method, these MOOCs adopt the similar methods to traditional ones, which are quite familiar to students and may be another reason for the great acceptance by them.

However, effective interaction is a real problem. Browsing the forums or discussion boards, we can hardly find meaningful questions or comments from students, except some related to the technical problems. Some students only type "Sign in" in order to get the grade of discussion. Sometimes, teachers are not the main role in the interactions with students. On Chaoxing, the responders to students' questions are not the teachers themselves, but the servicers or assistants of the platform. Accordingly, the current MOOC environment still lacks the ability to facilitate effective interactions. It is adverse to building good communication and relationship between teachers and students, let along the cultivation of character, value, emotion, etc.

4.4 Issues with Course

When MOOCs enter the local university as optional courses, on one hand, students can enjoy the opportunity of autonomous learning presented by MOOCs; on the other hand, their learning autonomy is also restricted by the school regulations and course requirements, for example, they have to finish the phased learning tasks of MOOCs to receive credits.

Integrated into the university system, MOOCs seem to go out of the shadow of low completion rate. In the latest three academic years, the completion rates of the MOOC optional courses in NBT all exceed 90%. Most importantly, these MOOCs are related to credits, so the students attach great importance to them. The high rates are also credited to the university's supervision and reminder. For the MOOC optional courses, the university will issue notices twice a term on the university website to remind students of completing learning tasks. For the MOOCs on ZJOOC, most of them are assigned as supplementary learning materials for the students and their teachers will check the learning results periodically. Interestingly, college credit granting can function as a good incentive to raise completion rate of MOOCs. If MOOCs could grant recognized accreditation, they may fulfill their potential better and be more accepted by learners.

Currently, MOOC certifications have still been narrowly accepted by Chinese society and they are not valued highly in employment market [31]. But most Chinese universities have actively integrated MOOCs with campus education and recognized MOOCs for credits, since Tsinghua University in 2014 transferred several basic courses from offline to the online MOOC platform and offered credits to those who passed the exams [23]. However, in China, cheating also appears in MOOC learning time and again. Based on NBT students' feedback, it is feasible for them to surf online for answers when they are doing MOOC exercises, quizzes and exams, which can partly explain why most of the students get high grades in MOOC optional courses.

5 Implication of MOOCs' Development on Chinese Local Undergraduate University

For Chinese local undergraduate universities which have difficulty in adapting to the needs of modern education in the face of insufficient teacher resource and less educational resource, making full use of MOOCs may be a good opportunity for them to deepen teaching reform, enhance teaching quality and develop teachers' professional skills. But how to effectively integrate MOOCs with current education of Chinese local undergraduate universities still needs to be explored in depth.

According to the above analysis, for Chinese local undergraduate universities, MOOCs cannot completely replace the traditional courses at present. They are mainly used as optional courses, supplementary resources to assist the face-to-face teaching, or valuable alternatives in times of pandemic. Policy encouragement and school guidance play a decisive role in bringing MOOCs into the local university teaching system. In contrast, most teachers there are not well prepared or qualified to make MOOCs. Due to a lack of relevant training, they still tend to create MOOCs based on the traditional teaching experience. Meanwhile, these chosen MOOCs are almost all made by prestigious universities, which also narrows the existing space of the MOOCs made by local undergraduate universities. Besides, though these MOOC optional courses are popular among the students, inefficient interaction and undiversified assessment instrument make up serious deficiencies of MOOCs used in local universities, which hampers MOOCs' advantages and influences their quality. Bound by the local university management system and inspired by credits, students take completion rate more seriously and make it largely increased, while the issues like cheating and low social approval of MOOC certification still need to be solved.

Some suggestions are raised for the improvement of MOOC teaching in Chinese local undergraduate university. Firstly, Chinese educational authorities should formulate the certification standards of MOOCs in higher education to guarantee their quality. They should establish a sound mechanism of MOOC credit recognition, conversion and certification to promote the standardization of MOOCs, which will also improve MOOCs' social recognition.

Secondly, local undergraduate universities should actively incorporate MOOC teaching mode and construction into the whole teaching system. They should provide teachers with practical and technical guidance on making MOOCs, improve their MOOC production ability and help them develop MOOCs with local characteristics distinct from those of elite universities. Meanwhile, with the help of big data technology, universities should construct a standardized management system, guide students to find and solve problems in MOOC learning process, and enhance students' autonomous learning ability.

Last, MOOC platforms should add more interactive activities to course content and assignments. Also they should optimize interactive activities such as forum communication, question-answering and so forth, so as to promote learners' motivation. Additionally, building cooperative learning teams is also a good attempt to improve communication and interaction. In order to ensure the fairness and effectiveness of MOOC learning results, MOOC platforms could introduce audio-visual recognition and other technical means to ensure the authenticity of learning as well as online monitoring and checking technology to ensure the reliability of the exam results. MOOC learning should be based on integrity. Only when the learning results truly reflect learners' learning achievements, can the fairness and justice of MOOC education be really realized.

6   Conclusion

The emergence of MOOCs represents a direction and evolution of higher education in the digital era. MOOCs, with their large-scale, open and online features, play a unique role in higher education. However, the current development of MOOCs in Chinese higher education is not mature enough and still in a developing stage, especially from the perspective of teaching content and method in which there is no thorough innovation. It is still too early to assert whether MOOC teaching mode will completely replace the traditional one since they have not fully demonstrated a disruptive power. In addition, some issues, especially validity of MOOC certification, call for more concern in the future.

All in all, MOOC is an innovative educational mode. Whether to be disruptive or not depends on its development. Disruption is something like a process rather than an event, which needs time to prove. What's more important is MOOCs do provide Chinese local undergraduate universities with developing chances. In order to be more focused, this paper mainly studies the MOOCs integrated in the university teaching system or supported by the school, so the MOOC materials used in classes by teachers privately are not taken into consideration. Further research may explore MOOCs in this aspect, considering blended learning and flipped classroom have also received much attention.

References

1. Zhao, H., Zheng, Q., Chen, L.: A study of the construction and development of MOOCs in China: development and reflections. Distance Educ. China **11**, 55–62 (2017)
2. The number and scale of MOOCS in China has ranked first in the world. http://www.xinhua net.com/politics/2020-12/12/c_1126851919.htm. Accessed 19 Jan 2021
3. Brooks, D.: The campus tsunami. The New York Times. https://www.immagic.com/eLibrary/ARCHIVES/GENERAL/GENPRESS/N120503B.pdf. Accessed 5 Feb 2021
4. Regalado, A.: The most important education technology in 200 years. MIT Technol. Rev. **116**(5), 61–62 (2013)
5. Kanenari, R.: MOOC and innovation of university education. Inf. Process. **55**(5), 475–481 (2014)
6. Baggaley, J.: Reflections on the upsurge of MOOC. Open Educ. Res. **20**(1), 9–17 (2014)
7. Auyeung, V.: To MOOC or not to MOOC: Issues to consider for would-be MOOC academic leads. High. Educ. Res. Netw. J. **9**, 64–71 (2015)
8. Kaplan, A.M., Haenlein, M.: Higher education and the digital revolution: About MOOCs, SPOCs, social media, and the Cookie Monster. Bus. Horiz. **59**(4), 441–450 (2016)
9. Porter, S.: To MOOC or Not to MOOC: How Can Online Learning Help to Build the Future of Higher Education? Chandos Publishing, Oxford (2015)
10. Atiaja, L., Guerrero-Proenza, R.S.: The MOOCs: Origin, characterization, principal problems and challenges in higher education. J. E-Learning Knowl. Soc. **12**(1), 65–76 (2016)
11. Gaebel, M.: MOOCs: Massive open online courses. An update of EUA's first paper. EUA Occasional Papers. http://www.eua.be/Libraries/Publication/MOOCs_Update_January_2014.sflb.ashx. Accessed 19 Dec 2021
12. New, J.: MOOC: Every letter is negotiable. https://www.ecampusnews.com/2013/10/17/letter-mooc-644/. Accessed 23 Jan 2021
13. Zheng, Y.: A review of MOOC research in the past five years and controversies behind it. Voice Yellow River **10**, 17–19 (2017)
14. Yuan, L., Powell, S.: MOOCs and open education: Implications for higher education (JISC CETIS white paper). http://publications.cetis.ac.uk/2013/667. Accessed 30 Jan 2021
15. Lane, J., Kinser, K.: MOOC's and the McDonaldization of global higher education. https://www.immagic.com/eLibrary/ARCHIVES/GENERAL/CHRON_HE/C120928L.pdf. Accessed 1 Jan 2021
16. Jung, I., Gunawardena, C.N.: Culture and Online Learning: Global Perspectives and Research. Stylus Publishing, Sterling (2015)
17. Laurillard, D.: The educational problem that MOOCs could solve: Professional development for teachers of disadvantaged students. Res. Learn. Technol. **24**(1), 1–17 (2016)
18. Altbach, P.G.: MOOCs as neocolonialism: who controls knowledge? Int. High. Educ. **75**(75), 5–7 (2017)

19. Lockley,P.: Open initiatives for decolonising the curriculum. In: Bhambra, G.K., Gebrial, D., Nişancıoğlu, K. (eds.), Decolonising the University, pp. 145–170. Pluto Press, London (2018)
20. Zakaria, F.: In defense of a liberal education. https://hadinur.net/wp-content/uploads/2018/06/fareed-zakaria-in-defense-of-a-liberal-education-2015-w-w-norton-company.pdf. Accessed 27 Jan 2021
21. Wang, J.: Research on the current situation and bottlenecks of MOOC development in China. Innov. Sci. Technol. **194**(4), 52–53 (2016)
22. Brown, J.S., Duquid, P.: The Social Life of Information. Harvard Business Press, Boston (2000)
23. Zeng, X.: From credit to degree: the integration of MOOC with universities. Comp. Educ. Rev. **308**(8), 78–84 (2015)
24. Lenox, M.: The imminent shakeout? Disruptive innovation and higher education. http://www.forbes.com/sites/darden/2013/03/29/the-imminent-shakeout-disruptive-innovation-and-higher-education/. Accessed 19 Jan 2021
25. Ansah, R.H., Ezeh, O.V., Teck, T.S., Sorooshian, S.: The disruptive power of massive open online course (MOOC). Int. J. Inf. Educ. Technol. **10**(1), 42–47 (2020)
26. Ho, A., et al.: HarvardX and MITx: The first year of open online courses, fall 2012 — summer 2013. http://dspace.mit.edu/bitstream/1721.1/96649/1/SSRN-id2381263.pdf. Accessed 27 Jan 2021
27. McAuley, A., Stewart, B., George, S., Cormier, D.: The MOOC model for digital practice. http://davecormier.com/edblog/wp-content/uploads/MOOC_Final.pdf. Accessed 30 Jan 2021
28. Santandreu, D.: Have Disruptive Innovations Arrived at the Gates of Academia?. Doctoral Dissertation, University of the West of England (2016)
29. Zheng, Q., Li, Q., Chen, L.: A survey of teaching model of MOOCs in China. Open Educ. Res. **21**(6), 71–79 (2015)
30. Zhang, Q., Rao, X., Wang, Y.: The thinking of MOOC and higher education connotation development: the problems and strategies of MOOC construction in China. Mod. Educ. J. **5**(1), 50–56 (2017)
31. Yang,L.: The critical thinking for MOOC and teaching of universities under the popularity of 'Internet Plus Education' in China. In: Proceeding of 2nd International Conference on Arts, Design and Contemporary Education, pp.1351–1355. Atlantis Press, Dordrecht (2016)

A Study of Students' Emotional Engagement in Blended Learning in the Post-epidemic Era-A Case Study of College English Course

Yuqi Lu and Huan Wang[✉]

NingboTech University, Ningbo, China
eletahuan@163.com

Abstract. With the advent of the post-epidemic era, blended learning, combining online and offline teaching, has become the choice of many university classrooms. How to improve student engagement in blended learning is therefore an issue worth investigating. This paper focuses on students' emotional engagement in blended learning, investigating its cognitive influences and its relationship with behavioral engagement items. Data analysis through SPSS 21.0 indicates that both learning motivation and self-efficacy may influence emotional engagement in blended learning, with self-efficacy as the mediating factor. It is also found that emotional engagement is significantly correlated with behavioral engagement items that are calculated through a combination of test score and screening time. These findings may imply some suggestion for the improvement of student engagement in blended learning context.

Keywords: blended learning · emotional engagement · behavioral engagement · learning motivation · self-efficacy

1 Introduction

Blended learning, a model combining online and offline teaching, emerged decades ago has been adopted widely in China by many university classrooms in post-epidemic era. Student-centeredness has been emphasized to encourage the creation in studies of blended learning and education, some focus on students' personal features [1], some on classroom context [2], both of with may influence students' satisfactory of learning, and in turn influence their learning engagement [3].

Students' learning engagement in blended context is presumed to be a dispensable topic. According to previous researches on student engagement, it can be regarded as one efficient predictors of learning, linking closely to students' academic achievement and dropout rates and is likely to be malleable according to the change in contextual features [4, 5]. Despite minor difference in classification, the multidimensional construct of student engagement consists of at least three interdependent and interactive components: behavioral engagement (how they perform during learning), emotional engagement (how student feel about learning), and cognitive engagement (how they reflect on learning) [4–6].

Emotional engagement has been referred to various emotional reactions caused by their identification to the courses, teachers, or schools [4, 5]. It is expected to stimulate students' participation and persistence in school endeavors [5]. In the cases of blended learning context, relevant researches have demonstrated that emotional engagement is linked to at least two cognitive factors: learning motivation and self-efficacy [7, 8].

It might be not so easy to understand emotional and cognitive engagements, as their assessments are usually conducted through self-report description like interview or think-aloud report [6]. But the monitor system of online learning platform offers various categories of data reflecting students' behavioral engagement online. By identifying the relationship between emotional engagement and online behavioral engagement, it might be more convenient to interpret students' online emotional engagement, and thus provide advice for the improvement of blended learning context.

As indicated in Ge's study, students' EFL online learning engagement might be significantly related to their motivation and mediated by their self-efficacy [9]. Such a conclusion might be challenged since the online learning engagement in Ge's research refers to a comprehensive engagement including behavioral, cognitive and emotional engagement. In addition, all the data in his research were collected via questionnaire instead of the more objective data from the online platform. Thus, a further study is needed to check the mediation value of self-efficacy, and to explore the relationships between cognitive engagement, emotional engagement and online behavioral engagement in blended learning context.

This research takes on emotional engagement as the research focus, examining cognitive factors that may influence emotional engagement and the correlation with behavioral engagement in terms of emotional engagement. Taking a college English online course as an example, this study aims to explore two questions: 1) What are the cognitive influence on emotional engagement? 2) What is the relationship between emotional engagement and online behavioral engagement?

2 Methodology

2.1 Participants and Setting

Altogether 100 non-English major freshmen in East China were included as participants in this study, including 58 female students and 42 male students. They were experiencing blended learning method in their college English course, where they were involved in various online/offline tasks both inside and outside classrooms. By offline learning, it means learning in traditional face-to-face lecturing, listening, reading and translation and writing class. By online learning, these participants were assigned to do tasks in http://www.chaoxing.com and https://welearn.sflep.com. They were supposed to complete self-regulated online tasks of listening and reading practices in these two websites or their mobile APPs outside of class. Once they click an online task, they would be recorded as "complete". In addition, these participants have also engaged in online learning tasks in class. Once a thematic discussion was launched by the teacher, they were supposed to post their idea online briefly, and then some were asked by teacher to express orally their ideas in detail. Their online learning record and discussion posts would constitute an important part in their final scores.

Outside of class, students were asked to study independently, pre-reading the text-book and reading the words offline, and online they would complete some practice questions, resource learning and news listening on the platform.

2.2 Questionnaire Design

A questionnaire was adopted in this study to the assess participants' English learning motivation, self-efficacy and evaluation on their own online English learning engagement. This questionnaire is designed by referring to three-section questionnaire in Ge's research [9]. What is different from Ge's questionnaire is that the third section only focus on emotional engagement data, leaving behavioral data to be collected from the learning platform.

All these 22 questions in this questionnaire can be divided in 3 sections (see appendix): learning motivation, self-efficacy, and online engagement. The learning motivation section is divided into five dimensions: effort (Question 1 and Question 8), intrinsic interest (Question 5 and Question 9), extrinsic need (Question 2 and Question 10), learning situation (Question 3 and Question 6), and learning value (Question 4 and Question 7). The self-efficacy section is divided into three dimensions: sense of course fit (Question 11 and Question 15), sense of goal confidence (Question 12 and Question 14), and sense of course competence (Question 13 and Question 16). The online learning engagement section is divided into three dimensions: cognitive engagement (Question 17 and Question 19), behavioral engagement (Question 20 and Question 22), and emotional engagement (Question 18 and Question 21). The responses to the questionnaire were provided on a 5-point Likert type scale ranging from 1 (Strongly Disagree) to 5 (Strongly Agree). At last, all the questions were uploaded into www.wjx.cn, a commonly used survey APP in China.

In order to ensure the reliability and validity of the questionnaire and to improve the scientific validity of the study results, the author conducted a pretest of the questionnaire. A total of 100 other non-English major college students were invited to attend this pretest. 100 responses returned, but with 2 invalid ones.

For each scale, a total score was produced by summing the numeric values of the individual responses on the questions making up that scale. The Chronbach's Alphas of the subscales, based on the current sample was 0.873 (Table 1).

Table 1. Questionnaire Reliability Analysis

Cronbach's Alpha	Cronbachs alpha based on standardised terms	Number of items
.873	.887	22

The KMO value for the overall validity of the questionnaire was 0.852, which was greater than 0.8, meeting the basic requirements of questionnaire validity. Meanwhile, the Bartlett sphericity test results showed that the overall questionnaire had a significant level value of 0.000 ($p < 0.001$), which shows that the intrinsic validity of this questionnaire satisfied the basic requirements of the questionnaire (Table 2).

Table 2. Questionnaire Validity Analysis

Kaiser-Meyer-Olkin metric for sampling adequacy		.852
Bartlett's test for sphericity	Approximate cardinality	2215.242
	df	528
	Sig	.000

2.3 Data Collection

The study was conducted at the beginning of the second half of the semester, when the participants had been engaged in blended learning for a whole semester. Three categories of data were collected from three sources respectively: 1) learning record from www.cha oxing.com, including percentage of tasks that have clicked and screening time they use in listening recording and video tasks. 2) Effort Value score from https://welearn.sflep. com, a comprehensive score of task-completion, test scores, and screening time; and 3) questionnaire scores, including the scores for motivation, self-efficacy, and emotional engagement.

The first two categories of data were collected at the end of that semester by the participants' teacher. The questionnaire was also delivered by the teacher informing them of research purpose and ensuring them that they could withdraw if they were unwilling to participate in this study. All the 100 participants responded validly. Then all the data were transferred anonymously to the researcher for data analysis.

2.4 Data Analysis

In order to investigate the correlation relationship between emotional engagement with emotion factors in blended learning and with behavioral engagement, SPSS21.0 was adopted in this study. These data were analyzed through the following steps:

1) The 1st Pearson correlation test was adopted to examine the correlation between three categories of data from questionnaire: emotional engagement, motivation, and self-efficacy.
2) Regression Analysis was applied to examine the mediation effect of self-efficacy between motivation and emotional engagement in blended learning, according to the intermediary effects test procedure initiated by Wen et al. [13].
3) The 2nd Pearson correlation test was adopted to calculate the correlation between emotional engagement data from questionnaire and behavioral engagement data from two learning websites, including screening time, percentage of task completion, and Effort Value.
4) In order to further explore the relationship between motivation and Effort Value, the 3rd Pearson correlation test was employed to examine the correlation coefficient between effort value and two dimensions in motivation to learn, namely extrinsic need and effort.

3 Results

3.1 Learning Motivation, Self-efficacy and Emotional Engagement are Correlated

By means of Pearson correlation analysis, learning motivation, self-efficacy and emotional engagement are highly correlated. The result (see Table 3) indicates that there was a strong correlation between emotional engagement and self-efficacy and motivation to learn, with correlation coefficients of 0.635 and 0.566 respectively with a significant p-value of 0.000, which is less than 0.01. This demonstrates that there is a significant positive correlation between self-efficacy, learning motivation and emotional engagement. In other words, students' self-efficacy and the state of their motivation to learn can greatly affect their emotional engagement, the higher the student's self-efficacy and learning motivation, the higher the emotional engagement in online learning.

Table 3. Correlation coefficients between emotional engagement, self-efficacy and motivation to learn

		Emotional Engagement	Self-efficacy	Learning Motivation
Emotional Engagement	Pearson Correlation		0.635**	0.566**
	Significance (two-sided)		0.000	0.000
	N		100	100
Self-efficacy	Pearson Correlation	0.635**	−5.29	
	Significance (two-sided)	0.000	15.71	
	N	100		
Learning Motivation	Pearson Correlation	0.566**		
	Significance (two-sided)	0.000		
	N	100		

**. Significantly correlated at the 0.01 level (two-sided).

3.2 Self-efficacy is a Mediating Variable Between Motivation and Emotional Engagement

In the separate regression analysis, emotional engagement, self-efficacy and learning motivation were entered in the equation. The equations were significant ($p = 0.000 <$

0.01) and according to the test steps for mediating effects, there were coefficients a and b and c', which were 0.420, 0.473 and 0.388 respectively. As a result, students' self-efficacy has a partially mediating effect. Table 4, Table 5 and Table 6 below demonstrate the mediating role of self-efficacy.

Table 4. Regression analysis of learning motivation and emotional engagement

Models		Non-standardized coefficients		Standard factor	t	Sig.
		B	Standard Error	Trial Version		
1	(Constant)	−.289	.985		−.293	.770
	Learning motivation	.206	.029	.586	7.163	.000

*. Dependent variable: Emotional engagement.

Table 4 tested the first equation depicted from Wen et al. (2004) [10]. As can be seen from the results, p = 0.000, meets the requirements for significance. The standardized coefficient c = 0.586, so the next test can be carried out.

Table 5. Regression analysis of learning motivation and self-efficacy

Models		Non-standardized coefficients		Standard factor	t	Sig.
		B	Standard Error	Trial Version		
1	(Constant)	7.455	2.787		2.675	.009
	Learning motivation	.373	.082	.420	4.581	.000

*. Dependent variable: Self-efficacy.

Test the second equation. According to the results, p = 0.000, satisfies the require-ments for significance. The standardized coefficient a = 0.420, consistent with the process of testing for mediating effects.

Table 6. Regression analysis of learning motivation, self-efficacy and emotional engagement

Models		Non-standardized coefficients		Standard factor	t	Sig.
		B	Standard Error	Trial Version		
1	(Constant)	−1.684	.870		−1.935	.056
	Learning motivation	.136	.027	.388	5.042	.000
	Self-efficacy	.187	.030	.473	6.145	.000

*. Dependent variable: Emotional engagement.

Test the third equation. Table 6 shows that p = 0.000 < 0.05 and meets the requirements for significance. The standardized coefficient b = 0.473, the standardized coefficient c' = 0.388, consistent with the process of testing for mediating effects.

3.3 Behavioral Engagement Correlates with Emotional Engagement

The third Pearson correlation analysis (Table 7) suggested that behavioral engagement correlates with emotional engagement. Three behavioral engagement data indicated different correlation with these emotional factors from questionnaire as follows:

Firstly, Percentage of task completion was not shown to be correlated with any of the emotional factors. The significance between percentage of task completion and emotional engagement, self-efficacy, and motivation to learn were 0.181, 0.906 and 0.881, which did not meet the correlation requirements.

Secondly, Video/listening screening time was also correlated with emotional engagement and learning motivation. And the correlation coefficients were 0.266 and 0.202 with the significance of 0.008 and 0.043 respectively.

Thirdly, Effort Value, a combination of test scores, length of study, completion of task, online screening time and number of logins, was highly correlated with emotional engagement with correlation coefficient of 0.276 and self-efficacy with correlation coefficient of 0.231, and they were significant at 0.005 and 0.021 respectively. But no significant correlation was found between effort value and motivation. The correlation coefficient between effort value and motivation 0.071, significant at 0.481.

However, the correlation coefficient between Effort Value and five sub-motivation items was examined, two further correlation was found: 1) Effort and effort value showed a positive correlation with a correlation coefficient of 0.222 and a significant p of 0.026. 2) There was a negative correlation between extrinsic need and effort value with a correlation coefficient of -0.199 and a significance of 0.047.

4 Discussions, Conclusion, and Limitation

Focusing on emotional engagement, this study examines its' relationship with cognitive factors and with behavioral engagement reflected in data collected from online learning platform.

Table 7. Correlation coefficients between emotional engagement and behavioral engagement

		Effort Value	Video/listening screening time	Percentage of task completion
Emotional Engagement	Pearson Correlation	0.276**	0.266**	0.135
	Significance (two-sided)	0.005	0.008	0.181
	N	100	100	100
Self-efficacy	Pearson Correlation	0.231*	0.119	0.012
	Significance (two-sided)	0.021	0.239	0.906
	N	100	100	100
Learning Motivation	Pearson Correlation	0.071	0.202*	0.015
	Significance (two-sided)	0.481	0.043	0.881
	N	100	100	100
Effort	Pearson Correlation	0.222*		
	Significance (two-sided)	0.026		
	N	100		
Extrinsic Needs	Pearson Correlation	−0.199*		
	Significance (two-sided)	0.047		
	N	100		

**. Significantly correlated at the 0 .01 level (two-sided).
*. Significantly correlated at the 0 .05 level (two-sided)

4.1 Correlations Between Learning Motivation, Self-efficacy, and Emotional Engagement

This result in Table 3 confirms the existence of a strong correlation between motivation, self-efficacy, and emotional engagement. Calculated by SPSS 21.0, this study also confirms that that self-efficacy plays a mediating role and has a crucial impact on both motivation and engagement in learning, which is in accordance with Ge's result that was conducted with AMOS 21.0 [9]. In addition, such a result is in accordance with that of Chen and Chen, advocating that there is a positive correlation between academic achievement in web-based autonomous learning and self-efficacy [11].

Since the twentieth century, the relationship between self-efficacy, motivation and student engagement have been studied by a number of scholars. Self-efficacy has been demonstrated to play a substantial role in predicting student engagement, motivation, and performance [12, 13], promoting students' self-efficacy is critical to increasing student engagement in blended learning. As discovered by Li, Yang, Cai and MacLeod (2017), there is a close relationship between students' computer self-efficacy, attitude, and satisfaction in the context of the model of blended learning and find that self-efficacy influence intrinsic motivation and attitudes [14]. Meanwhile, students with more positive academic emotions are also found to have higher self-efficacy for online learning, which can bring them more confidence to adapt to the online learning environment, and attend online learning activities, forming a virtuous cycle [15].

In general, this study demonstrates that self-efficacy plays a mediating role and has a crucial impact on both motivation and engagement in learning.

4.2 Correlations Between Emotional Engagement and Behavioral Engagement

It is found in this study that behavioral engagement data from online platform is not always significantly related to emotional engagement. That is, data such as task completion and screening time are not correlated with emotional engagement. A possible reason for weak correlation between emotional engagement and online behavioral engagement might be attributed to the easiness to be marked at "task completed" online. During the learning process, students are asked by teachers to complete these task points because these tasks are directly related to their grades. When students click to open the task online, they will be marked as "completed" soon. Such a practice cannot reflect the difference in students' emotional engagement.

Only those data that require long period of devotion are found to be closely correlated with emotional engagement, such as the video viewing time and a combination of test score and online screening time in this study. Usually, the length of viewing may indicate to some degree the students' self-determination in finishing this task. As indicated in Table 7, learning motivation is significant correlated with screening time. That means, students with higher learning motivation are likely to spending relatively longer time to viewing and listening these online materials. Considering their close correlation, motivation is likely to be transformed into student engagement under some friendly supportive conditions [8]. Flexibility in blended learning may bring students the sense of control and enhance their learning motivation and self-confidence [16].

A comprehensive score, combining online test and screen time, can function as a prominent indicator of students' emotional engagement. This result also confirms that emotional engagement is closely related to motivation and self-efficacy [12–15]. As is indicated in Table 7, the comprehensive score of Effort Value displays a significant correlation with self-efficacy. Students with a higher sense of self-efficacy may integrate into the learning process more quickly and are more engaged in their learning [9]. This comprehensive score also suggests a positive correlation with effort. On one hand, the portion of screening time requires students' devotion of time in learning; on the other hand, the performance in online test also demand students' self-study offline.

With a quantitative method, this study found that in blended learning context, students' emotional engagement is closely correlated with their motivation and mediated by self-efficacy. In addition, this study identifies a practical cue to monitor students' emotional engagement: That is, the degree of emotional engagement might be reflected in some online behavioral engagement data, e.g. the combination score with screening time and online test. This kind of data is to some degree related to self-efficacy and effort. Thus, promoting students' self-efficacy is critical to increasing student engagement in blended learning.

However, it is found in this study that the comprehensive score of online behavioral engagement does not indicates significant correlation with students' intrinsic need, but a negative correlation with extrinsic need. This result is not in accordance with the result of the study of Li, Yang, Cai and Macleod in 2017 [14]. This failure might be attributed to the difference in participant population or research setting. Further research is needed to be conducted on another group of participants or in other blended learning courses.

Acknowledgment. The authors gratefully acknowledge the research project supported by the Department of Education, Zhejiang Province Project (Project No. Jg20190584), and the research project supported by NingboTech University (Project No. NITJG-202084).

Appendix

Dear Students,
This is a survey on the emotional engagement of college students in blended English learning, aiming to understand the factors influencing the emotional engagement of college students in blended learning, so as to improve the teaching quality of blended learning. Please read each question carefully and fill it out carefully according to your actual situation. There is no right or wrong answer for each question, so answer as soon as you feel like it, without thinking too much. This questionnaire is for research purposes, and we hope you will actively participate in it, as your answers will be kept completely confidential.

Each question is followed by five levels, which are indicated by 5, 4, 3, 2, and 1, respectively, according to the degree of conformity. Please choose the level that best describes you according to the actual situation and select the appropriate option.

Note: Unless you think the other 4 do not really match your real thoughts, please try not to choose "I can't say".

1 = Very much incompatible 2 = Somewhat incompatible 3 = Impossible (neither compatible nor incompatible) 4 = Somewhat compatible 5 = Very much compatible.

1. I like to preview what I am going to study before I go to English class.
   A. Not very consistent   B. Somewhat not consistent   C. Not clear
   D. Somewhat consistent   E. Very consistent
2. I learned English because my parents/school wanted me to learn it.
   A. Not very consistent   B. Somewhat not consistent   C. Not clear
   D. Somewhat consistent   E. Very consistent
3. Good or bad test scores often affect my motivation to learn English.
   A. Not very consistent   B. Somewhat not consistent   C. Not clear
   D. Somewhat consistent   E. Very consistent
4. Learning English will help me gain more knowledge.
   A. Not very consistent   B. Somewhat not consistent   C. Not clear
   D. Somewhat consistent   E. Very consistent
5. The English online learning method has increased my interest in learning English.
   A. Not very consistent   B. Somewhat not consistent   C. Not clear
   D. Somewhat consistent   E. Very consistent
6. I like teachers who are inspiring and talk to their students a lot.
   A. Not very consistent   B. Somewhat not consistent   C. Not clear
   D. Somewhat consistent   E. Very consistent
7. English is a very important communication tool in today's society, and I want to learn it well.
   A. Not very consistent   B. Somewhat not consistent   C. Not clear
   D. Somewhat consistent   E. Very consistent
8. I like to take the initiative to participate in various teaching activities in English class and strive for question and answer opportunities.
   A. Not very consistent   B. Somewhat not consistent   C. Not clear
   D. Somewhat consistent   E. Very consistent
9. I like to learn English.
   A. Not very consistent   B. Somewhat not consistent   C. Not clear
   D. Somewhat consistent   E. Very consistent
10. The purpose of my English studies is to graduate successfully.
    A. Not very consistent   B. Somewhat not consistent   C. Not clear
    D. Somewhat consistent   E. Very consistent
11. I believe I can get good grades in English.
    A. Not very consistent   B. Somewhat not consistent   C. Not clear
    D. Somewhat consistent   E. Very consistent
12. I was able to adapt to the online English learning style very quickly.
    A. Not very consistent   B. Somewhat not consistent   C. Not clear
    D. Somewhat consistent   E. Very consistent
13. I believe I can grasp English grammar very well.
    A. Not very consistent   B. Somewhat not consistent   C. Not clear
    D. Somewhat consistent   E. Very consistent
14. No matter how good or bad my grades were, I never doubted my ability to learn English.
    A. Not very consistent   B. Somewhat not consistent   ·   C. Not clear
    D. Somewhat consistent   E. Very consistent
15. When I have some difficulty in English learning, I usually believe that I can figure it out if I try hard enough.
    A. Not very consistent   B. Somewhat not consistent   C. Not clear
    D. Somewhat consistent   E. Very consistent
16. I think I did a good job in completing the tasks assigned by the teacher.
    A. Not very consistent   B. Somewhat not consistent   C. Not clear
    D. Somewhat consistent   E. Very consistent
17. I have a reasonable study schedule in the online learning platform.
    A. Not very consistent   B. Somewhat not consistent   C. Not clear
    D. Somewhat consistent   E. Very consistent
18. I am highly motivated to use online learning platforms.
    A. Not very consistent   B. Somewhat not consistent   C. Not clear
    D. Somewhat consistent   E. Very consistent
19. I am not disturbed by other factors while learning in the online learning platform.
    A. Not very consistent   B. Somewhat not consistent   C. Not clear
    D. Somewhat consistent   E. Very consistent

20. I am always able to complete the tasks of the online learning platform on time.
    A. Not very consistent   B. Somewhat not consistent   C. Not clear
    D. Somewhat consistent   E. Very consistent
21. I am satisfied with the course resources and learning environment of the online learning platform.
    A. Not very consistent   B. Somewhat not consistent   C. Not clear
    D. Somewhat consistent   E. Very consistent
22. During the class, I will actively use the online learning platform to interact with the instructor.
    A. Not very consistent   B. Somewhat not consistent   C. Not clear
    D. Somewhat consistent   E. Very consistent

References

1. Hu, J., Peng, Y., Chen, H.: Differentiating the learning styles of college students in different disciplines in a college English blended learning setting. PLoS ONE **16** (2021). https://doi.org/10.1371/journal.pone.0251545
2. Yang, X., Zhou, X., Hu, J.: Students' preferences for seating arrangements and their engagement in cooperative learning activities in college English blended learning classrooms in higher education. High. Educ. Res. Dev. (2022). https://doi.org/10.1080/07294360.2021.1901667
3. Alshawisha, E., El-Banna, M.M., Alrimawic, I.: Comparison of blended versus traditional classrooms among undergraduate nursing students: a quasi-experimental study. Nurse Educ. Today **106** (2021). https://doi.org/10.1016/j.nedt.2021.105049
4. Fredricks, J.A., Blumenfeld, P.C., Paris, A.H.: School engagement: potential of the concept, state of the evidence. Rev. Educ. Res. **74**, 59–109 (2004)
5. Finn, J.D., Zimmer, K.S.: Student engagement: what is it? Why does it matter. In: Christenson, S.L., Reschly, A.L., Wylie, C. (eds.) Handbook of Research on Student Engagement, pp. 97–131. Springer, Boston (2012). https://doi.org/10.1007/978-1-4614-2018-7_5
6. Reschly, A., Pohl, A., Christenson, S.: Student Engagement, Effective Academic, Behavioral, Cognitive, and Affective Interventions at School. Springer, Cham (2020). https://doi.org/10.1007/978-3-030-37285-9
7. Manwaring, K.C., Larsen, R., Graham, C., Brigham, H., Halverson, L.R.: Investigating student engagement in blended learning settings using experience sampling and structural equation modeling. Internet High. Educ. **35**, 21–33 (2017)
8. Kim, C., Park, S.W., Cozart, J., Lee, H.: From motivation to engagement: the role of effort regulation of virtual high school students in mathematics courses. J. Educ. Technol. Soc. **18**, 261–272 (2015)
9. Ge, Z.: A Study on the Influence of High School Students' Motivation and Self-efficacy on Their Engagement in Online English Learning. Minnan Normal University, Zhangzhou (2021)
10. Wen, Z., Zhang, L., Hou, J., Liu, H.: The intermediate effects test procedure and its application. Psychol. J. **05**, 614–620 (2004)
11. Chen, Y., Chen, J.: A study on correlation between the achievement in web-based autonomous learning and self-efficacy. Technol. Enhanced Foreign Lang. Educ. **116**, 32–36 (2007)
12. Bong, M.: Academic motivation in self-efficacy, task value, achievement goal orientations, and attributional beliefs. J. Educ. Res. **6**, 287–298 (2004)
13. Choi, N.: Self-efficacy and self-concept as predictors of college students' academic performance. Psychol. Sch. **42**, 197–205 (2005)

14. Li, Y., Yang, H.H., Cai, J., MacLeod, J.: College students' computer self-efficacy, intrinsic motivation, attitude, and satisfaction in blended learning environments. In: Cheung, S.K.S., Kwok, L.-F., Ma, W.W.K., Lee, L.-K., Yang, H. (eds.) ICBL 2017. LNCS, vol. 10309, pp. 65–73. Springer, Cham (2017). https://doi.org/10.1007/978-3-319-59360-9_6
15. Lv, Y., Ding, M., Xing, Y., Cheng, D.: A study on the relationship between academic emotions and self-efficacy of online learning among university students in the post-epidemic era. Psychol. Mon. **01**, 37–39 (2022)
16. Tian, Y., Li, L., Zhao, H., Zhang, C.: A brief discussion on the motivation of military cadets in online and offline blended teaching. China Mod. Educ. Equip. **21**, 62–63+72 (2021)

A Portable Electrical Signal Generator for Active Learning

Zhi-Run Ye, Ming-Wei Wu$^{(\boxtimes)}$ ⓘ, Hong-Wei Tao, and Zheng Zhang

School of Information and Electronic Engineering, Zhejiang University of Science and Technology, Hangzhou 310023, China
wu_mingwei2004@aliyun.com, 195006@zust.edu.cn, zz.itee@msn.com

Abstract. As the electronic information and communication industry's demand for talents in universities continues to increase, more and more attention is paid to practical abilities of university students. Therefore, universities need to carry out project-based learning to strengthen students' practical abilities. Due to the problems of limited space and insufficient equipment in school laboratories, especially under the influence of the pandemic, conventional experiments using expensive and large equipment are no longer suitable. The students develop a portable electrical signal generator based on field programmable logic gate array to carry out project-based learning. The waveform is synthesized by direct digital synthesis Waveform switching and amplitude and frequency adjustment can be controlled by a hardware circuit. Lattice Diamond software is used for programming and simulation in experiments. This equipment and the development process not only improve students' practical ability but also facilitate students' independent learning.

Keywords: Field programmable logic gate array · Electrical signal generator · Project-based learning · Active learning Second keyword

1 Introduction

In the trend of teaching reform, project-based learning can not only make students memorize the theoretical knowledge points more deeply, but also broaden their horizons and improve their practical ability. Students' ability for independent learning and innovation plays a decisive role in their future development. We use FPGA to help students learn and understand the current hot topics in the industry, as well as cultivate their innovation ability and broaden their horizons.

This work is supported by 2020 Zhejiang Provincial-level Top Undergraduate Courses (Zhejiang Provincial Department of Education General Office Notice (2021) No. 195), Zhejiang University of Science and Technology (ZUST) Top Undergraduate Courses Development Project (Nos. 2022-k4, 2018-ky3), ZUST Teaching Reform Project (No. 2020-j12).

As is known to all, the experiment is an important part of science and engineering course. In the teaching, experiment equipment has a vital role in the experiment, the experimental apparatus quality can directly affect the efficiency of students' experiment. The signal generator is one of the basic experimental equipment in electronic information and communication laboratory, which plays an important role in the teaching of the corresponding specialty. At present, most of the signal generators in electronic information laboratories have the disadvantages of being heavyweight, expensive in price, difficult operation, and so on [1]. Therefore, it is of great practical significance to design a kind of electrical signal generator that is small, light, easy to use, and innovative.

FPGA [2] has the functional characteristics of high integration, high speed, and large capacity memory, so it can realize DDS technology quickly and stably [3], can maximize the efficiency of the electrical signal generator to generate a digital waveform, and greatly reduce the cost of the electrical signal generator [4]. DDS technology is a digital control method that can generate multiple frequencies from the reference frequency source. It is widely used in instrumentation and communication system. The signal produced by DDS has many advantages [5], such as high-frequency resolution, easy adjustment, fast switching speed, and high stability.

The project learning of a portable electrical signal generator can not only consolidate students' knowledge of hardware circuit programming and improve their ability for electrical signal analysis, but also improve experimental teaching. It is not only beneficial to cultivate students' ability for independent study and innovation but also beneficial to cultivate high-quality innovative talents in colleges and universities.

2   Project Design

The portable electrical signal generator is a simple instrument with an FPGA chip as the core and other hardware devices as auxiliary, as shown in Fig. 1. It can be divided into two parts: one is a control system composed of knobs, switches, and ADC0804 chipsets; The other part is a DDS system, which is composed of an FPGA chip, DAC(R-2R resistance network), and LPF.

The core programmable logic device (Field Programmable Logic Gate Array) is a 4000HC product of the MXO2 series of Lattice Company. The phase accumulator inside FPGA sends the new phase data which is generated after the last clock cycle as the sampling address value into the waveform memory and the waveform memory outputs corresponding waveform data according to this address. The device comes with 4 different waveforms, which can be adjusted for amplitude and frequency.

The project-based learning is designed to be finished by a group consisting of 5 members. The knowledge involved and personnel allocation are shown in Table 1.

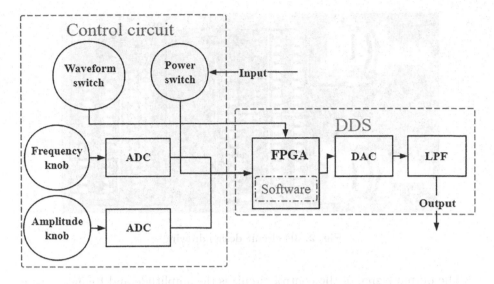

Fig. 1. The system block diagram

Table 1. Knowledge Involved and Personnel Allocation

Technology	Courses	Semester	Members
Diamond simulation	Analog circuit	3	1
R-2R resistance network	Digital circuit	4	1
Verilog language	Digital circuit	4	
A/D conversion	Digital circuit	4	1
Low pass filter	Analysis of Signals and Linear Systems	4	1
Circuit connection	The electronic circuit	4	1
FPGA	Programmable logic devices	7	

3   Portable Signal Generator Structure

The structure of a portable electrical signal generator based on FPGA is mainly divided into two parts, i.e. the amplitude and frequency control part which is composed of ADC0804 and knobs, and the waveform and power control circuit with buttons; The other part is the DDS system composed of FPGA, R-2R circuit and LPF.

3.1   Control Circuit

The control circuit can be designed by the students themselves so that the theory and practice can be combined in the teaching of electronic circuit technology so that the students can learn the theoretical basis and hands-on practice to consolidate knowledge at the same time. The circuit of the electrical signal generator is shown in Fig. 2.

Fig. 2. 3D circuit design drawing

The output signal of the control circuit is the amplitude and frequency control word, which is realized by chip ADC0804. By rotating the knob to change the voltage input value V_{IN}, sampling through ADC0804, FPGA receives the sampling data, according to the code to achieve different amplitude and frequency adjustments (accuracy of 8 bits). A/D conversion principle is shown in Fig. 3.

Using the dichotomy search method, the 8-bit A/D converter takes only 8 searches to complete the conversion action, where the input value represents the analog input voltage $V_{IN}+$.

3.2 DDS System

DDS is the abbreviation of Direct Digital Synthesizer, which is an important Digital technology of this equipment. As it is easy to learn and easy to study, this method is commonly used in modern teaching to realize waveform construction and output. Therefore, we choose DDS technology to realize the output of telecommunications. The signal synthesis principle of DDS is shown in Fig. 4.

It is mainly composed of FPGA(which mainly completes the function of phase accumulator and waveform memory), DAC(R-2R resistance network), and LPF. The key part of the DDS is phase accumulator, external clock control phase accumulator to read data address values, through the look-up table, the address is directly converted into digital signal waveform amplitude. And the D/A converter of the signal waveform amplitude digital sequence further into an analog voltage, finally transferred to the low pass filter. After filter processing, the unideal stepped waveform in the ADC is transformed into the desired smooth waveform.

FPGA Module: FPGA can output different waveforms through programming, adjust the amplitude and frequency of waveforms and realize waveform switching and other functions.

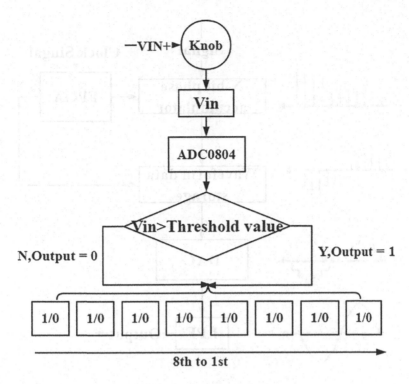

Fig. 3. A/D conversion principle

As the FPGA adopted by the device has its internal clock signal:

$$f_{\text{clk}} = 12\text{MHz} \tag{1}$$

Our sampling setting is k bit, so:

$$f_{\max} = 6\text{MHz} \tag{2}$$

$$f_{\min} = \frac{12\text{MHz}}{2^{k+1}} \tag{3}$$

Put k values of each waveform into formula (3), as shown in Fig. 5.

Waveform amplitude adjustment mainly involves amplitude control word A triggering and controlling the N value of the FPGA accumulator to adjust waveform amplitude, as shown in Fig. 6.

Since n points can be sampled in each cycle which can be set in the program, the original frequency of waveforms is f_c and the adjusted frequency is f_s, the control word f sent by ADC0804, the adjustment calculation formula is:

$$f_{\text{s}} = \frac{f_c n}{f} \tag{4}$$

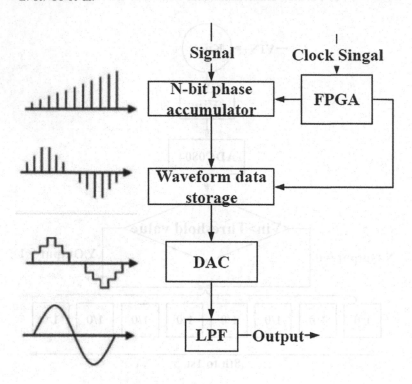

Fig. 4. DDS signal synthesis principle

Priority Module: The waveform switching is realized by four buttons, namely sine wave, square wave, triangle wave, and sawtooth wave. The output priority is: *Sine > Square > Triangular > Sawtooth*

DAC Module (R-2R Resistor Network): We adopt the DAC principle of an 8-bit R-2R resistance network, and D0-D7 is connected with FPGA for digital-to-analog conversion, as shown in Fig. 7.

When the high levels H from D0 to D7 are V_{cc} and the low levels L are 0, the ideal output expression of this V_{out} is:

$$V_{out} = \left(\frac{D7}{2} + \frac{D6}{4} + \dots \frac{D0}{2^8} \right) V_{cc} \tag{5}$$

LPF Module: LPF is a first-order RC low-pass filter consisting of a capacitor and an inductor. As shown in Fig. 8.

The principle of LPF is known from the knowledge of signals and linear [6]:

Time constant τ is:

$$\tau = R1C1 = \frac{1}{2\pi f} \tag{6}$$

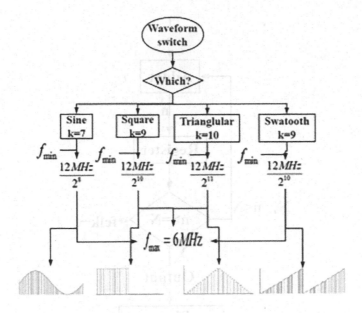

Fig. 5. Waveform flow chart

Amplitude and frequency characteristics:

$$f = \frac{1}{2\pi C1R1} \tag{7}$$

The relation between filter coefficient A and cut-off frequency f is:

$$A = \frac{T}{\frac{1}{2\pi f} + T} = \frac{1}{\frac{1}{2\pi fT} + 1} \tag{8}$$

4   Results

4.1   Simulation Results

Students can first use Diamond 3. 12 Software ModelSim simulation software, to simulate a sine wave, square wave, triangle wave, sawtooth wave, and other waveforms. They can also switch different waveforms and adjust the amplitude and frequency of the waveform.

Simulation of different waveforms is shown in Fig. 9. Waveform switching is shown in Fig. 10. Amplitude adjustment is shown in Fig. 11. Frequency adjustment is shown in Fig. 12.

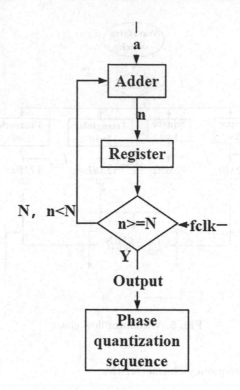

Fig. 6. Flow chart of accumulators

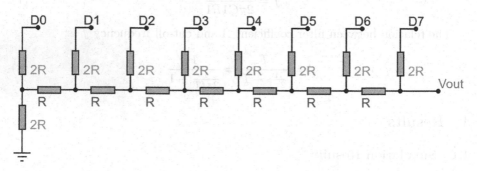

Fig. 7. R-2R resistance network

4.2 Hardware with Oscilloscope Waveforms (4 Types)

Students use oscilloscopes to practice, learning the generation, transmission, amplitude, frequency conversion, and other knowledge of electrical signals. Four types of waveforms are respectively shown in Fig. 13 a, b, c, and d.

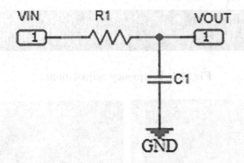

Fig. 8. First-order RC low pass filter

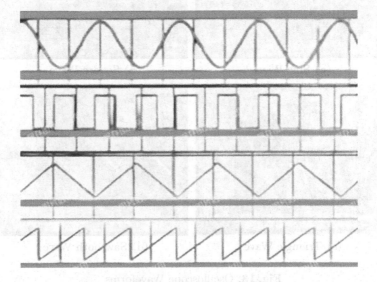

Fig. 9. Simulation output of four types of waveform: sine wave, sawtooth wave, square wave and triangle wave.

Fig. 10. Waveform switching

Fig. 11. Amplitude adjustment

Fig. 12. Frequency adjustment

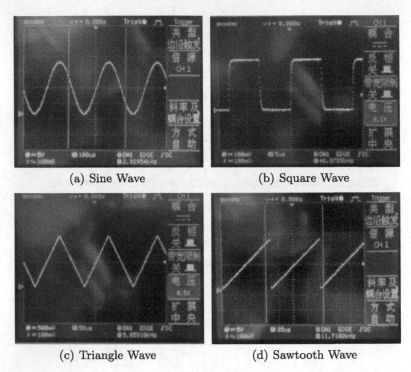

(a) Sine Wave

(b) Square Wave

(c) Triangle Wave

(d) Sawtooth Wave

Fig. 13. Oscilloscope Waveforms

4.3   The Learning Practice

We carry out 5-person group project learning in which students according to the electronic circuit, analog circuit, digital circuit, and other knowledge, independent design circuit, improve the program, debugging equipment.

An FPGA small foot chip, two 10 cm × 10 cm hole boards, two transformers, two ADC0804 chips, a 555 oscillator chip, five switches, some resistors, some porcelain capacitors, some wires, some rows of pins, a total of 270 yuan. Using skills in circuit welding design and welding, the signal generator is built, as shown in Fig. 14.

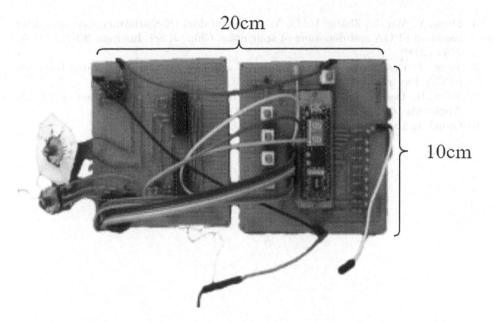

Fig. 14. Photo of the portable electrical signal generator

5   Conclusions

With the smooth development of the project-based learning with a group of 5 students, we are increasingly aware of the importance of practical ability for students and also realize the improvement of teaching and learning efficiency· by cultivating students' independent learning ability. Students designed circuits independently and installed welding circuits by themselves. Not only did we complete the device, which can be simulated in Diamond 3. 12, but it can also switch between four different waveforms in the oscilloscope and adjust the amplitude and frequency through the knob. This device can not only help students to learn and understand electrical signals independently but also solve the problem of insufficient signal generator instruments in the laboratory.

Due to limited time and skills, our portable signal generator inevitably has shortcomings, e.g. the appearance is not good enough, there is no matching portable oscilloscope, etc. We will continue to work hard to improve the device and strive to make it perfect.

References

1. Chang, N.: A novel non-linear load monitoring and identification scheme with FPGA implementation (2008)
2. Xu, M., Hu, J., Gao, Y.: FPGA-based design and implementation of arbitrary waveform generator (2011)

3. Deng, Y., Wu, L., Zhang, L., Li, Y.: Design of dual DDS arbitrary wave generator based on FPGA and denoising of spur noise. Chin. J. Sci. Instrum. **30**(11), 2255–2261 (2009)
4. Tang, J.: Design and implementation of arbitrary waveform generator based on FPGA. Electron. Technol. **5**, 37–38 (2010)
5. Yuan, H.: Design and implementation of digital signal generator based on FPGA. Application of Electronic Technique (2011)
6. Gabel, R.A.: Signals and linear systems. J. Wiley (1973)

Communication Principles Project-Based Learning: Smart Home Using Voice Remote Control and Visible Light Communication

Hao-Yuan Tang[1], Ming-Wei Wu[1]([✉])[iD], Ming Zhang[1], Xiao-Lan Wu[2], and Xue-Er Lin[1]

[1] School of Information and Electronic Engineering, Zhejiang University of Science and Technology, Hangzhou 310023, China
thyoff@163.com, wu_mingwei2004@aliyun.com, 463792192@qq.com, 18368600592@163.com
[2] School of International Studies, Zhejiang University, Hangzhou 310013, China
wuxiaolan@hotmail.com

Abstract. In order to deepen students' understanding of communication principles and improve their application skills after having learned the communication principles theoretical course, we propose a project-based learning case, building a voice-controlled visible light communication system. Through independent learning, application of multi-disciplinary knowledge and collaboration, a team of students complete a smart home model. Through this project-based learning experience, students apply theories learnt in lectures and gain a deeper understanding of basic communication principles.

Keywords: Visible light communication · Communication principles · Project-based learning

1 Introduction

The theoretical course "Communication Principles" teaches the structure of a communication system and how information is transmitted and received by the system. The key functions of a communication system are modulation and its inverse process, i.e., demodulation/detection. They are also the emphasis and difficulty of this course. Lecturing is the most commonly used teaching method in this course. Lecturers usually explain the principles of modulation and demodulation using a bit stream as an example: a bit stream is modulated into a baseband waveform, transmitted over the channel and demodulated and detected as

This work is supported by 2020 Zhejiang Provincial-level Top Undergraduate Courses (Zhejiang Provincial Department of Education General Office Notice (2021) No. 195), Zhejiang University of Science and Technology (ZUST) Classroom Teaching Reform Project (No. 2018-ky3), ZUST Top Undergraduate Courses Development Project (Nos. 2020-k11, 2020-k10, 2022-k4).

a bit stream. This method directly shows the basic principles of digital communication, but it is abstract and tedious and does not appeal to students. In addition, many students learn theoretical knowledge in a passive way. They need some vivid examples to understand the process and need an opportunity to apply the knowledge they have learned through practice [1].

Visible light communication [2] is a wireless optical transmission technology that uses low-power visible light for data communication. It uses the signal in the visible light band as the carrier and directly transmits optical signals in the air without the use of cable such as optical fiber. LED as a signal source is cheap, economical, and convenient for application. We can modulate a bit stream onto the optical signal, and transmit information by turning an LED on and off.

In 2021, Jiang Mengling designed an experiment setup based on visible light communication for the teaching of communication principles. It aroused students' interest in learning the course and improved learning outcome. The result was published in ICCSE 2021 [3].

However, after studying the communication principles course, communication engineering students still need further project application using a basic communication system. Therefore, we develop a project-based learning plan where students need to build a simple visible light communication system for smart home application. An Arduino Uno board is used at the transmitter, and three Arduino Pro Micro boards are used at the receiver respectively [4]. The transmitter sends optical signals by turning an LED on and off and transmits eight-bit instructions. The receiver receives the message through the optical receiving module and executes the corresponding instruction.

In the project-based learning plan, firstly, students need to send a bit stream and recover at the receiver, observe the LED light on and off to master the modulation and demodulation process. Secondly, instruction messages are sent from the transmitter and the receiver recovers the instruction. This shows students intuitively the process of formatting (source encoding), modulation, demodulation, and formatting (source decoding). Thirdly, a speech recognition module and various home appliances like a fan, a display screen, and a humidifier are added to build a smart home application [5] out of thin plywood and existing electronics. At this point, we can turn the home appliances on and off by giving oral commands.

2   Project and System Design

The project requires the knowledge of MCU, C programming language, digital circuit, and communication principles, which are compulsory courses for the communication engineering major. The semesters when the courses are offered in the curriculum are shown in Table 1. In Semester 5 or afterwards, students are divided into groups of 3 to work together on the project for 4 weeks [6].

As shown in Fig. 1, visible light communication is the core part of this communication system, so we need to ensure that the information can be modulated to the optical signal, and also demodulated from the optical signal. The LED

Table 1. Related Courses and Semesters

Technology	Course	Semester
Arduino Programming	C Programming	1
Circuit Design	Digital Circuit	4
System Design Based on Arduino	Microcontroller Unit	5
Modulation and Demodulation	Communication Principles	5

turning on and off gives students an intuitive understanding of modulation and demodulation.

Next, through formatting, the control message sent by the information source is converted into a bit stream which can be further modulated. At the receiver, the recovered bit stream is formatted into the control message which is further sent to the information sink. A communication system is thus constructed.

Finally, the speech recognition module as the information source and controlled home appliance modules as the information sink are then added on top of the communication system, to complete the voice-controlled smart home application.

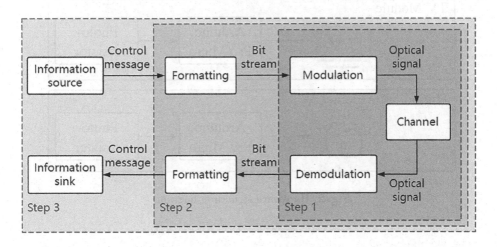

Fig. 1. Brief system design

The hardware system structure is shown in Fig. 2. The optical signal is sent out by the LED turning on and off at the transmitter, which is received by the photoresistor at each of the three receiver modules. The optical devices, e.g. the LED and the photoresistor are each controlled or accessed by an Arduino, which is in charge of modulation/demodulation and formatting. The information source is the speech recognition module which generates the control message. The information sinks are the home appliances.

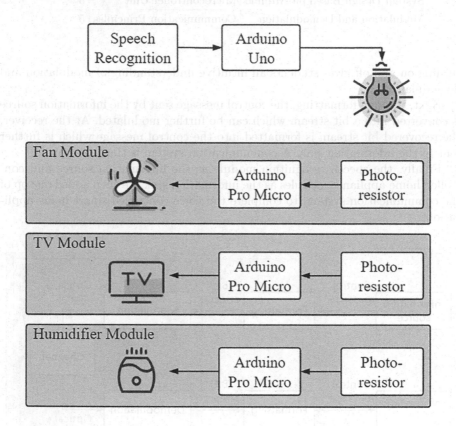

Fig. 2. Hardware structure diagram

3   Project Development

The specific development process is divided into three steps.

3.1   Modulation and Demodulation

Figure 3 and Fig. 4 show circuit design and connection diagrams of the modulator and the demodulator, respectively. The core of the project is visible light communication, in which a bit stream is modulated to an optical signal and demodulated from the optical signal. We can use the serial monitor and an oscilloscope to verify.

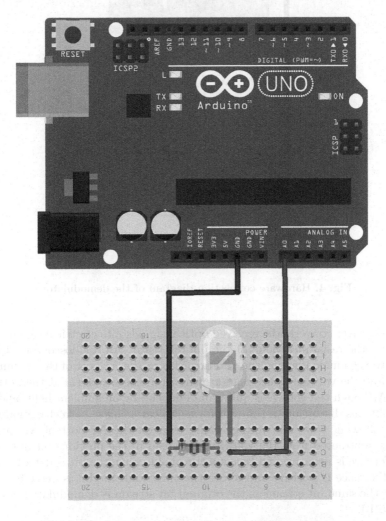

Fig. 3. Hardware connection diagram of the modulator

For example, a bit stream to be modulated is 10000110, as shown in Fig. 5(a). A "1" is modulated as a high voltage, switching the LED on, and a "0" is modulated as a low voltage, switching the LED off. As the LED is initially kept on for illumination purpose, an additional low voltage for a bit duration is sent as a flag to indicate the beginning of a message. Thus, the sequence of 9 light intensities LHLLLLHHL is transmitted, as shown in Fig. 6.

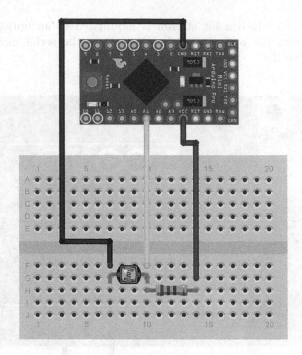

Fig. 4. Hardware connection diagram of the demodulator

The receiver converts the received optical signals into electrical signals by the change of the resistance value of the photoresistor. An oscilloscope is also connected to the pin connecting the photoresistor to the A1 port of the Arduino Pro Micro, and the voltage values read are shown in the waveform at the bottom of Fig. 6. Although the voltage is quite small depending on ambient light, and there exists obvious distortion in the waveform, we can achieve correct demodulation in the following way. The voltage value read on the A1 port of Arduino Pro Micro is subtracted from the voltage value read in the previous bit duration. If the difference is negative and below a threshold value, the bit is detected as "1"; if the difference is positive and above the threshold, the bit is detected as "0". Finally, the same bit stream as the original bit stream is demodulated, as shown in Fig. 5(b).

3.2 Formatting

A speech recognition module is the information source, and the control message sent by the source is a decimal number in Table 2. At the receiver, the corresponding operation is performed by deciding on the resulting decimal number. So, the formatting here is basically decimal-binary conversion.

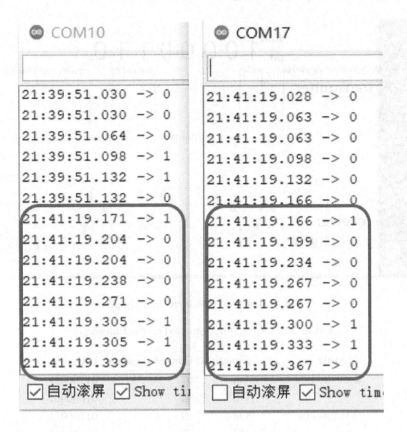

(a) Bit stream at the transmitter   (b) Bit stream at the receiver

Fig. 5. Bit stream information

For example, the control message to switch on the fan is a decimal 97. Using the bitread() function, the decimal is converted into 8-bit sequence 01100001. The least significant bit is transmitted first, resulting in the bitstream 10000110.

The receiver converts the 8-bit bit stream information into the corresponding control message according to Table 2.

3.3   Generation and Processing of Control Messages

The speech recognition module, as the information source, sends different decimal numbers (control message) to the transmitter, according to the voice commands. For example, to switch on the fan, the voice recognition module sends through the serial port to Arduino a decimal 97.

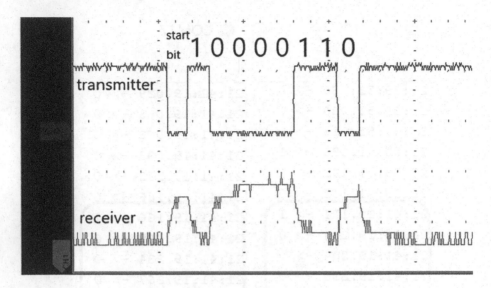

Fig. 6. Oscilloscope measured signals

Table 2. Module functions and control messages

Module	Function	Control message	Binary
Fan module	On	97	01100001
	Off	65	01000001
TV module	On	99	01100011
	Off	67	01000011
Humidifier module	On	101	01100101
	Off	69	01000101

After receiving the control message, the receiver looks up Table 2, and executes the corresponding instruction. There are three modules to control, so one team member is in charge of one module.

4   Results

The final completed smart home model is shown in Fig. 7.

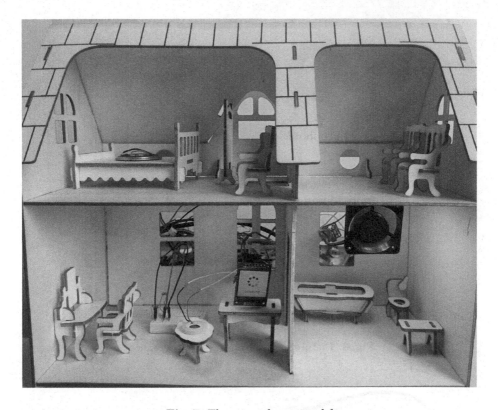

Fig. 7. The smart home model

Figure 8 shows the completed transmitter hardware consisting of a voice module, an Arduino Uno control board, and an LED.

Figure 9 shows a completed receiver module consisting of a photoresistor, an Arduino Pro Micro board, and a humidifier for example.

According to the setting of the voice module in advance, after saying a specific phrase to wake up the voice module, and then saying a specific statement, the voice module can send the decimal number corresponding to the statement to the Arduino board at the transmitter through the serial port. After transmission, the Arduino board at the receiver can select and execute specific functions. For example, when the user says, "turn on the TV" and "turn off the TV", the results are shown in Fig. 10.

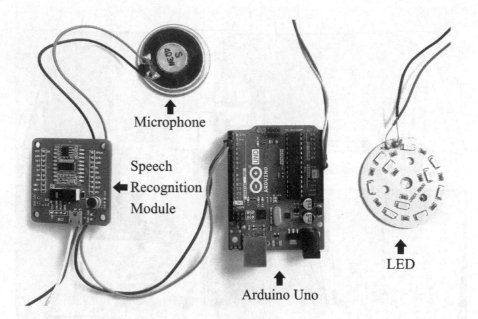

Fig. 8. Picture of the transmitter appearance

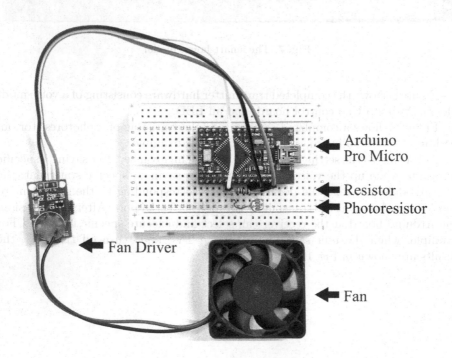

Fig. 9. Picture of the receiver appearance

(a) TV turned on   (b) TV turned off

Fig. 10. The TV turned on and off

5   Conclusions

In this project, we do not design a synchronization method. As a result, when the received signal is not sampled properly in a symbol duration, the receiver cannot demodulate properly. This observation raises the importance of synchronization for digital communications. A simple solution includes calculation of execution speed of programs at the transmitter and receiver, and adding suitable delay in the codes so that the local oscillators at the transmitter and the receiver are synchronized [7].

In the design of this system, the voice recognition module, TFT LCD screen, and other electronic components which are not taught in class are used, which requires students to independently search for materials and learn how to use them.

Through this project-based learning experience, students can connect theory with practical application and gain a deeper understanding of the basic steps of communication principles through the example of visible light communication. Voice control, visible light, and control of home appliances are three major catches of the project, among which visible light communication is the essential part as a basic communication system. The three parts are intuitive, interactive, and easily arouse students' interest and encourage them to apply theoretical knowledge and skills [8].

References

1. Grossman, P., Dean, C.G.P., Kavanagh, S.S., Herrmann, Z.: Preparing teachers for project-based teaching. Phi Delta Kappan **100**(7), 43–48 (2019)
2. Kumar, N., Lourenco, N.R.: Led-based visible light communication system: a brief survey and investigation. J. Eng. Appl. Sci. **5**(4), 296–307 (2010)
3. Jiang, M.L., Zhu, J.L., Chen, J., Wu, M.W., Wu, J.Q.: Research on experimental teaching of communication principles based on visible light communication. In: IEEE 16th International Conference on Computer Science & Education (ICCSE), Lancaster, pp. 1019–1023. IEEE (2021)
4. Liang, Y.W., Wu, M.W., Pan, Z.S., Cen, G.: Information and communication technology enabled active learning in college physics experiment. In: IEEE 16th International Conference on Computer Science & Education (ICCSE), Lancaster, pp. 1014–1018. IEEE (2021)
5. Kumar, A., Mihovska, A., Kyriazakos, S., Prasad, R.: Visible light communications (VLC) for ambient assisted living. Wireless Pers. Commun. **78**(3), 1699–1717 (2014)
6. Ye, Z.R., Wu, M.W., Tao, H.W., Zhang, Z.: A portable electrical signal generator for active learning. In: IEEE 17th International Conference on Computer Science & Education (ICCSE) (2022)
7. Scholtz, R.: Frame synchronization techniques. IEEE Trans. Commun. **28**(8), 1204–1213 (1980)
8. Wu, M.W., Zhang, M., Zhuo, H.H., Xu, Y.C.: 3D-LSTM wireless sensing gesture recognition-a collaborative bachelor and master project-based learning case. In: IEEE 17th International Conference on Computer Science & Education (ICCSE) (2022)

Image Stitching in Dynamic Scene for Computer Vision Project-Base Learning

Yizhen Lao, Yu Cao, Huiqing Zhang, and Yufeng Zhang[✉]

College of Computer Science and Electronic Engineering, Hunan University,
Changsha, China
{yizhenlao,yucao,huiqingzhang,yufengzhang}@hnu.edu.cn

Abstract. In this paper, we present a novel computer vision course project. The project aims to stitch images captured in the dynamic scene, which is challenging since traditional methods rely on the assumption of static scenes. However, it provides the opportunity to solve the frontier computer vision problem by using the theories and skills taught in the lectures. The proposed project has three milestones that cover most of the content in the course syllabus and require the students to use interdisciplinary CV techniques, including traditional and deep-learning-based ones. We provide a detailed description of the proposed course project, including the goal, milestones, schedule, and evaluation strategy. We believe it can serve as a practical CV education resource for other higher educators by applying to their CV-related courses.

Keywords: Computer Vision · Project-based Learning · Image stitching · Deep Learning

1   Introduction

Computer vision (CV) is an interdisciplinary scientific field that extracts information from images or video sequences. Typical CV tasks include acquiring (e.g., computational imaging), processing (e.g., photo enhancement), analyzing and understanding (e.g., image classification) images, and extraction of high-dimensional data from the real world (e.g., visual 3D reconstruction). With its board applications, CV theory and techniques basis drawn on computer science, signal processing, and several mathematical fields like geometry, statistics, and algebra.

In the past two decades, CV has progressively joined as required or elective courses in undergraduate and graduate computer science studies programs on a worldwide scale. More details of CV course and education were reviewed by [8, 24,27].

This work was supported by a grant from NSFC (No. 62102145 and 62002107) and Jiangxi Provincial 03 Special Foundation and 5G Program (No. 20224ABC03A05).

One proven effective method to let students learn the CV theory and skills is finishing a CV project that solves a practical problem [15,25,31,32]. Such an approach usually referred to as project-based learning (PBL) has been widely used in undergraduate and graduate engineering courses due to its significant advantages over the other traditional lecture-based schemes [15], namely:

- Students can gain hands-on experience related to the course.
- It motivates the student by unifying the theoretical and practical concepts with a single goal.
- Students can conduct self-learning and discover these new concepts beyond the course lectures.

In this paper, we present a CV course project which aims to include the subtopics of traditional and deep-learning-based CV techniques comprehensively with a single goal.

1.1   Context and Motivation

Table 1. Comparison of the course project of top-tire universities and our proposed one in project design scheme (MIP: multiple independent projects. SCP: single comprehensive project) and syllabus focus.

	Standford CS231n [4]	Standford CS231A [3]	MIT 6.819 [1]	Harvard CSCI-E25 [5]	Cornell CS6670 [2]	Ours: HNU CS06162
Project design scheme	MIP	MIP	MIP	MIP	SCP	SCP
Syllabus focus	Deep-learning-Based CV	Traditional CV	Deep-learning-Based CV	Deep-learning-Based CV	Deep-learning-Based CV	Traditional & Deep-learning-based CV

Multiple Independent Projects vs Single Comprehensive Project. There are two main types of PBL [17] in higher engineering education:

- *Multiple independent projects (MIP).* MIP-based PBL organizes the assignments as multiple independent tasks corresponding to subtopics of course content without needing to force connections between them.
- *Single comprehensive project (SCP).* SCP-based PBL requires the students to complete a single course project that integrates the course's multiple subtopics under one goal.

The works of [11,17] indicate that even though MIP can cover the subtopics of the course more entirely and precisely than SCP. However, SCP unifies most of the subtopics under a single object and requires the students to design and implement a more comprehensive and challenging solution. The survey in [17] also shows that SCP makes the students more motivated over MIP and is more inclined to encourage them to discover the knowledge and gain the skills beyond the course content and requirement.

As shown in Table 1, we surprisingly found out that most CV courses in top tire research universities conduct the PBL with the MIP scheme only. One of the explanations for such a setting is that the number of student attendances is large compared to the number of teachers and teaching assistance, and thus MIP which each sub-project covers one subtopic of the course with a small working load in evaluation, is more suitable to such case than SCP.

To be best of our knowledge, SCP for CV PBL is still absent from the literature and publicized CV courses. We believe that SCP for CV PBL is more feasible for high teacher-student ratio courses and brings more opportunity to the students to improve their ability to solve real-world compressive CV problems.

Traditional vs Deep-Learning-Based CV. We have witnessed that deep learning has revolutionized CV in the last decade. As a result, we can observe in Table 1 that most the CV courses now address deep-learning-based CV content significantly.

However, several problems and topics for which deep-learned solutions are currently not preferable over classical ones exist that typically involve a strong mathematical model [26] (e.g., camera calibration and geometrical 3D reconstruction). Thus, for a well-rounded CV education, a more comprehensive CV course that balances cover from a traditional CV to a deep-learning-based CV is valuable.

1.2   Contribution and Paper Organization

From the discussion above, we found out that an *SCP-based PBL* for CV course that *evenly cover both traditional and deep-learning-based CV content* is vital for CV education but still absent from the literature.

This paper presents a project assignment which is the core of the ***Pattern Recognition and Computer Vision*** course of the Bachelor's program in artificial intelligence (AI) at the Hunan University (HNU), Changsha, China. Specifically, we designed a course project that aimed to stitch two images filmed in a dynamic scene, a challenging but real-life CV problem. The proposed project has three milestones that cover most of the content in the course syllabus and require the students to use interdisciplinary CV techniques to develop such solutions, including traditional and deep-learning-based ones. The quantitative evaluation and feedbacks from the students and teachers verify that the proposed course project can effectively gain a deeper understanding of the course content and develop hands-on CV skills to solve complex real-life engineering problems. The main contribution of this work can be summarized as follows:

- To be best of our knowledge, this is the first work that presents a single comprehensive project for CV PBL that addresses both traditional and deep-learning-based CV techniques.
- Various evaluations demonstrate that the proposed course project can effectively gain a deeper understanding of the course content and develop hands-on

CV skills to solve a complex real-life engineering problem. The teachers in the CV or AI communities can easily merge and plug this project into related undergraduate and graduate study courses.

We detail how the project has been designed corresponding to schedule (Sect. 2.2), resource (Sect. 2.3), evaluation (Sect. 2.4) during the 2021–2022 term followed by the discussion to assessment methodology, feedback from students (Sect. 3.2) and instructors remark (Sect. 3.3).

(a) **Classical image stitching**   (b) **Image in dynamic scene**

Fig. 1. (a) Classical image stitching task aligns two images capture static scene [10] while the input images were filmed in dynamic scene (b) will be a challenge.

2   Image Stitching in Dynamic Scene Project

Fig. 2. Project milestones of the image stitching in dynamic scene prototype.

2.1   Project Design

Project Final Goal and Challenges. The proposed project aims to solve the image stitching problem in dynamic scenes (D-IS). Note that, as shown in Fig. 1(a) that classical image stitching solution [10] considers the static scene without any moving object. Thus the 3×3 homography matrix can be computed by using a simple linear 4pt solver [18] with RANSAC refinement [14] followed by homographic image warping to align two input images together.

(a) ORB

(b) SIFT

(c) SuperPoint

Fig. 3. An example of student experiment results to milestone 1, namely feature matching.

However, as shown in Fig. 1(b), nowadays, the image that contains dynamic content is common, which becomes a challenge for classical image stitching algorithms where simple 4pt-RANSAC can easily fail [20].

The proposed course project aims to investigate and address how to design and implement a novel image stitching solution that handles dynamic scenes. Note that this is a challenging but demanding problem since it can serve for many real-life applications such as video stabilization [16], pose estimation [23] and SLAM [30].

Milestone. As shown in Fig. 2 that the proposed course project development has three milestones, from the beginning of the course to the end, corresponding to the increasing functionality of the software prototype for D-IS:

– **Milestone 1.** The task of feature matching is to connect the corresponding points among two images that are projected by the same 3D points in the

(a) Classical RANSAC-based outlier filtering

(b) Detection-based outlier filtering

Fig. 4. An example of student experiment results to milestone 2, namely outlier filtering.

world. This a classical problem in CV community where extensively studies have been shown such as SIFT [22], SURF [7] and ORB [29]. Recently, deep-learning-based features (e.g., superpoint [12]) were demonstrated to be a good alternative option over the classical hand-craft feature descriptors. As shown in Fig. 3, in this milestone, we require the student to choose and re-implement one image feature descriptor fromSIFT [22], SURF [7], ORB [29] or Superpoint [12] by themselves and compare it to the rest with public-implementation in opencv [9].

- **Milestone 2.** To handle the dynamic scene, we require the students to detect moving objects (e.g., human and car) and filter the matched features among these dynamic objects as outliers [19]. Considering the limited computation resources, we recommend the students design and train a light CNN-based object detector similar to YOLOv3-tiny [6]. An example of student self-implement CNN-base dynamic outlier filtering results are shown in Fig. 4.
- **Milestone 3.** Milestone 3 is the final output of D-IS that stitches two images together. In this milestone, we require the students to self-implement a linear 4pt homography [18] solver and incorporate it into a self-implement RANSAC [14] refinement. An example of student self-implement CNN-base dynamic outlier filtering results are shown in Fig. 5.

2.2 Schedule

As shown in Table 2 the HNU CS06162 course lasts a 16-week term, with one theory lecture of 2 h and one project session of 1 hour per week. Students willingly

Table 2. Lectures schedule and their relevance to the proposed course project. Classical and deep learning computer vision related contents are highlighted in pink and green respectively.

Week	Lecture Topic	Relevances to proposed project	Techniques to implement
1	Introduction	1. Report writing 2. Resources acquire	-
2	1. Python introduction 2. linear algebra & calculus review	Coding and mathematical basis	IDE and 3rd party libraries preparation
3	Camera models	Pixel alignment between two images	Image warping and pixel interpolation
4	Camera calibration	Input image pre-processing	Rectify lens distortion using calibration information
5	Image processing basics	Feature matching	Image matching via hand-craft descriptors e.g. SIFT, ORB and SURF
6	Homography	3X3 homography estimation	Linear 4pt homography solver
7	Epipolar geometry and RANSAC	3X3 homography estimation	Robustify 4pt homography solver
8	Structure from Motion and SLAM	-	-
9	Classical machine learning basics	Detection-based outlier filtering	Training, testing and validation sets assignment
10	Neural networks	Detection-based outlier filtering	Neural network design
11	CNNs	1. Detection-based outlier filtering 2. Neural feature descriptor	Detection network encoder design
12	Training Neural Network	1. Detection-based outlier filtering 2. Neural feature descriptor	Detection network training
13	Classification, detection and segmentation	Detection-based outlier filtering	YOLO [28] or YOLO-tiny [6] re-implementation
14	GANs, Self-supervised learning and Transformers	Neural feature descriptor	SuperPoint [12] re-implementation
15	Traditional CV in the age of deep learning	Whole framework design and optimization	-
16	Oral presentation	Report writing and presentation skill	Academic document writing and academic presentation

(a) SIFT + 4pt-homography-RANSAC   (b) SuperPoint + 4pt-homography-RANSAC   (c) SIFT + detection-based outlier filter + 4pt-homography-RANSAC   (d) SuperPoint + detection-based outlier filter + 4pt-homography-RANSAC

Fig. 5. An example of student experiment results to milestone 3, namely final image stitching.

assign themselves to a team of three and must attend all the sessions. Please note that the teachers will indicate each milestone's goal and describe multiple potential solutions and the techniques they might have to use. However, they will not precisely instruct the students in detail to achieve the goal step by step.

Besides, it is essential to note that the milestones of the proposed project are strictly synchronized with the course lecture so that the students can make progress in theory learning and the course project simultaneously. We also want to highlight that the proposed project covers over 90% content of the course.

2.3   Resources

Dataset. All the student teams were provided with a dataset to facilitate each milestone's testing and serve as a common benchmark for all teams. For milestone 1, we use the number of inlier matches as the evaluation metric. In contrast, we use the number of remaining outliers after filtering as an evaluation metric for milestone 2. As to milestone 3, we use the visual inspection cross-team as an evaluation metric. The D-IS testing dataset is extracted from [20] that consists of 100 pairs of images.

For the two milestones related to deep-learning-based CV, we provide a sub-dataset of COCO image dataset [21] for training the superpoint [12] and VOC dataset [13] for object detector training.

GPU Support. We provide 8 Nvidia GTX 3080 Ti GPU (each team can be assigned at least one) to all the team, which we found can meet the requirement of training the neural networks needed in the proposed course project.

2.4   Evaluation

The course is graded as 50% for the course project D-IS, while a final written-based theory exam determines the remaining 50%. Specifically, the grade of the course project amounts to 20% for each of the three milestone deliverables, 20% for the final oral presentation, and 20% for the three reports of each Milestone and a final project report.

The instructors grade each team by evaluating source code, report, and a 10-minute Q&A session for each Milestone. Each Milestone and the final project grade is graded with an E (fail), D (pass), C (good), B (Very good), or A (excellent).

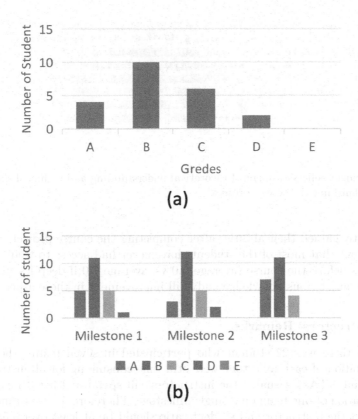

Fig. 6. (top) Distribution of the students' marks after taking into account deliverables, oral presentations, and intragroup evaluation. (bottom) Distribution of the grades (see legend) of the deliverables at each milestone.

3   Discussion

3.1   Marks

Figure 6(a) show the distribution of the final course project marks using the evaluation method described in Sect. 2.4. We can observe that most of the students achieve B and C (more that 50%), while only less than 20% get the highest score, A. Besides, the distributions of the marks of each milestone are shown in Fig. 6(b). Interestingly, the students perform better in traditional CV-related milestones than deep-learning-based ones.

3.2   Student Feedback

At the beginning and end of the course, the students were asked to fill in an anonymous assessment form on the project to self-evaluate their abilities related to the course content. As shown in Fig. 7 that the students believe that they have

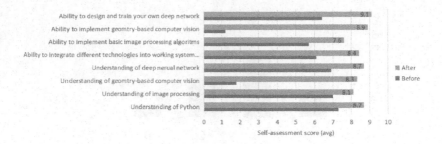

Fig. 7. Student self-assessment of theoretical understanding and technical skills before and after finishing the course project.

significantly gained their abilities after completing the course project. Specially, we point out that most of the students have never had access to traditional CV techniques before the course (average 5.0 vs. average 7.0 if deep learning), thus leading to an obvious knowledge and skill improvement in these aspects.

3.3 Instructors' Remarks

Although there was 22 student who participated in seven teams, the grading and evaluation of each milestone were still time-consuming for all instructors (1 teacher and 2 TAs). Usually, the instructors will spend at least 3 h completing the evaluation of one team on a single milestone. Therefore, in the future course, we suggest the instructor and student ratio should be at least over 0.5.

4   Conclusion

This paper presents a project on image stitching in the dynamic scene for a project-based learning computer vision course. The outcomes and assessment of the 2021–2022 year year term were dazzling: The students were satisfied due to their significant gain in the CV theories acquired from the lectures and the CV-related skill that can be used to solve challenging real-life problems. By the end of the course, they have designed and developed a complex vision system that can stitch two images in dynamic scenes, having researched numerous CV fields, read various state-of-the-art CV papers, and written several scientific and technical reports.

We provide a detailed description of the proposed course project, including the goal, milestones, schedule, and evaluation strategy. We believe it can serve as a practical CV education resource for other higher educators by applying to their own CV-related courses.

Acknowledgements. Please place your acknowledgments at the end of the paper, preceded by an unnumbered run-in heading (i.e. 3rd-level heading).

References

1. Advances in computer vision. http://6.869.csail.mit.edu/sp22/schedule.html
2. Cornell University: CS6670 - computer vision. https://www.cs.cornell.edu/courses/cs6670/2021fa/
3. CS231A: Computer vision, from 3D reconstruction to recognition. https://web.stanford.edu/class/cs231a/project.html
4. CS231N: Deep learning for computer vision. http://cs231n.stanford.edu/project.html
5. Harvard University: CSCI E-25 computer vision. https://canvas.harvard.edu/courses/96434/assignments/syllabus
6. Adarsh, P., Rathi, P., Kumar, M.: Yolo v3-tiny: object detection and recognition using one stage improved model. In: International Conference on Advanced Computing and Communication Systems (2020)
7. Bay, H., Tuytelaars, T., Gool, L.V.: Surf: speeded up robust features. In: ECCV (2006)
8. Bebis, G., Egbert, D., Shah, M.: Review of computer vision education. IEEE Trans. Educ. **46**(1), 2–21 (2003)
9. Bradski, G., Kaehler, A.: Opencv. Dr. Dobb's J. Softw. Tools (2000)
10. Brown, M., Lowe, D.G., et al.: Recognising panoramas. In: ICCV (2003)
11. Chen, C.H., Yang, Y.C.: Revisiting the effects of project-based learning on students' academic achievement: a meta-analysis investigating moderators. Educ. Res. Rev. **26**, 71–81 (2019)
12. DeTone, D., Malisiewicz, T., Rabinovich, A.: Superpoint: self-supervised interest point detection and description. In: CVPR Workshops (2018)
13. Everingham, M., Van Gool, L., Williams, C.K., Winn, J., Zisserman, A.: The pascal visual object classes (VOC) challenge. In: IJCV (2010)
14. Fischler, M.A., Bolles, R.C.: Random sample consensus: a paradigm for model fitting with applications to image analysis and automated cartography. Commun. ACM **24**(6), 381–395 (1981)
15. Geronimo, D., Serrat, J., Lopez, A.M., Baldrich, R.: Traffic sign recognition for computer vision project-based learning. IEEE Trans. Educ. **56**(3), 364–371 (2013)
16. Guilluy, W., Oudre, L., Beghdadi, A.: Video stabilization: overview, challenges and perspectives. Signal Process. Image Commun. **90**, 116015 (2021)
17. Guo, P., Saab, N., Post, L.S., Admiraal, W.: A review of project-based learning in higher education: student outcomes and measures. Int. J. Educ. Res. **102**, 101586 (2020)
18. Hartley, R., Zisserman, A.: Multiple View Geometry in Computer Vision. Cambridge University Press, Cambridge (2003)
19. Lao, Y., Yang, J., Wang, X., Lin, J., Cao, Y., Song, S.: Augmenting TV shows via uncalibrated camera small motion tracking in dynamic scene. In: ACM MM (2021)
20. Le, H., Liu, F., Zhang, S., Agarwala, A.: Deep homography estimation for dynamic scenes. In: CVPR (2020)
21. Lin, T.-Y., et al.: Microsoft COCO: common objects in context. In: Fleet, D., Pajdla, T., Schiele, B., Tuytelaars, T. (eds.) ECCV 2014. LNCS, vol. 8693, pp. 740–755. Springer, Cham (2014). https://doi.org/10.1007/978-3-319-10602-1_48
22. Lowe, D.G.: Object recognition from local scale-invariant features. In: ICCV (1999)
23. Lu, X.X.: A review of solutions for perspective-n-point problem in camera pose estimation. In: Journal of Physics: Conference Series (2018)

24. Maxwell, B.A.: A survey of computer vision education and text resources. Int. J. Pattern Recognit. Artif. Intell. **15**(05), 757–773 (2001)
25. Orhei, C., Vert, S., Mocofan, M., Vasiu, R.: End-to-end computer vision framework: an open-source platform for research and education. Sensors **21**(11), 3691 (2021)
26. O'Mahony, N., et al.: Deep learning vs. traditional computer vision. In: Arai, K., Kapoor, S. (eds.) CVC 2019. AISC, vol. 943, pp. 128–144. Springer, Cham (2020). https://doi.org/10.1007/978-3-030-17795-9_10
27. Panciroli, C., Rivoltella, P.C., Gabbrielli, M., Richter, O.Z.: Artificial intelligence and education: new research perspectives. Form@ re-Open Journal per la formazione in rete **20**(3), 43–67 (2020)
28. Redmon, J., Farhadi, A.: Yolov3: an incremental improvement. arXiv preprint (2018)
29. Rublee, E., Rabaud, V., Konolige, K., Bradski, G.: Orb: an efficient alternative to sift or surf. In: ICCV (2011)
30. Saputra, M.R.U., Markham, A., Trigoni, N.: Visual slam and structure from motion in dynamic environments: a survey. ACM Comput. Surv. (CSUR) **51**(2), 1–36 (2018)
31. Satılmış, Y., Tufan, F., Şara, M., Karslı, M., Eken, S., Sayar, A.: CNN based traffic sign recognition for mini autonomous vehicles. In: Świątek, J., Borzemski, L., Wilimowska, Z. (eds.) ISAT 2018. AISC, vol. 853, pp. 85–94. Springer, Cham (2019). https://doi.org/10.1007/978-3-319-99996-8_8
32. Seničić, M., Matijević, M., Nikitović, M.: Teaching the methods of object detection by robot vision. In: 2018 41st International Convention on Information and Communication Technology, Electronics and Microelectronics (MIPRO), pp. 0558–0563. IEEE (2018)

OneAPI Toolkits with Online Devcloud Platform for Teaching Heterogeneous Computing in Artificial Intelligence Specialty

Xing Liu[✉], Yabing Hu, Xinrong Wei, Shengwu Xiong, Xiaoyi Ye, and Ke Xu

School of Computer Science and Artificial Intelligence, Wuhan University of Technology, Wuhan, China
{liu.xing,xiongsw}@whut.edu.cn

Abstract. Data, algorithm and computing power are the three significant driving forces of artificial intelligence (AI). To increase the computing power, the heterogeneous computing (HC) architecture has been popularly applied. This architecture commonly consists of one general-purpose CPU and several specific accelerators such as GPUs, FPGAs or Neural network Processing Units (NPUs). For the students in AI specialty, it is essential to teach them the HC technology so that they can master the skills of accelerating the computationally-intensive AI algorithms. However, it is not easy to teach the HC technology as different accelerators have different development tools and different programming languages. To facilitate the HC development, the Intel corporation has launched oneAPI, which provides unified programming model across different accelerator architectures such as the CPU, GPU, FPGA and NPU, for the purpose of achieving faster application performance, more productivity and greater innovation. In this paper, the work on teaching HC technology for the students of AI specialty by using oneAPI toolkits, DPC++ programming and DevCloud experimental platform is presented. First, the background of HC technology is introduced. Then, the oneAPI toolkits and the teaching work of DPC++ programming is discussed. Following that, the experimental modules for teaching oneAPI by using DPC++ programming based on DevCloud online experimental platform are investigated. Later, a training project which uses oneAPI to accelerate Genome-Wide Association Studies (GWAS) algorithm based on CPU/GPU/FPGA HC platform is proposed. The above teaching work has been carried out in the AI specialty of Wuhan University of Technology, and the survey results show that this course can help the students easily and efficiently master the development technology of HC system.

Supported by Ministry of Education of China (MOE) & Intel Industry-University Cooperation Collaborative Education Project (Grant No. 220900015192812, 220800015230202) and Hubei Province Teaching Research Project (Grant No. 2020187).

Keywords: Heterogenous computing · OneAPI · DPC++ · Devcloud · Education teaching

1   Introduction

Data, algorithm and computing power are the three driving forces of artificial intelligence (AI) technology. To improve the computing power, the traditional methods resort to the ways of deploying large numbers of CPU processors and running these processors in parallelism. This way is effective in many cases. However, the CPUs are the general-purpose processors and are inefficient to run the computationally-intensive AI algorithms. In case of running the AI algorithms on CPUs, it can result in long execution time and high operating cost.

To solve the above problem, the heterogeneous computing (HC) technology is proposed [7]. This way commonly combines the general-purpose CPU with one or several domain-specific accelerators such as GPUs, FPGAs or neural network processing units (NPU). During the run-time, the CPUs work as the host and are responsible for processing the general-purpose tasks. The accelerators work as the devices and are responsible for running the computationally-intensive tasks that are offloaded from CPUs. In this way, the computing speed of the tasks can be accelerated while the energy cost can also be reduced.

Currently, the HC technology has been popularly applied in many AI applications. The CPU/GPU heterogenous architecture has been widely used to process the deep learning (DL) tasks [12], and show good performance due to the GPUs' high computing parallelism. However, GPUs have high energy cost, which limits their large-scale deployment in many applications. To achieve low energy cost, many studies resort to design AI accelerators based on FPGAs [1,11]. Compared with GPUs, the FPGA accelerators are more flexible and can achieve higher energy efficiency. However, its computing performance are commonly less than that of GPUs. In addition to CPU/GPU and CPU/FPGA architectures, the CPU/NPU architecture have also been developed in recent years, represented by the DianNao serials [2], google TPU [8,9] and Huawei Atlas, etc. These NPUs are designed specifically for DL applications, thus they can achieve high computing performance while also keeping high energy efficiency.

Different HC architectures have been developed in past years, and promot the development of AI technology. However, the developers of HC system need to meet a critical challenge, that is, different accelerators need to be developed by using different programming languages and different development tools, e.g., the Nivida GPUs need to be programmed by CUDA and developed by CUDA toolkits, while the Intel FPGAs need to be programmed by Verilog HDL and developed by Quartus toolkits, as is depicted in Fig. 1. Since the developers need to learn different programming languages and various development tools for different HC architectures, they waste a lot of time and efforts in the development process, and this has become a critical problem that needs to be solved in the research field of HC system.

To address the above challenge, it is essential to propose a standards-based unified programming model that can enable the developers to program on differ-

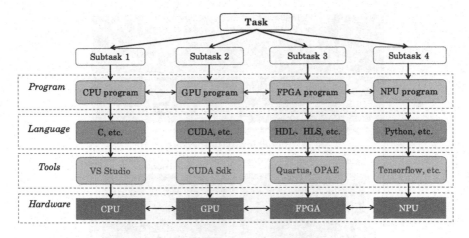

Fig. 1. Traditional way of developing heterogenous computing system.

ent accelerator architectures by using the same language, and the Intel oneAPI targets to achieve this mission [13]. With oneAPI, the HC developers only need to learn the DPC++ programming language and master the oneAPI development tools, then they can develop a program which can run across hardware platforms such as GPUs, FPGAs and NPUs, as is depicted in Fig. 2 and Fig. 3. Due to the above advantages of oneAPI, it is of great significance to teach the students in the AI specialty to learn to develop the HC system by using oneAPI.

In this paper, we present the work of teaching HC technology for the students in AI specialty based on oneAPI toolkits, DPC++ programming and online DevCloud experimental platform. First, the related work on teaching HC technology is introduced. Following that, the oneAPI toolkits are presented. Then, the teaching of oneAPI DPC++ programming language is discussed. Next, the experimental module and online DevCloud experimental platform are presented.

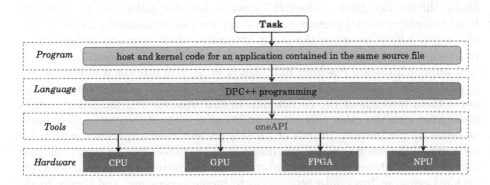

Fig. 2. The way to develop heterogenous computing system based on Intel oneAPI.

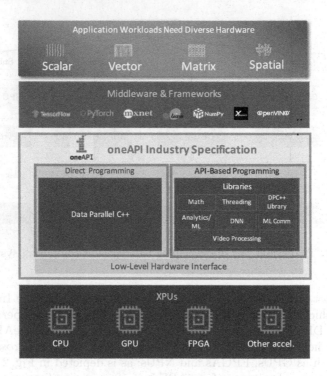

Fig. 3. The architecture of Intel oneAPI.

Later, a training project based on oneAPI is investigated. Finally, the conclusion is given.

2   Related Work

Many universities have opened HC courses for the undergraduate students. Frachtenberg et al. [4] present a case study for one semester-long class on the HC topic, which describes the goals, structure, challenges and lessons of the HC technology, for the purpose of promoting a conversation about a standardized approach toward teaching HC. Qasem et al. [16] propose a module-driven approach which can break the coverage of HC topics into smaller units and disperse them throughout the curriculum. In this way, the HC technology can be integrated with the other curriculum and taught without increasing the number of hours to graduation. Pfundt et al. [15] present their experience with a lab focusing on the design and programming of HC architectures for smart cameras, and this lab contains the implementation of a complete image processing application beginning from data acquisition to image processing, and finally to the embedded operating system.

Currently, the teaching work of HC technology is mostly based on the computing platform of either CPU/GPUs or CPU/FPGAs. Handayani et al. [6]

develop an e-Collab classroom for CNN practice on electrical engineering in Universitas Negeri Malang based on the CPU/GPU computing architecture. Wang et al. [20] discuss the parallelization and optimization of DNN models based on GPUs and discuss the online and offline mixed teaching evaluation of MOOC based on deep neural networks. Panicker et al. [14] present their work of a final-year undergraduate course on implementing a neural accelerator on a CPU/FPGA for edge computing. Malle et al. [10] present an open-source CPU/FPGA framework for designing and implementing a simple neural network targeting edge computing platforms for the purpose of providing the students with deep knowledge on how the neural networks perform their computations. Yang et al. [21] teach the students to design AI accelerators on the CPU/FPGA platforms aiming at exploring the ways to conduct AI education from the perspective of computing systems.

The above work effectively promotes the teaching effect of HC technology. However, there is almost no teaching work which pays much attention to the ways of simplifying the development complexity of HC systems. In this paper, we present the oneAPI teaching work to enable the students to program on different accelerator architectures by using one programing language and one development tool. This teaching work can help the students to master the HC development efficiently, make them to be more productivity and have greater innovation, and it is of great significance for the students in AI speciality.

3   OneAPI Toolkits

To facilitate the HC development process, oneAPI launches a series of development toolkits, which are designed for different kinds of developers.

The base toolkit is designed for most developers, and it can be used to develop the common applications which run across different computing architectures.

The high-performance computing (HPC) toolkit is designed for the HPC developers. It includes a series of components such as Intel C++/Fortran compiler, cluster checker and MPI library. It can be used to develop the HPC applications such as computational fluid dynamics, biological big data analysis and intelligent remote sensing.

The AI analytics tookit is designed for the AI developers and data scientists. It includes the Python distribution such as highly-optimized scikit-learn and XGBoost libraries. It also includes the Intel optimization for PyTorch, Tensorflow and so on.

The IoT toolkit is designed for the edge computing and IoT applications, and it includes an open embedded meta-intel layer for Yocto project.

The rendering toolkit is designed for the visual creators, and it provides a set of components such as Intel embree, open image denoise, openSWR and OSPRay.

The openVIN toolkit is designed for the DL inference developers. It includes the inference engine, openCV and DL streamer, and it can be used for the high-performance inference applications in the edge-cloud collaborative computing system.

Table 1. Teaching contents of DPC++ Programming

Chapter	Category	Contents
Ch 1–4	Foundation	- SYCL - Queues and Actions - Data movement - Parallelism expressing
Ch 5–12	Details	- Error handling - Buffer/Unified shared memory - Graph scheduling/data movement - Communications and Synchronization - Kernel defining - Vector types/interfaces/execution/parallelism - Device information
Ch 13–19	In practice	- Parallel patterns - Practical tips - Built-in functions/DPC++ libraries - Memory models/Atomic operation - Programming for GPUs/CPUs /FPGAs

When performing the experimental training, the students mainly learn how to use the oneAPI base toolkit, and generally understand how to use the AI analytics toolkit and IoT toolkit by means of two typical study cases. As for the other kinds of toolkits, they are left for the students to study with interest after the class.

4   DPC++ Programming Teaching

OneAPI simplifies the development process of programming on CPUs and accelerators by using the DPC++ language. DPC++ is an open source programming language based on SYCL, with a few extensions. SYCL is a cross-platform abstraction layer which enables the developers to program on the HC platform by using the standard ISO C++ [18]. SYCL can enable the host code and kernel code of a HC application to be contained in the same source file.

To teach DPC++ programming, the book 'Data parallel C++: mastering DPC++ for programming of heterogeneous systems using C++ and SYCL' [17] is used as the teaching material. This book is about programming for data parallelism using C++. It is suitable for the readers who are even new to the HC development or have never heard of SYCL.

This book contains 19 chapters, which can be divided into 3 sections, as is depicted in Table 1. Chapter 1 to 4 introduce some basic knowledge of DPC++. These four chapters lay a foundation for learning DPC++. Chapter 5 to 12 discuss the details of DPC++ programming. Chapter 13 to 19 present how to put the DPC++ into practice [17].

In case the teaching hours are limited, the instructors can focus on teaching the first eight chapters of this book, and this way can still enable the students to master the basic development skills of DPC++ programming.

Table 2. Devcloud experimental modules for oneAPI teaching (Part 1)

No.	Modules	Training Objective	Experimental Contents
1	oneAPI Introduction	- Master the workflow of Dev-Cloud - Master the framework of heterogenous programming using oneAPI - Understand the programming language and models of DPC++ - Use Jupyter notebooks for experiments	- SYCL Hello World - a sample for oneAPI programming model - Compile and Run a DPC++ program
2	DPC++ Program Structure	- Master the functions and usage of device selector - Learn to use basic parallel kernels and ND range kernels - Learn to use device selector and memory data management in simple cases - Learn to build a DPC++ application	- Selection of device selector - Data dependency and synchronization - Vector multiplication - Vector add
3	DPC++ Unified Shared Memory	- Use USM to simplify programming - Understand explicit and implicit data movement with USM - Understand data dependencies	- Implicit/Explicit USM - Data Dependency in-order/out-of-order queues
4	DPC++ Sub Groups	- Understand the benefits of subgroups - Learn to use subgroup to improve performance - Learn to use subgroup in ND-Ranges kernels - Learn to use subgroup shuffle	- Setting parameters of subgroup - Subgroup function

5   Experimental Module Design

The experiments are conducted on the Intel DevCloud platform. Intel Dev-Cloud is a free, online sandbox for developing cross-architecture applications with oneAPI [3], and it has the following features:

- full access to the latest Intel CPUs, GPUs and FPGAs.
- enable free access to the resources of oneAPI toolkits.
- connect remotely via a terminal or browser.
- provide training modules which can be operated by Jupyter Notebooks.

Currently, a serial of experimental modules have been designed for teaching DPC++ programming, as is shown in Table 2 and Table 3. Through these experimental modules, the students can understand the program structure of DPC++, and master the usage of DPC++ USM, SubGroup, Intel advisor tool, VTnue profiler tool, DPC++ library and so on.

Table 3. Devcloud experimental modules for oneAPI teaching (Part 2)

No.	Modules	Training Objective	Experimental Contents
5	Intel Advisor	- Understand how IntelR advisor works - Learn to use IntelR advisor command line syntax - Understand the optimization strategy	- Roofline Model - Analysis: Roofline Analysis Report - Effective Optimization Strategies - Options for GPU Roofline Analysis - Roofline Analysis on Intel GPU
6	Intel VTune Profiler	- Profile a DPC++ application using VTune profiling tool - Learn to use VTune command line options to collect data and generate reports	- What is VTune Profiler? - VTune Command-line Options - VTune profiling sample
7	DPC++ Library	- Understand DPC++ Library (DPL)v - Simplify DPC++ programming by oneDPL - Combination of oneDPL with Buffers and USM	- Simple oneDPL example - oneDPL with Buffer Iterators, USM Pointers and USM Allocators
8	DPC++ Reduction	- Understand reduction concept and learn to use reduction - Learn to use reduction in subgroups and workgroups - Learn to use reduction object and multiple reductions	- Reduction with kernel functions - Reduction in parallel_for USM and Buffers - Multiple Reduction in a single kernel

6   Project Training for DPC++ and OneAPI

Through the theoretical teaching of DPC++ and practical teaching of DevCloud, the students can master the DPC++ programming and understand the way to use oneAPI toolkits. Based on this foundation, a comprehensive oneAPI training project is further designed. This project requires the students to accelerate the Genome Wide Association Study (GWAS) algorithm by using oneAPI DPC++ programming based on the CPU/GPU/FPGA HC platform.

GWAS is a research approach used to identify the association between the genomic variants and a disease or a particular trait [19]. GWAS is selected for the design of DPC++ training case due to two reasons: First, the computing process of GWAS involves a large number of highly computationally-intensive tasks.

Second, different computationally-intensive tasks in GWAS are appropriate to be executed on different accelerators. The above two features make GWAS very suitable to run on the multi-core HC accelerating platform.

The computationally-intensive tasks in GWAS can be classified into two stages: (I) the creation of contingency table (II) statistical testing of each created table. The two stages show different computing features: the first stage has a large number of low-wide bit-bit logic operations, while the second stage has massively floating-point operations. Therefore, the first stage is appropriate to run on the FPGA accelerators, while the second stage is appropriate to run on the GPU accelerators [5]. In Fig. 4, the computing process of GWAS is depicted.

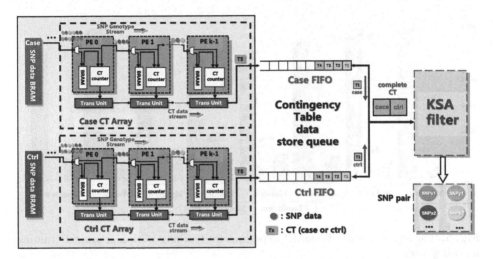

Fig. 4. The computing process of the GWAS which is appropriate to be accelerated by HC technology.

Since GWAS has the above features, this project requires the students to develop GWAS by using DPC++ programming and oneAPI toolkits based on the CPU/GPU/FPGA HC platform. Specially, the students need to use the DPC++ programming to offload the contingency table creation tasks of GWAS to the FPGA accelerators. Meanwhile, they need to use the same DPC++ programming to offload the statistical testing tasks of GWAS to the GPU accelerators. Through this project training, the students can deeply understand the following concepts: First, HC architecture can accelerate the executing speed of computationally-intensive tasks if compared with the general-purpose homogeneous computing architecture. Second, DPC++ can simply the development process of HC system since it enables to use the same programming language across different kinds of accelerators.

To help students to complete the development of this GWAS project, 3 subproject modules have been designed: (1) Sub-project 1 is in charge of reading and processing datasets. At this stage, the students only need to design the data structures to store datasets. (2) Sub-project 2 is in charge of creating the contingency table (CT) based on the read data. At this stage, the students need to use DPC++ programming to offload the CT creation tasks to FPGAs and generates the CT results. (3) Sub-project 3 is in charge of performing statistical operations based on CT. At this stage, the students need to use DPC++ programming to offload the statistical operating tasks to run on the GPUs.

The project results can show the students that the computing time of GWAS can be greatly shortened and meanwhile the energy efficiency of GWAS can keep high due to the usage of DPC++ programming and oneAPI toolkits on GWAS development.

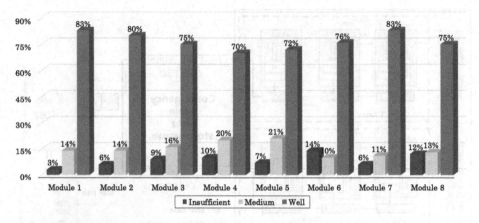

Fig. 5. The survey result of oneAPI experimental teaching work and project training teaching work.

7   Course Survey and Evaluation

The teaching work of this paper has been carried out through the intelligent computing system course in the AI speciality of Wuhan University of Technology. The course has 32 credit hours, including 12 credit hours for experiments.

The teaching objectives of the course include: understand the significance of HC technology; master the use of oneAPI tools and DPC++ programming; complete different modules of the DevCloud experiments; complete the migration of GWAS code from C code to DPC++ code.

The survey results show that 93% students think that they have understood the significance of using HC technology to accelerate the computationally-intensive tasks. 81% students think that they have mastered the usage of oneAPI basic toolkits and DPC++ programming. As for the training effects of different modules, it is shown in Fig. 5.

8   Conclusion

HC has emerged as a dominant technology in the field of intelligent computing. This paper presents the work of teaching HC technology based on the Intel oneAPI toolkits, DPC++ programming and Devcloud experimental platform. The teaching material of this course is introduced, the experimental modules are presented, and a DPC++ training project is also designed and conducted. The work of this paper has been carried out in AI specialty of Wuhan University of Technology, and the survey results show that this course can help the students efficiently master the development skills of HC system.

References

1. Ayachi, R., Said, Y., Ben Abdelali, A.: Optimizing neural networks for efficient FPGA implementation: a survey. Arch. Computa. Methods Eng. 1–11 (2021)
2. Chen, Y., Chen, T., Xu, Z., Sun, N., Temam, O.: Diannao family: energy-efficient hardware accelerators for machine learning. Commun. ACM **59**(11), 105–112 (2016)
3. Devcloud: Intel devcloud for oneapi - a development sandbox to learn about programming cross architecture applications (2022). https://devcloud.intel.com/oneapi/get_started/
4. Frachtenberg, E.: Experience and practice teaching an undergraduate course on diverse heterogeneous architectures. In: 2021 IEEE/ACM Ninth Workshop on Education for High Performance Computing (EduHPC), pp. 1–8. IEEE (2021)
5. González-Domínguez, J., Wienbrandt, L., Kässens, J.C., Ellinghaus, D., Schimmler, M., Schmidt, B.: Parallelizing epistasis detection in GWAS on FPGA and GPU-accelerated computing systems. IEEE/ACM Trans. Comput. Biol. Bioinf. **12**(5), 982–994 (2015)
6. Handayani, A.N., Zaeni, I.A.E., Kurniawan, W.C., Asmara, R.A., et al.: Development of e-collab classroom for CNN practice on electrical engineering, universitas Negeri Malang. In: 2020 4th International Conference on Vocational Education and Training (ICOVET), pp. 47–51. IEEE (2020)
7. Hennessy, J.L., Patterson, D.A.: A new golden age for computer architecture. Commun. ACM **62**(2), 48–60 (2019)
8. Jouppi, N.P., et al.: Ten lessons from three generations shaped Google's tpuv4i: industrial product. In: 2021 ACM/IEEE 48th Annual International Symposium on Computer Architecture (ISCA), pp. 1–14. IEEE (2021)
9. Jouppi, N.P., et al.: In-datacenter performance analysis of a tensor processing unit. In: Proceedings of the 44th Annual International Symposium on Computer Architecture, pp. 1–12 (2017)
10. Malle, N., Ebeid, E.: Open-source educational platform for FPGA accelerated AI in robotics. In: 2022 8th International Conference on Mechatronics and Robotics Engineering (ICMRE), pp. 112–115. IEEE (2022)
11. Mittal, S.: A survey of FPGA-based accelerators for convolutional neural networks. Neural Comput. Appl. **32**(4), 1109–1139 (2020)
12. Mittal, S., Vaishay, S.: A survey of techniques for optimizing deep learning on GPUs. J. Syst. Architect. **99**, 101635 (2019)
13. oneAPI: A new era of heterogeneous computing (2022). https://software.intel.com/content/www/cn/zh/develop/tools/oneapi.html

14. Panicker, R.C., Kumar, A., John, D.: Introducing FPGA-based machine learning on the edge to undergraduate students. In: 2020 IEEE Frontiers in Education Conference (FIE), pp. 1–5. IEEE (2020)

15. Pfundt, B., Reichenbach, M., Hartmann, C., Häublein, K., Fey, D.: Teaching heterogeneous computer architectures using smart camera systems. In: 2016 11th European Workshop on Microelectronics Education (EWME), pp. 1–6. IEEE (2016)

16. Qasem, A., Bunde, D.P., Schielke, P.: A module-based introduction to heterogeneous computing in core courses. J. Parallel Distrib. Comput. **158**, 56–66 (2021)

17. Reinders, J., Ashbaugh, B., Brodman, J., Kinsner, M., Pennycook, J., Tian, X.: Data parallel C++: Mastering DPC++ for Programming of Heterogeneous Systems Using C++ and SYCL. Springer, Berkeley (2021). https://doi.org/10.1007/978-1-4842-5574-2

18. SYCL: SYCL overview - The Khronos Group Inc. (2022). https://www.khronos.org/sycl/

19. Uffelmann, E., et al.: Genome-wide association studies. Nat. Rev. Methods Primers **1**(1), 59 (2021)

20. Wang, G., Chen, X.: Evaluation of the online and offline mixed teaching effect of MOOC based upon the deep neural network model. Wirel. Commun. Mob. Comput. **2022** (2022)

21. Yang, J., Gao, X., Zhao, W.: Towards systems education for artificial intelligence: a course practice in intelligent computing architectures. In: Proceedings of the 2020 on Great Lakes Symposium on VLSI, pp. 567–572 (2020)

GcnSV: A Method Based on Deep Learning of Calling Structural Variations from the Third-Generation Sequencing Data

Meng Huang, Han Wang, and Jingyang Gao(✉)

College of Information Science and Technology, Beijing University of Chemical Technology, Beijing, China

{2019200827,2021200811}@buct.edu.cn, gaojy@mail.buct.edu.cn

Abstract. The birth of the third-generation sequencing technology provides a large number of long-read data for calling structural variations (SVs). However, the existing calling tools for these long-read data have high precision but low recall. Therefore, to solve this problem, a new method called GcnSV is proposed in this paper. Firstly, GcnSV maps all reads in the genome sequencing data into corresponding graphs as the input of the graph neural network. Then, it uses these graphs to train the graph neural network in order to learn the characteristics of variations themselves and their upstream and downstream. Finally, a clustering algorithm is designed to obtain the final calling results. On the simulated and real data, we give the evaluation results of GcnSV and other calling tools. The experimental results show that GcnSV has higher recall and F1-score on different coverage depths and different variant lengths.

Keywords: graph neural network · structural variations · sequencing data · pruning · clustering algorithms · deep learning

1 Introduction

Structural variations (SVs) are considered to be closely related to some genetic diseases [1] and cancers [2]. At the same time, some studies have shown that biological evolution [3] will be affected by SVs to a certain extent. In order to explore the characteristics of SVs, it is necessary to provide a large number of gene samples with real variations. Therefore, many researchers are committed to designing more effective calling methods. The previous methods (such as Pindel [4], BreakDancer [5], Lumpy [6]) are based on the second-generation sequencing data in which reads are relatively short, so that their sensitivity is not satisfactory [7]. To overcome the shortcomings of the second-generation sequencing technology, Pacific Bioscience and Oxford Nanopore Technologies have developed their own third-generation technology, which is also known as single molecule sequencing technology. It has been proved that longer reads can be sequenced directly without PCR amplification, and errors such as GC bias will be greatly reduced. However, the third-generation sequencing data inevitably has a higher random sequencing error rate

© The Author(s), under exclusive license to Springer Nature Singapore Pte Ltd. 2023
W. Hong and Y. Weng (Eds.): ICCSE 2022, CCIS 1813, pp. 397–409, 2023.
https://doi.org/10.1007/978-981-99-2449-3_35

[8]. Therefore, how to give full play to the advantages of the third-generation sequencing data and abandon its disadvantages has become the focus of frontier research. In this paper, calling deletion variations is the key point.

At present, some calling methods for the third-generation data use traditional strategies. For example, Sniffles [9] uses split-read (SR) mapping strategy and read-depth (RD) analysis strategy, PBSV (https://github.com/PacificBioscien- ces/pbsv) uses SR mapping strategy. And some methods use innovative strategies, for example, CuteSV [10] uses strategy based on block division, NextSV [11] uses integration strategy. However, the common feature of them is that precision is high but recall is low, which leads to a small number of real deletion variations actually detected. Consequently, it can't meet the clinical needs of exploring disease diagnosis and genetic evolution.

Graphs are unstructured data, but graph convolution network (GCN) [12] won't be affected by their sizes. Compared with convolutional neural network (CNN), it can combine the characteristics of nodes and the structural information of graphs to learn new representation of nodes, which is especially suitable for the graphs with uncertain number of neighbor nodes. In recent years, GCN has been widely used in various research fields, such as social impact modeling [13], computer vision [14], traffic prediction [15], drug target interaction prediction [16], but it is rarely used to call SVs. There are three main theoretical sources for applying GCN to calling variations:

1) The information stored in Binary Sequence Alignment/Map Format (BAM) file is the factual basis of converting sequence text data into graphic data. The CIGAR field records the alignment relationship of each small base segment, including matching, deletion, insertion, soft clipping and so on. Among them, matching means that the corresponding base segments of reference gene and target gene are exactly the same. Naturally, it as well as the positional relationship upstream and downstream between continuous base segments jointly constitute the edges of graphs, and the nodes refer to the base segments.

2) The information of deletion variations upstream and downstream indeed has a certain impact on judging variations. For example, the necessary condition for judging homozygous variations is that there are a large number of soft-clipping parts near their breakpoints. Only considering the characteristics of deletion variations will lead to more missed detection, which is reflected as low recall. Fortunately, an advantage of GCN is that it can learn structural information of data and mine the related information between deletion variations and their upstream and downstream.

3) In the past, there have been calling methods that convert sequencing data into image data in order to extract variant features with CNN. The common problem of these methods is that in the face of super-long deletion variations, the input images have to be reduced and unified into the same size by dividing windows or compressing images. As a result, a large number of details suffer from loss and fuzziness. But GCN is not sensitive to the scale of graphs when training graphic data.

In this paper, we propose GcnSV based on GCN to call as many deletion variations as possible. And it is expected to capture additional features upstream and downstream of the variations to increase recall. On the simulated and real data (HG002, Skbr3), we evaluate the results of GcnSV and four other tools (Sniffles, NextSV, CuteSV and

PBSV). In terms of recall and F1-score, the results show that GcnSV performs better on both real and simulated data.

2   Methods

Generally, the overall process of GcnSV can be divided into two parts. In the first part, the sequencing data is transformed into graphic data, and then it's sent to GCN to accomplish the classification of graph nodes. In essence, each small base segment on each read is dichotomized, and all continuous base segments classified as deletion variations (0 represents non-deletion, 1 represents deletion) are spliced to form variation intervals as the output of the first part. The second part is to cluster the variation intervals detected in all the reads. If there are reads whose number exceeds the preset threshold in a certain area in which deletion variations are considered to exist, then take the mean value of all intervals in this area as the final output, otherwise it's determined that there are no deletion variations. These two parts are described in more detail below.

2.1   Converting Reads to Graphs

As is shown in Fig. 1, the generation steps of graphs are different in the training and testing stage. And the training stage will be taken as an example to be introduced in detail below. Due to the low probability of deletion variations, a large number of reads don't cover the variant areas. In order to reduce the amount of input data and eliminate the interference of non-variant areas as much as possible, so that the network model can focus more on learning the characteristics of variant areas, we firstly filter all reads. The specific method is to select the reads containing deletion variations from the BAM file according to the variant sites marked in the benchmark file.

The average length of reads in the third-generation sequencing data is more than 10kbp, while the average length of deletion variations is only about a few hundred bp, which is far less than the length of reads. Therefore, the base segments in variant areas still account for a very small proportion of the candidate reads, which actually reflects the data imbalance between variant areas and non-variant areas. A large number of experiments show that such data imbalance will increase the difficulty of training the deep learning model, and more importantly, it will make the model more inclined to learn the characteristics of non-variant areas, which is contrary to the original intention of building deep learning model in this paper. Consequently, in order to reduce the amount of data in the non-variant areas and reflect the relative size relationship of data volume between variant areas and non-variant areas to a certain extent, we perform a pruning operation for the candidate reads. Specifically, the length of a variant interval will be regarded as the unit length, then retain a unit length of non-variant base sequence in the upstream and downstream of deletion variations, and prune the part beyond this range at last. Such an operation actually reduces the ratio of data volume between variant areas and non-variant areas to 2:1.

After pruning, we mainly extract four types of field information including Mapping Quality, Reference Start, Read Length and the most important CIGAR. Among them, Mapping Quality is used to eliminate the reads that fail aligning, Reference Start and

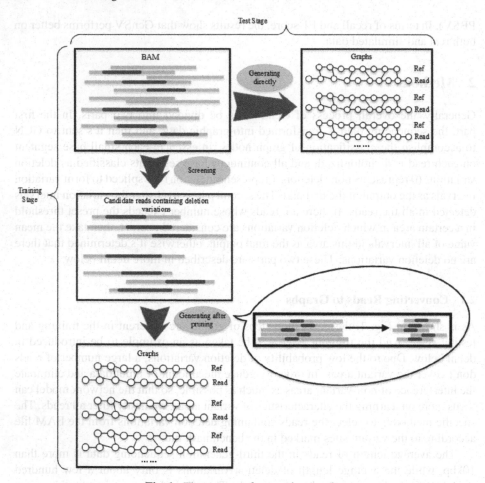

Fig. 1. The process of generating graphs.

Read Length are used to label the nodes of graphs and determine the pruning positions, CIGAR is used to construct the feature matrix. CIGAR consists of many tuples, each containing 2 elements. The first one has values 0, 1, 2, 4 and so on, which represent matching, insertion, deletion and soft-clipping respectively. The second one represents the length of the current base segment. In fact, these tuples are the nodes of subsequent generated graphs. When the corresponding base segments of target gene and reference gene are completely matched, one edge can be used to connect the two tuples. At the same time, the base segments of reference gene and target gene are extended in a stranded configuration, so positionally adjacent base segments can also be joined by edges. In this way, each read can be transformed into a graph, thus calling variations can be refined to each read. In order to distinguish four types of base segments, four colors (green, blue, red and yellow) are used to represent different types of tuples.

Figure 2(a) shows two graphs transformed from different reads in the same area where a deletion variation of about 800 bp exists. It can be seen that the sequencing performance of reads is very different, and the proportion of soft-clipping parts of some reads is too high. Besides, the deletion segments of quite a part of reads show fragmented distribution, which is particularly prominent in heterozygous deletion variations. That is why heterozygous deletion variations are more difficult to detect than homozygous deletion variations.

Figure 2(b) shows the loss curves of pre-pruning and pruning. Comparing the left and right pictures, it can be seen that pruning operation is indeed indispensable in the training stage of GcnSV. After pruning, when the value drops to the lowest point, it will not fluctuate up and down compared with pre-pruning, but can well converge to a minimum value close to 0. In addition, the pruning operation also effectively shortens the training time of each epoch. Previously, it takes more than 40 min to train the data of a whole chromosome, but now it only takes about 7 min.

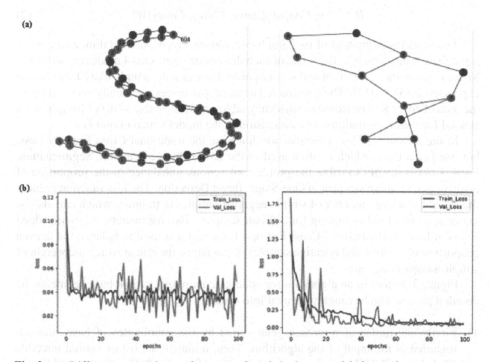

Fig. 2. (a) Different sequencing performance of reads in the same deletion variant area. (b) The loss curves, the left is pre-pruning, the right is pruning.

2.2 Constructing Network Model

Inspired by the idea that R-GCN [17] classifies and aggregates neighbor nodes when modeling heterogeneous graphs, the edges that reflect matching relationship between reference gene and target gene, and the chain edges that reflect their positional relationship of upstream and downstream, are converted into adjacency matrices A_1, A_2

and A_3 respectively in this paper. Then, the transpose of the characteristic matrix H^l is convoluted with them respectively, and the convolution results are spliced as the output of the current network layer. In this way, the output dimension will become three times as much as traditional convolution, making it easy to classify the features in the high dimension that are difficult to classify in the low dimension.

The traditional fourth-generation GCN firstly normalizes the adjacency matrix, and then updates the network layer parameters layer by layer:

$$H^{(l+1)} = \hat{D}^{-\frac{1}{2}}\hat{A}\hat{D}^{-\frac{1}{2}}H^l W^l \tag{1}$$

The convolution formula adopted in this paper is shown as (2), where $Conv_i = \hat{D}^{-\frac{1}{2}}\hat{A}_i\hat{D}^{-\frac{1}{2}}H^l i \in (1, 2, 3)$:

$$H^{(l+1)} = Concat(Conv_1, Conv_2, Conv_3)W^l \tag{2}$$

The model is composed of two graph convolution layers, and the dimension of the input feature matrices is 4. The value of each dimension represents 4 modes respectively: Matching, Insertion, Deletion and soft-clipping. For example, a tuple like (0, 34) can be expressed as (34, 0, 0, 0). The constructed adjacency matrices are usually very sparse, so the data of edges will be stored in adjacency tables, and the Sparse Matrix Multiplication is used for matrix operations. The dimension of the model's final output is 2.

In the selection of loss function, we don't use the traditional Cross Entropy Loss, but use Focal Loss, which is often used in the task of Image Semantic Segmentation. Focal Loss is mainly to solve the problem of serious imbalance in the proportion of positive and negative samples in One-Stage Target Detection. The loss function reduces the weight of a large number of simple negative samples in training, which can also be understood as a kind of mining for difficult samples. Two parameters (α, γ) are added in Focal Loss on the basis of Cross Entropy Loss, and α is used to balance the uneven proportion of positive and negative samples, γ can adjust the rate at which the weight of simple samples decreases.

Figure 3. Refers to an algorithm for splicing continuous variant base segments, its detailed process can be roughly divided into 4 steps:

1) Firstly, the tuples of reference gene sorted by the coordinates of base sites are regarded as the input of the algorithm. Then, initialize the list of variant intervals (Del_List) to NULL and the current index (Cur_Index) to 0. Finally, the coordinates of the starting site of reference gene are marked as POS.
2) The index begins to increase gradually from Cur_Index, whenever a tuple with category 0 is encountered, update the value of POS. Don't record the current value of POS as the starting site (DelVar_ST) of a deletion variation until encounter a tuple with category 1.
3) The index begins to increase gradually from Cur_Index, whenever a tuple with category 1 is encountered, update the value of POS. Don't record the current value of POS as the ending site (DelVar_ED) of a deletion variation until encounter a tuple with category 0.

4) If DelVar_ED - DelVar_ST > 50 is satisfied, then add a variant interval which starts
    with DelVar_ST and ends with DelVar_ED to Del_List. And repeat 2) and 3) until
    the whole read has been scanned.

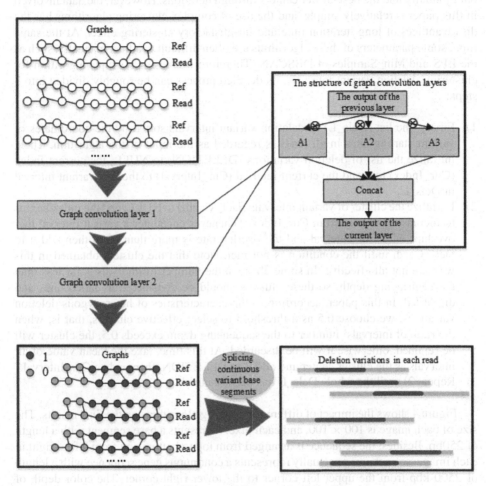

Fig. 3. The general framework of GcnSV.

2.3 Designing a Clustering Algorithm

After obtaining the deletion variant intervals in each read, it can be found that many
variant intervals will cluster around the same sites. In this paper, such sites are regarded
as the final output deletion variant sites, that is, the cluster centers of variant intervals
are regarded as deletion variant sites. In order to get the cluster centers, a clustering
operation needs to be introduced into the model.

We compare three existing mainstream clustering algorithms, including Affinity Propagation Algorithm [18], DBSCAN [19] which is a spatial clustering algorithm based on density, Mean Shift Algorithm [20]. The common feature of these three algorithms is that they don't need to manually specify the clustering number in advance, but gradually find the best cluster centers through iterations. However, the data involved in this paper is relatively simple, and the use of complex clustering algorithms has the disadvantages of long iteration time and unsatisfactory clustering effect. At the same time, some parameters of these algorithms are often difficult to adjust manually, such as the EPS and Min_Samples of DBSCAN. Therefore, we design a simple algorithm for clustering deletion variant intervals, its detailed process can be roughly divided into 3 steps:

1) Firstly, the list (Dels_L) of deletion variant intervals sorted by the coordinates of variant starting sites in all reads is regarded as the input of the algorithm. Then, initialize the list of deletion variations (DELETION) to NULL, the current index (Cur_Index) to 0 and the current interval (Cur_Interval) to the first variant interval in Dels_L.
2) Initialize the cluster of variant intervals (Del_ Candi) to NULL, and the index begins to increase gradually from Cur_Index. Whenever encounter a variant interval that overlaps with Cur_Interval and the overlap rate is more than 80%, then add it to Del_ Candi until the condition is not met. Note that the clusters obtained in this way are not all effective. In some clusters, the number of intervals is far less than the sequencing depth, so these clusters should be considered as failed ones and discarded. In this paper, according to the characteristics of heterozygous deletion variations, we choose 0.5 as a threshold to select effective clusters, that is, when the ratio of intervals' number to the sequencing depth exceeds 0.5, the cluster will be retained, otherwise it will be discarded. At this time, take the mean value of all intervals as the cluster center and add it to DELETION, then update Cur_Interval.
3) Repeat 2) until the whole Dels_L has been scanned.

Figure 4 shows the impact of different clustering algorithms on the final results. The size of each image is 100×100, and each pixel represents a base segment with a length of 250bp. Besides, the sequence is arranged from top to bottom and from left to right in each image, so each image actually represents a continuous gene sequence with a length of 2500 kbp from the upper left corner to the lower right corner. The color depth of each pixel represents the ratio of the variant part's length at the current base segment to 250bp. And the closer it is to 1, the darker the color is. In general, comparing Fig. 4(b), Fig. 4(c), Fig. 4(d) and Fig. 4(e) with Fig. 4(a), it can be found that the clustering effect of the newly designed algorithm is the best. Besides, the running time of it is relatively less because clustering can be realized without hundreds of iterations. On the contrary, the other three algorithms have the following problems more or less:

1) The color of pixels appears to fade and blur.
2) Some variant intervals fail to cluster.
3) Some large clusters are divided into small clusters.

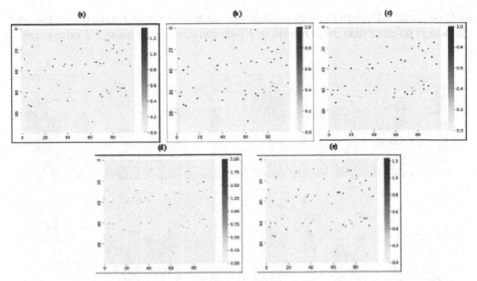

Fig. 4. The results of calling deletion variations obtained by different clustering algorithms. (a) is benchmark, (b) is Affinity Propagation Algorithm, (c) is DBSCAN Algorithm, (d) is Mean Shift Algorithm, (e) is the newly designed algorithm.

3 Results

In order to verify the effectiveness of GcnSV in improving the recall of calling deletion variations, the experiments are divided into two parts: one is for real data, the other one is for simulation data. There is no recognized benchmark, but a lot of sequencing noise in the real data sets, and the deletion variations in data are complex and diverse. In the simulation data sets, deletion variations are basically homozygous, and their length is generally very long. We select chromosomes 1 to 6 as the training set and chromosomes 7 to 22 as the test set, and randomly divide the training nodes and verification nodes in the graph nodes' classification task, with the division ratio of 8:2.

3.1 The Results of Real Data

The real data sets used in this paper are from the gene sequencing data of HG002_NA24385 and Skbr3 individuals which are published by GIAB (Genome In A Bottle), the depth of HG002 is 70X and the depth of Skbr3 is 100X. In order to obtain a credible benchmark, we refer to the idea of Dierckxsens N et al. [21], and then determine to absorb the advantages of CuteSV, SVIM [22], Sniffles and PBSV with combining their callsets.

For HG002, we use Samtools to get 4 kinds of data with different coverage depth of 28X, 42X, 56X and 70X through down-sampling operations, so as to verify the effectiveness of GcnSV under different coverage depth. As can be seen in Fig. 5, GcnSV exceeds 90% on all three evaluation indexes, which shows that GcnSV is least affected by the reduction of coverage depth. Besides, GcnSV is significantly better than other tools on recall. Although its precision does not reach the optimal, the maximum gap with the best is no more than 3%. Overall, its F1-score increases by about 5% on average.

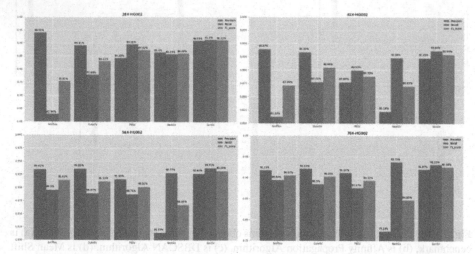

Fig. 5. The experimental results of the HG002 datasets with different coverage depth.

For Skbr3, after obtaining the data of 30X and 70X, we carry out deeper experiments for five different length ranges (50-200bp, 200-500bp, 500-1000bp, 1000-5000bp and more than 5kbp) on them, in order to explore whether GcnSV has a preference for longer deletion variations. The experimental results show that on the 30x data, only when GcnSV detects the variations of 500-1000bp, its recall does not reach the best (but its comprehensive F1-score is the best), but its recall and F1-score both rank first in other cases. On the 70X data, the recall of GcnSV increases by 3%–10% on average, and its F1-score increases by 2%–8%. Although the advantages of GcnSV are not significant when calling the variations above 5kbp, considering that the deletion variations below 5kbp account for more than 95% of the total ones in the real data sets, GcnSV's gap with CuteSV on F1-score above 5kbp is acceptable (Table 1).

3.2 The Results of Simulation Data

Generally, obtaining high-quality real data requires high financial support, and real data is often difficult to contain various types of deletion variations as much as possible, so calling variations in simulation data is also one of the means to test calling methods' effectiveness. In this paper, SURVIVOR [23], PaSS [24] and NGMLR [25] are used to simulate the third-generation sequencing data. Firstly, the reference genome files with variations are simulated by SURVIVOR, and then the FASTQ files are generated by PaSS. Finally, the BAM files are obtained by aligning the FASTQ files to the reference genome files using NGMLR. According to the above steps, we simulate four kinds of BAM files with low coverage depth: 10X, 20X, 30X and 40X, so as to evaluate the performance of GcnSV.

Table 1. The experimental results of the Skbr3 datasets with deletion variations of different length

30X_Skbr3					70X_Skbr3				
Length Ranges	Methods	Precision	Recall	F1-score	Length Ranges	Methods	Precision	Recall	F1-score
	Sniffles	93.10%	20.07%	33.02%		Sniffles	91.56%	71.21%	80.11%
	PBSV	75.28%	82.76%	78.84%		PBSV	85.55%	87.12%	86.32%
50-200bp	CuteSV	92.72%	39.03%	54.93%	50-200bp	CuteSV	90.03%	81.96%	85.80%
	NextSV	87.80%	40.89%	55.79%		NextSV	82.77%	82.42%	82.60%
	GcnSV	77.31%	84.55%	80.76%		GcnSV	87.98%	89.70%	88.83%
	Sniffles	100%	36.03%	52.98%		Sniffles	94.18%	88.32%	91.15%
	PBSV	79.85%	98.19%	88.08%		PBSV	90.78%	91.97%	91.37%
200-500bp	CuteSV	100%	58.55%	73.86%	200-500bp	CuteSV	91.76%	90.54%	91.14%
	NextSV	97.22%	61.26%	75.16%		NextSV	83%	95.62%	88.86%
	GcnSV	81.23%	99.10%	89.27%		GcnSV	88.82%	98.54%	93.42%
	Sniffles	100%	35.71%	52.63%		Sniffles	100%	86.30%	92.64%
	PBSV	58.82%	71.42%	64.51%		PBSV	88.88%	69.56%	78.04%
500-1kbp	CuteSV	100%	50%	66.66%	500-1kbp	CuteSV	96.71%	90.65%	93.58%
	NextSV	100%	50%	66.66%		NextSV	88.88%	86.95%	87.91%
	GcnSV	88.89%	64.29%	74.61%		GcnSV	92%	95.65%	93.79%
	Sniffles	100%	59.25%	74.41%		Sniffles	92.55%	88.61%	90.53%
	PBSV	78.78%	93.15%	85.36%		PBSV	91.89%	72.34%	80.95%
1k-5kbp	CuteSV	100%	59.25%	74.41%	1k-5kbp	CuteSV	91.44%	88.61%	90%
	NextSV	80.76%	77.77%	79.24%		NextSV	87.80%	93.61%	90.61%
	GcnSV	75.44%	99.30%	85.74%		GcnSV	90.42%	91.49%	90.95%
	Sniffles	100%	30%	46.15%		Sniffles	87.50%	87.50%	87.50%
	PBSV	83.33%	92.48%	87.66%		PBSV	92.85%	81.25%	86.66%
>5kbp	CuteSV	100%	30%	46.15%	>5kbp	CuteSV	100%	81.25%	89.65%
	NextSV	80%	70%	74.66%		NextSV	88.88%	87.50%	88.18%
	GcnSV	84.59%	95.63%	89.77%		GcnSV	90.37%	88.81%	89.58%

Table 2. The experimental results of the simulation datasets with different coverage depth

Benchmark	Methods	Coverage Depth			
		10X	20X	30X	40X
	Sniffles	0	2680	7042	10603
	CuteSV	0	2919	6840	9643
19568	PBSV	5112	8281	9697	10963
	NextSV	43	2320	6522	9682

Since the precision of all methods can basically reach 100%, we evaluate them based on the number of real variations actually detected. It can be seen from Table 2 that low coverage depth has a great impact on Sniffles, CuteSV and NextSV, but little on PBSV and GcnSV. On the 10X data, the first three only call very little variations, although the latter two's calling number also decreases, the decline range is still acceptable. Overall,

GcnSV detects more variations than others, and only slightly less than PBSV on the 20X data.

4 Conclusion

In this paper, a new method called GcnSV is proposed for calling deletion variations. Firstly, GcnSV maps sequencing data into graphs according to the designed rules, in order to establish the relationship between variations and their upstream and downstream. Secondly, GCN is introduced to learn graphs, so as to fully mine the information of variations upstream and downstream, and then enhance the features learned. Finally, calculate the cluster centers of variant intervals and regard them as the final variant sites. Compared with four existing tools, GcnSV has higher recall and F1-score, it means that GcnSV can provide more real variant samples for disease diagnosis and biological evolution. The idea of transforming reads into graphs isn't only suitable for calling deletion variations, but also can be extended to other types of structural variations. For example, for inverted variations, it may only need to construct directed graphs. Future work will focus on exploring the feasibility of extending the above thinking to other types of structural variations.

References

1. Stankiewicz, P., Lupski, J.R.: Structural variation in the human genome and its role in disease. Annu. Rev. Med. **61**, 437–455 (2010)
2. Yang, L., et al.: Diverse mechanisms of somatic structural variations in human cancer genomes. Cell **153**(4), 919–929 (2013)
3. Lupski, J.R.: Structural variation mutagenesis of the human genome: impact on disease and evolution. Environ. Mol. Mutagen **56**, 419–436 (2015)
4. Ye, K., Schulz, M.H., Long, Q., et al.: Pindel: a pattern growth approach to detect break points of large deletions and medium sized insertions from paired-end short reads. Bioinformatics **25**(21), 2865–2871 (2009)
5. Xian, F., Abbott, T.E., Larson, D., et al.: BreakDancer - Identification of Genomic Structural Variation from Paired-End Read Mapping. Wiley, Hoboken (2014)
6. Layer, R.M., Chiang, C., Quinlan, A.R., et al.: LUMPY: a probabilistic framework for structural variant discovery. Genome Biol. **15**(6), 1–19 (2014)
7. English, A.C., et al.: Assessing structural variation in a personal genome-towards a human reference diploid genome. BMC Genomics **16**, 1–15 (2015)
8. Goodwin, S., McPherson, J.D., McCombie, W.R.: Coming of age: ten years of next-generation sequencing technologies. Nat. Rev. Genet. **17**, 333–351 (2016)
9. Sedlazeck, F.J., Rescheneder, P., Smolka, M., Fang, H., Nattestad, M., von Haeseler, A., Schatz, M.C.: Accurate detection of complex structural variations using single-molecule sequencing. Nat. Methods **15**, 461 (2018)
10. Jiang, T., Liu, B., Jiang, Y., et al.: Long Read based Human Genomic Structural Variation Detection with cuteSV (2019)
11. Fang, L., Hu, J., Wang, D., Wang, K.: NextSV: a meta-caller for structural variants from low-coverage long-read sequencing data. Bioinformatics **19**, 180 (2018). https://doi.org/10.1186/s12859-018-2207-1

12. Kip, F.T.N., Welling, M.: Semi-Supervised Classification with Graph Convolutional Networks (2016)
13. Qiu, J., Tang, J., Ma, H., Dong, Y., Wang, K., Tang, J.: Deepinf: modeling influence locality in large social networks. In: Proceedings of the 24th ACM SIGKDD International Conference on Knowledge Discovery and Data Mining (2018)
14. Qi, X., Liao, R., Jia, J., Fidler, S., Urtasun, R.: 3D graph neural networks for RGBD semantic segmentation. In: Proceedings of the IEEE Conference on Computer Vision and Pattern Recognition (2017)
15. Li, Y., Yu, R., Shahabi, C., Liu, Y.: Diffusion convolutional recurrent neural network: data-driven traffic forecasting. In: Proceedings of the 7th International Conference on Learning Representations (2018)
16. Wen, T., Altman, R.B.: Graph convolutional neural networks for predicting drug-target interactions. J. Chem. Inf. Model. **59**(10), 4131–4149 (2019)
17. Schlichtkrull, M., Kipf, T.N., Bloem, P., van den Berg, R., Titov, I., Welling, M.: Modeling relational data with graph convolutional networks. In: Gangemi, A., et al. (eds.) ESWC 2018. LNCS, vol. 10843, pp. 593–607. Springer, Cham (2018). https://doi.org/10.1007/978-3-319-93417-4_38
18. Frey, B.J., Dueck, D.: Clustering by passing messages between data points. Science **315**, 972–976 (2007)
19. Ester, M., Kriegel, H.P., Sander, J., et al.: A Density-Based Algorithm for Discovering Clusters in Large Spatial Databases with Noise. AAAI Press (1996)
20. Comaniciu, D., Meer, P.: Mean shift: a robust approach toward feature space analysis. IEEE Trans Pattern Anal. Mach. Intell. **24**(5), 603–619 (2002)
21. Dierckxsens, N., Li, T., Vermeesch, J.R., et al.: A benchmark of structural variation detection by long reads through a realistic simulated model (2020)
22. Heller, D., Vingron, M.: SVIM: structural variant identification using mapped long reads. Bioinformatics **35**(17), 2907–2915 (2019)
23. Jeffares, D.C., Jolly, C., Hoti, M., et al.: Transient structural variations have strong effects on quantitative traits and reproductive isolation in fission yeast. Nat. Commun. **8**(1), 14061 (2017)
24. Zhang, W., Jia, B., Wei, C.: PaSS: a sequencing simulator for PacBio sequencing. BMC Bioinform. **20**(1), 1–7 (2019)
25. Sedlazeck, F.J., Rescheneder, P., Smolka, M., et al.: Accurate detection of complex structural variations using single-molecule sequencing. Nat. Methods **15**(6), 461–468 (2018)

Online Teaching of *Computer Fundamentals* Course During the Pandemic

Sanyuan Zhao[✉][iD], Zongji Zhao[iD], and Jingfeng Xue[iD]

School of Computer Science and Technology,
Beijing Institute of Technology, Beijing, China
{zhaosanyuan,zhaozongji,xuejf}@bit.edu.cn

Abstract. This work discussed the mindset and solutions for online teaching of the *Computer Fundamentals* course during the pandemic in spring 2020, and conducted teaching experiments and statistical data analysis. Through the combined use of multiple webcast platforms and multiple online teaching tools, the online theoretical course webcast, online experiments, online Q&A, online exams, and online course resource management and information statistics are realized. In the online teaching practice project, according to the student information fed back from the webcast platform and online teaching tools, we grasped the students' learning situation and status in time, adjusted the online teaching, and finally obtained relatively good student evaluation and course evaluation results.

Keywords: computer fundamentals · online teaching · computer education

1 Introduction

The outbreak of the COVID19 pandemic has brought a great impact on offline teaching recently. It has caused school suspension, learning suspension, and teaching suspension. The online teaching in the world is facing up to difficulties and moving forward in exploration, especially in China. Its massive-scale applications and developments have a profound impact on the future online teaching. In the process of the online teaching reform, we have also took the lead in the systematic practice of online teaching of the *Computer Fundamentals* course, providing effective solutions and experience for private online courses of large classroom scale. *Computer Fundamentals* is a compulsory course for the first-year students of different disciplines (*e.g.* arts, engineering and science) offered by most of the universities. This course is a public basic computer course with the integration of knowledge and practicality. The teaching content should keep in tune with time. As a common basic course, Computer Fundamentals usually adopts large class (about 90 to 150 students per teaching class). In this work, we take a total of 48 teaching hours for the liberal arts students, including 32 h of theoretical teaching and 16 h of experiments.

Due to the characteristics of this course mentioned above, its online teaching faces the following difficulties:

1. What kind of online teaching method is used for a larger scale audience of students, live webcast or recorded teaching video? Considered their learning background, the liberal arts students may have the following problems with science and engineering (such as computers): not interested in these courses, needing to further intensify thinking of science and engineering, having different levels of knowledge in engineering, *etc.* On the other hand, their thinking is active and their learning attitude is rigorous. In order to make classroom teaching more effective and enable teachers to receive feedback from students in time to adjust the rhythm of the classroom, we adopts online live webcast for both theoretical teaching and experimental teaching.

2. How to choose network platform for live teaching? What functions of the online teaching platform are necessary? The basic requirement of the platform used in this course is that when it broadcasts to about 150 people, the teacher can push the video stream in time, and the student can smoothly receive it. In addition, both the teacher and the students can interactive during the online teaching broadcasting. At the beginning, about spring of 2020, many online education service providers have a full set of online teaching solutions to provide small-scale consumers. However, when the online teaching demands enlarged to the range of nationwide, their load capacity becomes too heavy to satisfy the real-time educational requirement. Problems such as network stalling, disconnection, and the inability to provide new online course applications happens. As for software used in traditional online video conferences, its may show instability as the number of participants increases. At the same time, these software cannot synchronously perform teachers teaching demonstration, online check-in, online quiz, and online discussion, which are used to happen in a real classroom. Luckily, after one year practise, some of these softwares developed rapidly(such as DingTalk), providing a large capacity of online teaching consumers, large scale meetings, abundant online course management tools, and so on. Therefore, for a student size of about 150, choosing a commercial webcast platform with reliable network performance is the most important. Although some platform do not provide online teaching tools, we can adopt auxiliary third-party tools for online interaction and evaluation. However, even the most developed softwares used in online teaching, online meeting, or webcasting, online experiment is a problem that has not been solved in most of the conditions, because hardware devices in experiments cannot be shared via network. It limits the effect of online teaching.

3. How does the online exam work? A developed online examination platform should be used to conduct online course examinations. In the examination system, the major problem is no longer concurrency. Many MOOC service providers provide online examination functions. However, a MOOC course is open to the society, and its students vary greatly in capability. It is not

suitable to directly adopting a MOOC examination for a specific course of the school. In addition, online exams should enable teachers to obtain student data effectively and timely in the backstage of the exam system, such as the rate of progress, student answers, and the accuracy. Besides, it is necessary to prevent students from communication and other cheating behaviors during online exams.

Owning to the above considerations, we conduct online teaching practice for the course of *Computer Fundamentals*, and provide a complete strategy for its online course, including online teaching, online experiments, and online exam. Statistics demonstrate that our method has achieved a satisfactory teaching effect.

2   Related Work

With the informatization progress in education, online courses are developed rapidly, which are represented as Massive Open Online Courses(MOOC), Small Private Online Course (SPOC) and other forms. As resources of online courses becomes plentiful, the number of online learners keeps growing. There have been many researches in online learning, such as the innovation of online learning strategies [1], the quality of online education [2], synchronous online learning [6], the accessibility of online higher education [5], *etc.*

MOOC was born in Utah State University in 2007. It has attracted worldwide attention as a way to provide the society with increased chance of higher education and to improve university teaching qualities [4]. Since 2012, Stanford University, Massachusetts Institute of Technology, Tsinghua University, Fudan University and other well-known universities have successively built MOOC platforms and launched MOOC courses. The teaching procedure in a MOOC environment is not limited by time and place. Teachers publish a number of course resources to the platform, such as videos, coursewares, texts, quizzes, discussions, *etc.*. Learners can develop personal learning plan, freely decide when and how to use these teaching resources.

The SPOC concept was first proposed by Professor Fox from University of California, Berkeley, and is a new online and offline teaching model. Its teaching model can integrate online learning, traditional classroom teaching, flipped classrooms, cooperative learning, etc. Effectively using the rich and diverse online teaching resources, SPOC also ensures that teachers and students can communicate and interact in time. Yang *et al.* [9] integrates teaching concepts with teaching practice through SPOC, and explored on reasonable application and implementation of SPOC model.

At present, computer fundamental course reform in universities has gained many achievements. Many researchers explored teaching in terms of teaching concepts, teaching methods, and curriculum design. [3] summarized and reviewed the concept of designing and compiling university computer fundamental teaching material guided by Self-Directed Learning. Guided by deep learning thoughts,

[8] designed the computer fundamental application course including teaching goal, teaching content, teaching process, and teaching evaluation, to cultivate students' high-level thinking ability, complex problem resolution ability and innovation ability. [7] studied on context-based teaching of fundamental computer science concepts that connected to algorithmic thinking. [10] studied on how to integrate computer science concepts with game design courses, allowing students to deepen their understanding of concepts in practice.

3 Solution

3.1 Live Platform

Before the beginning of our course, we investigated several webcast and online education platforms that can be used for online teaching, such as XuetangX (Rain Classroom), Tencent Meeting, DingTalk, QQ, *etc.*. Among them, XuetangX (Rain Classroom) provides the most comprehensive teaching functions, such as flexible pre-class preview functions, pushing slides to students' WeChat, controllable class tests, and rich forms of online classroom interaction and various types of questions. However, due to the outbreak of the pandemic, the demand for live broadcast on the Rain Classroom platform was too large. The load capacity of its system was limited. At the beginning of the online teaching semester, there were obvious live broadcast jam problems. Tencent Meeting is a software that is suitable for online teaching. The software supports online meetings with a maximum number of 300 people. A meeting can support up to 60 participants to turn on the camera. The software interface of the PC displays 9 participants windows, the mobile phone software interface displays 4 windows, and all participants can speak and project screens, which is suitable for face-to-face questions and answers between teachers and students. However, too many participants turning on the camera will seriously affect the fluency of the live broadcast. In addition, participants may turn on video or voice, which will cause some interference to the online theory teaching process. DingTalk, QQ, and Zoom are also similar online conferencing softwares and have been adopted in many online teaching courses. Compared with educational-oriented platforms, commercial webcasting platforms that dedicates to live streaming have more stable network transmission capabilities, such as TikTok Live, Taobao Live, Douyu, etc. Among them, Taobao live has a relatively high entry threshold, requiring a Taobao shop to be opened and credit scores meeting certain star requirements. TikTok Live does not have the computer screen projection function, and can only use the webcam in 2020 spring. Douyu mainly focuses on game live, which has a computer screen projection function. During the webcast, the interface can be managed at layer level and pushed synchronously. In addition, its software can record webcast videos, which is convenient for playback after class. In summary, our course is based on the principles of stability. We choose the Douyu webcast platform for online theoretical teaching for the principles of stability and anti-interference, and choose the Tencent meeting to carry out online experiments for easy communication.

3.2 Online Interactive Tools

It is not enough to merely adopt a webcasting platform. Some auxiliary tools are needed in the online teaching process to realize functions such as online sign-in, online answering, and online discussion. The *Mooc Classroom* tool of icourse163 can be easily combined with any webcasting platform during online teaching. By opening a SPOC course in icourse163, you can enable the *Mooc Classroom* tool in the backstage, and use the WeChat mini apps to create a *Mooc Classroom* course, which can be associated with the SPOC course. Many types of teaching activities can be added to the *Mooc Classroom* course, including online check-in, online exercises, online questionnaires, *etc.*. What is more, it supports online scoring to evaluate students' answers in time. The webcast platform provides a bullet comments function. Students can send real-time comments during the class, the assistants in class also respond by bullet comments, and teachers can also answer students questions.

Table 1. Questionnaire survey on basic computer knowledge of students in Mu Classroom (from the statistics of *Mooc Classroom*).

Questions	Answers	
(1) Have you received computer knowledge education before?	Yes	No
	76/59.4%	52/4.6%
(2) If you have ever studied computer-related knowledge, what is the learning content?	-	
(3) What do you often do with a computer?	-	
(4) What computer software do you usually use?	-	
(5) Please recommend a software that you think is good	-	
(6) Please list the programming languages you know	-	

Table 2. Questionnaire survey on Python experiment (from WeChat voting statistics).

What do you think of the difficulty of python programming	Number of students
(1) The difficulty is very low, not challenging	0/0%
(2) Moderate difficulty, acceptable	11/10.2%
(3) The difficulty is high, can be completed independently after guidance	28/25.9%
(4) The difficulty is high, can not be done independently, but want to try	39/36.1%
(5) It's too difficult to learn	30/27.8%

Table 3. The score statistics of the true code, complement code, and ones-complement code test (from the statistics of *Mooc Classroom*).

Test	Number of submissions	The average score	Highest score	Lowest score
Ture code, Ones-complement code, and Complement code	114	5.48	8	0

3.3   Online Experiments

Our online experiment choose the textbook *University Computer Experiment* developed and published by the department of Computer Science, Beijing Institute of Technology. It provides a set of virtual experiment softwares for the course and is available for online experiments. Students can install the experimental software provided by the textbook on their own computers to perform virtual experiments. Since the content of the experimental class and the content of the theoretical class are not the same, the teacher may briefly explain the experimental content and demonstrate operating steps at the beginning of the class. After that, students perform experimental operations, record experiments results, fill in experimental reports and submit the report online. Since the process of the virtual experiment is a process that allows students to explore independently, students can directly ask for help by projected screen when meet with questions during the experiment, and the teacher and the assistant will answer via the online meeting. The experimental content of our course mainly includes:

1. Turing machine model
2. Virtual disassembly and assembly of computer hardware system
3. Data representation and calculation in computer
4. Character encoding and information exchange
5. The execution process of an instruction
6. Process management and virtual machine
7. File management and disk recovery
8. WAN communication and mail transmission
9. Word processing and document layout
10. Data processing and chart making
11. Report processing and slide production
12. Data management and database operation
13. Learning Python in one hour

3.4   Online Examination

The online exam session uses the LeXue platform developed by Beijing Institute of Technology. The platform only supports access by users on campus, which has a certain degree of closure and security. The LeXue platform provides a variety of exam question types, including multiple-choice questions, judgment questions, short answer questions, *etc.*. Before the exam, students sign the honesty agreement. In order to reduce the opportunities that students communicate during the exam, the online exam has a larger number of questions, and Tencent meeting software is used to supervise the students' behavior during the online exam.

3.5   Online Course Management

Because our course adoptes a variety of online teaching platforms and tools to achieve the above functions, the course needs a unified online course management method. Our course adopts the online course *Computer Fundamentals* opened on the LeXue Platform to share the course resources and information. At the same time, we construct the SPOC *Computer Fundamentals* on the platform of icourse. The former facilitates the connection of teachers and students when the students and teachers cannot communicate with each other at the beginning of the school year, and releases relevant notices of the course. The latter facilitates the use of *Mooc Classroom* the online teaching tools in SPOC, and can inherit all the teaching resources of the MOOC source course. In addition, due to the sudden outbreak of the pandemic, the students did not receive the textbooks in time. The teachers of the course, meanwhile as the textbook writers, applied to the Higher Education Press for free electronic textbooks, including both the theoretical textbook and the experimental textbook. Two electronic textbooks were published on the website of Higher Education Press for students to study online during the pandemic.

4   Practice Data Statistics

The final review of this course consists of four parts, namely, homeworks, assignments, experiments and final exam. The homework is composed of SPOC homework and LeXue homework. The assignments mainly includes the design of assembly computer scheme, ER diagram, and flow chart design. The experiment session requires the submission of experiment reports for the 12 experiments in Sect. 3.3. The Final Exam lasts for two hours with a score of 100, which accounts for 40% of the total course score. In this work, we have carried out statistics and analysis on information such as online assessment, questionnaire survey, and final review.

4.1   Questionnaire Survey

At the beginning of the first lesson, we investigate the students about their computer knowledge through a questionnaire survey. As shown in Table 1, the contents of the questionnaire included: 1) Have you received computer-related knowledge before? 59.4% of the students chose "Yes" and 40.6% of the students chose "No". 2) If you have ever studied computer-related knowledge, what is the learning content? Most students said that they have learned the simple

Table 4. The question data statistics of true code, complement code, and ones-complement code test (from the statistics of *Mooc Classroom*).

Question	The average score	Correct rate
(1) 0's complement (eight bits)	0.9	90.4%
(2) −1's complement (eight bits)	0.78	78.1%
(3) −128's complement (eight bits)	0.75	75.4%
(4) −9's complement (eight bits)	0.67	66.7%
(5) −12's complement (eight bits)	0.64	64.0%

Table 5. Questionnaire survey of the final exam (from WeChat voting statistics).

What do you think of the exam time setting and Internet speed.	Number of students
The exam can be completed in one hour to one and a half hours. Internet speed is normal.	0/0%
The exam can be completed within two hours. Internet speed is normal	10/8.4%
Barely finish the exam on time. The internet speed is normal	95/79.8%
Barely finish the exam on time. The Internet speed is slow	39/36.1%
Did not complete the exam, but the internet speed is normal	1/0.8%
Did not complete the exam, and the internet speed is too slow	0/0%

Table 6. Statistics on the grades of the course final evaluation (from the school educational administration system).

Score	Number of students	Grade
Over 90	14/10.22%	Excellent
80–89	95/69.34%	Good
70–79	22/6.06%	Medium
60–69	3/2.2%	Pass
60 or less	3/2.2%	Failed
Highest score: 95	Lowest score: 0	The average score: 81.01

operation of some software like Office and Photoshop, and a few students have learned programming such as Python, Java, and VB. 3) What do you often do with a computer? The answers are mainly reading or writing documents and videos, making slides, games, socializing, drawing pictures, writing novels, *etc.*. 4) What computer software do you usually use? The answers are Office, WPS, QQ, Taobao, UC, bilibili, Baidu, Google, TikTok, Weibo, PhotoShop, Audition, Zhihu, WeChat, Steam, Baidu Netdisk, Tencent Video, iQiyi, Email, NetEase CloudMusic *etc.* 5) Recommend a software that you think is good. The recommended ones are mainly WPS, other productivity tools such as 135 editor, Audition, Fotor, PhotoShop, Premiere, as well as software such as NetEase Snail Book, Tianxing Advertising Firewall. 6) List the programming languages you know. Most students answered Python, Java, C++, and others included VB, Ruby, PHP, HTML, CSS, *etc.*. The above statistical information shows that

签到信息

签到	签到时间	是否开启GPS定位	状态
第1次签到	2020年03月20日 14:58-2020年03月21日 14:57	否	已结束

签到情况

已签到 146人/ 迟到 1人/ 旷课 33人 ⊘

输入学生姓名/昵称进行搜索 🔍

学生信息	学号 ⇕	签到时间 ⇕	状态 ⇕	操作
BIT阿依波塔1120183770 _阿依波塔·赛力克	1120183770	2020年03月20日 15:05	已签到	修改状态
海盗ykt1469862087444 _雷正朗	3120110374	-	旷课	修改状态
BIT于溪源1120191636 _于溪源	1120191636	2020年03月20日 15:09	已签到	修改状态
bit-胡佳琦-1120151287 _胡佳琦	1120151287	2020年03月20日 15:05	已签到	修改状态
梓ykt1564328229787 _苏陵凡	1120193233	-	旷课	修改状态
BIT刘一烨1120193098 _刘一烨	1120193098	2020年03月20日 15:01	已签到	修改状态
BIT宋繁琼1120191976 _宋繁琼	1120191976	2020年03月20日 15:03	已签到	修改状态
bit1120190184 _依力达娜·色地克江	1120190184	2020年03月20日 14:59	已签到	修改状态

Fig. 1. Statistics of online check-in results (from the statistics of *Mooc Classroom*).

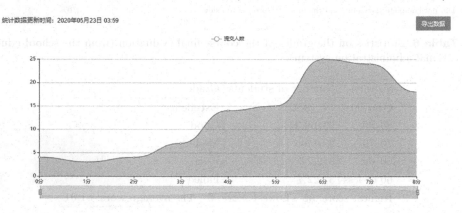

Fig. 2. The statistics of the true code, complement code, and ones-complement code test (from the statistics of *Mooc Classroom*)

most students have a certain computer foundation and apply them in daily life and study work, while a few students still lack the concept of computer.

Since 4 lessons of Python programming were added to the course for the first time, a questionnaire survey was conducted after the end of the Python-related lessons. This Python exercise contains a total of 13 basic cases and two high-level thinking questions. The knowledge points corresponding to the first 12 cases, including simple input and output, basic data structure (string, list), grammatical format (indentation), loop statement, function definition, function call. A total of 51.7% of students feedback that Case 13 and thinking questions are the most difficult. Case 13 involves Python class and inheritance. Thinking questions involve more complicated loop structure programming and algorithm design.

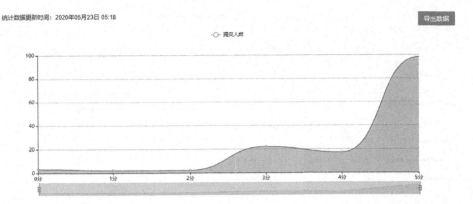

Fig. 3. The statistics of the logic operation test (from the statistics of *Mooc Classroom*)

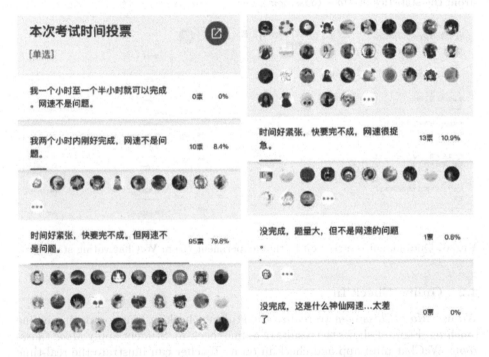

Fig. 4. Questionnaire survey of the final exam (from WeChat voting statistics)

36.1% of students said that Python programming is difficult, 27.8% of students said that it is too difficult, 25.9 students said that the difficulty is too high but can be completed independently after teacher guidance, only 10.2% of students said that the difficulty is moderate and acceptable. Using only 4 h (theory and experiment) can only enable students to master the basic Python grammar, while object-oriented and inheritance are high-level knowledge in Python and are not suitable for teaching content in this course.

Fig. 5. Questionnaire survey on basic computer knowledge of students in Mu Classroom (from the statistics of *Mooc Classroom*).

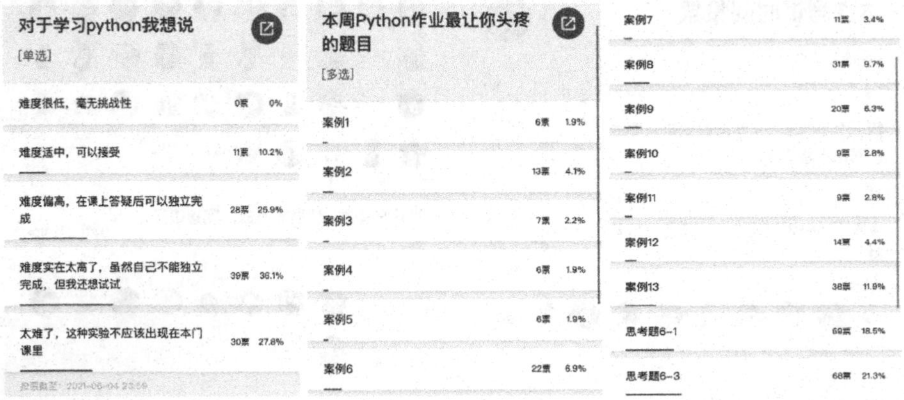

Fig. 6. Questionnaire survey on Python experiment (from WeChat voting statistics).

4.2   Online Check In

We use *Mooc Classroom* to realize the student check in function during online teaching. Figure 1 shows the results of online check-in. Student apply *Mooc Classroom* WeChat mini app and check in on it. Teacher can illustrate the real-time check in data on his/her screen and broadcast via the platform. According to statistics, a total of 146 students signed in on time, one student was late and 33 students were absent. Notice that account confusion occurred during *Mooc Classroom* account login process (that is, many students did not bind WeChat and icourse accounts). Therefore, the number of students in the *Mooc Classroom* is more than the actual number of classe, as some students use two accounts to join the class at the beginning of the course. (The accual number of students in this course is 133, and there are also individual students who resit or repeat this course.) Although it seems that there is a large number of absenteeism, the actual number of participants meets the requirement of the class.

4.3   Online Test

Using online test tools provided by *Mooc Classroom*, our course conducts online test of important knowledge points. In the chapter on number system and coding, our course is the first time to conduct an online test, a total of 8 test questions, 1 points for each question, the average score of the whole class is only 5.48 points as shown in Table 3. This is because we did not provide online textbooks and teacher courseware for students during this test, students only answer the questions based on the relevant knowledge they have heard in class. It is difficult to memorize new knowledge quickly and clearly (such as calculation formulas, encoding and conversion rules of true code, ones-complement code, and complemental code). Therefore, many students did not get good scores in this test. Some questions and corresponding average scores are shown in the Table 4. The score of most students is about 6 points, as shown in Fig. 2. Based on the feedback from the students during the webcast, we adjusted the teaching method in time and repeat the relevant knowledge points again.

Before the second test (logical operation), teachers pay attention to slowing down the teaching speed and provide teaching courseware to students. Therefore, in this test, most students scored a perfect score of 5, as shown in Fig. 3. As a result, through direct online communication, student feedback on teaching can be obtained in time, and classroom organization and teaching rhythm can be effectively adjusted to improve teaching effects.

4.4   Final Examination

For the final examination, students enter the exam system by visiting the LeXue platform. Because this is an internet online test, some students may have behaviors of cheating during the exam. Therefore, the amount of questions in this test is very large, so that students have no time to take care of other behaviors. After the exam, we used WeChat voting to conduct a questionnaire survey regarding the time of the exam and the internet speed during the exam. The survey results shown in Table 5 demonstrates that 79.8% of students think that the test time is tight and the internet speed is no problem; 10.9% of the students consider that the test time is tight and the internet speed is not good; 8.4% of the students think there is no problem with time and internet speed; only 0.8% of the students indicates that the test questions were not completed within the test time. It demonstrates that the amount of examination questions basically meet the expectations.

The final grade of this course is shown in Table 6. The average score of the whole class is 81.01, the good rate is 69.3%, the excellent rate is 10.2%, the rate of medium and pass are 18.26%, and the failed rate is only 2.2%. The reasons for the student's failure are that the homework is not done and the results of the final exam are not satisfactory. The results of the overall course evaluation show that this online teaching has achieved a good teaching effect.

5   Summary

During the recent epidemic, we explored the online teaching of the course *Computer Fundamentals* for liberal arts students. Through the investigation of a large number of online teaching platforms, we finally decided to adopt a mixed use of multiple online teaching platforms and tools to achieve online teaching, online experiments, online exams, online feedback, online course construction and management. We use the statistical information of the online teaching platform and tools to keep abreast of the students' learning situation and make adjustments timely to the online classroom. In the end, this course has gained good student evaluation and teaching effect.

References

1. Davis, D., Chen, G., Hauff, C., Houben, G.-J.: Activating learning at scale: a review of innovations in online learning strategies. Comput. Educ. **125**, 327–344 (2018)
2. Esfijani, A.: Measuring quality in online education: a meta-synthesis. Am. J. Distance Educ. **32**(1), 57–73 (2018)
3. Zhu, J., Gu, Y., Zhang, B.: Research on design of computer fundamental teaching material based on SDL. In: 2009 First International Workshop on Education Technology and Computer Science, vol. 2, pp. 729–732. IEEE (2009)
4. Jung, Y., Lee, J.: Learning engagement and persistence in massive open online courses (MOOCS). Comput. Educ. **122**, 9–22 (2018)
5. Lee, K.: Rethinking the accessibility of online higher education: a historical review. Internet High. Educ. **33**, 15–23 (2017)
6. Martin, F., Ahlgrim-Delzell, L., Budhrani, K.: Systematic review of two decades (1995 to 2014) of research on synchronous online learning. Am. J. Distance Educ. **31**(1), 3–19 (2017)
7. Nijenhuis-Voogt, J., Meijer, P.C., Barendsen, E.: Contextbased teaching and learning of fundamental computer science concepts: exploring teachers' ideas. In: Proceedings of the 13th Workshop in Primary and Secondary Computing Education, pp. 1–4 (2018)
8. Yang, Y., Yu, D.: Design of computer fundamental application course teaching to promote deep learning. In: Proceedings of the 2019 4th International Conference on Information and Education Innovations, pp. 78–81 (2019)
9. Yang, Y., Yu, D.: SPOC blended teaching of computer fundamental course. In: Proceedings of the 5th International Conference on Frontiers of Educational Technologies, pp. 24–29 (2019)
10. Cao, F., Ding, D., Zhu, M.: Introducing fundamental computer science concepts through game design. J. Comput. Sci. Coll. **34**(4), 90–96 (2019)

Effects of WeChat on English as L2 Mobile Learning and Teaching

Huiqiong Duan[1], Xiaoqian Wei[1(✉)], and Yanmin Li[2]

[1] Nanchang Hangkong University, Nanchang, China
1019873474@qq.com
[2] Industrial and Commercial Bank of China, Wuhan, China

Abstract. A convenient learning style is a constantly pursuit. This study examined the effects of using WeChat on English as L2 teaching and learning. 76 non-English major students participated in the quasi-experiment. WeChat groups, Moments, public platforms, mini-programs, and other aspects in Wechat were used in English as L2 teaching. Research results indicate that applying Wechat in English as L2 teaching has overcome the disadvantages of traditional English as L2 classroom teaching. Students' English proficiency in terms of English vocabulary, listening, reading and speaking has improved. Moreover, WeChat enhances the English learning flexibility, builds better autonomous learning and collaborative learning atmosphere. It provides a new direction for personalized, multi-level and full-time mobile teaching in English as L2 education.

Keywords: WeChat · Mobile learning · English as L2 · English teaching reform

1 Introduction

Many experts and scholars have studied the problems in the current English as L2 teaching in China. The students' ability to use the language is weak, especially in the less developed Western China. "Dumb English" and "deaf and dumb English" are still difficult issues. *China Youth Daily* published a series of articles aimed at placing higher education's role in achieving development goals under the spotlight and discussing the reform of English language teaching.

Zhang Jin [1] believes that the disadvantages of the current English as L2 teaching model are time-consuming, high input costs, and poor economic efficiency. The existing teaching system can not meet the social need in this field. First, English as L2 has become one of the most time-consuming and intensive courses. In addition to daily classroom learning tasks, many college students spend another 2 h a day learning English. They complained that English as L2 occupied other courses' time.

Secondly, English as L2 curriculum system has the problem of "one-size-fits-all" and it is difficult to meet the needs of students' individual development. College students' English proficiency is often unbalanced. Some students have large vocabulary and poor grammar. Some students have strong listening and speaking skills but poor reading ability. Regional differences in students' English ability are also significant. Clearly, students in southern China, especially those in the southeast coastal areas, have strong English comprehensive ability. Some non-English majors like spoken English and even beat some English majors in speech contests. In this situation, classroom teaching is hard to achieve differentiated teaching, and extracurricular learning lacks effective guidance for students at different levels.

Thirdly, incorrect teaching and learning concepts have hindered the English teaching development in China. Some universities do not know the essence of College English Test Band 4/6 (CET-4)/6 and only pay attention to its passing rate. During the teaching process, some teachers ignore the students' practical English ability and pay attention to their achievements. In addition, extracurricular exercises focus on how to answer questions in the CET4/6 exam. All these moves will put the students into a tedious cycle of English learning. Once they pass CET4/6, some students will not actively learn English.

Some scholars began to apply some SNS (social networking sites) to higher education. In Britain, Rachel Menzies, a renowned scholar at the University of Dundee, said that more and more people are focusing on SNS on students, such as Facebook, as an educational tool. Students often use Facebook for education, albeit in an informal manner. [2] The majority of the existing studies into the impact of WeChat on English as second language (L2) have been devoted to reading [3, 4], writing [5], speaking [6, 7], EFL Communicative Competence [8], mobile learning strategies [9] and vocabulary [10]. A few studies have yielded contradictory findings.

In view of the above studies, few studies have conducted on the comprehensive use WeChat in effectively solve the problems in current English as L2 learning in China. This paper attempts to apply WeChat, a new media communication tool, to the mobile learning of English as L2, and further investigate its effect on English as L2 teaching reform in China.

2 Research Design

2.1 Research Questions

This study addressed the following research questions. (1) How is WeChat, a new media communication tool, used to the mobile learning of English as L2 in China?

(2) What is the effect of WeChat on the comprehensive development of college students' English vocabulary, listening ability, reading ability and speaking ability?

2.2 Participants

The participants ($n = 76$), non-English majors from one University in Central China were recruited from the pool of the 213 English of L2. They attended the placement English test, and their English proficiency is between 60–75.The result shows that they are at the middle level of the whole school and have a certain representativeness. They are 18 or 19 years old. All of them have WeChat accounts. 74% of the students use mobile phones every day for more than 3 h, 60% of the students have the habit of checking WeChat News at anytime and anywhere, and 58% of the students will use the mobile phone to do something in the classroom that has nothing to do with the subject.

They were classified into two classes. One of the two classes is the control group, and the other class is the experimental group. These two classes are two parallel classes of the same major, so their teachers, teaching content, learning time, and learning conditions are exactly the same. Their score in the placement English test passes the independent sample T test, confirming that there is no significant difference in the English score of the two classes. During the experiment, there were no students who quit halfway.

Based on the English scores of the final exams, participants in the experimental class were divided into three groups. All groups were provided separately a set of experimental instructions and different English learning materials related to the subject of learning in the textbook.

2.3 Research Process

Prior to conducting the main study, 76 students were asked to complete a questionnaire about English learning and teaching. For the main study, weekly WeChat teaching activities will be clearly defined as the teaching content of the experimental class, and English vocabulary, listening, reading and speaking tests will be taken. The students in the experimental class are divided into 3 groups, voluntarily form WeChat sub-groups, and use WeChat once a week to conduct English non-instant voice chats and complete vocabulary, listening, reading and speaking exercises. The main teaching methods include starting an English teaching public account, uploading listening materials, correcting problems in students completed oral tasks, and pushing English articles with high attention. In order to minimize the influence of the communicator, the forms and contents of the test in the parallel class and the experimental class are completely same. The data analysis was conducted using SPSS28.0 software. At the end of the experiment, students were required to do a feedback questionnaire.

3 Results

3.1 WeChat Improves Chinese Students' English Lexical Diversity

Vocabulary is the foundation of English learning. It cannot be accumulated overnight. As British linguist Wilkins pointed out, "Without grammar, there is little to convey; no vocabulary, nothing to convey. [11] Linguist Laufer also said, "The most significant difference between foreign language learners and native speakers is vocabulary." [12].

Vocabulary learning is a basic part of language acquisition and plays a vital role in language use. Vocabulary amount directly affects the improvement of the overall language level. Most non-English majors have a poor English foundation and are not interested in learning English. In the process of learning English, most learners complain that their vocabulary is too limited to understand, read or speak properly. On the one hand, they find vocabulary learning boring and difficult to arouse their interest. On the other hand, they always find it difficult to remember English words but easy to forget them in a short time. Over time, they gradually lose interest and confidence in English learning. They feel frustrated and fall into a vicious circle of language acquisition.

The teacher of the experiment class asked their students to use MOMO App to encourage them to learn English vocabulary after class. This APP can match students' textbooks to strengthen students' position in learning and stimulate their interest in English learning. (See Fig. 1 screenshots of MOMO used in English vocabulary learning).

Fig. 1. Screenshots of MOMO used in English vocabulary learning.

Besides this, the teacher taught two or three words every day in the WeChat. See Fig. 2. Examples for words taught in four days.

Fig. 2. Examples for words taught in four days.

Before the start of the vocabulary learning experiment, students need to test their current vocabulary and choose suitable courses according to their original vocabulary levels. After a semester, they had another vocabulary test. By comparing and analyzing the scores in two vocabulary tests and the questionnaire survey results, it is proved that mobile learning based on WeChat helps improve the English vocabulary of college students.

The vocabulary surveys were carried out before and after the experiment. The results showed that 61.6% of the students' vocabulary increased by about 200 words, 16.7% of the students' vocabulary increased by 300 words, and 11% of the students' vocabulary did not change greatly, as shown in Fig. 3 below.

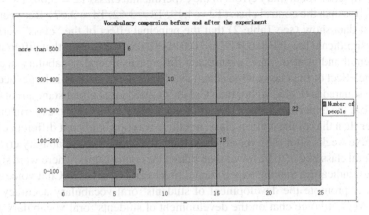

Fig. 3. The result of vocabulary survey.

WeChat's diverse functions and simple operation provide an excellent platform for vocabulary learning. WeChat breaks the limitation of time and space, and provides convenience for students to learn, share and use words with pictures, texts, audio and video. This combination of audio-visual learning method and vocabulary learning materials helps to consolidate and enhance vocabulary retention.

Table 1. Descriptive statistical results.

	Classes	Mean	Std. Deviation	Number
Lexical Error (T1)	Control Class	3.62	2.247	38
	Experimental Class	4.25	3.998	38
	Total	3.93	3.197	76
Lexical Error (T2)	Control Class	4.19	1.806	38
	Experimental Class	3.00	2.271	38
	Total	3.61	2.108	76
Lexical Error (T3)	Control Class	3.62	2.559	38
	Experimental Class	2.00	1.645	38
	Total	2.83	2.290	76
Lexical Error (T4)	Control Class	2.67	2.106	38
	Experimental Class	0.75	0.851	38
	Total	1.73	1.871	76

As can be seen from the descriptive statistics (see Table 1), the mean value of vocabulary errors in the experimental class in the first test was 4.25, higher than the mean of the vocabulary error in the control class 3.93, but the independent sample t-test showed no significant difference between the two ($t = -0.627, p = 0.534 > 0.05$). From the second test, the number of vocabulary errors in the experimental class (T2 $= 3.00$, T3 $= 2.00$, T4 $= 0.75$) is less than the control class (T2 $= 4.19$, T3 $= 3.62$, T4 $= 2.67$). Between-subject effects test data show (see Table 2) that the principal effect of the "class" variable has reached a significant level ($F = 6.609, p = 0.014 < 0.05$). It indicates that different classes (experimental and control) have significant differences in oral vocabulary accuracy of CET4. The effect of the class on the accuracy of spoken vocabulary is large, because the partial eta squared is 0.145, higher than Cohen's (1988) large effect standard of 0.140. In short, before the experiment, the number of vocabulary errors in the experimental class was higher than that of the control class, but there was no significant difference between the two. Five weeks after the experiment started, the number of vocabulary errors in the experimental class began to be lower than that of the control class. There were significant differences, indicating that the experimental processing (that is, WeChat voice chat) can significantly promote the development of students' oral vocabulary accuracy, and the effect of WeChat voice chat on the development of students' oral vocabulary accuracy is obvious.

Table 2. Testing of between-subject effects.

Source	Type III sum of squares	df	Mean	F	Sig	Partial eta squared
Intercept	371.713	1	271.713	228.790	0.000	0.854
Class	10.738	1	10.738	6.609	0.014	0.145
Deviation	63.363	39	1.625			

3.2 WeChat Enhances English Listening Ability

Listening course is always a bottleneck in English as L2 course. In college English course, students are at different levels (the college entrance examination English scores range from 130 to 70), but their listening materials are the same. This makes some students have lost interest in English listening: Some students find hearing materials too difficult to understand; other Students feel that listening materials are too simple to listen. Therefore, the reform of listening course has always been the key to the English as L2 development. The application of the WeChat platform on English as L2 teaching and learning has opened up new breakthroughs for listening courses.

In response to above situation, our study has adopted a hierarchical listening course to establish different WeChat groups for different levels of students in experiments. Teachers uploaded different listening materials in different WeChat groups, then students could do listening exercises directly with their own mobile phones.

The researchers have analyzed the questionnaire before conducting listening experiments and has proposed corresponding countermeasures.

We design a WeChat official account named "Sevenation". Then we upload some English learning materials (especially listening materials) in this official account.

Students can choose listening tasks as their will. (See Fig. 4. The official account "Sevenation".)

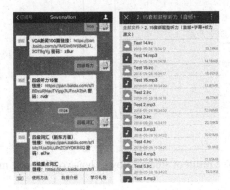

Fig. 4. The official account "Sevenation".

This method not only prevents students from using mobile phones in class, but also trains students based on their English proficiency. This can improve teaching efficiency and complete teaching tasks before the deadline. In the traditional English listening class, it is impossible for the teacher to play three different audio recordings in class to meet student's learning demands at the same time. This will not only waste time, reduce the efficiency of learning, but also make some students to generate ideas that "the content of the class has nothing to do with me."

Faced with the predicament of the development of China's college education, it is necessary to take actions from a new technical point of view. First, the teacher needs to send different listening materials to each group. Second, students can download their listening materials to their local mobile phones. Third, students can continue listening training outside the classroom.

The questionnaire survey shows that 84% of the 76 students believe that this method is better than the traditional method and are willing to continue to use WeChat for listening training (the result of students' own choice of listening materials can be seen in Fig. 5 below).

3.3   WeChat Increases English Reading Comprehension Efficiency

In English as L2 class, reading refers to intensive reading. The teaching process begins with the interpretation of new words. Then, teacher explains the general idea of reading materials and analyzes sentence structures or grammar. This teaching process is tedious. Students only do some reading practices. They do not know how to apply what they have learned to their daily lives. Besides, without the teacher's request, students seldom take the initiative to read extracurricular English reading materials, so it is difficult to create a language learning environment. In a questionnaire before the experiment, 87% of the students chose "Before the exam" when they answered the question "the time you will actively read English materials is". It can be seen that the inertial thinking formed by exam-oriented education has a great influence on the students' study habits.

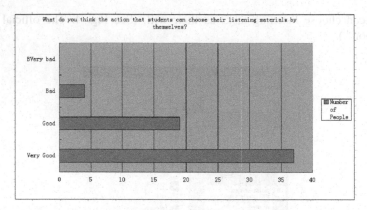

Fig. 5. The result of students' own choice of listening materials.

With the WeChat official account, teachers can upload the latest reading materials, teaching plans and current affairs to the public platform, and require students to subscribe. In addition, teachers can also send out the relevant reading material before class begins in order to broaden the students' horizons, or upload relevant background knowledge to speed up the teaching progress after class.

The questionnaire survey conducted before the experiment shows that 63% of the students often have WeChat checks and notifications. The result "What do you read most in your phone everyday" can be seen in Fig. 6. A survey shows that, the fans number of well-known English education WeChat official accounts, such as kkenglish (He Kaiwen English), China Daily Mobile (China Daily Bilingual News), 21st Century English, is over 1 million which is why their articles have a high click rate. In addition, there are a large number of WeChat official accounts on the Tencent platform that can provide articles related to English as L2 education.

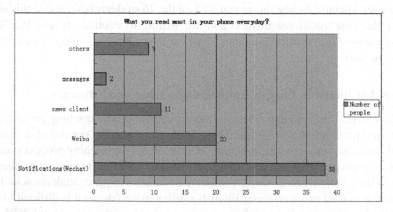

Fig. 6. The result of question "What do you read most in your phone everyday".

Churchill Daniel proposed a framework called RASE learning activities in the 2016 mobile learning environment. In this framework, R stands for resources and refers to resources for learning activities. A is the activity that refers to a series of learning activities designed to achieve teaching goals. S is support, which means that teachers provide help and support for students and achieve educational goals from the background of mobile phones. E is the evaluation, which refers to the reflection of students and teachers before and after the learning process [13].

According to this RASE framework, R (resources) represents various reading articles and articles related to English learning in WeChat teaching experiments. Teachers can choose articles that are closely related to the teaching content or provide the latest activities to broaden their horizons. For example, in March 2018, well-known media such as the Washington Post and Bloomberg published articles related to trade wars. After President Trump announced that he would start a large-scale trade war with China. Therefore, teachers could share the article with students.

A (activity) is the WeChat push subscriptions activity from the official account. On the basis of the reading materials shared by the teachers, students choose the learning content as their will, such as the use of the new words, the translation of the long difficult sentences and so on.

S (support) is very extensive in content. It includes the teacher's assistance throughout the reading process, such as explaining the background of the article, and modifying students' translation about difficult sentences.

E (evaluation) is an important part of all teaching methods. Teachers provide students with articles to read outside the class, then discuss relevant topics with students in class, and invite students to share their thoughts. This part is suggested to carry out in the way of self-evaluation, group evaluation and teacher evaluation.

The feedback of the post-questionnaire survey from the experimental class is very different from that of the pre-questionnaire. It shows that the WeChat official account has greatly changed students' reading habits and improved their interest in English reading.

3.4 WeChat Drives Chinese Students' English-Speaking Practice

The experimental methods of WeChat in vocabulary and listening classes are also applied to spoken English teaching. Although traditional classrooms establish group discussions and demonstrations to improve the students' oral ability, few of the students are able to perform even a simplest conversation in English. The teaching effect is not good.

WeChat is able to send out not only voice messages within 60 s, but also implement multi-user voice dialogues. Therefore, we used the WeChat groups to conduct layered oral teaching: teachers shared different verbal discussion topics in different WeChat groups, gave students some time to think, and then asked them to communicate via WeChat voice messages. The voice messages could be heard repeatedly, so students were able to find their own mistakes in terms of speech, syntax problems and so on. In addition, teachers asked students to send out voice messages every day, and supervised the teaching process. Each student's pronunciation mistakes are different, so Wechat voice message avoids the repetition of the oral teaching task. In this way, long-term WeChat teaching and learning experiments improved students' oral proficiency. In addition, teachers also uploaded some demonstration tasks through WeChat, allowing students to present and demonstrate in the classroom. In this way, WeChat increased students' participation in English course and achieved higher teaching goals.

For example, college English teachers shared a hot issue in WeChat groups, which was linked to students' real life and learning needs. In this way, students were willing to express their opinions in English. Teachers in the training process needed to strengthen the guidance and supervision of English expression, effectively point out their deficiencies. Only by this way could students improve English listening and speaking skills. Their English lexical diversity and grammar accuracy are enhanced.

WeChat launched mini-programs in 2017 to allow mobile phone users to scan QR codes and access a large number of different services, such as food ordering and bicycles, without having to download other separate mobile applications. Because of its convenience, it attracted more than 170 million daily users and included more than 600,000 mini programs. The famous English professional education programs, such as Oral ABC and Speak English Every day, can provide different services, including English conversation exercises, commenting on homework, giving users feedback and linking programs, and so on. Therefore, using the WeChat mini-program is a good way to learn and practice spoken English.

In our experiment, the teacher divided the students into three groups according to the students' oral proficiency. Then, she introduced a WeChat mini-program to these groups and asked the students to complete some related speaking tasks. Teachers could rate their oral tasks on the WeChat mini-program. In practical teaching, the teaching content should not be too difficult or too simple. In WeChat groups, teachers could not over-correct students' errors in grammar or pronunciation. If the teacher corrected a student too directly after he sent a voice message in the WeChat group, the introverted student may feel hurt. On the basis of praise, teachers should focus on encouraging and correcting mistakes. In this way, students who made mistakes would realize their own mistakes without losing faces. The specific operation is shown in Fig. 7.

Fig. 7. The specific operation of WeChat used for oral practice

4 Discussion

WeChat is a mobile chat software launched in 2011. By the end of April 2017, WeChat had 889 million users worldwide. The features of this App include allowing people to establish friendships, group chats and photo sharing, expand user's circle of friends, and share users' "moments" (a function just like twitter's). In addition, it has become more popular and trickier than ever before. It has quietly entered the new field of offline payments.

Tencent, the owner of WeChat, said that some of WeChat 's core users are 18–24-year-old students, but the number of users in other age groups has increased. According to a survey by Tencent Holdings, in 2016, one-third of its 889 million monthly active users spent four hours or more per day on this super-application, twice the number of a year ago. [14] The average daily time has also increased. It is now 66 min, which exceeds the Facebook average of 50 min in 2016.

For college students, WeChat is not only a communication APP, but also a lifestyle. This laid the foundation for WeChat to provide university students with a fragmented English learning environment, and proved the view that students use WeChat to inform their education, albeit in an informal way. Although students who spend more time on their mobile phones do not always score higher grades, teachers and students can share various learning materials, including all kinds of latest developments published in newspaper, books, and magazines. Yang Shaofa believes that WeChat is an important channel for information release and exchange. It conveys information to students with rich diversity and a combination of graphics and textures, enabling students to easily learn, participate and communicate with each other [15].

Therefore, WeChat has unique advantages in breaking the defects of traditional English teaching class.

4.1 Extending Teaching Platform from Classroom to Extracurricular Activities

Based on the instance and interaction of WeChat, students can not only talk about their own learning experiences through chat, but also gain knowledge of English learning through the following educational WeChat Subscripts.

For teachers, you can create an English study group chat, upload English learning materials, set up assignments and tasks, or improve students' oral English ability through WeChat's voice and group chat functions. Through the WeChat platform, the English class is no longer just 45 min of classroom instruction, but is permeated into students' daily life. WeChat not only extends the classroom from the blackboard to the mobile phone screen, but also makes full use of fragmented learning time.

4.2 Fully Mobilizing the Students' Learning Enthusiasm

Unlike traditional English classroom teaching, students are no longer passive recipients of WeChat, but are active participants. The relationship with teachers is equal. Through WeChat miniprogram learning and personal learning data analysis, students can see changes in their English ability, thereby mobilizing their subjective learning initiative, allowing them to increase their enthusiasm for English learning and develop their self-learning skills.

4.3   Making Personalized Education Possible

German educator Dieterweg said: "The starting point of teaching is to increase students' competence. Education must satisfy the need. In other words, it must be in line with the current situation." Zhang Meng said: "For each student's level of learning, junior high school English teachers need to teach students based on their talents in teaching practice." [16].

WeChat's instant communication function speeds up student feedback to teachers. On this basis, teachers can adjust teaching plans and teaching schedules accordingly, and design individualized learning tasks for different students, thereby, WeChat makes personalized education possible. It can improve students' learning efficiency. Compared with traditional classroom teaching, WeChat teaching methods are more flexible and richer in teaching materials.

5   Conclusion

This study explored the effect of WeChat on English as L2 learning and teaching from the aspects of vocabulary, reading, listening and speaking. The research results show that WeChat plays an active role in cultivating students' communicative competence and comprehension ability. Therefore, WeChat-based learning and teaching is a convenient, effective and creative way of mobile learning.

Research shows that the use of WeChat changes the traditional way of English as L2 learning. It helps to cope with the problems in the current English as L2 teaching in China, like "Dumb English". The students' ability to use the language is extremely weak, especially in the less developed Western China. Moreover, English as L2 curriculum system has the problem of "one-size-fits-all" and it is difficult to meet the needs of students' individual development. WeChat drives individual learning.

Regional differences in students' English ability are also significant. Clearly, students in southern China, especially those in the southeast coastal areas, have strong English comprehensive ability. Some non-English majors are good at spoken English and even beat some English majors in speech contests. In this situation, classroom teaching is hard to satisfy differentiated students, and students' extracurricular learning also lacks specific guidance. WeChat facilitates to tackle the problem that education resources are regionally distributed uneven.

College students' English extracurricular exercises focus on how to answer questions in the CET4/6 exam. This will put the students into a tedious cycle of English learning. Once they pass CET4/6, some students will not actively learn English. With WeChat, they will keep the habit of lifelong learning. It is consistent with the requirements of the English curriculum. WeChat helps students to learn English outside the classroom.

There are some defects of using WeChat in teaching. For example, teachers cannot supervise students to use mobile phones since the students are easily distracted by other information in their smartphones. This reduces their learning effect.

Appendix

附件1：《微信在大学英语教育中的应用研究》调查问卷(1)

一、个人信息调查

1.您的性别

（A）男生　　　　　　（B）女生

2.您的年级

（A）大一　　（B）大二　（C）大三　（D）大四

3.您的大学入学英语基础水平如何

（A）130分以上　（B）C.110分-130分（C）90分-110分　（D）90分以下

4.您现在的英语水平如何

（A）四六级过不了　（B）四六级很悬　（C）四六级稳过D）英语是优势

二、英语课堂调查

1.在课堂上，生词语法讲解频率是

（A）很经常　（B）经常　（C）有时　（D）从不

2.在课堂上，阅读文章结构分析讲解频率是

（A）很经常　（B）经常　（C）有时　（D）从不

3．在课堂上，长难句讲解频率是

（A）很经常　（B）经常　（C）有时　（D）从不

4．在课堂上，口语对话训练频率是

（A）很经常　（B）经常　（C）有时　（D）从不

5．在课堂上，听力训练语法讲解频率是

（A）很经常　（B）经常　（C）有时　（D）从不

6．在课堂上，句子翻译讲解频率是

（A）很经常　（B）经常　（C）有时　（D）从不

7.您觉得平时的英语课堂教学对您英语水平提高有帮助吗？

（A）帮助很大　（B）有一点帮助　（C）没有帮助

8.您觉得在英语学习中最大的瓶颈是什么？（多选）

（A）词汇　（B）听力　（C）写作

（D）口语　（E）语法　（F）长难句　（G）翻译

9.您觉得传统英语课堂的短板有哪些？（多选）

（A）教学方式单一

（B）教学内容太简单 我已经掌握

（C）教学内容太难 无法跟上老师节奏

（D）课堂上的学习内容对我一点帮助也没有

（E）听不进去 无法集中自己的注意力

（F）不喜欢自己的授课

（G）其他

10.您平时如何学习英语？（多选）

（A）背单词

（B）看美剧、听音乐等
（C）考试之前做相关的试卷
（D）完成老师布置的作业
（E）阅读外刊等英语阅读材料
（F）不会主动学习英语
（G）其他

三、微信使用调查

1．您平时使用微信的频率是：
（A）基本不看微信　　（B）有消息才会看　　　（C）沉迷微信 无法自拔

2．您每天微信的使用时间大概是：
（A）30分钟之内　（B）一小时之内（C）2-3小时　　（D）3小时以上

3．您觉得在微信里加上大学英语教学对您有帮助吗
（A）帮助很大　（B）有一点帮助　（C）没有帮助

4．如果有免费的英语学习平台（基于微信）您愿意参加吗？
（A）愿意　（B）不愿意

5．您平时有关注过新媒体英语学习平台吗？（多选）
（A）英语教育相关的微信公众号或者微信群
（B）帮助记忆单词的软件（例如百词斩、扇贝单词）
（C）英语教育专家的个人帐号（例如谷大白话、周思成、何凯文等）
（D）其他

附件2：《微信在大学英语教育中的应用研究》调查问卷（2）

1.您的性别
（A）男生　　　　　　（B）女生

2.您的年级
（A）大一　　（B）大二　（C）大三　（D）大四

3.您觉得微信应用在英语课堂教学中对您英语水平提高有帮助吗？
（A）帮助很大　（B）有一点帮助　（C）没有帮助

4.您愿意参与微信辅助大学英语学习吗？
（A）愿意（跳转题5）（B）接受（跳转题5）
（C）不愿意（跳转题6）

5.请您简述愿意使用微信学习大学英语的原因：
_____
_____

6.　请您简述微信辅助大学英语学习的弊端或者不便之处：
_____
_____

附件3：相关学习资源
链接：https://pan.baidu.com/s/1Mv4uXURDH88WLKtvkk3mxQ 密码：l9pv

References

1. Jing, Zh.: The Application of WeChat in College English Listening and Speaking Teaching. Northwest Normal University (2015)
2. Menzies, R., Petrie, K., Zarb, M.: A case study of Facebook use: outlining a multi-layer strategy for higher education. Educ. Inf. Technol. (1), 22 (2017)

3. Hao, B., Jingjing, H.: Research on the application of WeChat public platform in the field of college education. Educ. Inform. China (4), 4 (2013)
4. Yinjian, J.: An experimental study on english reading teaching supported by WeChat public platform. Technol. Enhanced Foreign Lang. Educ. (03), 169 (2016)
5. Yinjian, J.: An experimental study on WeChat public platform supporting English reading teaching. Foreign Lang. Teach. (3), 6 (2016)
6. Kexin, Z.: Research on college english writing teaching based on WeChat. Ph.D.thesis, Harbin University of Science and Technology (2021)
7. Junbo, M., Huhua, O.: An empirical study of WeChat-assisted oral english vocabulary accuracy development. Technol. Enhanced Foreign Lang. Educ. (02), 198 (2021)
8. Li, Y.: The promotion of unicom learning mode to EFL communicative competence – when flipped classroom meets WeChat. High. Educ. Explor. (05), 5 (2019)
9. Ning, M.: English mobile learning strategies in universities and colleges based on WeChat. China Educ. Technol. (03) (2016)
10. Junbo, M., Huhua, O.: An empirical study on WeChat's promotion of vocabulary accuracy in oral English. Foreign Lang. Teach. (2), 9 (2021)
11. Wilkins, D.A.: Linguistics in language teaching. Linguistics in language teaching(1972)
12. Laufer, B.: What's in a word that makes it hard or easy? Some intralexical factors that affect the learning of words. In: Vocabulary Description, Acquisition and Pedagogy (1997)
13. Daniel, C.: Educational applications of web 2.0: using blogs to support teaching and learning. Br. J. Educ. Technol. (2009)
14. Xichen, Z.: Decoding tencent annual report. Int. Finan. J. (016) (2018)
15. Yang, S.: Research on the application of Wechat in college ideological and political education. In: International Conference on Economics, Social Science, Arts, Education and Management Engineering (2016)
16. Meng, Zh.: How to maintain students' motivation—a sample analysis of WeChat application in middle school english teaching. Overseas English (10) (2015)

Developing Blockchain Learning Lab Experiments for Enhancing Cybersecurity Knowledge and Hands-On Skills in the Cloud

Mohamed Rahouti[1]([✉])(iD), Kaiqi Xiong[2], and Jing Lin[2]

[1] Fordham University, New York 10023, USA
mrahouti@fordham.edu
[2] University of South Florida, Tampa 33620, USA
{xiongk,jinglin}@usf.edu

Abstract. Blockchain technology has drawn significant attention from academia and industry. Such technology offers unique features and capabilities, including security and reliability. However, there needs to be more significant integration of blockchain into cybersecurity education curricula. Hence, it is of great interest to establish novel initiatives for designing and implementing hands-on learning modules and labs based on blockchain technology to support college cybersecurity education. Furthermore, with the dramatic increase in cybersecurity students' enrollment and hybrid courses, universities have faced many challenges, such as limited networking and computing resources, while trying to offer quality-based education. For this reason, we propose an emerging solution by leveraging a real-world testbed, such as the Global Environment for Network Innovations (GENI), a federated, heterogeneous, at-scale, programmable, and virtual infrastructure for hands-on experimentation in a broad range of computer engineering and science fields. This paper presents design methodologies for integrating blockchain technology into the GENI testbed in a cybersecurity course, with applied cryptography as an example. The presented learning modules can further be deployed in cloud-based facilities such as Cloud Lab and Chameleon. The primary design idea is to leverage blockchain technology with the GENI testbed to train students on advanced cryptographic modules, such as Public Key Infrastructure (PKI) and hash functions. This paper mainly focuses on educational aspects of blockchain and GENI testbed applicability to cybersecurity education, deployment challenges, and implementation design of the hands-on learning labs. Lastly, a partial analysis of students' feedback over a couple of lab modules is also included.

Keywords: Blockchain technology · cybersecurity · GENI · lab · applied cryptography

© The Author(s), under exclusive license to Springer Nature Singapore Pte Ltd. 2023
W. Hong and Y. Weng (Eds.): ICCSE 2022, CCIS 1813, pp. 438–448, 2023.
https://doi.org/10.1007/978-981-99-2449-3_38

1   Introduction

According to Gartner, a leading research and adversary firm, blockchain technology is one of the top 10 strategic technologies in 2020. Blockchain-based Service Network (BSN) has recently been launched to host all types of blockchain applications in China [22]. Digital Currency Electronic Payment (DCEP) is one example. These groundbreaking projects will inevitably increase the demand for blockchain developers in the market [11]. However, there is a lack of the current integration of blockchain technologies and applications into curricula for college education. Therefore, it is important for us to rethink and redesign hands-on learning modules and labs that incorporate blockchain technology.

Blockchain technology traces its origins to Stuart Haber and W. Scott Stornetta, who tried to time-stamp a digital document in 1991 [24]. The first implementation of blockchain technology is Bitcoin transactions [24]. In addition to this well-known application, blockchain technology has been deployed in the smart contract, Internet of Things (IoT), finance, supply chain management, voting, healthcare, insurance, etc. [6]. Recently, e-Yuan, a Chinese government-backed cryptocurrency, was released following Xi Jinping's remark on the important role of blockchain technology in the next round of technological innovation and industrial transformation in 2019 [13]. Overall, blockchain continues to gain attention due to its unique features, including decentralization, security, and reliability [15].

Despite this growing interest in blockchain technology, its intricacies are hard to grasp. As a result, there is an increasing need to include blockchain technology in education curricula [5,14]. In this paper, we present our developed lab experiments for students to practice and apply blockchain technology. We believe that only when students can build their own blockchain-based public key infrastructure (PKI) and smart contracts can they truly understand how blockchain works and get the benefits of blockchain technology.

However, there exists a range of challenges concerning blockchain education. First of all, student background knowledge and skills vary widely. Some cybersecurity students lack fundamental knowledge in computer networking, such as software-defined networks [21], blockchain technical knowledge implementations, and data structure. Similarly, general computer science students may lack a clear understanding of information security and cryptography, whereas blockchain technology utilizes public-key cryptography, hash functions, digital signatures, and block ciphers from cryptography. Last, the students enrolled in the computer science program or related programs have limited mathematical backgrounds.

In order to enable a good understanding of Blockchain, students should have good knowledge of distributed systems, networking, data structures, and cryptography. Besides, students are better have some experience in information technologies. The broad range of background requirements, financial and computing resources limitations, and lack of computing resource-efficient hands-on/real-world labs are key challenges hindering hands-on-oriented cybersecurity education [8]. Further, though the number of students enrolled in a computer science program has increased over the past few years, the school computing resources available to students are stalled. Another challenge is the platform in which blockchain education is deployed. In general, cybersecurity education is delivered either in-class, online, or a hybrid of two. It is significantly challenging to ensure that remote students have an equal opportunity to access computing resources as on-campus students. In this paper, we present the Global Environment for Network Innovations (GENI) testbed to overcome the last two challenges.

A cryptography course provides students with fundamental knowledge of public-key cryptography, hash function, digital signatures, etc. Besides, students are expected to understand cryptographic mechanisms for securing data. These pieces of knowledge are crucial in deploying blockchain technology. It is beneficial to incorporate blockchain technology into a class project or a final hands-on lab in which students can integrate all the concepts they learned in a cryptography course into an innovative real-world application. This not only helps students see the importance of cryptographic concepts presented in the lectures but also provides a comprehensive assessment of their learning outcomes.

Furthermore, most cybersecurity programs nowadays offer senior-year capstone design projects and/or courses. These projects and courses indeed serve as quality assurance before accreditation approval. In these capstone projects, senior students must integrate and apply their skill sets and knowledge acquired throughout their program study [16]. From the cybersecurity perspective (applied cryptography in particular), students can deploy and incorporate advanced paradigms and platforms, such as real-world federated networking testbeds and blockchain technology, into their project implementations while applying "know-how" from their expertise and past work experiences. Therefore, the integration of such advanced technologies and paradigms does not only improve the students' skill sets but can also allow promising research products, including framework prototypes, proofs of concept, and publishable manuscripts [9].

Lastly, the primary contribution of this education paper is the demonstration of novel educational learning modules for teaching applied cryptography concepts. In these hands-on-based learning modules, blockchain technology and GENI testbed facilities are incorporated to provide students with a flexible and convenient environment to apply various cryptographic concepts and modules (e.g., asymmetric-key cryptography and hash functions). These learning modules were anonymously evaluated and assessed by online graduate cybersecurity students discussed in Sect. 4. The developed lab modules incorporate key factors, components, and phases corresponding to the learning-teaching procedure. This effort has led students to establish or improve their knowledge and skillset in cryptographic concepts, cryptocurrency and blockchain implementations, and computer networking configurations.

It is essential to note that these pedagogical modules are currently deployed over GENI testbed facilities [20]. However, they can also be integrated into other current and future cloud-based laboratories such as Cloud Lab [2], Chameleon [1], and Fabric [3]. Importantly, Fabric, programmable adaptive research and education-based infrastructure for computer science and applications, will soon be released and is anticipated to be a strong fit for the learning modules presented in this paper.

The rest of this paper is organized as follows. Section 2 discusses our research efforts and contributions towards the development strategies for enhancing hands-on-based cybersecurity education with a focus on blockchain technology. Building upon the strategies, Sect. 3 presents our methodology for integrating blockchain technology into GENI testbed for cybersecurity education. This section further presents an overview of the developed lab modules for the hands-on-based cybersecurity curricula. Next, Sect. 4 provides a summary of key findings based upon student feedback and assessment of our learning modules that have been integrated into an existing cybersecurity course. Last, Sect. 5 provides concluding remarks along with future research plans.

2   Development Strategies

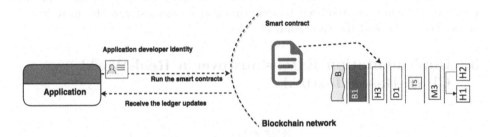

Fig. 1. A sample smart contract with FabCar [4].

Given that the vast majority of cybersecurity students lack fundamental knowledge in blockchain technology and the complexity of cryptocurrency-related teaching/learning processes, an introductory level learning lab was initially developed to assist these students with leveraging and comprehending how the technology operates and runs. We further discuss its details as follows.

Foremost, before launching into advanced technical blockchain labs, students must be familiarized with smart contracts. A contract is a written or spoken agreement inherited from the trust in legal systems and intended to be enforceable by law. However, with the emergence of technology paradigms, such as cryptocurrencies and blockchains, people started incorporating the concept of a smart contract into the blockchain. The developed learning modules herein allow students to program and save the terms of clauses for smart contracts in blockchain in a transparent and immutable way, as shown in Fig. 1. Moreover, given each Internet browser has a set of trusted Certificate Authority (CA) certificates already installed, students can adopt the role of CAs (e.g., Verisign and Symantec) to create root certificates and sign Certificate Signing Requests (CSRs) for other certificates.

Furthermore, we consider a scenario of a client who owns a domain and wants to use Secure Sockets Layer and Transport Layer Security (SSL/TLS) to get a certificate. If this client does not trust that certificate, they can refuse the connection. Therefore, students herein (as the client) can verify and validate a certificate they receive by looking at which CA signed it (i.e., if a trusted CA signed the certificate, then the communication would continue. Otherwise, there would be a chance that the certificate might be compromised. This case would permit an adversary to establish a trusted communication channel with the client.)

A further experimental scenario is developed based upon a live list of certificates. Once a CA claims that a particular certificate has been revoked, the certificate will be untrusted. To do so, the students, who play the role of a CA, will have to revoke the certificate through the blockchain and then generate a new trusted certificate (assuming that the blockchain is private and only those who possess the 'write' permissions can write to the blockchain, whereas anyone else is only allowed to act as a listener/end node on the blockchain and they do not have the 'write' permission). Lastly and most notably, in this learning module, students are required to experimentally demonstrate the usability of smart contracts and the validation of CAs.

3 Implementation Extensions over a Real-World Cloud-Based Testbed

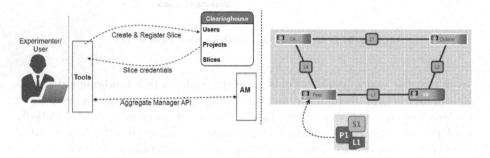

Fig. 2. (1: left-hand side) Layers of Interaction between GENI infrastructure resources and experimenters; (2: right-hand side) A use case of a blockchain peer network over GENI testbed resources consisting of peer hosts. Each peer entity in this blockchain network possesses ledgers and smart contracts' copies. The peer node in this GENI topology holds its own instance of the distributed ledger, who can use a chaincode to access its distributed ledger copy.

To date, virtual laboratory-based environments, such as SEED Lab [10], still play a significant role in offering interactive-enabled learning experiences via devoted experimental scenarios based upon desktop software and/or web platforms [19]. However, these virtual environments often fall short of guaranteeing realistic practice and experience (in cybersecurity education) concerning real-world learning requirements [12,18]. GENI is a vital alternative platform for both in-class and online engineering-related research and education curricula sponsored by the US National Science Foundation (NSF). GENI is a real-world, federated, heterogeneous, at-scale, repeatable, programmable, and virtual infrastructure for hands-on experimentation in a broad range of computer engineering and science fields including, but not limited to, computer networking, cybersecurity (e.g., applied cryptography and networking security), and high-performance computing [7,23]. Furthermore, deploying the GENI testbed in cybersecurity education in general and applied cryptography, in particular, will allow students to concurrently conduct multiple experiments via isolated slices over available GENI infrastructure resources [17].

Remarkably, the GENI testbed may be utilized as a virtual remote lab environment by educators in the STEM field, and it allows for carrying out real-world experimentation on flexible network topology, as shown in Fig. 2. Therefore, the testbeds, such as the GENI testbed, are considered for integration along with a broad range of blockchain-based lab modules to enforce different cryptographic concepts (e.g., public/private key cryptography, PKI, and hash functions). The primary reasons behind this integration are the facilitation of experimentation, overcoming the hardware and software resource limitations, enabling collaborative experiments among students (via shared experimental slices), and providing convenient access to various remote resources (for the desired allocation time). Moreover, throughout lab sessions, educators can monitor students' experiments via a dedicated real-time experiment console (e.g., identify active experiments and those awaiting available resources to run and successfully finish and submit experiments.)

Before we introduce students to GENI testbed-based lab modules, a set of introductory hands-on labs are delivered to help familiarize students with GENI facilities, resources, and features. These introductory labs range from creating and setting an account on the GENI testbed (including private and public keys and Privacy Enhanced Mail Certificate file) to allocating at-scale topologies over geographically distributed GENI sites. The following lab modules are being implemented to extend the perceived teaching process of applied cryptography concepts and modules through blockchain technology and the GENI testbed.

- Write-Your-First-Application lab: This learning module aims at providing students with an introductory tutorial to write their applications using Fab-Car. Specifically, students will dive into a broad range of hands-on programs to explore how the Fabric applications operate based upon collectively FabCar smart contracts. This learning module further enables an essential starting point to learn how permissioned blockchain hyperledger work (e.g., how to update and query ledgers through smart contracts and generate X.509 certificate files via CAs).
- Atomic Swap lab: This learning module uses python-bitcoinlib, an open-source python library mainly devoted to bitcoin transactions' simulation. This lab provides students with the opportunity to create cross-chain atomic

swap transactions. Students are first required to allocate a couple of nodes on GENI resources and then securely and efficiently exchange coins ownership over various ledgers.

- Create Bitcoin Transactions lab: This learning module also utilizes the python-bitcoinlib library and enables students to learn how to draft and develop blockchain transactions and place them on the Bitcoin testnet bitcoin blockchain, an alternative Bitcoin blockchain mainly used for testing.
- Decentralized Ethereum Applications lab: This learning module requires students to utilize multiple languages and platforms (e.g., web3.js to provide a set of libraries for interaction with a distant or local Ethereum entity and Solidity; an object-oriented programming language for implementing smart contracts over different blockchains, including Ethereum). This lab module further allows students to implement blockchain smart contracts and user access.

4   Assessment and Feedback over Learning Outcomes

Yes, I have.	8 respondents	26%
No, I have not.	22 respondents	71%
No Answer	1 respondents	3%
Very difficult	4 respondents	13%
Difficult	6 respondents	19%
Neutral	6 respondents	19%
Easy		0%
Very easy		0%
No Answer	15 respondents	48%
less than 1 hour		0%
between 1 and 2 hours		0%
between 2 and 3 hours		0%
between 3 and 4 hours	3 respondents	13%
between 4 and 5 hours	1 respondents	4%
between 5 and 6 hours	2 respondents	8%
between 6 and 7 hours		0%
between 7 and 8 hours	1 respondents	4%
between 8 and 9 hours		0%
between 9 and 10 hours	1 respondents	4%
more than 10 hours	2 respondents	8%
No Answer	14 respondents	58%

Fig. 3. Student feedback regarding the blockchain experiment in Spring 2021.

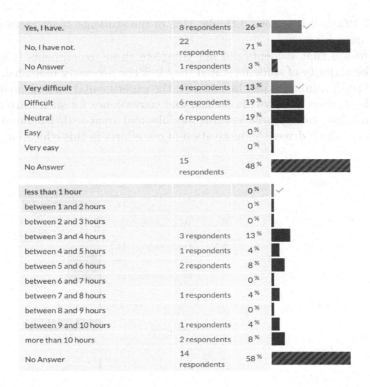

Fig. 4. Student feedback regarding the blockchain experiment in Summer 2021.

To assess how students benefit from our pedagogical learning mechanisms and modules, we first included a few tasks from these modules as optional experiments (where students get bonus credit upon their completion) in the Applied Cryptography course for Spring 2021 and Summer 2021. Figure 3 expresses students' feedback on the following questions related to the experiments.

– Have you completed the lab's optional/bonus task of the blockchain experiment?
– How difficult did you find the learning experiments by indicating the difficulty scale/level of the experiments?
– How many hours did you need to complete the experiments?

   The corresponding results on the top, middle, and bottom of Fig. 3 show students who finished the optional blockchain task, the feedback on the difficulty of the learning experiments, and the time spent to complete the block experiment, respectively. 26% of the students completed the optional blockchain learning modules, whereas no student thought these experiments were easy to conduct. The time spent to complete these modules was over 3 h (on average). Figure 4 shows students' feedback over these blockchain modules in Summer 2021. We can see that 30% of the students have completed the blockchain learning modules, and 19% feel it is very difficult. 11% of the students spent more than 5 h on these modules.

The reason that students did not complete these experiments is shown in Fig. 5. The majority of students stated they lack the necessary blockchain knowledge and programming skills. In contrast, the experimental virtual environment (virtual host) does not provide realism and convenience for such learning modules. Hence, integrating these learning modules and an at-scale federated testbed is necessary, which drives the motivation of our efforts in this educational study.

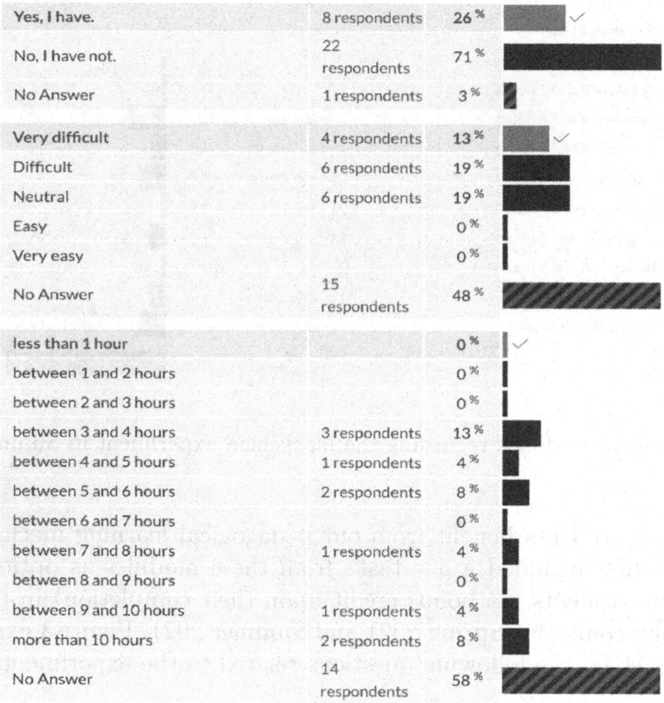

Yes, I have.	8 respondents	26 %	
No, I have not.	22 respondents	71 %	
No Answer	1 respondents	3 %	
Very difficult	4 respondents	13 %	
Difficult	6 respondents	19 %	
Neutral	6 respondents	19 %	
Easy		0 %	
Very easy		0 %	
No Answer	15 respondents	48 %	
less than 1 hour		0 %	
between 1 and 2 hours		0 %	
between 2 and 3 hours		0 %	
between 3 and 4 hours	3 respondents	13 %	
between 4 and 5 hours	1 respondents	4 %	
between 5 and 6 hours	2 respondents	8 %	
between 6 and 7 hours		0 %	
between 7 and 8 hours	1 respondents	4 %	
between 8 and 9 hours		0 %	
between 9 and 10 hours	1 respondents	4 %	
more than 10 hours	2 respondents	8 %	
No Answer	14 respondents	58 %	

Fig. 5. Student feedback regarding the blockchain experiment.

5   Conclusion

The decentralized blockchain technology has attracted remarkable attention from academic and industrial sectors over the last few years. This technology provides unique features and capabilities, such as data integrity, security, and reliability. However, on the one hand, a lack of notable deployment remains vital in cybersecurity education curricula. Therefore, elaborating on efficient academic initiatives for implementing and integrating hands-on learning modules using blockchain technology to support higher cybersecurity education is particularly interesting. On the other hand, the enrollment of cybersecurity students in face-to-face, online, or hybrid courses has been massively augmenting. As such, universities face various challenges, including, but not limited to, networking and computing resources. Thus, an alternative solution can be the integration of a real-world testbed, such as GENI, a federated and heterogeneous networking-enabled testbed, into cybersecurity curricula. This paper has proposed the design methodologies for integrating blockchain technology and the GENI testbed in a cybersecurity core course (i.e., applied cryptography). The presented design idea uses blockchain technology and GENI testbed facilities for training students on advanced cryptographic modules, such as PKI and hash functions. This paper has primarily focused on educational aspects of blockchain and GENI testbed applicability to cybersecurity education, deployment challenges, and implementation design of the hands-on learning labs. Lastly, a partial analysis of the course students' feedback over a couple of lab modules has demonstrated the approach efficiency and student satisfaction over learning outcomes.

Acknowledgements. We would like to acknowledge the National Science Foundation (NSF) that partially sponsored the work under grants #1633978, #1620871, #1620862, #1651280, #1531099 and BBN/GPO project #1936 through NSF/CNS grant. The views and conclusions contained herein are those of the authors and should not be interpreted as necessarily representing the official policies, either expressed or implied of NSF.

References

1. Chameleon Cloud. https://www.chameleoncloud.org/. Accessed 15 Apr 2022
2. Cloud Lab. https://www.cloudlab.us/. Accessed 15 Apr 2022
3. Fabric Testbed. https://fabric-testbed.net/. Accessed 15 Apr 2022
4. Hyperledger Fabric. https://www.hyperledger.org/use/fabric. Accessed 15 Apr 2022
5. Alammary, A., Alhazmi, S., Almasri, M., Gillani, S.: Blockchain-based applications in education: a systematic review. Appl. Sci. **9**(12), 2400 (2019)
6. Ali, A., et al.: Blockchain and the future of the internet: a comprehensive review. arXiv preprint arXiv:1904.00733 (2019)
7. Berman, M., et al.: Geni: a federated testbed for innovative network experiments. Comput. Netw. **61**, 5–23 (2014)
8. Cheung, R.S., Cohen, J.P., Lo, H.Z., Elia, F.: Challenge based learning in cybersecurity education. In: Proceedings of the International Conference on Security and Management (SAM), p. 1. The Steering Committee of The World Congress in Computer Science (2011)
9. Dascalu, S.M., Varol, Y.L., Harris, F.C., Westphal, B.T.: Computer science capstone course senior projects: from project idea to prototype implementation. In: Proceedings Frontiers in Education 35th Annual Conference, pp. S3J–1. IEEE (2005)
10. Du, W.: SEED: hands-on lab exercises for computer security education. IEEE Secur. Priv. **9**(5), 70–73 (2011)

11. Dumas, J.G., Jimenez-Garcès, S., Soiman, F.: Blockchain technology and crypto-assets market analysis: vulnerabilities and risk assessment. In: IMCIC 2021-The 12th International Multi-Conference on Complexity, Informatics and Cybernetics, vol. 1, pp. 30–37 (2021)
12. Fedynich, L.V.: Teaching beyond the classroom walls: the pros and cons of cyber learning. J. Instr. Pedag. **13** (2013)
13. Kshetri, N., Loukoianova, E.: Data privacy considerations for central bank digital currencies in asia-pacific countries. Computer **55**(03), 95–100 (2022)
14. Malibari, N.A.: A survey on blockchain-based applications in education. In: 2020 7th International Conference on Computing for Sustainable Global Development (INDIACom), pp. 266–270. IEEE (2020)
15. Martin, K., Rahouti, M., Ayyash, M., Alsmadi, I.: Anomaly detection in blockchain using network representation and machine learning. Secur. Priv. **5**(2), e192 (2022)
16. Prusty, N.: Building Blockchain Projects. Packt Publishing Ltd. (2017)
17. Rahouti, M., Xiong, K.: Board 128: understanding global environment for network innovations (GENI) and software-defined networking (SDN) for computer networking and security education. In: 2019 ASEE Annual Conference & Exposition (2019)
18. Rahouti, M., Xiong, K.: Board 129: facilitation of cybersecurity learning through real-world hands-on labs. In: 2019 ASEE Annual Conference & Exposition (2019)
19. Rahouti, M., Xiong, K.: A customized educational booster for online students in cybersecurity education. In: CSEDU (2019)
20. Rahouti, M., Xiong, K., Lin, J.: Leveraging a cloud-based testbed and software-defined networking for cybersecurity and networking education. Eng. Rep. **3**(10), e12395 (2021)
21. Rahouti, M., Xiong, K., Xin, Y., Jagatheesaperumal, S.K., Ayyash, M., Shaheed, M.: SDN security review: threat taxonomy, implications, and open challenges. IEEE Access **10**, 45820–45854 (2022)
22. Stockton, N.: China takes blockchain national: the state-sponsored platform will launch in 100 cities. IEEE Spectr. **57**(4), 11–12 (2020)
23. Thomas, V., Riga, N., Edwards, S., Fund, F., Korakis, T.: GENI in the Classroom. In: McGeer, R., Berman, M., Elliott, C., Ricci, R. (eds.) The GENI Book, pp. 433–449. Springer, Cham (2016). https://doi.org/10.1007/978-3-319-33769-2_18
24. Whitaker, A.: Art and blockchain: a primer, history, and taxonomy of blockchain use cases in the arts. Artivate **8**(2), 21–46 (2019)

The Metaverse Technology Empowered English Education—"Meta-course"

Haoyun Wang, Yilan Shi, Yi Cheng, and Yu Wang[✉]

Department of International Studies, NingboTech University, Ningbo, China
Bluefish1978@126.com

Abstract. A metaverse is a new form of the Internet in the future that integrates many new technologies. According to some practical applications of metaverse-related technologies in education, we innovate a new English education model-"meta-course." The Meta-course is a model that can diversify teaching, provide digital services, and meet individual needs through feedback and assessment in the form of nodes. It is divided into three parts: preparation before class, course of teaching, and feedback after class. Compared to traditional education methods, meta-course integrates immersive learning, personalized design, and intelligent feedback after class to solve the current problems of single-mode English education, lack of practice, and low efficiency.

Keywords: Metaverse · English education · Meta-course

1 Introduction

Nowadays, there are two apparent problems in English teaching in colleges and universities. Firstly, the teaching methods are relatively single, the teaching activities lack innovation, and the teaching atmosphere is weak. Secondly, the teaching lacks practicality. It seriously weakens the cultivation of the English ability of college students, which is detrimental to the realization of the comprehensive English quality of college students.

The education community has proposed some countermeasures to solve those problems. Based on AI techniques, some scientists propose a profound learning-assisted online intelligent English teaching (DL-OIET) system [1]. Others recommend multimedia teaching to overcome the drawbacks of traditional teaching [2].

However, most of these countermeasures can only solve one or a small part of the problems, but not completely. "Metaverse + education" may be able to break through the current bottleneck period of education fundamentally. The emergence and development of the metaverse have brought opportunities for the reform and development of university English teaching. In the future highly immersive and interactive education metaverse, the effect of education will also be significantly enhanced. Some of the high-tech technologies in the metaverse have been practically applied in some teaching scenarios.

W. Hong and Y. Weng (Eds.): ICCSE 2022, CCIS 1813, pp. 449–459, 2023.
https://doi.org/10.1007/978-981-99-2449-3_39

In China, Guangzhou Vocational College of Engineering and Technology has proposed a teaching reform of "borderless" management of teaching resources. Virtual reality technology will be introduced into the simulation room and "air classroom" according to the teaching needs of each major [3].

From the above case, we can see that applying metaverse technology in practical education is feasible, so this thesis assumes a new English education model based on the metaverse foundation—Meta-course. The following sections present the foundation of metaverse technology applied in English education and meta-course and the challenges of the meta-course.

2 The Foundation of Metaverse Technology Applied in English Education

2.1 Background of the Metaverse

Many media outlets are calling 2021 "the year of the metaverse," and the landmark event is Facebook changing its name to "Meta" and investing at least $10 billion a year in its "metaverse" division. Although the metaverse is still in its infancy, it has shown great potential for development.

The word metaverse first appeared in Snow Crash, a famous 1992 science fiction novel by the famous American science fiction author Neal Stephenson [4], which depicted a vast virtual reality world. Meta stands for transcendence, and verse stands for the universe and is intended to indicate that the Metaverse is a digital world in which the virtual and the real are seamlessly and deeply integrated.

Emerging education technologies represented by virtual reality and augmented reality have led the new direction of future education in recent years. The metaverse, which integrates virtual reality, artificial intelligence, and blockchain, provides a virtual learning environment for learners and potentially brings about new education and teaching changes [5].

2.2 Problems Encountered in English Education

With the impact of the pandemic, online education has become an essential part of the modern English education system in recent years. However, there are still many problems in current online English education, such as tedious web pages, which are difficult to motivate learning; simple human-computer interaction methods, which do not give students a strong sense of participation; incomplete learning data records, which make it difficult to evaluate the effectiveness of leaning. Due to the lack of teaching tools, it is difficult for teachers to obtain students' learning status in time and adjust the teaching pace according to students' learning situations. Teacher-centered teaching resources make teachers tired and are not conducive to improving teaching quality, while students are tired of such passive learning resources and quickly lose interest in learning, which dramatically affects teaching quality [6].

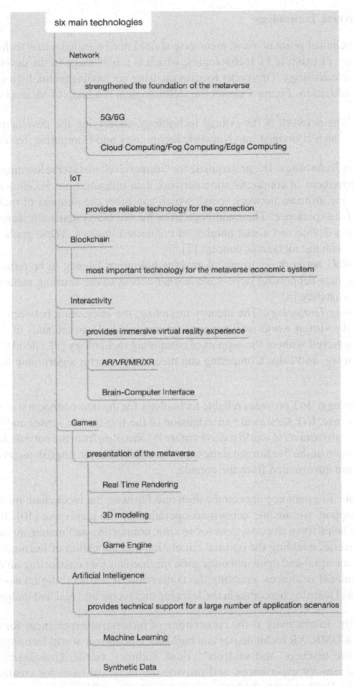

Fig. 1. The technological roadmap of Metaverse.

2.3 Metaverse Technology

From the technical point of view, metaverse should not be called a new technology but extensive use of existing IT technologies, which is a new stage in the development of information technology. This paper focuses on using six leading technologies in English metaverse education. Figure 1 shows the technological roadmap of Metaverse.

Network. The network is the critical technology underlying the development of the metaverse, which is divided into Network Technology and Computing Technology.

Network Technology. The prerequisite for "immersive" metaverse learning in English is the improvement of communication network data transmission. 5G allows people to experience the ultimate network speed, which can meet the demand of metaverse for an immersive experience. The main objectives for the 6G systems are incredibly high data rates per device and a vast number of connected devices. These goals are highly compatible with the metaverse concept [7].

The 5G/6G network environment enables hologram latency to be reduced to less than 20 ms, thus supporting large-scale learner access to the learning metaverse while meeting low latency [8].

Computing Technology. The identity modeling, the interaction between the natural world and the virtual world, will generate unimaginably large amounts of data, which cannot be achieved without the support of computing technology [9]. Cloud Computing, Fog Computing, and Edge Computing can meet the powerful algorithmic needs of the metaverse.

IoT Technology. IoT provides reliable technology for the interconnection of everything in the metaverse. IoT sensors are an extension of the five human senses and can ensure that the English metaverse world receives more information from the outside. IoT sensors are an extension of the five human senses and can ensure that the English metaverse world receives more information from the outside.

Blockchain. To guarantee decentralization and fairness, the blockchain must be introduced to support sustainable ecosystem operation in the metaverse [10]. Blockchain technology helps form an ecosystem for storing, connecting and managing information in the metaverse, enabling the optimal circulation and allocation of learning resources. It provides an equal and open authentication mechanism for constructing an ecology of open educational resources, enabling the conversion of learners' digital assets, virtual identities, and learning outcomes in the learning metaverse into real and imaginary ones.

Interactivity. Interactivity is the cornerstone of immersive experiences for metaverse users. VR/AR/MR/XR technologies can build realistic mirror-world learning scenarios, fully mobilize teachers' and students' visual, auditory, tactile, kinesthetic, and other multimodal sensory experiences, and provide the technical basis for creating immersive learning. Furthermore, the brain-computer interface (BCI) can connect computers directly to the metaverse to shape an idealized intentional learning experience.

Games. GameTech includes 3D modeling, 3D rendering, and simulation technology. Thanks to 3D technology, virtual characters can be constructed closely, resembling reality. With 3D rendering, computer graphics convert 3D wireframe models into 2D images with 3D photorealistic, or as close to reality, effects [11].

Artificial Intelligence. AI enables the personalization of needs in English learning, and the creation of particular incarnations of the user.AI can combine and even generate specially tailored content and experiences. When students put on a sophisticated, AI-enabled VR headset, its sensors will be able to read and predict their electrical and muscular patterns to know precisely how they would want to move inside the metaverse [11].

3   The English Meta-course Based on Metaverse Technology

Based on the problems mentioned above regarding English education, we have assumed a new type of English education model—meta-course, which incorporates the six technologies of the metaverse.

3.1   Definition

English meta-course is a course that can diversify teaching, provide digital services, and meet individual needs through feedback and assessment in the form of nodes. It empowers more flexibility and creativity among teachers and students. A meta-course is not simply an online course but a digital world in which students and teachers re-engage as a separate digital identity. Students are part of the virtual world in the course, and they can be creators or participants. Unlike regular online courses, meta-course is more comprehensive and intelligent. Currently available courses do not have the personalized design and virtual learning, or even intelligent feedback, that meta-course do.

3.2   Construction

The Meta-course is divided into three parts: preparation before class, course of teaching, and feedback after class. Figure 2 shows the roadmap of the Meta-course.

Preparation Before the Class
Procedure

- Create characters and learning scenarios: First, each student and teacher can create their avatar based on 3D scanning technology before the course starts. Students and teachers can also create their desired classrooms and extra-curricular teaching spaces. Teachers select or judge the learner identity conditions and scenario requirements required for a particular knowledge context and redesign them to guide learning in different learning scenarios based on their content and identity conditions [12].
- AI analyses data: Once created, students input their course learning objectives and study habits. AI technology calculates, stores, and analyses the student's accurate English level derived from previous exams and tests.

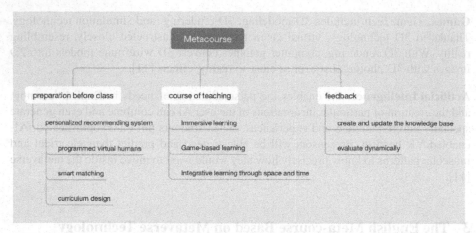

Fig. 2. The roadmap of the meta-course.

- Intelligent matching: The AI can achieve smart matching after creating the data context. It will accurately measure students' current level of language knowledge and place students with similar ability levels in the same class for instruction. In the future, Metaverse can even smarten up the teaching models and experiences of excellent English teachers and train them as virtual digital teachers of various styles to match the needs of different types of students.

Advantages. The creation of personalization can help solve the current problem of differentiated English teaching. Students in the same classroom have varying levels of English proficiency, but teachers use the same teaching techniques to teach. The use of technology allows teachers to tailor individual instruction, allowing teachers more time to provide targeted attention to struggling students or learners who are progressing faster than their peers, rather than being forced to "teach to the middle."

Cases. Based on the knowledge points from the previous step and the students' personalized characteristics, the Apriori clustering algorithm is used to complete personalized path recommendations and resource recommendations for the corresponding knowledge points [13].

Course of Teaching. After completing the above personalization, teachers and students can enter the meta-course for teaching and learning. Meta-course has the following main advantages.

Immersive Learning

- Virtual learning: Interactive teaching mode built mainly with VR/AR/XR/MR and other technologies. Teachers and students can wear devices such as VR helmets or do not need to wear any equipment anytime and anywhere to enter the classroom. It allows students to experience the realism of virtual space and immersive learning.

Cases: In training students' listening and speaking skills, students can communicate "face-to-face" with people from different countries to achieve real English conversation training. Mondly VR is a platform specifically designed for learning English, which can be downloaded and used with VR devices that support the Google Daydream platform. After putting on the VR device, users can engage in conversations with virtual characters in the scene. Also, Hodoo Labs is an English learning community that transposes more than 300 characters and approximately 4,300 scenarios into English conversation virtual reality scenarios. Users travel freely across five continents and more than 30 imaginary villages to improve their English skills [5]. (Fig. 3).

Fig. 3. English conversations in hodoo labs.

- Multisensory learning: Simultaneously, immersion learning is a kind of multisensory learning, breaking through the single audiovisual sensory experience, integrating visual, auditory, tactile, olfactory, and other multimodal sensory experiences to achieve the immersion effect of learners on the content of learning resources. The static content in the original paper textbook will be upgraded to 3D pictures, animations, audio, and video, thus strengthening cognition from the perspective of sight, sound and touch.

Cases: When students learn new words, they will no longer memorize them on paper, but the meaning of the words will be "visualized," and they can remember the words in the scenes. "MageVR" is a virtual reality learning product, providing nearly a thousand high-quality courses and immersive VR interactive experiences. The team combines the new curriculum series textbooks, Cambridge Young Learners English, New Concept English and other classic teaching materials with the virtual scenes, characters, and 3D elements of the MageVR platform to create an exclusive learning world for users. Currently, the platform offers nearly 1000 course contents, serving college students and English learners. Besides, Beijing Normal University's "VR/AR + Education" Lab and Tsinghua University Elementary School conducted a series of AR-based language learning activities, creating an augmented reality learning environment through AR applications. Figure 4 shows that students observed and interacted with the sun and the earth in English class while learning English [5]. Immersion learning can effectively solve the "lack of practical teaching" and "disconnect between theoretical and practical teaching" in English education today.

Fig. 4. English AR open class "the sun and the earth" at Tsinghua university primary school.

Game-Based Learning. Game-based learning enhances the learning process by incorporating game mechanics and elements into the curriculum and self-directed learning activities to enrich and diversify the learning content. The emergence of the Metaverse has broken the limitation of gamified learning as merely an auxiliary application or tool in a limited time or environment, and presents a normalized and highly immersive virtual-real interactive learning environment for gamified learning. Based on simulation and interaction, important knowledge points in each digital textbook may be gamified to promote students' enthusiasm for learning. Each new course students learn will almost follow a gamified process of playing and upgrading, and the various problems and challenges they encounter can be pulled up to learn the relevant knowledge points in time. In addition, the learning metaverse empowers gamified learning, which can also stimulate students' creativity and provide them with an exploratory learning experience process.

Cases: Abroad, Vergne et al. (2019) designed a live-action escape room game called Escape the Lab (2019). The Escape the Lab game dramatically enhances learners' immersion experience and learning participation [8]. Gamification of English teaching enriches the content and breaks through the bottleneck of the monotonous teaching mode.

Integrative learning through space and time. Integrative learning encompasses temporal integration as well as spatial integration.

- Time-bound parts: Students can rely on the metaverse to enter the virtual time to learn and review the corresponding knowledge for time-bound parts, such as history. For example, if a text involves relevant historical content, students can enter the virtual world and travel to a specific period to witness what happened in that scene, understand the history of the context and help students remember.
- Part of space limitations: For the part of space limitations, such as different regions and countries, teachers and students can also "travel" to specific virtual scenes to feel the experience. For example, when the teacher talks about the British system,

they can set the classroom in the British Parliament building and immerse themselves in the meetings of the British Parliament. This further improves the efficiency of learning resources, enriches learners' perceptions and experiences, and enhances their creativity. More importantly, after breaking through the limitation of students' learning space, universities can realize the dialogue and discussion in the virtual world and share English resources to effectively solve the uneven distribution of educational resources and promote equality in education.

Cases: Tourism English is a branch of English for Specific Purposes, and tourism English is the core course in its training program. After VR technology is introduced, the proportion of practical class hours can be appropriately increased, and high-quality technical talents who can quickly adapt to the position can be cultivated through the simulation platform [14]. Through VR, students can break the limitations of region, time and space by using VR materials of a tourist region as learning materials. During the learning process, students formed teams to simulate a tour guide in scenic spots. One student simulated a tour guide, several students simulated tourists, and several students simulated service personnel. With the help of VR technology, the tour guide was simulated, and problems were found and solved in the virtual practice process to improve their ability. Li Jie, associate professor of foreign Languages at Xinxiang University, used VR materials from Muye Huazhang Exhibition Hall of Henan Plain Museum as teaching materials when instructing students to learn museum guide. After theoretical teaching, she led students to start virtual tour, interactive communication and summary through VR equipment. Then guide the students to carry out the simulated tour guide training, experience the process through group activities, personal demonstration and other links, and complete the teaching objectives [15].

Feedback. After the class, Meta-course provides intelligent feedback and dynamic evaluation of students' knowledge mastery in that class based on blockchain pass technology and artificial intelligence technology. The Metaverse can save the level of knowledge that students have acquired, upload it to the cloud, and teachers can view it anytime and anywhere. This is more conducive to teachers fully preparing for their lessons and developing targeted teaching plans based on the different situations of the students.

Grammar has always been a complex problem for Chinese students to learn English, but through metaverse technology, it is possible to systematically build students' grammar knowledge base to identify what has been mastered and what has not. Secondly, the meta-course will record students' usual homework, exams, key behaviors, and other scores, optimizing students' learning and behavior guidance.

Cases: In an educational application of an artificial intelligence robot, the secondary school mathematics classroom "quadratic equation" is used as an example. At the end of the class, the AI education robot presents the teacher with the evaluation report of individual learners and the learning situation of the whole class in real time based on the feedback data from multiple terminals of the class, so as to understand the classification of students in the class and provide a reference basis for the next teaching design [16].

4 The Risks and Challenges of Meta-course

4.1 Ethical Risk Challenges

The ethical and moral issues in the Metaverse refer to the phenomena that arise in the Metaverse due to the lack of corresponding moral norms and confusion, which are in conflict with the moral norms of real society, such as integrity issues, the dissemination of false information, and so on. Although the Metaverse has given people new identities and created a new space of freedom, it also contains more complex social relationships. In creating the learning metaverse, the highly accessible and open virtual space may significantly impact human society's value, data, and algorithm ethics. How students will establish correct worldviews and values amidst different cultural outputs and false information brings challenges to the design of civilization rules in the learning metaverse [8]. In the process of constructing a learning metaverse, the ethical issues of role change between the learner's "self" and "virtual self" and the collaboration between the teacher and the "virtual teacher" need to be fully considered.

4.2 Lack of In-Depth Exploration of Teaching Applications

The application requirements of an educational metaverse in the classroom are much more than that, so there is a need to continue to strengthen the more bottomless construction of the course knowledge system. In addition, the current design of relevant teaching products is mainly technology-oriented, favoring the design and development of software while lacing systematic teaching theory support. In the new learning environment of the educational metaverse, producers of teaching applications need to consider how to combine embodied cognition theory and immersion theory to innovate the design of teaching contents and launch learning resources and teaching applications suitable for multimodal learning environments.

5 Conclusions

To make up for the shortcomings of traditional English education, this thesis assumes a new English education model—meta-course. We innovate from the construction of the meta-course that meets the individual characteristics and significantly promotes their motivation to learn. This model can encourage students to maximize their potential. Therefore, the traditional English teaching mode has been overturned. Even though there are still challenges in the practical application, such as ethical risks and lack of depth of content, the future of metaverse-empowered English education is still bright overall.

References

1. Sun, Z., Anbarasan, M., Praveen Kumar, D.: Design of online intelligent English teaching platform based on artificial intelligence techniques. Comput. Intell. **37**, 1166–1180 (2021)

2. Zhang, Z.: The use of multimedia in English teaching. US-China Foreign Lang. **14**, 182–189 (2016)
3. Peng, G.: Application of virtual reality technology in "virtual classroom" for higher vocational colleges. Hydraul. Pneumat. Seals **37**, 9–12 (2017)
4. Stephenson, N.: Snow Crash: A Novel. Spectra, USA (2003)
5. Cai, S., Jiao, X., Song, B.: Open another gate to education——application, challenge and prospect of educational metaverse. Mod. Educ. Technol. **32**, 16–26 (2022)
6. Xie, F.: Application and research of immersive classroom teaching based on virtual reality technology in 5G networks. Comput. Eng. Sci. **z1**, 14–17 (2019)
7. Chowdhury, M.Z., Shahjalal, M., Ahmed, S., Jang, Y.M.: 6G wireless communication systems: applications, requirements, technologies, challenges, and research directions. IEEE Open J. Commun. Soc. **1**, 957–975 (2020)
8. Lan, G., Wei, J., Huang, C., Zhang, Y., He, Y., Zhao, X.: Metaverse for learning empowering education:constructing a new pattern of internet+education application. J. Distance Educ. **40**, 35–44 (2022)
9. Wang, W., Zhou, F., Wan, Y., Ning, H.: A survey of metaverse technology. Chin. J. Eng. **44**, 744–756 (2022)
10. Duan, H., Li, J., Fan, S., Lin, Z., Wu, X., Cai, W.: Metaverse for social good: A university campus prototype. In: Proceedings of the 29th ACM International Conference on Multimedia, pp. 153–161. ACM, Virtual Event China (2021)
11. Mozumder, M.A.I., Sheeraz, M.M., Athar, A., Aich, S., Kim, H.C.: Overview: technology roadmap of the future trend of metaverse based on IoT, blockchain, AI technique, and medical domain metaverse activity. In: 2022 24th International Conference on Advanced Communication Technology (ICACT), pp. 256–261. IEEE, Republic of Korea (2022)
12. Li, X.: Learning in the metaverse: a future learning scene of integrating the identity, time and space of learners. J. Distance Educ. **40**, 45–53 (2022)
13. Zhou, X., Tan, R.: Construction of personalized learning model based on big data. Comput. Knowl. Technol. **17**, 54–56 (2021)
14. Xue, M.: Research on application of tourism experiment teaching based on VR technology. Real Technol. Manage. **34**, 13–15 (2017)
15. Li, J.: Development and application of "Tourism English" teaching resources based on VR technology. New Curr. Res. **11**, 111–113 (2018)
16. Wang, S., Fang, H., Zhang, G., Ma, T.: Research on the new "double teacher classroom" supported by artificial intelligence educational robots: discuss about "human-machine collaboration" instructional design and future expectation. J. Distance Educ. **37**, 25–32 (2019)

A Study on Online Game *Genshin Impact* and the Dissemination of Chinese Culture

Xiaomin Cai[1] ⓘ, Yidi Chen[2], Yuhan Mao[3], and Liang Cai[1(✉)]

[1] School of International Studies, Ningbo Tech University, Ningbo, China
violacxm@sina.com, 719675711@qq.com
[2] School of Economics and Management, Southwest Jiaotong University, Chengdu, China
1351946588@qq.com
[3] School of Economics and Management, Zhejiang Sci-Tech University, Hangzhou, China
13805850311@qq.com

Abstract. By examining the cross-cultural acceptance of *Genshin Impact*, a mobile hit game developed by Chinese -based miHoYo, this paper discusses the strategy of integrating Chinese culture into online games. This paper introduces the relationship between Chinese culture and gaming, together with the theoretical and practical significance of using games to disseminate Chinese culture. Secondly, it analyzes the international influence of *Genshin Impact* from three aspects: the latest rating on foreign websites, awards won, and revenue statistics. Furthermore, it explores the Chinese cultural elements as well as its cross-cultural acceptance in *Genshin Impact* and discusses the role of games in promoting Chinese culture. Finally, a further discussion is made on a combination of the theories of Hanvey and Jauss for a better achievement of using games to tell Chinese stories.

Keywords: Online games · *Genshin Impact* · Dissemination of Chinese culture · Cross-cultural communication

1 Introduction

The piling up of oriental elements in Hollywood film and television constructs the imaginary Chinese culture and values - whether it is Fu Manchu, the famous "evil genius of the East" in the British novel, or the brave and filial "Wonder Woman" Mulan, they are all essentially misinterpretations of Chinese culture under the skin of Western values. Orientalism essentially means a Western way of culturally controlling the East [1]. As the old saying goes: "Citrus grows in both sides of River Huai, rooting in the south for mandarins, but in the north for orange bitter". The "mirror image" that makes generalized conclusions based on limited material given to the person, which can lead to perceptual errors, preconceptions, and prevent correct evaluation of others by ignoring individual differences when perceiving others. How to break the "mirror image" and adhere to the original orientalist aesthetics is the mission issue of China's foreign communication for communication between China and the West. Former U.S. President George H.W. Bush [2] said in 1989, "No country in the world has yet found a way to import

W. Hong and Y. Weng (Eds.): ICCSE 2022, CCIS 1813, pp. 460–470, 2023.
https://doi.org/10.1007/978-981-99-2449-3_40

the world's products and technologies while keeping foreign ideas at its borders." With China's Opening-up Policy, the 1980s turned out to be a time when Bush's remarks have been fully testified. Consequently, the terminology of cross-cultural communication was introduced to China by the foreign language teaching community in the early 1980s. Many Western-related works and products found their way into China. However, communication is not a one-way process, and the 1980s also kicked off a golden age for China's cultural exchange with the outside world.

The turn of the 21st century witnessed the formation of a new picture of the world, during which globalization and national identity remarkably changed all areas of human life. [3]. In economic terms, globalization fosters fierce competition among countries to attract overseas investment. In cultural terms, the spread of technology and products across national borders leads to the dynamic exchange of ideas and values among different cultures [4]. The prosperous economic development has brought about the blossoming of cultural diversity. However, globalization does not necessarily mean the loss of national identity. In a sense, cultural products exported by a country reflect and affect the country's international image. Therefore, the culture industry becomes one of the determining factors for representing a country's culture and reshaping consumers' attitudes toward a particular culture.

As a medium, online game is a mass communication form of large-scale online production, group collaboration and human-computer interaction. The dialogue between Chinese culture and the world in the form of games can effectively convey the spiritual core of Chinese culture, eliminate misunderstandings and prejudices caused by cultural estrangement, and thus enhance the soft power of national culture.

With more and more online games going abroad, the influence and popularity of China's game industry in the world is also expanding. Since this year, the pace of Chinese games going abroad has further accelerated. In March, the top three global handheld game publishing companies in terms of revenue were once again swept by China, namely Tencent, NetEase and miHoYo. Indeed, on April 11, the National Press and Publication Administration officially announced a total of 45 game license numbers. Which means, the domestic game license number restarted to issue after 263 days. And the restart of game license approval will help restore industry confidence and promote stable development, allowing players to enjoy more quality games. Chinese games going abroad is a manifestation of the continued strengthening of Chinese cultural influence.

The 47th report of China Internet Network Information Center (2021) specifically mentioned the open-world adventure games represented by *Genshin Impact*, which creatively combined the open-world mechanism with online and mobile games to bring novel game experiences to domestic and foreign players. Therefore, based on the influence of Genshin Impact in foreign countries, The research is aiming to explore "how the game achieves cross-cultural communication".

2 Using Games to Disseminate Chinese Culture

2.1 The Significance of Games in Cross-Cultural Communication

Gaming signifies a very special branch of the culture industry. By definition, game is a "text" that requires input from the player to traverse it [5]. Games can also uncover particular cultural customs [6]. Game, with culture as its core connotation, is a unique medium that has become one of the biggest entertainment items in the world [7]. It is noted that the information age gives birth to online games, which can be categorized into three major types according to the different game terminals: client-side games, web-based games and mobile games. Client-side games mainly refer to games that can only be run by downloading relatively large software clients on computers. Web-based games refer to games that can be run by simply clicking on web pages and using plug-ins such as Flash Player, mobile games generally refer to games that can be run on mobile devices such as mobile phones. At present, China's cultural export is mainly concentrated on neighboring countries and overseas Chinese communities, which shows that China's cultural export enjoys a relatively small influence and there is still a long way to go in internationalization. Meanwhile, online games are the "ninth art" in comparison with the traditional eight arts, and the important feature that distinguishes them from other art categories is their "participation". Moreover, ethnocentrism is social psychology that no one can completely get rid of it in the process of cross-cultural communication. People often unconsciously use their own culture as the standard to judge another culture. Therefore, when engaging in cross-cultural communication, it is important to try to find the commonalities and similarities in culture between the two sides to build a platform for the effectiveness of communication. In this sense, online games are supposed to be a good approach for us to study, which have the commonality and relative stability of human thought and understanding. This is the first thing we should pay attention to seeking and discovering. With regard to games, internet availability brings more convenience for international game players and easier access to Chinese online games greatly promoting cross-cultural communication. After more than 20 years of development, Chinese online games have made remarkable achievements in the world market. In addition, "The Belt and Road Initiatives" has set out new demands for Chinese culture going global. Therefore, game-based technologies pave the way for a deeper understanding of Chinese culture [8].

With the increasing popularity of Chinese cultural products, the Chinese culture "going out" strategy has met unprecedented opportunities and challenges. Online games have become an important part of people's daily entertainment, especially for the younger generation. Online games not only bring players great pleasure but also build a global experiential learning space for Chinese culture. However, the reality is that both game developers and course designers may not be fully aware of the educational function of game-playing. In other words, how to make the best use of games to disseminate Chinese culture remains a pressing need for full recognition. In this sense, integrating online games into the learning process of Chinese culture is the research initiative of this paper.

2.2 Functions and Approaches of Using Games in Cross-Cultural Communication

Online game is a way of entertainment, and it bears its social essence. Maslow argues that there are seven different levels of human need, which are expressed with varying degrees of urgency at different times. The most urgent need is the main reason and motivation to motivate people to act. Human needs are the satisfaction from the outside gradually to the satisfaction from the inside. He believes that human beings, as an organic whole, have multiple motivations and needs, including physiological needs, security needs, love and belonging needs, respect & esteem needs and self-actualization needs. With reference to Maslow's hierarchy of needs, the social aspects of online gaming meet the third and fourth levels of psychological needs. The social learning mechanism represents the inborn capability of all human cultures and the great need to be engaged in a social and cultural event will generate a precious chance for self-cultivation and self-development. When players are immersed in a game with exotic cultures both mentally and physically, they are exposed to a brand-new world of knowledge. Today, the game operator will choose to set up domestic servers, Asian servers, and foreign servers (divided into Europe and the United States). Therefore, intentionally or unintentionally, the game integrated with culture will have a significant role in promoting cross-cultural communication.

Since communication is a basic social function of human beings, culture is unique to human beings, and cross-cultural communication is the process of spreading something from one culture to another. Therefore, the cross-cultural communication of Chinese cultural elements must occur in the field of social communication, including interpersonal communication, mass communication, and organizational communication. Then the spread of Chinese cultural elements also has these three channels. And online games have exactly these factors.

2.3 Online Games and Cross-Cultural Acceptance

When we describe gamer culture, the gaps between different countries and cultures cannot be ignored. Therefore, it makes sense to extend the study of gamer identity to other countries and cultures [9]. In 1976, the famous American linguist R. G. Hanvey [10] wrote in An Attainable Global Perspective that cross-cultural awareness is a learnable sense of thinking. He argues that the presence or absence of cross-cultural awareness, or its degree, will directly impact the effectiveness of cross-cultural communication. Also, Straubhaar [11] posits that people prefer local, provincial or national content first, given that its production values meet at least a minimum standard; restricted content second; and alien range third, which has the appeal of encompassing new ideas (for want of a better term, the exotic). In the past, when people were exposed to these Chinese cultural elements, they often had stereotypes, knowing one but not the other [12].

In this sense, online games can be utilized as an instructional strategy for teaching Chinese culture, in addition, acceptance will grow higher when learning happens in a meaningful society and cultural context.

3 A Study on the Cross-Cultural Acceptance of Online Game *Genshin Impact*

Genshin Impact is an action role-playing game developed by Chinese developer miHoYo Technology (Shanghai) Co., Ltd, which has more than 56 million players worldwide. The following two aspects introduce its international influences.

3.1 Rating Sites of Online Game *Genshin Impact*

First, I need to introduce these sites that appear in Table 1.

GameSpot delivers the best and most comprehensive video game and entertainment coverage. Based on GameSpot's resources, GameSpot provides gamers with the fastest, most rigorous and authoritative game information and industry news, and GameSpot's game review articles are an important reference for gamers to buy games.

IGN (Imagine Games Network) is a multimedia and review website for video games and has grown to become the world's largest gaming and entertainment media outlet. IGN editors write reviews of games and then assign a score from 0 to 10 on a scale of 0.1 plus or minus to determine the playability of the game. The score depends on various factors such as performance, graphics, sound, gameplay and appeal, but the total score is not calculated from these values but is independent.

Famitsu: It is a video game magazine published by Enterbrain and is considered to be the most authoritative video game news magazine. This weekly magazine focuses on reviewing video games and reporting on video game industry news.

Sensor Tower: It is a mobile app data analytics company that deals with mobile app data analytics.

By comparing the credibility of these rating sites in Table 1, IGN is the most authoritative and most cited game rating site, so its data is the most convincing. And the rating for *Genshin Impact* was a surprising nine out of ten. This is a testament to *Genshin Impact's* popularity and uncommon strength overseas.

Table 1. *Genshin Impact's* ratings

Sites	Ratings in China	Ratings abroad
GameSpot	/	7/10
IGN	/	9/10
Famitsu	/	35/40
Sensor Tower	4.1/5	4.2/5

3.2 Revenue Statistics on Online Game *Genshin Impact*

The basic data in Table 2 is from the App Annie & Sensor Tower. The "up" written in Table 2 refers to the number of countries or regions topped by the revenue reached by the characters appearing in Gacha, and it seems that *Genshin Impact* has achieved a completely unimpressive result. According to Sensor Tower, there is a monthly list of the top revenue earners for outbound mobile games, and *Genshin Impact* often tops the revenue list. We can also see that its annual sales were staggering around 29,924,280,000 yuan, which only calculates the mobile player's recharge data.

Table 2. *Genshin Impact's* Annual Sales in 2021

Characters	1st up	Sales (CNY/K)	2nd up	Sales (CNY/K)
Zhongli	39	¥ 2,392,050	8	¥ 1,456,500
Xiao	27	¥ 2,565,080	64	¥ 1,609,240
Ganyu	16	¥ 1,997,040	43	¥ 1,126,980
Hu Tao	28	¥ 2,315,230	32	¥ 2,926,460
	Year	2021	Total	¥ 29,924,280

4 An Analysis of Cross-Cultural Acceptance in *Genshin Impact*

The game is a comprehensive art that combines several art forms. The content in the game can be said to be the epitome of human society. Therefore, in a broad sense, any content in the game is a cultural element, and cultural elements can be understood from a variety of perspectives. This paper will be from the three levels of culture to understand the elements of Chinese culture embodied in *Genshin Impact*.

4.1 Chinese Cultural Elements in *Genshin Impact*

With strong Chinese characteristics, the Chinese-style city - Liyue- has impressed many domestic and overseas players. By cooperating with Zhangjiajie, Huanglong Scenic Area, and Guilin. By taking the beautiful landscapes of these three places as inspiration, the game has built a region with the Oriental fantasy beauty of Liyue, which is loved by global players. This is the charm brought by traditional culture to the game. Liyue worships the Geo Archon Rex Lapis (Rex means king in Latin, and Lapis means rock) and is the largest market harbor in Teyvat. Liyue harbor is presided over by the Liyue Qixing, a group of business leaders and ancient guardians known as Adepti, a class of magical beings including Rex Lapis himself.

There is no doubt that Zhongli is the most popular role in Liyue. As stated above in Table 3, Morax is the overlord Rex Lapis who rules Liyue and the Geo Archon of the Seven Archons. However, in Sect. 1: Act 2, he created a fake death of his own by holding the Rite of Parting. Through this, Morax has successfully transformed from a god revered by the people of Liyue to an ordinary person in Liyue, Zhongli. This means that he voluntarily retired from his millennial divine throne and released his power to Liyue Qixing, marking Liyue's shift from divine rule to human rule. Just as a child quickly matures after losing their parents, so has Liyue matured when faced with the death of its deity. As the character in *Genshin Impact* says: "The time of contracts between gods and Liyue has long since passed. Now is the time of contracts between Liyue and its people." Zhongli is not only able to create great land but also to guard his people. He could make wise decisions in literature and secure the country in arms, but he was not attached to power and retired in a hurry. While enriching Zhongli's persona, these episodes have attracted many overseas players' curiosity about Liyue. They want to learn how to pronounce Liyue's names of people and places, which are named in Chinese

Table 3. Characters in *Genshin Impact*

Characters	Affiliation	Notes
Xiao	Liyue Adeptus	A yaksha Adeptus who defends Liyue. Also heralded as the "Conqueror of Demons" and "Vigilant Yaksha." Rex Lapis liberated the yaksha and gave him the name "Xiao."
Zhongli	Liyue Harbor	He is Morax, the overlord Rex Lapis who rules Liyue and the Geo Archon of the Seven Archons
Guoba	Wanmin Restaurant	Marchosius, God of the Stove. He devoted all his life to Liyue and then became Xiangling's Guoba
Yun Jin	Yun-Hao Opera Troupe	She is a renowned Liyue opera singer who is skilled in both playwriting and singing

pinyin. So many instructional videos suddenly sprang upon foreign online media, with the highest video play count even reaching 2264k. In the setting of *Genshin Impact*, each character has a dish they're good at, and Zhongli is no exception. Slow-Cooked Bamboo Shoot Soup is his specialty. The dishes in *Genshin Impact* also have detailed recipes, which have attracted many foreign gamers to make replicas of them.

We should be brave enough to name something Chinese - Baozi is "Baozi" and Jiaozi is "Jiaozi". It is because Koreans insist on using the word "kimchi" that foreigners will blurt out the word when they mention kimchi. But when we introduce our Paocai to foreigners, we rarely say the word "Paocai" with confidence. In cultural communication, we cannot afford to be culturally intimidated. And *Genshin Impact* clearly shows this cultural confidence in this regard.

There are two traditional festivals in Liyue, one is the Moonchase Festival, and the other is the Lantern Rite. The Moonchase Festival was set to commemorate Marchosius, God of the Stove. From the launch date of this event, it is not difficult to guess that its prototype is China's Mid-Autumn Festival. Just as Zhongli said in the plot that "The moon is a carrier of countless emotions, so many things only seem to surface as we gaze up beneath its poignant glow. Wherever the moonlight shines, the heart is wont to follow. Fond memories of those no longer with us. Debts of gratitude to old friends. The meaning of ages past and gone. All wrapped up in the city that has existed for so many moons to date. All these things and more. They are why people chase the moon." Lantern Rite reflects the Spring Festival. On the first full moon of each year, the people of Liyue celebrate the Lantern Rite. At night, everyone in Liyue would put Xiao Lanterns and Mingxiao Lanterns into the bright night sky. With the quickening pace of people's lives, the realistic sense of the festival atmosphere becomes less and less. *Genshin Impact*, however, takes great care to combine the traditional festival with the game, giving the player a festive feeling. Hosting these two festivals has undoubtedly attracted a large number of foreign players who are curious about Chinese culture, which has led some of them to do in-depth research. These are the first two levels of what Hanvey said about cross-cultural awareness.

Genshin Impact has also created many extraordinary works on music, and each song has a style that fits its theme. A song called "The Divine Damsel of Devastation" is adapted from the story Li Ji beheads a snake in the book Anecdotes About Spirits and Immortals [13], performed by Yun Jin, a character with opera elements. Because of its popularity, the public's interest in opera has been driven by the singing of Mrs. Yang Yang, which is like a "piercing arrow" and has attracted many artists in the domestic opera field to "come and meet". Foreign players also have flocked to the Beijing Opera video released by China Global Television Network (CGTN) several years ago to learn, and the number of video plays has skyrocketed by more than 100,000 in just a few days. The number one hot comment was even taken by the player, which shows how popular it is. A game-developer at miHoYo introduces the designing concept, "If there is a chance to let more people know that there is a very good artistic crystallization of traditional Chinese opera through *Genshin Impact*, which is a more popular and easily accepted form of entertainment, and even become interested in this art and get close to the real essence of opera culture. We feel that it is already very worthwhile if it can serve as such a superficial introduction." Later, it is found that a combination of the game and traditional opera conveys traditional culture to players, enabling players to feel the charm of opera.

4.2 Evaluation on the Cross-Cultural Acceptance of *Genshin Impact*

The above survey gives us a concrete indication of how well overseas players accept the different levels of cultural elements in *Genshin Impact*. Chinese cultural elements presented by *Genshin Impact* have reached the first level of "curiosity" of cross-cultural acceptance, satisfying the aesthetic psychology of "curiosity" of cross-cultural gamers. Human beings have an innate curiosity to explore peculiar things that differ greatly from what they have experienced. Or something that varies greatly from what we have experienced. The popularity of the opera song "The Divine Damsel of Devastation" with elements of Beijing opera and the annual revenue of *Genshin Impact* illustrate the interest of Westerners in this unique Chinese art form. It is quite challenging to truly realize the whole four levels of cross-cultural awareness proposed by Hanvey. Still, in *Genshin Impact*, I see the possibility of reaching the first level and even reaching the third - a culture that can be accepted through reasoned analysis.

The fact that a growing number of foreign players are exploring the Chinese culture included in the game means that *Genshin Impact* has greatly achieved success in cross-cultural acceptance, showing that the game is indeed a great tool for cross-cultural communication in the present day. It's high time that a wider range of popular culture is integrated into Chinese learning, and it is not only a task for the game developer but a joint effort from all parties involved.

5 Implications for Teaching in Cross-Cultural Communication

5.1 Sharing Cultural Commonality is Fundamental for Cross-Cultural Communication

Not long ago, on 16 March, the New York Times published an article about *Genshin Impact*, in which Yusuke Shibata, a well-known Japanese Youtuber, was interviewed, and the article seemed to be an objective presentation of the facts, but the words were full of arrogance and prejudice against China and *Genshin Impact*. It was described cynically as total plagiarism rather than genuine inspiration and cultural exchange, and the interviewer's interview was altered. After reading the article, the interviewer stated that he was interviewed to spread the reputation of *Genshin Impact*, that the theme of the interview was "to find out the secret of *Genshin Impact's* popularity", and that he strongly regretted that the New York Times did not publish his positive interview. This is a common tactic of the foreign media to smear China by not reporting the truth and including personal information.

Hanvey describes cross-cultural awareness as cultural sensitivity or insight, and divides it into four levels: At the first level, when a communicator first encounters a foreign culture, he or she feels amused, peculiar and exotic when seeing its superficial and visible features. At the second level, when people are initially exposed to foreign cultures, they often feel curious and new about their superficiality and superficial cultural phenomena, but once their deeper core concepts are different from their own mother culture, they will feel incomprehensible and thus develop a mentality of disapproval or even resistance. The third level is similar to the second level, where it is believed that this level of cultural identity can only be accepted through rational analysis. The fourth level is the ability to achieve a sense of the other person's culture from their standpoint. It is the highest level of cross-cultural awareness. With it, everyone can feel the impact of culture and understand it. This is not limited to one culture but applies to any culture. And the above example clearly achieves the second level as described by Hanvey. Hanvey's second-level theory of cross-cultural awareness mentions that when people are initially exposed to foreign cultures, they often feel curious and new about their superficiality and superficial cultural phenomena, but once their deeper core concepts are different from their own mother culture, they will feel incomprehensible and thus develop a mentality of disapproval or even resistance. Therefore, in spreading Chinese culture, we should try to find the concepts that Chinese culture and other cultures share and then present these concepts in our cultural products to enhance the acceptance of these cultural products in the world. To progress or not to regress, always have to be new from time to time, or at least must be taken from foreign countries, if all kinds of scruples, all kinds of care, all kinds of nagging, do so that is against the ancestors, then do and like the barbarians, lifelong anxiety such as on thin ice, shivering is still too late, how will make good things to [14]. Combine the game and traditional opera so that players can feel the charm of opera and convey traditional culture to players, like the art of opera.

The themes of art, contract and trustworthiness embodied in Liyue are cultural concepts recognized worldwide. Throughout the world, these concepts can be found in all countries. Players of different cultures can identify with these concepts and empathize with them when playing the game, which naturally leads to a high level of acceptance.

5.2 Exploiting Profound Chinese Cultural Elements is Beneficial for Cross-Cultural Acceptance

Jauss's expectation horizon refers to the potential aesthetic expectations of existing works formed by the recipients based on their previous life experiences as well as aesthetic experiences. The expectation horizon is not fixed, it will change based on the original one with the influence of new art appreciation practices. While according to Hanvey's hierarchy of cross-cultural consciousness, people feel curious when they are initially exposed to the superficially visible features of a foreign culture, which is rich in exoticism. For example, westerners have long been interested in Chinese martial arts, food, Beijing opera, and other content. It is because they have this expectation horizon that the curiosity about exoticism comes later. And what *Genshin Impact* shows in the game is exactly what they are interested in ancient architecture. The language passed from mouth to mouth and words that have changed over the years are all carriers of culture, as are the sounds of street hawkers and street crafts. By using these profound cultures to appeal to foreign players with a view to attracting them to learn more about the real China.

5.3 Integrating Online Game is Essential for Promotion of Chinese Culture and Language

Genshin Impact's analytical discourse on international cross-cultural acceptance shows that today's society is equipped to use games to teach the Chinese language overseas. Whether learning Liyue's Chinese pinyin through video sites or learning about Chinese culture in games is just like the Confucius Institute, it is a way to comprehend Chinese culture. Also, it is important to pay attention to the cultural differences between people of different cultures to be fully understood and noted. According to the reasoning that conceptual forms have relative stability, international students, who have been educated and nurtured by their own country and nationality's culture since childhood, are bound to have different perceptions of Chinese culture from those of Chinese culture transmitters. Thus, game developers must pay great attention to cultural differences in Chinese international education activities while looking for cultural similarities.

Also, a game developer can't disregard what the players think. When Zhongli first showed up, many players complained that their Zhongli wasn't as powerful as it was inside the episode. They thought miHoYo had nerfed Zhongli and even flirted with the idea that their Zhongli was crippled. So, they didn't buy into it, which set off a wave of refunds at the time. The topic continued to heat up and caught the attention of miHoYo, who soon issued an apology and announced that improvements would be made concerning Zhongli's image. This incident tells game developers that they can't just keep their heads in the game, but they also need to be good at listening to players' ideas and making reasonable changes. The combination of the two can better spread Chinese culture.

6   Conclusion

The soul of a game lies in the values implied, without which players achieve little when they exit the games. The exploration of *Genshin Impact's* international acceptance suggests that players, at home or abroad, are more likely to be motivated by the culture integrated into the game, the inquiry into the Chinese culture will serve as a ladder for further pursuit of Chinese language. When entertainment turns up to be challenging and engaging enough for a younger generation, there is the possibility of developing it into an effective learning method. Years ago, learners in China developed their enthusiasm for English learning through western popular culture, books, magazines, comics, games, popular songs, movies, etc. Chinese culture has a chance to repeat the story by pedagogically using games to nurture Chinese lovers. *Genshin Impact* provides a good beginning for spreading Chinese culture, and online games are designed instructively for situated learning. Game is not only a way of entertainment but a functional educational force.

Acknowledgments. This paper is supported by 2022 Key Project for Professional Comprehensive Reform at NingboTech University: Construction of International-Communication-Capacity-Oriented Experimental Teaching System and Cooperative Education Mechanism for New liberal Arts.

References

1. Said Edward, W.: Orientalism, 351p. Random House, New York (1979)
2. Bush, G.W.: Public Papers of the Presidents of the United States, George Bush. Government Printing Office, Washington D.C. (1992)
3. Svetlana, S., Aleksandra, M.: semantic emergence as a translation problem. Vestnik Volgogradskogo Gosudarstvennogo Universiteta. Serija 2. Jazykoznanije 16(3), 48–57 (2017)
4. Najita, T.: On Culture and Technology in Postmodern Japan. Postmodernism and Japan, pp. 1-20. North Carolina. Duke University Press, North Carolina (1989)
5. Aarseth, E.J.: Cybertext: Perspectives on Ergodic Literature. Johns Hopkins University Press, Baltimore (1997)
6. Salen, K., Zimmerman, E.: Rules of Play: Game Design Fundamentals. Massachusetts Institute of Technology Press, Cambridge (2003)
7. Bachell, A., Barr, M.: Video game preservation in the U.K.: a survey of records management practices. Int. J. Dyn. Control 9(2), 139–170 (2014)
8. Gjicali, K., Finn, B.M., Hebert, D.: Effects of belief generation on social exploration, culturally-appropriate actions, and cross-cultural concept learning in a game-based social simulation. Comput. Educ. **156**, 103959 (2020)
9. Ćwil, M., Howe, W.T.: Cross-cultural analysis of gamer identity: a comparison of the United States and Poland. Simul. Gaming **51**(6), 785–801 (2020)
10. Hanvey, R.G.: An attainable global perspective. Theory Pract. **21**(3), 162–167 (1982)
11. Straubhaar, J.D.: World Television: From Global to Local. Sage Publications, California (2007)
12. Piao, Y.: Study on the spread of Chinese short video in South Korea against the background of cross-cultural communication. In: 2nd International Conference on Language, Communication and Culture Studies (ICLCCS 2021), pp. 325–330. Atlantis Press, Amsterdam (2021)
13. Bao. G., Huang, D., Ding. W.:(tran.). Anecdotes About Spirits and Immortals. Foreign Languages Press, Beijing (2004)
14. Xun, L.: Mirror-looking. In: Selected Works of Lu Xun: vol. 1. People's Literature Publishing House, Beijing (2005)

An Enabling-Oriented Blended Teaching and Learning Ecosystem—Take the Data Structure and Algorithm Course as an Example

Jiawei Luo(✉) ⓘ, Weilan Qu, Xiaobo Yang, Hongbo Jiang, Yan Xia, and Guanghua Tan

College of Information Science and Engineering, Hunan University, Changsha 410083, China
{luojiawei,qwlan,jt_yangxb,hongbojiang,xiayan,
guanghuatan}@hnu.edu.cn

Abstract. Based on the reform of online and offline blended teaching, this paper constructs an enabling-oriented 3324 blended teaching and learning ecosystem. Taking the data structure and algorithm course as an example, this paper expounds on the design and implementation process of the teaching ecosystem based on the teaching philosophy and goal orientation of this course and explains the application of these reform measures during actual teaching. This teaching and learning ecosystem highlights the deep fusion of enabling education and blended teaching and shows the effect of teaching reform according to the final multi-dimensional teaching evaluation results.

Keywords: online and offline blended teaching · enabling education · teaching and learning ecosystem · teaching design

1 Introduction

It is the main responsibility of universities to cultivate talents, and curriculum is the core element of talent cultivation, therefore, the quality of curriculum directly determines the quality of talent cultivation. In 2019, the Ministry of Education of the People's Republic of China promulgated the "Opinions on the Implementation of First-class Undergraduate Curriculum Construction" [1], which clearly elaborates the general requirements for "first-class curriculum construction". To build first-class undergraduate curricula that meet the requirements of the new era, it proposes the requirements of "Improving high-level", "Highlighting innovation" and "Increasing challenge" (IHI). Therefore, in the new era, it is imperative to build a new teaching model that meets the standards of IHI.

Based on the orientation of Hunan University, we take the course "Data Structure and Algorithm" as the research carrier, combine the Outcome-Based Education (OBE) engineering education concept with the requirements of online and offline blended first-class courses, build a 3324 blended teaching and learning ecosystem, and achieve the deep fusion of enabling education and blended teaching.

2 Enabling-Oriented Teaching Philosophy

Under the background of emerging engineering education in the new era [2], it is required to increase students' investment in learning, evaluate examinations strictly, and enhance students' sense of achievement in gaining ability and quality improvement through hard studying. The data structure and algorithm course, as a basic course in the second semester of freshman, needs to gradually cultivate students' ability to simplify the complex and the way of thinking in the transition from science to engineering.

The setting of curriculum goals, combined with the characteristics of the curriculum and professional requirements, emphasizes student-centered enabling education. The course goal is to adhere to the organic integration of knowledge, ability, quality, and to cultivate students' comprehensive ability and advanced thinking to solve complex problems.

The golden standard of IHI emphasizes breadth and depth, of course, breaks through habitual cognitive patterns, and cultivates students' spirit and ability to analyze, question, and innovate. The combination of cutting-edge technology content with case-based teaching reflects the "height" of the course; the combination of professional expansion content with group discussions reflects the "breadth" of the course; the combination of course key points with inquiry-based teaching reflects the "depth" of the course; The content of professional interviews and disciplinary competitions is combined with the construction of course resources to reflect the "hotness" of the course.

In the implementation of teaching, the cultivation of outstanding ability goals runs through the whole process of course teaching, while a single education model cannot meet the requirements of course teaching. Therefore, it is necessary to use the course platform to establish various course resources to assist teaching, such as MOOCs [3], which is a kind of "online" and "offline" blended teaching platform. Simple and easy-to-understand basic knowledge is learned independently by students by watching MOOC videos pre-class, while abstract and difficult theories are organized, explored, and integrated by teachers in class. Through the dynamic combination of these two teaching organization forms, course learning can be guided from shallow to deep, and the deep integration of enabling education and blended education can be achieved.

3 Teaching Goal Orientation

The teaching goals of the data structure and algorithm course follow the three-in-one education model which includes knowledge imparting, ability training, and value shaping. Through the combination of online and offline theoretical and practical learning, students can understand the principles of data structures, the ideas of algorithms, and the measurement method of algorithm complexity. And according to the characteristics of the applied data and the space-time constraints of the problem, they can choose a reasonable data structures and algorithms to control the complexity of time and space (simplify the complexity), which can cultivate and improve students' theoretical, abstract, and design abilities (computational thinking ability). Meanwhile, we can cultivate students' awareness and ability of independent learning, team communication, and adaptive development through the pre-class preview, small class discussion, group cooperation, and information retrieval. Teaching goals also include developing the ability to evaluate other people's programs and work and self-expression, and to independently analyze and comprehensively solve practical problems (engineering thinking ability).

Cognitive goals follow Bloom's cognitive classification rules. For example, when explaining the shortest path problem, cognitive goals are divided into four levels: memory, understanding, application, and analysis. The "memory" level requires students to recognize what is the shortest path problem. The "understanding" level requires students to understand the shortest path algorithm Dijkstra's algorithm and to explain the shortest path calculation method. The "application" level requires applying Dijkstra's algorithm to solve the shortest path problem independently. The "Analysis" level requires a Spatio-Temporal analysis of Dijkstra's algorithm.

In the new era, ability training follows the requirements of cultivating new engineering students, and cultivates students' "computational thinking ability", "innovative thinking ability", "self-learning ability", and "system thinking ability". For example, we can help students to understand the importance of systems thinking by analyzing and comparing the advantages and disadvantages between Dijkstra's algorithm and Freud's algorithm. In the aspect of value shaping, we focus on enabling students to establish a rigorous engineering attitude, a scientific academic attitude, and the spirit of craftsmanship of a great country that strives for perfection. With the national sentiment and mission of serving the country through science and technology, they can become engineering and technological talents in the new era with both political integrity and ability.

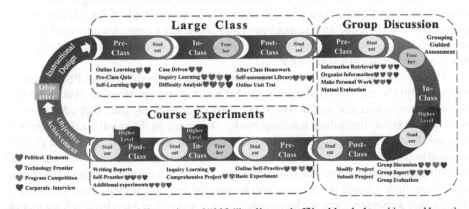

Fig. 1. Constructing an enabling-oriented "3324" online and offline blended teaching and learning ecosystem

4 The Construction of Teaching and Learning Ecosystem

Taking the data structure and algorithm course as an example, this paper constructs an enabling-oriented "3324" online and offline blended teaching and learning ecosystem, as shown in (Fig. 1). The course is enabling-oriented in teaching design and teaching implementation, based on the large cycle model of teaching units and supported by 3 teaching links (large class teaching, small class discussion, and course experiment). This teaching model runs through three stages: pre-class, in-class, and post-class to highlight the dual face-to-face teaching and online supplementary. Combined with the teaching philosophy of teacher-led and student-centered, we embedded the four aspects of ideological and political elements, technological frontiers, program competitions, and corporate interviews in the teaching content to achieve a deep fusion of enabling education and blended teaching.

The online and offline blended teaching and learning ecosystem is based on the large cycle of teaching units, which includes five classic algorithm design units: algorithm analysis, linear structure, tree structure, graph structure, search, and sorting algorithm.

4.1 "3" Teaching Links

The three teaching links include large class teaching, small class discussion, and course experiment. In order to realize the transformation from a "teaching"-based model to the "self-learning"-based mode, the online and offline blended teaching is carried out using the information resources of the course platform. In detail, offline class hours are allocated 46 h, 16 h, and 16 h respectively, and online class hours are allocated 10 h, 14 h, and 16 h respectively. Meanwhile, the class adopts the teaching model of "large class teaching and small class discussion".

The large class teaching adopts various teaching methods such as PBL, inquiry-based, BOPPPS, etc. It also integrates the MOOC resource platform to extend the theoretical class to extracurricular. The small class discussion uses the flipped classroom with online and offline mixed teaching mode. The theme of the small class course is to expand the course knowledge. The personal information submitted before the class is applied to the mutual evaluation among students. Each assignment is randomly assigned to 3 students for evaluation. The students will evaluate each other according to the rating scale (see Table 1), and the average will be divided into the grades of the small class. The practical course adopts the hierarchical online and offline blended teaching model, based on the characteristics of the freshman students with a weak programming foundation and the large differences. At the same time, we take into account the "high-level, innovative, challenging" goals of the course, and design multi-level experiments, which are divided into four levels from simple to difficult: preliminary experiments, basic experiments, comprehensive experiments, and additional experiments. An experimental question bank containing four levels is established on the experimental platform [4].

4.2 "3" Teaching Stages

Table 1. Data structures and algorithms profile rating scale

Indicator Item Name	Total Score	Comments	Score
Submit Specification and Content Correctness and Integrity	40	Submit the materials collected and prepared before the class as required, the report format is standardized and the content is complete	40
		Submit the materials collected and prepared before the class as required, the report format is relatively standardized and the content is relatively complete	32
		Submit the materials collected and prepared pre-class as required, but the report format is not standardized or the content is not complete enough	24
		Incorrect submission method (not submitted as attachment)	0
		The file format and name are incorrect (no pdf file was submitted or the file name is irregular or leaks personal information)	0
		The submitted content does not match the assignment task	0
Format of Document Content	10	Excellent typographic format	10
		Good typographic format	8
		Fair typographic format	6
		Wrong typographic format	0
Reference	10	Standard bibliography citation	10
		Relatively standard bibliography citation	8
		Basically standard bibliography citation	6
		Irregular bibliography citation	0
Report Material Content	30	The content material is reasonable and effective, and the explanation is clear	30
		The content material is relatively reasonable and effective, and the explanation is relatively clearer	24
		The content is effective and the explanation is basically clear	18
		The content material has major problems or is unclear	10
		Content does not meet requirements	0
Reporting Level	10	Be able to correctly use course knowledge such as data structures and algorithms to organize materials, and complete reports according to discussion requirements	10
		Be able to relatively correctly use course knowledge such as data structures and algorithms to organize materials, and relatively complete reports according to the discussion requirements	8
		Able to use course knowledge such as data structure and algorithms to organize materials, and basically complete the report according to the discussion requirements	6
		There are many obvious mistakes in the course knowledge of data structures and algorithms used	4
		Failure to properly use course knowledge such as data structures and algorithms to organize materials	0

The three teaching stages are pre-class, in-class, and post-class. Table 2 shows the teaching stages corresponding to the three teaching links.

Table 2. Each link stage of the big cycle of the teaching unit

Teaching stage Teaching link	Pre-class	In class	Post-class
Large class	Release preview tasks completed independently by students, such as watching the video, self-testing knowledge points, and online learning must-test tasks	Focus on guiding students' participation and inquiry, using PBL, inquiry, BOPPPS, and other teaching methods	Further consolidate knowledge through homework, discussion and posting, and self-assessment question bank
Group discussion	Complete personal information search, sorting, submission, and mutual evaluation	Group discussion and group presentation on extended knowledge	Use the smart teaching platform to conduct class evaluation and interaction, organize, and submit group reports post-class
Course experiment	Independently complete preparatory experiments and basic experiments, i.e., self-testing of verification experiments	Complete algorithm designing, code writing, compiling, debugging, and running of comprehensive experiments	Independently choose to complete additional experiments depend on students' abilities and interests

4.3   "2" Role Fliping

In order to help the freshmen gradually get rid of the memory-based tactics of high school, we design the ability-based training model and all teaching links are student-centered. The blended teaching model runs through all teaching activities. There are 10 full-online learning hours in the large class, and online learning tasks will be pushed to the students. Then, students will actively master the basic knowledge by watching the video of the MOOC pre-class and consolidate their foundation through the self-assessment question bank of knowledge points. And the classroom adopts an inquiry-based teaching model, which emphasizes inquiry and multi-interaction, to greatly mobilize students' learning enthusiasm and initiative. Meanwhile, small-class discussion topics cover advanced data structures and algorithms, highlight the difficulty and breadth of the major, and allow students to collect, organize, discuss and report, which improves students' ability to collect and organize information and self-learning. The experimental course highlights "hierarchical experiments" and the experiments are divided into preliminary experiments, basic experiments, comprehensive experiments, and additional experiments, which is conducive to selective practical training based on students' personality characteristics and knowledge reserves. It can allow students easily achieve success and improve their professional interest and sense of identity. Teachers play a guiding and auxiliary role, complete the reversal of the two roles of teaching and learning, and realize the transformation from teachers' "teaching" to students' "learning".

4.4 "4" High-Level Elements

The "4" high-level elements are ideological and political elements, technological frontiers, program competitions, and corporate interviews.

Table 3. Grade composition of data structures and algorithms course

Score Composition	Assessment Name	Proportion	Examination Content	Evaluation Method	Evaluation Subject
General Performance	Online learning	5%	Video viewing tasks	Automatic evaluation	Course Platform
	Post-class homework	5%	Solving method and process of questions	Teaching assistant review	Teaching assistant
	Online unit testing	10%	Comprehensive knowledge	Automatic evaluation / Manual review	Course Platform/ The teacher
	Small class discussion	3%	Personal information	Mutual evaluation	Student
		7%	Group class performance/Group report	Group evaluation/ Teacher assessment	Student/Teacher
	Course experiment	10%	Basic experiment/Code test/Everyone pass	Automatic evaluation	CG system
		10%	Comprehensive Experiment	Automatic evaluation/ Online review	CG Systems / Teaching Assistant / The teacher
Midterm	Midterm	10%	Knowledge, Application, Analysis, Synthesis	Manual marking	Teachers
Final Exam	Final exam	40%	Knowledge, Application, Analysis, Synthesis	Manual marking	Teachers

First, we combine the characteristics of the data structure and algorithm course and the actual situation of the disciplines to explore the ideological and political education elements in the course. For example, when explaining the introduction of algorithms, we will talk about the abacus from ancient times to the current supercomputer, which not only contains the wisdom of our ancestors, but also the hard-working spirit of contemporary scientific and technological workers. This is an independent development path with

Chinese characteristics, which enhances students' national pride and inspires students' feelings and responsibilities to serve the country through science and technology.

We integrate into various technological frontiers when telling the knowledge of each chapter of the course. For example, when explaining the hash function, it is introduced that SHA256 is the main cryptographic hash function used to construct the blockchain. Whether it is the header information of the block or the transaction data, this hash function is used to calculate the hash value of the relevant data to ensure the integrity of the data. In this way, it not only broadens students' knowledge but also enhances students' professional interest and sense of identity.

For freshman students, they usually use the blended teaching model to acquire theoretical knowledge. However, because the freshman students have a relatively weak coding foundation, are not exposed to many algorithms, and without programming skills, it is necessary to strengthen the learning of the algorithm and develop programming skills.

We organize the exercises of ACM competition and CSP programming certification into the application cases taught in the course, the classic example resource in the MOOC and the course experiments. For example, when describing the Kruskal algorithm of minimum spanning tree, we lead the students to solve the exercise of "Data Center of CSP-201812-4", the fourth question of CSP certification in December 2018. At the same time, we optimize and increase MOOC resources, and incorporate interview questions from technology companies into student practice and self-test sessions such as ByteDance, Huawei, Tencent, Microsoft, Ali, and Baidu.

Two high-level elements of program competition and corporate interview are implanted into the teaching content, which can greatly stimulate students' interest in learning, complete the cognitive practice of "integration of knowledge and action", and achieve the consolidation of knowledge.

5 Innovation of Evaluation Mechanism

We apply diversified ways to evaluate, highlight the process achievements, and synchronize the progress of the assessment and teaching. (1) Diversified evaluation contents include online learning, homework, unit tests, small class discussions, and course experiments. (2) Diversified evaluation methods include mutual evaluation between students and students, mutual evaluation in groups, system evaluation, teaching assistant, and teacher evaluation. (3) Diversified evaluation results include awards for excellent course performance, presentation of high-quality works and verbal real-name recognition, etc. We also develop a rating scale, which can automatically generate ratings and comments, as shown in Table 3.

6 Implementation Effect

Curriculum reform has been ongoing. In 2013, the teaching model of "large class teaching and small class discussion" was implemented, which took students as the center, using flipped classroom and inquiry-based teaching methods. The MOOCs was started to build in 2015 by gradually building teaching cases and question banks, and completed the construction in 2017 by officially launching online and offline blended teaching. In

2019, centering on the fundamental task of fostering integrity and promoting rounded development of people, the data structure and algorithm ideological and political brand course will be carried out.

The data structure and algorithm course has improved the teaching quality in six aspects. (1) Excellent course: The course is a school brand course, provincial excellent course, and provincial first-class online and offline blended course. It has a good foundation and insists on continuous improvement. There are 2 MOOCs courses And These MOOCs courses are convenient for students to watch internalized knowledge repeatedly. The classic example website covers knowledge series, classic example explanations, real postgraduate examination questions, real course examination questions, and interview questions. Multi-level example questions can expand knowledge, which can improve students' thinking ability to analyze and explore problems. (2) Excellent teachers: The teaching team includes well-known professors and returnee professors with research backgrounds, as well as basic-teaching teachers who are excellent in teaching and are most popular with students. They insist on teaching and educating people while actively teaching and researching. The structure of the teaching team is reasonable and can be very effective. And it can well integrate the frontier of science and technology into teaching and improve the height and breadth of the course teaching content. (3) Active Classroom: we use teaching methods and information technology to focus on "exploration" and "interaction", use Learning-Pass to carry out the interaction between teacher and student, and use smart classrooms and flipped teaching methods to improve students' participation rate and teaching quality. (4) Busy Students: we rely on ChaoXing platform and CG training platform to establish 2 large practical training question banks, which can help students to conduct self-training according to the teaching progress. And practical training question banks and blended teaching allow students to combine learning and practice. (5) Strict assessment: The diversified evaluation mechanism is synchronized with the teaching progress, highlighting the process assessment, strictly tracking each teaching link, and assessing each stage. (6) Good effect: The students' ability of theory, abstraction, design, and analysis has been steadily improved, and they have achieved excellent results in various program and algorithm competitions, such as the second place in International Parallel Computing Challenge (IPCC) in 2020, and the first prize of 2021 and second prize of 2022 in the ASC Student Supercomputer Competition.

7 Conclusion

Based on the large unit cycle of curriculum knowledge, we construct a teaching and learning ecosystem that is deeply fusion enabling education and blended teaching. The construction process is easily copied by other courses and has strong operability, which provides new teaching ideas in emerging engineering education background. Teaching practice shows that 3324 teaching and learning ecosystem can effectively improve teaching effect, highlighting the new teaching model centered on cultivating students' ability. Particularly, we through a "combination of learning and practice" to improve students' ability. And the integration of four high-level elements can better stimulate students' professional identity and learning interests. Further reform attempts will be made to the data structure and algorithm courses in the two aspects of "horizontal and vertical". The horizontal aspect is through the horizontal connection of courses in the entire subject system to promote the reform of other courses and form a series of curriculum reform models main-based enablement. In vertical aspects, it mainly aims at different students to carry out personalized stratified teaching. Based on the current experimental stratification, we implement stratified teaching in each stage of the course, so that some students with a poor foundation will not be affected by the difficulty of the course, and some students with a good foundation and outstanding learning ability have better room for display.

Acknowledgment. We thank the financial support from Hunan Province Online and Offline Blended First-Class Courses of "Data Structure and Algorithm", (Hunan Education [2021] No. 322; Serial number: 459).

References

1. Young, M.: The Technical Writer's Handbook. University Science, Mill Valley (1989). Ministry of Education of the People's Republic of China. Notice of the Ministry of Education on Printing and Distributing the "Implementation Opinions on the Construction of First-Class Undergraduate Courses" [EB/OL]. (24 Oct 2019). http://www.gov.cn/gongbao/content/2020/content_5480494.htm. Accessed 20 Feb 2020
2. Dekai, T., Xinwen, X., Xiaolin, G.: Exploration of college computer curriculum reform for enabling education under emerging engineering education background. Comput. Educ. **9**, 178–182 (2020)
3. Shuyan, W., Jiani, Z., Yan, W., et al.: Design and practice of a blended teaching model of "Enabling Education"—taking the data structure and algorithm course as an example. Comput. Educ. **4**, 110–113 (2020)
4. Weilan, Q., Xiaohong, L., Xiaobo, Y., et al.: Teaching reform and practice of data structure test based on "six-dimensional integration and innovative teaching closed Loop". Comput. Educ. **4**, 77–81 (2021)

Attention Cloud Map: Visualizing Attention Migration of Students' Debugging Process in Semantic Code Space

Jiayi Zeng, Wei Liu[✉], Ying Zhou, Xinyu Li, and Wenqing Cheng

Hubei Key Laboratory of Smart Internet Technology, School of Electronic Information and Communications, Huazhong University of Science and Technology, Wuhan 430074, China
{zeng_jiayi,liuwei,zhouyinghust,lixinyuhust,chengwq}@hust.edu.cn

Abstract. Researchers explored the cognitive process of students by analyzing their eye-tracking data in some specified computer programming tasks. Although there are some quantified analysis and data visualization methods proposed in this area, none of them is designed to visualize the attention migration in debugging task. In this paper, we designed a novel kind of chart, i.e. Attention Cloud Map (ACM), for this purpose. We model the semantic code space into a polar coordinate system, and map the code lines and functions of the test program are mapped into points and sectors. We put the bug line in the center point, and mark the relevant code areas in the code space. By plotting the heat map of the amount of eye fixation attention in given time slices, we can obtain a serial of attention distributions in the code space. Experiment results show that, such attention cloud map can enable us to observe the debugging strategy of individual student, and abstract the average progress of one student group, which can be provide some references for the evaluation of students' debugging performances.

Keywords: eye-tracking · visualization · debugging process · semantic code space

1 Introduction

Debugging tests are widely adopted in assessing the students' programming skills in computer education. Besides the submission results of source code, various kinds of measurements have been conducted to record the students' behavior during the debugging test, in which the eye tracking measurement is adopted to estimate the students' visual attention.

Researchers explored the cognitive process of students by analyzing their eye-tracking data in some specified computer programming tasks. For instance, Obaidellah et al. [1] recorded students' eye-tracking data, and performed an

W. Hong and Y. Weng (Eds.): ICCSE 2022, CCIS 1813, pp. 481–491, 2023.
https://doi.org/10.1007/978-981-99-2449-3_42

Area of Interest (AoI) sequence analysis to identify their reading strategies in programming tests. The measurement data of eye movement consists the two-dimension screen coordinates and time stamps. Due to the complexity of human behavior, it is not easy to analyze the eye tracking results by pure quantified methods. Therefore, visualization approaches are indispensable in eye-tracking analysis.

There have been various kinds visualization tools proposed for eye movement data, such as Attention heatmap [2], Timeline flow [3], AOI transition graph [4], and etc. They were adopted to analyse the different reading strategies and programming behaviors. However, none of the existing visualization tools is designed for the debugging task, and thus they ignore the relationships among the normal lines and the bug lines. They rely on the original code space, and they cannot represent the semantic information of the code.

The behavior of tracking source code is quite normal in debugging test. The visualization of students' attention on semantic code space will be helpful for the understanding students' debugging progress. To this end, we propose a novel visualization method named Attention Cloud Map (ACM). It incorporates semantic information of code lines and supports attention heatmap migration observations. Experiments show that our visualization method presents students' debugging behavior as an attention converging process that gradually gets close to the center of ACM.

The main work and contributions of this paper include:

- A novel polar coordinate system is proposed to model the semantic code space of one program. The code lines and functions of the test program are mapped into points and sectors.
- A layout scheme is adopted to highlight the logic clue of bug for the analysis of debugging progress. The bug line is put in the circle center, and the relevant code is marked by nearby sectors.
- A attention cloud map is present to visualize the migration of students' fixation attention in semantic code space. Different from the existing visualize tool, it is superimposable, which means it is applicable not only for an individual but also a group.

The remainder of paper is organized as follows: Sect. 2 reviews the existing visualizations. Section 3 states our test material and scenario. Section 4 introduces the design work. Section 5 presents some representative results, followed by the conclusion in Sect. 6.

2   Related Work

Various visualization tools were developed to enhance eye movement analysis [2]. Some of them have been utilized for the eye-tracking measurement in programming education.

Attention Heatmap [2]: It can visualize the counts of fixations, the number of users who fixed on different areas, the absolute or relative fixation duration, and etc. Abid et al. [5] generated attention heatmap to show programmers' visual attention distribution on line level.

Timeline Flow [3]: It plots fixation points along time, showing the programmers' reading path and even patterns along time. The code space is commonly compressed into line numbers [6]. Based on timeline flow visualization, Clark et al. [7] introduced the skyline visualization, which showed the duration of fixation and saccade in time.

AOI transition Graph [4]: It indicates the attention transition among multiple pre-marked area of interest (AOI) [8]. AOIs are placed in different segments in a circle, whose sizes are determined by the AOI dwell time. Peterson et al. [9] reported the AOI transition graph results of novices and experts in reading C++ code snippets.

Embedded Space Graph [10]: It map the functions to the semantic embedding space represented as a scatter plot on a two-dimensional coordinate system. The eye-tracking data of the participants is also mapped to the semantic embedding space in the form of scattered points. However, they only take into account the coarse-grained relationships of function calling, rather than the semantic relationships among lines.

In summary, none of the existing visualization tools is designed to visualize the attention migration in debugging task. They rely on the original code space, and ignore the relationships among the normal lines and the bug lines. Novel visualization tool is required for this purpose.

3   Testing Scenario and Material

We setup a test scenario of ten computers, to collect the students' eye tracking data during the debugging test. Each computer was installed with an Tobii EyeX eye tracker, and connected in the same LAN. We adopt the Eclipse IDE in test, and installed iTrace plug-in [11] with Eclipse to collect eye movement data.

We prepared a C-language program as our test material. Its purpose is to calculate the intersections of two integer arrays. It has four functions, including `main()`, `resetArray()`, `displayArray()` and `getInsectionSet()`. The bug is located on line 102 in function `getInsectionSet()`.

Figure 1 shows a part of the testing materials, in which two functions are shown but some lines are skipped and represented as "region". The bug is in line 102 of the function `getInsectionSet()`, which is a misuse of pointer type variable `interSize`. Tracing this bug requires reading the line 39 in the caller function `main()`. Although they are far away from the original code space, they are relevant in the view of semantic code space. Since the existing visualization methods for eye movement (such as [2–4]) utilized the original code space, the tracing behavior on these lines will be plotted discontinuously, and therefore not appropriate for observing the debugging process.

```
22      int *getIntersection( const int *array1, const int *array2, int *interSize);
23
24      int main( void )
25    ⊞ {region ...
37          int *interSet = NULL;
38          int interSize = 0;
39          interSet = getIntersection( array1, array2, &interSize );
40    ⊞     printf("intersection set: ");region ...
68    ⊟ int *getIntersection( const int *array1, const int *array2, int *interSize)
69    ⊞ {region ...
97    ⊟             if ( *interSize == 0 || *p3 != *p1 )
98                  {
99                      *p3 = *p1;
100                     printf("   *p3 = %d, *interSize = %d \n", *p3, *interSize );
101                     p3 ++;
102                     interSize ++;
103                 }
```

Fig. 1. Partial view of the tested C program

4 Visualization Method Design

4.1 Motivation

In the original code space, it is difficult to find the migration pattern that attention heatmaps convergent to a bug without manually consulting the test material. The semantic code space is more suitable to observe the students' tracing and debugging behavior. There have been some models to describe the semantic relationships of source code lines, such as Abstract Syntax Tree (AST) [10] and Control Flow Graph (CFG) [12]. AST is a logical tree that retains only the important branches of the program syntax structure. The code lines in the same control flow are in the same layer of AST. CFG is a kind of marked-directed graph obtained by simplifying the program flow diagram, which reflects the logical order of code execution. However, these tree-like models are not designed for the representation of semantic code space.

In this paper, we are motivated to propose a novel visualization chart to observe the students' attention in tracing particular source blocks. Our design objectives include: (1) to visualize the semantic code space of the test program, where the program execution logic could be observed; (2) to highlight the bug line in the space, which helps the observation of debugging process.

In order to address the above problem, we intend to represent the attention migration during debugging as a dynamic chart indicating the convergence to a central point, in which the center is the code line where the bug is located. We adopt a circle area to indicate the semantic code space and map the code lines in the points of different AoI sectors. By plotting the heat map of the amount of eye fixation attention, we can obtain a serial of attention distributions in the code space, which look like the satellite cloud map. Therefore, we name the serial of charts as Attention Cloud Map (ACM).

4.2   Visualization of Semantic Code Space

We visualize the semantic code space in the form of polar coordinates, with the bug line as its origin point. Each code line can be represented as a point in the polar coordinate system. The angle θ and radius r of one point indicate the physical distance and semantic distance of the corresponding line to the bug line. The basic design is illustrated in Fig. 2.

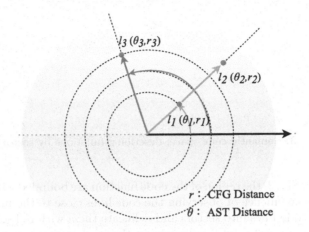

Fig. 2. Semantic code space: describing code lines by polar coordinates

Representation of Code Lines. For each line, we calculate its coordinates of θ and r by its physical and semantic distances to the bug line. We define CFG distance as the inverse of the weight of each code line vertices in the adjacency matrix generated by the CFG, and calculate one line's r by its CFG distance to the bug line. We define AST distance as the difference between two layers in the AST graph and calculate one line's θ by its AST distance to the bug line.

The relationships of θ and r values can be illustrated by some samples in Fig. 2. Given three lines l_1, l_2 and l_3, they are represented by three points in the semantic code space. Assuming that lines l_1 and l_2 are in the same if-conditional control statement brunch, thus they have the same direction, i.e. same θ. Assuming that l_3 is more close to the bug line, thus it has a smaller r than l_2 in the figure.

Representation of Functions. After the above processing, all code lines can be mapped into points in the semantic space. Then we manually label the code regions that are closely associated with bugs, and calculate their locations in the semantic code space. We start from the zero angle direction, and mark the region of each function according to their distance to the function having bug. One example is shown in Fig. 3.

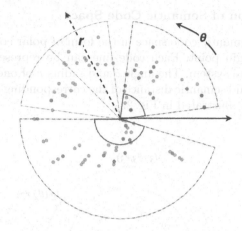

Fig. 3. Semantic code space: describing functions by sectors

As shown in Fig. 3, the region of the code function are bounded with red dashed lines. For the convenience of observing the code lines close to the bug, we cluster those relevant code lines into sectors and delineate them with red solid lines. The sectors bounded by red solid lines represent the most important regions for bug finding, we call them core areas. They provide semantic references for us to investigate when and how the students' attention approaches the bug-related regions.

4.3   Visualization of Eye Fixation Attention

In order to generate the serial of attention cloud map, we need to divide the whole debugging process into T equal slices. Without lossing the generality, we set T as ten in our practice. We use the same method as Andrienko et al. [2] to accumulate the eye-tracking data and plot the attention heatmap in the generated semantic code space. Figure 4 is an example.

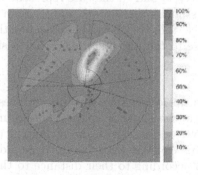

Fig. 4. Attention Cloud Map: eye fixation attention heat map

As shown in Fig. 4, each function is marked by a circular sector with dotted lines. The colorbar on the right shows the coloring scheme. The percentage in the colorbar represents the ratio of the student's amount of eye fixation to the whole process. Such one chart can help us observe where the student's attention distributes, and the time serial of these charts can describe the student's attention migration during the debugging process.

5   Experiment and Result

5.1   Generation of Attention Cloud Maps

We mapped the code lines into semantic code space. The final result is shown in Fig. 5. The mapping range details of each function are listed in Table 1. Among the five functions in the program, the most important function is getInsection(). The partial view of its mapping result is indicated in Fig. 6.

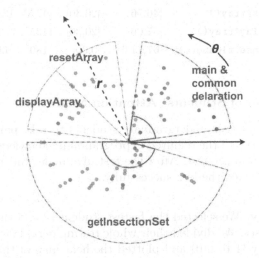

Fig. 5. Visualization result of semantic code space: function sectors

We take the code blocks from line 99 to 101 as an example. Their distance to the bug line 102 is decreasing, thus their r decrease sequentially. They are in the same if-conditional control statement brunch (see Fig. 1), therefore they share the same direction θ. Code line 98 only contains a meaningless bracket, thus sharing the same r with line 99 in Fig. 6.

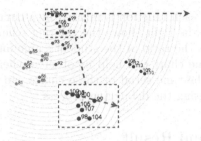

Fig. 6. Visualization result of semantic code space: particular lines

Table 1. Visualized code space of the test program

Code block	line range	r range	θ range
common declaration	[1,23]	[5,30]	[7.5°, 82.5°]
main()	[24,45]	[5,30]	[7.5°, 82.5°]
resetArray()	[46,56]	[20,30]	[97.5°, 135°]
displayArray()	[57,66]	[20,30]	(135°, 172.5°]
getInsectionSet()	[67,113]	[0,30]	(180°, 343.7°]

5.2   Observation of Students' Attention Migration

We recruited 10 first-year undergraduate students to take part in the test. All
the students had learned the required C programming knowledge, and they were
numbered s1 to s10 in the test. After the test, five male students (s1, s2, s4, s7,
and s9) found and fixed the bug successfully.

Individual Study. We selected the fastest student s2 and the slowest student
s7 as our study cases. We divided their whole testing period evenly into ten time
slices (indicated by t1 to t10) and plotted the heat map of their eye attentions
in our proposed chart. The results are presented in Fig. 7.

The relevant code space of the bug line is marked by a red circle in each ACM
chart. By observing the time slice when one student's attention came into or left
this bug-related circle, we could estimate their progress in the whole debugging
mission. As shown in Fig. 7(a), student s2 began to put his attention on the bug
area at time slice t2, and stayed there until the end of the test. These cloud maps
imply that he was quite efficient in finding the bug, and only spent 10% of the
total time. In contrast, as shown in Fig. 7(b), student s7 focused the bug area as
late as time slice t8. His attention was distributed counterclockwisely from t1 to
t7, which implies he was tracing the source code in functions one by one in the
linear sequence.

Group Study. As indicated by the case study results, we can observe different
debugging strategies of the students through the serial of ACM charts. In the

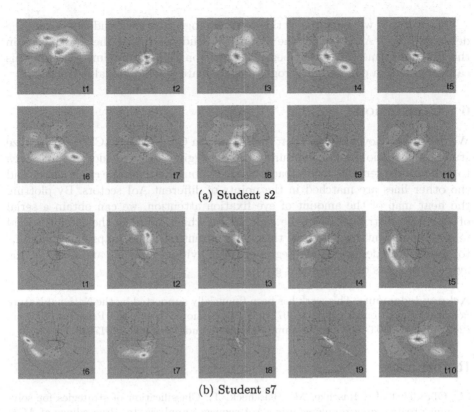

(a) Student s2

(b) Student s7

Fig. 7. Attention migration of two students: the fastest student s2 and the slowest student s7

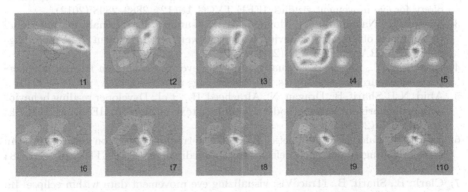

Fig. 8. Attention migration of the group of five students

following experiment, we investigate the common features of students' attention migration by plot the sum of their fixation attentions in ACM charts. The result is provided in Fig. 8.

From Fig. 8, we can observe the average progress of five students during the debugging test. As shown in the figure, the students traced the source code in the first four time slices, and began to focus on the bug in time slice t5. This can provide us a comparable progress to evaluate the individual performance.

6   Conclusion

We designed a novel kind of chart, i.e. Attention Cloud Map (ACM), to visualize students' attention migration during the debugging test. We adopt a circle area to indicate the semantic code space, where the bug line is in the circle center and the other lines are matched in the points of different AoI sectors. By plotting the heat map of the amount of eye fixation attention, we can obtain a serial of attention distributions in the code space, which look like the satellite cloud map. Experiment results show that, such attention cloud maps can enable us to observe the debugging strategies of an individual student, and abstract the average progress of one student group.

Acknowledgment. This work has been financially supported by the National Nature Science Foundation of China (61977064), the National Key R&D Program of China (2021YFC3340803) and the Teaching Research Funds of HUST (2017049).

References

1. Obaidellah, U., Raschke, M., Blascheck, T.: Classification of strategies for solving programming problems using AoI sequence analysis. In: Proceedings of ACM ETRA, pp. 1–9 (2019)
2. Andrienko, G., Andrienko, N., Burch, M., Weiskopf, D.: Visual analytics methodology for eye movement studies. IEEE TVCG **18**(12), 2889–2898 (2012)
3. Uwano, H., Nakamura, M., Monden, A., Matsumoto, K.-I.: Analyzing individual performance of source code review using reviewers' eye movement. In: Proceedings of ACM ETRA, pp. 133–140 (2006)
4. Blascheck, T., Sharif, B.: Visually analyzing eye movements on natural language texts and source code snippets. In: Proceedings of ACM ETRA, pp. 1–9 (2019)
5. Abid, N.J., Sharif, B., Dragan, N., Alrasheed, H., et al.: Developer reading behavior while summarizing java methods: size and context matters. In: IEEE/ACM ICSE, pp. 384–395 (2019)
6. Sharif, B., Falcone, M., Maletic, J.I.: An eye-tracking study on the role of scan time in finding source code defects. In: Proceedings of ACM ETRA, pp. 381–384 (2012)
7. Clark, B., Sharif, B.: iTraceVis: visualizing eye movement data within eclipse. In: Proceedings of IEEE VISSOFT, pp. 22–32 (2017)
8. Blascheck, T., Raschke, M., Ertl, T.: Circular heat map transition diagram. In: Proceedings of Conference on Eye Tracking South Africa, pp. 58–61 (2013)
9. Peterson, C.S., Saddler, J.A., Blascheck, T., Sharif, B.: Visually analyzing students' gaze on C++ code snippets. In: Proceedings of IEEE EMIP, pp. 18–25 (2019)
10. Zhang, L., Sun, J., Peterson, C., Sharif, B., et al.: Exploring eye tracking data on source code via dual space analysis. In: Proceedings of IEEE VISSOFT, pp. 67–77 (2019)

11. Shaffer, T.R., Wise, J.L., Walters, B.M., Müller, S.C., et al.: iTrace: enabling eye tracking on software artifacts within the IDE to support software engineering tasks. In: Proceedings of ESEC/FSE (2015)
12. Arora, V., Bhatia, R.K., Singh, M.: Evaluation of flow graph and dependence graphs for program representation. Int. J. Comput. Appl. **56**(14), 18–23 (2012)

Research on the Database Construction of Talents for Professional Chinese in the Energy Industry

Zeng Xiaoyan(⊠) (iD)

China University of Petroleum-Beijing, Beijing, China
xiaoyan03zeng@cup.edu.cn

Abstract. At present, the supply of professional Chinese talents in the energy industry is inadequate to meet the demands of the national energy strategy and energy cooperation under the background of "Belt and Road Initiative". The training units lack a comprehensive and systematic understanding of the type and quantity of required talents, preventing them from conducting systematic research on talent training systems for professional Chinese. Therefore, this paper proposes using the theory of complex dynamic theory and big data method to extract the characteristics and relevant parameters of talents for professional Chinese required by energy cooperation in "Belt and Road Initiative", to build a database for the cultivation of talents for professional Chinese in the energy industry, and to provide a reference for the cultivation of talents for professional Chinese in other domestic colleges.

Keywords: Professional Chinese in energy industry · Database · Talent training · Chinese + vocational education

1 Introduction

Energy cooperation is an important aspect of "Belt and Road Initiative" and the training of language talents is a major factor in the success of energy cooperation. Strengthening the training of language talents for professional Chinese in the energy industry conforms to the needs of national strategy as well as the development of the times. Therefore, a targeted database of talents for professional Chinese in the energy industry should be built to quickly search for high-quality Chinese language talents for energy enterprises. Since "Belt and Road Initiative" was put forward, Zheng Tongtao and other scholars have published the first book about the training of professional talents in "Belt and Road Initiative" at home and abroad. Based on research and the collection, collation and analysis of data, Zheng explores how to dovetail the concept, approach, mode and mechanism of nationalized talent training for "Belt and Road Initiative". He forms a strong synergy for talent training for "Belt and Road Initiative", and promotes the development of education and economic and trade cooperation on the "Belt and Road" in parallel [1]. "National Database of Foreign Language Talent Resources" and "National

Database of Language Volunteers" built by Beijing Foreign Studies University have taken shape. These two databases mainly investigate the current situation of foreign language talent resources in major universities in China, determine the criteria for high-end foreign language talents, and build a national database of high-end foreign language talents, a national database of foreign language teachers and students, and a national database of information on the supply and demand of foreign language talents. These talent databases are dominated by language talents from domestic universities but has not been expanded to serve the energy cooperation of "Belt and Road Initiative".

The research questions of this paper are as follows: firstly, what is the purpose of database construction of talents for professional Chinese in the energy industry? Secondly, what are the needs for cultivating talents for professional Chinese in the energy industry? Thirdly, how to build the database for the cultivation of talents for professional Chinese in the energy industry? Fourthly, what are the applications of the database for the cultivation of talents for professional Chinese in the energy industry?

2   The Purpose of Building Database

2.1   To Mutually Verify Theories and Practices of Talent Training

Many research results in this field still remain at the macroscopic conceptual level, and lack of research on the demand for high-level industrialized talents in professional fields in China. This study can provide specific data and trends needed for both theoretical and practical research.

2.2   To Fully Understand the Characteristics of Talent Demands in the Energy Industry

At present, there is a lack of comprehensive and systematic researches on talent demands and training situations, which leads to the difficulty of accurately grasping the characteristics of talent needed for professional fields in China, particularly in the field of energy cooperation. In addition, there has been no in-depth and systematic research conducted on the talent training system, including training objectives, targets, curriculum system and training evaluation etc.

2.3   To Improve the Quality of Teaching Reform

Building a special database can promote talent training for professionals in the energy industry in China to be more precise, which leads to the improvement in the quality of training.

2.4   To Serve Energy Cooperation Projects

By utilizing the theory of complex dynamic systems theory and adopting a demand-orientation approach, it is possible to broaden the research scope and depth of Chinese talents for the energy industry.

3 Demand Research for Database Construction

3.1 Lack of Teaching Resources for Talent Training

With the increasing energy cooperation between China and the countries along the "Belt and Road", the shortage of high-level talents is becoming increasingly prominent. In particular, a large number of talents for professional Chinese with cross-cultural communicative skills who are well versed in international energy rules can solve the problems of cross-border energy transmission laws, coordinated regional energy development, cross-border gas pipeline trade and international investment in energy projects [2]. Specifically, there is an acute shortage of high-level talents who know foreign languages, cultures, policy and energy. In addition, there has several serious issues with the current talent training system, such as time-consuming and inefficient teaching resources, curriculum reform and so on [3]. Therefore, there is an urgent need of improving the training of professional Chinese talent and curriculum in energy-related universities [4, 5].

3.2 Lack of Research on the Construction of Talent Training System

Strengthening the cultivation of energy talents is of great strategic importance for enhancing China's international energy discourse and promoting the construction of the "energy community with a shared future" [4]. At present, most research is limited to concept and awareness with very little research on how to cultivate language talents for energy cooperation in "the Belt and Road". Therefore, the construction of a large database can provide much-needed data support for the talent training system for professional Chinese in energy industry.

4 Construction of Database

4.1 Overall Design of the Database

The database mainly collects information and data related to talent training for professional Chinese, talent demand, talent training unit information, talent training teacher, talent training evaluation, talent training teaching resources (including the database of multilingual parallel energy cooperation basic terminology, paper teaching resources for professional Chinese in the energy industry, digital teaching resources for professional Chinese in energy industry), energy policies and regulations, energy cooperation project case, and so on. The database of talents for professional Chinese in the energy industry is integrated through data screening, cleaning, and extraction. With this database and a demand-oriented approach, research on talent training for professionals in the Chinese energy industry can be carried out promptly.

4.2   Construction Thoughts

The database is constructed along the following lines (see Fig. 1 and Fig. 2).

- Construct the structure of the database under the guidance of the complex dynamics theory.
- Explore effective implementation measures according to the division of labor of the database architecture.
- Write fieldwork outlines, and then has fieldwork and statistical analysis, and write survey reports according to the division of labor.
- Discuss and determine the sources and means of data, and solve technical problems arising in the construction of the database.
- Collect data, screen data and input data.
- Update relevant data in real-time and establish the correlation of each sub-database.

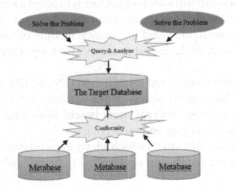

Fig. 1. A diagram of construction thoughts of targeted database

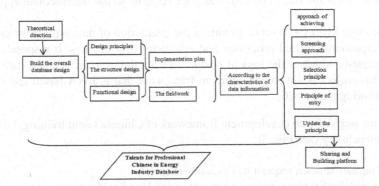

Fig. 2. Construction of Chinese talent training database in energy industry

4.3 Structure Design

First, determine the information interaction between the front-end and back-end of the database. Next, select the database web development framework. Then, design the main control process for the search function, as well as design the using functions such as the query dictionary and the administrator system.

Information Interaction Between Front-End and Back-End. For the support system, a B/S structure is used in the design of the system structure, while a combination of C/S and B/S for the digital interactive system. The B/S structure reduces the workload of the system administrator and allows for an unlimited number of users on the front-end.

The mainstream choice of software architecture is to adopt a network structure model with Browse/Server as the main structure and Client/Server as a supplement. In the database information system, the aided preparation module of talent training planning can adopt the C/S structure, while daily data is processed, input and update modules can use the B/S structure.

The mainstream choice of software architecture is to adopt a network structure model with Browse/Server as the main structure and Client/Server as a supplement. In the database information system, the aided preparation module of talent training planning can adopt the C/S structure, while daily data is processed, input and update modules can use the B/S structure.

The database has been constructed using hybrid C/S and B/S software architecture. External users do not have direct access to the database server, helps to ensure the database's security. In contrast, internal users benefit from strong interactivity and a rapid response time when querying and modifying data.

The database adopts the B/S model which adopts a three-layer mode frame structure (B/S model) to achieve the interaction between the front-end and the back-end (Fig. 4 and Fig. 5).

Presentation layer (browser) serves as the visual interface, which is the interface through which the user interacts with the database. The user observes data information through the visual interface and issues service requests to the intermediate application layer.

Application layer (web server) realizes the interaction of data with front-end commands, implements formal processes and completes logical rules. It responds to user service requests which is the logical bridge between the user service and data service layers. This project is a web development framework that is JAVA-based and operates in the following manner [6].

Specific steps of web development framework of Chinese talent training database in the energy industry (see Fig. 3):

Step 1, The user sends a request to DispatcherServlet;
Step 2, DispatcherServlet receives a request to call HandlerMapping;
Step 3, HandlerMapping finds the specific processor based on the request URL, generates the HandlerExecutionChain (including processor objects and processor interceptors), and returns it to DispatcherServlet;
Step 4, DispatcherServlet obtains the corresponding adapter according to Handler;

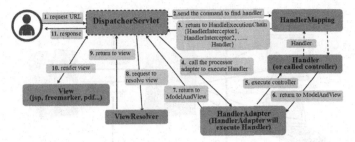

Fig. 3. Database web development framework (Spring MVC)

Step 5, HandlerAdapter calls Handler;

Step 6, After Handler completes execution, Handler returns to ModelAndView;

Step 7, HandlerAdapter returns to ModelAndView;

Step 8, DispatcherServlet uniformly sends the returned ModelAndView to ViewResolver for parsing;

Step 9, ViewResolver parses and returns to View;

Step 10, Render view;

Step 11, Dispatcherservlet responds to the user.

Data layer (DB Server) is the underlying database. The database service layer can realize all typical data processing activities, mainly including data acquisition, modification, update and other related services.

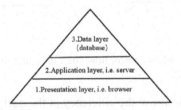

Fig. 4. Structure of information interaction between front-end and back-end

Main Control Process for Search Functions. With a clear front or back-end interaction model (B/S structure) and the web development framework (Spring MVC) in place, the next step is to define the main control process of the database search function. We de-fine the main control process of the database search function as follows (Fig. 6): First, the user enters a query field based on the input field. Next, the input field is assessed to 7 determine what type of query it belongs to. Following this, the judgment result is out-putted (if it does not match the query settings, the query is automatically ended), The command is then submitted to the database, and the query result is provided, which is shown to the user through the feedback mechanism of Spring MVC.

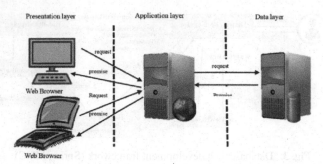

Fig. 5. Front-end and back-end interaction structure of the database of talent training for professional Chinese in energy industry

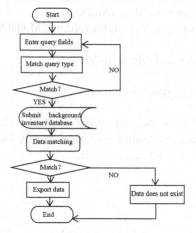

Fig. 6. Main control flow chart of search function

3) Query Dictionary. To improve the efficiency of the query function, we have implemented both "Exact Search" and "Fuzzy Search". "Exact search" requires a dictionary to be set up in advance, while "fuzzy search" is an indiscriminate full-field search of the database. The former being more efficient than the latter.

Considering the intricacies of talent training research for professional Chinese in the energy sector, we have designed the dictionary structure in two levels. The first-level dictionary is the "country dictionary", which can be used for the search function of any database containing country information. The second-level dictionaries are set up with specific query dictionaries according to the different level sub-databases. The followings are presented separately.

The secondary dictionaries designed for the "Research Literature Database" are "keywords", "name of journal", "title of paper or work", and "field of study".

The secondary dictionaries designed for "Talent Demand Database" are "name of the organization", "nature of the organization", "programmatic documents" and "publications of the editorial office".

The secondary dictionaries designed for "Training Unit Information Database" are "designation of school", "establishment time", "nature of school", "nature of operation", "level of operation", "medium of instruction", "number of teaching staff", "number of teachers", "structure of faculty", "main courses offered".

The secondary dictionaries designed for "Teaching Resource for Talent Training Database" are "title", "publisher", "book type", "book format", "country", "applicable course type", "applicable course", "nationalized textbook".

The secondary dictionaries designed for "Talent Training Faculty Database" are "name of faculty training", "type of training (distance or on-site)", "venue", "time", "organization ", "number of trainees", "content of training", "duration of training".

The secondary dictionaries designed for "Energy Policy Database" are "name of energy policy", "issuing entity", "main content", "issuing time".

The secondary dictionaries designed for "Cooperation Case of Energy Projects Database" are "name of project", "type of project", "form of exchange or cooperation", "visitor", "receptionist".

Administrator System. A three-tier administrator system is designed to facilitate back-end database management. The super administrator is granted the highest authority and can appoint or dismiss any second or third-level administrator, and audit the data of any database. The second-level administrator's authority is limited to a specific sub-data-base and can only appoint or dismiss the third-level administrator of that sub-database and audit the data of that sub-database. The third-level administrators have the lowest authority and can only appoint or dismiss the third-level administrator of that sub-data-base and audit the data of that sub-database.

4.4 Shared Platform Building

To enhance the sharing and building of energy professional Chinese talent training resources, we should utilize new information technology and communication means. Additionally, we should promote relevant work by leveraging social media to disseminate information about the relevant services and actively guide more users to participate in the sharing and building. The functional structure of the database sharing platform (see Fig. 7) [7].

The database system for energy industry professionals' talent has a co-construction and sharing function, and requires network system security management to be implemented. To ensure the security of network system, technical control and management should be integrated in the construction of network information security protection system. For example, password authentication can be applied to terminals to prevent unauthorized access.

The database sharing platform employs a layered architecture (see Fig. 8). The shared platform system mainly comprises of two subsystems (user use system and data management system). During the construction of the talent database system for energy industry professionals, the actual situation should be considered and a scientific way should be adopted to promote the realization of system operation objectives.

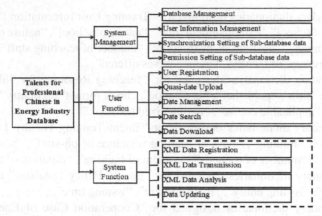

Fig. 7. Functional structure of the database shared platform for the talent cultivation for professional Chinese in the energy industry

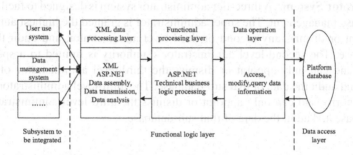

Fig. 8. Hierarchical structure in this database system

4.5 Functions and Roles of the Database

The hierarchical structure of the master database and the level 1 sub-database of the Chinese language training database for the energy industry is as follows (see Fig. 9).

Research Literature Database. It mainly contains literature on research on Chinese education, including journal papers, conference papers, books, newspapers, dissertations, national projects, ministry of Education projects, and so on. It requires suitable methods to obtain literature and adopt the correct manage mental methods of editing, adding, deleting, sorting, categorizing and searching literature materials to achieve effective analysis and rational use of literature information. Its management methods include editing, adding, deleting, sorting, categorizing and searching. Literature information analysis and use of these functions can be sorted by the number of literatures included in the catalog statistics, the number of times they have been read, the number of times they have been downloaded, or by the phonetic order of the authors of the documents, their nationality, and so on.

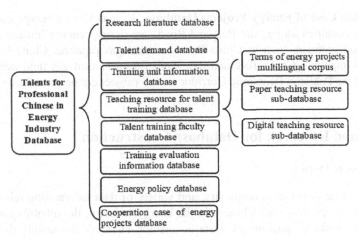

Fig. 9. Hierarchical structure of the general database and sub-database of Chinese talent training in the energy industry

Talent Demand Database. It mainly contains recruitment information and job requirements of companies in the domestic and overseas energy industry. The survey includes information on the type, quantity, language and ability of energy professional Chinese talent required by companies, as well as information on highly qualified professional Chinese talents, including nationality, professional background, education or training experience and overall quality.

Training Unit Information Database. It investigates the training and supply situation in universities, research institutes, language service providers and other sectors, including training objectives, curriculums, types and numbers of talents, employment situation, distribution of talents and so on.

Teaching Resource for Talent Training Database. It includes "Terms of energy projects multilingual corpus", "Paper teaching resource sub-database" and "Digital teaching resource sub-database". It mainly contains information about teaching materials and aids used by the main units of training issued by official institutions in overseas countries.

Talent training Faculty Database. It mainly collects information about teachers and their related training in countries along the Road. The aim is to gain a deeper understanding of the current situation, training methods, and training contents of such teachers' training, to provide a reference for improving the quality of training faculty.

Training Evaluation Information Database. It mainly includes subjects, objects, contents, standards, methods or instruments of evaluation.

Energy Policy Database. It includes units or departments that formulated the relevant policy, the policy name, the release time, the main content and so on.

Cooperation Case of Energy Projects Database. Researches on energy cooperation projects in countries along "the Belt and Road" are mainly energy infrastructure and energy trade projects, such as China-Russia natural gas pipeline, China-Kazakhstan natural gas pipeline, China-Turkmenistan Amu Darya natural gas field development project, China-Pakistan Economic Corridor energy project cooperation, and so on.

5 Demand Research for Database Construction

5.1 Access to Data

Due to the wide coverage, complexity, and variety of data information related to talent training for professional Chinese in the energy industry, the reliability and validity of data should be guaranteed. Data acquisition channels are mainly divided into two categories: Internet resources and paper resources, including a network of energy cooperation, websites of domestic educational institutions, publications, journal papers, academic dissertations, conference papers, newspapers, conference information, various research reports, research projects, survey reports, Chinese education yearbook, etc.

5.2 Data Filtering Method

Filtering by Country. Energy cooperation projects are mainly concentrated in Saudi Arabia, Kazakhstan, the United Arab Emirates, Thailand, Turkmenistan, Algeria, the Philippines, Morocco, Libya, Indonesia, Romania, Cambodia, Malaysia, and so on.

Overall Filtering by the Sub-database Thematic Content. The construction of energy professional Chinese talent cultivation can be divided into 8 thematic content sub-databases: "Research literature database", "Talent demand database", "Training unit information database", "Teaching resource for talent training database", "Talent training faculty database", "Training evaluation information database", "Energy policy database", "Cooperation case of energy projects database".

Filtering by the Specified Field. The nine sub-databases of talents training for professional Chinese in the energy industry have set fields respectively. See the following table for details of the fields set in each sub-database (Table 1).

Table 1. Field settings of talent training for professional Chinese in the energy industry database sub-database

Name of Sub-database		Main Field
Research literature database		Literature name, keywords, author, publication institution, project support, project level, publication time, literature type, data source, etc
Talent demand database		Country, language, category, number of employees, job responsibilities, disciplines involved, types of data sources, data sources, etc
Training unit information database		Name, country, start time, founder (institutions), location, nature, education form, education level, the main language, the main source of funds, the number of students, teaching media, the main teaching materials, teachers, teaching venue (lease, its own), the main courses, course number, weeks of classes, school total class hour, presence of cooperation colleges and universities, colleges and universities, data Source type, data source, etc
Teaching resource for talent training database	Terms of energy projects multilingual corpus	Chinese names of professional terms, language names of professional terms (English, French, Spanish, German, Russian, etc.), foreign language explanations of professional terms, common collocations of professional terms, Chinese explanations of professional terms, illustrations, etc

(*continued*)

Table 1. (*continued*)

Name of Sub-database	Main Field
Paper teaching resource sub-database	Title, press, author, press, types of books, teaching materials, books, examination, teaching, digital media), book form (new or revised, multilingual, and other binding), medium (paper), comments, whether for national teaching materials, language, country, suitable objects (preschool, elementary, middle and high school students, college students, the adult society), applicable grade, applicable level, applicable class type, applicable course, teaching nature, data source type, data source, etc
Digital teaching resource sub-database	Title, press, author, press, books, teaching materials, books, examination, teaching, digital media), book form (new or revised, multilingual, and other binding), medium (multimedia, network, mobile terminal), comments, whether for national teaching materials, language, country, suitable objects (preschool, elementary, middle and high school students, college students, the adult society), applicable grade, applicable level, applicable class type, applicable course, teaching nature, data source type, data source, etc

(*continued*)

Table 1. (*continued*)

Name of Sub-database	Main Field
Talent training faculty database	Faculty unit, gender, highest education level, major, teaching type, teaching years, salary, etc Name of teacher training activities, remote training/field training, location, host institutions (host/host/sponsor institution name), hold time, long, long/short, training staff's countries and regions, the number of trained personnel training school, the main contents of training, the types of data source, data sources, etc
Training evaluation information database	Evaluation subject, evaluation object, evaluation content, evaluation standard, evaluation method or means, etc
Energy policy database	Name of energy policy and regulation, issuing entity, main content, issuing time, original text, etc
Cooperation case of energy projects database	Project name, project signing time, project duration, main project area, project type, project content, cooperation mode, both parties involved in the project, capital input, type of talents, expected results, etc

6 Database Application

6.1 Application Value of Database

Firstly, to improve the quality of relevant academic research and serve the "going global" strategy of national culture. Secondly, to improve the scientific decision-making level of professional Chinese talent cultivation. Thirdly, to promote the reform and innovation of core curriculum. Fourthly, to provide the basis for the formulation of international Chinese education policy. Fifthly, to meet the actual needs of the teaching in international energy professional Chinese talent cultivation. Sixthly, to meet the actual needs of international energy professional Chinese talent. Seventhly, to improve the research and development quality demand of the teaching material in talent training for professional Chinese in the energy industry. Eighthly, to serve international energy cooperation projects. Ninthly, to promote cooperation between enterprises, universities and research institutes.

6.2   Usage of Database

The main usages of the database are as follows: Firstly, to accurately understand the demand for talents for energy enterprises or energy cooperation projects along "the Belt and Road". Secondly, to understand the current situation of energy professional Chinese along "the Belt and Road". Thirdly, the implementation of precision, customized cultivation in talent trainings for professional Chinese in the energy industry. Fourthly, to understand the level of the teaching staff of talent cultivation. Fifthly, to study the training mode, method, approach and characteristics of talent cultivation for professional Chinese in the energy industry. Sixthly, to make country comparative study with professional Chinese talent cultivation mode, methods and approaches in the energy industry. Seventhly, to get research and development of professional Chinese. Eighthly, to be the guidance basis of national teacher training. Ninthly, to build professional Chinese talent cultivation system in the energy industry. Tenthly, to analyze typical cases of energy cooperation in order to better serve international energy cooperation projects.

6.3   Construction of Talent Cultivation for Professional Chinese in the Energy Industry Based on Database

The cultivation of talent for professional Chinese in the energy industry requires a comprehensive training system consisting of "target first, clear target, course following, teaching guarantee, evaluation and supervision, and teacher-oriented (Fig. 10)".

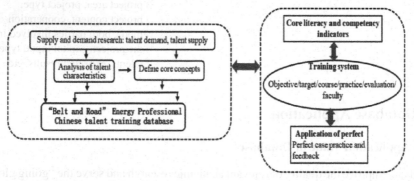

Fig. 10. Relationship between database and training system of Chinese language talents in the energy industry

Cultivation Objectives.   On the basis of investigation, research and database. Research on talent cultivation could clarify core ability and accomplishment indicators, and develop cultivation objectives, curriculum objectives and teaching objectives of talent cultivation.

Cultivation Objects. ① Broaden the cultivation objects: Chinese students whose foreign language is English or the language of "the Belt and Road" countries, international students, overseas Chinese and localized employees of energy enterprises of "the Belt and Road" whose foreign language is Chinese; ② Establish selection mechanism to screen high quality students by setting selection criteria of different types and grades.

Curriculum Construction. The core curriculum system is planned across seven dimensions of curriculum design, curriculum content, curriculum organization, curriculum implementation, curriculum management, curriculum development and curriculum evaluation. Four courses are set around the core literacy and competence indicators required for energy cooperation in "Belt and Road initiative": "Basic language skills and interlinguas transfer skills training courses", "Big data interlingua conversion processing skills courses", "Professional knowledge related to energy cooperation affairs", "Intercultural communication ability of energy cooperation parties courses", such as *"The Belt and Road Intercultural Communication Course for energy countries"* and "Intercultural Communication Teaching Resources for energy Industry in the Context of new liberal arts". The curriculum incorporates various engaging learning formats, such as text, pictures, audio, and video, to improve learning efficiency [8].

Teaching Practice. It will give full play to the resource advantages of universities with industry characteristics. Depended on the World Alliance of Energy Universities, energy enterprises and training institutions, we need to strengthen the flowing education between schools-enterprise, interschool and between government universities and enterprises. By setting up multinational transnational industry-university-research cooperation bases and transnational practical training platforms, so as to create a variety of practice platforms, and strengthen practical teaching.

Teaching Evaluation. To develop a new model combining formative evaluation and summative evaluation, and to form a mechanism combining teacher evaluation, student self-evaluation and mutual evaluation and third-party evaluation.

Faculty Building. Create interdisciplinary faculty teams, make full use of the World Energy University Alliance, promote teacher training and exchange programs, optimize the joint faculty training mechanism between universities and energy enterprises, and establish inter-university and transnational exchange mechanisms for teaching teams.

7 Conclusion

Energy universities, energy enterprises, and their training units, as the key player in talent cultivation, need to study the unified demand and supply of the energy industry to effectively guide the cultivation of professional Chinese talent and support the reform of talent cultivation in universities. Firstly, to promote the construction of the world Energy University Alliance energy education community. Secondly, to promote the transformation of traditional language talents cultivation in China's vocational universities. Thirdly, to establish the energy professional Chinese talent cultivation system.

Fourthly, to establish the assessment standard and evaluation system for the energy professional Chinese talent cultivation. Fifthly, to explore the talent practice program in energy international organization. Sixthly, to cultivate specialized researchers engaged for professional Chinese in the energy industry and related talent cultivation theory and application research.

Acknowledgment. This paper was supported by National Social Science Fund of China (No. 18CYY027), Cooperative education project of the Ministry of Education (No. 202102122014), Science Foundation of China University of Petroleum-Beijing (No. 2462020YJRC002), and Science Foundation of China University of Petroleum-Beijing (No. 2462020YXZZ010).

References

1. Tongtao, Z.: The Belt and Road Research on the Nationalized Talent Demand and Talent Training. World Book Publishing Guangdong Co. Ltd., China (2018)
2. Xiongguan, Z.: Community of energy destiny: China's plan for global energy governance. Thinking **46**(01), 140–148 (2020)
3. Rochman, Y., Levy, H., Brosh, E.: Dynamic placement of resources in cloud computing and network applications. Perform. Eval. **115**(10), 1–37 (2017)
4. Shilei, Z.: On the versatile foreign language talents training measures in the service of belt and road initiative: a case study in energy field. Meitan Higher Educ. **35**(02), 42–46 (2017). https://doi.org/10.16126/j.cnki.32-1365/g4.2017.02.010
5. Yingjie, G., Xiaomeng, J., Juan, A., Weiwei, W.: SINOPEC international talents training practice and outlook. J. Sinopec Manage. Inst. **20**(6), 6–11 (2018)
6. Spring MVC-Diagram execution process. https://blog.csdn.net/jiadajing267/article/details/81010741. Accessed 5 May 2022
7. Kaiyu, W.: Research on the co-construction and Sharing of University teaching resources database system. Inf. Technol. Informat. **05**, 215–217 (2018)
8. Benlian, A., Kettinger, W.J., Sunyaev, A., Winkler, T.J.: The transformative value of cloud computing: a decoupling, platformization, and recombination theoretical framework. J. Manage. Inf. Syst. **35**(3), 2–24 (2018)

Exploration and Research on the Construction of New Generation Information Technology Specialty Cluster for Application-Oriented Universities

Yingyan Teng[✉] and Zonggang He

The School of Computer Science, Guangdong University of Science and Technology, Dongguan, China
tengyy@foxmail.com

Abstract. In order to adapt to the vigorous development of the new economy characterized by new technologies, new industries and new models, there is an urgent need for a large number of emerging engineering education application-oriented talents with good industry literacy, comprehensive engineering practice ability and innovation and entrepreneurship ability. Therefore, it is necessary to explore and build a specialty cluster for the new generation of information technology. Strengthen the cross integration of various majors, realize complementary advantages, scientifically and reasonably allocate educational resources, optimize the construction of teachers, and complete the complete connection between the talent training chain and the new generation of information technology industry chain, which will avoid internal friction caused by professional homogeneity and provide talent guarantee for serving regional economic development and industrial cluster layout reform.

Keywords: Specialty Cluster · Application-oriented Universities · New Generation of Information Technology

1 Introduction

In 2015, the guidance on guiding the transformation of some local ordinary undergraduate colleges and universities to application-oriented was issued, requiring local colleges and universities to build specialty clusters and improve the structure and process of talent training, so as to meet the needs of local industrial chain and innovation chain. In 2015, the guidance on guiding the transformation of some local ordinary undergraduate colleges and universities to application-oriented was issued, requiring local colleges and universities to build specialty clusters and improve the structure and process of talent training, so as to meet the needs of local industrial chain and innovation chain. Driven by the policy, specialty cluster has become an important breakthrough in the transformation of Application-oriented Universities and a strategic choice for the optimization of specialty structure and the adjustment of specialty layout.

In 2019, the CPC Central Committee and the State Council issued the outline of the development plan of Guangdong Hong Kong Macao Bay area, which proposed to build a modern industrial system with international competitiveness, with emphasis on cultivating strategic emerging industries. Develop and expand a new generation of information technology, biotechnology, high-end equipment manufacturing and new materials as new pillar industries.

In the development plan of key emerging industries in Dongguan (2018–2025), it is emphasized to focus on five emerging fields and break through ten key industries. Seize the development opportunities of the new generation of information technology, accelerate the implementation of the intelligent strategy, vigorously develop the digital economy, carry out technical research in the fields of artificial intelligence, information communication, intelligent terminals and core components, seize the high-end links such as 5G network, Internet of things, big data and cloud computing, and accelerate the transformation from manufacturing to intelligent manufacturing.

The school of computer science in Guangdong university of science and technology now offers six undergraduate majors: software engineering, network engineering, Internet of things engineering, data science and big data technology, information system and information management, and intelligent science and technology. The degree of correlation between majors is high, which is easy to form a specialty cluster of symmetrical and mutually beneficial integrated symbiotic model. Therefore, it is considered to rely on software engineering and take the emerging majors of Internet of things engineering, data science and big data technology and intelligent science and technology as the core, transform the majors of network engineering, information system and information management, and build a new generation of information technology specialty cluster. Strengthen the cross integration of various majors, realize complementary advantages, scientifically and reasonably allocate educational resources, optimize the construction of teachers, and complete the complete connection between the talent training chain and the new generation of information technology industry chain, which will avoid internal friction caused by professional homogeneity and provide talent guarantee for serving regional economic development and industrial cluster layout reform.

2   The Composition of the New Generation of Information Technology Specialty Cluster

The new generation of information technology includes next-generation communication network, Internet of things, triple play, new flat panel display, high-performance integrated circuit and high-end software represented by cloud computing. According to these six aspects, the corresponding key industrial fields are sorted out, and the key industrial fields are divided into three categories: information and communication, intelligent hardware, software and services. Based on this classification, a new generation of information technology specialty cluster is constructed, as shown in Fig. 1. Software engineering, information management and information system and data science and big data technology correspond to the software and service industry, Internet of things engineering and intelligent science and technology correspond to the intelligent hardware industry, and network engineering corresponds to the information and communication industry.

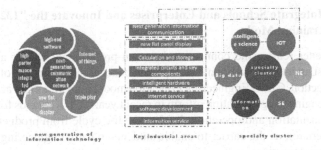

Fig. 1. Composition diagram of new generation information technology, key industrial fields and specialty clusters

3 Construction Path of New Generation Information Technology Specialty Cluster

3.1 Building a New Generation of Information Technology Specialty Cluster

Firstly, the construction of specialty cluster is an educational problem. Secondly, because it is closely related to industrial development, it is also an economic problem. Finally, as a specialty organization form of advantageous resource agglomeration, specialty cluster are still a management problem. Therefore, at the theoretical level, we should deeply understand the relevant theories and methods affecting and supporting specialty cluster from the perspective of pedagogy, economics, management and other disciplines, so as to lay a scientific theoretical foundation for the construction of specialty cluster.

At the practical level, the construction of specialty cluster should refine the technical links according to the post requirements of the industrial chain and innovation chain in the new generation of information technology industrial clusters, and organically combine several disciplines with the same or similar disciplines in the same or similar fields of engineering technology and application according to the principle of advantageous resource agglomeration.

According to the working links of the industrial chain of the new generation of information technology, it is divided into four aspects: perception layer, network layer, execution layer and application layer. The technology link oriented by the perception layer is mainly the sensing technology and information acquisition technology, corresponding to the Internet of things engineering and intelligent science and technology. The network layer is responsible for information processing and network transmission, corresponding to the network engineering discipline. The executive layer focuses on various intelligent solutions, corresponding to the specialty of intelligent science and technology. The application layer is mainly software and information services and data analysis and prediction at the top of information technology, corresponding to software engineering, information system and information management, data science and big data. See Fig. 2 for details.

3.2 Deeply Integrate Schools and Enterprises and Innovate the "1321" Applied Talent Training Mode

In order to better realize the connection between professional cluster and industrial chain, we must update the traditional educational concept in the process of professional cluster construction. CDIO Engineering Education model is an important achievement of international engineering education reform in recent years. CDIO stands for conception, design, implementation and operation. It takes the life cycle from product R & D to product operation as the carrier to enable students to learn engineering in an active, practical and organic way.

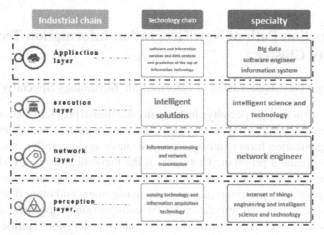

Fig. 2. Specialty cluster based on industrial chain

3.3 Deeply Integrate Schools and Enterprises and Innovate the "1321" Applied Talent Training Mode

In order to better realize the connection between professional cluster and industrial chain, we must update the traditional educational concept in the process of professional cluster construction. CDIO Engineering Education model is an important achievement of international engineering education reform in recent years. CDIO stands for conception, design, implementation and operation. It takes the life cycle from product R & D to product operation as the carrier to enable students to learn engineering in an active, practical and organic way.

Based on CDIO Engineering Education Ideas and methods, build a "1321" ring talent training mode with information technology characteristics, namely: 1 goal (training goal), 3 training dimensions (knowledge, ability and quality), 2 training routes (in class main line and extracurricular auxiliary line), and a set of completion requirements achievement evaluation system.

Track the regional economic development and the development trend of the new generation of information technology industry, understand the changes of talent demand structure, investigate and analyze stakeholders (enterprises, graduates, students in school, professional teachers and brother colleges), and clarify the professional training objectives in combination with the characteristics of each specialty. On this basis, clarify the knowledge, ability and quality required by professionals, and refine the requirements for graduation ability in combination with professional guiding norms. Based on this, the integrated curriculum system is designed.

Considering the characteristics of the new generation of information technology industry, in the process of talent training, it is not limited to the teaching of vocational skills and industry experience, and fully consider the cultivation of talent system thinking mode, professional quality and innovation and entrepreneurship ability. Based on this, the integrated curriculum and project system is designed to form two training routes: in class main line and extracurricular auxiliary line.

Change the current situation of judging the quality of students by their grades, build a diversified evaluation system for the achievement of graduation requirements, and verify the rationality and effectiveness of talent training path.

The new generation of information technology specialty cluster is built based on different links of the industrial chain. Therefore, in the process of specialty cluster construction, we should cooperate to build a talent training mechanism on the basis of win-win needs of schools and enterprises. Enterprises and schools reach a consensus, actively participate in the whole process of talent training, jointly set up talent training objectives and graduation requirements (ability) indicators, including formulating and revising training plans, teaching plans, jointly discussing talent training methods, planning and designing practice and training systems, curriculum groups and knowledge systems, participating in Curriculum teaching, training projects, special lectures, innovation and entrepreneurship activities, guiding discipline competitions College Students' innovation and entrepreneurship training program, as well as guiding graduation design, internship, employment and other links. Finally, according to the evaluation of teaching effect, feedback the graduation requirements (ability) indicators that students meet.

3.4 Optimize the Curriculum System of Specialty Clusters

Through the correlation matrix between graduation requirements and courses and teaching activities, optimize the curriculum and enrich curriculum resources; Due to the similarity of specialties in the specialty cluster, the basic courses of general education, discipline and specialty should be highly consistent to realize the sharing and co construction of resources. Specialty compulsory courses and specialty elective courses are determined according to the talent training objectives of various majors. Some specialty elective courses can also be selected and recognized by each other.

3.5 Building an Integrated Practical Project Teaching System with Progressive Layers

Closely combined with the requirements of solving complex engineering problems in engineering education certification, aiming at cultivating students to analyze, design and realize complex engineering projects, organically connect technical knowledge, specialty ability and specialty interest, and form an integrated practical teaching system with comprehensive training projects as the main line, semester practice projects as the support and curriculum practice projects as the basis.

Taking the typical modern enterprise value chain as the background, taking the industrial employment standards and industrial needs as the entry point, determine the comprehensive training project; Guided by the theory and technology development of modern information technology specialty, it is divided into semester practice projects and curriculum practice projects of major courses.

a) Design and research of comprehensive training project: By means of questionnaire survey and discussion with stakeholders and enterprises, starting from the employment position corresponding to the graduates trained in the major, and combined with the characteristics of the discipline, determine the requirements of professional core technical ability and non-technical ability to be trained. Introduce real enterprise projects, and effectively cut and restructure them according to the characteristics of students and practical environment, so as to form teachable practical training projects. It is a project designed based on the training of the whole process of product project conception, design, implementation and operation. After completing professional course learning and relevant semester project training, students use their knowledge to systematically experience the whole process of software product or project design.

b) Design and research of semester practice project: The semester practice project based on the curriculum group design is organized and implemented at the end of each semester to guide students to apply the knowledge of the curriculum group to practice. Each semester project is a subset of the abilities required by the comprehensive training project. The semester project should support the comprehensive training project, which includes a variety of meanings, the support of project content and the support of project training ability.

c) Design and research of curriculum practice project: Curriculum practice project is a curriculum project set up by a single course to enhance the realization of the ability goal of the course. This project guides students to use the key points of knowledge and ability learned to form ideas and methods to solve practical problems. Each curriculum project serves the specialty talent training and plays a specific role in the talent training system.

d) Design and research of unit group project and unit project: The unit group project is designed to strengthen the course ability goal based on the ability requirements of more than two units of a curriculum. Unit project is designed to enhance ability training in a unit of a curriculum. The unit project serves the unit group project, and the unit group project serves the curriculum project. The completion of the curriculum project is the achievement of the curriculum training goal.

In the implementation of project teaching, the enterprise engineer, the person in charge of training scheme, the person in charge of project training, the person in charge of semester practice project and the person in charge of curriculum and other professional teaching related parties cooperate with each other to clarify the relationship and progression between training scheme, project training, semester practice and curriculum practice, so as to consider the design of practice project from the overall perspective.

After the design is completed, all professional teaching parties will participate in the demonstration, implementation, feedback and continuous improvement of the project to ensure the achievement of the final training goal.

3.6 Build a Outstanding faculty with Multi-disciplinary Integration

The construction of specialty cluster involves many disciplines such as pedagogy, economics and management. Therefore, it is necessary to build a outstanding faculty with the combination of schools and enterprises, full-time and part-time, reasonable structure and multi-disciplinary integration.

Teachers should have high professional ideal and sound personality characteristics, innovative and entrepreneurial education concept, complete knowledge structure and professional skills, high teaching monitoring ability and strong management art. Teachers can absorb the latest educational scientific information, creatively discover and put forward the problems existing in practical education and teaching, creatively plan, organize and implement educational and teaching activities, have unique opinions and find effective new laws and methods of education and teaching, practice and apply educational and scientific research achievements, and be good at organically combining teaching work with empirical research on scientific research topics, Be able to use modern information technology to improve the efficiency of education and teaching. Be able to study the latest technologies, tools and development trends of the industry, and improve the ability of application innovation.

Strictly implement the teacher access system: Strictly control the entrance of teachers according to their academic standards, engineering practice and innovation and entrepreneurship practice experience, and hire industry experts with enterprise practical experience and teaching ability who love the teaching profession to enter the teaching team, so as to ensure the quality of the faculty. Formulate relevant policies to attract talents with solid basic knowledge, creative thinking and innovative and practical scientific research achievements to teach in Colleges and universities. High quality talents with successful entrepreneurship experience inject new vitality into the specialty. Establish an enterprise human resources database that can participate in the teaching of the specialty, and clarify the courses, projects, special topics and activities that engineering and technical personnel, marketing personnel and management personnel can participate in.

Develop training plan: Cultivate teaching backbones through academic exchanges, on-the-job training, project funding, regular study and exchange in enterprises and participating in innovation and entrepreneurship practice in social industries. Select young and middle-aged teachers who are willing to innovate and start a business from among teachers, set up the first echelon according to the technical direction, provide them with innovation and entrepreneurship training, participate in roadshows of various innovation and entrepreneurship activities, and cultivate teachers' innovation and entrepreneurship awareness and ability by means of temporary training in Enterprises, participating in horizontal projects and projects with independent intellectual property rights. After 1–2 years of training, industry experts are invited to evaluate and assess them. Qualified teachers train other teachers in the way of replication to achieve the growth of the faculty.

Set up an application R &D team: The specific application purpose of applied research is to determine new methods and approaches to achieve specific and predetermined goals.

Although applied research is also to obtain scientific and technological knowledge, this new knowledge is obtained on the basis of opening up new application ways. It is an expansion of existing knowledge, comes to solve practical problems, and has a direct impact on application. Teachers in specialty cluster should pay more attention to applied research in order to emphasize the transformation of scientific research achievements into actual productivity.

3.7 With the Goal of Improving Students' Innovative Practical Ability, Build a Practical Environment Inside and Outside the School

Take students as the center, reform and improve the construction of practical education base in the school. Build a practical education base working system with associations as the core, extracurricular interest groups and training camps as the support, college students' entrepreneurship center as the extension and effective linkage with scientific research, so as to realize the comprehensive improvement of teachers' and students' professional ability, technical level, innovation ability and professional quality.

Based on the operation mechanism of resource sharing, cost sharing and process management, this paper studies the mode and method of cooperation between practice and it industry to build an off campus practical education base. Based on the operation mechanism of resource sharing, cost sharing and process management, the mode and method of practice and it industry cooperation in the construction of off campus practical education base are studied.

4 Guarantee Mechanism for the Construction of a New Generation of Information Technology Specialty Cluster

The orderly construction of specialty cluster needs the guarantee of good operation and management mechanism. Set up a professional Cluster Construction Committee, which is composed of the vice president in charge of teaching and scientific research of the computer college, the principals of various majors, relevant teachers of the academic affairs office, enterprise engineers, backbone teachers and teaching managers. The Construction Committee has a director and three deputy directors of teaching, scientific research and school enterprise cooperation according to the business line. The Construction Committee is responsible for formulating the construction plan and implementation plan of professional clusters, focusing on the three aspects of teaching, scientific research and innovation and entrepreneurship practice, and uniformly allocating resources such as teachers, laboratories and funds.

Establish the evaluation measures for the construction of specialty cluster, the management and assessment measures for the process of specialty cluster and other institutional measures, and strictly implement the implementation of the management system. Innovate the school enterprise cooperation mechanism and attract well-known enterprises to invest in the construction of specialty cluster. In view of the changes of new business forms in the development of information technology, build a dynamic adjustment and optimization mechanism of professional clusters, timely adjust the layout of specialty clusters, add new majors related to the needs of the industrial chain, and delete the old majors with poor adaptability, so as to adapt to the changes in the demand for talents in the new generation of information technology industrial chain.

5 Conclusion

Build specialty cluster according to the principles of demand orientation, industrial docking, system construction and personality development, which can realize the rational allocation and utilization of teaching resources and platform environment, and maximize the benefits of various resources.Cultivate high-quality application-oriented talents with high fit with the development of the new generation of information industry, wide industrial chain knowledge and strong professional skills, which can effectively enhance students' adaptability to the job market and professional competitiveness, and truly reflect the student-centered education concept.Effectively connect the new generation of information technology industrial clusters, integrate into the industrial chain and innovation chain, highlight the concept and function of serving the society, and provide human support for regional economic development and industrial transformation and upgrading.

References

1. Wang, H.C.: Specialty cluster: prospect and challenge of application-oriented universities. Jiangsu High. Educ. **2022**(04), 75–81 (2022) https://doi.org/10.13236/j.cnki.jshe.2022.04.011
2. Gu, Y.A.: Research on the theoretical basis and application of specialty clusters in applied universities. J. Chengdu Normal Univ. **37**(4) (2021)
3. Gu, Y.A.: Applied undergraduate major cluster: an important breakthrough in the transformation and development of local colleges and universities. China Higher Educ. **22**, 35–38 (2016)
4. Wang, J.L.: Research on the construction of cross-border new business professional clusters in Russia -- Taking Heilongjiang University as an example. .Heilongjiang Educ. (Research and Evaluation of Higher Education) (12), 19–21 (2020)
5. Cheng, Q.L.: Research and thinking of the cluster of new engineering. Educ. Teach. Forum **24**, 33–36 (2021)
6. Zhang, H.G.: Research and practice of cluster construction of IIT. J. Heilongjiang Coll. Teach. Dev. **40**, 11–14 (2021)
7. Wu, R.H.: Research on the construction of professional cluster in applied undergraduate universities. Res. Higher Eng. Educ. (6), 98–102 (2016)
8. Yang, B.L., Wu, L.P.: Research on the construction strategy of specialty cluster in application-oriented Universities. Henan Educ. (Higher Education) (07), 43–45 (2021)

A Study on Behavioral Engagement of College English Learners in Blended Teaching Model

Huihui Li and Huan Wang(✉)

NingboTech University, Ningbo, China
eletahuan@163.com

Abstract. The issue of student behavioral engagement in the blended teaching mode has become increasingly significant to ensure students' learning outcome. This study focuses on the features of college English learners' online behavioral engagement in a blended teaching context: gender difference, major difference, and its correlation with academic achievement. A sample of 106 first-year college non-English students were involved in this study. All the collected valid data were analyzed by software SPSS 22.0, including independent-sample t-tests, Pearson correlation analysis and regression analysis. This study found that (1) there are significant differences in behavioral engagement and academic achievement between male students and female students, and the behavioral engagement and academic achievement of females are significantly higher than those of males. (2) international business students' behavioral engagement and academic achievement are significantly higher than science & engineering students. (3) students' overall behavioral engagement was significantly related to midterm, final and CET-4 scores, but not significantly related to CEE scores. (4) student's effort value for online listening practice, midterm and final scores can predict 66.6% of the variance of the CET-4 score.

Keywords: Behavioral Engagement · College English Learners · Blended Teaching Model

1 Introduction

Appeared decades ago, researches on student engagement have demonstrated its relationship with academic achievement or dropout rate. Student engagement is considered as a combination of behavioral engagement, emotional engagement, and cognitive engagement [1–3]. It might change with the shift of school context [2]. Behavioral engagement in learning is an important factor in academic performance [2, 4–8]. Promoting appropriate learning behavior can raise student academic performance [9].

Given the prominence of information technology, blended learning has become a significant part of English as a foreign language (EFL) learning and has been recognized as an efficient learning mode in this setting. In recent years, students' engagement and blended learning has been paid increasing attention. Especially in the context of the Covid-19, blended learning can meet learners' academic needs in a larger way [10]. It

W. Hong and Y. Weng (Eds.): ICCSE 2022, CCIS 1813, pp. 518–530, 2023.
https://doi.org/10.1007/978-981-99-2449-3_45

can be seen that online or distance learning has become an urgent necessity for higher education institutions [11].

The network environment provides effective support for blended teaching and learning, extending teachers' teaching behaviors from inside the classroom to outside the classroom, which can considerably promote students' learning efficiency and learning effectiveness [12]. Chen and Liu [13] took advantage of SPSS to analyze data and construct models, and found that constructive learning behavior can promote English learning. Ji et al. [14] proposed that the quality of online education and the learning effect of learners can be ensured by analyzing student behavior data, including the number of visits to courses and discussions, and the progress of learning. Wang [15] made use of an online English education learning behavior model to collect student behavior data, built a data mining model, and filtered the collected behavior data. It can save learners' time to fill in the questionnaire. Moreover, the behavior data is more objective and real. Besides, the use of automatic recognition methods can dynamically acquire learners' learning styles according to changes in behavioral data and provide several learning support services" [15]. Therefore, this study provides new insights into the behavioral engagement of college English learners in blended learning model.

2 Methodology

2.1 Question

Accordingly, this study aims to explore behavioral engagement in blended learning teaching model with the following contributing questions:

(1) Are there gender and major differences in online learning behavior engagement and academic achievement?
(2) Are there any significant correlations between students' behavioral engagement and their academic achievement?
(3) Can online behavioral engagement predict academic achievement in test score?

2.2 Subjects

The subjects selected for this research were106 non-English major university freshmen, including 44 males (41.51%) and 62 females (58.49%) all from a university in East China. These participants were divided into two categories according to their majors: international business majors (48, 37 females and 11 males) and science & engineering majors (58, 26 females and 33 males). The students were enrolled in September 2021. During the first semester of freshman year, their English teacher implemented a blended teaching mode, That is, they had a semester of blended learning experience, a combination of offline learning and online learning.

College English is a comprehensive course, including an intensive reading section and a listening-speaking section. In this case study, two online systems were adopted, one for intensive reading, and the other for the listening-speaking section. In online learning section, participants were supposed to do self-study including listening to textual, audio and video materials, participating in class discussions, and doing vocabulary quizzes. Besides, they were also involved in offline learning in traditional face-to-face teaching in classrooms.

2.3 Data Collection

Quantitative methodology was adopted in this study. Four kinds of data were collected from their online learning platforms: the duration of audio and video learning (E1), discussion (E2), study frequency of chapters (E3), and online vocabulary quiz score (E4). One data effort value (E5), was collected from another listening learning platform. It was a comprehension of the duration of audio and video learning, and listening exercise scores. In addition, traditional academic achievement data were offered by their teacher, including scores of College Entrance Examination (CEE), midterm examination scores, final examination scores, and scores of College English Test-Band 4 (CET-4). Since two male students did not participate in the first CET-4, their data were invalid. As a result, the total number of valid records is 952.

2.4 Data Analysis Procedure

Following data collection, these data were analyzed with SPSS 22.0 in three steps. First, a descriptive analysis was used to describe the relationship between students' academic achievements in College Entrance Examination (CEE), midterm examination, final examination, and College English Test-Band 4 (CET4). Second, independent-sample t-test analysis was employed to analyze the differences in behavioral engagements and academic achievements among different genders and majors. Third, Pearson correlation analysis was used to analyze the correlation between students' behavioral engagements and academic achievements, to investigate whether the correlations are significant. Finally, regression equation was established through a regression analysis.

3   Result

3.1 Descriptive Statistics

As displayed in descriptive statistics of academic achievement (see Table 1), CEE scores of the subjects are $122.179 + 4.7264$, with a relatively small standard deviation. The midterm scores are $63.703 + 11.4773$, and the final score are $77.014 + 9.3649$. The CET4 score are $503.30 + 59.449$, with a relatively big standard deviation.

In addition, the scattered plot (see Fig. 1) shows that there seems to be little significant correlation between CEE scores (indicating the English proficiency before the semester) and CET-4 scores (indicating their English proficiency after the semester). The subject with lowest CEE score has achieved higher score in CET4 than the subjects with highest CEE score. Among the four subjects who had got the score of 125 in CEE achieve different scores in CET 4, one is higher than 550, two are between 500 and 550, and one is below 400, which is lowest in all the subjects. This suggest that it is meaningful to investigate whether there is a correlation between students' learning engagement and their academic achievement.

Table 1. Descriptive statistics of academic achievement

	N	Minimum	Maximum	Mean	Std. Deviation
CEE	106	114.0	139.0	122.179	4.7264
Midterm	106	34.5	89.5	63.703	11.4773
Final	106	48.5	93.5	77.014	9.3649
CET4	106	353	642	503.30	59.449

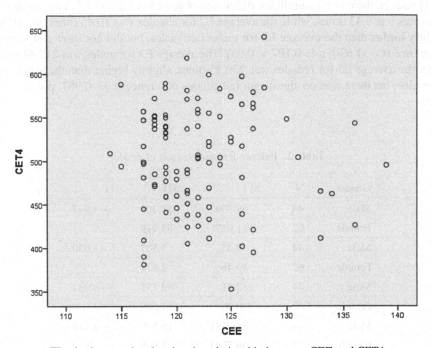

Fig. 1. Scatter plot showing the relationship between CEE and CET4

3.2 Difference Analysis

Gender Differences in Students' Behavioral Engagement and Academic Achievement. To detect the gender differences between students' behavioral engagement and academic achievement, the paper conducted independent-sample t-tests on the full sample. As shown in Table 2, although there is no significant difference in males' and females' CEE score (t = -0.744, p = 0.458 > 0.05), female students' midterm scores, final scores and CET-4 scores are significantly higher than those male students. The average midterm score of females was significantly higher than that of males (t = -2.386, p = 0.019 < 0.05). The average final score of females was significantly higher than that of males (t = -2.436, p = 0.017 < 0.05). The average CET-4 score of females was significantly higher than that of males (t = -2.032, p = 0.045 < 0.05).

In addition, female students' behavioral engagement for E1, E4, and E5 are also significantly higher than that of male students. The average E1 of males was 68.309 min, while the average E1 of females was 111.037 min, which was much higher than the average E1 of males, showing a significant indigenous difference (t = -3.947, p = 0 < 0.01). The average E4 score of males was 51.3291, while the average E4 score of females was 66.3703, which was slightly higher than that of males, showing significant difference (t = 4.839, p = 0 < 0.01). What's more, the average E5 of males was 3924.95, while the average E5 score of females was 4193.21, which was slightly higher than that of males, showing significant difference (t = -3.019, p = 0.003 < 0.01).

However, there is no significant difference observed in E2 and E3. The average E2 for males was 9.43 times, while the average E2 for females was 10.45 times, which was slightly higher than the average E2 for males into males, but did not show a significant difference (t = -1.630, p = 0.107 > 0.05). The average E3 for males was 212.61 times, while the average E3 for females was 230.35 times, slightly higher than the average E3 for males, but there was no significant indigenous difference (t = -0.987, p = 0.326 > 0.05).

Table 2. Independent samples test of gender

	Gender	N	M	SD	t	p
E1	Male	44	68.309	38.703	−3.947	0
	Female	62	111.037	63.919		
E2	Male	44	9.43	3.507	−1.630	0.107
	Female	62	10.45	2.634		
E3	Male	44	212.61	99.735	−0.987	0.326
	Female	62	230.35	84.648		
E4	Male	44	51.3291	15.586	−4.839	0
	Female	62	66.3703	15.895		
E5	Male	44	3924.95	575.892	−3.019	0.003
	Female	62	4193.21	335.736		
CEE	Male	44	121.773	4.209	−0.744	0.458
	Female	62	122.468	5.076		
Midterm	Male	44	60.614	11.093	−2.386	0.019
	Female	62	65.895	11.324		
Final	Male	44	74.443	9.725	−2.436	0.017
	Female	62	78.839	8.726		
CET4	Male	42	489.12	57.356	−2.032	0.045
	Female	62	512.90	59.365		

Major Differences in Students' Behavioral Engagement and Academic Achievement. To determine whether there are significant differences in behavioral participation and academic performance among students from different majors, an analysis of the participants in different categories of majors was performed.

Table 3 suggest that CEE score of students majoring international is business significantly lower than that of students majoring science and engineering (t = -2.344, p = 0.021 < 0.05). The average score of students majoring international business in CEE (m = 121.773) is relatively lower than that of students majoring science and engineering (m = 123.138), but with a smaller standard deviation. However, international business students got significantly higher scores in either midterm examination (t = 4.643, p = 0 < 0.01), final examination (t = 4.227, p = 0 < 0.01) or CET 4 (t = 3.952, p = 0 < 0.01). In addition, students majoring international business got significantly higher performance than students majoring science and engineering in either E1(t = 3.193, p = 0.002 < 0.01), E4 (t = 5.040, p = 0 < 0.01), or E5 (t = 3.592, p = 0.001 < 0.01).

Table 3. Independent samples test of international business students and science & engineering students.

	Gender	N	M	SD	t	p
E1	International business	48	112.458	70.477	3.193	0.002
	Science& Engineering	58	77.447	40.821		
E2	International business	48	10.63	2.863	1.851	0.067
	Science& Engineering	58	9.53	3.141		
E3	International business	48	233.38	96.096	1.067	0.288
	Science& Engineering	58	214.40	86.798		
E4	International business	48	68.546	16.054	5.040	0
	Science& Engineering	58	53.159	15.304		
E5	International business	48	4251.92	351.408	3.592	0.001
	Science& Engineering	58	3941.12	506.934		
CEE	International business	48	121.021	3.9221	−2.344	0.021
	Science& Engineering	58	123.138	5.138		
Midterm	International business	48	68.906	9.751	4.643	0
	Science& Engineering	58	59.397	11.072		
Final	International business	48	80.938	8.369	4.227	0
	Science& Engineering	58	73.767	8.951		
CET4	International business	48	526.58	50.365	3.952	0
	Science& Engineering	56	483.34	59.768		

3.3 Correlation Analysis

The Pearson correlation was used to analyze behavioral engagements and academic achievements to examine whether the correlations were significant. Table 4 illustrates the correlation statistics between behavioral engagement and academic achievement.

Table 4. Correlations of Behavioral Engagement and Academic Achievement

	E1	E2	E3	E4	E5	GEE	Midterm	Final	CET-4
E1	1	0.268**	0.491**	0.456**	0.330**	0.131	0.276**	0.270**	0.189
E2	0.268**	1	0.254**	0.230*	0.184	0.005	0.145	0.109	0.156
E3	0.491**	0.254**	1	0.445**	0.387**	0.070	0.316**	0.282**	0.191
E4	0.456**	0.230*	0.445**	1	.568**	0.052	0.699**	0.675**	0.577**
E5	0.330**	0.184	0.387**	.568**	1	−0.081	0.541**	0.507**	0.542**
CEE	0.131	0.005	0.070	0.052	−0.081	1	−0.024	−0.017	−0.027
Midterm	0.276**	0.145	0.316**	0.699**	0.541**	−.024	1	0.673**	0.735**
Final	0.270**	0.109	0.282**	0.675**	0.507**	-0.017	0.673**	1	0.742**
CET4	0.189	0.156	0.191	0.577**	0.542**	−0.027	0.735**	0.742**	1

a. **. Correlation is significant at the 0.01 level (2-tailed).
b. *. Correlation is significant at the 0.05 level (2-tailed)

It is shown that E1, E3, E4, and E5 are significantly related to midterm and final performance ($p < 0.01$). The correlation coefficients ranged from 0.270 to 0.699 ($p < 0.01$). Moreover, the correlation among E4, E5, and CET-4 are virtually strong with each other ($p < 0.01$). Furthermore, midterm and final scores have significant correlation with CET-4 ($p = 0 < 0.01$). However, there is less significant correlation between CEE and behavioral engagement and academic achievement in college ($p = 0 < 0.01$). It reveals that after a semester of college English learning, students' language level has been altered.

3.4 Regression Analysis

According to the results of the Pearson correlation analysis, only E4 and E5 have significant correlations with CET-4. Therefore, the author didn't take the other factors into the regression analysis in this part. The following tables (Table 5, Table 6, and Table 7) show that only the E5, midterm, and final scores were significantly correlated with CET-4 ($p < 0.05$). After excluding other irrelevant variables, the linear regression was repeated once more and the results were as follows:

It can be seen that only 3 significant variables entered the regression equation with a multiple regression number of 0.816 when predicting the CET-4 score with the length of E5, midterm, and final score. The joint explained variance is 0.666, which means that E5, midterm, and final score can predict 66.6% of the variance of the CET-4 score. This resulted in a standardized regression equation:

$$CET - 4\ Score = 77.216 + 0.019\ E5 + 2.195\ Midterm\ Score + Final\ Score \quad (1)$$

Table 5. Model summary[b] of academic achievement and behavioral engagements

Model	R	R Square	Adjusted R Square	SE	DW
1	0.816[a]	0.666	0.653	35.028	2.002

a. Predictors: (Constant), E4, E5, Final, Midterm,
b. Dependent Variable: CET4

Table 6. ANOVA[a] of academic achievements and behavioral engagements

Model		Sum of Squares	df	Mean Square	F	Sig
1	Regression	242551.885	4	60637.971	49.421	0[b]
	Residual	121469.875	99	1226.968		
	Total	364021.760	103			

a. Dependent Variable: CET4
b. Predictiors: (Constant), E4, E5, Final, Midterm,

Table 7. Coefficients[a] of academic achievements and behavioral engagements

		Unstandardized Coefficients		Standardized Coefficients	t	Sig
Model		B	Std. Error	Beta		
1	(Constant)	77.216	38.738		1.993	0.049
	E4	-0.321	0.310	-0.092	-1.035	0.303
	E5	0.019	0.009	0.151	2.082	0.04
	Midterm	2.195	0.464	0.417	4.735	0
	Final	2.928	0.565	0.447	5.185	0

a. Dependent Variable: CET4

4 Discussions and Conclusions

This study used quantitative research methods, through descriptive analysis, independent sample t-test, Pearson correlation coefficient analysis, and regression analysis, to study the behavioral engagement of college English learners in blended teaching mode. It is concluded that there are significant differences in behavioral engagement and academic achievement between male students and female students, and the behavioral engagement and academic achievement of females are significantly higher than those of males. Meanwhile, international business students' behavioral engagement and academic achievement are significantly higher than science & engineering students. In addition, this study found that students' overall behavioral engagement was significantly related to midterm, final, and CET-4 scores, but not significantly related to CEE scores. Moreover, student's effort value for online listening practice, midterm, and final scores can predict 66.6%

of the variance of the CET-4 score. Therefore, more insightful decisions can be made regarding how to promote students' behavioral engagement to enhance their level of English learning.

4.1 The Significant Difference of Students' Behavioral Engagement and Academic Achievement

The Significant Difference of Students' Behavioral Engagement and Academic Achievement in Gender. The present research investigated different genders and majors of College English learners' behavioral engagements across five aspects in blended learning mode. The results revealed female students achieved better than male students in E1 (the duration of audio and video learning), E4 (vocabulary quiz), E5 (effort value for online listening practice), midterm, final and CET-4.

Previous studies have documented that there was a wide range of gender differences in student behavioral engagement and that females were more involved [12, 16, 17]. Moreover, this paper draws the same conclusion as previous studies that there were significant differences between males and females in CET-4 scores, and the average score of females was significantly higher than that of males [18, 19].

Kimura [20] pointed out that from the perspective of neurolinguistics, female's language proficiency is stronger than male's because the male language center is primarily concentrated in the left hemisphere of the brain, while female makes full use of the left and right hemispheres of the brain to coordinate their work in language learning.

The Significant Difference of Students' Behavioral Engagement and Academic Achievement in Major. This study revealed a significant difference between international business major students and science & engineering major students in behavioral engagement and academic achievement in blended learning, revealing that international business major students achieved better than science & engineering major student students in these dimensions.

Although the CEE scores of international business students are lower than those of science and engineering students, their behavioral engagement and academic achievement are significantly higher than those of science & engineering students. It can be seen that there is a correlation between international business students' behavioral engagement and academic achievement, and behavioral engagement may have a crucial influence on academic achievement.

According to Bai [21], there are two main reasons for the fact that the CET-4 scores of international business major students are significantly higher than that of other majors: First. The nature of the major determines that students must pay attention to foreign language learning; Second, more female students in international business majors that their motivation and effort are generally higher than male students.

The analysis results of gender differences and major differences are not much different, which may be due to the incoordination of the proportion of men and women in international business majors. According to research subjects, the male-to-female ratio of international business majors is 11:37, while that of science & engineering majors is 12:11.

4.2 The Correlation of Students' Behavioral Engagement and Academic Achievement

The Overall Behavioral Engagement is Significantly Related to Academic Achievement Except for CEE. This paper inferred that the correlation between students' CEE scores and their entire behavioral engagements in blended learning during college is not significant, which is similar to the findings supposed by Zhang [22]. A few explanations are feasible for this outcome:

- The gap of students' English scores in the college entrance examination is tiny. Among the samples selected in this study, the difference between the highest score and the lowest score is only 25 points. Such a gap is not able to precisely reflect the distinction of students' competence.
- The sample size is small. The data to measure student engagement in blended learning in this paper is limited to online. However, students who are highly engaged in online learning may not necessarily be highly engaged offline.
- Midterm and final exams are the test of students' learning level and effort during college, which can precisely reflect students' behavioral engagement. Consequently, they have significant correlation with behavioral engagements. Zhang [22] found that students with amazing CEE scores may have poor performances during college, and students with relatively low CEE scores may also have amazing performances during college.

Different Correlation Coefficients of Different Factors. E1 (the duration of audio and video learning) and E3 (study repetition of chapters) were not significantly correlated with CEE, but were significantly correlated with midterm and final scores. The Pearson correlation coefficient among them were low. Several explanations are feasible as follows:

- The contents of midterm and final exams were relevant to online learning. According to the teacher, some of the questions in these two examinations were related to the text content, while the students' online learning content was also related to the text.
- Through interaction with teachers, it is found that E1 and E3 were components of students' usual performance. In order to obtain higher scores, students might try to learn online resources, but they might not really engage in them.

Only E4 (vocabulary quiz), and E5 (effort value for online listening practice) are significantly correlated with all the academic achievements in college, including midterm, final, and CET-4. The possible reasons for the high correlation coefficient among E4, E5, midterm, final, and CET-4 scores are as follows:

- E4 is related to students' extracurricular learning engagement. The acquisition of E4 scores required students to make more effort after class, by reading the text and memorizing the vocabulary. Generally speaking, students who could take vocabulary seriously in the text were also prepared for the midterm final examination and the CET-4 preparation in earnest. Academic engagement is reliably and directly associated with student achievement and high school graduation [23]. Therefore, the E4 could better reflect the students' intrinsic motivation.

• E5 is a relatively comprehensive online behavior engagement data, which can more precisely reflect the real behavioral engagement of students. Moreover, the amount of time that students involve engaged in academic activities is reliably and consistently associated with student achievement; more time translates to higher achievement [24].

The possible reason for no significant correlation between E2 and academic achievements is possibly related to the intrinsic motivation of the students. According to the teacher of these learners, E2 was primary for students to participate when they were in offline class, and students could generally engage seriously, therefore, there is not much discrimination.

4.3 The Prediction on Students' CET-4 Scores

Overall, this study demonstrated that the E5 (effort value for online listening practice), midterm and final scores generally had significant predictive abilities on CET-4. They have a high Pearson correlation coefficient with CET-4 and can predict 66.6% of the variance of the CET-4 score. As previous researches noted, academic achievement in College English is highly correlated with the performance of CET-4 [21, 22, 24]. Furthermore, the effort value has a significant predictive ability on CET4 [25]. The overall effort of students is more precisely reflected in academic achievement and E5. It could be seen that students who take the initiative to learn English well are more likely to get high marks [25]. Therefore, students who want to attain impressive results in CET-4 must strengthen the accumulation of knowledge and upgrade their behavioral engagement in curriculum learning. Moreover, they should conduct a great number of listening and speaking training during the usual learning process, as well as strengthen their basic language skills training and enhance their sensitivity to the language.

In conclusion, on the one hand, this study underlines the gender and major differences in online behavioral engagement. This indicates the necessity of teachers' awareness on these differences in mixed classes. On the other hand, the correlation between behavioral engagement and traditional academic performance suggests that online behavioral engagement (the duration of audio and video learning, and study repetition of chapters) can serve as indicators of students' online performance to arise teachers' attention to students' online learning engagement. In addition to the purely online behavioral engagement indicators described above, this study suggests that online vocabulary quiz and effort value (a combination of behavioral engagement and listening quiz) shows a high correlation with students' traditional academic achievements. This finding suggests that online exercises are of importance to urge students to improve their language skill.

On balance, this study aims to explore the behavioral engagement of college English learners in blended teaching mode, hoping to offer suggestions for both teachers and students in blended learning context. It may offer English teachers some help in allocation online tasks in the post-Covid-19 situations.

Acknowledgment. The authors gratefully acknowledge the research project supported by the Department of Education, Zhejiang Province Project (Project No. Jg20190584), and the research project supported by NingboTech University (Project No. NITJG-202084).

References

1. Jimerson, S.R., Campos, E., Greif, J.L.: Toward an understanding of definitions and measures of school engagement and related terms. Calif. Sch. Psychol. **8**, 7–27 (2003)
2. Fredricks, J.A., Blumenfeld, P.C., Paris, A.H.: School engagement: potential of the concept, state of the evidence. Rev. Educ. Res. **74**, 59–109 (2004)
3. Yazzie-Mintz, E.: Voices of students on engagement: a report on the 2006 high school survey of student engagement. Cent. Eval. Edu. Policy Indiana Univ., Bloomington (2007)
4. Lahaderne, H.M.: Attitudinal and intellectual correlates of attention: a study of four sixth-grade classrooms. J. Educ. Psychol. **59**, 320–324 (1968)
5. Anderson, L.W.: Student involvement in learning and school achievement. Calif. J. Ed. Res. **26**, 53–62 (1975)
6. Finn, J.D.: Withdrawing from school. Rev. Educ. Res. **59**, 117–142 (1989)
7. Birch, S.H., Ladd, G.W.: The teacher–child relationship and children's early school adjustment. J. Sch. Psychol. **35**, 61–79 (1997)
8. Johnson, M.L., Sinatra, G.M.: Use of task–value instructional inductions for facilitating engagement and conceptual change. Contemp. Educ. Psychol. **38**, 51–63 (2013)
9. Durbrow, E.H.: Learning behaviours, attention and anxiety in Caribbean children. Sch. Psychol. Int. **21**, 242–251 (2000)
10. Bordoloi, R., Das, P., Das, K.: Perception towards online/blended learning at the time of Covid-19 pandemic: an academic analytics in the Indian context. Asian Assoc. Open Univ. J. **16**, 41–60 (2021)
11. Iman, O., Tariq, E.: The impact of COVID-19 on learning: Investigating EFL learners' engagement in online courses in Saudi Arabia. Edu. Sci. **11**, 473–492 (2021)
12. Yu, S.Q., Lu, Q.L., Chen, S.J.: Blended teaching in network environment – a new teaching mode. China Univ. Teach. **10**, 50–56 (2005)
13. Chen, L., Liu, X.: A correlative study of the influence of higher vocational students' learning behavior on English effective learning based on SPSS. J. Wuhan Polyt. **19**, 63–67 (2020)
14. Ji, Q.Y., Li, D., Ming, Y.: Research on psychological characteristics and behavior law of college students' online learning in the new era. In: International Conference on Information Technology, Education and Development, vol. 68. Francis Academic Press (2021)
15. Wang, C.X.: Analysis of students' behavior in English online education based on data mining. Mob. Inf. Sys., 10 (2021)
16. Zeng, Q.: Primary school students participation in classroom learning and role difference. Edu. Res. Exper. **2**, 60–64+73 (2000)
17. Liu, X.Q.: Gender differences and teaching strategies of undergraduate class engagement. University (Academic) **4**, 50–58 (2018)
18. Yuan, F.S., Xiao, D.F.: On the gender differences of the relationships between the behaviours and CET4 scores. Foreign Lang. Teach. **8**, 22–25 (2003)
19. Shi, Y.Z.: Gender difference in foreign language reading anxiety and its relations to CET4. Foreign Lang. China (2), 46–49+53 (2008)
20. Kimura, D.: Are men's and women's brains really different? Can. Psychol. **28**, 133–147 (1987)
21. Bai, L.: Analysis on CET- 4 influential factors in western area and ways to improve. J. Hunan Univ. Human. Sci. Technol. **5**, 141–144 (2012)

530   H. Li and H. Wang

22. Zhang, T.: Research on correlation analysis of university student's score based on data mining. Beijing University of Posts and Telecommunications, p. 41 (2017)
23. Reschly, A..L.., Pohl, A..J.., Christenson, S..L.. (eds.): Springer, Cham (2020). https://doi.org/10.1007/978-3-030-37285-9
24. Sheng, P., Zhang, L.S.: A study on the correlation between academic achievement and CET-4 scores. Educ. Res. Exp. **2**, 84–87 (2015)
25. Wen, Q.F., Wang, H.X.: The relationship between learner factors and CET-4 scores. Foreign Lang. Teach. Res. **4**, 33–39+80 (1996)

Data Analysis of Online Judge System-Based Teaching Model

Yuting Zhang, Zheng Li, Bin Du, Yonghao Wu[✉], and Heng Jiang

College of Information Science and Technology, Beijing University of Chemical
Technology, Beijing, China
lizheng@mail.buct.edu.cn, dubin@buct.edu.cn, appmlk@outlook.com

Abstract. For Computer Science and Technology students, the development of practical programming skills is crucial. In order to cultivate students' practical programming skills, Online Judge (OJ) system has been developed rapidly and widely used by many universities. However, the OJ system-based teaching model has not been sufficiently analyzed in terms of teaching effectiveness. Therefore, in this paper, we analyze the problems in teaching programming courses, the current application status of OJ systems and teaching models in many universities. We propose a teaching model of programming courses based on OJ system in Beijing University of Chemical Technology (BUCT). Besides, we apply this model to the course teaching of Computer Science and Technology in BUCT for nearly 10 years and accumulate a large amount of raw data of programming practice activities. After scientific and reasonable data analysis, it is proved that the teaching model has achieved good teaching effect. The results of the experiment show that students' use of the OJ system was positively correlated with their scores in the programming course. The more students practiced programming in the OJ system, the higher the students' scores in their programming courses.

Keywords: Online judge · Programming education · Practical teaching efficiency

1 Introduction

The problem of high failure rate of novice programmers in learning programming courses has been a hot topic in the field of programming education. Many researchers have conducted detailed analysis of programming courses and their teaching models in order to identify the reasons for these problems [4].

Programming courses are characterized by difficulty of introduction, serious polarization, and strong practicality. Most universities rely on computer program experiments and integrated course design to allow students to do programming practice. This is used to develop students' ability to analyze problems and solve practical problems with programming ideas. However, the teaching effect of the above-mentioned practical teaching models is not satisfactory, and the main problems are summarized in the following aspects [1].

Limitations on Large Class Teaching. Programming courses are generally taught in large classes, with one teacher instructing hundreds of students in computer program experiments at the same time. Teachers work under great pressure and are unable to keep abreast of each student's experiment completion. This results in students not getting timely guidance when they encounter programming problems, which can greatly discourage students in programming. In addition, teachers do not have the time and energy to verify students' programming assignments one by one. This leads to a serious phenomenon of plagiarism, which is not conducive to the development of students' programming skills [13].

Limitations on Programming Practice Time. Each programming course typically has less than 15 computer program experimental sessions, and each session typically lasts between two and four hours. It can only be used for the purpose of consolidating and understanding class theoretical knowledge, but not for effective training of programming skills. This leads to poor practical programming and debugging ability of students [14].

Limitations on the Type and Number of Programming Practices. The cases for conducting computer program experiments are usually provided through textbooks or courseware. However, computer-related technology iterates and evolves rapidly, and it is difficult to fully cover the contents of textbooks or courseware. So students do not learn the latest computer-related technology [3]. This is not conducive to the development of students' practical programming skills and innovative abilities [15].

Therefore, how to meet the needs of the development on programming education and how to improve the teaching effect of practical teaching are the urgent problems for teachers to solve. To this end, we apply the Online Judge (OJ) system of Beijing University of Chemical Technology (BUCT) to the practical teaching of programming in Computer Science and Technology, and propose a teaching model based on OJ system. This teaching model helps teachers to keep track of students' learning and also helps students to do more programming practice. Based on the scientific and reasonable statistics and analysis of the collected large amount of raw data of practical teaching activities, it is concluded that the teaching model based on OJ can stimulate students' learning interest and improve the teaching quality.

The contributions of our study can be summarized as follows:

- We propose an adaptive teaching model based on the OJ system according to the shortcomings and problems of BUCT in programming education.
- We analyze the usage of the OJ system at BUCT over the last 10 years and the variability in behavior of students using the OJ system.
- We analyze the relationship between student answer data on OJ system and students' performance. The experimental results show that the correct use of the OJ system for programming practices contributes to the improvement of students' performance.

The rest of the paper is organized as follows. Section 2 introduces the background and related work. Section 3 introduces our proposed teaching model based on OJ system. Section 4 provides a detailed description of the experimental and analysis of the results. Section 5 summarizes our study and discusses potential future work.

2   Background and Related Work

2.1   Current Application Status of Online Judge System

The OJ system originated from the ACM International Collegiate Programming Contest (ACM/ICPC) [7,8]. After nearly 40 years of development in the ACM competition, many universities have developed their own OJ systems. The OJ systems of well-known universities are the UVA OJ system[1] of the University of Virginia in the United States, the SGU OJ system[2] of Saratov State University in Russia, and the URAL OJ system[3] of Ural State University in Russia.

Among the well-known OJ systems in China, the first university to develop an OJ system is Zhejiang University, named ZOJ[4]. The OJ system with the highest number of submissions is POJ[5] of Peking University [12]. ZOJ from Zhejiang University and HustOJ[6] from Huazhong University of Science and Technology have high practicality as open source OJ systems. In addition, Beijing University of Chemical Technology has also developed its own OJ system based on the open source HustOJ system, named BUCTOJ[7]. These OJ systems are not only widely used in competition training and programming courses, but also open for registration for other universities' programming enthusiasts.

In the above OJ systems, students can participate in programming competitions, complete programming assignments issued by teachers, and engage in various programming practices. Moreover, the OJ system can provide students with timely and accurate programming feedback. As a result, students' practical programming skills can be effectively improved.

2.2   Teaching Model Based on Online Judge System

Currently, OJ systems are widely used in programming courses in many universities [5,17]. Its existing teaching model can be concluded by the following three aspects: experimental teaching, course scope and teaching effectiveness evaluation.

---

[1] http://acm.uva.es/.
[2] http://acm.sgu.ru/.
[3] http://acm.timus.ru/.
[4] http://acm.zju.edu.cn/home/.
[5] http://poj.org/.
[6] http://www.hustoj.com/oj/.
[7] https://buctcoder.com/.

In the Aspect of Experimental Teaching. The OJ system is directly applied to the computer program experimental teaching of programming courses in many universities. According to the experimental content and specific requirements of the programming courses, the teachers set the programming assignments reasonably. For example, the teacher adds new questions or selects suitable questions from the question bank for students to practice programming skills [16]. After writing and debugging the program, students submit the program to the OJ system for judgment. Each question has a given set of test input cases and test output cases. It is used to determine whether the student program meets the requirements of a particular question. The OJ system first compiles and runs the program, inputs the test input cases into the program, and gets the actual output cases. Then it compares the actual output cases with the test output cases. Finally the OJ system gives the judging results. Since the OJ system can give the students real time assignment completion status, the teacher can understand the students' performance in real time and give guidance [11]. Therefore, the OJ system allows the teacher to instruct several classes at the same time, which greatly reduces the teacher's work pressure. The use of the OJ system also prevents plagiarism in assignments, as the OJ system has a built-in source code plagiarism detection function. In addition, after the class, students can continue to log into the OJ system to finish the assignments. It ensures the continuity of teaching and improves the quality of teaching [6].

In the Aspect of Course Scope. The application of the OJ system mainly focuses on the teaching of practical programming courses. Such as C, C++, Python, Java [10]. And for programming theory courses, such as Introduction to Computer Science, Principles of Computer Composition, Compilation Principles, Database Principles are rarely involved.

In the Aspect of Teaching Effectiveness Evaluation. Before using the OJ system, many universities generally use comparative data on course grade point average or survey reports to evaluate teacher's teaching effectiveness [2]. These data do not effectively reflect students' programming skill. After using the OJ system, the data from the OJ system can accurately reflect the students' programming skill, so a more scientific and powerful data analysis can be conducted to show whether the OJ system has substantially helped students improve their programming skills.

3   Our Approach

3.1   Design of Online Judge System in BUCT

In order to effectively help students improve their programming skills, our school developed an OJ system based on the improved open source system HustOJ[8] in

---

[8] http://www.hustoj.com/oj/.

2011, named BUCTOJ[9]. BUCTOJ is mainly used for students to participate in ACM competition training, weekly competitions and monthly competitions organized across campuses, and programming exercises of our programming courses.

BUCTOJ is developed in php language, the database uses MySQL, and the system adopts B/S architecture. The main system modules include system maintenance, question database management and training, real-time status and ranking, competition and assignment management, famous school league, BUCT programmer forum, data statistics, etc.

BUCTOJ supports C/C++, C#, Java, Python and other common programming languages. In the process of use, we pay great attention to the management of the question bank. After continuous enrichment and improvement, BUCTOJ's question bank has more than 6000 questions. The question types cover the main knowledge points of several courses such as Data Structure, Programming Fundamental, ACM/ICPC Programming Methodology and Practice, etc. And to meet the practice needs of students at different levels, the questions are divided into five levels according to the difficulty coefficient, which stimulates students' interest in learning programming courses.

The data statistics module uses data visualization techniques. Meaningful data is obtained from the database, and the data analysis results are graphically displayed through highcharts, thinkphp and other technologies. This provides a more visual understanding of student BUCTOJ usage.

3.2 Application of OJ System-Based Teaching Model at BUCT

After nearly 10 years of teaching practice, our school has formed a teaching model for programming courses based on BUCTOJ. It includes four aspects: practical teaching, teaching effectiveness, assessment and evaluation mechanism, and incentive mechanism.

Interactive Practice Teaching Model with Real-Time Assessment and Feedback Regulation. Through the status display function of the BUCTOJ, the teacher can check the students' assignment completion, track the students' progress in real time. The teacher can also give timely and targeted guidance to the common problems encountered by students in the process of question solving, and can also provide focused guidance to students who are at the bottom of the ranking. In order to meet the learning needs of students at different levels, teachers can adjust the difficulty and number of programming assignments in a timely manner according to the students' knowledge mastery. Thus, the purpose of improving the effectiveness of classroom teaching can be achieved.

Simplify Assignment Access to Improve Teaching Effectiveness. The teacher submits the assignment to BUCTOJ and sets the start and end time of the assignment. Students submit their assignments through the BUCTOJ

---

[9] https://buctcoder.com/.

according to the time requirements. BUCTOJ will count the number of submissions and passed answers. The completion of the assignment is ranked and can be exported to an excel file. Teachers can easily access all students' work on each question, summarize the common problems encountered by students, and provide targeted explanations in classroom teaching. After students submit their assignments, BUCTOJ will quickly provide the results of the evaluation. Students are informed of the completion status of their assignments and can make subsequent revisions and resubmissions. Compared with the traditional model of sending and receiving assignments, BUCTOJ shortens the feedback cycle and stimulate students' learning potential and enthusiasm.

Fair and Objective Assessment and Evaluation Mechanism. The use of BUCTOJ for programming course assessment is easy to operate and implement, and the judging results are fair and objective. By using BUCTOJ, students can systematically manage the content of each assessment, find out the weak parts of current course learning, and take the initiative to make up for the deficiencies. Each assignment ranks students based on the number of passed answers and time spent, which can make students aware of the learning gap, so that they can put forward higher requirements for themselves, and motivate students to study.

Create a Scientific and Reasonable Learning Incentive Mechanism. BUCTOJ will give an overall ranking based on the number of answers submitted and the percentage of answers passed. This will encourage students who are lagging behind to catch up and motivate those who are at the top to keep up. In addition, in each course, we set up a prize for "the most correct answers award", "the most difficult answers passed award". Introduce the ACM competition mechanism into the practical class teaching. Every semester, we conduct variety of programming competitions, such as monthly and weekly competitions. Through the above different forms of incentives, students are motivated to learn, guided to develop good study habits and form a positive learning atmosphere, thus promoting the improvement of teaching quality.

4   Experimental Analysis

In a total of 10 years of practical teaching of programming courses from 2012 to 2021, the practical classes of programming courses have been incorporated into the OJ system. Such as Data Structures, Java Programming, Assembly Language Programming. To evaluate the effectiveness of the BUCTOJ-based teaching model in programming teaching at BUCT, we design the following RQs.

4.1   RQ1: How the BUCTOJ has Been Used in Recent Years at BUCT?

To answer RQ1, we compare and analyze the number of submitted answers by grade level and by month of the year.

A comparison of the number of submitted answers by grade level is shown in Table 1. We can see that there is an overall increasing trend in the number of submitted answers for each grade level. Grade 2019 has the highest number of submissions and the best use of the BUCTOJ. Grade 2012 is in the initial stage of experimentation with the BUCTOJ because the teaching model has not been fully transformed. Grade 2021 has been used for a relatively short period of time. Therefore, the number of submissions for the Grade 2012 and Grade 2021 is low. In addition, the correct submission percent gradually decreased and then increased from 2012 to 2021. This shows that the programming ability of students has been improved after teachers as well as students have gradually adapted to and made reasonable use of the BUCTOJ.

Table 1. Comparison of the number of submitted answers by grade level.

Grade	The number of submitted answers	The number of passed answers	Percent correct %
2012	39247	16385	41.7
2013	79940	32024	40.1
2014	50857	17294	34.1
2015	56846	20762	36.5
2016	93192	24893	26.7
2017	117251	34321	29.3
2018	200372	59832	29.9
2019	289896	71115	24.5
2020	252948	83353	33.0
2021	38168	17486	45.8

Figure 1 lists the change pattern of the total number of submissions in different months in the three years of 2018, 2019 and 2020. The total number of submissions dipped in June, November and December 2018 as students prepared for their final exams. In 2019 students are significantly more motivated to practice programming during the course compared to last year and the total number of submissions is at a higher level overall. The total number of submissions peaked in May, June and October 2020. This is because the teacher summarized the students' programming practice in 2018 and 2019. In 2020, teacher adjusts the teaching and assessment scheme, increases the teaching of practical courses, and applies the BUCTOJ to the practical teaching in the primary term.

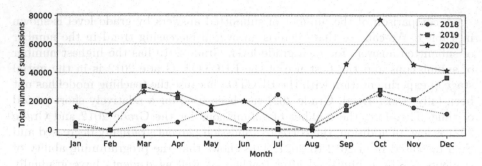

Fig. 1. The curve of the total number of submissions in different months of the year.

4.2   RQ2: What is the Variability in Behavior Among Students Using the BUCTOJ?

To answer RQ2, we compare and analyze the answer submissions of each class, the answer submissions of male and female students within the class, and the answer submissions of each dormitory.

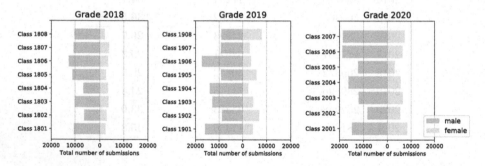

Fig. 2. Comparison of answers submitted by students in each class and comparison of answers submitted by male and female students within a class

Figure 2 shows the answer submissions for each class and the answer submissions for male and female students within the class in the Grade of 2018, 2019 and 2020. According to the survey, the class teacher of the class with the highest total number of answer submissions had guided the students to do programming exercises on the BUCTOJ after school. So the learning enthusiasm of the class was strong and the students with strong programming ability were mostly gathered in these classes.

As seen from Fig. 2, the ratio of the number of answer submissions for males and females in the Grade 2018, Grade 2019 and Grade 2020 was 3.27:1, 2.52:1 and 2.37:1, respectively. In the Grade 2018, Grade 2019 and Grade 2020, the ratio of male to female students is 3.51:1, 3.47:1, and 2.5:1, respectively. It can be seen that the average number of submitted answers by female students is always slightly higher than that of male students. As you can see, the programming practice of the girls has also been improved by using BUCTOJ.

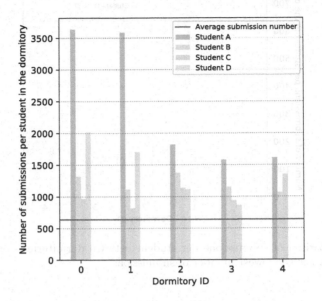

Fig. 3. Comparison of submissions per student between dorms - one student in the dorm has the highest number of submissions

A total of 10 dormitories in the Grade 2019 are surveyed in this experiment, with five dormitories each containing a student with a top overall submission ranking and another five dormitories each containing a student with a bottom overall submission ranking. Notably, the number of submissions per student in the Grade 2019 is 639. As shown in Fig. 3, dorms with one top student in the dormitory have better overall submissions, and everyone in the dormitory has a higher than average number of submissions. As shown in Fig. 4, the dormitory containing one poor student has a poor overall submission profile, with only two students of the five dormitories having a submission count above the average submission count. Therefore, it is suggested that at the end of the first year, the school can reasonably allocate the dormitory members according to all the students' answer submission. So as to enrich the students' daily study life and stimulate their team consciousness, thus achieving the effect of improving the whole dormitory study condition.

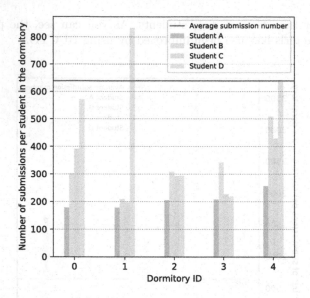

Fig. 4. Comparison of submissions per student between dormitories - one student in the dormitory has the lowest number of submissions

4.3   RQ3: What is the Correlation Between Student Answer Data on BUCTOJ and Student Performance?

To answer RQ3, we compare and analyze the correlation between student answer data on BUCTOJ (include the number of submitted answers, the number of passed answers and the number of corrected answers passed) and student performance (include GPA and the scores of each subject).

Table 2 lists the correlation coefficients between student answer data on BUCTOJ (include the number of submitted answers, the number of passed answers and the number of corrected answers passed) and student performance (include GPA and the scores of each subject) in the Grade 2019 and Grade 2020. In particular, $N_{correct} = N_{pass} - N_{plagiarize}$, where $N_{correct}$ is the number of corrected answers passed, N_{pass} is the number of passed answers, $N_{plagiarize}$ is the number of plagiarized answers passed. The correlation coefficient is calculated as follows:

$$\rho_{X,Y} = \frac{cov(X,Y)}{\sigma_X \sigma_Y} = \frac{E(XY) - E(X)E(Y)}{\sqrt{E(X^2) - E^2(X)}\sqrt{E(Y^2) - E^2(Y)}} \tag{1}$$

where $\rho_{X,Y} \in [-1, 1]$. cov is the covariance. σ_X, σ_Y is the standard deviation. E is the mathematical expectation [9]. The variables X is the number of submitted answers, the number of passed answers or the number of corrected answers passed. The variables Y is the scores of each subject or GPA for each student. A larger $\rho_{X,Y}$ means a stronger correlation between X and Y.

Table 2. The correlation between student answer data on BUCTOJ and student performance.

Course Type	Course	The number of passed answers	The number of corrected answers passed	The number of submitted answers
	GPA	0.39	0.39	0.3
Theory Course	Introduction to Computer Science	0.15	0.15	0.15
	Database Principles	0.20	0.20	0.3
	Principles of Computer Composition	0.22	0.24	0.28
Practical Course	Programming Fundamentals	0.32	0.37	0.27
	Algorithm Design and Analysis	0.32	0.33	0.36
	Object Oriented Programming	0.36	0.38	0.34
	Operating System Principle	0.36	0.37	0.4
	JAVA Programming	0.37	0.37	0.43
	High-level Language Programming	0.38	0.43	0.3
	ACM/ICPC Programming Methodology and Practice	0.38	0.4	0.31
	Assembly Language Programming	0.47	0.5	0.5
	Data Structure	0.5	0.53	0.41

As seen from Table 2, the correlation between the students' GPA, final scores in practical courses (such as JAVA Programming, High-level Language Programming, ACM/ICPC Programming Methodology and Practice, Assembly Language Programming, Data Structure) and student answer data on BUCTOJ is strong. The correlation coefficient of all of them is greater than 0.3, and the correlation coefficient of the Data Structure course is the largest at 0.53. Because, the Data Structure course is the course that uses the BUCTOJ most frequently, and the number of data structure-related questions in the BUCTOJ is the largest.

The correlation between the final scores in theory courses (such as Introduction to Computer Science, Database Principles, Principles of Computer Composition) and student answer data on BUCTOJ is weak. The correlation coefficient for the Introduction to Computer Science course is the smallest at 0.15. Because the Introduction to Computer Science course is offered in the first semester of the freshman year and students generally did not have programming fundamentals at the time of the class. There is a weak correlation between the scores in the programming courses and student answer data on BUCTOJ. Courses such as Database Principles and Principles of Computer Composition are less relevant because there are fewer relevant exercises in the question bank and students do less questions in the BUCTOJ. Therefore, it is necessary to continue to enrich the question bank of the BUCTOJ for the relevant courses, set the corresponding questions according to the course content, play the role of the BUCTOJ in these courses.

From Table 2, it can be seen that the correlation between the number of corrected answers passed and student performance is higher than the correlation between the number of passed answers and student performance. This shows that it is crucial for students to complete programming questions independently to improve their programming skills in practice.

5 Conclusion

After 10 years of teaching practice proved that the teaching model of programming course based on BUCTOJ proposed in the paper has achieved good teaching effect. By using BUCTOJ in teaching, students' practical programming skills have been well practiced. However, the teacher's role of macro control and guidance and supervision cannot be ignored. Although the application of the BUCTOJ shifts students' learning from passive acceptance to independent learning, the system cannot be overly relied on. If teachers do not provide timely guidance and supervision, it may lead to students' lack of innovation, excessive self-management, or itchy and formal learning. On this basis, further research is needed on how to give full play to the teaching application value of the BUCTOJ. We hope that the research results of this paper can provide help and reference for the teachers of programming courses in various universities.

Acknowledgements. The work is supported by the National Natural Science Foundation of China (Grant nos. 61902015, 61872026 and 61672085), and Educational research projects of Beijing University of Chemical Technology (Grant nos, 2021BHD-JGYB16 and G-JG-PTKC202107).

References

1. Alturki, R.A., et al.: Measuring and improving student performance in an introductory programming course. Inform. Educ. Int. J. **15**(2), 183–204 (2016)
2. Arthur, W., Jr., Tubré, T., Paul, D.S., Edens, P.S.: Teaching effectiveness: the relationship between reaction and learning evaluation criteria. Educ. Psychol. **23**(3), 275–285 (2003)
3. Brusilovsky, P.: Webex: learning from examples in a programming course. In: Web-Net, vol. 1, pp. 124–129 (2001)
4. Gomes, A., Mendes, A.J.: An environment to improve programming education. In: Proceedings of the 2007 International Conference on Computer Systems and Technologies, pp. 1–6 (2007)
5. Kurnia, A., Lim, A., Cheang, B.: Online judge. Comput. Educ. **36**(4), 299–315 (2001)
6. Luo, Y., Wang, X., Zhang, Z.: Programming grid: a computer-aided education system for programming courses based on online judge. In: Proceedings of the 1st ACM Summit on Computing Education in China on First ACM Summit on Computing Education in China, pp. 1–4 (2008)
7. Mu, Y., You, D., Dou, Y.: CDIO training mode of programming ability for software engineering students based on ACM/ICPC competition standard. In: Proceedings of 11th International CDIO Conference (2015)

8. Sun, D., Wang, L., Zou, Z.: ACM ICPC in China: learning from contests. In: Proceedings of the International Conference on Frontiers in Education: Computer Science and Computer Engineering (FECS), p. 1. The Steering Committee of The World Congress in Computer Science, Computer (2013)
9. Taylor, R.: Interpretation of the correlation coefficient: a basic review. J. Diagn. Med. Sonogr. **6**(1), 35–39 (1990)
10. Wang, R.: Design and practice of the blended learning model based on an online judge system. Int. J. Contin. Eng. Educ. Life Learn. **27**(1–2), 45–56 (2017)
11. Wang, T., Su, X., Ma, P., Wang, Y., Wang, K.: Ability-training-oriented automated assessment in introductory programming course. Comput. Educ. **56**(1), 220–226 (2011)
12. Wen-xin, L., Wei, G.: Peking university oneline judge and its applications. J. Changchun Post Telecommun. Inst. **2** (2005)
13. Wu, H., Liu, Y., Qiu, L., Liu, Y.: Online judge system and its applications in C language teaching. In: 2016 International Symposium on Educational Technology (ISET), pp. 57–60. IEEE (2016)
14. Wu, J., Chen, S., Yang, R.: Development and application of online judge system. In: 2012 International Symposium on Information Technologies in Medicine and Education, vol. 1, pp. 83–86 (2012). https://doi.org/10.1109/ITiME.2012.6291253
15. Yadin, A.: Reducing the dropout rate in an introductory programming course. ACM Inroads **2**(4), 71–76 (2011)
16. Zhao, W.X., Zhang, W., He, Y., Xie, X., Wen, J.R.: Automatically learning topics and difficulty levels of problems in online judge systems. ACM Trans. Inf. Syst. (TOIS) **36**(3), 1–33 (2018)
17. Zhou, W., Pan, Y., Zhou, Y., Sun, G.: The framework of a new online judge system for programming education. In: Proceedings of ACM Turing Celebration Conference-China, pp. 9–14 (2018)

Design and Practice of Multi-level Programming Experimental Teaching for Emerging Engineering Education

Hua Lv, Ye Zhu, Yingchun Guo, Gang Yan[✉], Yang Yu, and Xiaoke Hao

Hebei University of Technology, Tianjin 300401, China
yangang@hebut.edu.cn

Abstract. Programming courses should not only cultivate the students' programming ability, but also should guide the students' ability to analyze and solve complex engineering problems. The Programming Teaching Assistant (PTA) is adopted to design different types of experiments with different levels of difficulty based on output, guided by the course objectives and centered on students. Exploring the multi-level experimental teaching system of Basic Experiment of Programming in Emerging Engineering Education, and analyzing the data collected in the platform, can further improve the teaching methods, enhance the teaching quality, and provide a better basis for the reform of other programming courses in the future.

Keywords: Emerging Engineering Education · Multi-level teaching System · Programming · teaching reform

1 Introduction

Engineering education is an important part of China's higher education, aiming at cultivating a large number of high-quality engineering and technical talents with strong innovation ability and meeting the needs of economic and social development. In February, 2017, the Ministry of Education promoted the Emerging Engineering Education construction to help build a powerful country in higher education [1–3]. In order to meet the connotation requirements of the "Emerging Engineering Education" construction and quickly change and improve the training quality of engineering talents, in addition to consolidating the professional theoretical knowledge of the students, the existing experimental teaching should be reformed and put into use to fully train and improve students' practical operation ability and engineering innovation ability on account of the development and demand of the industry and students' ability [4].

"Experiment of Programming Foundation (Python)" is a basic experimental course for the majors of artificial intelligence and mathematics in Hebei university of Technology, which aims at stimulating students' interest in computer learning, establishing computational thinking, and using computers to solve practical engineering problems.

This practical course requires students to have strong logical reasoning ability and mathematical foundation, the abilities of analyzing and solving problems and practical operation are also indispensable. Students need sufficient practice to fully understand and flexibly use theoretical knowledge to write programs and improve their ability to solve problems. The traditional experimental teaching method did not use teachers to grasp students' experimental situation in time, As a result, teachers and students can't synchronize effectively, and some students' experimental results are not ideal.

The Programming Teaching Assistant (PTA) will be applied in Basic Programming Experiment (Python) teaching reform, which will be guided by the course objectives, and student-centered concept, design different types of experiments with different levels of difficulty based on the output, and explore the hierarchical experimental teaching system of Basic Programming Experiment in the Emerging Engineering Education. Through this system, students with a poor foundation can get a necessary training; students with a good programming foundation can also receive an advanced training. In the process of programming training with perfect contents and an applicable difficulty, students can gradually build up their computational thinking, develop a serious working attitude, and cultivate their innovative thinking and design ability and lifelong learning awareness and ability.

2 Problems in Traditional Experimental Teaching

"Experiment of Programming Foundation" (Python) is a basic experimental course for the majors of artificial intelligence and mathematics in Hebei university of Technology. Each class has 60 ~ 70 students, and students have different learning abilities and programming foundations. In the theoretical teaching, the teaching can be enhanced by modern methods such as massive open online course, Rain Classroom and Learning Pass, but the traditional offline teaching method lacks effective supervision tools and means in the practical teaching, and it is difficult for teachers to be synchronized with students effectively. Some students are afraid of the computer operation experiments, which leads to unsatisfactory learning results. At the same time, it is difficult to train students' programming ability at different levels because of the limitations of the topic and the subjectivity of the assessment methods.

3 Construction of Multi-level Experimental System

Guided by the course objectives and student-centered concept, the experimental teaching contents with different levels of difficulty are designed and the multi-level teaching is carried out on the basis of the output. Deeply decompose and refine the existing experimental teaching contents, compile experimental contents that can be updated iteratively with the same problem, and establish a complete experimental teaching content system. Through Programming Teaching Assistant(PTA) with questions and topics of different levels of difficulty, students can explore the experimental content step by step according to their own abilities, which can not only help students with poor foundation get necessary training, but also help students with good programming foundation get improved training, and effectively implement hierarchical programming training.

The cultivation of complex engineering problem solving ability is stressed. Each part of the experimental content selects a typical programming case based on task-driven concept, designing solutions from simple to complex to guide students to combine theoretical knowledge with practical application, and effectively expand practical contents, which cultivates students' comprehensive application ability of professional knowledge, and gradually strengthens their ability to solve complex engineering problems.

students' process assessment and individualized counseling are strengthened. Through Programming Teaching Assistant(PTA) online evaluation system, students' login information, submission status, correct answer rate and pass rate of questions, students' submission code and other information can be viewed in real time. By tracking and analyzing these teaching data, students' basic information such as the completion of experimental content and weak links can be known in time. Consequently, problems can be intensively analyzed and discussed and students with weak foundation and lagging progress can be instructed by individual targeted guidance.

Various means are set up to ensure the continuous improvement of teaching quality. Through two-way communication between teachers and students, and timely analysis of teaching platform and questionnaire data, effective and timely feedback on teaching can be formed; the experimental content, the experimental progress and experimental methods can be adjusted in combination with the feedback to ensure the continuous improvement of the course. In the experiment, professional norms of the computer programming are integrated, which encourages students to try different programming ideas to solve the same problem, cultivates students' flexible programming ideas, guides students to develop serious and rigorous study and work attitude, and cultivates students' lifelong learning consciousness and ability.

4   Project Implementation

Relied on the school of Artificial Intelligence of Hebei University of Technology, the project adopts Programming Teaching Assistant(PTA). Taking the course "Experiment of Programming Foundation(Python)" as an example, the auxiliary teaching platform of PTA programming experiment is used to further promote students' experimental operation ability, effectively evaluate the progress and quality of students' experiments, and cultivate students' subjective initiative of independent learning, and realize multi-level experimental teaching.

"Experiment of Programming Foundation (Python)" is a disciplinary foundation course for artificial intelligence and big data majors, and a public practice session for intelligence majors and big data majors, which is an essential practice session for students to further master and deepen the theoretical knowledge they have learned. Through hands-on experiments, students will be able to use IDLE or other Python development environments proficiently, and Python basic data types such as lists, meta-groups, dictionaries, sets and related list derivatives, slices and other features to solve practical problems; they will master Python branching structure, loop structure, function design and use, be skilled in different fields of Python extension modules in different fields and develop the ability to solve practical problems in the fields of file manipulation, data analysis, scientific computing, etc. At the same time, students will develop and improve their scientific literacy, scientific style of seeking truth from facts, serious working attitude, active research spirit and awareness of code optimization and safe programming.

"Experiment of Programming Foundation(Python)" cover the following main parts:

(1) Python syntax basics: be familiar with the basic data types of Python, master the rules of Python arithmetic operations and expression writing methods and the application of basic input/output statements.
(2) Control structure programming: master the statement format and execution rules and the use of branch and loop structures.
(3) Application of strings: understand and master Python string functions and be able to solve related problems.
(4) The application of functions: master the use of functions, learn to write programs with functions and reuse code
(5) The application of combined data types: master the use of Python's three mainstream combined data types, and learn to write programs that deal with a set of data.
(6) File and data formatting: understand the file and data representation from the Python perspective, and learn to write programs with file input and output.
(7) Comprehensive application: be familiar with Python extension modules in different fields and be able to initially have the ability to solve practical problems in the fields of file manipulation, data analysis, scientific computing, etc.

PTA (Programming Teaching Assistant) is an experimental teaching platform for programming courses, which is led by Zhejiang University, managed and operated by Hangzhou Baiteng Education Technology Co.Ltd, and jointly constructed by university teachers all over the country [5]. The system has three main groups of users: administrators, teachers and students. Teachers can create new topics, create and share their own topic sets, create classes, add students, assign homework, view students' homework submissions, count grades and conduct data collection and analysis, etc. Students can login to the system to complete the exercises according to the tasks assigned by the teacher, check the completion status of the exercises and their scores, and check their ranking in the class to understand their position in the class, so that students can adjust their study attitude and study plan in time. The PTA platform enables the sharing of national resources, easy management and accurate data analysis, which can help teachers analyze students' experiments and carry out targeted teaching and guidance, thus promoting the improvement of students' programming ability.

4.1 Reconstruction of Experimental Content and Construction of Experimental Question Bank on Programming Teaching Assistant(PTA)

A "project-led, task-driven" curriculum reform model is established. Taking typical practical application cases or real scenes as the carrier, the practical teaching content of the course is reconstructed, emphasizing the combination of theory and real scenes, learn and master programming in real scenes, which will improve their application ability, and truly turn knowledge into ability. The course group has reorganized the content of the experimental course, designed and selected the typical questions of different difficulty levels with the same content according to the knowledge points, and built its own database of experimental questions on Programming Teaching Assistant(PTA). A complete experimental question bank with wide content coverage and multiple levels of difficulty coverage has been established. The experimental content arrangement follows the principle of easy to difficult and gradual progress. The width and depth of the experiment are equal, covering a wide range. First, start with the easy-to-learn content, and combine with typical daily cases to stimulate students' enthusiasm for learning. For students without any programming foundation, they can quickly master the foundation and application of programming. Then, the experimental content should be deepened continuously to meet the learning needs of different students and realize the hierarchical training of students. The interface of the student exercise set is shown in Fig. 1.

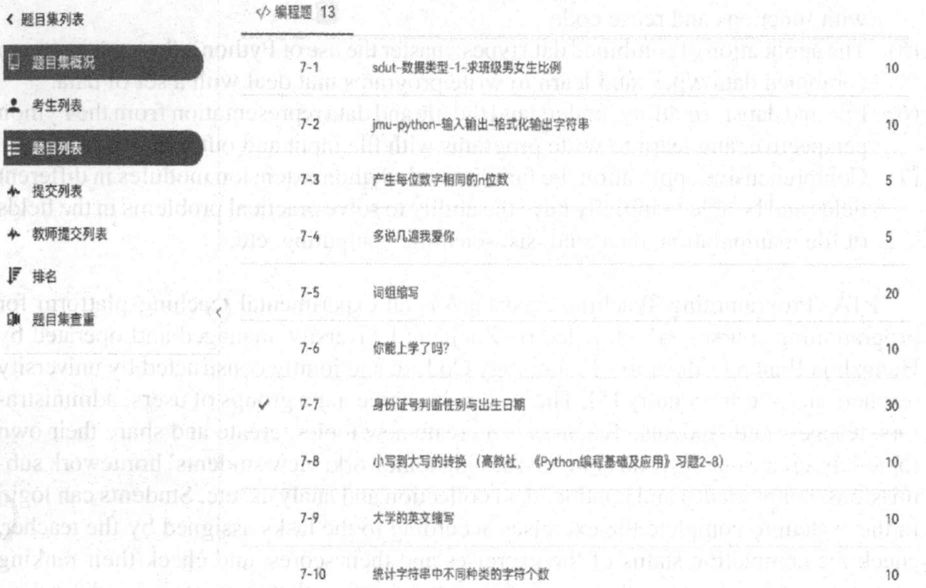

‹ 题目集列表	‹/› 编程题 13		
☐ 题目集概况	7-1	sdut-数据类型-1-求班级男女生比例	10
♟ 考生列表	7-2	jmu-python-输入输出-格式化输出字符串	10
☰ 题目列表	7-3	产生每位数字相同的n位数	5
➤ 提交列表	7-4	多说几遍我爱你	5
➤ 教师提交列表			
⌒ 排名	7-5	词组缩写	20
▣ 题目集查重 ‹	7-6	你能上学了吗?	10
	✓ 7-7	身份证号判断性别与出生日期	30
	7-8	小写到大写的转换（高教社,《Python编程基础及应用》习题2-8)	10
	7-9	大学的英文编写	10
	7-10	统计字符串中不同种类的字符个数	10

Fig. 1. The interface of the exercise set

4.2 Formulate Process Assessment Standards, Establish Comprehensive Evaluation System, and Strengthen Students' Process Assessment and Individualized Counseling

The process assessment should be strengthen by formulating clear process assessment standards and organically combining process assessment with achievement assessment to form a scientific and reasonable comprehensive evaluation system. A sound and reasonable comprehensive evaluation system should be established by collecting and analyzing students' experimental data in time. The interface of student performance ranking is shown in Fig. 2.

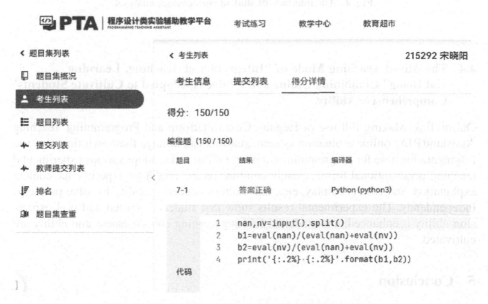

Fig. 2. The interface of student performance ranking

A comprehensive evaluation is set up in multiple links to effectively cover the course objectives, combining the process evaluation with the outcome evaluation, so that students' achievements can effectively reflect the achievement of experimental teaching. The interface of the code submitted by the student is shown in Fig. 3.

Fig. 3. The interface of the code submitted by students

4.3   Experimental Data Analysis and Continuous Improvement

Teachers can download and analyze the student experiment data obtained on PTA, and conduct comprehensive data analysis and visualization from multiple dimensions such as the positive answer rate of questions, submission, transcripts, and code quality, combined with questionnaires to form an effective feedback mechanism for subsequent continuous improvement.The interface for student performance analysis is shown in Fig. 4.

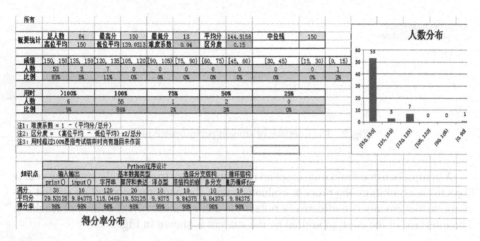

Fig. 4. The interface of student performance analysis

4.4   The Mixed Teaching Mode of "Integration of Teaching, Learning and Doing" Combining Online and Offline is Adopted to Cultivate Students' Comprehensive Ability.

Online link: Making full use of Hegong Cloud Platform and Programming Teaching Assistant(PTA) online evaluation system, students can arrange their own time and use fragmentation time for programming training. Offline links: adopt various experimental teaching organizational forms, closely combine on-the-computer experiments, content explanation, and results display, etc., and exercise students' ability to solve problems independently. The experimental results show that students' written and oral expression ability is enhanced, and students' lifelong learning consciousness and ability are cultivated.

5   Conclusion

In Emerging Engineering Education, this paper analyzes the role and significance, the direction and content of teaching reform of Basic Experiment of Programming, formulating the implementation plan of teaching reform from the aspects of experimental system construction, experimental content design and construction, and the experimental implementation, and implementing it with the help of Programming Teaching Assistant(PTA).Through abundant experimental resources with different levels of difficulty closely combined with the scene, students' learning enthusiasm can be stimulated, and their initiative in autonomous learning can be developed, resulting in the improvement of programming and hands-on practice ability, and students' all-round development. In a word, a new direction and goal can be provided for the experimental teaching reform of programming.

References

1. Zhong, D.: Connotation and action of emerging engineering education construction. High. Eng. Educ. Res. (3), 1–6 (2017)
2. Lin, J.: Future-oriented emerging engineering education construction in China. Tsinghua Univ. Educ. Res. **38**(2), 26–35 (2017)
3. Lin J.: Curriculum system reform and curriculum construction of emerging engineering education majors. High. Eng. Educ. Res. (1), 1–13 (2020)
4. Dong, G., Zhao, G., Wang, G., Zheng, C.: Design and practice of hierarchical experimental teaching system for emerging engineering education. Exp. Sci. Technol. **18**(x), (2020). The first paper on the Internet
5. Sun, X.: Teaching reform and practice of C language programming based on programming teaching Assistant(PTA). J. Shenyang Norm. Univ. (Natural Science Edition) **38**(3), 377–380 (2020)

The Reform and Practice of PYTHON Programming Teaching in the Context of Emerging Engineering Education

Ye Zhu, Yingchun Guo$^{(\boxtimes)}$, Hua Lv, Tingting Zhang, Yang Yu, and Yi Liu

Hebei University of Technology, Tianjin 300401, China
guoyingchun@hebut.edu.cn

Abstract. In order to adapt to the talent cultivation system in the field of artificial intelligence and carry out the talent cultivation mode of "Artificial Intelligence + X" in the context of emerging engineering education, the course of Python programming is used as an example for reform exploration and practice. In this paper, we focus on cultivating students' ability, reforming student-centered teaching methods, building online and offline teaching resources and integrating curriculum ideology and politics, and explore the application of two properties and one degree in the Python course reform. This paper divides the course content into three modules: Python introduction, Python ecological understanding, and Python ecological application. Besides, project-based driving and course thinking integration teaching methods are applied to enhance learning interest and cultivate their computational thinking skills with specific project-based teaching. Furthermore, this course reform method provides course reform ideas for various majors to cultivate composite talents.

Keywords: AI + X · PYTHON programming teaching · Content reform component · Curriculum ideological and political education

1 Introduction

In recent years, China has continued to pay attention to the development of artificial intelligence, and policy promulgation has been promoted, as is shown in Table 1. The Ministry of Education released "the Action Plan for Artificial Intelligence Innovation in Higher Education" in 2018, which pointed out that it was necessary to improve the talent training system in the field of artificial intelligence, strengthen professional construction [1]. Besides, the universities should actively carry out research and practice of "Emerging Engineering Education", and explore the talent training mode of "AI + X" [2].

Most colleges and universities use C programming as the first programming language course that freshmen are exposed to. However, the mathematical and logical thinking training at the high school level is not enough to support students' learning of computational thinking, and the complex syntax structure of C language further increases the difficulty of learning.

Table 1. The policy promulgation of artificial intelligence.

Time	Administration	Policy	Policy Content
2015.05	State Council	Made in China 2025	Proposed "to promote intelligent manufacturing as the main direction"
2015.07	State Council	Internet Plus action plan	Artificial intelligence as one of the eleven key layout areas of "Internet +"
2016.05	National Development and Reform Commission	"Internet +" Artificial Intelligence Three-year Action Implementation Plan	Support pilot demonstrations of AI applications in manufacturing, education, environment, transportation, business, health care, cyber security, social governance and other important areas
2016.07	State Council	the 13th Five-year Plan on Technology and Innovation	Proposed to "focus on the development of big data-driven human-like intelligence technology approach"
2017.07	State Council	Development Planning for a New Generation of Artificial Intelligence	Improve the AI education system, strengthen the talent pool and echelon construction, especially accelerate the introduction of global top talents and young talents, and form a highland of AI talents in China
2017.12	Ministry of Industry and Information Technology	Three-year Action Plan to Promote the Development of Artificial Intelligence Industry (2018–2020)	Promote the integrated application of intelligent products in industry, medical care, transportation, agriculture, finance, logistics, education, culture, tourism and other fields
2018.04	Ministry of Education	Action Plan for Artificial Intelligence Innovation in Higher Education	The artificial intelligence in the field of education should be accelerated, which can support the innovation of talent training model, reform of teaching methods, and improve the educational governance capacity
2019.02	State Council	China Education Modernization 2035	Accelerate the transformation of education in the information age, build intelligent campuses, and coordinate the construction of integrated intelligent teaching, management and service platforms

Moreover, for students of Data Science and Big Data, an emerging cross-composite major in mathematics, statistics and computers, the application scenario of C language in future work or graduate study is less, and students' active learning motivation is poor [3]. Therefore, the course of Data Science and Big Data Technology in the context of the emerging engineering education is built, and the course Python programming is offered as an introductory programming language course for students [4]. Python language syntax is simple and closer to natural language, which reduces the difficulty of learning programming language and enhances students' interest in learning. Moreover, Python supports both process-oriented and object-oriented programming ideas. It is the mainstream language of artificial intelligence, and contains a large number of third-party function extension libraries, and has a perfect ecological environment, which is suitable for students majoring in big data for employment or further study. However, the current Python course has the problems of single teaching method, emphasis on syntax and lecture, and classroom PPT teaching focusing on knowledge points, resulting in students' poor ability to solve complex functional problems. Therefore, this project explores the course construction reform of Programming Foundation (Python) for Data Science and Big Data Technology majors in the context of the engineering education.

2 Programming Foundation (Python) Course Reform Design

The reform of the course of Foundation of Programming (Python) is carried out in four aspects: reform of teaching contents to meet the needs of big data majors, reform of teaching methods focusing on cultivating students' abilities and student-centered teaching methods, construction of online and offline teaching resources and integration of course ideology and politics, cultivating the ability of big data majors to solve complex problems and exploring the application of "two properties and one degree" in the reform of Python course.

2.1 Python Course Content Reform for the Big Data Major in Emerging Engineering Education

This project divides the Python course content into three modules: Introduction to Python, Python Ecological Understanding, and Python Ecological Application, and its structure is shown in Fig. 1.

- In the stage of Introduction to Python, the methods and skills of Python language programming are systematically taught, using various methods such as electronic lesson plans, multimedia teaching, and traditional board books, combining knowledge lectures with actual program running demonstrations, and combining class discussions and exercise explanations to improve the amount of classroom teaching information and enhance the teaching effect.
- In the stage of Python Ecological Understanding, four third-party libraries, Request, Numpy, Pygame and Pytorch, are used as examples. Help students master the installation and use of third-party libraries and become familiar with Python extension modules for different domains. In the stage of Python Ecological Application, with four major practical directions of web crawling, data analysis, computer games, and deep learning, students choose group practice through their interests and are initially equipped with the ability to solve practical problems in the fields of data analysis, scientific computing, and artificial intelligence.

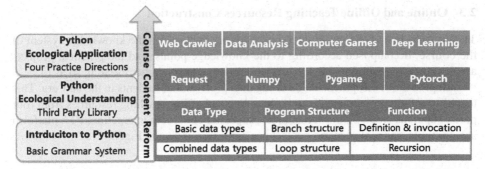

Fig. 1. The reform structure of the course content of "Programming Foundation (Python)".

2.2 Reform of Student-Centered Teaching Methods

In the teaching process, with the help of the information platform, a combination of online and offline teaching methods is used, with 60% of the students' funded learning in class and 40% of the teachers' teaching guidance in class. Teaching is student-centered, with timely feedback on student learning effects and process-oriented assessment. Students can practice, interact and discuss in class through Super Star Cloud Platform, and review their knowledge points with the help of PTA platform and MOOC resources in class. The course is driven by project practice, combined with online Q&A, timely checking of students' homework progress and problems, timely making new adjustments to lecture content, methods and progress according to students' problems, and strengthening the weak links of students' knowledge mastery, as is shown in Fig. 2.

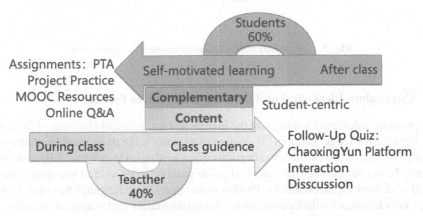

Fig. 2. Reform of student-centered teaching methods.

2.3 Online and Offline Teaching Resources Construction

The construction of the teaching resource library is based on the knowledge system of the course, decomposed according to the knowledge points, and the practical projects are designed according to the needs of enterprises and scientific research, so as to.

adapt to the development needs of big data professional students in the new era. This teaching reform project intends to build online and offline teaching resources from four parts: superstar cloud platform resources, superstar classroom interaction, PTA platform assignments, and real scenario project practice, as is shown in Fig. 3.

Fig. 3. Online and offline teaching resources construction

2.4 Curriculum Ideological and Political Education in Python

The program is designed to integrate the ideological and political elements of the course in different knowledge modules [5]. In the syntax knowledge point module, students are strictly required to follow the specifications when writing code, test carefully and meticulously before submitting the code, and guide students to be willing to explore and not afraid of difficulties and setbacks. Python as an open source language has over 120,000 third-party libraries for data connectivity, data computation and statistical analysis, data mining, data visualization, and other application scenarios. With such a complete Python ecosystem, students have a vast amount of resources to apply, guiding them to stand on the shoulders of giants to learn and progress quickly.

In the stage of Python Ecological Application, through group practice, on the one hand, students can develop good communication and collaboration skills, and on the other hand, they are trained to read the requirements carefully, analyze them carefully, and not be afraid of difficulties and setbacks when solving the complex problems.

2.5 Personalized Education

Teaching students in accordance with their aptitude is the foundation of educational theory, and a student-centered individualized learning model to cultivate innovative spirit is the goal of educational model and the original intention of individualized education. According to the needs of national policy and social, individualization education is combined with students' own interests, learning experiences and other humanized information, which can formulate learning contents that vary from person to person. With the rapid development and wide application of artificial intelligence, we can make full use of big data in education industry for analysis, and personalized education has occupied a place in the field of artificial intelligence.

Through the analysis of intelligent teaching system, we can solve the problem of accurate teaching process. Collect all students' behavior data, basic information data and academic data, conduct big data analysis and intelligent technology processing, form portraits of individual students and students as a whole, generate visual academic situation analysis reports and provide them to teachers. Teachers can accurately grasp the learning situation of individual students, the learning atmosphere of the whole class, the weak distribution of knowledge points and other information, make personalized learning plans, and submit them to the learning situation analysis service; The learning situation analysis service accurately plans the teaching path and designs the teaching strategy through the background teachers according to the index data in the learning situation report. Thereby realizing the precision of the teaching process (Table 2).

Table 2. Case design of ideological and political teaching of programming foundation (Python) course

Course Knowledge Modules	Ideological and political elements	Moral Education Objectives
Combined data type text word frequency statistics	Statistics on the frequency of the term "socialist ideology with Chinese characteristics" in the "Resolution of the Central Committee of the Communist Party of China on the Major Achievements and Historical Experiences of the Party's Centennial Struggle"	Understand the major achievements of the Party's century-long struggle and adhere to the ideology of socialism with Chinese characteristics
Python Third-party library applications	Huge amount of resources available for application	Guiding students to stand on the shoulders of giants to learn and progress quickly
Python Syntax specification	Promote the spirit of craftsmanship in the new era	Cultivate excellent professionalism and broaden students' international perspective
Applying Python Ecology Grouping Practice	Good communication and collaboration skills	Learn to communicate and collaborate, read the requirements carefully, analyze them carefully, and be unafraid of difficulties and setbacks

3 Conclusion

According to the requirements of the Emerging Engineering Education construction, through the research of the course reform of "Programming Foundation (Python)" in Data Science and Big Data Technology, the reform of teaching contents that meet the needs of the society, the transformation to a student-centered teaching method, the construction of online and offline teaching resources, and the condensation of practical projects in the direction of big data. The course ideology and political education reform the traditional teaching mode, and cultivate the Python based project development ability and quality, as well as professionalism of Big Data students.

The cultivation of students majoring in data science and big data technology in the context of Emerging Engineering Education is different from that of traditional computer science majors, so it is necessary to study and analyze the needs of big data professionals, study the reform of the course teaching content of Programming Foundation Python, stimulate students' learning interest and cultivate computational thinking and problem-solving abilities for the characteristics of non-computer science students. In the teaching method, students are guided to change the learning style of only listening to the teacher's lecture in high school, and the students' independent learning is the main focus, and they are guided to learn to solve computing problems with programming thinking by using problems in learning, life and production. In addition, combining Python's unique computing ecological resources and excellent cases with students' interests, stimulating students' creative thinking and innovation ability, and effectively improving teaching quality by continuously adjusting and optimizing teaching contents and teaching methods, achieving the education goal of cultivating computing thinking and innovation ability, and laying a solid foundation for improving the learning quality of big data professionals in the context of Emerging Engineering Education.

References

1. Homepage.   http://www.moe.gov.cn/srcsite/A16/s7062/201804/t20180410_332722.html. Accessed 23 Feb 2023
2. Hwang, G., Tu, Y.: Roles and research trends of artificial intelligence in mathematics education: a bibliometric mapping analysis and systematic review. Mathematics 9(6), 584–589 (2021)
3. Wu, Y., Chen, W., Li, Z., Li, Y., Shi, L., Liu, Y.: Exploration of teaching reform for c programming course based on OBE-BOPPPS model and rain classroom. In: 2021 International Conference on Education, Information Management and Service Science (EIMSS), pp. 467–470. IEEE, Xi'an, China (2021)
4. Kroustalli, C., Xinogalos, S.: Studying the effects of teaching programming to lower secondary school students with a serious game: a case study with Python and CodeCombat. Educ. Inf. Technol. 26(5), 6069–6095 (2021). https://doi.org/10.1007/s10639-021-10596-y
5. Li, H., Zhang, M., Li, C.: Research on the entry point of curriculum ideology and politics in the teaching of computer programming. In: 2nd International Conference on Education, Knowledge and Information Management (ICEKIM), pp. 286–289. IEEE, Xiamen, China (2021)

Exploration and Practice of High-Quality Engineering Teaching Process Evaluation System of College-Enterprise Cooperation in Colleges

Shulin Yuan[1] , Huixia Shu[2]([envelope]) , and Yimei Yang[2]

[1] College of Marxism, Huaihua University, Huaihua 418000, Hunan, People's Republic of China
[2] School of Computer Science and Engineering, Huaihua University, Huaihua 418000, Hunan, People's Republic of China
shuhuixia@126.com

Abstract. We present the results of a case study concerning the introduction of collaborative and cooperative education key process evaluation system of "Four synergies" strategies based College-Enterprise Cooperation (CEC) in local colleges. In this paper we point out CEC is an effective way of high quality engineering education, and the key element of the evaluation system should be positioned in the students' practical working ability, and a "win-win" mode that focuses on the quality of training, college learning and enterprise practice, and resource and information sharing between college and enterprise. We explore the construction and practical significance of high-quality engineering teaching process evaluation system of CEC in colleges such as joint formulation of training plan, joint implementation of training process, joint development of teaching resources and joint supervision of teaching quality, and puts forward new thoughts on the innovative management mechanism of college enterprise cooperation and collaborative education.

Keywords: College-enterprise Cooperation · Process Valuation · Innovative Management · Talent –training

1 Introduction

At present, school-enterprise cooperation and collaborative education has become an effective way for local colleges to cultivate applied talents and key to the engineering education reform of new engineering construction. Through school-enterprise cooperation and industry education integration, it can effectively enhance students' practical ability in solving engineering projects, stimulate students' ability to analyze and solve problems, improve students' ability to adapt to post development, and improve the quality of talent training to meet the requirements of social development [1]. However, with the deepening of school-enterprise cooperation and the diversification of industry education integration, the new problems and contradictions faced by various management

W. Hong and Y. Weng (Eds.): ICCSE 2022, CCIS 1813, pp. 560–566, 2023.
https://doi.org/10.1007/978-981-99-2449-3_49

mechanisms are also highlighted. The existing school enterprise cooperation management mechanism needs to be improved, innovated and adapt to the requirements of the new situation, explore new school-enterprise cooperation management paths, and provide effective guarantee for the in-depth development of school -enterprise cooperation from the institutional system.

From the perspective of school-enterprise cooperation and collaborative education evaluation system, there are mainly the following problems to be solved: first, we should strengthen the construction and sharing of resources between schools and enterprises, solve the bottleneck encountered in the process of school-enterprise collaboration and in-depth integration, and provide resource support for talent training through the reform of the supply side of educational resources between schools and enterprises; Second, we should strengthen the active connection between schools and industries, enterprises and institutions, comply with the development of the industry in the process of talent training, include industry research, industry planning and vocational skill assessment into the scope of the evaluation system, and promote the organic coordination between schools and enterprises; Third, we should strengthen the innovative management mechanism of schools and enterprises, strive to explore, actively practice, establish a perfect sustainable development mechanism, and build an evaluation system for the whole process of talent training [2]. Therefore, in the process of deepening school-enterprise cooperation and collaborative education, we should actively think and continue to research and practice in the following aspects: first, actively carry out theoretical research on innovation management, think and explore the cooperation mode, system framework, management mechanism, process evaluation and other main contents of school enterprise cooperation and collaborative education, and deeply realize that these research contents are not a point or just a chain, But a system with its own internal coordination structure and external interaction. Second, actively carry out the research on the evaluation system of the whole process of talent training based on the joint construction of school-enterprise resources, information sharing and the combination of work and study, strengthen the teaching concept of joint construction, common maintenance and common development of internal and external resources of schools and enterprises, and explore a new talent training mode combining in-school learning and out of school enterprise project practice [3]. Third, we should actively carry out and explore the research on the construction of the evaluation system in the whole process of school enterprise cooperation and collaborative education, carefully grasp and analyze the internal needs, internal elements, internal relations and internal laws of the cooperation between the two sides, and build and explore a new evaluation system for the key process in the joint formulation of talent training plan, joint implementation of talent training process, joint development of teaching resources and joint supervision of teaching quality [4].

2   Constructing the Key Process Evaluation System

Some colleges have also gradually established school enterprise cooperation evaluation index system in line with the actual situation of the school, which generally includes teaching quality evaluation, student quality evaluation, training base evaluation and so on. Focusing on the construction of new engineering, in the process of promoting the deepening and integration of school-enterprise cooperation and collaborative education, actively explore the establishment of an application-oriented talent training mode combining work and learning, and form a key process evaluation ecological system of school-enterprise cooperation and collaborative education through jointly formulating talent training plan, jointly implementing talent training process, jointly developing teaching resources and jointly supervising the construction of the key process evaluation system teaching quality, Realize the organic integration and coordinated development of innovation and entrepreneurship education, professional qualification certification and professional vocational skill education; Explore the establishment of "Three Abilities" training modules, namely: general ability module, professional ability module and development ability module, and explore the realization of "four docking" teaching ideas, namely: curriculum matching enterprise industry needs, curriculum content matching career development, teaching process matching project process, professional education matching employment and entrepreneurship; Through regular evaluation of the rationality of training objectives, timely understand and analyze the changes of various internal and external needs and conditions, and organize enterprises and industry experts to participate in the evaluation and revision of talent training programs, so as to ensure that the evaluation and revision can better reflect the talent needs of the industry, better strengthen the professional quality requirements, better implement innovative education, and better enhance students' practical ability, so as to achieve the goal of training applied talents [5] (Fig. 1).

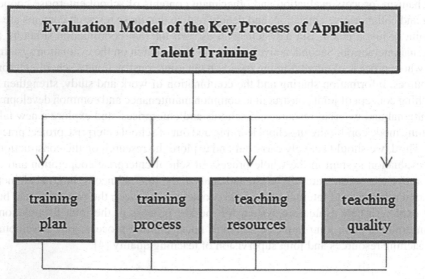

Fig. 1. Evaluation system of the key process of "four synergies" in school-enterprise cooperation

A. *JointlyFormulate Training Plan.* According to the characteristics of specialty construction and the needs of curriculum construction, both schools and enterprises jointly formulate talent training plans. In order to deepen the teaching reform, promote the integration of industry and education, and cultivate applied talents that meet the development requirements of production, management and service industries, both schools and enterprises jointly discuss and jointly build the curriculum system of talent training scheme, determine the new technology curriculum of school-enterprise cooperation, and clarify the curriculum construction and resource construction. In view of the changes of new technology development and the needs of industry development, both schools and enterprises will jointly study the new problems, new situations, new changes and new requirements encountered in the implementation process, and jointly discuss the supplement, improvement and revision of the scheme on the existing basis. Introduce the teaching methods of enterprise and professional training into the school, and promote the teaching mode of enterprise and professional training, such as the development of teaching materials and practical training, to promote the depth of enterprise and professional training, so as to promote the teaching mode of enterprise and professional training, As the focus of the construction of school enterprise cooperation and collaborative education demonstration base, build a demand oriented talent training mode through the base construction.

B. *Jointly Implement the Training Process.* Both schools and enterprises constantly optimize the teaching implementation process, standardize the management of the teaching process and ensure the teaching effect by regularly discussing the training plan. The main links of joint training include the following parts:

- Implementation of professional theory courses.
- Implementation of professional practice.
- Implementation of employment training.
- Implementation of graduation practice.
- Implementation of innovative education
- Implementation of graduation design.

C. *Jointly Develop TeachingRresources.* Schools-enterprises jointly develop teaching resources in curriculum teaching, project cases, MOOC courses, textbook construction and other aspects to realize the co construction, sharing and sharing of resources. Both schools and enterprises jointly develop teaching resources. On the one hand, through the innovative and entrepreneurial education practice by means of platform support, discipline competition, innovative projects, activity guidance and tutor drive, it enriches education and teaching methods, promotes the construction of education and teaching resources and promotes education and teaching reform; On the other hand, through the collaborative education practice of jointly building professional teaching resources, jointly building curriculum system network resources, jointly building joint laboratory project resources and sharing various educational resources of school enterprise cooperation, it not only deepens the depth of industry university research cooperation and realizes the sharing of teaching resources, but also takes market demand as the guidance, engineering technology as the main line and double qualified team as the guarantee The joint development and construction

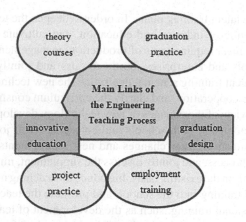

Fig. 2. Main links of joint implementation of engineering teaching process

of teaching resources aimed at serving social and economic construction, through the innovation and reform of curriculum system with professional ability training as the core, has improved the quality of education and teaching and highlighted the school running characteristics of applied talent training.

D. *Jointly Supervise the Teaching Quality.* Both schools and enterprises jointly supervise the teaching quality, formulate, revise and improve various quality standards and management requirements for various teaching links such as theoretical teaching, experimental (practical training) teaching, internship teaching, curriculum design, examination and graduation comprehensive training, and establish quality standards for main teaching links, which has laid a solid foundation for implementing the training objectives of applied talents and ensuring the teaching quality. By analyzing and studying the management mechanism, operation mechanism and supervision mechanism of school-enterprise cooperative and collaborative education, including teaching management mechanism, student management mechanism, student training, internship mechanism, graduation design guidance mechanism, curriculum resource construction mechanism, school enterprise cooperative system guarantee and evaluation incentive mechanism, we adopt a dynamic way to build a comprehensive evaluation system of the whole process of school enterprise cooperative and collaborative education, Highlight the new evaluation system for the cultivation of applied talents (Fig. 2).

3 Conclusion

School-enterprise cooperation behavior is accompanied by the whole process of high-quality engineering education construction, and the closeness of cooperation between schools and enterprises is bound to be reflected in all links of professional construction. Based on the clear construction principle of evaluation purpose, the collaborative and cooperative education evaluation system is mainly positioned in three aspects: students, schools and enterprises. The establishment of the engineering teaching key process evaluation system in school-enterprise cooperation is the internal requirement of school-enterprise cooperation, collaborative education and sustainable development. For the construction of school-enterprise cooperation mechanism, both schools and enterprises integrate them by jointly building training base platform, teaching resource platform and innovation and entrepreneurship base, so as to form a new model of application-oriented talent training process of enterprise integration, build an evaluation mechanism for innovative management of school enterprise cooperation and collaborative education teaching process, and through the mutual connection, mutual supplement, mutual support and mutual integration of each link of the each process. The mutually constructed practice platform enables students to enter all levels of training or participate in all training according to their own characteristics, which effectively improves students' innovative practice ability and their ability to solve practical engineering problems.

Practice has proved that technical exchange projects with industries and enterprises can more effectively help students understand the new trend of industrial transformation and upgrading, grasp the cutting-edge information in the application field, and also help the mutual connection between the course content and the requirements of engineering education standards, Through in-depth research on the key elements of cooperation, local colleges should build a reasonable high-quality engineering teaching evaluation system of school-enterprise cooperation, effectively guide the majors of colleges to effectively serve enterprises, and realize the deep integration of schools and enterprises in the real sense.

Acknowledgment. This study was supported by the Hunan Education Science Planning Project:(NXJK19CGD065). School enterprise cooperation and collaborative education project of the Ministry of Education:"Exploration and Practice on the construction of management mechanism of Huaihua University Nanjing yun chuang school enterprise cooperation big data practice base" (201901168012), "Exploration and Practice on the construction of management mechanism of Huaihua College JEP software school enterprise cooperation and collaborative training base for College Students" (201801224022), "Exploration and Practice on the construction of the whole process evaluation system of school enterprise cooperation and collaborative education between Huaihua University and Jiepu software" (201902167038).

References

1. Xiao-qian, L., Jun, C.H.: On the key elements of school-enterprise cooperation evaluation system in higher vocational colleges. J. Liaon. High. Vocat. **2**, 25–27 (2018)
2. Jin-cui, Y., Hong-jie, F., Renjie, Q.: Research on the development path of school-enterprise integrated collaborative education under the background of new engineering education. Educ. Teach. Forum (30), 50–51, July 2020
3. Rong, Z., Wu-xiu, D.: Construction of school-enterprise cooperation curriculum teaching quality evaluation system in applied undergraduate colleges. J. Henan Inst. Educ. (Philos. Soc. Sci. Ed.) **40**(1), 13–17 (2021). https://doi.org/10.13892/j.cnki.cn41–1093/i.2021.01.003
4. CI-yan,Z.H.: Study on the training model of collaborative education in local colleges and universities under the background of emerging engineering education. Educ. Teach. Forum (9), 5–8, March 2021

5. HUI-xia,S.H., Shu-lin, Y., Feng, K.J.: An study on the whole process evaluation system of "Four Tongs" based college enterprise cooperation for local colleges, vol. 34, pp. 46–48 (2021). Agenc. **9** , 5–8 (2021). https://doi.org/10.19392/j.cnki.1671-7341.202123056

Teaching Reform and Practice of University Computer Foundation Course Based on Python

Zhenyu He[1], Haihu Zhao[2(✉)], and Zhenfeng He[3]

[1] College of Information Science and Technology, Jinan University, Guangzhou, China
[2] School of Foreign Language and International Business, Guangdong Mechanical and Electrical Polytechnic, Guangzhou, China
zhh256058@126.com
[3] Administrative Office, Guangdong Tobacco Huizhou City Co., Ltd., Huizhou, China

Abstract. In view of the serious disconnection between the theoretical content and practical teaching of the existing university computer foundation courses, this paper proposes a teaching reform model for the university computer foundation course based on the Python language, and explores the teaching method of integrating computer foundation theories with programming. This paper takes Python language as a tool to reconstruct the theoretical and practical teaching system of university computer foundation courses, focusing on building multi-level innovative practices, so as to strengthen the verification and understanding of theoretical knowledge, and enhance the ability to research and solve practical problems. The results of the pilot teaching reform show that the reform of the curriculum can effectively improve the in-class teaching effect, enhance the course assessment performance, stimulate students' innovative consciousness, so as to realize the practical implementation of computational thinking training.

Keywords: University Computer Foundation Course · Python · Computational Thinking · Teaching reform

1 Introduction

As a common information processing tool, computers have been widely used in various industries and fields with the development of computer technology. The university computer foundation course is a general course in the current higher education stage, and the objective of this course is to cultivate college students' basic computer knowledge and important pathway to information literacy competencies [1].

Nowadays, the university computer foundation course system in colleges and universities mainly includes two parts, one is the basic theoretical knowledge of computer-related fields, such as development history, system structure, information processing methods, operating system principles, database technology and network applications, etc., and the second is the training of computer operation skills, which is generally based on the use of commonly used software, especially Office. The content of the first part is rather extensive, involving various fields of computer, with many complex concepts, and requirements for the content are mainly based on preliminary understanding. Therefore, students often feel that they are marvelous but difficult. The second part mainly focuses on software operation and use, and it has nothing to do with the theoretical content. Besides, computer is mostly regarded as a modern information processing tool. All these leads to the misunderstanding of "tool class" in basic computer courses. Due to this, it is difficult for the original teaching content to meet the needs of students, which puts forward new requirements for computer foundation courses in colleges and universities. Therefore, teachers of university computer foundation course begin to explore new teaching content and teaching modes.

Professor Jeannette M. Wing at Carnegie Mellon University in the United States, proposed the concept of Computational Thinking (CT) in 2006 [2]. Once Computational Thinking was put forward, it aroused resonance in the computer teaching community, and also it showed a new direction for the current basic teaching of computer science in higher education [3]. In Sep. 2010, the nine-university alliance's joint statement on the development strategy of computer foundation teaching reiterated that computer foundation teaching is an indispensable and important part of cultivating the comprehensive quality and innovation ability of college students [4]. At the same time, it takes "cultivation of computational thinking ability" as the core task of basic computer education. Therefore, at this stage, computer teaching should focus on cultivating students' universal computer application ability through the learning of courses, and guide students to learn to use computers to solve practical problems in their professional fields. Therefore, we propose that on the basis of learning basic computer knowledge, the university computer foundation course should focus on enhancing students' information literacy and computational thinking ability. While optimizing teaching content and innovating teaching mode, the programming language Python is added to the university computer foundation course content system, exploring a new teaching mode of computer foundation courses with the cultivation of students' computational thinking ability as the main line.

2   The Rise of Python Language and Its Advantages

During the 70 years from the mid-20th century to nowadays, computers have experienced rapid development, and many different programming languages have appeared, such as Pascal, Fortran, C, C++, Java, PHP, C#, etc. These different languages all reflect different design philosophies and the features of different times. However, every programming language has its limitations. Guido von Rossum, the designer of Python, wanted a language not only can call computer functional interfaces as C easily, but also can be programmed as easily as some scripting languages, and it is against this background that Python was created. Compared with languages such as C/C++ and Java, Python has the following advantages [5]:

(1) **Simplicity**. Python is a language that represents the thought of simplicity with simple syntax and it is easy to learn. This enables students to focus on problem solving rather than learning the language itself.

(2) **Interpretability**. Programs written in Python do not need to be compiled into binary code and it can be run directly from the source code. This makes Python simpler and more portable.

(3) **Object-oriented**. Python supports both procedural and object-oriented programming.

(4) **Scalability**. In order to improve running efficiency, C/C++ can be sued to write key codes, and then used in Python programs.

(5) **Mixed programming**. Python is called the glue language because it can be easily mixed with other languages for programming. In this way, various existing toolkits can be conveniently used, and the development efficiency can be improved.

(6) **Rich library**. Python has a strong standard library, and the Python ecosystem is beginning to expand into third-party packages such as web.py for web frameworks, numpy for scientific computing, and matplotlib for data visualization etc.

As a cross-platform programming language, Python has been ported to many platforms represented by Linux, Windows, Mac, and Android. Due to the openness of Python, it is supported by a wealth of mature libraries from the open source community, so that various tasks can be done based on Python, such as data acquisition (such as web crawler), image processing, machine learning, scientific computing, data visualization, etc.

3   The Practice of Integrating Python into the Teaching of University Computer Courses

In view of the above-mentioned features and advantages of Python language programming, this course teaching reform aims to incorporate Python language programming into the teaching of non-computer majors in our university, researching and exploring suitable teaching content and teaching methods. In the process of teaching reform of computer courses, Python language, with rich third-party libraries, can be widely used in a variety of programming fields, and application cases can be introduced into each module of computer courses [6, 7].

3.1   The Construction of a Computer Foundation Course System Based on Python

Although computer is a rapidly developing subject, it has not changed the basic principle of computer. The teaching of basic theory in university computer foundation courses is still the cornerstone of the course, such as the proposal and application of stored programs in von Neumann architecture, the binary digitization methods of various forms of information, and the locality principle of cache applications in storage systems Wait. Currently, computer science is no longer an independent discipline, but more as a tool discipline intertwined with other disciplines. It should not simply take theoretical knowledge as the focus of teaching, but should enable students to acquire the ability to use computers to solve problems in their professional fields on the basis of understanding the basic theories and concepts of computers, and promote the cultivation of students' thinking ability and innovation ability. Thus, the practical ability cultivation is also crucial.

Therefore, we divide the university computer foundation course into two parts: theoretical teaching and practical teaching. In terms of course content, both basic computer knowledge and computational thinking are taken into account, and knowledge such as information representation and processing, computer systems, networks, and database multimedia are used as teaching content. Then this theoretical knowledge is taken as the research object of using computational thinking to solve problems, and the practice is implemented to apply computer thinking to solve problems in various fields. Ultimately, it is hoped that through the study and practice of problem solving, students will be able to take the initiative to use computational thinking methods and skills in their professional learning to solve problems and practical problems with a certain degree of difficulty while understanding the basic knowledge of computers.

Thus, we organize the teaching content according to the core principles of computer centering on the syllabus of university computer foundations and the teaching objects of course implementation. The teaching object of computer foundation course in our university is freshmen. We select non-computer major students majoring in science and engineering, such as physics, chemistry, civil engineering, as pilots. After the survey before school starts, it was found that some of these students have a certain understanding of computers, and some students even have participated in information competitions in high school. However, there are still some students who have no basic understanding of computers. Therefore, the teaching content must be set according to the teaching object and teaching goals. For undergraduate students, the main theoretical content and the distribution of class hours are shown in Table 1.

Table 1. Main theories and time distribution.

Theories	Class hours (theories + practices)
Computer system composition and structure	4 + 2
Information encoding and data representation	6 + 4
Algorithms and logic	8 + 4
Operating system	4 + 4
Database and its application	6 + 4
Computer network	6 + 4
Information processing and multimedia technology	4 + 4

The practice content corresponds to the theoretical content, and the theoretical knowledge is understood through the practice. Using the Python language as a tool, a multi-level innovative practical teaching system has been constructed, that is Python programming practice (PPP), basic theoretical knowledge verification (BTKV) and comprehensive case innovation practice (CCIP). The main practice content is shown in Table 2.

Table 2. Practice content.

Practice content	Practice in detail	Type of practice
Basic syntax of Python	Variables, data types, expressions, branches, loop structures	PPP
Algorithm design of Python	Use Python to implement common algorithms such as searching and sorting	PPP
Information representation	Conversion of number system, character encoding, string encryption and decryption realizing by Python	BTKV; CCIP
Operating system programming	Obtain the management information, such as hardware information, process status, storage capacity and utilization, file directory and operation of the computer through the API interface in the pushil module in Python	BTKV
Database design	Use the pymysql module of Python to connect the database system, and realize basic operations such as adding, removing, modifying, and querying	BTKV; CCIP
Computer network programming	Use Socket, smtplib and urllib modules in Python to implement TCP communication, mail sending and receiving, as well as web crawler programming	BTKV; CCIP
Information processing and multimedia technology	Use matplotlib module to draw pictures, and use pillow module to process images	BTKV; CCIP
Comprehensive practice	Use Python to realize the work. The content of the works covers the main key knowledge points of the course: such as networks, operating systems, algorithms, programming languages, etc	CCIP

3.2   Practice Case of Python

Conversion of Number System. The computer application field is ever-changing, but the most important application is still data processing. In computer field, various types of data are all represented in the form of "numbers". One type is the "number system" that can directly perform mathematical operations. The other type is "code system" used to represent different object properties. Therefore, number system and code system are the most basic parts of the computer field. In order to deepen the understanding of different conversion methods of data, we ask students to use Python programming to convert decimal numbers into binary numbers. The code is shown in the Fig. 1.

```
def dec2bin(n):
    a=[]
    while n>0:
        n,r=divmod(n,2)
        a.append(r)
    a.reverse()
    print(a)

n=eval(input("Please enter a decimal number"))
dec2bin(n)
```

Fig. 1. Code of number system conversion.

Use Python to Write Web Crawler. Presently, our life is inseparable from the Internet, because a lot of data required in work and life is obtained from the Internet. Therefore, it is the basic ability of college students to master related technologies such as network data acquisition, analysis and processing. The Python language provides a rich library of web crawler functions, including urllib, wget, scrapy, requests, beautifulsoup4, etc. The following is an example of requesting access to a web page through the requests library (Fig. 2).

```
import requests
def getHTMLText():
    try:
        r = requests.get(url, timeout=30)
        r.raise_for_status()
        r.encoding = 'utf-8'
        return r.text
    except:
        return ""
url = "http://www.baidu.com"
print(getHTMLText(url))
```

Fig. 2. Code of web crawler.

Data Visualization. Rich visual data graphics can better display data. Using data visualization is conveniently for analysts to understand the shape and distribution of data from a macro perspective, or to display the final results. Python provides rich data visualization tools such as pandas, Seaborn, Bokeh, matplotlib, etc. The Fig. 3 takes matplotlib as an example to illustrate how to use Python to complete data drawing and visualization. The result of running the program is as Fig. 4.

```
from mpl_toolkits.mplot3d import Axes3D
from matplotlib import cm
from matplotlib.ticker import LinearLocator, FormatStrFormatter
import matplotlib.pyplot as plt
import numpy as np

fig = plt.figure()
ax = Axes3D(fig)
X = np.arange(-5, 5, 0.25)
Y = np.arange(-5, 5, 0.25)
X, Y = np.meshgrid(X, Y)
R = np.sqrt(X**2 + Y**2)
Z = np.sin(R)
surf = ax.plot_surface(X, Y, Z, rstride=1, cstride=1, cmap=cm.coolwarm,
        linewidth=0, antialiased=False)
ax.set_zlim(-1.01, 1.01)
ax.zaxis.set_major_locator(LinearLocator(10))
ax.zaxis.set_major_formatter(FormatStrFormatter('%.02f'))

plt.show()
```

Fig. 3. Code of data drawing.

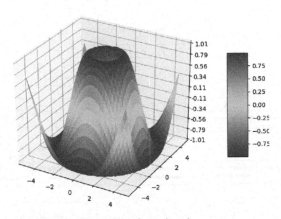

Fig. 4. The result of running the program.

Comprehensive Practice at the End of the Semester. We use a variety of process-oriented assessment methods. The focus of the assessment is gradually shifted from the "result" assessment to the "process", so that students can seriously participate in each process of learning, avoiding rote memorization for final exams, and cultivate students' good study habits of self-management, self-discipline and self-control. There is a comprehensive practice at the end of the semester, which is done in groups, and each student's contribution in the group is used as a part of the assessment. Below is an example of a comprehensive practice. Figure 5 shows the software requirements analysis, and the overall design framework of the system is shown in Fig. 6.

Develop a book resource management software with Python. The functions of the soft are as follows:

- To realize the inquiry, addition, deletion, borrowing and returning of books.

- The information of each book includes: author, book title, remaining quantity, lending quantity, etc.

- The client/server network programming mode is adopted. The server program is used for administrator operation, and the client program is mainly used for borrowing and returning books.

- Users can borrow and inquire about their own books through the client program.

- Administrators can manage user information and book materials

---

Fig. 5. Software requirements analysis.

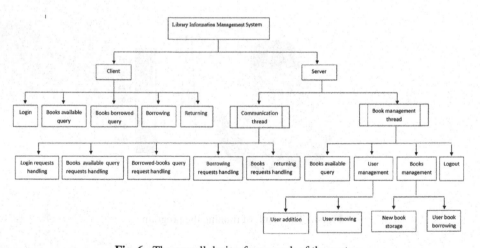

Fig. 6. The overall design framework of the system.

4 Analysis of the Effect of the Pilot Reform

Since September 2014, Jinan University began to introduce Python language teaching into the university computer foundation course for freshmen majoring in science and engineering. We have reconstructed the teaching content and designed a multi-level innovative practice based on Python. This teaching reform has been piloted for 8 years, and in 2015, the supporting experimental textbook Computer Science Basic Practice Course was published [8]. At present, this textbook is popularized and applied in many colleges and universities. Compare the previous pilot reforms with the traditional university computer foundation teaching methods, Python-based teaching helps to promote students' active learning, enhance the learning effect of in-class practice, improve the course assessment scores, and stimulate students' innovative consciousness.

Students' Energy Input for Practice Increases. According to the statistics of the practice test platform, the average time for students to use the platform for practice after class is 4 h per week. Due to the increasing difficulty and rich content of the course practice, the participation and concentration of the students and completion of the practice in practice class have been significantly improved. Classroom discipline violations have been eliminating.

The Test Scores have Improved Obviously. Due to the addition of Python content in the course teaching, the Python programming content in the final exam paper accounts for about 25%. Besides, the final comprehensive practice accounts for 20% of the test scores. Due to the adoption of more flexible and diverse assessment methods, students' assessment scores have improved significantly. The average final scores of all the students at the end of the semester each year are above 80, which is 5% higher than that before the reform.

Students' Innovation Ability has been Enhanced Extraordinarily. The course is designed with comprehensive practice, and students can comprehensively apply the operating system, computer network, database and other knowledge learned in class, and use Python programming to realize a complete work. The difficulty and innovation of the works have been continuously improved over the years. Through this method, the cultivation of students' innovative and practical ability has been strengthened, which has won great praise from the university leaders and teaching supervision experts.

5 Conclusion

For traditional college computer foundation courses, there is a serious disconnect between theoretical content and practical teaching, and the courses lacks conceptual thinking, high-level system, content matching and difficulty challenge. By adopting Python, this paper reconstructs the theoretical teaching content and supporting practice content by combing theories with practice to promote teaching reform. Using the Python language as a tool, a multi-level innovative practice, including Python programming practice, basic theoretical knowledge verification and comprehensive case innovation practice has been constructed, and a number of Python practice cases are illustrated. According to the pilot teaching reform of Jinan University students starting in 2014, the university computer foundation courses teaching based on Python can promote students' more energy input, improve the effect of in-class practice, enhance course assessment results, stimulate students' innovative consciousness, as well as to cultivate students' application of theory to practice, so as to realize the practical implementation of computational thinking training.

Acknowledgment. This work is supported by the following funding: Jinan University Teaching Quality and Teaching Reform Project ("Reform and Practice of College Computer Course for Overseas Students", 2023); Guangdong Provincial Higher Education Teaching Research and Reform Project ("Teaching Reform and Practice of Programming Course Integrating Application Demand Orientation and OBE Concept", 2021); Research on Information Technology in Education Project of China (No. 186140100).

References

1. Xia, F., Ying, R., Lina, W.: Computational thinking-oriented python case application in computer foundational curriculum. J. Shenyang Normal Univ. (Nat. Sci. Ed.) **38**, 572–576 (2020)
2. Wing, J.M.: Computational thinking. Commun. ACM **49**(3), 33–35 (2006)
3. Peizeng, G., Zhiqiang, Y.: Computational thinking training in computer foundation teaching. Chin. Univ. Teach. **5**, 51–54 (2012)
4. Joint Statement for Computer Foundation Teaching Development Strategy of C9 League, vol. 9. Chinese University Teaching (2010)
5. Tian, S., Tianyu, H., Xin, L.: Basics of Python Language Programming, 2nd edn. Higher Education Press, Beijing (2017)
6. Sainan, Z., Changyou, Z., Yuanyuan, J.: Hongyu: reform and research on university computer foundation driven by programming for the training of computational thinking ability. Softw. Eng. **22**, 48–50 (2019)
7. Fuliang, G., Gang, Z., Yongjie, L., Liangzhong, C., Zhao, W.: Computer foundation course system of military academies with python as the main line. Softw. Guide **19**, 214–216 (2020)
8. Yujuan, Q., Zhanrong, C., Liu Xiaoli, H., Yan, L.L.: Foundations of Computer Science in Practice. People's Post and Telecom Press, Beijing (2015)

Data Mining Series Experiment Design and OJ System Development Based on R Language

Xuqing Luo[1], Wei Zhou[1(✉)], Xiaoyan Jin[1], Yongji Wang[2], Binyue Cui[3], Yunbao Zhou[1], and Haonan Yu[1]

[1] School of Computer and Information Technology, Beijing Jiaotong University, Beijing 100044, China
wzhou@bjtu.edu.cn
[2] School of Science, Beijing Jiaotong University, Beijing 100044, China
[3] School of Management Science and Engineering, Hebei University of Economics and Business, Shijiazhuang 050061, Hebei, China

Abstract. Based on a comprehensive analysis of the existing Online Judge (OJ) evaluation systems at home and abroad, this paper designs and implements a new R language data mining online evaluation system based on HUSTOJ with reference to the characteristics of R language and data mining model algorithms. The overall system architecture is roughly divided into front-end, display layer, business layer, data layer and other parts. OJ System functional design includes OJ user system design, OJ question bank system design and OJ question judgment system design. Likewise, an accompanying experimental checklist and instructions are also developed. To a certain extent, the system solves problems of online test of data mining algorithms and lack of R language learning methods. At the same time, it also provides references for the designers and developers of related online referee systems. In the future, we look forward to the prospect of the system, such as how to ensure the security of the system, add automatic evaluation mechanism, and add natural language processing algorithms.

Keywords: Online Judge · Data Mining · R language · Online Evaluation · System Development

1 Introduction

Due to the wide application of modern database systems and the rapid development of Internet information technology, content management technology has entered a new period of development, that is, it has developed from only processing a few basic numbers in the past to being generated by computers for different reasons. It contains complex information in various forms such as graphics, images, sounds, electronic documents, web pages, etc., and the amount of information is also increasing. However, too much invalid statistical information will lead to information distance and lack of actual scientific research knowledge inevitably. Therefore, people are eager to analyze the massive statistical data, dig out and extract the hidden data information content, so as to make the best use of these data resources. Under these circumstances, data mining technology came into being. In recent years, data mining technology has received great attention in the electronic information industry. Since the first international academic conference on knowledge discovery and data mining abroad in 1995, the field of data mining and cognitive mining have become the hot spot gradually [1]. There are many research institutions or universities, such as the famous KDnet, NCDM, ACM, etc., and formed a lot of industrial results, such as RapidMiner, SAS, WEKA and so on. In contrast, the domestic research on this aspect is slightly slower, and it has not yet formed an overall rationale.

In the same way, the development of R language is very different between international and domestic. In the world, R language is already an authoritative language in the field of data analysis and professional statistical analysis [2]. There are various development forums based on R language, various auxiliary tools such as online running platforms in foreign countries. The Resources column on the website of RStudio covers many contents from basic entry to advanced R programming. A Variety of websites, take Kaggle and Data Camp for example, provided learning resources from online entrance courses to project design practice platform [3]. However, in China, R language teaching started late, and due to some factors, such as few users and no relevant authoritative organizations to promote. No professional R language online teaching materials and practice methods, people who want to study R, but cannot find more resources and open-source platforms. Therefore, there is an urgent demand for learners or users to have online learning and training platforms supported by R language to meet the growing business demand of data analysis and data mining [4].

Among the various network learning resource platforms of R language, OJ system is a relatively unique platform. The OJ system is also known as an online evaluation system. After the user submits the program source code online, the source code is compiled and run in the background, and the accuracy of the program source code is checked by the test dataset in advance. This technology is now widely used in the programming training of college students around the world, the training and screening of competition personnel, the teaching of various programming competitions or algorithm courses, as well as the automatic analysis and judgment of exercises, etc. The degree of mastery of an algorithm model or data structure, and the degree of mastery in different situations of different students is highly evaluative and inspiring.

Therefore, this research will try to build an online evaluation system for data mining based on R language [5]. Through small-scale trials, we try to solve the problem of lack of learning resources for data mining algorithms, hope to bring some inspiration to the design and development of related OJ systems [6].

2   System Overall Design

2.1   System Architecture Design

OJ System Architecture Design Model. According to the characteristics of data mining and R language, the basic architecture design management mode - MVC can be used to build an Online evaluation system for data mining [7]. The overall system architecture is roughly divided into front-end, display layer, business layer, data layer and other parts.

The data layer is based on a MySQL single database. The overall system is built on the virtual cloud server host [8] (Fig. 1).

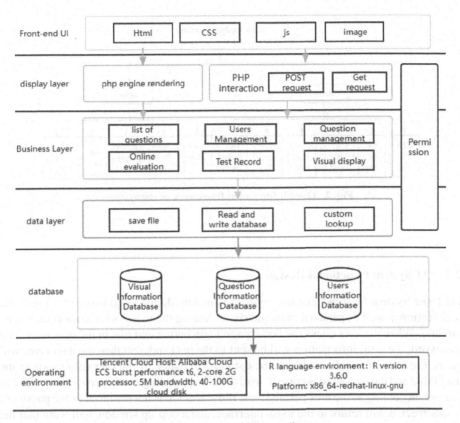

Fig. 1. OJ system architecture diagram

Overall Design of OJ System. In this project, the entire online evaluation website can be divided into students' online evaluation use design, teacher management student topic design, and administrator overall debugging background design. There are three types of role permissions in this system: students, teachers, and managers. Student users can click the "Login" button to complete the registration and enter the personalized operation page. Students may edit their personal data on the personalized page and are allowed to blog; the user can enter the visualization interface, browse visualization operations, and publish personal visualization codes; users may also enter the topic list page, view the topic information, and complete the course tasks arranged by the teacher. After completing uploaded questions, users can take the online test or examination. After the teacher logged in, the teacher can publish teaching topics, manage students' personal data, and add, delete, adjust, manage the contents of the question bank information. After entering the background of the website database, the administrator is able to manage the personal data of students and other users, the class arrangement information of teachers, the contents of the question bank information and the evaluation pass rate [9] (Fig. 2).

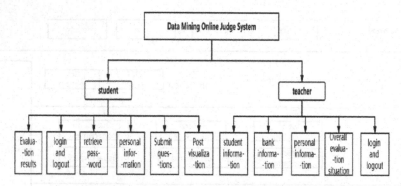

Fig. 2. Overall functional framework of the system

2.2 OJ System Functional Design

OJ User System Design. The user system is mainly divided into two parts: login and registration as well as personal main interface. Among them, login is the most important module. When the user clicks the home page login button and fills in the user name and password, the form information will be sent to the backend, and then the data layer will query the user information table in the database to match, if the user data exists in the user table and the password is correct, load the corresponding user's personal interface of the user according to the user permissions, if the account is not retrieved or the password is incorrect, it will return to the login interface, and a pop-up window will warn that the user does not exist or the password is incorrect.

OJ Question Bank System Design. The topic system mainly includes the topic list interface, and the topic details display interface. This function is mainly designed for student users and teacher users. After the teacher user logs in, click the New Question button from the question list interface, fill in the relevant data of the question according to the prompt information, select the corresponding data set or upload a new data set, submit, and save to complete the update of the question bank. After the student user logs in, browses the basic information and various labels of the questions in the question table, the user can select the appropriate exercises to practice, which needs to download the corresponding data set, design the corresponding locally according to the requirements of the question, and then submit the saved R file, tested by the system.

OJ Question Judgment System Design. The premise of the question judgment function is that the question is selected, and the student user needs to log in to the system first, and then select the question that needs to be completed in the assessment exercise from the question list box. Then choose the programming language and start evaluating the current problem by uploading the language code the user designed locally. The evaluation process of the exercises is illustrated by Fig. 3.

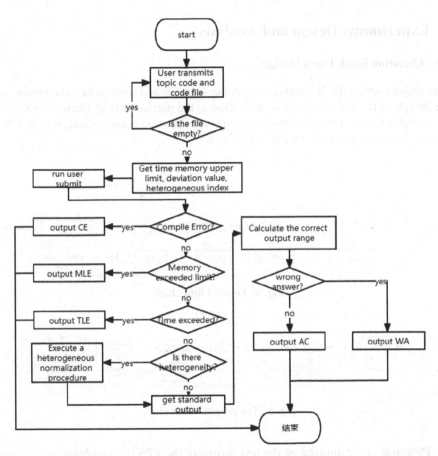

Fig. 3. Evaluation flow chart

2.3 Database Design

The database of this OJ system mainly realizes the construction of the database system through MySQL, and realizes the online visual management through phpMyAdmin. According to the selected analysis and functional analysis, the important entities applied in MySQL are designed as student entity, teacher entity, administrator entity, visualization module entity, topic entity and evaluation information entity. Now let's take students' online evaluation exercises as an example, and use students, teachers, and topics as entities to display the E-R diagram corresponding to each entity. The student entity includes attributes such as user ID, username, password, class, personal profile, and the number of visual uploads. Teacher entities include ID, username, password, manage class, personal profile, overall student status, etc. The subject entity includes attributes such as subject serial number, subject title, subject content, subject description, output format, visual display position, dataset serial number, and other prompts [10].

3 Experiments Design and Analysis

3.1 Question Bank Form Design

This project serves the R language algorithm learning and training of data mining, and the design of the question bank as well. Due to the particularity of the service objects, the overall process of the evaluation system is not the same as the normal process, which will evaluate the process from Fig. 4 to Fig. 5.

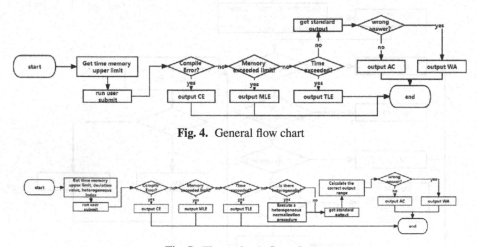

Fig. 4. General flow chart

Fig. 5. The project's flow chart

Therefore, after drawing on the text format of the FPS (free problem set) question bank for model design, the form design of the question has also been modified to a certain extent. The topic template of the modified FPS in this project also includes two parts: the topic data template and the sample visual display template.

The fields of the question data model include question number, question title, question description, time and memory limit, data set description, input and output format description, etc. The data model is shown in Table 1.

Table 1. Item data model parameter table

Column Name	Description	Data Types
ID	topic number	Integer
Title	topic title	String
Description	Topic description	String
Timelimit	time limit	Integer
Memorylimit	memory limit	Integer
InputSize	input size	Integer
Inputformat	input file format	String
OutputIndex	output indicator	SampleTestcase
OutputFormat	Sample output	SampleTestcase
MapTest	output legend	File
DataSet	data set	File
DataSetDescription	Dataset Description	String
Hint	other information	String
testCaseInfo	Evaluation data information	TestCaseInfo
Provider	Topic uploader information	User
deviation	Deviation of the result allowed	Integer
Heterogeneous	Whether there are heterogeneous indicators	Boolean

The design of data samples also has certain changes in data mining algorithms. Since the actual use process of data mining algorithms is more inclined to graphical display, the sample design of this project generally provides one or more sets of input and output [11]. The field is modified to display the visual display of the results after the running algorithm of the data set, as well as the description of the evaluation indicators. The specific model design is shown in Table 2.

Table 2. Item sample model parameter table.

Column Name	Description	Data Types
Output	output	String
Map	Visual result placement	File
deviation	Allowed result deviation value	Integer

3.2 Experiment List Design

Since the online judge system designed in this project is a full-time system mainly serving R language and data mining algorithm model training, the experiment list and data design need to meet the application scenarios and usage habits of R language and data mining.

In the basic part of R language, a series of topics are designed to meet the teaching demands of R language from introduction to simple use and finally to being able to perform certain data processing, mainly including R language input and output, basic operations, file opening and use, data preprocessing Orientation design with simple drawings. For each direction, this project has designed some basic questions, so that users can directly use it for teaching practice without filling the question bank by themselves [12].

The current list of design topics for the basic part of the built-in R language is shown below (Table 3):

Table 3. Basic part of the experiment list

No	Question Title	Difficulty Level	Tag
1	hello world; input and output; Basic operations; functions and files	Simple	R language basics
2	Pie Chart; Bar Chart; Line Chart; Scatter Chart	Simple	Visualization Basics
3	data preprocessing; Basic Statistical Analysis Methods; Sampling and permutation testing	medium	Data Analysis Fundamentals
4	Advanced Plotting; Regression Algorithms; Time Series	difficult	Advanced data analysis

P.S.: The data set of all the questions in the basic practice part is the iris data set

In the data mining algorithm part, it mainly focuses on the basic application and result display of various data mining algorithms. As we all know, data mining algorithms are complex, so the classification of algorithms in this section will imitate other OJ systems. Instead of a qualitative algorithm classification, it uses the form of labels. An algorithm will have more than one label. Algorithm labels for independent selection [13].

Similarly, this project also has some basic algorithm models built into the system for users to get started quickly. The list of internal topics is as follows (Table 4).

Table 4. List of data mining questions and experiments

No	Question Title	Difficulty Level	Tag	Data Set
1	K-means Clustering	Simple	Clustering	Iris Data Set
2	Bayesian Classification Algorithm1	Simple	Classification	THUCNews
3	Bayesian Classification Algorithm 2	Medium	Classification	THUCNews
4	Bayesian Classification Algorithm 3	Difficulty	Classification	THUCNews
5	OLAP Algorithm 1	Simple	Comprehensive	Jingdong Electric Dataset
6	OLAP Algorithm 2	Medium	Comprehensive	Jingdong Electric Dataset
7	OLAP Algorithm 3	Difficulty	Comprehensive	Jingdong Electric Dataset
8	Decision Tree Algorithm	Medium	Classification	Iris Data Set
9	KNN Classification Regression Model	Simple	Classification, Regression	CIFAR10 Dataset
10	Apriori Algorithm	Difficulty	Association rules	Jingdong Electric Dataset
11	EM Algorithm	Simple	Classification	Iris Data Set
12	Adaboost Algorithm	Difficulty	Integrated learning	Iris Data Set
13	Collaborative Filtering Algorithm	Difficulty	Comprehensive	Jingdong Electric Dataset
14	PageRank Algorithm	Difficulty	Comprehensive	Hillary's mail door Dataset
15	LOF Algorithm	Medium	Abnormal Detection	Jingdong Electric Dataset
16	Isolation Forest Algorithm	Medium	Abnormal Detection	Jingdong Electric Dataset
17	PCA Algorithm	Simple	Base	Jingdong Electric Dataset
18	DAGMM Algorithm	Difficulty	Abnormal Detection	Jingdong Electric Dataset

3.3 Dataset Selection

Due to the service objects and application scenarios of this project, the data set selection process will be more inclined to the world's public data sets. Similarly, without affecting the integrity of the algorithm expression and the matching degree between the algorithm and the data set. In order to improve the coherence of students' learning, the data sets used in the built in questions will select the same data set as much as possible. In this project, the entire R language basic training based on a unified iris data set. The various data sets selected in the data mining algorithm experiment have also been shown in the table, and it will not be repeated here [4].

4 System Testing and Discussion

4.1 User System Testing

The user registration is the first part before entering the system test. The user can access the homepage of the OJ system and the web page of the question bank without registration. Then, we complete the registration by logging in the user information. You can only enter the operating system when the account and password are correct. The background of the system database also implements permission distribution according to the account entered, so that users with different rights can get different permission and enter different interfaces. The user information should have been authorized by the administrator. After completing the registration, the normal application of the OJ system can be implemented, and the online topic training can be completed [14].

4.2 Question Bank System Testing

The question bank system mainly includes new modules for test questions and question upload modules. When select a topic on the main page, obtain the main page of the problem details, enter the required elements, and after selecting and submitting, return to the question list item to implement the upload of this question.

During the actual use of the OJ system website, nearly 40 practice questions will be uploaded in this assessment question bank, which will be introduced with the example of the k-means question test. By uploading the source code of the question, if it reflects "correct" in the result interface, it means that this source code has passed the system evaluation. If the result interface displays WA, CE, TLE, etc., it means that this source code failed the test. Importantly, refer to the Table 5 for the correspondence between the returned labels and their specific meanings.

4.3 Analysis and Discussion

The overall goal of the OJ system at the beginning of product design is: teachers support learners to achieve free computer training, providing a training platform for data mining teaching; reduce evaluation pressure for teachers, because the method of adding question banks is used to train different learners. The implementation of tracking training evaluation can effectively improve the training effect of the trainees. At the same

Table 5. Evaluation system judgement feedback result table

tags	specific explanation
AC	Accepted
WA	Wrong Answer
CE	Compilation Error
RE	Runtime Error
TLE	Time Limit Exceeded
MLE	Memory Limit Exceeded
OLE	Output Limit Exceeded
PE	Presentation error

time, the teacher also uses the OJ system to arrange program training tasks in a targeted manner, and students can use practice questions to complete online practice and learn freely. At present, this series of evaluation services has completed the evaluation of the R language source code and can use the inspection of the test samples to draw evaluation conclusions.

5   Conclusion and Prospect

5.1   Conclusion

With the emergence of R, the number of learners of R is also increasing rapidly, and with the advent of the era of big data analysis, the driving effect of data mining on the development of various disciplines has gradually become obvious. Nowadays, "Internet + education" is being vigorously promoted, if the teaching of R language is still in accordance with the traditional way of teaching code demonstration by teachers, the data mining algorithm is still unified by the traditional mode of looking at pictures and speaking by classifying content in other fields. It is possible that the development of R language and data mining in China will be seriously affected. This paper implements the R language data mining online evaluation system. After a period of testing and practical use, it is found that this OJ system can not only solve the problems of the R language learning fever, talent shortage, and single knowledge approach to a certain extent, but also can promote the development of R in China better, and provides a new method form of data mining learning to another extent.

Based on a comprehensive analysis of the functions of mainstream online evaluation systems at home and abroad, according to the characteristics of R language and data mining models, public data sets are collected and organized from Graviti, UCI, Kaggle and other websites, and R language-based K-means, Naive Bayes, Apriori are designed and implemented. There are nearly 20 data mining algorithm models. By comparing and analyzing the realization difficulty of various algorithms, the evaluation index of the results is established, and the experiment list question bank is developed. Then design and implement the R language online evaluation system based on HUSTOJ and deploy the network cloud server to use and test the designed OJ system.

5.2 Prospect

Since the system has not been officially launched, we will first name the OJ system for data mining in R language, and then adjust it after the OJ system is officially launched. Further plans and prospects of the system are listed below.

(1) Put the existing system into the network test, collect various actual operation results, and modify the system after comprehensively sorting out the actual operation situation.

(2) As a system, the security and stability of the system must be further improved, and the data loss in the event of an attack should be minimized.

(3) At present, the functional development of this system is not completely simple. The next step is to improve the automatic evaluation of the R language, combined with a more secure and reliable evaluation mechanism, and at the same time implement the display and enrichment of visual modules.

(4) Some NLP algorithms can be incorporated to exclude the use of truancy methods such as direct package adjustment, plagiarism, and card constants.

(5) Encapsulate the overall code to a certain extent and establish a visual management tool to facilitate subsequent maintenance and version upgrades by developers and maintainers.

Acknowledgments. The research is supported by Key Research and Development Program of Hebei province (No. 21373902D).

References

1. Chen, L., Zhang, F.: The application of Python data mining in the introduction of talents in colleges and universities. China Educ. Inform. (15), 52–54 (2019)
2. Chen, Q., Jiang, G.: Review of "how to use R for linguistic research: data exploration and statistical analysis." J. Beijing Int. Stud. Univ. **41**(05), 126–132 (2019)
3. Deng, X., Jia, Q., Yang, Y.: Construction of R language data visualization learning platform. China New Commun. **23**(04), 52–53 (2021)
4. Xu, T., Li, B., Liu, L., Hu, W., Yao, W.: Multi-perspective data mining and comprehensive analysis of graduate teaching data. Mod. Electron. Technol. **44**(19), 95–99 (2021)
5. Dash, S., Pani, S.K., Balamurugan, S., Abraham, A.: Biomedical Data Mining for Information Retrieval: Methodologies, Techniques and Applications. Wiley, New York (2021)
6. Manimannan, G., Priya, R.L., Arumugam, A., Poompavai, A.: Comparative study of data mining classifiers with different features and different databases domain. Int. J. Data Mining Emerg. Technol. **10**(1) (2020)
7. Qu, C.: Research on big data mining course construction based on R language. Wirel. Internet Technol. **15**(04), 91–93 (2018)
8. Yue, Q., Hu, Z., Wen, J., Zhao, Q.: Experiment design of data mining course based on R language. Microcomput. Appl. **32**(05), 31–34+37 (2016)
9. Meng, S., Meng, S., Yin, Z.: Data mining and visualization method of auto-mobile consumption based on R language. J. Ningbo Inst. Technol. **27**(04), 17–23 (2015)

10. Li, B.: Construction of DNA microarray data analysis and mining platform based on R language. Master, Chongqing University (2013)
11. Sonja, P.: R language in data mining techniques and statistics. Am. J. Softw. Eng. Appl. **2**(1), 7–12 (2013)
12. Yin, X., Lang, H.: Research on application security of unified service plat-form based on big data. Mod. Electron. Technol. **44**(23), 117–120 (2021)
13. Gou, R., Ye, X., Luo, X., Wang, B., Hu, Y.: Design of teaching evaluation system based on fuzzy evaluation and data mining. Inf. Technol. (09), 19–23 (2021)
14. Weng, A.: Research on the Development of Online Judge System for Middle School Informatics Olympiad. Master, Qingdao University (2019)

Author Index